MW01707411

Aboriginal Peoples and Natural Resources in Canada

Claudia Notzke

CAPTUS UNIVERSITY PUBLICATIONS

Aboriginal Peoples and Natural Resources in Canada

Copyright © 1994 by Centre for Aboriginal Management Education and Training (CAMET), Claudia Notzke and Captus Press Inc.

All rights reserved. No part of this book may be reproduced, stored in a retrieval system, or transmitted, in any form or by any means, electronic, mechanical, photocopying, recording, or otherwise, without prior written permission of the copyright holders. Correspondence can be sent to: Captus Press Inc., York University Campus, 4700 Keele Street, North York, Ontario M3J 1P3

Canadian Cataloguing in Publication Data

Notzke, Claudia, 1952–
Aboriginal peoples and natural resources in Canada

Includes bibliographical references and index.
ISBN 1–895712–03–3

1. Native peoples — Canada. 2. Natural resources — Government policy — Canada. I. Title.
E78.C2N67 1993 333.7'089'97071 C93–095589–7

This book was sponsored by the BESS Program (Business Enterprises and Self-Governing Systems of Indian, Inuit and Metis Peoples) and by CAMET (the Centre for Aboriginal Management Education and Training) at the University of Lethbridge, Alberta, Canada. The fieldwork was made possible by a research grant from the National Geographic Society, Washington, D.C.

0 9 8 7 6 5 4 3 2
Printed and bound in Canada

This book is dedicated to my parents.

Contents

Commentary on the Cover

The Oldman River controversy in southern Alberta is representative of aboriginal people's resource-related concerns across Canada. With the construction of the Oldman River Dam in the 1980s, the Peigan witnessed their treaty and aboriginal rights threatened, as well as their religious freedom and economic prospects. They have fought this threat by negotiation, litigation and civil disobedience.

On a cold day in February 1988, native and non-native people gathered on the banks of the river in a spirit of prayer and protest to participate in a Blessing-of-the-River ceremony, conducted by Peigan Elder and spiritual leader Joe Crowshoe and spiritual Elder from the Blood Indian Reserve, Harry Shade. When Joe Crowshoe concluded his blessing and prayer for the river, a golden eagle materialized in the sky. At that moment all of us knew that, somehow, our actions had been acknowledged.

Preface

The idea for this book was conceived at a crucial time for aboriginal territory: 1990 was the year of Oka and of the Lonefighters' stand on the Oldman River. It was also a year of important court rulings, such as *Sparrow* and *Sioui*. Across the country aboriginal people were asserting themselves, and in many cases the land and its resources were at the centre of their struggle.

Nevertheless, *Aboriginal Peoples and Natural Resources in Canada* started out rather inconspicuously. Doug Elias, who was then working on his book *Development of Aboriginal People's Communities*, suggested that I research and write some modules on selected natural resources for his book. Since this fitted nicely with my training as a geographer and my deep interest in land, resources and environmental management in general, I gladly agreed. I started out with a module on water resources, followed by another on fisheries. But after the "fish chapter," in particular, it became obvious that what started out as a rather modest research project was somehow "getting out of hand". At this stage, Doug Elias, Ken Nicol, then Head of the BESS Program and myself, made the unanimous decision that I should write my own book.

This decision sent me off on a two-year journey through aboriginal people's territory, much of it on paper, but some of it — the most interesting part — on the land itself. Many people contributed in numerous different ways to the success of this journey.

In British Columbia I should like to express my thanks first and foremost to the Gitksan and Wet'suwet'en people. Their hospitality and cooperation not only helped me gain invaluable insights in their initiatives to regain ownership of and jurisdiction over their House Territories, but they also provided me with some first-hand experience of these Territories. I am grateful in particular to Maas Gaak (Don Ryan), Speaker for the Hereditary Chiefs of the Gitksan, Wii Seeks (Ralph Michell), Skanu'u (Ardythe Wilson), and Goo tsa gin (Art Loring), all from the Office of the Hereditary Chiefs of the Gitksan and Wet'suwet'en People. You certainly showed me just how much is at stake.

In Haida Gwaii I appreciate the cooperation of Miles Richardson, President of the Haida Tribal Society, of Guujaw, and Russ Jones of the Haida Fisheries Program. Special thanks to John Broadhead and Roger Hamilton, Superintendent of the South Moresby/Gwaii Haanas National Park Reserve.

In my home province, Alberta, I am grateful to the Peigan Nation. The Lonefighters and other band members, once again, allowed me to share their lives. My special thanks to all of you.

My visit to Fort Smith, N.W.T., would not have been the same without Shannon Cumming, who personified the South Slave Research Centre. His support made a relatively short visit not only unusually productive, but also very enjoyable. Special thanks are extended to Lloyd Binder and Sam Ransom of the Government of the N.W.T., Chief Henry Beaver of the Fort Smith Native Band, Doug Stewart, Superintendent of Wood Buffalo National Park, George Kurszewski, aboriginal Chairperson of the Northern Buffalo Management Board, Gilles Paquin, Coordinator of the Fort Fitzgerald Buffalo Management Program, Kenny Hudson, President of the Fort Smith Hunters and Trappers Association and Manager of the Hanging Ice Buffalo Ranch, Eddy Powder, trapper and member of the Beverly-Kaminuriak Caribou Management Board, and Sonny MacDonald, master carver.

In Yellowknife, Gordon Hamre of the Canadian Parks Service and Kevin McCormick of the Department of the Environment as well as member of the (Inuvialuit) Wildlife Management Advisory Committee, generously shared their time and experience.

In Inuvik I would like to acknowledge the support received from the Inuvik Research Centre, particularly Manager Gary White. Many individuals helped me gain an understanding of the implementation of the Inuvialuit Final Agreement, as it pertains to resource management: Norm Snow and Richard Binder of the Joint Secretariat; Gary Wagner, then Secretary of the Environmental Impact Review Board; Marshall Netherwood, then Secretary of the Environmental Impact Screening Committee; Michael Fabijan, Inuvialuit Harvest Study Coordinator; Bill Smith, Chief Park Warden of Ivvavik National Park; John Nagy and Bruce McLean of the N.W.T. Department of Renewable Resources; and Lois Harwood and William Day of the Department of Fisheries and Oceans. In Tuktoyuktuk special thanks to Charles Klingenberg, Assistant Land Administrator in the Inuvialuit Land Administration and Sandra Schlachter of the Hunters and Trappers Committee.

In Iqaluit, the Iqaluit Research Centre was not only a comfortable place to stay, but also a valuable source of information. A very special thank you is due to Manager Bob Longworth. Further thanks are extended to Jim Noble, Regional Superintendent, Renewable Resources, and to Tim Suretti, Area Manager for the Department of Fisheries and Oceans.

In Pangnirtung the local Parks Canada Office is a welcoming place to everybody, local and visitor alike. I want to express my heartfelt appreciation to Bruce Rigby, Superintendent, Eastern Arctic District National Parks, and Sakiasie Sowdlooapik, Visitor Service Officer, for the interest they expressed in my research and the valuable contributions they made in terms of shared information and experience. Further thanks are extended to Rebecca Mike, Pangnirtung MLA, and to Japodee Akpalialuk, Mayor of Pangnirtung. A final thank you to Stuart Innes, research scientist of the Department of Fisheries and Oceans, for interesting "beluga conversations".

In Manitoba I would like to thank Chief Harvey Nepinak and Raymond Marion of the Waterhen First Nation, and Harvey Payne and Karen Stock of Winnipeg, for sharing "wood bison experiences" with me.

In Ontario I would like to express my appreciation to Dean Jacobs, Research Director, and Nin.Da.Waab.Jig, the Walpole Island Research Centre. Nin.Da.Waab.Jig represents a unique example for an aboriginal research institution and producer of data. Thanks also to Dean for the information regarding the aboriginal participation in the Ontario Round Table on Environment and Economy.

An earlier research association with the Confederated Salish and Kootenai Tribes in Montana gave me access to an unusual example — to date without a Canadian counterpart — of an aboriginal "park": the Mission Mountains Tribal Wilderness. I extend my deep appreciation to Tom MacDonald, Program Manager of the CSKT Wildland Recreation Program, for a wealth of shared experience and documentation.

Many of the individuals encountered on my travels read selected draft chapters of this book, and offered their opinion, constructive criticism and advice either to myself or to the publisher. Thank you so much for your contribution. Other people with an interest and expertise in the field assisted the same way: Margaret Anderson of the University of Northern British Columbia, Prince George; Peter Burns, lawyer in Cranbrook, B.C.; Martin Weinstein, consultant in Comox, B.C.; and Beverly Bird of the National Aboriginal Forestry Association (NAFA), Ottawa. I thank each and every one of you.

Finally, I would like to consider my "home base", the University of Lethbridge. My profound gratitude goes to my colleague Doug Elias, who not only provided me with some important "grey" literature, but who also was a constant source of encouragement and inspiration throughout this project. I would also like to thank Karen Davies and Lynn Mather who pointed out interesting pieces of information which they came across in their research or travels. And last, but certainly not least, thanks are due to Fran Olivier, for the successful management of office details and "computer crises" as only she can do it!

The contributions of my friends, colleagues and readers are greatly appreciated, but the responsibility for the final result is mine.

1

Native Perspectives on Natural Resource Management

INTRODUCTION

The myth of a pristine pre-columbian landscape, untouched by human influence, is a popular one (Denevan 1992), but there is ample evidence to suggest that before the arrival of Europeans, aboriginal people not only used their resources but manipulated, impacted and sometimes in a very real sense "managed" their resources and environment. After Europeans appeared on the scene, most of the historical relationship between native and non-native people was characterized by competition for land and resources.

An important exception to this state of competition was the Canadian fur trade, which was essentially based on a partnership between native and European groups for the cooperative exploitation of the fur resource. When the fur trade era came to an end (which in large parts of the country happened in 1870, with the transfer of Rupert's Land and the Northwestern Territory from the Hudson's Bay Company to the Dominion of Canada), so did whatever partnership that had existed between native and non-native groups. The following century was characterized by intense competition for land and resources and a continuing erosion of native rights.

It has only been during the last two decades that aboriginal people have made substantial progress in regaining some of their use and management rights to land and resources. Along with this progress has come the prospect of a new partnership between aboriginal and non-aboriginal people, this time not a partnership of resource exploitation, but rather a partnership for resource management and conservation.

RESOURCE MANAGEMENT: THE CONCEPT

Although everyone seems to know what "natural resource management" means, the term is not easily defined or comfortably used, particularly in the aboriginal context.

> The concept of "resource management", given the relationship of many Native people to the natural environment, is as foreign to them as the courts in which they have argued their rights to lands and "resources". The words "resource" and "management" imply a human superiority incompatible with the holistic values expressed by many traditional Native people. (Shapcott 1989:72)

The term "resource management" is firmly rooted in the traditions of western industrialized society and thus carries much ideological baggage.

> A resource is something that is useful and valuable in the condition in which we find it. In its raw or unmodified state, it may be an input into the process of producing something of value, or it may enter consumption processes directly and thus be valued as an amenity.... "Resource" is a dynamic concept, and the possibility always exists that changes in information, technology and relative scarcity may make a valuable resource out of that which previously had no value. Second, things that are produced under human guidance in processes that combine resources, capital, technology, and/or labor, are not themselves called resources, although resources are always among the inputs used to produce them. (Randall 1981:13f)

The concept of resources is thus a dynamic one, and it is culturally circumscribed. Not without reason, Erich W. Zimmermann states that "resources are not, they become." (Zimmermann 1964:21). Resource management is a complex decision-making process which ideally involves inventory, assessment, goal formulation, policies, programs, legislation, administration and managerial strategies. It comprises biophysical, economic, social, political, legal, institutional and technological perspectives as well as temporal and spatial dimensions (Krueger and Mitchell 1977:6f).

It needs to be acknowledged that many aboriginal people, particularly the elders, are uncomfortable with the term "resource management", not only because there is no equivalent term in aboriginal languages, but also because it implies a sense of superiority over nature and a sense of apartness from it. Many non-native environmentalists express the same concerns. Nevertheless, native people have traditionally employed and are still employing measures of resource manipulation and conservation which would normally be associated with what is referred to as resource management. Therefore, if the term "resource management" is utilized in this book for those actions and decision-making processes which concern the assessment, allocation and utilization of elements of the natural environment by man, it is done strictly for pragmatic reasons and for lack of a different term in the English language that is equally comprehensive and universally understood. It should not be taken as an endorsement of and subscription to the attitude that is commonly associated with it.

SIGNIFICANCE OF NATURAL RESOURCES IN THE ABORIGINAL CONTEXT

With regard to natural resources, native people in Canada are looking back on a history of exclusion and denial of power. In the past this denial was explicit and blatant, as exemplified by the Colonial Land Ordinance of 1870, which specifically prohibited any Indian from claiming a right of land pre-emption (Mathias and Yabsley 1991:35). In a similar vein, the Indian Act of 1876 barred Indian people from the acquisition of land in Manitoba and the North-West Territories. Section 70 of that Act provided that:

> 70. No Indian or non-Treaty Indian, resident in the province of Manitoba, the North-West Territories or the territory of Keewatin, shall be held capable of having acquired or acquiring a homestead or pre-emption right to a quarter section, or any portion of land in any surveyed or unsurveyed lands in the said province of Manitoba, the North-West Territories or the territory of Keewatin, or the right to share in the distribution of any lands allotted to halfbreeds. (ibid.:36)

In Yukon, the Game Ordinance of 1923 was amended to refuse licensing Indians as commercial big-game hunting outfitters. The intent behind this amendment was the elimination of Indians as competitors of non-aboriginal and often non-Canadian outfitters already in the business (Elias 1991:43).

In the late twentieth century, restrictions on aboriginal people's access to natural resources are less blatant, but aboriginal people are still operating in an "environment of constraint" (ibid.). Legislative devices, such as the Indian Act, the Indian Oil and Gas Act and the Regulations, made thereunder vest control, management and disposition of Indian lands and resources in the Department of Indian Affairs. These Acts and Regulations make no allowance for aboriginal self-government or even self-management, and this legislation remains essentially unchanged (Bartlett 1990:136). Indian treaty rights have a tradition of restrictive interpretation and have certainly not assisted Indian people in gaining access to off-reserve resources. Metis and non-status Indians have historically been denied any special rights. By and large, provincial and federal political agendas have tended to favour aboriginal people's competitors for natural resources.

However, before this background, the 1980s and 1990s have been witnessing a redefinition of the relationship between native and non-native Canadians, and as part of it, a restructuring of power and responsibility with regard to natural resources. This restructuring has been acted out in many different arenas and on many different fronts: at negotiating tables and in the political arena, in the courts and out on the land.

Several key events and developments set things in motion. The entrenchment of aboriginal and treaty rights in the Canadian Constitution Act of 1982 by means of Section 35 has focused increased attention on contents and substance of these rights, particularly as they pertain to renewable resources. The 1980s and early 1990s also witnessed the negotiation of Agreements-in-Principle, Umbrella Final Agreements and Final Agreements with aboriginal people of Yukon and the Northwest Territories, and the ratification of the Inuvialuit Final Agreement, the Nunavut Land Claims Agreement and the Gwich'in Agreement. Northern comprehensive claims settlements invariably feature access to and control over natural resources as one of their principal elements.

In 1990 the Supreme Court of Canada ruling on *Sparrow* (R. v. Sparrow [1990] 3 C.N.L.R. 160) sent shockwaves not only through British Columbia but through the entire nation. Federal and provincial government departments — particularly those concerned with resource management — are still grappling with the implications of this ruling. Also in 1990, after a century of denial, the government of British Columbia decided to acknowledge the validity of comprehensive claims in that province, a step which is already transforming the resource management regime of the region. In the summer of 1990, aboriginal people all over Canada turned out in force on land, rivers and sea with the message that, should they fail to attain their goal of increased control over their land and their resources in the courts and through negotiation, they would proceed to assert their rights. And finally, control over land and resources is also considered an integral part of the First Nations' inherent right to self-government as brought into the discussion of constitutional reform in the 1990s.

With regard to aboriginal people's thrust towards a right to resources — no matter whether we are concerned with treaty rights, aboriginal rights, or rights evolving from comprehensive claims settlements — it is important to realize that native groups do not just want access to and a fair share of the resources in question, but they also strive for participation in the management of these resources. They want to share in the power to make decisions about the fate of the land and the resources it supports. Native people are also interested in opportunities to contribute their traditional knowledge to the resource management regimes they helped to set up. In short, they want to be partners in resource management. The arrangement which has been used to pursue this goal has become known under several names, such as co-management, joint management or joint stewardship. Further discussion will indicate that it has experienced its greatest proliferation with regard to wildlife.

SIGNIFICANCE OF ABORIGINAL RESOURCE MANAGEMENT

In this age of environmental crisis the significance of past and present aboriginal resource management practices transcends immediate aboriginal concerns of economic development, maintenance of traditional socio-economic systems, definition of rights, claims settlements, etc. A recognition of the need to fundamentally rethink established western resource use practices and power structures is gradually permeating many sections of North American society. Such rethinking has opened many communication channels between aboriginal and non-aboriginal stakeholders in the environment and has rendered a two-way exchange of environmental knowledge increasingly attractive and feasible.

In 1980 and 1987 respectively, the World Conservation Strategy and the World Commission on Environment and Development coined the term "sustainable development". The Brundtland Commission acknowledged the contribution which aboriginal people are able to make in this area and endorsed aboriginal self-government with regard to natural resources.

> Sustainable development is development that meets the needs of the present without compromising the ability of future generations to meet their own needs. (The World Commission on Environment and Development 1987:43)
>
> These communities [so-called indigenous or tribal peoples] are the repositories of vast accumulations of traditional knowledge and experience that links humanity with its ancient origins. Their disappearance is a loss for the larger society, which could learn a great deal from their traditional skills in sustainably managing very complex ecological systems. It is a terrible irony that as formal development reaches more deeply into rain forests, deserts, and other isolated environments, it tends to destroy the only cultures that have proved able to thrive in these environments.
>
> The starting point for a just and humane policy for such groups is the recognition and protection of their traditional rights to land and the other resources that sustain their way of life — rights they may define in terms that do not fit into standard legal systems. These groups' own institutions to regulate rights and obligations are crucial for maintaining the harmony with nature and the environmental awareness characteristic of the traditional way of life. Hence the recognition of traditional rights must go hand in hand with measures to protect the local institutions that enforce responsibility in resource use. And this recognition must also give local communities a decisive voice in the decisions about resource use in their area. (ibid.:115f)

The Brundtland Report's popularization of the concept of sustainable development has engendered a voluminous literature on the subject. Not surprisingly, there has been much overuse and abuse of the term. However, this should not distract from the significance of the concept, nor should it disguise the fact that for many aboriginal communities there is nothing new about sustainable development. This becomes evident from statements by Norma Kassi of Old Crow, Yukon, and Peter Green of Paulatuk, Northwest Territories.

> So in spite of all the threats to our way of life, I have to be optimistic about the prospects for the basic ideas of conservation and even though scientists like to use big words when they talk about conservation — words like sustainable development, biological diversity, and ecological stability — to my people of Old Crow, it all means **survival** to us. All the fancy concepts in the world conservation strategy come down to that one idea in communities like Old Crow — **survival**. There really is no acceptable alternative to conservation for my people — at least if we want anything like our present lifestyle and if we want a future which follows our tradition. (Kassi 1990:97, emphasis in original)
>
> Conservation is ensuring that if we take caribou, there will be caribou the next year and the year after that. The same for anything else. This applies to all uses of the land: if it is used and enjoyed now, it must be left and preserved so that it will be there for the next year and for future years. (Peter Green, Paulatuk Conservation Working Group, in The Community of Paulatuk and The Wildlife Management Advisory Council [NWT] 1990:6)

While sustainable development may not be new to many aboriginal communities, something else is: a growing opportunity to practise, develop, preserve and share their ideas and experiences in this field. While this is still a slow process not devoid of numerous obstacles, government resource managers and policy makers are increasingly willing to listen to what aboriginal resource users want to say and to devolve part of their decision-making power. This is evident in the numerous co-management regimes currently being established throughout the country.

There are other signs. In the late 1980s the Inuit Regional Conservation Strategy was developed, representing the first attempt by an indigenous people to devise a conservation strategy (Doubleday 1990:83). Regional as well as individual community-based conservation plans were a direct outcome of the implementation of the Inuvialuit Final Agreement, the Paulatuk Conservation Plan being the first one to be completed.

In Ontario in 1991, a Native People's Circle on Environment and Development was established as an integral part of the Ontario Round Table on Environment and Economy to explain the native perspective on sustainable development. In the early 1990s the Hudson Bay Program was set up, which was a joint initiative of CARC (Canadian Arctic Resources Committee), the Rawson Academy of Aquatic Science and the Environmental Committee of Sanikiluaq (Belcher Islands) to study the cumulative effects of development projects on Hudson Bay. One important element of this program is the examination of traditional environmental knowledge in Inuit and Cree communities around Hudson Bay (Okrainetz 1992:14f).

TRADITIONAL ENVIRONMENTAL KNOWLEDGE

All these developments — improvement in aboriginal people's access to natural resources, aboriginal participation in resource management through joint management regimes and native people's participation in national and international conservation and sustainable development initiatives — have brought the importance of indigenous peoples' traditional environmental knowledge (TEK) into sharp focus. They have resulted in joint efforts to preserve this knowledge for the future and to make it accessible to resource users and managers.

> Knowledge is the condition of knowing something with familiarity gained through experience or association. The traditional knowledge of northern aboriginal peoples has roots based firmly in the northern landscape and a land-based life experience of thousands of years. Traditional knowledge offers a view of the world, aspirations, and an avenue to "truth", different from those held by non-aboriginal people whose knowledge is based largely on European philosophies. (Department of Culture and Communications, Government of the Northwest Territories 1991:11, quoted in Bielawski 1992:6)
>
> Traditional knowledge is the accumulated knowledge and understanding of the place of human beings in relation to the world in both an ecological and spiritual sense. (Hobson 1992:2)

However, as Mary Simon, President of the Inuit Circumpolar Conference, points out, several questions and challenges remain after the acknowledgement of the value of traditional knowledge.

> What exactly is traditional knowledge?
>
> How can it be made available outside of the oral tradition of indigenous peoples?
>
> How can indigenous peoples be assured control of their knowledge?

and very importantly,

> Is it itself a "sustainable" resource, or is it, like the environment around us, deteriorating under the assault from often overwhelming external social and cultural forces?
>
> ....
>
> It must also be fully accepted that this knowledge base is the intellectual property of indigenous peoples and not, as have their lands, a resource to be exploited. Non-indigenous institutions, agencies or governments becoming involved in this process must come to it from a position based on support and respect, not appropriation.
>
> ....

> The mentality that underlies any initiative, however, must not be driven by a simple desire to "salvage" a disappearing knowledge base. Rather it must be driven by an understanding why traditional knowledge is important in a modern context. (Simon 1991:1f)

The documentation of traditional environmental knowledge is a burgeoning field of research which is primarily controlled and directed by aboriginal people, with outside agencies providing technical advice and administrative support. The Dene Cultural Institute Pilot Project is an example of a participatory community project that is designed to document the traditional environmental knowledge of the people of Fort Good Hope and Colville Lake. In the early 1990s a team of local researchers, a biologist and an anthropologist have started developing methods to document TEK. The ultimate goal of this project is to integrate TEK and western science for the purpose of community-based natural resource management (Johnson 1992:3).

CONCLUSION

With regard to natural resource use and management, Canada's aboriginal people are still operating within an environment of constraint, while at the same time the last decade has constituted a period of extremely rapid change. The 1980s and early 1990s have witnessed an increasing empowerment of aboriginal people which has been brought about by closely interconnected developments on many different fronts, such as constitutional development, court decisions, policy changes and the claims process. As a catalyst for these developments the last two decades have also witnessed a gradual transformation in the ideas of social justice and environmental consciousness on the part of mainstream society and, concurrently, an increased degree of politicization of aboriginal people.

The efficient use of land and resources such as water, fish, forests, wildlife and non-renewable resources, constitutes an important component of many aboriginal development strategies. In these rapidly changing times aboriginal people, therefore, face a maze of options in terms of what is legally possible, economically feasible, socially acceptable and culturally appropriate.

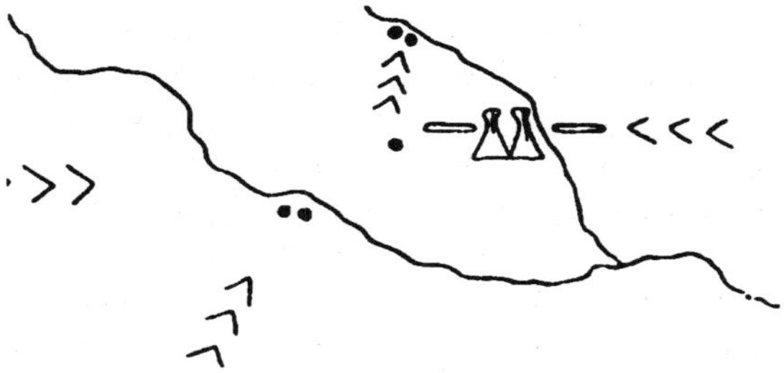

2 Water Resources

INTRODUCTION

> Water — aside from our own children — is the most valuable resource we have. (Dan Boggs, Blackfeet Tribal Council, Montana, May 23, 1991, Intertribal Water Resources Conference, Sarcee Reserve, Alberta)

> I am part of that water, and water is part of me. (Chief Gordon Antoine, Coldwater Indian Band, British Columbia, June 25, 1991, Indian Water Rights Workshop, Vernon, British Columbia)

> Quebec is a vast hydro-electric plant in the bud, and every day, millions of potential kilowatt hours flow downhill and out to sea. What a waste! (Robert Bourassa 1985, quoted in Linton 1991:28)

In the context of natural resource use by aboriginal peoples and constraints thereof, water occupies a unique position. Water in itself constitutes a distinct "resource" in the narrower Euro-Canadian sense, for consumptive and non-consumptive use for irrigation, hydroelectricity, recreation and domestic purposes. Water also functions as an all-pervasive life-force for native people, in a physical sense as habitat for wild rice, fish, waterfowl and game, thus supporting a harvesting, fishing, hunting and trapping way of life, and in a less tangible spiritual sense, which has been documented by native people's testimony in such diverse environments as British Columbia's west coast, the Oldman River in southern Alberta and the Mackenzie River. It is obvious, therefore, that a lack of definition and protection of native water rights is bound to have equally all-pervasive and potentially disastrous consequences.

At the same time, native rights to ownership and management of water resources, as compared to other natural resources, are even less well defined or documented by case law. In Canada there is no comprehensive native water law in existence. For this reason and in view of the fact that Indian water law in the United States is founded on the principles of interpretation of treaties and statutes which have also been recently endorsed by the Supreme Court of Canada in *Nowegijick* and *Simon* (Bartlett 1989:180f),[1] it seems appropriate to briefly consider the native water rights situation south of the border.

---

[1] In the landmark case of *Nowegijick* v. *The Queen*, a unanimous court decision declared that "treaties and statutes relating to Indians should be liberally construed and doubtful expressions resolved in favour of the Indian." (*Nowegijick* v. *The Queen* [1983] 2 C.N.L.R. 89 (S.C.C.) at 94, 46 N.R. 41)

Due to reasons of physical geography as well as historical factors (resulting in the present distribution of the Indian population in the United States), water rights issues in connection with Indian lands have always held a greater significance in the United States than in Canada. Over 80 per cent of Indian lands are concentrated in 11 western states with an arid or semi-arid climate. Protection and guarantee of sufficient water resources are considered vital to the economic survival of reservation communities. United States Indian water rights are defined by the so-called "Winters' Doctrine," which is based on a 1908 federal court decision. The Winters' Doctrine acknowledges every Indian reservation's implied right to sufficient water to make it economically viable. This ruling runs counter to most western states' water-related legislations ("Doctrine of Prior Appropriation": "First in time, first in right"; "use it or lose it"). Riparian rights are only recognized in the eastern United States. Its inherent problem is the fact that such water right is "open-ended". Its quantification and the question of state involvement in its adjudication pose innumerable problems. Although theoretically the Winters' Doctrine puts native groups in a favourable position to negotiate with other water users, throughout this century it has failed to protect Indian people from the most disastrous consequences of non-Indian water developments, mostly federally funded megaprojects, such as the Salt River Project in Arizona (1907), the "Pick-Sloan Plan" for the Missouri River (1944–1966) (Lawson 1985) and the San Juan Chama Project, which was authorized by Congress in 1962. The United States government invariably ignored the Winters' Doctrine and its own role as a federal trustee, thereby allowing the impoverishment of western Indian reservations by state diversions of water, inundation of tribal lands and the destruction of Indian agricultural resources. As C.P. Morris (1985:244) concludes, "Like the taking of Indian land, the taking of Indian water has underwritten much of western United States economic development." Moreover, in recent years native people in the United States have been subjected to an erosion of their water rights both by court decisions and through the policies of the Federal Government (Corke 1985:142). Thus the existence of Indian water rights in the United States has so far proven to be more symbolic than real.

In Canada there have been no precedential court rulings on native water rights, but legal scholars agree that native people do indeed have some water rights deriving from different sources (Barton 1985; Bartlett 1988). The situation, however, is extremely complex and subject to considerable variation from region to region.

SCOPE AND ORIGIN OF NATIVE WATER RIGHTS IN CANADA

Native water rights in Canada derive from three distinct sources. First, they are an integral part of native people's aboriginal title to their ancestral lands. Second, Indian water rights result from the establishment of a reserve, either by treaty or by executive action (Order-in-Council). Third, native people enjoy riparian rights derived from their occupation of lands adjoining a body of water. Aboriginal and treaty rights to water are uniquely native rights, while riparian rights are common law rights held by all Canadians. (The French civil law provides similar rights to landowners in Quebec.)

Aboriginal Rights to Water

The landmark case *Calder v. Attorney General of British Columbia* ([1973] S.C.R. 313, [1973] 4 W.W.R. 1, 34 D.L.R. (3d) 145) left little doubt that native water rights are indeed an aspect of aboriginal title. Justice Hall described aboriginal title as "a right to

---

This ruling was confirmed by a unanimous Supreme Court of Canada in *R.* v. *Simon* (1985), 62 N.R. 366 (S.C.C.) at 377.

occupy the lands and to enjoy the fruits of the soil, the forest and of the rivers and streams." (Bartlett 1988:7) Thus aboriginal title includes but does not distinguish between land and water. While we may thus assume that the concept of aboriginal title recognizes water rights as a part of the title, Richard Bartlett (1988:8) notes that it also suggests significant qualifications as to its scope. Water rights derived from aboriginal title may be limited to historic and traditional uses. Court decisions have tended to confirm this conclusion. For example, in *Attorney General for Ontario v. Bear Island Foundation* ([1985] 1 C.N.L.R. 1 (Ont.S.C.), 49 O.R. (2d) 353), Judge Steele determined that "the essence of aboriginal rights is the right of Indians to continue to live on their lands as their forefathers lived." He further concluded that aboriginal title was confined to "traditional uses for basic survival and personal ornamentation." (ibid.:8f) They included the right to fish and to trap, as well as the right to use water for transportation, traditional irrigation, and domestic consumption. The judge clearly did not consider that aboriginal title to water authorized modern uses for production of hydroelectric power or for irrigation. While the language of various court proceedings in Canada as well as the United States is far from consistent, a comprehensive analysis prior to 1990 did suggest that aboriginal title to water is confined to traditional uses, and that more extensive rights only arise upon the establishment of a reserve, whether by treaty or otherwise (ibid.: 13). But even this limited right could be sufficiently powerful to restrain the development of any major water resource project. It was the existence of the aboriginal title of an indigenous population which compelled the Quebec Superior Court to issue an interim injunction restraining the James Bay Hydro Project, eventually resulting in the James Bay and Northeastern Quebec Agreements.

The Supreme Court of Canada ruling on *Sparrow* (Sparrow v. R. [1990] 3 C.N.L.R.) in 1990, however, shed a different light on the situation. The ruling states explicitly:

> An existing aboriginal right cannot be read so as to incorporate the specific manner in which it was regulated before 1982. The phrase "existing aboriginal rights" must be interpreted flexibly **so as to permit their evaluation over time**. (Sparrow v. R. [1990] 3 C.N.L.R.: 161, emphasis added)

In the light of *Sparrow*, legal counsel for the Peigan Nation in its water rights case against the Province of Alberta, Gary Nelson, feels that the aboriginal right to water is highly flexible and adaptable. The right is neither quantified nor qualified, but it must be viewed in a modern context and negotiated according to a "living tree principle" (Gary Nelson, May 23, 1991, Intertribal Water Resources Conference, Sarcee Reserve, Alberta). Bartlett agrees that *Sparrow* would favour "contemporary" rather than only traditional use of water resources by aboriginal people (Richard Bartlett, Indian Water Rights Workshop, Vernon, British Columbia, June 24, 1991).

Treaty Rights to Water

Although treaties (or other agreements or executive orders) do not expressly mention water rights, it seems reasonable to infer that they were intended to guarantee Indian bands at least enough water for the development of their reserve lands, particularly agricultural development (Barton 1985:18; Bartlett 1989:179). This is considering the purpose for which reserves were set aside, namely to enable aboriginal people to become settled and "civilized" people in the European mold, and to encourage the adoption of non-traditional uses of the land and water. This conclusion was reached in the landmark water rights case *Winters v. United States* (207 U.S. 564 (1908), 52 L.Ed. 340, aff'g 143 F. 740 (9th Cir. 1906)) which resulted in the formulation of the "Winters' Doctrine". This type of Indian water right is very significant, since it covers present as well as future needs of water, and theoretically can be used for all beneficial purposes. The unique character of the treaty right to water also entails numerous pitfalls which is borne out by the developments in the United States.

Three issues in particular have dominated the controversy: the quantum of volume of the Indian right, the legitimate uses to which the water guaranteed by the right can be put and the priority of the right in relation to the rights of non-Indian users. (Hundley 1985:79) Historically, the most important basic measure of need was the irrigable area of a reserve. This quantification and the question of state involvement in the adjudication have always been (and still are) extremely problematic for Indian people. This is even more so after the *Arizona v. California* case (373 U.S. 546 (1963), 10 L. Ed. 2d 542) where the term "practicably irrigable" was adopted (Corke 1985:143). The Supreme Court used the term extensively without ever defining it. In recent years the departments of Justice and Interior have tended to impose their notion of economic feasibility on native people in their interpretation of "practicably irrigable", which has resulted in a further reduction of Indian water rights.[2] Also, since Indian reserves in Canada ,as well as in the United States, were devised, either explicitly or implicitly, to transform native people into farmers in the European mold (unless they already followed a farming way of life), there has been a tendency to view native water rights exclusively in terms of irrigation needs. If these rights were to be conceived within the wider framework of (socio) economic viability and development of tribal homelands, other traditional as well as innovative water uses by the native communities would have to receive more attention, including hunting and fishing, wild rice harvesting, recreation and hydroelectricity.

As a result of constitutional developments and the *Sparrow* ruling it is possible, however, that some problems encountered in the United States may be avoided in Canada if or when the notion of "reserved water rights" becomes operative in this country. With regard to quantification and qualification of such rights, the *Sparrow* ruling is likely to affect not only aboriginal rights but also treaty rights, which would imply a flexible common sense approach to the interpretation of reserved rights to water. Furthermore, Gary Nelson explains that, in contrast to the United States, a priority date of water rights is of no consequence in Canada, since treaty and aboriginal rights enjoy constitutional priority. He also stresses that Indian water rights in Canada should be free from provincial regulation, since Canada has no legislation equivalent to the American McCarran Amendment of 1952, which was the crucial piece of legislation whereby the federal government relinquished its exclusive responsibility for water rights issues on federal lands. (Intertribal Water Resources Conference, Sarcee Reserve, Alberta, May 23, 1991)

While the cession of aboriginal lands and the establishment of reserves were core elements of most treaties, they also promised the native signatories continuing rights to hunt and fish throughout the unoccupied lands of the treaty area. Barry Barton (1985:19) suggests that without adequate habitat protection such rights would be useless, and therefore Treaty Indians must possess implied rights to prevent damage to wildlife habitat, including the aquatic habitat. During the Intertribal Water Resources Conference in 1991, Gary Waters, INAC General Director, admitted that the federal government has not defined its position vis-à-vis an intervention in favour of hunting, trapping and fishing rights on unoccupied Crown lands: "The jury is out as to what our role may be." He did feel, however, that there might be "a good case for Indian water jurisdiction." (Gary Waters, Intertribal Water Resources Conference, Sarcee Reserve, Alberta, May 23, 1991)

The only reported Canadian case concerning a treaty right to water use was tried in British Columbia in 1987. In *Saanichton Marina Ltd. v. Claxton* ((1987), 18 B.C. L.C. (2d) 217 (B.C. S.C.), [1987] 4 C.N.L.R. 48) the treaty right to use water to maintain a traditional fishery was upheld (Bartlett 1989:180). The Tsawout Indian Band on Vancouver

---

[2] For further discussion of the implications of the usage of Practicably Irrigable Acreage for the quantification of water rights, see Franks 1991.

Island succeeded in preventing the construction of a marina in a bay which band members had traditionally fished. This court decision could have far-reaching implications. Bartlett (1988:36) hypothesizes that "It may well be that in Canada the treaty right to water will first be addressed by the courts in the context of hunting, trapping, and fishing, rather than agriculture. The principles of interpretation are, of course, the same."

Legally, there are no indications either in Canada or the United States that any particular native use of water is excluded from the consideration of treaty rights to water. Agriculture, including stock-raising and wild rice harvesting; and hunting, fishing, and trapping are obviously within the contemplated objectives of the treaties (ibid.:67). The most economically rewarding use of water today, which is the generation of hydroelectricity, poses some questions. No reported case in the United States has contemplated the rights of native people to use water for hydroelectric power. But a corollary of such right was upheld in *United States v. 5,677.94 Acres of the Crow Reservation* (162 F. Supp. 108 (D. Mont. 1958). The District Court ruled that the Crow Tribe was entitled to just compensation for the water power value of reservation land that was expropriated. In agreement with Bartlett (1988:67), it is safe to conclude that "Entitlement to compensation for expropriation of water power suggests the right to use water for such purposes." According to common law in Canada, a riparian landowner is entitled to use the water flowing by his/her land for power generation provided it does not interfere with the rights of other riparian landowners. The landowner is entitled to make use of the difference between the level where the water first enters the land and where it leaves. According to Bartlett (ibid.:68), it would seem appropriate in this context to conclude that Indian water rights set apart by treaty or executive order extend to the generation of hydroelectricity, thus permitting sale to users off reserve lands.

A 1905 Canada-Ontario agreement pertaining to Treaty No. Nine (1905) sought to exclude all lands having a water power capacity in excess of 500 horsepower from reserves set apart by this treaty. In 1915 Ontario unilaterally sought to exclude similar lands from reserves set apart in accordance with Treaty No. Three (An Act to confirm the title of the Government of Canada to certain lands and Indian Lands, S.O. 1915, c.12) in 1873, but provided for compensation of 10 per cent of all purchases and royalties. In 1924, Canada and Ontario negotiated another agreement concerning the development of reserve lands in that province (An Act for the settlement of certain questions between the Governments of Canada and Ontario respecting Indian Reserve Land, S.C. 1924, c.48). The Agreement declared that no water power on a reserve exceeding 500 horsepower could be disposed of by the Dominion except in agreement with the province and on such terms as were agreed upon, respecting the division of royalties and purchases. This provision was also applied to reserves in Manitoba, Saskatchewan and Alberta by the Natural Resources Transfer Agreements in 1930, although the Prairie Provinces were not given the right to share in the proceeds with respect to the development of hydroelectricity on reserves set apart prior to 1930. These federal-provincial agreements indicate an accepted understanding that Indian water rights set apart by treaty or by executive appropriation extend to hydroelectricity generation both for on-reserve use and for sale to other users (Bartlett 1988:69).

British Columbia occupies a special position in Canada with regard to the setting aside of Indian water rights in conjunction with reserve lands. Unlike other provinces in Canada, the issue was subject to a prolonged dispute between the province and the federal government. With the exception of the province's northeast corner and southern Vancouver Island, no treaties were ever signed with British Columbia's First Nations. By the time settlement expanded and the provision of reserve lands became necessary, the Colony had joined Confederation, but under terms which gave the province ownership and jurisdiction over public lands and waters. Reserves could only be allocated by the federal government upon agreement with the province. Nevertheless, the Joint Commission for the settlement of Indian reserve questions established in 1876, unlike anywhere else in Canada, proceeded to expressly ater rights along with the appropriation of reserve lands. These water allocations ally took place in the more arid interior agencies of Fraser, Kamloops-Okanagan, Williams Lake; there were none in the Kootenay, Kwawkewith, North West Coast or vest Coast agencies. The allotments of water made by the Commissioners usually noted the source and quantity of water allocated for each reserve, and were invariably made subject to the prior recorded rights of white settlers (Bartlett 1988:48). However, the province has never recognized the Commission's allotment of water, claiming that it was beyond the Commissioners' authority to make such grants. Despite the fact that the province passed an Order-in-Council approving the Minutes of Decision of the Commission in 1878, the province has maintained that this approval applied only to land grants and not to water allotments (Doran 1982:3).

Riparian Rights

Riparian rights are the third source of rights for native people to take and use water, in addition to their aboriginal and treaty rights. According to Barton (1985:19f), riparian rights

> ...may simply be described as rights to water that may be enjoyed by any owner or occupier of land by virtue of the fact that the land adjoins a lake or a river, whether or not it includes the bed of the lake or river. They are common law rights, which may be varied or abolished by statute....Riparian rights include only limited rights to make use of water, but correspondingly they include rights for a downstream riparian owner to have the flow of water and the quality of water to remain substantially unaffected....Their main significance in the present context is that they provide a legal basis for protecting waters from disruption of the natural state of a watercourse upstream. Pollution, water diversion or water storage are the types of activity that would affect riparian rights and would therefore give rise to a right to sue — in the absence of statutory authorization for that activity.

Riparian rights are significant for native people since notably many of the reserves provided for in the treaties were to be located on the banks or shores of specified bodies of water, or to include a particular lake or bay. Native water rights based upon a treaty, agreement, or the executive appropriation of reserve lands are substantially broader in scope than those derived from riparian ownership of land. But riparian rights do pose a formidable constraint on upstream users. Commercial and industrial uses that deplete water supply, disturb its flow or impair its quality will breach the rights of a riparian landowner. According to Bartlett (1988:57), riparian rights, like aboriginal title, suffice to protect the traditional and domestic uses of water by aboriginal people.

Whether we are dealing with native water rights based on aboriginal title, treaty or riparian land ownership, it is crucial to emphasize that in common law, water itself cannot be the subject of ownership (ibid.:76). Native water rights imply rights of occupation and use, but not ownership of the water itself. Canadian court cases have not considered this question, but United States decisions confirm the conclusion that Indian water rights are "usufructuary" and not rights of ownership.

A different but equally important right associated with water is the right of ownership of the water bed or foreshore of a river, lake or sea. This right confers control over such projects as the construction of dams, weirs, bridges or wharves. It also brings with it the exclusive right of trapping and fishing and often includes ownership of underlying mineral resources. Courts in Atlantic Canada, Ontario and British Columbia have adopted the so-called "English rule", and have recognized the presumption of ownership of the water bed of navigable as well as non-navigable water bodies by the riparian owner (ibid.:83). This right of ownership applies to lakes as well as rivers, but has never been applied to the St. Lawrence River or the Great Lakes. In Quebec and the Prairie Provinces, navigable waters are exempted from the presumption of riparian ownership. This denies native people some of their most significant traditional waterways: The Red, Pembina, Winnipeg, Saskatchewan,

Assiniboine, Ottawa, and Gatineau rivers. They have all been held to be navigable. The same applies to the Churchill River and Lake Winnipeg. Also, no Indian band may assert ownership of the foreshore or bed of tidal waters on the basis of their riparian location.[3]

Where native ownership of the water bed is unimpaired, it does endow its holders with significant powers. Governments cannot undertake major water control projects on reserve lands without Band Council authorization, based on the Indian ownership of the land and s.81(f) of the Indian Act. Section 81(f) empowers a Band to make by-laws respecting "the construction and maintenance of water courses". The only exception would be in the case of expropriation under s.35 of the Indian Act which, however, requires the consent of the Governor in Council. In the event that a water-control fixture was constructed upon the Indian-owned water bed, it would become the property of the owner of the bed as, for instance, the diversion weir on the Oldman River on the Peigan Reserve, Alberta.

REGULATION AND ABROGATION OF NATIVE WATER RIGHTS

The previous section has shown that aboriginal people do in fact have substantial water rights which, if properly protected, could provide a powerful safeguard for traditional as well as modern water uses by native communities. But how safe are these rights, particularly from provincial interference and takeover? As Bartlett (1988:121) indicates,

> There is little room for the application of provincial legislation with respect to aboriginal waters. First, the Indian Act has provided for federal government and Band Council control of 'waters and watercourses' and of 'fishing and trapping', and secondly, the regulation of water rights is 'of the essence of' the jurisdiction with respect to 'lands reserved for Indians'.

Prior to 1982 it was generally assumed that the federal government was empowered to unilaterally abrogate aboriginal rights and title (ibid.:122). Yet since the passing of s.35 of the Constitution Act, 1982, it seems that "existing aboriginal and treaty rights" may only be extinguished by a constitutional amendment or by agreement with the aboriginal people.

Public water resources policy was not developed in Canada until the end of the nineteenth century. Several provinces proceeded at that time and thereafter to vest ownership and administration of water rights and riparian lands in the Crown. By that time many Indian reserves had already been set apart. As in the past, the provinces are in no position to regulate or abrogate existing aboriginal water rights, as that would be an invasion of federal jurisdiction under s.91(24) of the Constitution Act, 1867. No such inability hindered the federal government until the enactment of s.35 of the Constitution Act, 1982. The degree to which native water rights have been left intact by the legislatures varies considerably from province to province, and particularly between the eastern and western part of the country.

Eastern Provinces

In eastern Canada — the Atlantic provinces, southern Quebec and Ontario — Indian water rights are substantially unimpaired. There has been no vesting of government ownership and administration of water resources in southern Quebec, New Brunswick and Prince Edward Island (ibid.:142, 211), and restrictions on the granting of riparian lands occurred too late to prevent Indian ownership. Nova Scotia, Ontario, and Newfoundland have enacted general legislations aimed at the abrogation of water rights, but these legislations were also passed after most reserves were already established and after Confederation; hence, too late to have any significant effect on Indian water rights.

---

[3] For a detailed legal history of the Ad Medium Filum Aquae Rule determining title to the water bed in Ontario, the Prairie Provinces and British Columbia, see Wuerscher 1982.

Prairie Provinces

The situation is more complex in the Prairie Provinces. The provincial governments commonly assert that Indian water rights were abrogated by legislation (Bartlett 1989:184). The legislation invoked for this statement is the Northwest Irrigation Act of 1894 and its successors. The Northwest Irrigation Act was passed when Parliament still had unrestricted legislative powers in the region. It was designed to abolish riparian rights which might stand in the way of major irrigation diversions. The Act (which excluded southern Manitoba) deemed all property and rights of use in any river or body of water to be vested in the Crown, except to the extent that an inconsistent private right of use was established. Any person holding previous water rights was required to obtain a licence, failing which the rights were forfeited to the Crown. After the passing of the Act, acquisition of water rights by riparian title or Crown grant was barred. The statute effectively abrogated the common law notion that water was not the subject of ownership and the common law concept of riparian rights to water appropriation.

The question of whether the Northwest Irrigation Act is applicable to Indian water rights on the Prairies has never been conclusively answered. Apparently, the Department of Indian Affairs did not apply for water licences to protect the reserves' water rights. It may, however, be argued that the Act is not applicable to native water rights. As Bartlett (ibid.) points out, the question is one of the intention of Parliament. The recent Supreme Court of Canada rulings (see footnote 1) suggest the need for a "clear and plain indication" to abrogate Indian property rights, specific rather than general wording, and the resolution of ambiguities in favour of the Indians. The Northwest Irrigation Act does not explicitly refer to Indian reserves or Indian water rights and, therefore, does not suggest any "clear and plain indication" to abrogate these rights.

To date there is no Canadian court decision considering the relationship between the Northwest Irrigation Act and Indian water rights. However, the United States Supreme Court has ruled on a legislation very similar to the Irrigation Act, the Desert Lands Act of 1877, and has concluded that this Act is not applicable to native water rights (*Winters* Decision 1908). The provisions of the Irrigation Act ceased to apply upon the enactment of the Natural Resources Transfer Agreements in 1930. The Agreements transferred the Crown's interest in land and resources — including the Crown's interest in waters under the Northwest Irrigation Act — to the administration of the Prairie Provinces.

If the Irrigation Act is indeed held to be applicable to Indian water rights, then the Act forfeited the water rights attached to reserves established before July 1, 1896, essentially in the area covered by Treaties Nos. Four, Five, Six and Seven. The Act would also have denied water rights to reserves established after that date, which are essentially those in the northern parts of the Prairie Provinces.

British Columbia

In British Columbia, native water rights were decisively affected by legislative restrictions passed before Indian reserves were established, and by the terms of agreement for the transfer of lands for Indian reserves from the province to Canada. Such legislation as there was to the effect of allocating water rights to riparian landholders — even if it substituted common law riparian rights with statutory rights — for example, the Land Ordinance of 1865, explicitly barred Indians from these rights without special permission of the Governor. While the allocation of Indian reserve lands was still going on (until 1938), British Columbia's water rights legislation culminated in the Water Privileges Act of 1892. This Act unequivocally declared that all unrecorded water in the province was vested in the Crown and thus severely restricted, if not totally obliterated, common law riparian rights. In 1916 and 1925, riparian rights and all private rights to water resources, respectively, were declared to be retroactively abrogated (Bartlett 1988:175).

Based on his analysis of British Columbia's provincial water rights legislation, Bartlett (ibid.:176) concludes that the Reserve Commissioners were indeed empowered to appropriate water rights and that these rights are beyond the power of the province to regulate and abrogate. But this matter is by no means free from doubt or controversy. Barton (1985:23) arrives at a different conclusion, namely that it was after the passage of the Railway Belt[4] Water Act in 1912 (and only in that area specifically) that the federal government was empowered to unilaterally allocate water resources to Indian reserves. While the validity of these water rights was confirmed by an amendment to the Act in 1913, they were made subject to administration by the province (Barlett 1988.:183). Due to the urgent need to resolve water rights questions outside the Railway Belt, and because of federal pressure, the Province of British Columbia enacted the Indian Water Claims Act in 1921. The Act conferred jurisdiction upon a (provincial) Board of Investigation to pass judgement on Indian reserve water claims and to confirm or disallow them by the issuance of a licence. Built-in restrictions of water rights thus attained were significant: The priority could in no case "be earlier than the date on which the Indian water claim was filed or published" and the quantity of water could in no case exceed the quantity stated in the claim (ibid.:184). Moreover, licences issued under the Act remained subject to provincial legislation.

Today the approximately 600 Indian water licences in British Columbia are beset by numerous problems. Provincial water rights legislation does not address the question of water quality. Permanent water licences make no allowance for population increases of reserve communities. Some bands (for example, the Columbia Lake Band) are threatened with the removal of their water licences because of the "use it or lose it" policy of the provincial Water Management Branch (Columbia Lake First Nation 1991). In other cases, water bodies are overlicensed, such as the Whiteman's Creek, which flows through the Okanagan Indian Band Reserve, thus limiting the growth potential in that community (Chief Archie Jack, circular letter 1991). There seems to be no procedure in place for the return of revoked water licences. To address water-related issues, British Columbia's First Nations established the Indian Water Rights Committee in 1990. Its objective is to pursue the following mandate: "protect present water rights, licences, etc.; get back what we lost; guarantee future supply." (ibid.)

Thus, in British Columbia, riparian rights of most reserves have been effectively abolished, and native water rights attached to reserves as well as those based on aboriginal title are expressly disallowed. The existing limited water rights are in force only by virtue of provincial legislation and, as a result, hold no security whatsoever. On the other hand, it must be remembered that for most of the province aboriginal rights to land and water have never been surrendered.

Northern Territories

The Territorial Lands Act of 1950 constituted the first legislation that provided for Crown administration of water resources in Yukon and the Northwest Territories. It determined the reservation of a strip of 100 feet of riparian land bordering on the sea and navigable waters from every grant. The Act also provided that no grant or disposition, subject to express provision to the contrary, could convey an exclusive right to the use of waters bordering on or passing through the land subject to the transfer. In 1970 the Northern

---

[4] Under the Terms of Union (1871), article 11, British Columbia was to transfer large tracts of land to the Dominion government for the purpose of constructing a transcontinental railway to the Pacific coast. Over 1,400,000 hectares were granted to the railway in the Peace River District of the province, as well as 64 kilometres adjoining the track along its right of way over some 800 kilometres to the Pacific terminus. The Railway Belt, as this land came to be known, became the focus of provincial/Dominion land and administrative disputes for many years. (Doran 1982:2)

Inland Waters Act declared that the property and the right to use the water resources of the Territories was vested in the Crown, and that no waters could be used or diverted without a licence. The Yukon Territorial Water Board and the Northwest Territories Water Board were the agencies empowered to issue licences for water use, based on a system of priorization of use and prior appropriation similar to that employed by the Irrigation Act. Domestic uses were exempt from the operation of the Act.

In Yukon small reserves were set apart in the early 1900s, and in 1974 a reserve was purportedly established at Hay River in the Northwest Territories. Treaty No. Eight (1899) encompasses the Mackenzie River Basin south of Great Slave Lake while Treaty No. Eleven (1921) covers the western half of the Northwest Territories and the southeast corner of Yukon. As Bartlett (1988:170) argues, however, the issue here is not whether the rights derived from such reserves and treaties have been abrogated by these two federal statutes. The case of *Re Paulette* (6 W.W.R. 97 [N.W.T.S.C.]) suggested in 1973 that the treaties had not extinguished aboriginal title in the Territories. As a result, the federal government has acknowledged its obligation to negotiate for a comprehensive claims settlement for Yukon and the Northwest Territories.

The crucial question that arises in the Territories is whether the Territorial Lands Act and the Northern Inland Waters Act have extinguished or limited aboriginal title to water. Based on the *Hamlet of Baker Lake* decision (Hamlet of Baker Lake v. Minister of Indian Affairs and Northern Development, (1979) 107 D.L.R. (3d) 513 (F.C.,T.D.), [1979] 3 C.N.L.R. 17) in 1979, Bartlett (1988:170ff) tentatively suggests that neither statute has extinguished aboriginal title to water, and that this title can only be considered abrogated in the event of the issuance of water licences inconsistent with the maintenance of aboriginal water title. Moreover, it is more than likely that "domestic uses" under the Northern Inland Waters Act include all those water uses associated with aboriginal title, even if restricted to traditional forms of sustenance.

MEGAPROJECT PSYCHOLOGY AND ITS IMPACT ON NATIVE WATER RIGHTS

In many parts of the country, particularly in eastern and northern Canada, native water rights appear to be on a relatively secure legal footing. In British Columbia, Indian water rights have been severely crippled and are hardly stable. In the Prairie Provinces, pending a precedent-setting court decision, open questions remain with regard to implications of the Northwest Irrigation Act of 1894. Like British Columbia, provincial governments of the Prairies have a tradition of being aversive to native interests, particularly in the field of natural resource management.

Having briefly considered the legal and jurisdictional situation of aboriginal water rights in theory, one question remains: What is the Canadian track record with regard to protecting and respecting aboriginal rights to water resources? The commonality and interjurisdictional nature of water resources creates tremendous problems with regard to the adjudication of native water rights. In the United States this situation resulted in the development of a "comprehensive" water rights adjudication system and an institutionalized negotiating process (which has turned out to be anything but a panacea). In Canada, the adjudication of aboriginal water rights is proceeding to date on an ad hoc basis, through negotiation, mediation and litigation.

As Peter McLoughlin of the Canadian Environmental Advisory Council stated, Canada has been consumed by a "megaproject psychology" in its approach to water management (Struzik 1990:33), a fact which has had severe consequences for aboriginal people and the environment. It is significant that by and large the provinces have proceeded with water-resource related projects without considering native people's aboriginal title-based, treaty or riparian rights to water. Nowhere is this more evident than in relation to hydroelectric development. While small-scale water power projects with only limited environmental and social impacts have been common throughout the country for a long time, an era of hydro megaprojects was ushered in a few decades ago (Waldram 1988:7). Enormous dams and control structures have been designed to provide power on a regional, national and even international scale. These new developments are mostly located in the northern provinces on the major river systems, where they wreak havoc upon the sensitive ecosystems and the lives of people depending on them. In these relatively remote regions it is mostly native people who bear the brunt of the impact, while southern-based industries and consumers reap the benefits of the development of relatively inexpensive power. Throughout the country, native people have shared in similar devastating experiences.

Eastern Provinces

The James Bay Project in northern Quebec has tended to overshadow all other hydro developments in the country with regard to native rights, and the James Bay and Northern Quebec Agreement of 1975 has been hailed by some observers as a landmark and model for outstanding claims settlements. This shall be further discussed in a later section of this chapter. The James Bay Cree and Inuit though have not been the only ones affected by Hydro Quebec's development initiatives. By the late 1980s there were also 13 large power plants and five hydro reservoirs in the hunting territories of the Montagnais Indians to the east of the James Bay Cree. According to Waldram (1988:10), the Montagnais have, until recently, expressed little objection to these developments. However, like the Cree to the west of them, the Montagnais claim aboriginal title to their land. During the past few years they have begun to organize politically and have created the Conseil Attikamek-Montagnais. The group has indicated that it will not follow the model of the James Bay settlement.

Despite enormous potential, Ontario has actually built very few hydroelectric dams, as the energy production here seems to have concentrated more on the province's nuclear power generating program. The northern Ontario Ojibway communities of Grassy Narrows and White Dog have acquired sad fame as victims of water pollution in the late 1960s, when mercury was discharged from a paper mill in Dryden into the English-Wabigoon river system. Today these communities have not yet recovered from the devastating physical and social impact of this incident. Less known is the fact that, prior to the mercury pollution, these two communities along with other native groups in the region had also experienced the negative effects of hydro dam construction. These effects ranged from the flooding of graveyards over a loss of fur production to enforced relocation of 15 Ojibway families from the settlement of One Man Lake to the White Dog Reserve (ibid.).

Moreover, wild rice harvesting, which is a traditional economic activity very important to northern Ontario's native population, has been adversely affected by hydro power production. Lake of the Woods, traditionally an Ojibway ricing area, is part of a huge water system now managed by a control board representing both national and provincial interests (Vennum 1988:279). The system, administered by engineers of Environment Canada, the Ontario Ministry of Natural Resources, Ontario Hydro and Manitoba Hydro, is charged with ensuring multiple use of the water "for domestic and sanitary purposes, navigation, fishing, power, irrigation and reclamation." Under their control, Lake of the Woods serves as a holding tank for water, producing 30 per cent of power for northwestern Ontario and 25 per cent for Manitoba. The control board is allowed water level variations up to 5 1/4 feet. Water level fluctuations have drastic effects on wild rice growth, and as a result, the crop fluctuates in size annually according to the whims of the board (ibid.). During the 1970s the raising of water levels to generate hydroelectric power resulted in several crop failures. Ironically, this happened at a time when the government was using the argument of Indian underproduction to urge the development of a wild rice industry.

There are numerous open questions with regard to the special wild rice harvesting rights of native people (and resultant ways of dealing with the impact of non-native water resource developments). The official version of Treaty No. Three, which was signed in 1873 with 25 bands of Ontario Indians, mostly Ojibway, does not mention ricing rights, but the Indians possess a document that, they claim, does (Vennum 1988:278). Signed by two Metis interpreters for the Ojibway during the treaty negotiations, it states explicitly that "The Indians will be free as by the past for their hunting and rice harvest." The native position was further weakened in 1888, when a court ruling gave jurisdiction over natural resources including wild rice to the province rather than to the federal government. The 1959 Wild Rice Harvesting Act did nothing to clarify the issue.

Prairie Provinces

Northern Manitoba

Hydroelectric development in Manitoba has involved four river systems: the Winnipeg, the Saskatchewan, the Nelson and the Churchill. The first major hydro project to affect native people was the Grand Rapids Dam on the Saskatchewan River, which was completed in 1964. The Indian bands at Grand Rapids, Moose Lake, The Pas and particularly Chemawawin, whose residents had to be resettled to a new location, Easterville, experienced a variety of negative impacts as a result of the development. Virtually no political opposition was offered at the time, as these communities were relatively isolated and largely unaware of their options of resistance. However, after the construction of the dam the native residents felt its actual impact and began to investigate the circumstances surrounding this project. They hired lawyers and initiated legal action for compensation. Their initiatives resulted in numerous "letters of intent" on the part of Manitoba Hydro and a protracted negotiation process which failed to reach a satisfactory settlement (Waldram 1988:98).

A decade later, in 1974, the Churchill-Nelson River Hydro Project was completed. It entailed the diversion of most of the Churchill River south at Southern Indian Lake into the Nelson River system, where generating facilities were constructed. Since the early 1970s seven gigantic hydroelectric dams have been put into place on the Nelson and Churchill river system, and another 11 generating stations have been proposed (Krotz 1991:38). The landscape of northern Manitoba has been irreversibly transformed. The Churchill-Nelson Project constituted the first large-scale river diversion and lake impoundment in widespread permafrost. At the time of planning, the implications of this fact were suspected but unproven (Robert Newbury, in Krotz 1991:41). During the next two decades, the lakes that were tampered with became subject to a continued cycle of erosion and slumping, with no shoreline stabilization in sight. Vast areas were flooded. Habitat and migration patterns of animals and birds were severely altered. Forests turned into swamps and mercury, leached from the soil, has been released into the food chain. As a result, diet, economy and the lifestyle of communities along the Nelson and Churchill rivers were changed forever, with their fishery ruined and their trapping and hunting disrupted.

The project directly affected some 10,500 Indian and Metis people, including three reserves along the diversion route and two on the upper Nelson (Barton 1985:32). These people were largely engaged in trapping, hunting and fishing. Floods covered 4,730 hectares of reserve land, and one village had to be relocated. From the outset Manitoba Hydro only accepted responsibility for facilities directly affected by the project, leaving it up to the province to deal with impacts on fishing, hunting, trapping and transportation. However, the province did not assume this responsibility. There was neither consideration of social impacts nor mitigation or compensation of losses. No consultation took place with the native population, and crucial information was intentionally withheld from them (Barton 1985:32; McCullum and McCullum 1975:113). Throughout the entire process the federal government remained passive. It was only in 1974, when the project was a fait accompli, that the native communities formed the Northern Flood Committee which entered into a prolonged process of mediated negotiations with the federal and provincial governments for a proper settlement. As a result the Northern Flood Agreement was signed in 1977 by the Northern Flood Committee, Manitoba Hydro, the Manitoba Government and the federal government. The Agreement provided for a land exchange, trappers' compensation, mitigative measures and a cash settlement. Its implementation, however, has been plagued by tremendous difficulties.[5]

With regard to the Churchill-Nelson Hydro Project, the struggle of one native group in particular is noteworthy and well documented (Waldram 1988:115–170; McCullum and McCullum 1975:102–124). The community of South Indian Lake counted approximately 900 residents, three-quarters of whom were treaty-status Indians (Cree). The remainder were primarily non-status Indians who referred to themselves as Metis (Waldram 1988:116). The Treaty Indians were descendants of those who had signed the adhesion to Treaty No. Five in 1908, and were members of the Nelson House Indian Band to the south. The community of South Indian Lake itself was not a reserve, despite the preponderance of Treaty Indians living there, but was located on provincial Crown land. As a result the Manitoba Government regarded them as "squatters" on provincial land. People had moved there on account of favourable hunting and fishing conditions, and since the 1940s, had established a flourishing commercial fishing business. It was this self-reliant community of South Indian Lake which would be the most severely affected by the hydro project, which initially purported to raise the water level of Southern Indian Lake by 10 metres.

As a result, since 1968 and throughout the licence application and construction phases, the local people organized themselves and employed legal counsel. What followed during the subsequent seven years can only be described as an odyssey of legal and political actions which accomplished absolutely nothing. It is significant that the Indians' lawyers, in their Statement of Claim, did not employ the question of treaty rights held by the majority of the South Indian Lake residents. They probably erroneously assumed that treaty rights were only reserve-based. While at that time the whole concept of treaty rights was not too clearly defined, the people themselves readily invoked them as the reason for their legal action (ibid.:137). Despite being repeatedly approached for funding and intervention by the band and its lawyers, the Department of Indian Affairs steadfastly refused to get involved. Indian "rights", it seemed, were only in effect on reserves (ibid.:139). In an internal document (ibid.), Indian Affairs admitted, "...that such a drastic change as that feared with respect to the South Indian Lake fishery could lead to the almost total disintegration of community, family and personal relationships and life." Nevertheless, the federal trustee declined any assistance, since no "special Indian rights" were violated. No mention was made of hunting and fishing rights guaranteed by Treaty No. Five. By the time the Northern Flood Committee was formed in 1974 — this time with financial assistance by Indian Affairs, as bona fide reserves were involved (and as Waldram [1988;149] suggests, no doubt under the influence of the *Calder* decision) — the people of Indian Lake had given up. Many had succumbed to Manitoba Hydro's divide and conquer strategies and had settled individually with the hydro company. A final irony is the fact that South Indian Lake, the community most severely affected by the Churchill-Nelson River Project,[6] is not even mentioned in the

[5] The compensation to the five Indian bands whose lands were flooded and whose fishing and trapping livelihoods were disrupted, increased from a rough sum of $35 million in 1973 to an actual pay-out of $180 million by 1989. It is estimated that the total cost of compensation will have amounted to $500 million, when all claims are finally settled (Krotz 1991:43f).

[6] Since 1973, there has been a complete reversal in the diet of people at South Indian Lake. In the early 1970s, wildlife provided 75 per cent of their food. By 1989, it contributed only 25 per cent to their diet, the major part now being expensive, store-bought processed food from the south (Krotz 1991:43).

Northern Flood Agreement. While many residents are covered by the Agreement by virtue of their membership in the Nelson House Band, the status of the community under the Northern Flood Agreement remains a controversy (Waldram 1988:162).

Northern Saskatchewan

Native people in Saskatchewan have similarly been subjected to detrimental effects of hydro developments, principally on the Churchill and Saskatchewan river systems. The Island Falls Dam on the Churchill River (1928) and the Whitesands Dam on the Reindeer River, a tributary of the Churchill River (1942), had debilitating effects on the land-based economy of the Cree and Metis of Sandy Bay and the Peter Ballantyne Band of Southend respectively. The latter had over 240 hectares of the shoreline of their reserve lands flooded by the operation of the dam. The province and the power companies have never offered to compensate the Indian and Metis people for the damage inflicted upon them.

The Cumberland House Metis community (population: 1,100) and Swampy Cree Indian Band (population: 244) sustained a drastic impact on their way of life and economy, when the Squaw Rapids Dam (now known as the E.B. Campbell Hydro Electric Station) was constructed on the Saskatchewan River in 1964, creating a large forebay out of the river, which is now known as Tobin Lake. The native residents were neither consulted nor were they allowed to offer any resistance to the dam during construction, but they soon became aware of its disastrous effects:

> The impact described by the band includes reductions in summer water flows, increases in winter flows, sudden unannounced changes in water levels, mercury pollution, loss of flood peaks, and a general lowering of water levels. The consequences of such changes include the drowning of muskrat and beaver lodges, trapping of moose on 'false islands', freezing of water in the lake which kills fish, greatly reduced wildlife and fish habitat, difficulty and damages in boat travel, loss of equipment, loss of income from hunting, trapping, fishing and guiding, and loss of an unpolluted water supply. The dams on the river have severely disturbed its natural flow and damaged the traditional means of sustenance of the Indians. The Saskatchewan Delta at Cumberland House is regarded as one of the most significant wildlife habitat areas in North America. (Bartlett 1989:188f)

After this realization the local community initiated extensive political action in pursuit of both mitigative measures and compensation. The only result was two decades of studies accompanied by little action. In frustration the Cumberland House Local Community Authority in 1983 and then, in 1985, the Cumberland House Indian Band announced their intention to commence litigation against the Saskatchewan Power Corporation and the Government of Saskatchewan. In 1986, the latter declared its willingness to enter into mediated negotiations. As a result, both lawsuits were put on hold. A settlement was finally reached in 1989.

During the entire dispute, the federal government was conspicuous by its absence, even though there were an Indian band and reserve land in the downstream impact area. These facts did not prevent the Cumberland House Indian Band from pursuing their legal action separately from the Metis, as they hoped for a better chance of settling their claim, if they used their treaty rights under Treaty No. Five as a lever. Waldram (1988:79) also draws attention to the fact that procrastination and reluctance over the years of the Government of Saskatchewan and the Saskatchewan Power Corporation to deal with the Cumberland House people clearly reflect the province's attitude toward the Metis people in general. The expeditious manner in which the concerns of non-native farmers in the Tobin Lake area were addressed contrasts sharply with the protracted struggle undertaken by the Metis. How little has really changed is demonstrated by the fact that no environmental impact assessment and consultation with the community took place in the Cumberland House area for the Nipawin Dam, which was constructed 50 kilometres upstream from the E.B. Campbell Hydro Electric Station in 1986.

Central Alberta

In Alberta the case of the Bighorn Dam on the North Saskatchewan River on the eastern slope of the Rocky Mountains — though the focus has been on the violation of land, rather than water rights — is a tragic example of how hydro development can rob a native community of its livelihood. This situation is particularly complex because the area flooded or otherwise directly affected is subject to a land claim, as yet unresolved. The area in question is the Kootenay Plains, northernmost ancestral territory of the three Stoney Bands who today occupy a reserve at Morley, halfway between Calgary and Banff.[7]

Through oversight and manipulation, this band's traditional territory was not covered by Treaty No. Seven. After the establishment of the Morley Reserve (intended for all three Stoney Bands), one-third of the Goodstoney Band moved out of the reserve and returned to their ancestral hunting grounds along the banks of the North Saskatchewan River in 1894. Against many odds and constantly petitioning the federal government for a reserve under the terms of Treaty No. Seven in this region, the Goodstoneys persisted in their traditional territory. In 1948 an Order-in-Council established the Bighorn Reserve, located just north of the Kootenay Plains and totally inadequate in both quality and quantity. There, the Stoneys' existence was made bearable by their continuing use of the Kootenay Plains. During the following decades though, they were subjected to continuous harassment, their horses killed by forestry officials and their traditional lands invaded by seismographic surveyors and road construction. The fatal blow to the Bighorn Stoneys' remaining self-sufficiency was dealt by the provincial government and Calgary Power Limited in the early 1970s. The construction of the Bighorn Dam on the North Saskatchewan River virtually inundated the entire claim area of Kootenay Plains, thereby flooding cabins, graves, campgrounds and pastures. Moreover, it eliminated the Stoneys' livelihood derived from hunting, guiding hunters and fur trapping. About 95 per cent of the Bighorn Stoneys, formerly the most self-reliant section of the tribe, have been on welfare since the dam was completed in 1972.

Observations

In his study of three native communities in Manitoba and Saskatchewan — Cumberland House, Chemawawin (Easterville) and South Indian Lake — as they experienced the impact of hydroelectric developments, Waldram (1988.:171–183) makes some interesting observations, which in their applicability are most likely not confined to those three cases under investigation.

It appears that the Department of Indian Affairs invariably assumed the role of an "interested observer" (ibid.:99) rather than lived up to its role as a trustee. While showing utter indifference towards Metis and non-status Indians, the federal government even seemed to be unable or unwilling to fully support the rights of treaty-status Indians. It never ventured more than feeble objections against the provincial governments and invariably backed down when pushed by the latter. The federal government always found reasons to moderate its interventions: The Metis and non-status Indians of Cumberland House were not within federal jurisdiction; South Indian Lake was not a reserve; and funding of the Northern Flood Committee was stipulated to be used for negotiation purposes only, not for legal action.

It also became very clear that in all three communities the Metis truly were a "forgotten people" (ibid.:177). This is obvious in the manner by which Cumberland House has continued to be dealt with. The Metis of Easterville and South Indian Lake were not considered separate from the Indians. They were allowed all of the "benefits" of compensation agreements signed with the Indians, but not permitted to negotiate their own agreements. In the Cumberland House case, the Metis were not even accorded general rights as provincial citizens in the light of the great attention paid by the Saskatchewan government to non-native residents in the impact area.

---

[7] The struggle of the Bighorn Stoneys is detailed by Getty and Larner 1972 and by Getty 1975.

Finally, Waldram observes that contemporary compensation agreements bear an unsettling resemblance to the historical treaties: They are done belatedly, as an afterthought, with the project a fait accompli, and with little negotiation. Opposition to both treaties and dams would have been fruitless. In the treaties and the modern hydro agreements, native people were asked to surrender their land and resources in the interest of non-native developments, in the name of the "common good". Divide and conquer strategies have been commonly employed in treaty and hydro negotiations. And finally, there is an ongoing debate about the extent to which the federal and provincial governments have fulfilled the terms of the treaties and the hydro agreements, and the degree to which they have lived up to the spirit and intent of these pacts.

Such compensation agreements or settlements, however belated, unsatisfactory and poorly implemented, have only come about as the result of a determined threat of litigation on the part of native people. As will be discussed later on, the necessity to assume a strongly confrontational stance to achieve something is borne out by native experiences in the southern part of the country as well.

British Columbia

In British Columbia the circumstances surrounding the construction of the Kemano I Dam by Alcan (Aluminum Company of Canada) on the Nechako River in 1956 have to date resulted in three specific claims submitted by the Haisla Band, the Carrier-Sekani Tribal Council and the Cheslatta Indian Band (Cheslatta Carrier Nation 1990). In 1950 the British Columbia government granted Alcan the right to virtually all of the water of the Nechako River above Cheslatta Falls so that the company could divert water into its reservoir. This hydroelectric project caused widespread environmental damage, particularly to salmon stocks, and significant human dislocation. Nevertheless, three decades later, B.C. Hydro and Alcan embarked upon the Kemano Completion Project, which is designed to utilize the remaining power potential of the Nechako River. The 1987 Kemano Agreement between Alcan and the federal Fisheries Department was challenged in court by native and environmental groups. In the early 1990s they were still embroiled in controversy concerned with the question of a full environmental impact assessment (*Globe and Mail*, June 14, 1991; *Ha-Shilth-Sa*, October 14, 1992:9; *Windspeaker*, February 1, 1993:3).

Another example was the W.A.C. Bennett Dam, which was completed in 1968 as part of B.C. Hydro's Peace River Hydroelectric Project. Flooding behind the dam created one of the world's largest artificial lakes, known as Williston Lake, covering some 1,600 square kilometres. The project has caused extensive environmental disruptions downstream, particularly in the Peace-Athabasca Delta, which has resulted in vigorous protests by native groups and environmentalists in British Columbia, Alberta and Saskatchewan (Waldram 1988:16).

The W.A.C. Bennett Hydroelectric Dam on the Peace River illustrates the kind of callous disregard for native people that has accompanied so many other developments. Hugh Brody (1981:134f) comments that while consideration was given to the concerns of homesteaders, white trappers, tourists and even moose who lost some winter habitat, the only reference to Indians in the major impact report was a comment by one Indian, who was reported as saying, "By the time the water comes, I find some other place." Several Sekani Indian bands lost their entire traditional homeland, including their principal hunting, trapping and fishing territories to flooding. Downstream, particularly in the Peace Athabasca Delta area, reduced river flows severely disrupted habitat conditions for fish, waterfowl, muskrat and bison, and along with it the domestic economy of the Cree and Chipewyan of Fort Chipewyan, Alberta. A lawsuit against B.C. Hydro was launched in 1970 by these two bands and by the Metis Association of Alberta on behalf of the community's Metis residents, but they never made it to court. Now the native community of Fort Chipewyan is concerned about a new B.C. Hydro Project which would further affect the flow of the Peace River: Another dam, usually referred to as the Site-C project, presently in its planning stages, is to be constructed downstream from the W.A.C. Bennett Dam, in the Fort St. John area (Kubish 1990:24f).

British Columbia is also the testing ground for an innovative "use" of water which could have a significant effect on aboriginal people's water rights: bulk water export. Native people could become players in this new game, or they may be exposed to the environmental impacts of these ventures. Canada has roughly 30 per cent of the world's fresh water, and schemes to export some of it originated more than a century ago with plans to rope icebergs and tow them south by barge (Noble 1991:63). Over the decades, these water ploys evolved into gigantic engineering projects to reroute river systems south by interbasin transfer. Ottawa has, for now, declared a ban on diversion projects. Exporting fresh water in tankers, however, has been viewed as a provincial matter of natural resource management, which in the mid-1980s resulted in the British Columbia government's decision to grant export licences. The attention of the various promoters immediately focused on the water crisis in southern California. In 1990 Tzela Creek in Toba Inlet, in the traditional territory claimed by the Klahoose First Nation, was targeted by Snowcap Waters Ltd. for water export by supertanker. When initially approached by the proponent with the suggestion to become a joint venture partner, the band expressed a cautious interest and proceeded with gathering information on the issue of water export and with a preliminary environmental impact assessment (Francis 1992:4). It soon became clear, however, that the process of involvement and consultation, in which the Klahoose people thought they were participating, was more apparent than real, and that crucial decisions about licensing were made by the provincial government behind closed doors without any public screening or consideration of environmental effects (ibid.:6).

Once this became obvious, the Klahoose First Nation concentrated on publicizing its opposition to the venture and the industry in general, an opposition which quickly spread to other Coast Salish bands. With their claims unsettled, First Nations are strongly opposed to the government's licensing to private commercial interests the last uncommitted "resource" within their territories (ibid.:9). Furthermore, the potential environmental consequences of a water export industry are completely unexplored. Chief Kathy Francis of the Klahoose First Nation expresses great concern about the cumulative environmental impact of water withdrawal on shellfish and salmon stocks, super tanker traffic in narrow inlets, water pollution by dumped ballast water and accidental oil spills, and the impacts of structures and facilities for water storage and loading (ibid.:10).

In June 1991 the provincial government announced a moratorium on water export licences until the end of the year, which in 1992 was extended until June 30, 1994. Many British Columbia First Nations would like to see this moratorium extended until after the settlement of comprehensive claims, along with a moratorium on the alienation of other natural resources. In view of the unsuccessful attempts to ignore First Nations concerns with respect to two California export proposals, and after the election of a new provincial government in 1991, Chief Kathy Francis expresses the hope that maybe "the proposed water export industry will be the first in this province where First Nations rights are not ignored or overridden by the short term economic desires of private commercial interest." (ibid.:12)

The Struggle for Indian Water Rights: The Peigan and the Oldman River

The Peigan Reserve is located in southern Alberta. In terms of natural resources, its main assets are its land base and its location on the Oldman River, a body of water that is of vital importance for irrigation purposes. A contentious issue between the Peigan and the Province of Alberta concerns the question of who owns the Oldman River water bed (The Oldman River is considered a non-navigable river). The controversy arose in 1979 when the Peigan claimed that facilities of the Lethbridge Northern Irrigation District (L.N.I.D.) system — a canal and a diversion weir — were located on unexpropriated Indian land, and, therefore were constructed illegally. They demanded retroactive compensation and the imposition of a yearly fee system. This dispute developed into a three-year confrontation which culminated in the Peigan's blockade of the weir, thus cutting the irrigation district off its water supply. The conflict was resolved when the tribe's rights to the land were finally acknowledged with the payment of $4 million plus an annual cash payment of $300,000 (Notzke 1985:41–43).

In the early 1980s Peigan and provincial negotiators failed to reach an agreement on the location of a major on-stream storage facility on the Oldman River on the reserve. The Three Rivers Dam was since constructed — under ongoing controversy — 20 kilometres upstream of the reserve. On account of these developments, the Peigan have raised the question of their water rights. Initially, they insisted on their right to control the entire flow of water through their reserve, thereby claiming a water right going far beyond the United States "Winters' Doctrine". Since then they have moved towards some form of reserved water right, which would have to be quantified. The Peigan argue that the tribe has aboriginal rights to the Oldman River, including the waters, river bed and shore, and the continued maintenance of its present water quality and flow characteristics (these rights are identical with riparian rights). All these are altered by the dam upstream. In addition, the Peigan claim water rights and title to the Oldman River as part of their reserve which was set aside by Treaty No. Seven. They feel that their water rights and title to the Oldman River were held in trust for them by the federal government and were never legally transferred to the Government of Alberta by the Alberta Natural Resources Transfer Act (*Environment Law Centre Newsletter*, Vol.14, No.2, 1987). On the other hand, the provincial government is currently claiming ownership of the water, all sections of the Oldman River water bed, and even ownership of the permitted land within the reserve, in blatant disregard of its own 1981 agreement with the Peigan.

In 1986 the Peigan submitted a Statement of Claim for a case against the Province of Alberta. It has been held up by technical hurdles and inadequate funding for several years. The Peigan also filed a court injunction in a provincial court to halt construction of the dam which was, however, denied (September 24, 1988). In their call for an injunction, the Peigan invoked their right to religious freedom, as the valley contains religious sites as well as flora and fauna essential for Peigan religious practices (*Kainai News*, June 15, 1988 and May 17, 1989).

In August 1990 the Peigan's lawyer, Louise Mandell, in defence of their water rights drew an interesting analogy between water and fish, saying both were resources that moved into and out of Indian lands. The Supreme Court decided in *Sparrow* that Indians had first rights to fish, and the Peigan want the same status accorded Indian water rights (Louise Mandell, interview on C.B.C. "Eye-opener," August 17, 1990). The Peigan are determined to settle the question of their water rights in the courts, which would be the first court case of its kind in Canada. And with the dam a fait accompli, the Peigan's case against the province is concerned not only with control over water, but also with potential benefits from the dam.

While a precedent-setting settlement of Peigan water rights through the legal system seems unavoidable, it may be a long time in coming. In the meantime, with their legal efforts frustrated or at least delayed, and the dam project nearing completion, a group of Peigan, the Lonefighter Society[8], opted for extraordinary tactics and asserted jurisdiction

[8] The name "Lonefighter Society" is not without controversy within the Peigan community. Reggie Crowshoe of the Oldman River Cultural Centre contends that traditionally the Lonefighters were not a society but

over on-reserve waters. In August 1990, they set up camp in the river bottom and proceeded to divert the flow of the river around the irrigation weir, an action aimed to cut off water from the L.N.I.D. system and thwart the purpose of the dam upstream. They justified their action by referring to a 1984 water by-law approved by the federal government, which allows the band to construct water projects on reserve lands. The protest action lasted throughout the remainder of 1990. During the ensuing months, the Lonefighters were subjected to armed police raids, vilified by irrigation supporters, served with court injunctions and eventually had one of their leaders jailed. Smouldering Peigan discontent continued during the early 1990s, with Peigan participation in the farcical EARP hearings in 1991 and continuous rumblings among the Lonefighters during 1992.

In 1991 the Peigan Nation took the lead in establishing an international Indian Water Rights Coalition endorsed by First Nations and Tribes in Canada and the United States. This coalition is intended to further the protection and advancement of native water rights in both countries by means of information exchange and common strategy development.

INDIAN USE OF WATER RESOURCES: WILD RICE HARVESTING

Next to fishery, wild rice production is likely the most important benefit which aboriginal people derive from water resources. This wild crop is an important resource not only in traditional wild rice areas, but also for aboriginal people who turn to wild rice as an innovation to boost or replace threatened trapping or fishing economies.

Traditionally, wild rice grew and was harvested in the so-called wild rice bowl, an area extending from west of Lake Superior into southern Manitoba and to Wisconsin and Minnesota in the United States, but the heart of wild rice country was northern Ontario's Lake of the Woods region. For the Anishnaabe (Ojibway), "Manomin" (wild rice) once occupied a central place in tribal life. The plant was endowed with spiritual attributes and was used in ceremonies as well as for food, while its harvest promoted social interaction in late summer each year (Vennum 1988:1). Today Manomin is still important, although its social and cultural significance has been modified by new economic factors, and Indian ricing activities are being affected by external regulatory forces. Furthermore, as already discussed, Manomin's habitat is severely threatened by competing water uses such as hydroelectricity, since the plant is extremely sensitive to water level fluctuations during various stages of its growth (Stevenson 1988:15).

As previously mentioned, Indian ricing rights in Ontario are still surrounded by controversy. The 1959 Wild Rice Harvesting Act created 10 "block areas" as wild rice harvesting sections, which native people interpreted as government recognition of their harvesting rights. In fact, however, the Act did nothing to clarify the issue (Vennum 1988:278f). The late 1970s witnessed various attempts by the non-native lobby to open up traditional Indian harvesting territory on Crown land for economic exploitation, until in 1980, the Ontario government announced a moratorium on non-native harvesting licences. It remains in effect in the early 1990s, despite periodic challenges (Thurston 1992:26).

During the late 1980s a conservative estimate given for the number of harvesters participating in the northwestern Ontario wild rice harvest was 2,000 individuals. The majority were of native ancestry, harvesting on block areas licensed to their respective bands (Stevenson 1988:29). The average total income per individual, estimated from the average price paid

---

a clan.

In 1993, independently from their protest action, members of the Lonefighters established themselves as a cultural organization in Calgary, sometimes competing for funds with the Oldman River Cultural Centre on the Peigan Reserve (Reggie Crowshoe, personal communication, August 20, 1993).

per kilogram, was $476.00. For the people involved in the harvest ricing constitutes a seasonal activity which supplements other income sources.

With the establishment of Kagiwiosa Manomin Inc. by the Wabigoon Lake Ojibway Nation in 1987, aboriginal people in Ontario entered the wild rice processing industry. Kagiwiosa Manomin is a cooperative enterprise, which uses traditional wood fire parching and purchases its rice from Indian bands that have received organic certification from the Organic Crop Improvement Association (Kagiwiosa Manomin Inc. fact sheet; *Dryden Local Express*, September 6, 1988:8; *Weekender*, February 9, 1989:10). The company thus capitalizes on Anishnaabe wild rice traditions in both its harvesting and processing practices.

In neighbouring southern Manitoba, too, Anishnaabe First Nations are trying to translate their wild rice tradition into a modern means of sustenance. In 1984 the Manitoba government introduced the Manitoba Wild Rice Act. While the Act granted exclusive harvesting rights to native cooperatives in Whiteshell Provincial Park, set apart lakes traditionally harvested by five Indian reserve communities and introduced a provincially funded affirmative-action program to assist Manitoba's Indian people in entering the industry, it also gave the government the right to regulate the industry. As a result the Act dissatisfied both native and non-native groups. Twenty-five Anishnaabe bands claimed that the provincial government's assertion of regulatory power constituted an infringement on their treaty and aboriginal rights. The Manitoba Wild Rice Farmers' Association challenged the policy as unconstitutional (Thurston 1992:26).

In the early 1990s, northern Manitoba is poised to supplant — at least economically — the more traditional ricing areas in southern Canada. Here, in what constituted a virtual rush, not unlike those usually associated with minerals, wild rice was sown into lakes which offer favourable growth conditions. Here, too, aboriginal people are seeking entry into the industry, although there is no wild rice tradition among the native people of the northern provinces. As a result, cultural considerations are overridden by economics. In the late 1980s when the rush peaked and northern Manitoba was declared "open territory", most wild rice prospectors were non-native, because native trappers found it difficult to finance entry into the industry at a time when rice-seed prices were at historic highs and fur prices at an all-time low (ibid.). In some cases, native trappers were even faced with non-natives leasing lakes on their traplines (ibid.:32).

Today most of the lakes accessible by road have been claimed, and rice that must be flown out from remote lakes is only marginally profitable. The amount of risk capital that needs to be invested — most of it for an airboat, since ricing northern style is not carried out by canoe — is prohibitive for many aboriginal people. Hoping that wild rice will provide a boost to the declining trapping and fishing economies of northern Manitoba's aboriginal communities, the Manitoba Indian Agriculture Program offers free test seed, assists in processing leases to rice lakes and arranges loans to Treaty Indians. Surprisingly enough, in Manitoba non-status Indians seem to have been more successful than Treaty Indians in establishing themselves in the industry (ibid.).

In 1991 the Manitoba Aboriginal Justice Inquiry recommended that the province recognize the harvesting of wild rice as an aboriginal right and negotiate co-management agreements with native groups for harvesting off-reserve. Jim Smith of Swampy Cree Holdings Ltd., the economic arm of the Swampy Cree Tribal Council, came up with an idea for a possible solution to the shortage of suitable rice lakes. His scheme envisages non-native growers selling surplus lake leases to native individuals interested in entering the business. In many cases the maximum number of leases, which is eight lakes, proves to be more than one person can handle, and Smith feels that those producers may be willing to sell back some of their lakes to aboriginal people. However, considering the market value of rice leases, any publicly funded buy-back scheme might prove prohibitively expensive (ibid.).

Wild rice production has also established itself in northern Saskatchewan (Lac La Ronge) and, more recently, in northern Alberta (Lac La Biche), with native people striving to claim their share of the resource.

NATIVE WATER RIGHTS IN CONTEMPORARY AGREEMENTS

Since 1973 when the federal government changed its policy towards aboriginal title, several aboriginal title claims have been negotiated under what is known as the comprehensive land claims process. With regard to the question of native water rights, the settlements attained so far fundamentally differ from one another.

The James Bay and Northern Quebec Agreement

The first contemporary agreement was the James Bay and Northern Quebec Agreement of 1975. It is unique among the comprehensive claims settlement processes in so far as it concerns lands and resources within provincial boundaries. The James Bay and Northern Quebec Agreement was negotiated by the Cree, the Inuit, the Government of Canada, the Government of Quebec and the provincial Crown corporations engaged in hydro development in northern Quebec. The Agreement was necessitated by the claim of the Cree and Inuit to unextinguished aboriginal title in northern Quebec and by the province's desire to proceed with large-scale hydro developments in that region. As Bartlett (1988:220) explains, the latter purpose is strongly reflected in the terms of the Agreement. It is much more explicit in spelling out the rights of the province with respect to water resources and the water bed than those of the Cree and Inuit.

As summarized by Bartlett (ibid.:220–222) and Barton (1985:37–39), under the Agreement, "the seashore, beds and shores" of the major lakes and rivers in the region are excluded from lands set aside for the Cree and Inuit under Category I (i.e. under exclusive native control), along with 200 feet in depth along the shores of the lakes and rivers (except for one mile in either direction from the centre of a community). These lands exempt from native control, including the intertidal zone, were classified as Category II lands, held by the Crown in the right of Quebec. Native people have exclusive hunting, trapping and fishing rights over these lands, whereas the province retains general control plus the right to use them for developmental purposes (providing replacement Category II land or compensation).

The Agreement authorized the James Bay Energy Corporation and Hydro Quebec to proceed with their development plans. As perceived by the province, these included the first and ongoing stage, the La Grande Complex, and further stages which would affect other river basins in the region. The Agreement further committed the developers to minimizing ecological impacts and made the authorization of the project subject to conditions with regard to the control of water levels; the clearing of reservoirs and forebays; erosion control; supplying communities with hydroelectricity and water, remedial works to alleviate the negative impact on hunting, trapping and fishing; relocation of burial sites; and preference for project employment and contracts.

The Agreement also created environmental and social protection agencies with substantial Cree and Inuit representation. These provisions, however, only provide native people with advisory, consultative and administrative functions but not with a veto power over developments. The only areas over which the Cree and Inuit exercise a real measure of control, Category I lands, constitute a minute fraction of the region, and their boundaries are designed to reduce native control over major waterways. Thus Bartlett's (1988:222) conclusion that "The Agreement is more a statement of the rights of the James Bay hydro project than it is of the rights with respect to water of the Cree and Inuit," hardly seems exaggerated.

Today, 18 years after the signing of the James Bay and Northern Quebec Agreement, the Cree and the Inuit are painfully aware of their lack of power to control impending developments. It is the Cree view that the native signatories only recognized construction of one major hydro project, specifically the La Grande Complex. This opinion was voiced in 1981 by Phillip Awashish from Mistassini (*Akwesasne Notes*/Late Spring 1982:19) and echoed in 1990 by Grand Chief Matthew Coon-Come (quoted in *Edmonton Journal*, February 24, 1990:E10) in an impassioned plea against a future hydroelectric project on the Great Whale River north of La Grande. The Cree feel that the existing project on the Grande River created far more environmental hazards than they had ever anticipated; hence, they are desperately opposed to future projects in the region which they claim they have never approved.

The "environmental cost of reshaping the geography of northern Quebec", as Peter Gorrie (1990:21) puts it, has indeed been tremendous. Damage to the environment is most concentrated along the edges of water bodies, which constitute the richest habitat for plants and wildlife. A reworking of the region's hydrological regime has resulted in "unnatural" erosion and sedimentation patterns and the drying up of waterways and flooding of terrestrial habitats. Spawning grounds are destroyed and waterfowl habitat is eliminated.

Profound changes have occurred in estuaries, where river flows have been reduced or increased. Patterns of water temperature, the length and extent of ice cover in winter and the mixing of fresh and salt water are all altered. Changes in water salinity at various locations in James Bay and Hudson Bay are likely to affect fish and mammals requiring specific nutrient levels or water conditions at certain times of the year to prepare for migration, reproduce or survive the winter (Gorrie 1990:24; Corelli 1990:58). The same is true for changes in coastal marshes and tidal flats, which are of vital importance for migratory birds.

The rate of flow in James Bay Rivers is normally highest in spring during melt-off and lowest in winter. Hydro Quebec is reversing this natural cycle for waterways below powerhouses. Water is stored above dams during spring and released in winter when power demand is highest. Not only does this springlike flooding of rivers in midwinter flush away fish and their fertilized eggs, but an abnormal water regime is also likely to have contributed to the disaster that befell 10,000 caribou attempting to cross the Caniapiscau River in 1984 (Busby 1991:12).

These are only some examples of impacts already incurred or immanent. Perhaps the single most devastating effect of the project, and certainly the most insidious one, has been mercury contamination of fish. Mercury commonly occurs in rocks in an insoluble form. However, bacteria associated with decomposition of organic matter (proliferated by the creation of new reservoirs) transform it into highly toxic methyl mercury, which vaporizes, enters the hydrological cycle and the food chain, and reaches its highest concentration in predatory fish species. For the local population such fish, for example, pickerel, pike and lake trout, constitute the most reliable source of high quality protein. On the La Grande, levels of mercury in fish downstream from the dams increased to six times their normal levels within months of the project's completion. A 1984 survey of Cree living in the village of Chisasibi at the river's mouth revealed that 64 per cent of the people had unsafe levels of mercury in their bodies (Gorrie 1990:27; Coon-Come 1992:8).

To date no human deaths have yet been contributed to mercury contamination, but for the land-based economy and Cree society its impact has been even more devastating than the flooding of thousands of square kilometres of traplines and hunting territories.

> Nimass aksiwin (lit. "fish disease", or methyl mercury poisoning) strikes at the very heart of our society. It's like being told that armageddon has started, and people are scared as hell. The scientists come in here and tell us we're getting better (by eating less fish), but, hey, you can't measure...nimass aksiwin by taking hair samples. How can you measure a man's fear? How can you measure your way of life coming to an end? (George Lameboy, Cree trapper, quoted in Coon-Come 1992:8)

As Cree Nation representatives pointed out at the Second International Water Tribunal in Amsterdam in 1992, loss of confidence in country food is easily induced, has profound consequences, and is difficult to remedy, resulting in severe stress on subsistence as a social and economic system.[9] The collective effect of this reaction and other prodigious changes that Cree society has been forced to undergo at a precipitous pace as a result of the hydro project all too often manifests itself in social pathologies and general social disintegration (ibid.).

In the 1970s all these direct and indirect impacts of the hydro project were not foreseen in their full extent either by the Cree and the Inuit or the project proponents. Today, however, James Bay II, which comprises the Great Whale project and eventually the Nottaway-Broadback-Rupert project, is being assessed by the aboriginal and environmental lobbies in the light of what the La Grande project has done to the people and to the environment, and in a socio-political climate fundamentally different from what it was two decades ago.

The Inuvialuit Final Agreement

The Western Arctic or Inuvialuit Final Agreement of 1984 does not show much inclination to entrench paramount aboriginal water rights either, but the circumstances surrounding its implementation were profoundly different from the James Bay situation. The Agreement provides for the grant of the most expansive territory ever set aside for aboriginal peoples in Canada, and includes the "beds of all lakes, rivers and other water bodies found in Inuvialuit land." (Government of Canada 1984:6) All waters are, however, reserved to the Crown. This, together with a clause subjecting Inuvialuit lands to all laws of general application to private lands, indicates that the government regulates all aspects of water allocation and water quality on Inuvialuit lands under the Northern Inland Water Act (Barton 1985:40). It would appear, therefore, that the Agreement bestows additional powers on the government rather than the aboriginal landholders. The Agreement also authorizes Canada to retain the right to manage and control water bodies for the purposes of fisheries, migratory birds, navigation, flood control and the like. According to Bartlett (1988:222), federal powers do not extend to authorizing hydroelectric development. But such a project could be authorized by the unfettered powers of expropriation conferred upon the Governor in Council by the Agreement.

There is no explicit reference to Inuvialuit rights to water. As previously mentioned, ownership of the water bed normally entails exclusive hunting, fishing and trapping rights in the waters above such lands. The Agreement, however, expressly denies the Inuvialuit any "proprietary interest in fish" or "exclusive right to harvest fish". With regard to fisheries, wildlife and environmental matters, they only have advisory powers. The grant of lands to the Inuvialuit includes the "beds of all lakes, rivers, and other water bodies found in Inuvialuit lands". Bartlett (ibid.:223) notes a very crucial point in this context: "The descriptions of the lands granted, and the accompanying maps, however **exclude** (emphasis in original) the offshore from the Inuvialuit lands." Also, the native people have only preferential, not exclusive, rights to fish in the offshore. It appears, therefore, that the Inuvialuit are unable to derive any true power to control offshore activities and developments from their land ownership. For this purpose they must rely on the impact of land use planning agencies on which they are represented, and on the advisory powers of the Wildlife Management Advisory Council and the Fisheries Joint Management Committee. Bartlett (1988:224) further suggests that the extent of federal and territorial government jurisdiction

---

[9] An important reference for this phenomenon is Peter J. Usher's revealing study on "Socio-Economic Effects of Elevated Mercury Levels in Fish on Sub-Arctic Native Communities" (Usher 1992c).

over water resources and other matters indicates an assumption which may explain much of the nature of the Agreement: that the Government of the Northwest Territories will be under aboriginal administration.

The Nunavut Land Claims Agreement

The Nunavut Land Claims Agreement represents a clear departure from the James Bay and Western Arctic agreements in its approach to aboriginal water rights. The Final Agreement was signed in May 1993 by the federal government and the Tungavik Federation of Nunavut, representing the Inuit of the Eastern Arctic. It was preceded by an Agreement-in-Principle in 1990. It entails a much clearer appreciation of water as a resource, provides for a greater aboriginal role in the administration of water resources, and contains an unequivocal declaration of rights (ibid.:224f). It also puts a strong emphasis on the integration of water management with land use management. The provisions of the Agreement call for the statutory establishment of a Nunavut Water Board with "responsibilities and powers over the regulation, use and management of water in the Nunavut Settlement Area on a basis at least equivalent to the powers and responsibilities currently held by the Northwest Territories Water Board under the Northern Inland Water Act." (Government of Canada and the Tungavik 1993:123)

All nine members of this Board are to be appointed by the federal government, but four must be nominated by the Inuit and two by the Northwest Territories Government. Thus the Nunavut Water Board entails joint aboriginal-government administration of the water resources of the Eastern Arctic. The Agreement also makes an explicit statement as to the rights of the Inuit with regard to water resources. Its provisions declare that the Inuit have the exclusive right to the utilization of water in Inuit lands, the right to have the water "flow through Inuit-owned lands substantially unaffected in quality and quantity and flow" (ibid.:169), and that Inuit lands include the banks of all water bodies. The Nunavut Water Board is empowered to authorize projects within Inuit lands which may substantially affect water resources, but only if a compensation agreement has been reached with the Inuit or compensation has been determined by the Board. In determining compensation, the Board will take into account the adverse effects of the water use on the land, the disruption of the renewable resource economy, and various social and cultural implications (ibid.:170). The provisions of the Agreement also strive to seek such consideration with respect to projects outside Nunavut by means of agreements with other jurisdictions.

The declaration of water rights embodied in the Nunavut Agreement is founded upon the principle of riparian rights and its implied rationale of the protection of the natural flow and state of the water. As previously mentioned, the doctrine of riparian rights affords substantial protection to traditional uses of lands and waters, and it is those uses, which the Inuit of the Eastern Arctic have chosen to emphasize. Richard Bartlett (1988:228) feels that the Nunavut Agreement is much more likely than the James Bay or Western Arctic agreements to serve as a model for other native agreements. It entails an innovative approach to joint aboriginal-government administration of water resources and does justice to the essence of aboriginal water rights.

An element of Inuit "land" claims which is hardly ever fully appreciated is the fact that the Inuit are a maritime people for whose interest management of marine areas is of paramount importance. With the exception of Baker Lake, all Canadian Inuit communities are located on coastlines and are dependent on the sea for their sustenance. In Nunavut the average percentage of the community hunting areas which are marine is 34 per cent, ranging from a low of 0 per cent for Baker Lake to a high of 88 per cent for Sanikiluaq (Riewe 1991:4f). These extensive community hunting territories overlap one another to the effect that virtually the entire land-fast ice region in Nunavut is currently utilized. The Nunavut Land Claims Agreement provides for the extension of the application of various components of the Agreement to marine areas, such as wildlife management, land use planning, impact assessment, resource royalty sharing, parks and conservation areas and some other elements. Inuit will not be in a position, however, to own sea bed as part of their land quantum (Government of Canada and the Tungavik 1993:135).

CONCLUSION AND OUTLOOK

A poignant statement by Trelease (Maxfield et al. 1977:212), while intended for the United States, is equally applicable in Canada: "...the Indians have had the water rights but the white men now have the water."

Native people in all parts of Canada (with the exception of Metis and non-status Indians) do have substantial water rights, which are derived from different origins than those of non-aboriginal persons and which are in addition to those of non-natives. Theoretically, these rights are legally secure, as they have not been effectively abrogated by legislation. However, we must exclude British Columbia from this generalization and merely speculate with regard to the Prairie Provinces.

In practice the situation looks much more gloomy. Almost everywhere in the country, provincial governments have proceeded with high-impact water development projects without the slightest pretence of regard for native rights. This is particularly evident in (though not confined to) the area of hydroelectric developments. Citing the case of Saskatchewan as an example, Bartlett (1989:191) shows that it has taken nearly 30 years for the provincial government and the Saskatchewan Power Corporation to start providing compensation for the damage inflicted by hydroelectric dams on Indian people in that province. This is not due to lack of legal rights which might compel such a result. As the author points out, "Rather it is the disparity in the abilities of Indian bands to assert their legal rights compared to that ability of the utility companies to resist." (ibid.) Experiences in the United States and in Canada suggest that settlements are furthered by a determined litigation strategy.

Waldram (1988:179) even views recourse in legal action rather dismal in its prospects. Based on his case studies in Manitoba and Saskatchewan, he concludes that despite injunction applications, the filing of statements of claim, and the real threat of litigation, no substantial action ever made it to court. The growing sophistication on the part of native communities, as well as the actions of their lawyers, have been countered by the increasing sophistication of the provincial governments in their endeavours to undermine opposition to their plans and to keep compensation to a minimum. Experiences of native people anywhere in the country seem to indicate that unequivocal threats of litigation or even physical confrontation (for example, the Peigan case) along with effective public lobbying are indispensable preconditions for settlement of their interests.

In the legal arena, the passing of Section 35 of the Constitution Act, 1982, the landmark decisions of 1983 and 1985 pertaining to treaties and statutes, and the implications of the 1990 *Sparrow* ruling shed a new and cautiously optimistic light on many issues relating to Indian water rights. The jury is still out on the implications for Indian water rights of the court decisions on Rafferty Alameda and the Oldman River Dam (see chapter 9).

North of Sixty the provisions for water use and management agreed to by the Tungavik Federation of Nunavut and the Government of Canada in 1993 may provide a potential model for other agreements. It genuinely addresses the issue of aboriginal rights regarding the use of water and provides for joint aboriginal-government administration of the resource.

Finally, an agreement signed on March 18, 1993, between the newly created Dogrib Power Corporation and the NWT Power Corporation, seems to indicate the dawn of a new era. The Dogrib Nation is planning to finance, build and own two hydroelectric dams within its traditional territory, which are to supply power to communities around Great Slave Lake (*Windspeaker*, April 12, 1993:8). Construction, engineering and environmental management will be locally controlled. There is an awareness of a rather tenuous balance of traditional native environmental values and the perceived need for jobs, as expressed by Eddie Erasmus, former chief of the Treaty Eleven Dogrib Nation, and a member of the Dogrib Power Corporation board:

> The environment has always been our concern. We know that we have to protect our land, our waters and our wildlife. It's part of our custom, our culture....But, in order to get into economic development and create jobs for our people, we have to give something in order to gain. (*Windspeaker*, April 12, 1993:8)

3

Fisheries

INTRODUCTION

> We, the Ehattesaht and Nuchatlaht Chiefs are reverting back to our Aboriginal Right to plan, manage, harvest and take true conservation measures in conjunction with Nature to ensure sustainable returns of all aqua-resources within our "Ha Holthe". This Aboriginal Right flows from total control and jurisdiction over a Hereditary Chief's "Ha Holthe" — Mountains, Lands, Rivers, Streams, Beaches, Foreshores, Reefs and Deep Seas. (Reprinted in *Ha-Shilth-Sa*, November 30, 1988)

The situation of native fisheries in Canada is an extremely complex topic, since key variables affecting it are subject to considerable regional variation. Among the key variables suggested are the following:

- The "aboriginal" significance of fishing, i.e. its economic as well as socio-cultural importance;
- The legal basis of native fishing rights: treaties, Natural Resources Transfer Agreements, aboriginal rights, contemporary agreements;
- The "state of the resource", i.e. quality and quantity of fish and their habitat; and
- The "economics of fishing" on a macro- and micro-scale.

The first two variables are uniquely native attributes, whereas the last two have an impact on fishing activities, no matter what group or locality is involved. With respect to native people, however, these first two factors are very important in determining the manner in which the latter two affect fishing activities, regardless of whether subsistence or commercial fisheries are involved.

As Erhard Rostlund mentions in his monograph on "Freshwater Fish and Fishing in Native North America", the importance of fish in the food economy of any North American tribe depended primarily on three factors: the kind of fish resource that was available to the tribe, the type of fishing equipment and degree of skill possessed by the tribe, and people's attitude toward fish as food (Rostlund 1952:145). Accordingly, the significance of the fishery resource for Canada's First Nations in aboriginal times varied widely from region to region.

With regard to the country's west coast peoples, it may be said without exaggeration that marine resources in general, and the salmon in particular, constituted not only people's economic staple but also provided the very essence of their social fabric and the basis for their territorial organization. Today fishing still is the economic activity around which life essentially revolves.

Fish has never played a comparable role for the tribes of the eastern seaboard, such as the Micmac, Montagnais or Malecite. Fishing constituted a very important seasonal activity, but hunting was much more significant here than among the west coast peoples; the Malecite were also maize farmers in aboriginal times (Jenness 1932:270). Thus, on the east coast, fishing constituted an essential part of people's land-based economy. The seashore and river mouths were visited and exploited as part of a seasonal cycle, but were not the site of permanent villages as was the case on the west coast. Today, fishing is still important to individuals and selected villages, but does not appear to be the economic base for the east coast's native population (with the possible exception of some Inuit groups in northern Labrador [CARC 1988:75]).

Similarly, fish was one of the staples for the tribes around the Great Lakes, whom Rostlund (1952:152) refers to as interior coastal tribes, e.g. the Hurons, Iroquois and Ojibway. The importance of fish varied over time and from place to place, depending on the availability of the resource and that of other staples, such as wild game, wild rice and cultivated crops.

To a lesser degree, fishing constituted an important part of the land-based existence of native people almost everywhere else in Canada: the interior of British Columbia, the northern provinces, and the subarctic and arctic regions of the territories. The only area where fish — not an abundant resource in any case — was hardly utilized was on the plains. The majority of the Blackfeet even regarded fish as unclean, although the Fish Eaters band of the Blood Indians derived their name from their custom of eating them (Ewers 1958:87).

This brief glimpse of aboriginal economies brings us to the rather obvious conclusion that fish was an important resource to most native societies in Canada, in some cases even the crucial resource. This raises another question: How accessible are fishery resources to native people nowadays?

Native fishing rights are closely interwoven with native hunting rights, and in numerous treatments of this topic they are lumped together (Cumming and Mickenberg 1972:207–226; Sanders 1974:45–62; Woodward 1989:317–338). Native fishing rights, i.e. rights to the fishery resource held by native people over and above rights accruing to non-native Canadians, may be based on treaties, Natural Resources Transfer Agreements in the Prairie Provinces, aboriginal title and on contemporary agreements. All these alternatives will be further explored in the appropriate regional sections of this chapter. A preliminary look at the nature of these rights shall serve as a general introduction.

Native fishing rights are usually limited geographically and with regard to the purpose of fishing. A treaty like the Vancouver Island treaty, which was considered by the British Columbia Supreme Court in *Saanichton Marina Ltd. v. Claxton* (1987), 18 B.C.S.C. (2d) 217 (B.C.S.C.) [1987] 4 C.N.L.R. 48), protects the fishing rights of a small band within the tract of land and water surrendered. The area where these rights can be exercised is very limited. The same applies to other Vancouver Island treaties (a total of 14) entered into immediately after 1850, and other treaties negotiated with bands and localized groups in southern Ontario prior to 1850 (Sanders 1974:49). In contrast, the Robinson Treaties of 1850 provide that the Indian tribes have

> ...the full and free privilege to hunt over the Territory now ceded by them, and to fish in the waters thereof, as they have heretofore been in the habit of doing. (ibid.:50)

Here the geographical area within which fishing (and hunting) is protected is the treaty area. An Indian only needs evidence that he/she is from a band covered by the treaty to establish a treaty-protected right in the treaty area, although he/she may be outside the territory that his/her band has traditionally used. As Sanders (ibid.) points out, this is of great practical significance in terms of rendering unnecessary expert evidence as to the traditional hunting and fishing territory of the band, a task which is particularly complex in areas of older colonial settlement.

Similarly, the last of the numbered treaties, Treaty No. Eleven, signed in 1921, provides that

> ...they shall have the right to pursue their usual vocations of hunting, trapping and fishing throughout the tract surrendered as heretofore described. (Sanders 1974:50)

The geographical area covered by Treaty No. Eleven is approximately half of the mainland area of the Northwest Territories. A further territorial extension of traditional harvesting rights is affected in each of the Prairie Provinces by the Natural Resources Transfer Agreements:

> ...the said Indians (the Indians of the Provinces) shall have the right, which the Province hereby assures to them, of hunting, trapping and fishing game and fish for food at all seasons of the year on all unoccupied Crown lands and on any other lands to which the said Indian may have a right of access. (British North America Act, 1930, Schedule 2, R.S.C. 1970, Appendices No. 23. Quoted in Sanders 1974:50)

These rights are province-wide. The Natural Resources Transfer Agreements of 1929 conveyed the ownership of natural resources from the federal government to the provinces of Alberta, Saskatchewan and Manitoba. All other provinces entered the confederation with the ownership of their natural resources (Sanders 1974:54). These agreements were incorporated into the British North America Act of 1930 and are therefore part of the Canadian Constitution. The guarantees of native harvesting rights under the agreements are strictly confined to personal use and have never been interpreted as permitting trading or barter (Bennett 1982:9). This matter is less clearly defined with regard to treaty rights.

An Ontario Provincial Court Judge (in R. v. Penasse (1971), 8 C.C.C. (2d) 569) has held that Indian rights to fish, protected by the Robinson Treaties with the words "as they have heretofore been in the habit of doing", gave the Indians a defence to a charge of failing to have a commercial fishing licence (Sanders 1974:57). The accused had been selling the fish to a non-Indian. The judge ruled that the Crown failed to prove that the Indians were acting outside the scope of their treaty rights, as there was the distinct possibility that native people of that area had been involved in some commercial exploitation of fish by 1850, the date of the Robinson Treaties.

In *Regina v. Cardinal* (Cardinal v. A.G. Alta., [1974] S.C.R. 695 [Alta]), an Indian was charged under provincial law for selling big game on a reserve. The Supreme Court of Canada upheld the conviction on the basis that the Natural Resources Transfer Agreements made provincial laws respecting game applicable on reserves in the Prairies, unless the Indian was hunting for food. It may be assumed that the same ruling would apply to fishing activities. Therefore, in this case an argument such as used in *R. v. Penasse* would not be available in Manitoba, Saskatchewan or Alberta, even if commercial exploitation of the resource at the date of the appropriate treaty could be proven (Sanders 1974:49, 57).

To what degree are off-reserve fishing rights based on treaties and Natural Resources Transfer Agreements protected from infringement by provincial and federal legislation? As a rule, the courts have tended to protect native fishing (and hunting) rights from provincial encroachment (Cumming and Mickenberg 1972:209). Even before the enactment of Section 88 of the Indian Act, provincial laws regulating fishing (and hunting) were considered inapplicable on Indian reserves, and Indian treaties served as a bar to legislative infringements on the right to fish and hunt.

Section 88 of the Indian Act reads as follows:

> Subject to the terms of any treaty and any other Act of the Parliament of Canada, all laws of general application from time to time in force in any province are applicable to and in

> respect of Indians in the province, except to the extent that such laws are inconsistent with this Act or any order, rule, regulation or by-law made thereunder, and except to the extent that such laws make provision for any matter for which provision is made by or under this Act. (Indian Act, 1985, c.I-6, s.88)

In other words, what this section seems to say is, that where there are treaty-protected fishing rights, provincial legislation cannot affect them. Regarding the question of what constitutes a treaty, case law seems to uphold a relatively liberal interpretation of this term (Cumming and Mickenberg 1972:210). In *Regina v. White and Bob* ((1965), 50 D.L.R. (2d) 613, 52 W.W.R. 193 (B.C.C.A.), aff'd (1966), 52 D.L.R. (2d) 481 (S.C.C.)), the document in question was informal and inconclusive as to whether its signatory, Governor Douglas, was acting in his capacity as Chief Factor of the Hudson's Bay Company or as governor of the colony. Nevertheless, the British Columbia Court of Appeal ruled that the document represented a binding treaty within the meaning of s.88. This decision clearly overrules an earlier holding by the Nova Scotia County Court in *Rex v. Syliboy* ((1928), 50 C.C.C. 389), which precedes the enactment of s.88. That judgement holds that the hunting rights claimed are non-treaty and therefore not protected against provincial law (Sanders 1974:52f). Moreover, *Regina v. White and Bob* concluded with the ruling that in a situation of conflict between an Indian treaty and a provincial game law, treaty provisions would prevail.

In the case of the Natural Resources Transfer Agreements, the phrase "which the province hereby assures to them" has been interpreted to mean that the rights are protected against provincial laws, but not against federal laws. Contentious issues pertaining to these agreements focus on the meaning of "unoccupied Crown lands" and "other lands to which the said Indians have a right of access" (for discussion see chapter 5).

The courts have consistently upheld that Indian fishing (and hunting and trapping) rights are subject to federal laws. One major piece of federal legislation which affects native fisheries is the Fisheries Act, which has been held to apply to Indians (for example, *R. v. Derrikson*, [1976] 2 S.C.R.V. [B.C.]; *R. v. Francis* (1970) 10 D.L.R. (3d) 189; Sanders 1974:47). Several of the regulations under the Fisheries Act make special provisions for native people. There are separate regulations for each province and territory, and the regulations are in fact drawn up by the province or territory concerned and not by the federal government (Sanders 1974:47). This explains the difference in the treatment of native people in the various regions. The regulations for Manitoba, Nova Scotia, Newfoundland and Prince Edward Island make no special provisions for Indians. The regulations for New Brunswick and Ontario make special provisions only for certain bands. Quebec has a provision for issuing special licences to Indians and Inuit which completely exempts the licensee from the regulations. Saskatchewan, Alberta and the Northwest Territories each permit an Indian to fish for food for himself and his family. British Columbia and Yukon have a similar provision, but it is subject to restrictions that may be written into the licence. In Alberta and the Northwest Territories, an Indian may fish for food for his dogs. In Yukon an Indian may fish for food for his band. In Alberta the rights are also granted to "Metis" defined as persons having not less than one-quarter Indian blood. In the Northwest Territories the rights are granted to the Inuit and "persons of mixed blood" defined as individuals having no less than one-quarter Indian or Inuit blood. In Quebec the special provisions also apply to the Inuit, and a special definition of Inuit is modeled after the Indian status definition system in the Indian Act (Woodward 1989:324–331; Sanders 1974:47).

The case of *The Queen v. George* ([1966] S.C.R. 267, 55 D.L.R. (2d) 386) established conclusively that s.88 of the Indian Act does not include federal legislation. Accordingly, in *Regina v. Cooper* ((1969) 1 D.L.R. (3d) 113 (B.C.S.C.)), the British Columbia Supreme Court upheld the conviction of three Treaty Indians for fishing violations under the federal Fisheries Act, even though the agreement which contained the guarantee of fishing rights relied upon by the defendants, constituted a binding treaty (Cumming and Mickenberg 1972:219).

Many of the numbered treaties with the Indians of western Canada contain an express clause subjecting native fishing and hunting rights to government regulations. In Treaty No. Eight, for example, the relevant clause reads as follows:

> And Her Majesty the Queen hereby agrees with the said Indians that they shall have the right to pursue their usual vocations of hunting, trapping and fishing throughout the tract surrendered as heretofore described, subject to such regulations as may from time to time be made by the Government of the country, acting under the authority of Her Majesty, and saving and excepting such tracts as may be required or taken up from time to time for settlement, mining, lumbering, trading or other purposes.

(For discussion see chapter 5.)

Section 88 of the Indian Act makes no reference to non-treaty or aboriginal fishing and hunting rights. The major non-treaty areas are British Columbia, Yukon, Quebec and the Maritime Provinces. There are no treaties with the Inuit and Metis. Case law regarding the conflict between provincial or federal legislation and claims to native fishing and hunting rights rooted in the concept of aboriginal rights, including the Royal Proclamation of 1763, is extremely sparse and was, prior to 1990, inconclusive. Generally, no off-reserve fishing or hunting rights were recognized in the non-treaty areas of the country. Lately, though, there have been some revolutionary developments in this area, occasioned by court rulings, such as *Sparrow* and *Denny* as discussed in the later sections of this chapter.

THE WEST COAST

For several reasons a major portion of this chapter is devoted to the west coast:

1. Hardly anywhere else in this country do native people's lives revolve around one economic activity to the degree that west coast Indian people depend on fishing: economically, socio-culturally and spiritually;
2. At the same time they are faced with more constraints and uncertainties in their utilization of fishery resources than native people elsewhere; and
3. The crisis situation of the west coast fishery and the unsettled state of affairs with regard to aboriginal claims create a unique challenge as well as an opportunity for future schemes of shared resource management.

West Coast Fishery

In British Columbia the commercial fishery ranks fourth among the province's resource-based sectors (after forestry, mining and tourism-recreation) in terms of aggregate economic impact, but this ranking seriously understates the significance of the fishery for the livelihood and lifestyles of British Columbians (Cassidy and Dale 1988:36). This is particularly true for native people: Almost all native communities depend on fish for food, intercommunity trade, sales or employment in the commercial fishing subsector.

Unlike the Atlantic, the Pacific Ocean has a narrow continental shelf, for which reason most fishing takes place on a relatively narrow coastal band (Clement 1986:35). Salmon is by far the dominant species in the west coast fishery, and the fish are captured on their spawning runs to the rivers. Halibut, herring and assorted groundfish are of lesser importance.

The west coast fishery did not become commercial until canning techniques were developed, but when they were, the canneries spread rapidly along the Fraser River and north to virtually all coastal communities as far as Alaska. Thus the commercial fishery began not with fishers and raw fish but with processors and canned fish (Marchak 1987a:23). In the late 1870s canneries were established by brokerage firms, and then by companies already involved in the Atlantic fishery and in the United States. They sought a fishing labour force through offers of daily wages and family employment: women and children at the cannery and men on the rivers and on coastal vessels. Such arrangements "captured" Indians in northern areas and Japanese-Canadians further south.

Large factory vessels so common in the offshore Atlantic fishery were never technically feasible or cost-effective in British Columbia's inland waters where the salmon fishery is concentrated. As early as the turn of the century (and somewhat later in northern waters), there was an increasing trend for independent fishers to enter the industry and supply the canneries. These were mostly gillnetters and trollers, whereas, until the 1970s, much of the seine boat fleet was company-owned (McMullan 1987a:37). Various considerations induced the processors to welcome the entry of independent fishers into the industry: the undesirability of tying up capital in vessels and gear; producing profit only on a seasonal basis; the risk costs associated with obsolescence and loss of vessels; labour costs and problems of supervision; variable harvests and variable markets (Marchak 1987:24). Although the majority of fishers are independent, companies have retained ownership rights in some vessels, as well as shares in vessels ostensibly owned by independents. This practice ensures a guaranteed minimum catch and a way of providing processors with information about runs, cash buyers and any other fishing conditions that might affect their supplies from independent fishers.

During the 1970s surplus returns to independent fishers were abnormally high. A large proportion was reinvested in the vessels as fishers strove to further increase their catch through purchase of new and expensive technology. By the late 1970s the British Columbia fishing fleet was vastly overcapitalized relative to the supplies of fish. The result was a situation aptly summarized by Patricia Marchak:

> Thus we arrive at the 1980s with a depleted resource, state managers striving to reduce the fishery, native fishers demanding aboriginal rights to greater allocations, sports fishers claiming special rights more in line with the increasing economic importance of their industry, and numerous disunified groups of commercial fishers mounting legal battles against these special claims on the specific grounds that the resource belongs to everyone. (Marchak 1987a:29)

Fishery Jurisdiction

Jurisdictional issues relating to the fishery are much more complex than they are for other renewable resources. Section 91 (12) of the British North America Act, 1867, grants to the federal government legislative jurisdiction over "sea coast and inland fisheries". This jurisdiction is exercised through the Fisheries Act, administered by the Minister of Fisheries and Oceans and his department. Section 91 provides the basis for the federal government to regulate fishing activities with closures, gear restrictions and limits on catches. An important 1985 decision of the Federal Court of Appeal suggests that the federal government may take allocation measures not just for conservation purposes, but also to allocate the available harvest among various user groups for socio-economic purposes (Cassidy and Dale 1988:39).

In waters outside of British Columbia, where the seabed is owned by the Crown in the right of Canada, the right to fish is owned by Canada, but since these waters are tidal and sea waters by definition, this right to fish is subject to the overriding public right of fishing (British Columbia Aboriginal Peoples' Fisheries Commission, n.d.:Appendix 4:2f).

The Constitution Act assigns to provincial legislatures jurisdiction over "the management and sale of the public lands" (s.92 [5]). As this implies all ownership rights, including the right to fish, this division of legislative power is, to say the least, confusing (ibid.). The provincial government, for the most part, owns the bed (solum) of non-tidal waters in the province (Cassidy and Dale 1988:42). As a matter of common law, the owner of the solum has the exclusive right to the fishery on non-tidal and non-navigable waters. Consequently, this right is provincial property and subject to provincial legislation. The province can grant fishing rights in non-tidal waters and may also establish closed seasons for these waters.

The owner of the bed underlying tidal and navigable waters does not have these rights for, as a matter of common law, there exists a public right to fish in these waters (Cassidy and Dale 1988::43).

Another very important aspect of provincial power over fisheries lies in provincial ownership of areas of fish habitat and the surrounding uplands. This severely curtails the federal government's ability to protect the environment of spawning fish. The Supreme Court of Canada has placed a limit on the use of federal power to protect fish habitat by striking down a section of the Fisheries Act which prohibited any deposit of logging debris into streams inhabited by fish; in the future, actual harm to the habitat would have to be established (ibid.).

A third source of provincial authority over the fishery derives from general powers over property and civil rights. These enable the province to regulate processing and intraprovincial marketing of fish.

A final source of provincial power is delegated by the federal government. The Fisheries Act empowers the Governor in Council to make fisheries regulations, such as controls on gear and the timing of fishing. These are passed for each province, but with regard to non-tidal water fisheries, the province has the delegated authority to amend the regulations.

Provincial leasing policy has far-reaching implications for the disposition of near-shore resources, including those near Indian settlements and within "sea claim" areas outlined by many coastal groups (ibid.). This is particularly significant for aquaculture operations. The province generally owns the foreshore (the area between low and high water) and, in any case, most if not all aquaculture operations will likely be land-based. Operators therefore need to purchase or lease provincially owned land. Since 1986 preliminary permits, referred to as Section 10 licences, have been automatically granted for a period of one year, which enables aquaculturalists to carry out detailed site surveys and production planning. The ensuing "goldrush" of site applications has alarmed many native observers.

The scope of federal jurisdiction in fisheries matters is considerably more limited than the broad language of Section 91 (12) of the Constitution Act would indicate. Patricia Marchak (1987a:15f) strikes at the core of the matter when she states that the federal government "may make rules governing the capture of fish but it cannot control the context of fishing." And even if this were otherwise, it is unlikely that fisheries would have precedence since, for the provincial as well as for the federal government, the chief property owners and most powerful voices are to be found in forestry and mining, not fisheries (ibid.).

Indians in the Fishery

The fishery may rank as a comparatively low priority in the provincial economic context, but it is of paramount importance to British Columbia's First Nations. This goes for both the subsistence or food fishery and commercial fishery. This distinction is highly arbitrary and controversial, and native people generally hold that a distinction between food and commerce is neither valid nor any business of outsiders (Cassidy and Dale 1988:41).[1] Nevertheless, governments and fisheries managers insist upon it.

The Pearse Report (Berkes 1990:37) indicates that some 25,000 people benefited from the **subsistence** harvest. Because of extensive food-sharing networks so prevalent among

[1] Polly Wheeler (1988) reports on an interesting example from Alaska where the distinction between subsistence and commercial fishery is made quite clearly by native people. In the Lower Koyukon Athabaskan fishing system, subsistence fishery and commercial fishery are governed by totally different value systems. It appears that subsistence fishing is a functional, self-regulating system both directed at and resulting in "conservation" and sustained yield. State regulations pertaining to subsistence fishing are perceived as intrusive and unnecessary. On the other hand, commercial fishing is viewed as an externally introduced activity, which is understandably regulated by the state. It is an opportunity to be exploited.

native people, Evelyn Pinkerton (Berkes 1990:37f) estimates that about three-quarters of the total native population of 57,000 (i.e. 43,000) may actually be its beneficiaries. The practice of subsistence fishing varies widely among bands, from the retention of a fairly intact system of traditional property rights, harvesting and distribution patterns with the Gitksan and Wet'suwet'en (see later section on The Aboriginal Right to the Fishery Resource) to a situation prevalent with numerous bands, where the food fishery has been reduced to several days of the year when Indian people obtain special permits from the Department of Fisheries and Oceans to take fish with commercial gear for home consumption (Pinkerton 1987:254f). Many of these groups are actively involved in the commercial fishery, and their systems of property rights have been quite differently affected. These bands also tend to perceive the focus of their struggle for recognition of aboriginal rights in terms of access to commercial high seas fishing licences and fishing areas (e.g. the Nisga'a).

But even when they have fully entered into the **commercial fishery**, native people have enough grounds beyond their claim of aboriginal rights to act as a special status group.

> Because they are legally wards of the state without the right to offer reserve land as collateral, Indian fishers have not had the same access to capital as many non-Indians, and have thus developed special relations of dependency with fish-processing companies. Programs to assist Indians in acquiring their own vessels have existed only in the last seventeen years and have helped mainly the most well established. In addition, the continuation of traditional cultural forms (often modified) has influenced the way many Indians act as commercial fishers, creating different patterns of capture, utilization of product and vessel, investment in vessels, and hiring of crew. These distinctive patterns, including the cooperative sharing of benefits within Indian communities, may have been important in bringing about a situation in which Indian fishers lost both licences and vessels. Tribal and pantribal organizations have formed to represent the special needs and interests of Indian fishers and Indian communities. These have created institutions to support aboriginal rights, cultural heritage and community life, and a desire to maintain a position in the fisheries, all simultaneously. In sum, aboriginal rights to fish, separate cultural traditions and communities, and a long history of dependence on the industry, especially in relations with processors, have caused Indians to perceive themselves as a special status group with unique interests and concerns in the fishery. (Pinkerton 1987a:249f)

From the start there was a strong mutual dependence between Indians and processing firms. In the nineteenth century, canneries would locate near Indian communities for the explicit purpose of utilizing native labour for both fishing and shorework, if those communities were near a particularly large salmon run. Canners would also buy the majority of fishing licences under the Indians' names. For example, in 1892, 3,000 to 3,500 Indians fished on the Fraser, a mere forty of whom owned their own licences in their own names (ibid.:255). All the others made less money because they sold their catch at wage rates and used company boats and/or licences bought by the companies. Many refused to pay for their licences, arguing that fishing was their right.

This dependency pattern was further accentuated in the 1920s when fishing became a more capital-intensive undertaking. Forbidden to mortgage reserve land, Indians were seldom in a position to purchase outright a fishing boat and net. At the same time, canners were becoming less interested in direct ownership of boats, but more willing to lend Indian fishers money for boat purchases, in return for guaranteed delivery of all their fish. In practice, however, few Indians actually benefited from this opportunity to become vessel owners. Cultural factors such as the contrast between a kin-based community life and an individually-based competitive life in an industrial setting, undoubtedly had something to do with this failure. But the fact that processors actively fostered the relationship of indebted vessel owners was at least as important (ibid.:257). The inability of native people to successfully compete in the labour market outside the fishing industry enabled cannery owners to exploit the ethnic position of Indians.

The fishing industry thus became an enclave for Indians, where they could acquire credit and job security largely unattainable elsewhere. As described by Evelyn Pinkerton, long-term relations of patronage developed between cannery managers and individual fishermen (Pinkerton 1987a:257). The reward for a long and dependable delivery record with a cannery included job opportunities for other family members. Such relationships very likely inhibited questioning about the canners' handling of licensing, boat ownership and payment arrangements, as well as curbing the development of entrepreneurship.

Indian vessel ownership seems to have declined from more than 50 per cent to about 12 per cent of all vessel owners between the First World War and 1983. At the latter date, Indians held 11.6 per cent of all the salmon gillnet, troll and combination vessels and 12.5 per cent of all the salmon seine vessels. When the vessels acquired by three Indian tribal councils in 1982 are included, Indians owned 14 per cent of all salmon vessels, as well as 28 per cent of the roe herring personnel licences (ibid.:258).

The year 1982 marked the establishment of the *Northern Native Fishing Corporation* (NNFC). One common share is held by each of the Nisga'a, Gitksan-Wet'suwet'en and North Coast Tribal Councils. The creation of this corporation took place primarily in response to a plan by B.C. Packers Limited to sell its large northern gillnet fleet (Cassidy and Dale 1988:51). The purchase of the fleet was financed through an $11.7 million federal grant.

Initially, the NNFC leased the fleet of some 250 boats and licences to native fishermen, but in 1983 the corporation began to negotiate sales exclusively to members of the three tribal councils. As the NNFC has sold its original fleet, it has continued to acquire other vessels with the intention of functioning as something like a "boat-bank" for would-be native vessel owners (ibid.).

The creation of this corporation constitutes a concerted effort to break away from the patterns of patronage so firmly established on the west coast. It also represents an attempt to merge individual entrepreneurship with tribal interests. That old habits persist is illustrated by the fact that, in 1987, fishermen still delivered to B.C. Packers and borrowed money from the company (Pinkerton 1987a:265). The NNFC tries to counteract this dependency by maintaining control of the fishing licences while endeavouring to extract a commitment to the corporation from fishers by requiring them to purchase the vessel attached to the licence. In return for access to commercial fishing privileges, loans, training programs in accounting and vessel maintenance, current NNFC members subsidize the entry of more fishers into the corporation.

While fostering the development of entrepreneurship, the corporation attempts to minimize the disruptive effects of elite formation and stratification within native communities. The tribal councils, through the corporation, are the actual owners of the licences, and maintain control of access to the licences in a manner not unlike the aboriginal system (ibid.). Through various measures, fishers are encouraged by the corporation to develop entrepreneurial attitudes, but within a structure of responsibility to the larger group.

The NNFC does contain a certain contradiction within itself, by virtue of the fact that it advances vessel ownership as the driving force of community development. With some tribal groups, such as the Gitksan-Wet'suwet'en of the upper Skeena River (who constitute part of the corporation), commercializing the food fishery is a major hope for a viable economic future as presented in a later section. This involves fishing with nets in the river some 200 kilometres inland, instead of using vessels at sea. Vessel owners and corporation members in this tribe constitute only a small percentage of the workforce, and they fish commercially outside their traditional territories.

The Native Brotherhood (see p. 42), has supported the idea of Indians acquiring territorial fishing rights organized around terminal river fisheries, where salmon would be taken as they enter their "home" territories. Terminal salmon fisheries are also favoured by many Department of Fisheries and Oceans policy makers as a preferential form of management, reducing some mixed stock problems and diminishing overcapitalization of vessels (Pinkerton 1987:266). In some tribal groups far fewer people have access to vessels than to river nets, for which reason the vessel-owning route of the corporation benefits these groups less. A potential conflict may thus be created even within the same tribal group, among members working toward vessel ownership and members trying to capture the same fish by different methods upstream.

Native shoreworkers find themselves in a position fundamentally different from that of vessel owners, with few opportunities for upward mobility. Early on in the development of the industry, however, native shoreworkers just like native fishers found the commercial fishery to be more accommodating and acceptable than any other industry. Particularly in the first few decades, the organization and the seasonal nature of cannery work permitted native people to retain many aspects of their traditional social and economic life (ibid.:260). For many workers, processing jobs were available only during a six-week period at the height of the season. In some cases, the timing of the salmon runs in different areas permitted Indians to finish the canning season in an urban centre and return home in time to process their own winter supply of salmon. As long as the canners were dependent on native labour, they accommodated the Indians' traditional social and economic arrangements. Hiring patterns, work arrangements and living accommodations at the early canneries were adapted to native labour. An Indian "cannery boss" or contractor with appropriate language skills (usually one per company per tribal area) arranged the hiring and housing of entire kin units who moved to the canneries for the two- to three-month season. Whole villages were reported to have relocated in this manner. In outlying areas, many of these arrangements continued into the 1960s.

In interviews conducted during the 1980s, Evelyn Pinkerton (1987a:260) found that Indian shoreworkers of all ages expressed a preference for fish-plant work over other jobs, despite the fact that this type of work often involved the pain associated with tendonitis, carpal tunnel syndrome and back problems. Their refusal to complain may be related to fear of losing high-seniority jobs. Moreover, like fishermen, Indian shoreworkers were often unable to obtain jobs in other industries, whereas fish-plant work enabled them to take advantage of family connections in fishing and shore work. Family structure and the year-round cycle of activities were less disturbed by this industry than by others.

When the processing industry went through a phase of centralization in the late 1960s, many fish plants in the more isolated areas of the coast closed down, thus eliminating critical seasonal employment for the local workforce. By 1970, Indians comprised only 1,500 of the 3,700 shoreworkers (Pearse 1982, quoted in Pinkerton 1987a:261).

An interesting observation by Pinkerton during her fieldwork in the 1980s concerns the fact that virtually all Indian shoreworkers are members of the United Fishermen and Allied Workers Union (UFAWU), and appear to assume a more militant and consistent **trade-union** stance than Indian fishers. Also, those interviewed felt they had more in common with non-Indian shoreworkers than with Indian fishers in the Native Brotherhood.

The UFAWU allows small but not large-scale boat owners to join, thus creating a division among vessel owners and between large-vessel owners and crew. On the other hand, the Native Brotherhood of British Columbia includes all classes of fishers, since it began as an organization concerned with the promotion of Indian health, education and aboriginal claims. In addition, it hopes to improve the Indian position in the fishing industry. Nevertheless, the effect that government programs have had on native fishers has rather served to divide the ranks of native fishermen. Programs like the Indian Fishermen's Assistance Program (1967–1979) have tended to benefit the more successful and relatively wealthy fishers who could, for example, afford to make the 12 to 20 per cent qualifying downpayment to acquire a vessel (Pinkerton 1987:258,262). As one successful Indian boat owner puts it: "Most Indians can't even get into the economic system, because the bottom two rungs of the ladder are missing." (ibid.:262) Those at the lower rung of the hierarchy tend to be attracted to the trade union movement.

The Native Brotherhood continues to present itself as an advocate for Indians as a status group whose interests are not adequately represented by the UFAWU. Indian vessel owners who had borrowed large sums of money in the 1970s to purchase newer and larger vessels identified themselves principally as owners, rather than workers, and preferred to ally themselves with others in the same situation. They needed to keep their boats working to keep up payments. Strikes over minimum prices and shorework wages were seen as most beneficial to fishers not owning their vessels and shoreworkers as well. The ambiguous and often tumultuous relationship between the Union and the Native Brotherhood has been documented by various writers (Marchak 1987b; Clement 1986). However, the rank and file of the native organization — composed of small and less upwardly mobile vessel owners, rental skippers and crew — continue to feel at least some solidarity with union ideology, rather than acting solely as a status group in native interests.

Native People and Aquaculture

In view of the shrinking employment base provided by the fishing industry, native people have also looked towards aquaculture to provide a much needed economic base for their communities. In the 1980s aquaculture was considered by many as one of the major growth industries of the next several decades and the great government panacea to British Columbia's salmon problems (Hunter 1985:59; Beaudry 1992:62).

In British Columbia, salmonoid aquaculture activities mostly originated from the Department of Fisheries and Oceans' Salmonid Enhancement Program (SEP), which is further discussed in a later section. In the mid-1980s, native people's involvement was limited to the operation of about 20 out of 69 enhancement facilities. No commercial salmon farm had been initiated by Indian entrepreneurs, but they had three unsuccessful oyster projects (British Columbia Aboriginal Peoples' Fisheries Commission n.d.:4–6).

Through their involvement in the SEP many native people have had a chance to familiarize themselves with the concepts and technology involved in the operation of fish farms and hatcheries. But their participation in commercial aquaculture is still hampered by some major obstacles, foremost among them resource access and development capital.

As described earlier, the provincial government controls land-based resources and most of the foreshore. Much of this land is effectively controlled by large corporations (forestry, mining, fishing, transportation) holding various rights through leases, licences and permits (ibid. Appendix 2:1). In the 1980s a veritable "goldrush" among non-native applicants staking provincial section 10 aquaculture leases on the remaining sites took place. Many Indian reserves are located close to areas with excellent aquaculture potential, and native people are encouraged to join in the application rush. But for some native groups, f.e. the Musgamagw Tribal Council on northern Vancouver Island, the aquaculture issue is a complex one (Cassidy and Dale 1988:60).

While there is a feeling of urgency for identifying locations of high potential before they are alienated, there is also some concern about the implications of following provincial regulations (i.e. acknowledging provincial jurisdiction over the foreshore and inland waters by applying for licences) for future land claims negotiation or litigation. Moreover, in many cases, there are potential resource use conflicts and competition for sites between aquaculture and more long-standing marine activities, such as traditional intertidal harvesting of shellfish. Commercial fishermen have tended to oppose rapid aquaculture development for various reasons, such as the potential transfer of diseases from cultured to wild stocks. Also, native people (Ryan 1985:15) as well as non-native biologists (P. Paquet, quoted in van Dyk

1990:29) have warned of other negative effects on wild stocks, including genetic erosion and salmonoid replacement. The critics' worst fears were substantiated in 1988 when a delegation of commercial fishers visited Norway, the world leader in farmed salmon production, on a fact-finding mission. Briefed by officials of Norway's Directorate for Nature Management, they discovered that the fish-farming business in Norway was severely endangering that country's remaining stocks of wild salmon through disease, parasites and genetic pollution (Beaudry 1992:62).

Problems associated with funding native aquaculture projects are summarized by the British Columbia Aboriginal Peoples' Fisheries Commission:

> The availability of funds from private lending sources for the purpose of new Native business development has always been limited, particularly when resources are sought for the purpose of purchasing assets that will be located "on reserve". In addition, the innovative and high risk nature of aquaculture activities make debt financing from conventional sources difficult even for non-native participants. Given, the operational risks, the long-term nature of the industry, the Native developmental setting and the alternative opportunities for private investment capital, it is predictable that low cost, long term debt funding will be required to initiate development of the Indian aquaculture enterprises. (British Columbia Aboriginal Peoples' Fisheries Commission, n.d., Appendix 2:5)

As a result, native people require special federal government assistance to participate successfully in this industry. A further potential source of development capital could arise from compensation for their comprehensive claims, but this does not appear to be forthcoming in the foreseeable future.

There is no need for aquaculture to be limited to salmon enhancement, and there are many indications that the former could contribute much to the well-being of British Columbia's native communities. This is borne out by the experience of the Lummi Indian community in Washington. Their aquaculture project, which in a decade turned their whole tribal society from one of welfare dependency to self-sufficiency, is eloquently described by Vine Deloria Jr.

> After the United States government had finished with the Lummi Indian tribe, all that the Lummi had left was the land that lay exposed between low tide and high tide. A mud flat. Yet clinging to this mere fragment of aboriginal existence, the tribe conceived one of the most advanced programs any community has ever created. (Deloria 1978:90)

The nucleus of their development was an aquaculture project, cultivating various species of fish and oysters, and marketing them on a national basis. But this project caught the imagination of virtually the entire community. Through various multiplier effects it had a positive impact on most aspects of community life: Spin-off industries were established; advanced training was provided in such diverse fields as marine biology, administration and clerical work; a reservation-wide housing program was undertaken by a Lummi construction company; new institutions for research, education and economic development were established; and various social programs were initiated. All these were demonstrable derivatives from the aquaculture project. As Deloria (ibid.:152) puts it, "Instead of categorizing Lummi aquaculture as a profit-making venture, one could more adequately characterize it as a generating source of development and social service funds."

The Aboriginal Right to the Fishery Resource

Earlier it has been mentioned that there are many divisions among native people involved in the west coast fishery. An Indian may be a subsistence fisher, a shoreworker, a crewman, a rental skipper, a small-vessel owner or a seine boat owner and, as such, he or she may pursue different interests and also be drawn into groups that include non-Indians. A unifying force, however, based on their ethnic status is native people's common claim to the fishery resource as an integral part of their aboriginal rights. Acknowledgement and assumption of these rights will have different implications for the diverse native interest groups, but since the claimed right does not only include a larger share of the resource, but also responsibility for its management, everybody will be affected.

With the exception of several groups on Vancouver Island[2], most British Columbia Indian nations never signed treaties or in any other form relinquished their aboriginal rights. On the other hand agreements made with Indians prior to the establishment of canneries, subsequent negotiations with the Department of Fisheries and Oceans (DFO), and the commissions that set up Indian reserve lands all recognized Indian rights to capture and sell fish (Pinkerton 1987a:249). Direct competition for fish between commercial canners and Indian domestic fisheries first made itself felt around the turn of the century. Ironically, this was a time period when Indian fishing rights were officially recognized and confirmed by both federal and provincial governments, mostly because of disagreements over the size of Indian reserves. Acreage and location of reserve lands were determined by joint Indian Reserve Commissions operating from 1876 to 1877, 1879 to 1880, 1880 to 1898 and by the joint Royal Commission operating from 1913 to 1916. The province succeeded in persuading federal officials that Indians in British Columbia did not require reserves as large as those set aside in other provinces, as long as native fisheries were protected. Indians, for their part, agreed to the small reserves allocated them on the understanding that their rights to the fishery were guaranteed (Lane and Lane 1978, quoted in Pinkerton 1987a:251). It did not take long, however, for the Fisheries Department to be sensitive to pressure from the canneries, as a result of which it insisted that native people's aboriginal rights did not exempt them from regulation under the Fisheries Act. The Department of Fisheries and Oceans maintains that the Fisheries Act supersedes any obligations incurred under treaties or commissions, whereas the Department of Indian Affairs upholds the rights of Indians to pass their own band by-laws for "the preservation, protection and management of fur-bearing animals, fish and other game on the reserve." (Indian Act 1985, c.I-5, s.81 [o]). Both the courts and the federal Department of Justice have taken the position that where there is an inconsistency between band by-laws and the federal Fisheries Act, the former will prevail.

Hence, band councils have the option to prescribe for themselves a less restrictive regime than that laid out in the Fisheries Act and Regulations. There are two major restrictions on the utility of the by-laws. First, band by-laws must be submitted to the Minister of INAC for a 40-day period during which the Minister may disallow the by-law. This has been a severe impediment for numerous British Columbia bands. Second, by-laws apply only within the confines of the reserve.

Until fairly recently these by-laws rarely constituted a challenge to federal authority, but the situation changed as tensions grew between the DFO and native groups in the late 1970s (Cassidy and Dale 1988:45). A notable example of the new more assertive use of band by-laws is the Squamish Band's By-law 10, which was passed to provide a legal basis for band members to fish without DFO regulation. This by-law differs from DFO regulations in the kinds and numbers of fish allowed to be taken, the fishing methods used, and the permissible times and locations of fishing. An even more controversial case of native fisheries regulations arose in 1986 after several Gitksan-Wet'suwet'en bands enacted by-laws. The circumstances surrounding this situation will be discussed further in this chapter.

Prior to 1990, no special native fishing rights were recognized in British Columbia outside the boundaries of reserves. Like other provincial citizens, native people were subject to DFO legislation and were allocated a quota together with other user groups by the DFO. These quota were also determined by international considerations, as dictated by the

[2] See chapter 2 for Saanichton Marina Ltd. v. Claxton (1987), wherein a treaty right to maintain a traditional fishery is upheld.

Canada/U.S. Pacific Salmon Treaty. Restrictions on time, place and gear type were imposed. This placed severe restraints on all aspects of native fishing activities: food fishing for domestic consumption and ceremonial or cultural occasions, small-scale traditional river and coastal fisheries, and commercial fishing vessels.

It is a long-professed federal policy — reiterated in the DFO's "Policy Proposal for a B.C. Indian Community Salmon Fishery" of 1986 — that next to conservation, the native food fishery is to have highest priority. This is a matter of policy and not based on a recognition of aboriginal rights. Moreover, "allocations for Indian community fisheries, in excess of those for traditional food fisheries must be determined when the TAC (total allowable catch) is allocated by the Department of Fisheries and Oceans in consultation with all user groups." (Government of Canada, DFO 1986:4, quoted in Cassidy and Dale 1988:40). In practice, native domestic fisheries have suffered de facto loss of fish to commercial fishing pressure, as the DFO is empowered to allocate fish to other user groups before they reach their rivers of origin (and Indian fishers). As a result, native people contend, stocks may be drastically reduced by the time they reach traditional native fishing sites.

In the last two decades, the legal arena has produced crucial court rulings which have already profoundly transformed the scene of native fishing rights. The landmark case Calder v. Attorney General of British Columbia (1973) left no doubt that native fishing rights are an aspect of aboriginal title. Justice Hall (Bartlett 1988:7) described aboriginal title as "a right to occupy the lands and to enjoy the fruits of the soil, the forest and of the rivers and streams."

In December 1986 the British Columbia Court of Appeal made a far-reaching decision in the case involving a native fisherman who had been convicted of illegal fishing in an earlier trial. In this case which has come to be known as the *Sparrow* case (Sparrow v. R. (1986) 9 B.C.L.R. 300), the court ruled that native people have an unextinguished right to fish for food, and also held that the term "food fishery" should be given a broad interpretation. This native fishing right should be given priority over other users' rights, subject only to federal authority to ensure conservation of stocks. In 1990 the Supreme Court of Canada confirmed this ruling and sent the case back for retrial on the basis of aboriginal rights (R. v. Sparrow [1990] 3 C.N.L.R.160). This acknowledgement of aboriginal rights in British Columbia by the highest court in the country has far-reaching implications for the whole concept of comprehensive claims in this province. It has already had an impact on court rulings on fishing rights in other parts of the country (f.e. Nova Scotia), as explained in a later section.

In the early 1990s all parties involved in British Columbia's salmon fishery are grappling with the consequences — real and imagined — of the implementation of the *Sparrow* ruling. In 1992 the DFO introduced an Aboriginal Fisheries Strategy on a pilot project basis which, for the first time in almost a century, allows the sale of fish caught in the native fishery (*Windspeaker*, December 21, 1992:1; *Ha-Shilth-Sa*, March 31, 1993:1,16). Not surprisingly, as a result, native people are the first ones to be blamed by non-native interest groups for the continued decline of the fishery resource. In summer 1992 they were held responsible for the mysterious disappearance of more than half a million sockeye from the Fraser River system. Although government officials expressed the opinion that an inaccurate prediction of the salmon run was likely responsible for much of the shortfall, non-native commercial fishers, processors and sportfishing groups charged aboriginal people with overfishing and petitioned the British Columbia Supreme Court to halt the native fishery. At the same time, native people and small-time commercial fishers, native and non-native, feel extremely threatened by the rapid proliferation of sportfishing lodges (Beaudrey 1992:59f).

A federally commissioned report by University of British Columbia's Peter Pearse blames "unusually intensive" fishing for the salmon's decline, without accusing any party in particular. There are indications that the native fishery worked well in some areas but invited abuses outside agreement areas (*Windspeaker*, December 21, 1992:1).

In recognition of the problem, 97 bands throughout the Fraser River watershed signed a Memorandum of Understanding on March 25, 1993, among themselves, to restore order to their fishery and to ensure mutual respect of First Nations' territorial fishing rights. The accord commits each signing First Nation to more effective watershed management and conservation efforts, and includes

- A clear recognition that First Nations communities bear a responsibility to "protect, conserve and enhance" Fraser Basin Fisheries;
- A commitment to work cooperatively, on a consensus basis, in developing co-ordinated fishing plans;
- A provision for an annual fisheries management plan to include harvest management, enforcement, conservation, allocation, habitat protection and enhancement; and
- Systems to resolve disputes. (*Windspeaker*, April 12, 1993:2)

In the meantime, negotiations between aboriginal groups and the DFO over the implementation of Ottawa's Aboriginal Fishing Strategy are continuing.

In 1994 the first appeals dealing with the interpretation and application of the *Sparrow* decision will be heard in the British Columbia Court of Appeal. The two cases, which will be heard simultaneously, both raise the management question of how to conserve a stock which must pass through commercial fishing areas on its way to a native river fishery. In *Regina v. Sampson* (Regina v. Sampson [1992] 3 C.N.L.R.) and *Regina v. Jack* (Regina v. Jack [1992] 1 C.N.L.R.), the DFO asserted that there was a conservation problem at the terminal area. The Indians charged with illegal fishing stated that other user groups had accessed the salmon prior to their return to the natal river and that, therefore, the fisheries department could not claim a conservation problem at the river. In his 1992 judgement at the British Columbia Supreme Court, Justice MacDonnell sums up the dilemma all parties are faced with.

> The management of the fisheries by the D.F.O. upheld in *Sparrow* cannot work if the D.F.O. is required to conserve for Indian use adequate amounts of every stock, no matter how small, before allowing the offshore commercial fisheries to proceed. Aboriginal people have the right to fish....Such a right cannot extend to the fishing of any stock no matter how small or endangered. Therefore there was a valid legislative objective and the infringement is justified.
>
> ....
>
> It would not be possible to protect all wild chinook salmon without serious effects on the commercial fishing industry. The chinook intermingle with hatchery-produced spry and a large and abundant population of other species of salmon before they return to spawn. The time that these stocks can be most effectively dealt with, in conservation terms, is when the chinook is not co-mingled with other salmon species, but separate in their natal rivers. In addition, it is at terminal fisheries that the chinook are most vulnerable and at their greatest reproductive potential. (R. v. Jack [1992] 1 C.N.L.R.:127)

Leading up to *Sparrow*: The Assertion of Aboriginal Rights

The developments which eventually resulted in the *Sparrow* ruling are due exclusively to native people's enduring persistence in asserting their aboriginal rights to the fisheries resource. Indians have asserted their rights by pursuit of fisheries elements and/or "sea claims" within the comprehensive claims process and by passage of fishing by-laws under the Indian Act that intentionally conflict with provisions of the Fisheries Act. They have also asserted their rights on a more personal level by simply pursuing their timeless harvesting activities or taking personal initiatives to protect sensitive habitat areas from the adverse impact of indiscriminate logging activities.

In July 1988 Hereditary Chief Earl George of the Ahousaht Band was arrested for refusing to obey a Supreme Court injunction granted to British Columbia Forest Products preventing protesters from shutting down the construction of a logging road in Sulpher Pass about 40 kilometres north of Tofino (*Ha-Shilth-Sa*, July 20, 1988). The protest focused on the effect of logging on traditional fishing camps of the Ahousaht, one of the 14 Nuu-chah-nulth bands on the west coast of Vancouver Island.

During the summer of 1987 — the year following the *Sparrow* case — more than 100 charges were laid under the Fisheries Act against Tseshaht and Opetchesaht (Nuu-chah-nulth) native fishers alone (*Ha-Shilth-Sa*, April 28, 1988). A notable example was a case involving eight charges under the Fisheries Act against native fishermen Richard Watts and William Sam. The two Tseshaht band members from Port Alberni were convicted of fishing at a time when the area in question was closed to the native fishery while the sports fishery was open. The two accused based their defence on their constitutionally entrenched aboriginal right to fish and on the fact that the native fishery has first priority after conservation, as was confirmed in the *Sparrow* case. The court proceedings conveyed the distinct impression that political considerations and sensibilities of the sports fishery (whose share of the total catch in the region has multiplied over the last two decades) played a dominant role in DFO decision-making. After the appeal in the Vancouver Island County Court the convictions were overturned. The judge ruled that "The Department of Fisheries made decisions that were contrary to the proper conservation and management of the chinook run....Instead of recognizing the procedure that was constitutionally protected of the appellants' right to fish, priority was given to the sports fishery." (*Ha-Shilth-Sa*, July 20, 1989).

In 1987 and 1988, 204 charges of illegal fishing (involving 102 individuals) were laid against members of the Tseshaht and Opetchesaht bands. On January 26, 1990, the Federal Crown dropped 150 of the charges; on May 22, 1990, a further 32 were dropped. Eight of the cases were won by the Indians in County Court, four of which were appealed by the Federal Crown to the British Columbia Court of Appeal, and the last 14 of the charges awaited a decision in August of 1990 (*Ha-Shilth-Sa*, June 30, 1990). In view of the federal government's rather meagre success rate in obtaining convictions and its practice of dropping charges "at the last possible minute" (ibid.), one is left with the impression that the government was waging a "war of attrition". The two bands incurred expenses for legal and anthropological reports, well in excess of $100,000 on this matter. In a letter to the then Minister of Fisheries, Bernard Valcourt, the band leadership called for an end to the harassment of their fishermen and for compensation for court expenses.

In what might have been considered a test case on the aboriginal right to sell or barter fish, on August 19, 1988, in the Port Alberni Provincial Court, charges were laid against the Nuu-chah-nulth Tribal Council (NTC) Smokehouse Ltd. for buying and selling Indian food fish, and the maximum fine of $5,000 was imposed for each charge. The charges stemmed from a 1986 food fishery sale in which 119,000 pounds of spring salmon were sold to the smokehouse by native fishers from the Tseshaht and Opetchesaht Bands. In his ruling, Judge Macleod agreed that there was no doubt that the Tseshaht Band has an aboriginal right to fish on the Somass River, and that native people traded fish with other tribes prior to the arrival of Europeans, and sold fish to early settlers. However, Fisheries regulations of 1888 prohibiting the sale of food fish still stood, according to the judge, and these regulations took precedent over a Tseshaht Band by-law that allows the sale of food fish (*Ha-Shilth-Sa*, September 1, 1988).[3]

---

[3] This case was heard in British Columbia's Court of Appeal in 1992 along with six other fishing and hunting rights appeals in conjunction with the *Delgamuukw* appeal. In June 1993 the Court ruled 4:1 to

Some tribal and band governments make a concerted effort to educate their membership as to what it takes to prove, assert or practise their aboriginal right to marine resources. For example, when a new type of licence for commercial clam harvesting was introduced by the DFO in 1989, the Nuu-chah-nulth tribal newspaper (*Ha-Shilth-Sa*, November 30, 1989) printed an article dealing in detail with such issues as to what it will take to prove in court that commercial clam digging is an aboriginal right; how to anticipate and counter likely DFO arguments; and, last but not least, how to get around buying a licence while still being able to sell clams. Further instructions on appropriate strategies to assert aboriginal rights to harvest and sell clams was promised for an upcoming conference.

Native and anthropological evidence alike has proven beyond doubt that there was a complex and adaptive aboriginal system of fisheries use and governance. While the social organization varied from group to group, property rights to fish were generally vested in the kin-based group or extended family as a collectivity, or in the highest ranking member of the group. In either case, access of group members was regulated. An individual's personal status was largely a function of his/her redistributive activity within the community and to other groups. Thus the aboriginal system of property rights functioned to "manage" the resource, to regulate access and to provide for the distribution of surplus (Pinkerton 1987a:251). The pre-contact existence of a well-established and complex system of resource management and utilization rights underlies much of the modern claim that British Columbia's native people make for fisheries governance (Cassidy and Dale 1988:38).

With Vancouver Island's Nuu-chah-nulth people, these rights are embodied in the concept of "Ha Holthe", meaning "rights of the chieftainship". On November 16, 1988, the Hereditary Chiefs of the Ehattesaht and Nuchatlaht bands issued the following statement to the Department of Fisheries and Oceans.

> We, the Ehattesaht and Nuchatlaht Chiefs are reverting back to our Aboriginal Right to plan, manage, harvest and take true conservation measures in conjunction with Nature to ensure sustainable returns of all aqua-resources within our "Ha Holthe". This Aboriginal Right flows from total control and jurisdiction over a Hereditary Chief's "Ha Holthe" — Mountains, Lands, Rivers, Streams, Beaches, Foreshores, Reefs and Deep Seas.
>
> We, the Ehattesaht and Nuchatlaht Chiefs will re-establish traditional enforcement and protection of resources within each chief's Ha Holthe.
>
> We further declare that Beaches, Reefs and Foreshores within our Ha Holthe are closed until permission is sought and given to harvest aqua-resources. (Reprinted in *Ha-Shilth-Sa*, November 30, 1988)

On February 27, 1990, the Nuu-chah-nulth Tribal Council, British Columbia Premier Bill Vander Zalm and his Advisory Council on Native Affairs met in Port Alberni to discuss the unresolved land question. Nuu-chah-nulth Tribal Council Chairman George Watts made his understanding of the issue as it pertains to resources perfectly clear.

> ...we are not just interested in hunting, fishing and picking berries. We want to exercise full jurisdiction on our lands above and below the ground. It is a bit of racist assumption to say that we would not have fully utilized our resources if this land was not colonized. Therefore we do not accept the concept of partial use of our lands.
>
> One of the most important issues to us is the management of the sea and river resources. We are not just interested in "taking our share" which seems to be emphasized in the media. We are interested in managing the resources as equal managers so that we can pass them on to future generations to manage. (Excerpt from George Watts' prepared statement, reprinted in *Ha-Shilth-Sa*, March 20, 1990)

---

reject the aboriginal right to fish sales for the Tseshaht and Opetchesaht Bands. Furthermore, Mr. Justice Wallace rejected the contention that the Tseshaht fish by-law applied to the fishery in the Somass River, which is adjacent to but not on the reserve.

The federal government has revealed its willingness to expand the native share of both the fishery and the decision-making about the fishery. With regard to the latter, however, there is no indication that a partnership of equals is envisaged (Cassidy and Dale 1988:42). Advisory functions and limited direct decision-making on the part of the Indians, in the federal view of the future, must be clearly subsidiary to the final authority of the Minister of Fisheries and Oceans. The problems foreseen in extending true joint authority in fisheries management include interference with Canada's international policies and obligations; increased management costs through bureaucratic expansion and duplication; fragmentation of management authorities; and potentially, above all, further exclusion of non-natives from decision-making.

Prospects for Native/Non-Native Fisheries Co-Management

When reading and hearing about Canada's Pacific fisheries, one cannot help but notice a general sense of crisis. There are numerous environmental factors which depress stock levels far below the original productive capacities of river systems, such as the impact of hydroelectric dams, poor logging practices and pollution. Above all there is the problem of chronic overfishing. Economists tend to define the problem as one of "too many boats chasing too few fish" (ibid.:37). The excessive efficiency of the present commercial fleet resulting from overinvestment renders it capable to take the annual harvest in a matter of hours.

It is often argued that habitat destruction rather than overfishing is the primary reason for the decline of B.C. salmon in this century. Don Ryan for the Office of the Hereditary Chiefs of the Gitksan and Wet'suwet'en people concedes that habitat problems unquestionably have caused the collapse of certain stocks, but he feels that overfishing probably affects more stocks overall (Ryan 1985:10). He also raises the crucial point that there is an important interaction between overfishing and habitat destruction.

> It is politically difficult to protect fish habitat that is not being fully utilized. When a stock is overfished, its escapement is not sufficient to use all of the available freshwater spawning and rearing habitat. All of the habitat is necessary if the stock in question is ever to be restored to its full natural production potential, but a proponent of an alternative use for the vacant habitat may well argue that empty fish habitat has no value. This is precisely the effect of the Aluminum Company of Canada's position that it is responsible for compensating only for any loss of fish production **below current levels** that might be caused by the company's proposed hydroelectric development in the Nanika/Morice River system. Alcan has strongly resisted the notion that it might be responsible for fish production potential based on available but currently underutilized habitat, even though it appears that current salmon escapements to the system are substantially reduced by overfishing below the numbers the system could accommodate. (ibid.:10–11, emphasis in original)

Within this wider context the native fishery is undergoing a crisis of its own. Indian people's domestic harvesting activities are severely affected by the dismal state of the resource as well as by restrictive and unsympathetic legislation. Since the 1960s, largely as a result of the controversial Davis Plan, the native commercial fleet has undergone considerable reduction in size, with many of the remaining vessels being marginal. British Columbia's First Nations are hard-pressed to issue any praise to the DFO for its track record in managing the fisheries resource. They are doubly motivated to take on the challenge themselves to restore aquatic resources to a healthier state and to improve their own position in their staple economy. As Frank Cassidy and Norman Dale (1988:81) observe in their discussion of the resource management scenario "After Native Claims", "...comprehensive claims settlements might create fisheries management in some areas of British Columbia totally unlike the present regime."[4]

---

[4] For details of the Davis Plan (1968), see McMullan 1987b:125–126.

Today there are numerous initiatives on the part of natives and non-natives aimed at enhancing the use and management of aquatic resources and at improving the position of Indian people in the fishery. These initiatives and actions (Cassidy and Dale 1988:49–79) cover a wide spectrum. Some are taking place in an atmosphere of cooperation between native and non-native people and can be accommodated within the institutions and distribution of power that characterize the status quo. Others constitute a determined assertion of self-regulation on the part of native groups, an approach that has mostly failed to elicit any government support.

Despite their variety many of these initiatives are often described under the collective heading "co-management".

> Co-management regimes work by altering the relationship among the actors in the fishery — primarily those between fishermen and government, but also those among individual fishermen and among fishermen's groups. Basically, by instituting shared decision-making among these actors, co-management systems set up a game in which pay-offs are greater for co-operation than for opposition and/or competition, a game in which the actors can learn to optimize their mutual good and plan co-operatively with long-term horizons. (Pinkerton 1989:4f)

In general terms, the goals sought by participants in fisheries co-management are more appropriate, more efficient and more equitable management (ibid.:5). But there are very significant secondary goals or consequences, such as community development, decentralized decision-making and participatory democracy. The priority accorded any one of those depends very much on the people involved (ibid.).

Another very important, if not the most important aspect of co-management, is raised by the Haida Nation. Miles Richardson and Bill Green write:

> Our relationship to the resources of Haida Gwaii cannot be managed by governments of another culture, with a different set of values. This is perhaps the most important reason for co-management — to provide a means for different cultures with conflicting values to share in a resource. Management of fisheries resources by one culture results in the almost complete loss of the ability of the resources to provide for the values of another culture. (Richardson and Green 1989:259)

Numerous so-called co-management systems could be labelled "incomplete" in so far as not every management function is shared that theoretically could be. Evelyn Pinkerton (1989:6) distinguishes seven categories of management functions:

- Data gathering and analysis;
- Logistical harvesting decisions, such as licensing, timing, location, and vessel and gear restrictions;
- Harvest allocation decisions;
- Habitat protection;
- Enforcement of regulations or practices guiding harvesting logistics, allocation, and resource protection;
- Enhancement and long-term planning; and
- Broad policy decision-making.

The Salmonid Enhancement Program

In the native context the role of co-management as a route to community-based development is a particularly important aspect. This connection is quite explicit in the DFO-operated Salmonid Enhancement Program (SEP), which started in 1977. The program has the overall purpose of reversing historic declines in salmon stocks and fostering economic development for the entire region. An integral part of SEP is the Community Economic Development Program (CEDP) which is primarily concerned with native communities. In this approach, native bands are involved on a contract basis in projects, such as constructing hatcheries and spawning channels, clearing streams of debris and barriers, doing biophysical inventories, and establishing monitoring and tagging programs (Cassidy and Dale 1988:52). While native people are fully in charge of individual project management (with DFO staff providing no more than technical support), they have no input in the overall planning aspect whatsoever. Pinkerton (1989:10) expresses the opinion that for long-term benefits to be realized, fishers may need to be involved on a regional and local basis in the location, size and species aspect of enhancement.

Most SEP funding is directed towards the seemingly efficient and cost-effective strategy of constructing and operating a small number of large hatcheries, contrary to fishers' and community advice and requests for fewer large projects and more small ones. The unfortunate by-product of the DFO strategy is that many smaller stocks have continued to be overfished, or even threatened with annihilation when taken by mixed stock fisheries. With little input into the overall planning process from individual fishing communities on a local or regional basis, the government tends to develop policies that seem aimed at satisfying the "average" fisher or the largest constituency, or highly mobile fishers in the short run, overlooking the fact that such strategies have a hidden cost.

The Salmonid Enhancement Program, the issue of special native licences (as part of the Davis Plan), the establishment of native-owned companies (such as the Northern Native Fishing Corporation) with government support, the granting of special harvesting rights to native groups for fish provided by over-escapements — all these initiatives, while clearly favouring native participation in the fishery, do not constitute any challenge to the status quo, as they can readily be accommodated by the present power structure and institutional framework, even though they may be challenged (and have been challenged) by other interest groups. While hardly qualifying for the term "co-management," these initiatives may be viewed as occupying one end of the spectrum of measures designed to benefit both the fishery resource and native people.

Gitksan and Wet'suwet'en Initiatives

The opposite end of the spectrum features initiatives not by the government but by native groups; in their essence, an assertion of aboriginal self-regulation with regard to the fishery resource. A good example is the Gitksan-Wet'suwet'en approach. The Gitksan and Wet'suwet'en people, through their Office of the Hereditary Chiefs (OHC), claim "ownership, protection and control" over more than 50,000 square kilometres in northwestern British Columbia on the Upper Skeena watershed (Cassidy and Dale 1988:215). They assert that their traditional political, legal and social system for managing their resources — the system of House Chiefs — has remained intact and functional. In their fishery, the Gitksan-Wet'suwet'en find themselves in competition for the same stocks with a large ocean fleet and a riverine sport fishery, which are both in a position to intercept fish before they reach Gitksan-Wet'suwet'en territory.

Gitksan and Wet'suwet'en people have a tradition of defying governmental regulation of access to their resources. Until 1977, native challenges to DFO authority mostly took the form of individual violations of fishery regulations — fishing out of season, without a licence or with illegal gear. In 1977, in response to a major undercover operation by the DFO, the Tribal Council (today known as OHC) began providing financial and legal aid to those charged under the Fisheries Act, very successfully for the most part.

As a result of the 1977 court cases — where the Crown was unable to obtain convictions on any of the charges — the DFO and the Tribal Council agreed to negotiate a mutually acceptable management system for the fishery of the Gitksan-Wet'suwet'en territories. Negotiations began in 1979 and have been ongoing ever since. More than a decade later, no resolution has been achieved. It was clear from the outset that the two parties entered into the negotiations with totally different objectives.

> The DFO negotiators' primary concern was to obtain Indian agreement to annual fishing plans and regulations in order to reduce the tension and eliminate the confrontational situation between fishers and fishery officers on the river. The Tribal Council's top priorities were to secure DFO recognition of the management authority of the House Chiefs under Indian law and to rehabilitate salmon stocks depleted under DFO management. (Morell 1989:246)

Over the years the Gitksan-Wet'suwet'en have maintained their fundamental position: Ultimate authority for fisheries management, including the allocation of resources, in the traditional tribal territory is the right and the responsibility of the hereditary chiefs. This position remains unacceptable to DFO and to most non-native user-groups of the region (Cassidy and Dale 1988:76).

In 1985 the Gitksan-Wet'suwet'en Tribal Council completed a six-year study of the Skeena fishery and a detailed management proposal for the fishery resource within the tribal territory. As the author of the study report points out,

> ...the Chiefs acknowledge that the fish migrate outside of their jurisdiction and that there is a need to co-ordinate management inside the territories with management outside. The Chiefs are prepared to integrate Gitksan and Wet'suwet'en management plans with the plans of Indian and non-Indian groups with jurisdiction over other areas, but this integration must be achieved through negotiations among equals. The House Chiefs will not accept a subordinate role. (Morell 1989:244)

The most important ingredient of the Gitksan-Wet'suwet'en proposal is its focus on stock-by-stock management. The bands argue that all wild stocks have both resource and spiritual value, and that consequently none can be considered expendable (Cassidy and Dale 1988:76). Harvesting must therefore take into consideration optimum escapement of the weakest stock. Such "management of the weakest stock" capitalizes on the structure of traditional native river fisheries, where highly discriminatory Indian techniques would make stock-by-stock management feasible, something that could not be achieved in this manner by the mixed-stock ocean fisheries.

Acknowledging that no progress was being made in the negotiating process, the Tribal Council in 1983 started a new strategy to strengthen the position of Indian authority in Canadian law. Several of the Gitksan-Wet'suwet'en member bands used Section 81 of the Indian Act to pass band fishing by-laws. The key elements of these by-laws were that they empowered the bands on behalf of the hereditary chiefs to manage and regulate their fisheries, and that they explicitly allowed the sale of fish taken in the Indian fisheries. The initial by-laws were disallowed by the Minister of Indian Affairs, and subsequent variations on these original by-laws suffered the same fate.

In February 1986 four bands of the Tribal Council passed revised versions of the by-laws. They still contained the essential elements mentioned above, but added a commitment on the part of the Tribal Council to meet with DFO and other user groups to discuss an integration of Gitksan-Wet'suwet'en management plans with the overall management of Skeena fisheries. This time the by-laws were allowed to stand by INAC (Morell 1989:247) and would have become effective by June 15, 1986. On June 13, the Supreme Court of British Columbia issued an injunction prohibiting the implementation of the band by-laws. The injunction was granted in response to the argument of the province that "the reserves extend only to the riverbank and that the bed of the river belongs to the province", and accordingly the by-laws could not apply to the fishery (Bartlett 1988:113). An appeal was dismissed on December 17, 1986 (Attorney General of British Columbia v. Wale [1987] 2 C.N.L.R. 36 (B.C.C.A.)).

In the meantime the bands ignored the injunction, and confrontations between native fishers and DFO enforcement personnel continued (Morell 1989:247). The band by-laws were regarded primarily as an interim measure, based upon rights asserted in the Gitksan-Wet'suwet'en comprehensive claim, and necessitated by the lack of progress on the claim (Cassidy and Dale 1988:78). The Gitksan-Wet'suwet'en pursued their goals on various fronts. Their comprehensive claim to their ancestral territory was accepted for negotiation by the federal government in 1977. On October 23, 1984, 54 hereditary chiefs, representing 76 houses, launched a land title action against the government of British Columbia in the Supreme Court of British Columbia seeking a declaration of continued ownership and jurisdiction over their 57,000 square kilometres. The case of *Delgamuukw v. The Queen* (Delgamuukw et al. v. The Queen in Right of British Columbia and Attorney General of Canada [1991] unreported) began on May 11, 1987, and ended on June 29, 1990. On March 8, 1991, Chief Justice Allan McEachern ruled in favour of the Crown, announcing that aboriginal title was extinguished in 1858. On June 25, 1993, the British Columbia Court of Appeal overturned key findings of this ruling to the effect that Gitksan and Wet'suwet'en aboriginal rights had not been extinguished; however, the court's majority conclusion as to the nature and extent of these rights was ambiguous and very unsatisfactory for the Gitksan-Wet'suwet'en. The case is likely to proceed to the Supreme Court of Canada (*Windspeaker*, July 5, 1993:R1; *Globe and Mail*, July 9, 1993:A17).

And finally, while pursuing their claim through the courts, the Gitksan-Wet'suwet'en signed a Self-Government Framework Agreement with the federal government in January, 1990 (*Windspeaker*, January 19, 1990). In the subsequent negotiations aimed at an agreement-in-principle, the Gitksan-Wet'suwet'en's main goal was to have their traditional form of government recognized in Canadian legislation (*Transition*, Vol. 3, No. 3:2).

The opposite sides of the spectrum of fisheries initiatives are thus characterized by the federal government's position of allowing token input by native groups at best, and by the Gitksan-Wet'suwet'en's assertion of total self-regulation. There are numerous native proposals and initiatives that fall somewhere in-between. Like the Gitksan-Wet'suwet'en, the Nisga'a Tribal Council and the Kwakiutl District Council demand considerable autonomy and for all intents and purposes assert their aboriginal right to manage their fishery. Unlike the Gitksan-Wet'suwet'en, however, their proposals call for the establishment of an intergovernmental co-management body (Cassidy and Dale 1988:71–77). The Haida Nation's 1984–85 proposal for their ocean fishery shares with the Gitksan-Wet'suwet'en a thrust towards "decentralized, localized, fine-grained harvest regulation" (Pinkerton 1989:18), but is phrased explicitly as a "co-management initiative".

> We proposed a form of co-management between the federal Department of Fisheries and Oceans and the Haida Fisheries Commission in which the Commission would undertake all management functions for a specific set of stocks. Management would be cooperative in that a general framework of management objectives would be negotiated between the federal government and the Commission. (Richardson and Green 1989:258)

The government's response to the Haida co-management proposal required the development of province-wide policies regarding native fisheries as a pre-condition to negotiation of any agreement. In 1986 the federal ministers of Indian Affairs and Fisheries and Oceans released their proposed policy paper on co-management and development of native community salmon fisheries (Government of Canada 1986). The Council of the Haida Nation considered this policy proposal as so inadequate that it withdrew the co-management initiative (Richardson and Green 1989:259). The Haida have since assumed a more assertive stance (Cassidy and Dale 1988:62).[5]

---

[5] Evelyn Pinkerton (1987c) describes an interesting informal and de facto co-management system which was established at Alert Bay to protect the Nimpkish River sockeye salmon stocks. The "social drama" described

The Boldt Decision

Since the early 1970s interested parties in the native/non-native fisheries conflict have been keen observers of events south of the border. In February 1974 Judge George Boldt of the U.S. 9th District Court made a historic ruling affirming the rights of 22 Washington tribes to use and manage fish (U.S. v. Washington 384 F. Supp. 312 (D.1974)). British Columbia's First Nations have studied the Boldt Decision and its consequences intensely and have maintained close contacts with Washington State native fisheries managers. Non-native fishery users and particularly INAC and DFO display a similar interest but tend to view the allocation and resulting co-management system that grew out of the Boldt Decision as a nightmare that should be avoided at any price.

While the Boldt Decision came about within an ecological and socio-cultural system very similar to that in British Columbia, its historical and legal context is fundamentally different. The Boldt Decision was litigated on the basis of treaty rights, not aboriginal rights. Also, the jurisdictional setting of American fisheries management is quite different from that in British Columbia. For these and other reasons, the British Columbia Court of Appeal ruled in the *Sparrow* case that American case law could not be used as a basis for adjudication of Canadian fishing conflicts (Cassidy and Dale 1988:66). But this does not prevent the Boldt Decision from exercising a powerful influence on the fears and expectations of all British Columbian groups in the fishery.

Under treaties negotiated in Washington in the 1850s, 22 Indian tribes residing in the Pacific northwest ceded most of their traditional lands to the U.S. government and reserved to themselves the right to fish on and off the new reservations at "usual and accustomed fishing places" "in common with" other citizens. These places were primarily in Puget Sound and Washington coastal streams and rivers (Ancona 1985:52). Over the next century, Indians found themselves constantly battling for their fishing rights, in the courts as well as on the rivers (Cohen 1986:52–82). When the issue reached the courts again, Judge Boldt ruled that the treaties would have to be interpreted as guaranteeing the native tribes a 50 per cent share of those salmon runs which would, without prior interception, return to tribal "usual and accustomed fishing places". Before the Boldt Decision, the state had managed the fisheries so that virtually the entire harvest was taken before reentering the waterways. As a result, few fish that were not needed for spawning got back into the rivers where "usual and accustomed places" were located.

The court's ruling met with an extremely hostile reaction from state resource managers and non-native fishing interests. As a result Judge Boldt took the unusual step of placing the fisheries under his court's jurisdiction. As pointed out by Janet Harper (1985:75), "There are a lot of pitfalls to a legalistic approach, especially in the absence of cooperation and willingness to make the court decision work." It took ten years and 366 more court cases to tire all parties of almost weekly confrontations in the courts during the fishing season. In 1984 the first true "Joint Management Projects" were initiated, and 1986 was the first year that tribes negotiated with the Department of Fisheries over how the whole fishing season would operate (*Ha-Shilth-S*a, December 20, 1988). According to Frank Cassidy and Norman Dale (1988:67), it is not exaggerated to say that the Boldt Decision has caused an almost revolutionary change in the governance structures and processes for the fishery. Along with increased shares in the harvest, native people acquired new management responsibilities which compelled them not only to deal with the government and non-native user groups but they also carried the additional onus of reaching agreements with other tribes and enforcing regulations within their own communities.

---

by Pinkerton also illustrates the workings of "self-management" in a modern Kwakiutl community with a vested interest in both commercial and food fishery.

According to Janet Harper (1985:75), as a result of the Boldt Decision

> Participation in the fishery has been increased, the level of community viability and the general well-being of the tribes has been improved significantly. The tribes, in general, have gained in terms of wealth and expertise and influence.

A final positive element of the Boldt Decision must not go unmentioned. The judge asserted that treaty fishing rights ought to imply that the tribes are empowered to halt environmentally destructive actions. The impact of this ruling has been considerable, as several of the larger timber, mining and hydroelectric developers have begun to negotiate with native groups on project proposals. The 1980 Northwest Power Planning Act treats Indian tribes as co-managers of fisheries in the Columbia Basin, and Northwest tribes are actively involved in reviewing Federal Energy Regulatory Commission licences for dams. Washington State tribes were instrumental in negotiating the Timber/Fish/Wildlife Agreement which was conceived to reduce conflicts over logging near spawning streams. Treaty Indian tribes have law enforcement authority on both on-reservation and off-reservation rivers (CRITFC News, Special Supplement, June 1988). Cassidy and Dale (1988:69) go so far as to suggest that "In the long run, the added leverage that the affirmation of native fishing rights provides in controlling habitat destruction may be the most important of all consequences."[6]

A Legacy of *Sparrow*: Co-Management Initiatives in the 1990s

Some of the most recently initiated co-management regimes in British Columbia may be viewed as a direct result of the Supreme Court of Canada's ruling on *Sparrow*. These regimes are not confined to fisheries, but are the tangible expression of an altogether changed relationship between aboriginal and non-aboriginal people in this province.

With regard to resource management in general, the most important and innovative elements of *Sparrow* are the tests for determining if any specific regulation affecting aboriginal rights is justified. The first step is the identification of a valid legislative objective, such as conservation and resource management, or the prevention of harm to society or to aboriginal peoples themselves. The Court makes it clear that the legislative objective must be "compelling and substantial" (R. v. Sparrow [1990] 3 C.N.L.R.:183).

The second step focuses on the question whether the honour of the Crown in its dealings with aboriginal peoples is being upheld. The courts will consider the regulation in light of the fiduciary obligations of the Crown to native people, and unless this standard is satisfied, the regulation will be invalid. Only valid conservation concerns are entitled to priority over the aboriginal right (ibid.:184).

The Court listed other factors that may be taken into account when the Crown attempts to justify limitations on aboriginal rights:

- Is the right infringed upon as little as possible?
- In the case of expropriation, is fair compensation provided?
- Have the aboriginal groups affected by the regulation been consulted? (ibid.:187)

In each case, the onus will be on the Crown to prove that any regulation of aboriginal rights is justified, a task that the Court describes as a "heavy burden" (ibid.:186).

> Sparrow indicates that aboriginal fishing rights consist not just of a claim to a share of the harvest, but also of a stake in the conservation and management of the resource. The positive approach for governments would be to give recognition and force to aboriginal systems of tenure, management, harvesting, and utilization, by entering into co-management or

---

[6] Evelyn Pinkerton (1992) gives a detailed account of the process of implementing the Boldt Decision.

> self-government arrangements. The alternative is to engage in long and costly skirmishes in court, which aboriginal people would appear to have a good chance of winning, on the facts. (Usher 1991b:21)

In 1990, in the wake of *Sparrow*, the government of British Columbia decided to acknowledge the validity of comprehensive aboriginal claims in this province. This decision and the election of an NDP government in 1991 set the stage for a redefinition of the relationship between the province's Indian people and mainstream society. Clearly, such redefined relationship was to have far-reaching consequences for the management of British Columbia's natural resources.

The reshaping of the provincial government's relationship with British Columbia's First Nations and its expression in resource matters is currently in the formative stages. The matter is complicated by the involvement of numerous stakeholders, such as various provincial government agencies, the federal government and third parties. It is also hampered by fiscal constraints. Nevertheless, British Columbia's Aboriginal Affairs Ministry and B.C. Environment have formulated their ideas of cooperative resource management, pending the eventual negotiation of contemporary treaties.

> We've also talked about joint stewardship, a mechanism through which we can, through cooperation, in the period leading up to treaty negotiations or parallel with treaty negotiations, form a new relationship, a cooperative relationship in terms of the stewardship of resources within this province on a cooperative basis. (The Honourable Andrew Petter, Minister of Aboriginal Affairs, First Nations Summit, Vancouver, May 14, 1992, Verbatim Proceedings:74)

> Cabinet has approved a comprehensive aboriginal policy framework, which begins to translate into action the fundamental shift of relationships. Within that framework, two discrete, but related, sets of policy development processes will be used: those focused on treaties and related matters; and those focused on a series of parallel, or pre-treaty, issues. The latter will include social policy, economic development policy...and natural resource policy. Natural resource matters outside formal treaty processes will be referred to as joint stewardship arrangements. (B.C. Environment 1992:6)

> Joint stewardship expresses British Columbia's recognition that aboriginal rights constitute a *sui generis* interest in land, the Province's obligation to protect those interests, and First Nations' inherent right to self-government. As such, joint stewardship policy will provide a framework to ministries and agencies for the new government-to-government relationship with First Nations on all aspects of land and resource management within traditional territories, including cultural resources such as archaeological and heritage sites. The joint stewardship policy will encompass all First Nations in British Columbia, including those who have entered into a treaty, such as Treaty 8 or the Douglas Treaties. The policy will aim to achieve overall provincial consistency in decision-making processes, yet maintain current flexibility for tailoring specific resource programs to local community needs and resource conditions. (ibid.:7)

In the early 1990s details of the joint stewardship policy[7] are being worked out and several pilot projects are being selected to test the principles and provide feedback to the policy

---

[7] The early 1990s gave rise to a second type of natural resource-related agreement with B.C. First Nations. Interim Protection Measures Agreements must be viewed within the context of contemporary treaty negotiations. On July 31, 1992, a one-year Nisga'a Comprehensive Land Claims Interim Protection Measures Agreement was signed by the Nisga'a Tribal Council, British Columbia and Canada. This Agreement is intended to guarantee Nisga'a input into any new development proposals within the Nisga'a claim area while treaty negotiations are underway. Areas in which the Nisga'a Tribal Council will assess new development proposals and make recommendations to the province include fisheries, forestry, wildlife, parks, agriculture, mining, energy, environment, highways, and residential, recreational, commercial and industrial initiatives involving public lands in the claim area. The Agreement will be in effect until an agreement-in-principle is reached or September 20, 1993, whichever comes first. (November 27, 1992 Press Release by the Government of

development process (B.C. Environment 1992:13). Naturally, the initiatives of the 1990s are being informed by the legacy of the 1970s and 1980s. As was shown in an earlier section of this chapter, there have been numerous initiatives on the part of native and non-native parties aimed at enhancing the use and management of aquatic resources and at improving the position of Indian people in the fishery. These initiatives and actions cover a wide spectrum.

In co-management terminology, one end of the spectrum is characterized by token input in resource use planning by native groups (as exemplified by the DFO-operated Salmonid Enhancement Program), whereas the opposite end features initiatives by native groups, in their essence, an assertion of aboriginal self-regulation. This approach has been most effectively demonstrated by the Gitksan and Wet'suwet'en people with regard to fisheries as well as forestry. There have been numerous native proposals and initiatives that fall somewhere in-between, and accordingly each First Nation dealing with the provincial government under its new Joint Stewardship policy is influenced by its own resource use history and perception.

Interestingly enough, one of the early joint stewardship agreements was signed with the Haida Nation in July 1992, and took its cue from a unilateral political initiative on the part of the Haida in 1990 to control the sports fishery in their homeland Haida Gwaii. For two years the Haida had successfully implemented their management plans for the commercial recreational fisheries in Haida Gwaii, enforcing their measures by means of their watchman program. Eight Haida "watchmen" establish a presence on the water, provide public relations and monitor catches by the fishing lodges (Russ Jones, Chairperson, Haida Fisheries Committee, personal communication, July 1, 1992). The Joint Stewardship Agreement of July 1992 between the provincial government and the Haida Nation for the management of the recreational fishery in Haida Gwaii fully endorsed the 1992 Haida management plan. Provincial signatories to the Agreement included the Minister of Aboriginal Affairs, the Minister of Agriculture, Fisheries and Food, the Minister of Environment, Lands and Parks, the Minister of Tourism, and Minister Responsible for Culture. An invitation was extended (but not accepted) to the federal DFO, since the federal government has jurisdiction over the management of tidal fisheries.

Russ Jones of the Haida Fisheries Committee feels, that apart from the sports fishery, the fisheries situation in Haida Gwaii is better described by the term "cooperative management" than the term "co-management". The Haida Fisheries Program was established in October 1989 under the auspices of the CEIC (Innovations Program and Canadian Jobs Strategy), as the "Haida Program". It was primarily geared towards job creation and related socio-economic matters. To date no co-management institutions are in place, and co-management procedures are only slowly evolving. Access to information, however, has improved and more pro-active initiatives have been encouraged. Haida input into fisheries management is strictly local. The Haida plan and execute their own projects, addressing stock assessment, habitat issues and enhancement. But even now, regulatory changes are not discussed with them, as exemplified by the controversial issue of the introduction of halibut licensing. This 1989 measure, along with an individual quota system introduced in 1991, has virtually eliminated the First Nations halibut fishery (Council of the Haida Nation 1991:5f).

The Gitksan and Wet'suwet'en people have traditionally pursued their goal of "ownership and jurisdiction" (Wii Seeks, Office of the Hereditary Chiefs, personal communication, June 23, 1992) over their traditional House Territories on many different fronts, engaging in litigation and negotiation as well as asserting control over their resources out on the land. Not surprisingly, they, too, are involved in resource-related negotiations with the provincial government. In January 1992 a Memorandum of Understanding was signed (the federal

---

Canada, the Province of British Columbia, and the Nisga'a Tribal Council; Nisga'a Comprehensive Land Claims Interim Protection Measures Agreement, July 31, 1992)

government was invited to participate but refused), and in May 1992, a Memorandum of Agreement. The latter was signed by the Minister of Aboriginal Affairs for British Columbia and by the Speakers for the Gitksan and Wet'suwet'en Hereditary Chiefs respectively. This Memorandum was not so much concerned with the development of a joint stewardship agreement for a particular area or resource as it was with the establishment of "alternative dispute resolution processes regarding land and resources" "in a way which favours negotiation rather than litigation". For this purpose a Joint Committee was to be formed to conduct discussions.

Since 1991 the Gitksan and Wet'suwet'en (either directly or indirectly through the Skeena Fisheries Commission) have also been involved in the negotiation of various Working Agreements, Sub-Agreements or Framework Agreements with the DFO, which have at times started out at a very low level of mutual agreement with a mere declaration of intent for a new relationship. The Gitksan and Wet'suwet'en leadership remains extremely guarded vis-a-vis joint stewardship or co-management agreements, which are viewed strictly as interim measures and only as a small part of their overall strategy, or as Richard Overall puts it: "Keep putting a foot in the door." (Gitksan-Wet'suwet'en Chiefs' Meeting, June 24, 1992). After decades of experience, Don Ryan (Maas Gaak), Speaker of the Gitksan Hereditary Chiefs, has come to the conclusion that most envisaged joint management schemes contain what he refers to as a "God clause" ("The Minister has final say") and a "greed clause" ("Everything has to make economic sense") (Personal communication June 18, 1992). For this reason, joint management strategies are not viewed as part of a final solution.

With regard to fisheries, the Gitksan and Wet'suwet'en people place much emphasis on the development of their river fishery. Don Ryan feels that the commercial ocean fishery is collapsing, and that "things are coming full circle": On economic grounds, the traditional aboriginal river fishery will undergo a revitalization and commercialization. This process is the focus of envisaged agreements between the Gitksan and Wet'suwet'en Watershed Authorities and the individual Houses, as well as of a Sub-Agreement with the DFO.

For some other First Nations in British Columbia, joint stewardship agreements and "interim measures agreements" (to be distinguished from interim protection measures agreements) are more important and more specific. In August 1992 a seven-year Interim Measures Fisheries Agreement or Framework Agreement was concluded between the Nuu-chah-nulth Tribal Council and the federal DFO. The Agreement is intended to protect Nuu-chah-nulth fishing interests in the years preceding a settlement of their land and sea claims.

It makes considerable concessions to the Nuu-chah-nulth in terms of financial assistance, elimination of catch ceilings for Nuu-chah-nulth fisheries, delegation of enforcement powers, etc. and also provides for a Joint Management Committee with equal numbers of Nuu-chah-nulth and DFO representatives. The Agreement is viewed very positively by the Nuu-chah-nulth, whose negotiators are hopeful that parts of the Agreement will become "building blocks" for the fisheries part of treaties which will eventually be negotiated between the Nuu-chah-nulth and the governments of Canada and British Columbia (*Ha-Shilth-Sa*, February 12, 1992:10; May 6, 1992:5; September 22, 1992:1, 3).

British Columbia's Joint Stewardship Agreement initiative is a highly flexible program, which has resulted in agreements with very different focuses, contents and consequences. It is no more and no less than a translation into policy of a new (government-to-government) relationship. The resultant agreements are being viewed and used quite differently by the various First Nations, who become party to them, depending on their experiences, the issues affecting them, and their political agenda. Third parties — most notably the forestry industry — view these new developments with some trepidation, as expressed in a letter dated July 23, 1992, by the Caribou Lumber Manufacturers' Association to the Minister of Aboriginal Affairs, in reaction to a Joint Stewardship Agreement and Memorandum of Understanding with the Xax'lip First Nation.

EASTERN SEABOARD AND QUEBEC

East Coast Fishery

Canada's Atlantic fishery is profoundly different from the west coast fishery in history and character which at least partly explains its different significance for native people. In contrast with the British Columbian situation, the fishery and related industries are of paramount importance for the economy of the Atlantic provinces, but they do not play a very significant role for the region's native communities.

The importance of fishing for the region is revealed in a statement of the Economic Council of Canada (Clement 1986:34) that "during the 1980s, 75 per cent of all the communities in the Atlantic provinces had some connection with the fishery, and 20 per cent of them had no other local industry." A major part of the fishery is conducted over shallow "banks" which extend to more than 500,000 square kilometres. The Grand Bank (more than 100,000 square kilometres) is the most important cod-fishing ground in the world. In addition the banks yield halibut and haddock. There are also vast areas of inshore fishing grounds, where catching of oyster, shrimp, prawn, crab and lobster takes place. Scallop, smelt and sardine fishing is carried out as well.

Newfoundland is responsible for the bulk of production (42 per cent), although Nova Scotia has the largest share of value (47 per cent), while New Brunswick has about 10 per cent of each category and Quebec about 8 per cent. Prince Edward Island contributes only 3 per cent of the volume but 6 per cent of the value (ibid.:33). Nova Scotia has a high share of the value because of the scallop fishery, which constitutes only one-sixth of its volume but one-third of its value. Nova Scotia's catch is worth about twice that of Newfoundland, and roughly equals that of British Columbia. Ignoring the relative importance of fishing to each province, British Columbia and Nova Scotia have been the major Canadian producers since the Second World War, followed by Newfoundland, New Brunswick, Quebec and Prince Edward Island.

Since 1946 lobster has surpassed cod (and all other species) in value. Especially since the mid-1950s scallops have been increasingly profitable, joining these two species, which are followed, at about half the respective value, by herring, redfish, and haddock. In Newfoundland, cod is the most important commercial species; in the Maritime Provinces, the fishery is more heterogeneous, although subregions may depend on a single species.[8]

Historically, the Atlantic fishery goes back more than 500 years as commercial fishing was the reason for early European forays into what became Canadian waters. The establishment of permanent European fishing villages did not occur prior to the seventeenth century. The fishery started as trade in salted fish, which was replaced by frozen fish in the 1940s. The eighteenth- and nineteenth-century Newfoundland and Nova Scotia fishery was organized on a feudal basis, with the fish merchants owning the means of production and employing fishermen to catch the fish, using schooners and dories (Clement 1986:18f). There were several variations of this theme. In the twentieth century, with increasing industrialization, the producers changed from being locally controlled merchants to externally dominated industrial firms. Commercial fish production shifted to the wet fish trawler for its main source of year-round supply.

East coast fishing does by no means take place entirely on a grand scale. For Nova Scotia, R.W. Heber (1986:170) distinguishes between a "big boat fleet" and a "small boat fleet". Vessels in the former category are owned and operated by individual companies that integrate fishing, processing and marketing activities within one enterprise. The crews are hired as employees of the companies. The second fleet consists of small boats which are

[8] Atlantic salmon — the species important for native people — is not mentioned in the literature. Undoubtedly, it is an important species for the sports fishery.

owned and operated by private entrepreneurs who sell their catch, for the most part, directly to onshore processing plants of which there are about 200 in the province. These boats operate out of small communities that are generally supported primarily by fishing. Crews, from one to three people, are typically made up of community residents along kinship and friendship lines. According to Heber (ibid.:172), almost 13,000 individuals are involved in small boat fishing in Nova Scotia which means that this sector accounts for the majority of fishing employment in the province.

Indians in the Fishery

There is an astounding lack of information on native involvement in any type of fishery or native employment in fishery-related industries in the Atlantic provinces. The abundant literature on the east coast fishery (f.e. Crerar 1969; Clement 1986; Heber 1986) does not mention native people with even one single word. Neither do there appear to be data on subsistence fishing in this region. In Fikret Berkes' recent work "Native Subsistence Fisheries: A Synthesis of Harvest Studies in Canada" (1990:36,37), the Atlantic region is the only area not represented by a single study.

Information gleaned from Fred Wien's work on the Micmac of Nova Scotia (1986) is sketchy at best. Studying trends in Micmac labour force employment figures, Wien (1986:68) discovers a decline of the proportion engaged in fishing, hunting, trapping and related activities from 6.5 per cent in 1971 to 1.4 per cent in 1981. He suggests that the collapse of several Micmac fishing operations, especially the oyster farming projects in Cape Breton, is responsible for these numbers. The reasons for these failures are not clear. According to Wien (ibid.:131), Indian spokesmen express the opinion that

> ...the projects began without significant planning and substantial investment; rather it was a case of taking advantage of existing short-term funding in an attempt to create employment for reserve residents. The terms of the available funding programs precluded a longer-term approach. Oyster farming, however, requires long-term planning and substantial capital investments.

On the other hand, there were commercial fishers among the approximately 150 Micmac considered as self-employed in the province in 1980 (ibid.:125). Compared to the west coast situation, however, in the absence of special government programs, relations of patronage with the processing industry, and powerful native organizations with a stake in the industry, it is easy to imagine that Indians face even greater obstacles on the east coast than on the west coast, when trying to enter the commercial fishing industry.

Fred Wien (ibid.:135) calls our attention to the fact that generally speaking, the natural resource-based projects funded by the Department of Indian Affairs have a much higher success rate (fishing, 62 per cent, 1971–1981) than those in the manufacturing and service sectors. Gasperaux and eel fishing were among the ventures being discussed within the Micmac community (ibid.:132). That the fishery resource is not inconsequential to native people of this region is evidenced by the fact that the issue of Indian fishing rights in the Maritimes keeps cropping up in the courts.

Indian Fishing Rights in the Maritimes

The Maritime Provinces are usually labelled as "non-treaty provinces". This label is correct only in so far as there were no land-cession treaties with Indian people of the Maritimes. There were, however, several treaties of peace and friendship (f.e. in 1722, 1752, 1779) which explicitly recognized native fishing and hunting rights. Consequently, maritime Indian fishing rights must be considered from the viewpoint of treaty rights as well as from that of aboriginal rights.

The record of legal recognition of treaty rights in the Maritimes is anything but encouraging. Several court decisions have for the most part tended to ignore or question the legal force of these treaties. One of the leading cases has been that of *Rex v. Syliboy* (1929). The court construed the treaty of 1752 very narrowly in finding that it did not apply to the defendant because he was from Cape Breton (an area considered as not covered by the document). The judge also questioned the nature of the agreement as a treaty (Cumming and Mickenberg 1972:98). The promises of hunting and fishing rights in the treaty of 1752 were dealt with again in the case of *Regina v. Simon* ((1958) 124 C.C.C. 110 (N.B.S.C.)). A Micmac Indian of the Big Cove Reserve was accused of breaking New Brunswick Fishery Regulations. The court in convicting the defendant relied on *Rex v. Syliboy* and affirmed that part of the earlier ruling which held that the treaty was not made with the Micmac Nation as a whole, but only a small portion of it.

A third case, *Francis v. The Queen* ((1969), 1 N.B.R. (2d) 886 (N.B. Cty. Ct.)) dealt with hunting and fishing rights promised in several Maritime treaties. This incident involved a band member of the Big Cove Reserve who had breached federal fishery regulations. This time the New Brunswick County court was willing to concede that the treaties of 1725, 1752, and 1779 were signed by the defendant's predecessors and that therefore the rights to fish and hunt given by those treaties devolved on the defendant. The judge ruled, however, that any special fishing rights granted by the treaty of 1752 had been taken away by the federal Fisheries Act. According to Cumming and Mickenberg (1972:99), the importance of this court decision is not the conclusion, but the recognition of the legal force of the early treaties. Mr. Justice Leger had stated unequivocally:

> All of these treaties, agreements or proclamations were made before Confederation and are valid unless changed by legislation properly enacted under the powers granted to the Government of Canada by Section 91 of the British North America Act. (ibid.)

On appeal the New Brunswick Court of Appeal upheld the lower court's decision but did not support the judge's conclusions as to the validity of the treaties. Mr. Justice Hughes denied the applicability of the two earlier treaties to the *Francis* case altogether. The treaty of 1779 was viewed as applicable to the Micmac Indians residing in the area in question. However, despite a clear and express provision that the Indians were to remain "...free from any molestation of any of His Majesty's Troops or other his good subjects in their Hunting and Fishing," the judge found it "...impossible to construe the treaty as conferring, either expressly or impliedly, any right of fishing or hunting." (ibid.:100).

Until recently, aboriginal rights to the fishery resource or other natural resources did not fare any better for maritime native people. Although the Royal Proclamation was considered as applying to the Maritime Provinces — as decided in the otherwise highly questionable *Warman v. Francis* case ((1959–60), 43 M.P.R. 197 (N.B.S.C.)) — the procedures outlined therein for the extinguishment of aboriginal title were never followed (Cumming and Mickenberg 1972:105). There is no indication that the federal government of today has any intention of rectifying this situation. In its statement on its policy on native claims settlement, "In All Fairness" of 1981 (referred to by Canadian Bar Association 1988:8), the government has specifically declined to extend its policy for dealing with unextinguished aboriginal claims to long-settled areas such as the Maritimes. The government justifies its position by arguing that in these areas all remnants of aboriginal title have been "superseded by law".

In view of a recent court decision, however, the government may have to change its position on this matter. In *R. v. Denny* (N.S.C.A., [1990] 2 C.N.L.R. 115), three Nova Scotia Micmac Indians were convicted of violations of the Fisheries Act and regulations under the Act. They had fished for food off reserve and out of season. The Nova Scotia Supreme Court, upon appeal, overturned the convictions on the grounds of aboriginal rights. Drawing heavily on *Sparrow*, Judge Clarke argued that the three natives had an aboriginal right to fish for food in the waters in question, and that this right had not been extinguished by a treaty, any other agreement or legislation. Since an existing aboriginal right was thus confirmed, it was found unnecessary to determine whether the appellants also had a right to fish as protected by a treaty.

The aboriginal right in question was defined using the words of the court in *Sparrow*: "It was in the beginning a regulated, albeit self-regulated, right. It continued to be a regulated right and on April 17, 1982, it was a regulated right." (R. v. Denny [1990] 2 C.N.L.R.:129f) However, the federal power to regulate the protected aboriginal right under s.35 of the Constitution Act is not absolute. It is limited. The goal of conservation is to receive paramount consideration, while the Indian food fishery is given secondary priority. In the case in question, the judges found, that while there was a surplus of salmon, after provision was made for conservation, there was no evidence of any priority given to the needs of the Indian food fishery over other user groups, such as sports fishermen. This case makes it very clear that *Sparrow* has established, once and for all, that in the future the priority of the Indian food fishery is to be understood as a constitutionally protected right, and not as a matter of DFO policy.

The Indian Fishing Rights Issue in Atlantic Quebec

No treaties had been signed with native people in the Province of Quebec prior to the James Bay and Northern Quebec Agreement of 1975. The history of Quebec in relation to its native population was a complex one with repeated boundary extensions in 1774, 1898 and 1912. Even though the old Province of Quebec passed into English hands in 1760 with a history of non-recognition of Indian title (by the French), the inherent land rights of native peoples have been reaffirmed since by, among other things, the 1760 Articles of Capitulation, the Royal Proclamation of 1763, the instructions to Quebec governors in 1763 and 1775, the Imperial Order-in-Council of 1870 and the Quebec Boundaries Extension Act of 1912 (Cummings and Mickenberg 1972:91). From this history the Dorion Commission (Rapport de la Commission d'Etude sur l'Integrité du Territoire du Québec: le Domaine Indien/Dorion Commission Report, Vol. 4.1, 1971:253–255, quoted in Cummings and Mickenberg 1972:91) has concluded that native people have "effective and incontestable rights over the greater part of the territory of Quebec."

As a consequence, Indian fishing rights in Quebec derive from aboriginal rights as well as from the occupation of reserve lands. The rights and interests associated with reserve lands in Quebec are not uniform as they may vary according to the origin of the reserves. Reserves were granted under French sovereignty to religious missions to the Indians; others (like Restigouche) were granted to native people after the Royal Proclamation of 1763 on the basis of aboriginal title. Further reserves were established under statutory authority of the Province of Canada in 1851, and of the Province of Quebec in 1922. The Indian interest in the reserves is described as "usufructuary" (Bartlett 1984:42), which includes fishing rights. As Indian water rights in (southern) Quebec are essentially unimpaired, we may assume that the Indian reserve fishing rights situation is less ambiguous and more uniform than some other resource issues on Quebec reserves (particularly minerals).

Information on the reality of Indian fishing rights and Indian fishing activities in Quebec, on- or off-reserve, is rather sparse. One incident, involving salmon fishing rights of the Micmac Indians of Restigouche, on the border to New Brunswick made the headlines in 1981, and was documented in a film by Alanis Obomsawin ("Incident at Restigouche", National Film Board of Canada, 1984). While presenting a vivid picture of the violent confrontation between Restigouche Micmac Indian fishers and Quebec provincial police and fisheries officers, the film understandably leaves us with numerous questions. The incident in question was apparently not the first, since previous confrontations with the province seem to have taken place in 1972 and 1973. The Restigouche Micmac Indian Band appears to occupy a rather prominent position among Atlantic native fisheries since, according to the film commentary, of the 22 tons fished by east coast Indians in 1981, the Restigouche Micmac took 6 tons.

The Restigouche River forms part of Quebec's border with New Brunswick and is known as one of Eastern Canada's finest salmon streams. The Micmac Indian Reserve is located near the mouth of the river. While the Band Council is entitled to pass by-laws affecting fisheries on reserve lands, the question whether the Restigouche River is part of the reserve has been subject to dispute, since it forms the reserve boundary (*IWGIA Newsletter*, October/December 1981:41). Although the salmon fishery is usually regulated by the DFO, Quebec was given regulatory power over its fishery by a 1922/23 federal-provincial agreement.

Within this regulatory framework, the Restigouche Micmac are entitled to a food fishery using nets. The Micmac are opposed to provincial attempts to enforce fishing restrictions, and they make no secret of the fact that they fish in order to sell their catch. As justification they invoke their aboriginal rights and reserve-based rights as well as economic necessity.

The "Incident at Restigouche" was triggered on June 9 in 1981, when Lucien Bessard, then Quebec Minister of Recreation, Fish and Game, sent a telex to Restigouche Chief Alfonse Metallic, requesting the removal of Indian fishing nets from the Restigouche River within 36 hours. At the same time the federal government on the New Brunswick side lifted the ban on commercial offshore fishing. The Indians were to restrict their fishing activities to three 24-hour periods per week, rather than the accustomed six 12-hour night fishing periods.

When the Indians failed to comply with the provincial orders on June 10, riot police and fisheries officers stormed the reserve, seizing and destroying Indian fishing nets and violently arresting a dozen band members, minors among them. A second raid took place on June 20. During the two raids fishing equipment worth about $75,000 was confiscated by the police. Lucien Bessard visited the reserve on June 23, 1981. Then Indian Affairs Minister John Munro also visited the scene, stating that band by-laws on fishing on a reserve override provincial legislation. He also called for a review of the federal-provincial agreement giving Quebec control over its fishery.

A trial of several band members took place in New Carlisle, Quebec, on May 3, 1982. Judging from the comments of Micmac witnesses, it can only be described as a "mock trial", in which native and non-native testimony for the defendants was openly ridiculed, and attempts were made to discredit witnesses. Several individuals were convicted.

Nevertheless, a fisheries co-management agreement between the Micmac and the province was reached in 1982. An internal memorandum of the federal Department of Fisheries and Oceans referring to this very agreement was chosen by Evelyn Pinkerton as the opening statement for her book on "Co-operative Management of Local Fisheries".

> Attached is a copy of an agreement recently executed in Quebec between the Micmac Band of Restigouche and the Government of Quebec. In view of the fact that there was a state of war between the Indian people and the Quebec Government over salmon fishing last year, I find this agreement quite remarkable. Does it provide a useful model for similar agreements here between the Government of Canada and Indian Bands? (Internal Memorandum, Department of Fisheries and Oceans Canada, 15 June 1982, quoted in Pinkerton 1989:3)

As a final note, in 1983, following an appeal, the Quebec Superior Court overturned the 1982 convictions. The judge commented that, had it not been for serious errors in fact and law, the accused would most likely have been acquitted in 1982.

What happened at Restigouche in 1981 was not an isolated incident. Further north, on the northern Gaspé coast, 200 Montagnais Indians clashed with the police and local whites over fishing rights (*IWGIA Newsletter*, October/December 1981:47).

With regard to developments in Montagnais country in 1977, Quebecois journalist Remi Savard (1979:59–64) describes what he terms "la bataille du saumon" ("the battle of the salmon"). Members of several Montagnais communities of the Atlantic north shore, such as Sept-Isles, Natashquan, La Romaine and St. Augustin, were involved over the years in confrontations with federal fisheries officials. Their 1977 initiatives, such as trespass onto the property of a private fishing club, were principally directed against the sports fishery which was perceived as depleting the resources of Montagnais ancestral territory. Once again, we do not learn much beyond the "newsworthy", but all these events serve to show us that in Atlantic Canada, too, native people are asserting their fishing rights, on reserve as well as off-reserve.

Fishery Co-Management under the James Bay Agreement

As Richard Bartlett (1988:220) notes with regard to native water rights under the James Bay and Northern Quebec Agreement of 1975, the provincial intention to proceed with large-scale hydro development is strongly reflected in the terms of the Agreement. It is much more explicit in spelling out the rights of the province with respect to water resources and the water bed than those of the Cree and the Inuit. This has obvious implications for the fishery resource.

Prior to the hydro development, the James Bay Cree had maintained a relatively undisturbed subsistence lifestyle, largely based on hunting, trapping and fishing. Their fishery was totally self-regulated and, according to Fikret Berkes (1977:305), showed biological evidence of what might be called good management. In their negotiations the Cree placed high priority on the protection of their subsistence resources. The resultant Agreement deals with fisheries and wildlife together, so that co-management institutions, harvesting studies, allocation procedures, etc. apply to fish as well as wildlife. The Cree themselves do not perceive hunting, fishing and trapping as distinct and separate activities (Berkes 1989:191). Among the provisions of the Agreement to protect these activities are the following (ibid.:191–194):

- Reservation of lands for exclusive native harvest;
- Designation of certain fish species for exclusive native use;
- Guaranteed levels of native harvest, as well as the principle of priority for native harvesting;
- An income security program to supplement the cash income of hunters, fishermen and trappers;
- The establishment of an advisory body representing native people and various federal and provincial agencies: the "Coordinating Committee on Hunting, Fishing and Trapping" as the key co-management institution;
- Recognition of certain Cree self-regulatory institutions such as Cree tallymen and traditional territories; and
- Preferential treatment of native people in resource-related economic development opportunities.

After his analysis of the resources co-management in the James Bay area, Berkes (1989:194–205) feels that by and large the Agreement has succeeded in preventing the overall erosion of Cree harvesting rights and their rights to manage harvesting activities. Serious problems have been encountered, nevertheless. Among them is the failure of the Coordinating Committee to reach an agreement on appropriate guaranteed harvesting levels. Also there is the unresolved dilemma of generating proper data about the impacts of developments or data on species which may be threatened by increased pressure and competition from outsiders. On one hand, many Cree distrust scientific data and methods; on the other hand, there is a serious lack of scientific information, particularly the kind of information needed to demonstrate to government officials the undesirability of certain developments.

Government funding to support this and certain other aspects of the Agreement has failed to materialize. Moreover,

> the Coordinating Committee, as the main co-management institution, has the disadvantage of being a white man's institution run by white man's rules. This effectively prevents the traditional fishermen-hunters from participating, and limits representation to articulate, southern educated people who are comfortable in committee settings. (ibid.:195)

The Coordinating Committee is large and cumbersome as it is, but it does not represent all user groups. Sport fishing and hunting groups are not represented, but they are vocal and politically powerful. Less well known but equally problematic is the exclusion of native groups, which have not yet signed agreements with the government. The implementation of the Agreement strained relations, for example, between the Naskapi (who signed the Northeastern Quebec Agreement in 1978) and their southern neighbours, the Montagnais, whose land claims have not yet been settled (ibid.:204). Problems have also occurred between the Cree and their neighbours to the south and southeast.

With regard to the impact of the James Bay hydro development on Cree fishing activities, Berkes provides us with some observations in 1982, although he concedes that a complete understanding of the biological impact on the fishery resource was yet to come (Berkes 1982:529). Four years after the first interruption of the LaGrande river flow in November 1978, Berkes claims that the biological impacts of the hydroelectric development on the fish stocks of the LaGrande have been relatively small. Such changes as did occur (in distribution of fish, for example) seemed to be relatively easy to adapt to for the local fishermen. More problems were created by other environmental impacts, such as delays in freeze-up.

Socio-economic factors affected the fishery as well. One such factor was the gas subsidy program which encouraged fishermen to move from the river to other areas. The relocation of the community of Fort George was another factor as it tied up much of the labour force of the village for most of 1980. The cash income from this employment enabled many families to purchase vehicles and to travel relatively long distances along recently opened roads. The availability of new roads was a very important factor by itself.

By 1980 much of the fishing activity of the whole community had shifted from the lower LaGrande and the adjacent James Bay coast to lakes and rivers along the roads. The magnitude of this shift and its impact on the domestic economy has yet to be documented. From an impact-assessment point of view, Berkes concludes that

> ...what actually happened to the fish and fishery in the period 1979–81 had little resemblance to what had been predicted in earlier impact assessments....
>
> While these...studies differed considerably from one another in their approaches and conclusions, they were similar in omitting those considerations which, in retrospect, affected the native fishery most profoundly: the physical environmental changes that limited the harvestability of the fish, and social and economic changes that facilitated a switch of the major harvest area. (Berkes 1982:530)

The most insidious effect of the LaGrande Project, namely methylmercury contamination of fish, has already been discussed.

Previously, the general assumption had been that mercury contamination is exclusively caused by industrial pollution and that hydroelectricity is an environmentally clean source of power. However, the identification of a link between reservoir formation and methylmercury contamination in northern Manitoba and its confirmation in northern Quebec have prompted a re-examination of this view. According to Robert E. Hecky (1987:8), the "'environmentally clean' reputation of hydroelectricity has been seriously damaged by the events and research of the past decade."

In the case of Quebec, the extensive flooding has caused dramatic increases in mercury concentrations in fish (ibid.:9). In fact, fish from some James Bay reservoirs have methylmercury concentrations comparable to those in polluted Ontario Lakes. The threat presented by this situation is particularly great for northern native communities due to their greater dietary dependence on aquatic food chains. The Canadian limit for domestic marketing is 0.5 milligrams of mercury per kilogram of fish. It must be borne in mind, though, that marketing limits are set to protect the majority of consumers, which for Canadian commercial fisheries means residents of southern Canada and the United States. Medical authorities have expressed concern that the marketing limits may be too high to protect northern Canadians who consume fish more frequently than southerners (ibid.:8).

ONTARIO

While there is no comprehensive documentation on the issue, it is safe to say that a considerable proportion of Ontario's reserve communities is involved in some aspect of fishing, be it the food fishery, the commercial fishery, or recreational fishing. This is particularly true for the North but also applies to several southern reserves. Many of the issues already reiterated with regard to the west coast, the Atlantic Seaboard and Quebec, reoccur in Ontario: intense-user group conflicts, with the sports fishery featuring as the prime opponent to native fishing rights; and a refusal on the part of the provincial government to recognize Indian treaty and aboriginal rights to the fishery resource. These closely interrelated issues are aggravated in many parts of the province, particularly in the Great Lakes drainage basin, by severe pollution stress on the fishery resource.

Native Fishing Rights

Historically speaking, in contrast to the situation in Quebec and the Maritimes, developments that resulted in the formation of Ontario were characterized by an adherence to the principles of the Royal Proclamation. As a result, Ontario is covered by a patchwork of agreements, surrenders and treaties spanning a time period from 1764 to 1929. These treaties (using this collective term as a matter of convenience) considered the issue of Indian resource use in general, and fishing rights in particular in a variety of ways.

In the late eighteenth- and early nineteenth-century, Indian people found themselves in a strong bargaining position. Consequently, when the chiefs of the Mississauga Nation agreed to cede their aboriginal title to more than 28,000 hectares near Lake Ontario in 1805, the Indians were able to reserve to themselves "the sole right of the fisheries in the Twelve Mile Creek, the Sixteen Mile Creek, the Etobicoke River...[and] also the sole right to the fishery in the River Credit." (Hansen and McNab 1986:5, quoted in Driben 1987:22).

By the mid-nineteenth century the position of native people had weakened, but they were still protected by the Royal Proclamation. The Robinson Treaties of 1850 covering the area north of lakes Superior and Huron provide for an unqualified Indian right to hunt and fish on unoccupied Crown land (Cumming and Mickenberg 1972:116). The subsequent numbered Treaties (Three, Five and Nine) make the right "subject to such regulations as may from time to time be made by Her [Majesty's] Government of Her Dominion of Canada" (Treaty No. Three, quoted ibid.:315). As previously mentioned, courts have generally ruled that treaty rights take precedence over provincial laws, but not over federal law. We have also seen that, to complicate matters, provincial fishing regulations are almost always adopted as federal law, giving them priority over treaty promises.[9]

[9] Two revealing historical studies paint a disturbing picture of nineteenth-century "protection" of Indian treaty fishing rights. John J. Van West (1990) describes, how nineteenth-century fisheries management policies and jurisdictional disputes, along with the uncontrolled development of the non-native commercial fisheries, caused the collapse of the self-sustaining Ojibway sturgeon fisheries of the Lake of the Woods and the Rainy River in less than three decades.

In Ontario two pieces of legislation bear on the issue of native fishing rights — the Ontario Fishery Regulations, which are drawn up under the federal Fisheries Act, and the Ontario Game and Fish Act. Most conflicts arise from the enforcement of the Ontario Fishery Regulations, which makes no provision for Indian fisheries (Marchand 1986:75). In 1979 the provincial government issued hunting and fishing guidelines for Treaty Indians that reflected the policy of the Ontario Ministry of Natural Resources (OMNR), but which had not involved any native consultation. The province unequivocally holds that the federal Fisheries Act and the regulations made thereunder override Indian treaties in Ontario and can be enforced against Treaty Indians wherever they are, including on their own reserves. The one concession the provincial government has been prepared to make is to allow food fishing as long as it occurs on unoccupied Crown land, and to direct conservation officers to be lenient when enforcing federal law in this area (ibid.). But even this provision is limited by a requirement that each individual must obtain a permit under the federal Fisheries Act. Traditional Indian fishing techniques, such as spearing, netting, trapping and the use of weirs, are prohibited under the Ontario Fishery Regulations.

Where a treaty is silent on the question of hunting and fishing, native people assume that these rights were not dealt with in the treaty and as a result remain intact and unsurrendered. The province, on the other hand, tends to interpret this silence as implying the surrender of hunting and fishing rights (Berkes and Pocock 1983, quoted in Marchand 1986:75).

Treaty No. Three (1873), which covers the southwestern corner of northern Ontario, is characterized by its own peculiar set of problems. They involve the "headland to headland" dispute and focus on Indian ownership of the water bed in the context of fishing and ricing rights. All the reserves set apart by Treaty No. Three are located on rivers or lakes. The descriptions of the reserves selected pursuant to the treaty do not explicitly refer to the land under the water, but describe the boundaries as following the "banks" or "coasts" of rivers or lakes, or describe the land as being located on the "side" of a lake or a bay (Bartlett 1988:101). The headland-to-headland principle arose from native concerns over certain developments on the Lake of the Woods in the late 1880s, where commercial fishing and dam construction caused a depletion of the fish supply and losses of wild rice respectively. The intergovernmental Agreement of 1894 (An Act for the settlement of certain questions between the Governments of Canada and Ontario respecting Indian Lands, S.O. 1891, c.3, and An Act for the settlement of certain questions between the Governments of Canada and Ontario respecting Indian Lands, S.C. 1891, c.5) committed the provincial government to the headland-to-headland principle, "unless some good reason presents itself for a different course."

> 4. That in case of all Indian reserves so to be confirmed or hereafter selected, the waters within the lands laid or to be laid out as Indian reserves in the said territory, including the land covered with water lying between the projecting headlands of any lake or sheets of water, not wholly surrounded by an Indian reserve or reserves, shall be deemed to form part of such reserve including islands wholly within such headlands, and shall not be subject to the public common right of fishery by others than Indians of the band to which the reserve belongs. (Id., Sch., s.4 quoted in Bartlett 1988:104)

That the Ontario provincial government had no intention to comply with this agreement became very clear in 1915 when the province enacted "An Act to confirm the title for the Government of Canada to certain lands and Indian lands". The Act provided for the transfer of the reserves to Canada and confirmed Dominion title to such lands, all purportedly pursuant to the Agreement of 1894. Section 2 of the Act declared:

In a similar vein, Victor P. Lytwyn (1990) recounts the demise of the native fisheries in Lake Huron and Georgian Bay around Manitoulin Island. In less than twenty years they were transformed from thriving commercial enterprises to marginal subsistence activities.

> The land covered with water lying between the projecting headlands of any lake or sheets of water not wholly surrounded by an Indian reserve or reserves and islands wholly within such headlands shall not be deemed to form part of such reserve, but shall continue to be the property of the Province and The Bed of Navigable Waters Act shall apply, notwithstanding anything contained in the fourth paragraph of the agreement hereinbefore mentioned. (Bartlett 1988:106)

Commenting on the refusal of the province to acquiesce in the Agreement, Richard Bartlett writes:

> It is suggested that the action of the province is not only a violation of the 1894 Agreement but also a violation of Treaty No. Three. The 1894 Agreement may be taken to have confirmed the undertakings given in Treaty No. Three. The Crown is liable for breaches of treaty, and it is suggested that the Crown, in the right of the province, is liable for breach of the fiduciary obligation where conditions attached to the surrender of aboriginal title are not met and it lies within the power of the province to fulfill them. (ibid.:107)

Since 1915 the matter of the headland-to-headland boundaries of the reserves set apart by Treaty No. Three has intermittently arisen between the federal and provincial governments. In the early 1970s the Grand Council of Treaty No. Three became increasingly active in seeking the confirmation of headland-to-headland boundaries. The matter remains the subject of negotiation and discussion among the three parties.

With regard to the Great Lakes fishery, Thomas H. Whillans and Fikret Berkes observe:

> Native fishing communities have watched their fishing rights erode and harvests diminish over the years. Some native leaders concede that they have lost out to both of the other user-groups [commercial and recreational]. Many feel cheated and have an ambivalent attitude as to whether they should fight for their rights or to pull out of the white man's game in which they can never win anyway. (Whillans and Berkes 1986:15)

On Manitoulin Island, Ojibway and Ottawa fishers are badly "outnumbered and out-muscled" by sport anglers, and are reduced to short, special "open seasons" in which they can legally fish traditional, non-game species such as whitefish (ibid.:15f). There can be little doubt that the five bands on Manitoulin Island are pursuing several claims with the fishery in mind. One such claim by the United Chiefs and Councils of Manitoulin (UCCM) concerns 90,000 acres (36,423 hectares) of surrendered but unsold land, mostly lakefront property and lake bottom that was surrendered to the Crown in the 1800s, but never sold. Manitoulin bands are seeking its return or compensation (*Manitoulin Expositor*, April 19, 1989). The United Chiefs and Councils of Manitoulin also lay claim to all 23,000 islands of Lake Huron and Georgian Bay which they feel they never surrendered. In 1974 and 1984 the Council of Wikwemikong, Manitoulin's largest band who maintains a substantial fishery, formally reclaimed the islands off the eastern coast of Manitoulin, an action which was supported by the UCCM (UCCM 1988:3).

Impact of Pollution on Native Fisheries

In Ontario, more than elsewhere, the problems associated with user-group competition and native rights questions are aggravated by severe pollution stress.

> What is rapidly diminishing in supply is not fish, it is environmental quality. Rather than emphasizing the "supply side" of fishery management, it makes sense to divert relatively more effort to Great Lakes ecosystem rehabilitation and sustainable redevelopment. For without this, there may be no fish for the user-groups to compete over or for the fishery managers to manage. (Whillans and Berkes 1986:16)

The impact of this state of affairs on native people has been devastating in some cases, and the full extent of the impact may not even be fully known at this stage. By far the most serious problem has been mercury contamination, which is not confined to the Great

Lakes ecosystem. The Wabigoon-English River system in northwestern Ontario and eastern Manitoba may be described as one of the most severely mercury-polluted waterways in the world (Marchand 1986:69). The Ojibway communities of Grassy Narrows and White Dog have not yet recovered from the devastating physical and social impact which they suffered after mercury had been discharged into their waterways from the Dryden Pulp and Paper Mill in the late 1960s. The bands relied on fish from this river system for subsistence, as well as commercial purposes. They also acted as guides for sport fishermen, mostly from the United States. Due to the high mercury concentrations in fish, commercial fishing was banned in 1971.

The Lake St. Clair fishery suffered a similar fate. In 1970 both the commercial and sports fishery on this lake were closed as a result of mercury contamination from an upstream source. Although the sports fishery ban only lasted for a few months, the commercial fishery remained closed for ten years. The main polluter in this case was the Dow Chemical chlor-alkali complex downstream from Sarnia (ibid.:36). Chlor-alkali plants were by far the most important sources of mercury to the aquatic environment in Canada. Regulations for mercury discharges from chlor-alkali plants were issued under the Fisheries Act in 1972, and since these regulations have been in force, six of the seven Ontario chlor-alkali plants have ceased operation (ibid.:35). Such actions by government and the industry in the early 1970s have virtually eliminated mercury discharges from major industrial sources, but much of the inflicted damage was irreparable, and there were important secondary effects, as is shown by the experience of the Walpole Island native community.

The 1970 closure of the Lake St. Clair fishery had a significant negative impact on Walpole Island's economy, since the community had been involved in all aspects of fishing. Before 1970 there had been several commercial family fisheries, which were eliminated by the closure. The Walpole Island sports fishing industry was also affected through loss of permit revenue and guide incomes. The native food fishery suffered, when fish customarily caught by band members had to be replaced by purchased goods. The only part of the Walpole Island fishery that was considered for compensation was the commercial fishery. Financial compensation materialized primarily in the form of interest-free loans from the provincial government under the Fisheries Loans Act (1970) (which were ultimately forgiven) and a token sum from the polluter, Dow Chemical (ibid.:52).

This hardly compares with the lost growth potential of the Indian fishery and spin-off economic benefits which existed prior to the closure. Although the commercial fishery on Lake St. Clair was reopened in 1980, commercial fishing on Walpole Island has never been the same ever since, due to the Ontario Ministry of Natural Resources' strict management regime that accompanied the reopening (Marchand 1986:87). No more than 10 commercial licences were issued on the lake, compared to 34 which existed before the ban. Despite reassurances that Indian people would be given priority in the allocation of the fishery resource, only one native applicant (out of three) was successful in obtaining a commercial licence, and he does not fish due to the uneconomic nature of his operation. The fishery no longer appears to be viable due to strict quotas and size restrictions on fish to be caught because of unsafe levels of contaminants, such as mercury and PCBs. Furthermore, larger capital investment is required, and markets have been lost after the absence of the Lake St. Clair fishery over a 10-year period (ibid.:56).

While being fully aware of the need for conservation measures, Walpole Islanders are disillusioned and frustrated with the provincial government over its handling of the Lake St. Clair fishery closure, and they question government-imposed restrictions, particularly the tight quota system which so obviously favours the sports fishery. Their suspicions were verified when in December 1985, the provincial government bought out nine of the ten remaining commercial fishermen (leaving Walpole Islander Roger Williams who wanted no part in the deal). This enabled the government to shift the commercial allocation (of yellow pickerel) to the sports fishery (ibid.:57).

> Thus, it can be said that mercury contamination of the St. Clair system created an opportunity for the imposition of a management regime on Lake St. Clair which has resulted in further infringement of aboriginal rights, through quota restrictions on the native sustenance fishery and the nonviability of Indian commercial fishing. (ibid.:83f)

The Indian Fishing Agreements Dispute in Northern Ontario

Tripartite agreements on fisheries management (between both levels of government and native groups) have been considered as a possible solution to the escalating conflict between user groups in Ontario since the late 1970s. After a period of nearly five years, negotiations finally resulted in the signing of an agreement in 1982 between the organizations that comprise the Chiefs of Ontario and the Six Nations of the Grand River Band and the Ontario Government. However, at the last moment, the federal government refused to ratify the agreement which it had participated in negotiating. Certain provisions of the agreement, such as native "harvest fishing" without a licence, the zoning of some lakes for Indians' exclusive use, and band involvement in the management of fisheries, resulted in much controversy and caused a public outcry particularly in northern Ontario. The Tory government immediately yielded to not-too-subtle political threats by municipal and business leaders (Marchand 1986:80f; Driben 1987:19f).

In 1986 the provincial government announced again its intention to negotiate fishing agreements with the province's Indian organizations and the federal government. This time both levels of government made a concerted effort to solicit input from the public before the negotiations began. Over and above the predictable opposition of such organizations as the Ontario Federation of Anglers and Hunters (OFAH) and the Northern Ontario Tourist Outfitters Association (NOTO), unprecedented outbursts of hostility took place, where people made it perfectly clear, as one concerned citizen put it that "non-Indians will not stand quietly and have our rights taken away" (*Dryden Observer*, February 11, 1987, quoted in Driben 1987:21).

Matters were not helped by the public position of the Grand Council of Treaty No. Three. In a report released to the public in June 1986, the Council stated that as a result of more than a century of mismanagement, the federal and provincial governments had "morally forfeited any claim...to regulate the Indian fishery" which its members rely on for income and food. However, it also said that it was "prepared to work with those governments to establish an entirely new system of fisheries management...[in which the] overall consideration will be preservation and renewal of the fish population" in accord with the treaty their ancestors signed (Grand Council of Treaty No. Three 1986:59, quoted in Driben 1987:19).

The Council also expressed the view that Treaty No. Three guarantees that its members' right to fish takes precedence over all other uses, and accordingly access to the fishery in Treaty No. Three area should be ordered along the following lines: Indian people first, local non-Indian sports and commercial fishers second and third, and non-Indian non-residents last (ibid.). The proposal was endorsed by the Chiefs of Ontario, an umbrella organization that includes the Council, the Nishnawbe-Aski Nation, the Union of Ontario Indians, and the Association of Iroquois and Allied Indians, and also by the Assembly of First Nations.

By the late 1980s nothing had been resolved in Ontario. As Driben (ibid.:24) points out, from the province's standpoint, negotiations are a concession to necessity. When the Davis government came to power, it endeavoured to have the courts prove that Indian treaty fishing rights are subject to Ontario's fish and wildlife regulations. Accordingly, the Ministry of Natural Resources was instructed to lay charges against Treaty Indians who hunted and fished for their own consumption without regard to the regulations. The strategy backfired.

Consistently and almost without exception, the courts ruled in the Indians' favour. By 1979 the government was ready to change its game plan. Rather than pursuing the matter in the court, it decided to seek a political solution by entering into negotiations with the province's Indian organizations.

The federal government was similarly motivated. In 1987 Dennis Watson, the federal negotiator, was quoted as saying: "...the point we have made repeatedly [in public meetings] is that we either negotiate an agreement or the whole thing is thrown into the courts." (*Globe and Mail*, May 16, 1987) There can be little doubt that for both levels of government the spectre of the Boldt Decision served as a powerful motive to seek a negotiated agreement. The fact that Ontario is covered by treaties — even though these are by no means uniform — creates a situation that is much more akin to that in Washington than British Columbia.

Nevertheless, it was the *Sparrow* decision which after years of stalling set things in motion in Ontario. In rulings on cases, such as *R. v. Jackson* [1992] 4 C.N.L.R. 121 and *R. v. Bombay* [1993] 1 C.N.L.R. 92, the Ontario Court of Appeal decided that *Sparrow*'s findings were applicable to treaty rights as well as aboriginal rights. Even more significantly — and in contrast to the subsequent British Columbia Court of Appeal ruling on the Nuu-chah-nulth Tribal Council Smokehouse case — Judge Fairgrieve of the Ontario Provincial Court found in favour of an aboriginal and treaty right to fish commercially, to which the principles set out in *Sparrow* were applied. In *R. v. Jones* [1993] O.J.No.893 (Ont. Prov. Div.), the Ontario Provincial Court struck down a quota on the amount of fish which the Chippewa of Nawash Band could catch and sell under the authority of a band-held commercial fishing licence. Band members had been charged with selling fish in excess of their quota, and they used the legal principle set out in *Sparrow* to argue that such a quota was an unjustified infringement of their right to fish commercially. The court ruled that the imposition of a quota caused hardship for a subsistence economy based on fishing and that it infringed on the treaty and aboriginal right of the band to fish commercially. The judge also pointed out that the recognition of aboriginal rights does not preclude the recognition of treaty rights, and that both can exist side by side, and that, in fact, treaty rights may be viewed as confirming pre-existing aboriginal rights (*The First Perspective*, June 15, 1993:8). The concession of the Crown that the Nawash Band had "an aboriginal right of some sort to fish commercially" and that this right had not been extinguished, sets a highly significant precedent (Woodward and Jordan 1993:2f), even though it is only a lower court decision. This ruling is not being appealed.

In 1991 the Government of Ontario released a number of policy documents in order to implement *Sparrow*. An important example is the Interim Enforcement Policy on the Aboriginal Right to Hunt and Fish for Food (IEP), which was released in May 1991.

> ...recognizing the impact of the *Sparrow* and other judicial decisions, the Government of Ontario wishes to minimize the number of instances where aboriginal people are in conflict with the Government of Ontario in the application of the Game and Fish Act, the Fisheries Act, the Migratory Birds Convention Act, and the regulations enacted pursuant to those Acts, consistent with public safety and conservation objectives. (Government of Ontario 1991:1)

Under this Policy, status Indians who are fishing or hunting for food in the area covered by their treaty or in their traditional harvesting territory will not be subject to enforcement procedures (Clairman 1993:11).

Another initiative undertaken by the Government of Ontario is an Interim Measures Agreement (IMA) with the aboriginal groups north of Lake Superior, signed in August 1991. Similar agreements have subsequently been negotiated with the Robinson-Superior Treaty bands as well as the groups in the Treaty No. Five and Treaty No. Nine areas. These agreements spell out formalized procedures to ensure that aboriginal people are informed of developments on Crown land which are likely to have an impact on them. Many questions as to the potential effectiveness of this "consultation" remain open and, furthermore, mining activities have been exempted from the notification requirements (ibid.:13). Nevertheless, as in British Columbia, a variety of agreements and policy initiatives signify a new government-to-government relationship between Ontario and aboriginal groups.

THE PRAIRIE PROVINCES

In Manitoba and the central and northern parts of Saskatchewan and Alberta, fishing makes a major contribution to native people's livelihood, for subsistence as well as for commercial purposes. Under the terms of the Manitoba, Saskatchewan and Alberta Resource Transfer Agreements of 1930, status Indians have assured access to fish for domestic purposes, whereas non-status Indians and Metis are excluded from this provision. But even the Indian subsistence fishery is indirectly regulated, due to the necessity under the provinces' multiple-use policy to allocate the available supply among all user groups: domestic, commercial and sports fishery. The fish resource is finite, and the demand for fish exceeds the sustainable supply. Even though the Indian domestic fishery may have priority relative to alternative uses, provincial management regimes determine the absolute amount of fish available for each use. The lack of reliable data on the food fishery precludes sound management of the resource with regard to this user group. Like in other parts of the country, no aboriginal person — Indian, non-status Indian, or Metis — has an inherent right to engage in any form of commercial harvesting of fish.

Manitoba

Native people became involved in the development of the commercial fishing industry in the 1880s, as reported by Frank Tough (1984) for central Manitoba. His example shows how the commercialization of the fishery adversely affected the local subsistence economy, and within a decade led to non-sustainable resource use patterns. It appears that initially many native people were somewhat ambivalent about the commercial exploitation of whitefish, but "In a manner similar to the fur trade, Indians were drawn into the fish trade by the prospect of obtaining goods." (ibid.:305) Numerous requests were made by Indian bands for exclusive fishing reserves. Patterns of overexploitation became evident at an early stage. When Indian agents attempted to prevent commercial fishermen from exploiting the spawning grounds, their jurisdiction was undermined by fisheries officers in Winnipeg.

> Therefore, Indians may have engaged in the fish trade as one alternative to exclusive exploitation by white fishermen. It appears that Indian involvement in the fish trade may have been motivated by trade goods, extra income from winter fishing, and the fact that an element of participation may have meant some control. This participation by Indians may have been in conflict with their long-term interests. Quite possibly there was no alternative to participating, aside from sitting on the banks and watching white commercial fishermen scooping up fish. (Tough 1984:306f)

By the late 1880s native people were facing a crisis as the collapse of their subsistence fishery and the uneven returns from commercial fishing caused serious social disruption. The situation was aggravated by the fact that these communities had no other economic sectors to fall back on, since the rapid development of the commercial fishery had served as a disincentive for potential agricultural development of reserve lands. "For this region, the underdevelopment of native communities was conditioned, in part, by the development of a commercial fishery." (ibid.:308) At the same time, the commercial fishing industry was still expanding, enabled to do so by its better equipment, but the continual northward shift of the operation of the fish companies was an indication that overfishing was occurring.

Continued pressure from both Indians and their agents in 1890 resulted in an investigation of the fishing conditions on Lake Winnipeg by Samuel Wilmot from the Fisheries Branch in Ottawa. Wilmot introduced certain conservation measures to protect whitefish spawning grounds. Some of his suggestions became regulations, such as a commercial and domestic licensing system and restrictions on where commercial companies could operate. He was also agreeable to providing the Indians with exclusive fishing grounds, but advised against assisting them with more capital for fishing. This was an important decision, since as Tough (ibid.:312) points out, "The control over capital would eventually determine who would control the fish resources."

Today both commercial and domestic fishing are very important activities for Manitoba's native population. A preliminary screening of INAC's 1988 Indian Reserve Community Profiles for the Manitoba Region (Government of Canada 1989) revealed that 24 out of 60 Indian communities are involved in the commercial fishery, an even larger number engage in subsistence fishing. Numerous native fisheries in this province, however, have been very adversely affected by hydroelectric developments. The most significant example is Southern Indian Lake, which prior to its impoundment in 1976 was northern Manitoba's largest commercial fishery (Hecky 1987:9). Southern Indian Lake is presently plagued by severe mercury contamination. A federal-provincial study of the reservoir-related mercury problem was completed in 1987, and a major claim by five affected Indian reserves under the Northern Flood Agreement was pending.

Saskatchewan

In Saskatchewan the dependence of native people on the fishery resource for food as well as income is substantial, particularly in its central and northern part, as was shown by a 1986 study (Murray and Clouthier 1986). The Natural Resources Transfer Agreement guarantees status Indians a free food fishery, but this is not to imply that their activities are not regulated. Indians may catch fish for personal consumption by angling or with gill nets. They do not require angling licences but instead require permits, which are issued free of charge, to fish for food with nets. The permits indicate the lakes and species being fished and thus enable the province to maintain a database on fishing activities. Indian anglers must abide by the same regulations as other anglers, that is, they cannot fish during closed seasons, in closed areas or take more fish than allowed by the angling regulations. Indian subsistence fishermen may fish the lakes specified on their permits at any time of the year (ibid.:2f).

In Saskatchewan the so-called domestic fishery represents a subsistence fishery for non-status Indians, Metis or non-Indians. Licences are available for $5 each. Domestic licences are only issued on the basis of need, i.e. an applicant must prove that due to financial hardship, geographical isolation or other pressing reasons he/she is dependent on access to the fishery resource. It is not a matter of rights or culture, and may even depend on the amount of surplus harvest available (Murray and Clouthier 1986:29).

For 1985, according to Murray and Clouthier (ibid.:7), 599 permits were issued to 519 Indians, but the researchers observed discrepancies between the numbers of permits issued and the numbers of respondents who fished, indicating that the number of permits underestimates the number of Indian fishermen. The same is true for domestic licences, 479 of which were issued in 1984. It is more than likely that the majority of recipients is native and living in the central or northern part of the province (ibid.:ii).

Although there was an implicit acceptance by subsistence fishers that the resource was finite, the majority of community leaders interviewed by Murray and Clouthier (ibid.:25, 28) perceived the regulations controlling the subsistence fishery as a constraint. Restrictions on lakes that could be fished, especially while trapping, and on the numbers of Indian permits and domestic licences issued, seemed most important. Some interviewees felt that their treaty rights were violated. In view of the discrepancy between permits and licences issued and actual fishing activities, Murray and Clouthier suggest that

> ...the matter of regulations as a constraint may be more artificial than real in the Northern and Central Management Zones....Thus given the vastness of northern Saskatchewan, the large number of lakes there, and the few Resource Officers, it seems likely that regulations are not a constraint to most native northern subsistence fishermen. (ibid.:28)

The authors indicate that, in their view, the most crucial obstacle to optimum management of the fish resource with regard to the subsistence fishery is the lack of information on the users, their harvest and the impact of other fisheries on fish populations (ibid.:29). One is tempted to ask whether more adequate information would result in politically unpopular reallocations of the (finite) fishery resource.

Native participation in Saskatchewan's commercial fishery is very substantial. In 1984–85, 63 per cent of the province's commercial fishermen were native. Native people comprised 98 per cent and 93 per cent of the commercial fishers in the Northern and Central Management Zones respectively, but only 5 per cent of commercial fishermen in the Southern Zone (ibid.:30). There were an estimated 620 native commercial fishers in the Central and Northern Zones in 1984.

Saskatchewan's commercial fishery faces numerous problems, most of them due to its distance from the major North American markets and its resultant inability to compete with the coastal and Great Lakes fisheries. This situation necessitates heavy subsidies.

> Subsidies are important to native commercial fishermen because they enable them to fish remote lakes and their products to compete in the marketplace. The withdrawal of the subsidy program would mean the virtual cessation of commercial fishing in northern Saskatchewan. There are two aspects to this. First, the commercial fishery is believed to be viewed by natives as a traditional occupation as well as a means of sustaining and promoting their culture. The loss of this tradition could have a serious impact on a socially disadvantaged people. Second, the commercial fishery is used to keep people employed in an area that lacks employment opportunities. The loss of a major source of income for many native northerners would be both socially and economically devastating and increase the number of welfare recipients. The coupling of social development issues to resource management problems makes an economic rationalization of the industry difficult to achieve. (ibid.:56)

Alberta

The situation in Alberta exhibits similarities to Saskatchewan. Subsistence fishing still has a role to play in the North, and there are some substantial commercial freshwater fisheries. One example is Lac La Biche, where commercial fishing is one of the most important economic activities in the region, and the majority of commercial fishermen are of native origin, status Indian or Metis. The Lac La Biche Fishermen's Co-Operative is one of the largest suppliers of freshwater fish in the province (Government of Alberta 1986:53). In the late 1970s the co-op in cooperation with the Regional Economic Development Council (REDC) started experimental production of caviar made from whitefish roe, a labour-intensive operation which became an instant success and remained so during the following years (McArthur 1986:165). Lesser Slave Lake also supports a commercial fishery, with Indians and Metis comprising approximately 75 per cent of the 300 licensed commercial fishermen (*Native Network News*, May 1990).

Similar to its neighbour to the east, Alberta's commercial fishery faces many problems. Within the overall economic picture of the province, it is a very minor industry and must compete with the tourist and recreational fishery industry, which is supported by strong lobbies (McArthur 1986:166). There is concern among native people about overfishing the northern lakes (*Native Network News*, May 1990). An even greater threat to domestic and commercial fisheries — usually minimized by official sources, but promulgated by native testimony — is the increasing pollution of Alberta's major northern river systems, the Peace and the Athabasca, by pulpmills and oil sands plants.

THE NORTH

Domestic Fishery

The domestic fishery is of great importance in northern Canada. A sizeable proportion of the residents of most, if not all native communities in the territorial north and Labrador still pursue an essentially land-based way of life. In such land-based economy, fish is quite often the most reliable and abundant source of sustenance and, as a result, the subsistence fishery tends to be the most persistent segment of the traditional renewable resource-based economy (Berkes 1989:39). Studies at various northern Canadian locations have found fish to account for from 25 to 53 per cent of aboriginal people's diet (Hopper and Power 1991:272). Arctic char above the tree line and whitefish below are the species preferred for human consumption; others such as northern pike are utilized for dogfood. In recognition of the importance of this fishery, DFO regulations determine that subject to conservation requirements, the first priority for fisheries use is native subsistence, followed by sports and commercial use (CARC 1987:7).

As perceived by the government, the northern subsistence fishery poses certain managerial challenges due to its special characteristics. The native domestic fishery is essentially unregulated. It has socio-cultural as well as economic significance and constitutes an aboriginal right. It operates outside the cash economy. The combined effects of these characteristics make it largely invisible to government management agencies (Yaremchuk and Wong 1989:1). The Department of Fisheries and Oceans lacks a comprehensive program for the collection, publication and storage of statistics on native domestic fishing locations and harvests in the Northwest Territories (ibid.:2).

Changes to the status quo, for example, licensing or the introduction of a regulatory quota, have traditionally been opposed by aboriginal people. Another contentious issue is the native request for removal of restrictions on the disposition of domestic fisheries products to allow for intersettlement trade (ibid.:4).

As shown by the Inuvialuit Final Agreement (IFA), the settlement of comprehensive claims creates a different managerial environment for the northern fishery, including the domestic fishery. The IFA provides for the allocation of subsistence or domestic quotas, based on conservation and community needs. This allocation relies on the recommendations of an advisory Inuvialuit-government co-management board, the Fisheries Joint Management Committee (FJMC) (see chapter 5 for IFA co-management structure). Within a framework of consultation, aboriginal people appear to view subsistence quotas and Total Allowable Harvest "as a method for safeguarding an entitlement, rather than as an unwarranted restriction." (Yaremchuk and Wong 1989:5)

Other responsibilities of the FJMC include management of the public right to fish on Inuvialuit lands, monitoring of fish harvesting within the Settlement Region, recommending harvestable quotas for Inuvialuit commercial fisheries, and advising the Minister of Fisheries and Oceans on all aspects of fishery management within the settlement region (Government of Canada 1984:29). The IFA includes provisions allowing the Inuvialuit to sell or barter the products of subsistence fisheries to other Inuvialuit or other aboriginal people within the settlement area (ibid.:26). Inuvialuit are allowed to fish without a licence, and where a licence is required for conservation purposes, they receive it without payment of a fee. Here, like in other areas of the North, native harvest surveys replace licensing as a management tool.

Commercial Fishery

According to Pierre Asselin, DFO, (CARC 1987:7) "On a value-per-pound basis, sport fishing provides a higher return than any other method, except perhaps for high-value marine species like shrimp and scallops that show some promise in the eastern Arctic." In 1985, 49 sport fishing lodges were operating in the Northwest Territories (Government of the

NWT 1986:77). There are no data on native participation in this sector, either as employees or entrepreneurs, but native people do seem to have made some inroads (Keith et al. 1987:2). In the late 1980s the Labrador Inuit Development Corporation purchased a resort facility, and native entrepreneurs in northern Quebec, the Northwest Territories and Yukon are also pursuing such opportunities.

While the commercial freshwater fishery in Yukon is relatively small (confined to 20 large lakes) due to lack of local markets, the commercial salmon fishery constitutes an important part of the Dawson economy (Government of Yukon 1986:41), in particular Han Fisheries, owned and operated by the Dawson Indian Band. By and large, the northern commercial fishery has led a rather tenuous existence. In the Northwest Territories the industry provides about 400 jobs and in 1989 produced an estimated $2.1 million, 75 per cent of which were accounted for by Great Slave Lake Whitefish (Legislative Assembly of the NWT 1989:14; Sibbeston 1986:155). Arctic char from the eastern arctic make up most of the rest. During the 1980s the industry declined due to falling prices and high costs of production. According to Nick Sibbeston (ibid.), the whitefish industry on Great Slave Lake was particularly hit hard, and many fishermen felt that part of their problem stemmed from inadequate marketing of their product by the Freshwater Fish Marketing Board. The commercial fishery is heavily subsidized, and the most viable fisheries appear to be those for arctic char at Cambridge Bay and Rankin Inlet.

There have been some innovative initiatives to boost the commercial fishery and native people's participation in it. One example is a joint venture between Qiqiqtaaluk Corporation, the corporate arm of the Baffin Regional Inuit Association, and Farocan, an Ottawa-based company. Since 1987 an offshore shrimp fishery has been providing approximately $1 million in income for Baffin Inuit crew members (Government of the NWT 1990:13). The DFO issues licences to people living in proximity to the resource. Qiqiqtaaluk holds the licence to fish, and Farocan, with no licence, provides the two-factory freezer trawlers, as well as the management and technical know-how. By the early 1990s the venture had been joined by Makivik Corporation of northern Quebec, holding a second licence. A third licence is held by Unaaq Fisheries Incorporated of Iqaluit, a joint venture between Qiqiqtaaluk and Makivik Corporation. The enterprise creates employment for 90 people. There is also the opportunity for the Inuit to buy interests in the boats. The product is sold wherever the market is best, usually in Greenland. To date no spin-off industries have developed (Jim Noble, Regional Superintendent, NWT Department of Renewable Resources, personal communication, August 6, 1992).

In summer 1992 Unaaq and another Inuit controlled company, the Cumberland Sound Fisheries of Pangnirtung, ventured into the Greenland halibut fishery (*News North*, August 3, 1992:A11). The fact that 14 Greenland halibut licences had been allocated to the Maritimes and only two to Baffin Island caused much indignation in Pangnirtung (Rebecca Mike, Pangnirtung MLA, personal communication, August 11, 1992). Traditionally, the northern turbot (Greenland halibut) fishery has been a winter fishery, giving Baffin Inuit a monopoly on fresh fish during that season.

Another major native/non-native venture is partly based on the shrimp fishery. Torngat Fish Producers Co-operative serves more than 400 Indian, Inuit and non-native members on the northern Labrador coast (Jackson 1984:15f). The co-op leases a vessel for shrimp fishing and runs plant and collector boat operations. In addition to processing salt cod, Torngat has shipped fresh and frozen char, salmon and sea trout to Canadian markets.

E.T. Jackson (ibid.) points out that although co-operatives have an impressive record of creating jobs and wealth under local control, their development has been restricted by a number of obstacles. Marketing has proven to be a major hurdle and was apparently the main challenge facing Torngat in the early 1980s.

> One of the elements of Inuit co-operatives' successful marketing efforts in the south has been the co-operatives' strong links with the marketing expertise and advice of the co-operative movement at large and their understanding that the co-operative movement itself provides key domestic and international markets. However, there has been no comprehensive attempt by co-operatives, together with governments, to develop long-range, creative, and aggressive marketing strategies in the fishery. (ibid.:16)

Significant expansion of the northern commercial fishery in the foreseeable future is unlikely (Topolniski et al. 1987:10). The resource does not lend itself to intensive exploitation and is easily overharvested due to relatively slow growth, depressed productivity and comparatively low abundance characteristic of arctic fish resources. Development has also been constrained by the fact that northern producers are remote from the places where most consumption occurs and the production of other goods takes place. Moreover, for many of the species of commercial interest, there exist lower-cost sources of supply. A more feasible prospect for the future is an expansion of the inter- and intra-settlement trade for country food. A fishery in this context does not face the economic and logistical constraints of the export fishery (ibid.:8). Quite likely it would integrate well into the existing domestic economies.

Similar to the situation in the midnorth of the Prairie Provinces, a fundamental public policy issue concerns the question to what extent the development of the northern fishery should proceed on both economic and social grounds. The future of the northern fishery resources and their beneficiaries will eventually be determined by the outcome of the comprehensive claims settlements. In her examination of the Inuvialuit Final Agreement under the aspect of resources co-management, Nancy Doubleday reaches the conclusion that

> ...the Inuvialuit Final Agreement contains all the required ingredients for a co-management regime. It recognizes preferential or exclusive harvesting rights, control of access to the resource, participation in management, relevance of traditional knowledge, and modern scientific approaches to conservation — all of which represent elements of special status and self-government necessary for the survival of indigenous peoples. (Doubleday 1989:221)

However, it is also felt that the Agreement fails in one very important criterion which would truly reflect the aboriginal right to self-government in resource management: the deregulation of native rights subject to a conservation principle. "The weight within the joint management bodies will be on the side of regulation acceptable to government, rather than deregulation of native harvesting rights." (Doubleday 1989:221) Regulation is still not decentralized, and final decisions are invariably made by government ministers.

The Nunavut Final Agreement, based on its provisions for water resources management and its stance on aboriginal water rights, offers more potential for aboriginal fisheries management, but it is too early to judge its implications.

CONCLUSION AND OUTLOOK

In the context of his study of the Great Lakes fishery, Fikret Berkes (1985) suggests a model in which living resources management can be conceptualized in terms of a "life cycle". This model is equally applicable to other kinds of renewable resources.

> The cycle starts with the steady-state, low-level exploitation of the resource. More often than not, the resource is utilized communally under some kind of common-property management institution.
>
> At some point in time pressure builds to exploit the resource, not for the benefit of the local community, but for individual profit. The situation may be complicated by population pressure and/or the availability of more effective exploitation technologies. At this phase of the cycle or shortly thereafter, the original community of users may be displaced or marginalized by the movement of more effective exploiters into the area. For this to happen, open access conditions have to be created; colonizers have usually been very successful at this. In the resource development phase of the life cycle, the fishery is no longer steady-state but

> growing. Growth is sustained not by husbanding the individual stocks that comprise the resource but by "mining out" (like a non-renewable resource) a succession of stocks from a succession of geographical frontiers.
>
> When this "sequential exploitation" phase of the cycle ends, the local community is once more able to control the resource, at least to some extent, because the depleted stocks are no longer attractive to developers who, by then have started looking elsewhere for short-term profits. The local community is faced with the necessity of managing the common property resource or what is left of it. The developers do not have this problem because they can move on. It may be expected at this phase, as a logical ecological response to the problem of too many users, that de facto use rights would start to emerge or to evolve, even without government intervention. These de facto rights may be new arrangements or, if the community consists of the descendents of the original users, they may be derived from a restoration of traditional practices. In this phase, the fishery is likely to become a sustained-yield operation rather than one based on the mining of stocks. It will tend toward steady-state.
>
> The post-development fishery is the last phase of the life cycle. Some post-development fisheries can become quite successful....But this can be a liability, because a successful fishery will attract new developers, and the cycle may start all over again. (ibid.: 205–206)

Elements and stages of the life cycle in this admittedly idealized and simplified model can be found in fisheries all over the country. In some cases the resource life cycle was completed very rapidly (and probably more than once) like, for example, on Lake Winnipeg and neighbouring lakes, as described by Frank Tough (1984). In many parts of the country, native people find themselves and the resources they depend on caught up in what Berkes terms "the resource development phase of the life cycle", and they anticipate and try to intercept the continuation of events. In British Columbia and Ontario, but also in the North, the struggle over "native fishing rights" (or wildlife including fish in the North) is not so much about a "fair share" of the resource, but about the right to manage this resource. The resource management envisaged by most native people would draw on traditional or neo-traditional practices. This intensified thrust towards aboriginal resource management not only stems from a feeling of entitlement but is also born out of concern and the conviction that, despite the government's limited access resource management, the fishery (and other renewable resources) are still being "mined" and altogether mismanaged. Looking back at the government's track record, many native people simply feel that they can do a better job, and equally important, that time is running out.

Events in British Columbia seem to indicate that native people are not alone with this opinion. On July 11, 1990, the First Nations Congress agreed to launch a massive flotilla of fishing boats to protest against the violation of a Haida fisheries management plan by several commercial sport fishing lodges. "Authority doesn't come through negotiation. Authority must be taken," Ralph Michell, a hereditary chief of the Gitksan-Wet'suwet'en, declared (*Globe and Mail*, July 12, 1990). The Haida had successfully implemented an unofficial salmon management program in their homeland Haida Gwaii, the region of the Queen Charlotte Islands. This program was endorsed by most non-native commercial and sports fishing operations in the area. It enforced a drastic reduction in the allocation to the sports fishery and was financed by fees charged to sports fishing lodges and commercial fishermen. The protest was triggered by the refusal of the Charlotte Princess, a floating lodge, and several other lodges to participate in the Haida management program. More than 80 commercial salmon fishermen — native and non-native —, Haida and native leaders from across the province jammed Parry Passage with about 100 boats, successfully preventing the arrival of new customers on the Charlotte Princess.

Dana Doerksen, the director of the Northern Trollers Association who participated in the protest, is quoted as expressing the opinion that the federal Fisheries Department has "totally mismanaged" the salmon fishery, and that the Haida "have the full support of all the commercial fishermen in all of British Columbia." (*Globe and Mail*, July 13, 1990). Two years later the Haida management initiative was endorsed by a provincial Joint Stewardship Agreement.

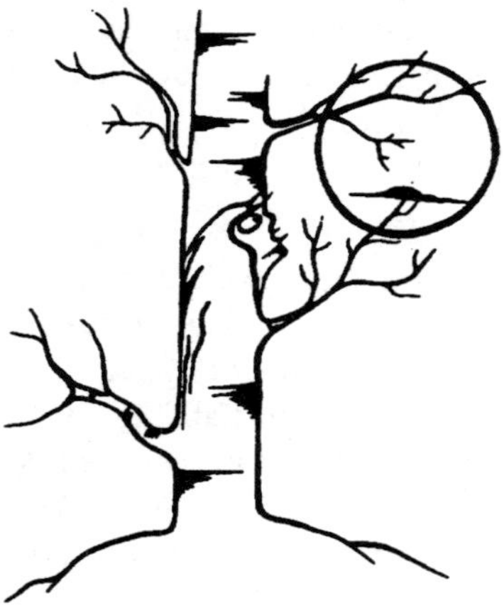

4

Forestry

INTRODUCTION

> I have used wood from trees growing on Meares Island. I cut young cedar about 36 feet tall for fishing poles around Mosquito Harbour. I used to look for long straight cedars, the less branches the better, about six inches in diameter. I used driftwood for firewood. I have made two canoes on Meares Island. One canoe was made of driftwood and one was made of wood from Vargas Island. My wife made baskets from cedar bark gathered on Meares Island. Yew tree wood is used mostly for making paddles. Cedar, yellow cedar, and fir are used for making oars. Yellow cedar is harder to find than red cedar. (Roy Haiyupis, Nuu chah nulth Elder, Affidavit for Wah nah jus/Hilth hoo is [Meares Island] Trial, 1991, quoted in *Ha-Shilth-Sa*, November 13, 1991:3)

> Canada's forests are its most valuable natural resource, with economic, social and environmental benefits. The forest covers nearly one-half of Canada's land mass. Productive forests, which supply timber for pulp, paper, plywood, lumber and other products, occupy 2.2 million square kilometres.
>
> Canada is the world's largest exporter of forest products, with 22 per cent of all these products traded in world markets. The industry ships $30 billion in goods per year and adds more to Canada's positive trade balance than any other industry. (Statistics Canada 1990, quoted in *Globe and Mail*, April 28, 1990)

This brief excerpt from *Globe and Mail* clearly shows that the importance of Canada's forests for the country can hardly be overstated. It also invites the hypothesis that such significance creates considerable resource development pressures and constraints that affect native groups' designs on the resource. The importance of forests and forest ecosystems for Indian people is equally significant but frequently at odds with the purposes and practices of the Canadian forest industry. Places such as Meares Island, the Stein Valley, South Moresby, Temagami and Barriere Lake, recall the more media-worthy native/non-native confrontations over forestry-related issues. The landmark *Sioui* court ruling on treaty rights in 1990 (R. v. Sioui [1990] 3 C.N.L.R. 127) was occasioned by Huron Indians' traditional use of the forest in Quebec's Jacques-Cartier Provincial Park. The summer-long stand-off at Oka in 1990 originated from the Mohawks' determination to protect their sacred pine forest, planted by their ancestors and considered as one of the oldest hand-planted forests in North America (MacLaine and Baxendale 1990:26).

First Nations' traditional and non-traditional use of forest lands on-reserve as well as on ceded and unceded ancestral territories has over time been faced with numerous disincentives and constraints. Conflicts between native and non-native user groups are multifaceted and often involve issues not traditionally dealt with within the framework of Canadian forestry institutions and forestry policies. A brief overview of Canadian forestry shall provide the background for a discussion of these issues.

FORESTRY IN CANADA: AN OVERVIEW

Like Canada's fishery resource, the country's forests are faced with a crisis. According to Jim Richardson, Forestry Canada's coordinator of forest biology research, "We're approaching the limit of the natural forest resource, and in some parts of Canada, have reached the limit." (Wylynko 1991:28). The cause for this impending shortfall lies in a history of mismanagement of the resource, a history which in the mid-1980s has been well documented by authors like Donald Mackay (1985), Ken Drushka (1985) and Jamie Swift (1983). According to Hamish Kimmins, a forest ecologist at the University of British Columbia, forest management evolves through three distinct phases.

> The first of these is familiar enough to Canadians. It involves the unrestrained exploitation of the resource, with little regulation and no concern for the principles of forestry or future forest yields. Canada has only just recently emerged from this primitive period and has entered a second phase, which Kimmins refers to as an administrative type of forest management. This phase is based on recognition of the need to do something in the area of forest renewal; that need, however, has been translated into a non-biological approach to forest management. This attitude toward the problems of forest renewal must, in Kimmins' view, eventually give way to a third type of forestry: one based on an appreciation of the highly variable, biologically-complex nature of the forest. (Swift 1983:162f)

Each of the provinces and northern territories shares in the country's forest wealth. The regional distribution in terms of area is shown in Table 1 as follows:

TABLE 1
Distribution of Canada's Forest

	Per Cent
Atlantic Provinces	13
Quebec	18
Ontario	17
Prairie Provinces	22
British Columbia	15
Northern Territories	15
Canada	100

(Reed 1980:18)

The importance of the forest sector for these regions can be fully appreciated after an examination of regional employment profiles with regard to the four primary sectors: forestry, agriculture, mining and fisheries (ibid.:20). In eastern Canada the forest sector ranks first as an employment generator in New Brunswick, second in Nova Scotia and Newfoundland, and third in Prince Edward Island. Out of 16 economic regions, the forest sector ranks first or second in 10, while fishing is first or second in only eight. Moving to central Canada, the forest sector ranks first or second in eight of Quebec's nine economic regions, and first or second in all six of those in Ontario. Among the 21 economic regions in the Prairie Provinces, forestry only manages to place second in three. In sharp contrast, in British Columbia the forest sector is first in eight regions and second in only two where mining and smelting dominate.

A comparison of the annual allowable cut (AAC) figures with the actual timber harvest in each area reveals a disproportionate reliance on the forests of specific regions. The

Atlantic provinces, with 8.4 per cent of the Canadian annual allowable cut, provide 9.7 per cent of the annual harvest. Quebec, with 14.8 per cent of the allowable cut, contributes almost 22 per cent of the Canadian harvest. The Prairie Provinces have 15.9 per cent of the allowable cut, but account for only 7.1 per cent of the harvest. Ontario has 23.9 per cent of the allowable cut, but provides only 13.4 per cent of the actual volume. British Columbia, with an estimated 36 per cent of the annual allowable cut, contributes 48 per cent of the Canadian timber harvest each year. Given the disproportionate concentration of the Canadian forest industry in British Columbia, it is not surprising that some of the most intense conflicts are encountered in that province (Drushka 1985:16). As Reed (1980:20) concludes, forest land is without question the most valuable natural resource possessed by Canada, and its fate is going to affect the lives of countless people.

One of the key factors determining forest management is the situation of forest ownership. In Canada, provincial governments own 87 per cent of the over 2 million square kilometres of forest land. The federal government's 5 per cent ownership consists mainly of the untapped forests of Yukon and the Northwest Territories. No more than 8 per cent of the national total is privately owned. The only provinces with significant portions of their forests in private hands are Nova Scotia (76 per cent) and New Brunswick (56 per cent). In Quebec and Ontario, less than 10 per cent of the productive forest is privately owned. A negligible amount of private forest land exists in the three Prairie Provinces, and the government of British Columbia holds about 94 per cent of that province's forests (Drushka 1985:15).

The most powerful tool of forest management is the tenure system.

> Forest policy and politics come together at no point more critical than this — the government's legal and administrative apparatus giving private interest access to timber on publicly owned lands. Tenure not only defines the mechanics of the process but can — as it has in British Columbia for the past thirty-five years — determine who may or may not obtain this access. In some cases, it can entail rights over the forest land itself, beyond the mere acquisition of timber. (ibid.:64)

Across Canada there are 42 major tenure systems used to grant property rights to forest operators. While there appears to be a spectrum of tenure systems ranging from the comprehensive freehold to the non-exclusive common property rights, a pattern does emerge.

> The entire menagerie of forest tenure systems can be grouped into three forms of tenure, namely; forest management agreements, forest licences, and timber permits. Forest management agreements are long-term agreements (20–25 years), negotiated between [sic] a resource user willing to make major capital investments. The agreements usually grant fairly extensive property rights in exchange for undertaking major forest management activities.
>
> Forest licences are generally competitively tendered granting a limited set of property rights over a shorter time period (5–10 years). Also, the firms receiving forest licences make smaller investments and the Crown generally retains a larger portion of the forest management responsibilities. Resource users tend to directly pay for a portion of the forest management through fees and royalty payments. Finally, timber permits tend to be very short-term (1–5 years), application-based tenures granting individuals or firms very limited and site specific property rights. Under the timber permit, the Crown assumes all responsibilities for forest management. (Heartwell 1988a:6)

Whereas the government essentially plays the role of landlord, virtually all of the timber harvesting and forest products manufacturing are being conducted by the private sector. Forest tenure arrangements have become the major instrument for implementing public forest policy. Almost every government declares sustained yield as its explicit goal, and in some cases as the primary goal (ibid.:9).

While the federal and provincial governments had identified the need for reforestation and sustained yield management in the early 1900s, the truth is that Canada's forests continued to be mined like a non-renewable resource until the 1970s. After his investigation of the question of timber supply and the track record of forest management, forest economist Les Reed in 1978 formed the following opinion:

> I came to the conclusion that virtually nobody could claim good marks in forestry. With few exceptions there had been negligence. Industry had been very short-sighted. The provinces had milked the resource. The federal government had turned its back on Canada's most important natural asset. (MacKay 1985:181)

The 1980s brought some tentative improvements at the provincial level, particularly in New Brunswick and to a lesser extent in Ontario and British Columbia (ibid.:191), and a federal commitment to a major push to increase timber supplies through intensive forest renewal and management. The proposed mechanism for program delivery was a new series of federal/provincial Forestry Resource Development Agreements (FRDAs). Negotiations with the provinces began in late 1982, and by 1985 agreements had been signed with all provinces except Newfoundland.

But in the early 1990s the sense of crisis has by no means diminished. Due to a combination of overcutting, underutilization, inaccurate inventories and insufficient regeneration efforts, Canada's most important natural resource still is in serious jeopardy. And there are more deeply rooted causes for the increasing controversy surrounding the resource, causes which have much to do with the basic structure of the industry and fundamental values expressed in the premises of forest management.

One of those fundamental values is the "holy cow" of sustained yield. In simple terms, sustained yield forest management means "management of forest land for continuous production with the aim of achieving a balance between net growth and harvest." (Expert Review Panel 1990:122) The classic sustained yield theory developed in Germany during the eighteenth and nineteenth centuries is explained as follows.

> In order to sustain productivity, employment and a constant flow of forest products, the annual cut should equal the annual growth. The growth would occur on the younger trees; the harvest would come from the older, mature trees on which growth had slowed. One did not cut more than the annual growth in a given year since this would bring about future shortages. Nor did one cut less, for this would tie up land that could be stocked with young, fast-growing trees.
>
> In practice, this theory was applied to a management unit, which might be a private estate or a state-owned forest. For example, if this unit were 10,000 ha in area and consisted of uniformly productive land that grew trees which matured at an age of one hundred years, then 100 ha would be harvested annually. If each hectare produced 10 m^3 of wood each year, the annual harvest would be 100,000 m^3. Deduction from this volume would be made for losses due to fire, disease and insect damage. Increases in the cut could be made only if productivity were increased through the application of various silvicultural practices that would boost the growth rate. After a century of this type of management, the forest would contain an even distribution of age classes, and each year 1 per cent of it would be harvested and planted. German foresters called this a "normal" forest. Creation of a normal forest was one of the primary objectives of their forest policies. Once achieved, the normal forest would sustain itself perpetually. (Drushka 1985:39)

When this European concept was transplanted to North America and introduced in British Columbia legislation in 1947, its application met with social, economic and physical difficulties which persist to the present day. Sustained yield theory was introduced to North America at a time when the bases of the forest industry were speculation and exploitation. "One did not invest money in the growing of trees when the continent was covered with a natural forest that grew itself gratis." (ibid.:40) Moreover, the Canadian forest, consisting of millions of square kilometres of unmanaged timberland, was as different as it could possibly be from the European concept of a "normal forest". Consequently, sustained yield forestry saw (and sees) its ultimate goal in the liquidation of the "abnormal" natural forest in order to replace it with the scientifically managed "normal" forest.

As no nineteenth-century European estates were available in twentieth-century British Columbia to serve as convenient management units, sustained yield forestry gave rise to the tenure system as we know it today. In the late 1940s two major types of sustained yield management units were created. Forest Management Licences (later Tree Farm Licences, or TFLs) were to be managed by private industry and were issued to individual companies to supply the timber needs of a particular processing mill or complex. Public Sustained Yield Units (PSYUs) were managed by the provincial Forest Service and their timber sold to private companies. By 1980 when there were 34 Tree Farm Licences and 84 Public Sustained Yield Units, the latter were reorganized into 33 Timber Supply Areas, acknowledging the concentration of the timber processing industry which had occurred since the 1940s (Drushka 1985:45).

Strong criticism has been directed against sustained yield forestry as it has been practised during the past five decades. Much of this criticism has focused on the problem of calculation of annual allowable cut in the absence of adequate inventory data, upon the issue of enforcement of cut controls and reforestation, and on the prevalence of the practice of clear-cutting, which accounts for more than 85 per cent of all logging in Canada (MacKay 1985:166). Also, while public input and multiple-use criteria are considered key elements of proper forest management by most jurisdictions, few have instituted formal systems for accommodating these criteria (Heartwell 1988a:16).

> The monolithic corporate structures and the industrial apparatus created in response to the adoption of sustained yield forestry in the province were designed to maximize control of timber rights and facilitate the harvesting of that timber. They were designed for the management of large logging operations rather than the long-term management of forest land. The only silvicultural practice of any significance was tree planting, and even that did not exist on the scale required by the volume of timber being harvested. (Drushka 1985:224)

More recently, a new form of criticism of sustained yield policy has emerged, growing in volume and sophistication during the 1970s and 1980s. This criticism reflects what may be called the ecological perspective and calls for ecosystem-specific management and an enlargement of the sustained yield vision to embrace sustained ecological systems (Drushka 1985:52ff; Swift 1983:166; Findley 1990:112). Even with lip-service being paid to "management on a sustained-yield basis, but with values other than forestry taken into account" (Louis Fortier, CPPA's [Canadian Pulp and Paper Association] spokesperson, quoted in Wylynko 1991:3), the fact is that most industrial forestry consists in monoculture, that is the cultivation of one (or two, or three at the most) particular species grown for a specified purpose. A current fact sheet by Forestry Canada states unequivocally:

> The primary objective of vegetation management for forest renewal is to enhance the competitive ability of desired tree species in relation to the associated vegetation. (Pacific Forestry Centre, n.d.)

The premise is that by reducing the number of variables, the forest can most easily be managed towards a predicted and profitable culmination, or harvest. In this context many forest managers pin their hopes on new, genetically improved tree species with shorter rotations, on plantings, thinning, fertilization, pest and disease control. Under the general heading of "intensive forestry" they envisage a kind of agro-forestry or "green revolution" in the woods (Swift 1983:167). The most serious objection to monoculture focuses on the perception of what actually constitutes the resource.

> The common view has been that trees are the basic resource: hence the stumpage-based practice of charging for the volume of trees cut, not to mention the unqualified belief in the virtues of tree planting or reforestation. An alternative view is that the basic resource is the land itself, with its ability to sustain a whole complex of life forms, including trees. The objection to monoculture in this instance is that, even though it sustains a population of trees, it will weaken the ability of the land to produce the volume and range of products of which it was once capable. (Drushka 1985:227f)

One of the major concerns about agro-forestry centres around soil impoverishment (Swift 1983:167). Another is the erosion of the genetic base (Drushka 1985:228f). The eradication of old growth forests — viewed by some as a throwing away of nature's blueprint (Findley 1990:136) — and their replacement by fibre-producing tree plantations or insufficiently regenerated "junk forests" is part and parcel of the controversy.

The basic premises expressed in current Canadian forest management, which so obviously fails to acknowledge the ecological diversity of the resource, are deeply rooted in the structure of the industry.

> By the early 1980s, an organizational structure and a management approach that are complementary and mutually sustaining thoroughly dominate the forestry business in North America....Monolithic corporations and government agencies seem able to practise only monocultural forestry. The lack of diversity and variety in organization is reflected in the growing uniformity of the forests being grown. (Drushka 1985:230)

> One of the problems in British Columbia is that so much of our land is owned and administered by a single level of government. As a result you tend to get uniform regulations over a wide range of conditions, instead of regulations best suited to the circumstances of particular forest sites. (Peter Pearse, quoted in Drushka 1985:90)

Such situation not only results in a separation of ecological and economic considerations, but also creates a system which is characterized by an "isolation from consequences" (Drushka 1985:222), a system in which no one is quite responsible, where all the participants can blame the system for anything that goes wrong.

It is, therefore, hardly surprising that many critics of corporate concentration and bureaucratic centralism call for more local control over resource management. This is nowhere more clearly expressed than in the conclusion of the Slocan Valley Community Forest Management Project study (1974).

> The local community represents the only visible group with a binding interest in the long-term sustenance of this valley's resources, for it is they who will have to live with the results of our management policies, good or bad. (Swift 1983:224)

What is surprising, is the conspicuous absence of any mention of native people in the abundant literature highly critical of contemporary forest management practices, critical from a social viewpoint as well as from an ecological perspective. Indian groups are not included in the listing of resource users for example in British Columbia, who clash over the forestry resource (Drushka 1985:135). There is no mention of the system's constraints of native people's traditional and modern utilization of forest ecosystems, nor is there any consideration of potential Indian contributions to a resolution of Canada's current forest management crisis.

INDIAN RESERVE FOREST LANDS: PROBLEMS AND ISSUES

Overview and Regulatory Framework

It is estimated that aside from very small holdings of less than 20 hectares, 85 per cent of Indian bands in the provinces have reserve forests totalling some 1,122,000 hectares of productive forest land as indicated in Table 2 (Mactavish 1987:17). This asset is divided among 1,172 reserves. While many of these forests are too small to provide more than occasional income, they must not be discounted, for they may, after all, be the single most important asset of many bands. Some reserve forests, on the other hand, are quite expansive and, if properly managed, capable of yielding a steady income and employment base to band members. There are 240 bands whose productive forest areas exceed 1,000 hectares.

TABLE 2
Indian Reserves with Productive Forests[1]

	No. of Bands	*No. of Forested Reserves*	*Area in ha*	*Total Forest in ha*
B.C.	196	689	337,000	150,400
Alberta	40	80	514,400	177,700
Sask.	61	105	493,000	205,600
Manitoba	48	72	202,900	88,600
Ontario	100	155	649,600	450,390
Quebec[2]	22	23	75,100	61,800
N.B.	16	20	17,600	14,400
N.S.	13	25	11,200	8,300
P.E.I.	3		520	670

(Mactavish 1987: 18)

While these lands have the potential of constituting a substantial resource for native people, Indian forests at present are generally in poor condition, as a result of a long history of overcutting, lack of reforestation, inadequate site tending and overall mismanagement (Mactavish 1987:18; Hopwood 1988:2). This situation has been compounded by a lack of Indian involvement (except in the case of timber harvesting) due to the way the trust responsibility of the federal government has been implemented. This state of affairs is due in large part to the shortcomings of the regulatory regime of Indian forestry, as a result of which Indian and Northern Affairs Canada (INAC) has no program, mandate, budget or database pertaining specifically to forestry.

The sections of the Indian Act dealing with natural resources are very brief, and they only address the removal of material from the reserves. According to Section 57

> The Governor in Council may make regulations
> (a) authorizing the Minister to grant licences to cut timber on surrendered lands, or, with the consent of the council of the band, on reserve lands;
> (b) imposing terms, conditions and restrictions with respect to the exercise of rights conferred by licences granted under paragraph (a).

The second regulatory tool is provided by the Indian Timber Regulations. Like the provisions of the Indian Act, these regulations, too, merely serve to govern harvesting of timber on reserves. In his analysis of Indian forest resources management, John Mactavish points out that even if timber was to be treated as a non-renewable resource and its removal regulated accordingly, both the Act and the Regulations raise practical problems and some of the regulations are *ultra vires* in the opinion of the Standing Joint Committee of the Senate and House of Commons on Regulations and other Statutory Instruments[3] (Mactavish 1987:37f). The restriction of licensing authority to the Minister makes for a time-consuming and

---

[1] Reserve Forests > 20 ha, from Summary of Federal Forest Lands in Canada. Canadian Forestry Service 1986.

[2] Excludes Category I-A and I-AN lands as defined by the James Bay and Northern Quebec Agreements.

[3] Views of the Standing Joint Committee are drawn from a letter from E.G. Eglington of the Committee to John C. Tait, Assistant Deputy Minister, INAC, dated September 7, 1982.

cumbersome process, so much so that bands tend to ignore it. Even the smallest volume of timber or a Christmas tree to be sold off the reserve is supposed to be licensed.

The drafters of Regulations 4 and 5 may have recognized this problem. These two regulations provide for the local "superintendent" to issue permits to band members or bands to cut timber for domestic use or sale. The Standing Joint Committee, however, has identified this delegation of authority as *ultra vires* under the Indian Act. Section 3 of the Act restricts delegation to the deputy minister or chief officer in charge of Indian Affairs. There are numerous other flaws and omissions in the Regulations, which altogether fail to provide for even the most elementary premises of forest management.

In practice, implementation of the Indian Timber Regulations varies widely across the country. In the Prairie Provinces and in Quebec they do not appear to be applied at all. In Ontario they are used in the Treaty Three area. In the Maritimes an effort is made to apply them in order to insure at least that the timber cut is paid for and dues credited to the appropriate band's capital account. Indian Timber Regulations are used in British Columbia, and here we find the only example of INAC going beyond its most basic requirements.

> In British Columbia, regional INAC staff have developed two detailed permit forms, one for band members to be responsible for all phases of the logging operations, the second for band members directly undertaking only certain phases of the operation with a purchaser-partner completing the operation. The latter type of permit has proven useful when Indians do not own the expensive capital equipment necessary to remove felled logs from the logging site. Both types of permits are signed by the band member as permittee and the log purchaser as contracts between themselves and as permit-contracts with the Crown.
>
> These permits go well beyond the usual interpretation of the Regulations, and in addition to the basic requirements, specify several important measures. Logging plans must be submitted for approval of logging sequences, road locations and proposed log landings, dumps and booming grounds. Maximum stump heights and minimum top diameters of logs are specified. Log lengths to maximize utilization are required. Young growth is to be protected. The permittee is required to comply with the provisions and regulations of the British Columbia Forest Act dealing with timber scaling and marking. Lastly, measures are included to protect streams and lakes from logging and road construction debris.
>
> Obviously, the permit goes much further toward protecting the interests of the bands than does the standard departmental permit (1A-401) that simply specifies the name of the permittee, location for logging, products to be logged for, species, quantity and stumpage dues to be collected. (Mactavish 1987:41f)

The inadequacy of the status quo of the regulatory regime governing Indian forest lands becomes overt when viewed in the context of the Crown's responsibilities to Indian people. John Mactavish develops his reasoning in reference to the *Guerin* decision (Guerin v. R. [1985] 1 C.N.L.R. 120). He feels that a much clearer definition of INAC's responsibilities emerges, when forests are recognized as part of the land, as in common law (Mactavish 1987:4–9); the key issue in the *Guerin* case was the Crown's obligation to the bands with respect to their land.

One of the most important conclusions of the case was that native people's right to occupy and possess reserves "gives rise upon surrender to a distinctive fiduciary obligation on the part of the Crown to deal with the land for the benefit of the surrendering Indians" (Supreme Court of Canada 1984:30, quoted in Mactavish 1987:6). In a quotation from the United States case *Johnson v. McIntosh* (1823) it is also noted that the Indians' rights of occupancy and possession of reserves include the right to use them "according to their own discretion" (op. cit.:23, quoted, ibid.).

> These quotations seem to indicate that a band is free to log timber on its reserve for its own use as it sees fit, but that the Crown's protective role comes into play when it is proposed to sell reserve timber to off-reserve interests. The question is whether or not the licensing process to cut timber involves the equivalent of a surrender of the resource by the band.
>
> While only the consent of the band council is necessary to authorize the Minister to grant licences to cut timber, the responsibility to act in the best interests of the band remains. The Minister would have to make an independent judgement that a proposed licence was for the benefit of the band as a whole. This means that **the Minister must be satisfied that the band has been counselled with enough information to make an informed decision, to decide what is in its own best interests. This is the primary obligation.**
>
> Since the forest is a resource capable of producing a variety of wood and other products, informed timber disposal decisions must be based on forest land management plans. These plans should discuss alternative management strategies and the results to be expected from each in terms of product mix, quantities and value. Plans must respond to the objectives of bands for wood, cattle, wildlife, furbearers, or fish and provide for their integrated management. Prerequisite for such plans is a forest inventory estimating the amounts of timber and other resources present and the land's capability to produce them.
>
> **The Minister then must insist that the band has based its decision to have timber logged on a forest management plan.** (Mactavish 1987:7f, emphasis in original)

John Mactavish (ibid.:44–49) and Allen Hopwood (1988:55) both agree that there is an urgent need to revise the Indian Act and the Regulations to provide for forest management and not just harvesting. Mactavish (1987:45f) suggests that the most effective way would be an amendment to the Indian Act, deleting Sections 57 (a) and (b), and substituting a general authority to fulfil INAC's responsibilities. The new section might read as follows:

> "S.57 The Governor in Council may make regulations
> (a) providing for the management of forests, including the harvesting of timber, on surrendered lands, and with the consent of the band council, on reserve lands."
>
> An amendment of this nature offers the advantage of clearing the stage completely for a new regulatory regime to be developed with band representatives. Licensing could encompass all aspects of forest management. The licensing authority could be assigned to INAC regional or district levels instead of the Minister. Forest management authority could, in turn, be assumed by bands under terms of multiple-year licences, with renewals contingent on fulfilment of management plan obligations. (ibid.)

An alternative would be the creation of a regulation authorizing the Minister to grant licences to bands to cut timber in accordance with the terms of management plans approved by the band and by INAC. Such licence could be for an extended period of time, perhaps five years, and be renewable, contingent on the band fulfilling the terms of the management plan. This concept has the potential of essentially transferring forest management authority to those bands who wish to assume it (ibid.).

Progress in the 1980s

Notwithstanding INAC's inaction, in the 1980s Indian bands received help from another federal department that assisted them in at least establishing the groundwork for a rehabilitation of their forest lands. In 1982 the federal government published its policy statement on "A Framework for Forest Renewal" in which it recommended to the provinces and industry an initial five-year cooperative forest renewal program. Throughout the 1980s this policy was implemented through federal-provincial agreements under the umbrella of the Economic Regional Development Agreements (ERDAs). Though not identical, these Forest Resource Development Agreements (FRDAs) provided for programs for inventories and planning to reforest the backlog of non-satisfactorily restocked lands, intensively manage selected forest stands on more productive sites and support forest research. Most of these agreements had expired by 1989, but by 1991 new ones were in the process of being negotiated.

More importantly for native people, a link between these policies and programs and Indian forest lands was established in 1983 when the Canadian Forestry Service (CFS) made public its Policy for Indian Land Forestry Programs (Government of Canada 1983). The policy statement identified Indian reserve lands as eligible for forestry programs under the FRDA program with direct delivery by the CFS. Such programs would include advice and support for forest inventories, preparation of forest management plans, forest renewal and silvicultural projects, as well as training.

> The FRDA program offers INAC both opportunity and challenge in fulfilling its forest related responsibilities to bands...and contributing to its objectives.... At the same time it brings with it two vital elements that are in short supply within INAC — money and the professional forestry advice it can purchase.
>
> The opportunity is to offer full support to CFS by encouraging bands to participate in the program and to make full sustained use of the results. The challenge is to develop a forest policy and program for integrated forest management in conjunction with the bands and to supplement the financial resources available through CFS with direct contribution and coordination of funded programs of other agencies in related fields like training and employment generation. (Mactavish 1987:16f)

Canadian Forestry Service assistance has been widely sought by Indian bands all over the country, and much progress has been made in laying the groundwork for forest rehabilitation on Indian lands. In British Columbia in particular the FRDA contained an Indian Forest Lands Program as a specific component, and during the first four years of the program, FRDA had contributed $4.1 million to assist 97 Indian bands in treating 4,270 hectares and surveying 208,000 hectares (Forestry Canada Information Booklet, n.d.:50). One of its most important positive steps has been without doubt its financial assistance to the establishment of the Intertribal Forestry Association of British Columbia (IFABC). This organization was initiated by native representatives on the FRDA-Indian Lands Program advisory board in 1986, and registered as a Society in 1988. Its primary mandate is

> ...to protect, maintain, enhance and develop First Nations' forestry resources for the use, benefit and enjoyment of First Nations of today and tomorrow.
>
> To establish and fulfil the rights and responsibilities of British Columbia First Nations with regard to First Nations forestry resources. (IFABC 1990)

The organization views itself as a "result-oriented institution" with a focus on integrated resource management. Its practice is to avoid the issues of land claims and aboriginal rights, as it is felt that those matters should be dealt with by bands and tribal councils (IFABC Fact Sheet). Its constitution commits the Association to objectives that "will not prejudice the Aboriginal title, treaty rights and those other inherent rights confirmed by law" (IFABC Constitution:3).

While the Indian reserve lands component of the FRDAs has served to ameliorate a desperate situation, it has not been an unmitigated success with regard to native goals. Hopwood (1988:54) observes that a fundamental problem common to all government programs associated with Indian forestry is that these programs are rarely flexible enough to make allowance for or support multiple use of forest lands or non-traditional forestry practices. He points to the otherwise highly successful Indian Forest Lands component of the Canada-British Columbia FRDA as an example, since it excluded such forest land management practices as Christmas tree farming and range enhancement. It appears that the government's objectives in these programs rarely coincide with Indian bands' land use and socio-economic priorities.

In the case of the Ontario FRDA, Don Jones, Vice Chairman of the Indian Forestry Development Program in Ontario, characterized its efforts as a "great start but only a start" (Infolink Consultants Inc. 1989:6). Fifty-three of 125 First Nations in this province were involved in the agreement, with eligibility based on commitment to long-term forest management. Jones emphasized the fact that Indian leaders were concerned about their role or lack of role in the process, indicating that many of the problems associated with the program were administrative in nature.

In north-central Saskatchewan the experience of bands with Forestry Canada assistance under the Canada-Saskatchewan FRDA seems to have been predominantly positive. Numerous bands in this region worked with Forestry Canada staff in Prince Albert to complete timber inventories and forest management plans. These plans took a multiple-use approach, aiming to integrate timber harvesting interests with fish and wildlife, water, recreational, aesthetic and spiritual values (Timberlines No. 10, Summer 1989:2).

These developments in the 1980s culminated in the establishment of the National Aboriginal Forestry Association (NAFA), which was conceived at a landmark conference on native forestry in 1989 (The National Native Forestry Symposium, November 22–24, 1989, Vancouver), and then spearheaded by the Intertribal Forestry Association of British Columbia. NAFA's overall goal is the promotion and support of increased aboriginal involvement in forest management and related commercial activities. In pursuing this goal, NAFA is committed to "holistic or multiple-use forestry" which takes into account not only fibre production for timber, pulp, paper and other wood by-products, but also wildlife habitat protection, the protection of furbearers and traditional food, cultural and spiritual use, and recreation and tourism. The "[k]ey to the concept of holistic forestry is the idea of community-based strategies for transforming this resource ethic into reality." (NAFA Fact Sheet, n.d.)

One of NAFA's first moves was to address the shortcomings of legislation for aboriginal forestry activities. In the early 1990s a "First Nations Forest Resources Recognition Act" is in the final preparatory stages. This new law, which is a joint initiative of IFABC and NAFA, is designed to provide First Nations with an alternative to the Indian Act, and to enable them to manage their own forest resources according to community direction. Once finalized the new legislation is intended to be optional and interim. It will be applied only to First Nations who request that it apply to them, and it will be interim in the context of constitutional negotiations on the inherent right to self-government (*NAFA Quarterly* 1(1), 1992:1f).

Selected Examples

In the development of their reserve forestry resource, native people are fully occupied trying to cope with a legacy of forest mismanagement and to revitalize their crippled forests. Nevertheless, even at this stage, there have been some noteworthy initiatives and developments.

There are 196 Indian bands in British Columbia holding 1,606 Indian reserves with a total area of 337,000 hectares. In accordance with their geographical location and the overall orientation of economic potential towards integrated resource development, the bands have begun to focus their socio-economic development strategies on the management of their forest lands (Hopwood 1988:2f). Approximately half of their total land base is classed as productive forest land, as it will produce commercial crops of timber within a "reasonable time period" (in line with provincial Ministry of Forests standards). The productivity of the coastal reserve forest lands, in terms of tree growth, is well above average compared to British Columbia as a whole, while the interior reserves are below average.

Currently, the province's Indian bands receive little economic return from their timber lands because of their limited involvement in the manufacturing side of the forest industry and the fact that most of the logging on reserve lands is done by outside operators. The bands' net revenues from harvesting are limited to the profits derived from the sale of logs, to stumpage paid to and held in trust for them by the federal government, and wage and contract payments earned by individuals from harvesting and, in some cases, tree planting.

Before this background, the *Nuu-chah-nulth forestry program* is one of the most comprehensive forestry initiatives yet undertaken by a native group in the province (Cassidy and Dale 1988:110). The Nuu-chah-nulth Tribal Council (NTC) represents 14 member bands with a combined population of about 5,100. They hold a total of 164 reserves encompassing approximately 4,800 hectares. These reserves are scattered over most of Vancouver Island's west coast. Typically, an individual band's population is concentrated in one or two communities; the band's remaining "reserves" constitute strategic fishing spots on river mouths, inlet banks or islands.

The Nuu-chah-nulth Tribal Council forestry program was initiated in 1978, prompted by Nuu-chah-nulth misgivings over the condition of reserve and off-reserve forest lands in their traditional territory. In 1978 the Ahousaht Band approached the NTC for help in organizing opposition to local logging. The Tribal Council held a community meeting and determined that there was a need for a comprehensive forestry analysis. INAC was approached for funding and agreed to a test study. There were four major study components:

- Determination of past and present involvement of the Nuu-chah-nulth bands in the British Columbia forest industry;
- Determination of the on-reserve and relevant off-reserve forestry resource base;
- Community consultation; and
- Development of a long-range Nuu-chah-nulth forestry program.

The study was executed by West Coast Information & Research Group and completed in 1980. As regards on-reserve forest lands, Nuu-chah-nulth holdings constitute only 0.43 per cent of the study area (i.e. the Nuu-chah-nulth comprehensive claim territory), of which almost 800 hectares are located within Pacific Rim National Park and therefore alienated from timber harvesting. The forest resource base on Nuu-chah-nulth reserve lands is small and far-flung, a fact complicating the management of the timber resource (West Coast Information & Research Group 1980:20). Moreover, the tribe's forests have been severely depleted under past INAC mismanagement and failure to apply even the most basic silvicultural practices. The consultants go so far as to suggest that the Nuu-chah-nulth may have sufficient grounds to sue the federal government for its failure to live up to its trustee's responsibility in managing the Indian timber resource (ibid.:21, 54). In their present state the forests do not constitute a viable economic resource but are in sore need of a rehabilitation program.

The study contained five main recommendations to the Tribal Council. They were advised to hire a forestry manager, undertake a detailed forest inventory, initiate a site rehabilitation program, develop a training program for Nuu-chah-nulth band members and negotiate a takeover of INAC's trusteeship for native forest lands. The NCT immediately responded to the first recommendation by hiring a forestry manager in 1980. Throughout the 1980s a wide array of other activities was initiated. Harvesting activities were limited, but progress was made in several aspects of silviculture, although lack of funding was a constant obstacle. Small-scale business development in forestry took the form of silvicultural contracting, the acquisition of portable sawmills and the establishment of two Christmas tree farms (Cassidy and Dale 1988:112). The NTC Forest Nursery which became operational in 1984 was the most successful of the tribe's forestry-related ventures. Its main customers are large firms with Tree Farm Licences, such as MacMillan Bloedel and British Columbia Forest Products. Training in forestry was another priority successfully pursued by the bands since 1980.

In their endeavour the Nuu-chah-nulth have placed much emphasis on a community-based approach (Kuiper 1985, quoted in Cassidy and Dale 1988:113). In response to the significant geographic distances between member bands, coordination has been achieved through a forestry committee, which gives direction to the NTC's forestry manager. As Frank Cassidy and Norman Dale point out (Cassidy and Dale 1988), "co-management" with regard to reserve lands is well developed among the Nuu-chah-nulth far-flung bands. Access to and input into the management of off-reserve lands is quite a different story.

Indian lands in the province of Ontario total 703,735 hectares, 450,390 hectares of which or 64 per cent, are productive forest. In 1986 there were an estimated 93 Indian-operated businesses in the forestry sector, two-thirds of which were in the logging and/or sawmilling business. A typical firm employed six to eight people and worked as logging subcontractor for one of the major leaseholders (Mactavish 1987:21). The overexploited condition of reserve forests in Ontario manifested itself in declining log production by Indian enterprises. While overall production is estimated to have remained fairly constant, the proportion drawn from reserve forests declined from about 84 per cent to 28 per cent during the 1970s. This state of affairs has led to declining harvesting opportunities but, on the other hand, has created new opportunities for investment in rehabilitation programs, which are mostly labour-intensive and capable of providing on-reserve training and employment. In the longer term, these investments will yield the raw materials for logging and manufacturing businesses (ibid.:20).

By far the most important provincial region in terms of forest management is northwestern Ontario. Not surprisingly, it was here, in the *Treaty Three area*, where native forestry activities have received the most attention. Beginning in 1962 under the Canada-Ontario Provincial Resource Development Agreement, an Indian Logging Program (ILP) was set up and operated by the Ontario Ministry of Natural Resources to assist bands in obtaining Crown timber licences from the province and industrial licensees, to prepare operating plans and generally to assist Indian bands with forestry advice. In the late 1970s the emphasis of the program shifted from logging assistance to the provision of management and silvicultural plans with a focus on forest rehabilitation (ibid.:31).

In the mid-1980s the ILP structure was changed. Renamed the Indian Forestry Development Program (IFDP), and more recently, Mitigonaabe Forestry Resources Management Inc., it is now federally funded with INAC providing the core and administrative budget and some project funding coming from CFS through the Canada-Ontario FRDA. The organization is managed by a native-owned corporation, with a very small professional and technical staff and advisory support from federal and provincial agencies.

Mitigonaabe Forestry Resources Management Inc. serves as a forest management advisory group to some 25 bands on 62 reserves that constitute Treaty Three. These reserves comprise a total productive forest area of 93,100 hectares in the Kenora-Fort Frances area, about one-third of the productive Indian forest in the province. Interest among the bands in rehabilitating and managing their forests for the future is strong, and their demand for projects far outstrips Mitigonaabe's ability to provide them. A major obstacle to the group's successful operation is the year-to-year uncertainty as to the availability of funds, which makes it difficult to develop the longer term operational plans necessary for forest management (ibid.:32).

In the agriculturally and industrially more developed southern part of Ontario, Indian reserves sometimes constitute islands of relatively undisturbed natural woodlands. The Six Nations Reserve and Walpole Island are examples. The *Walpole Island Indian Reserve* deserves particular attention. Not only is it likely to be the largest single forested area in Essex, Kent and Lambton Counties (Jacobs 1986:9), but it also contains one of the last sizeable tracts of Canada's Carolinian forests. About 90 per cent of the original forest cover of this type have been cleared, and it constitutes one of Canada's five most threatened habitats. There are more endangered, threatened and rare species in the Carolinian zone than in any other ecosystem in Canada (Price, WWF, 1984, quoted in Hildebrand 1985:33). It is obvious that this situation poses a special challenge to Walpole Island's resource managers.

In 1985 under the direction of Nin.da.waab.jig, the Walpole Island Research Centre, a woodlot utilization plan was developed for 178 hectares of public forest on Walpole Island. This plan considered such diverse options as supplantation (clear-cutting and replacement of the original cover with a more profitable crop), preservation (non-use), implicit conservation (e.g. single purpose use for hunting or recreation), explicit conservation (for example, multiple-use management for wood products, recreation and education), and the integration of the woodlot into a reserve conservation plan (i.e. identification of zones of environmental and cultural significance on the reserve, publicizing their existence, and making them available for study). After examining all these possibilities, Nin.da.waab.jig identified the fourth option with its multiple-use approach as the most desirable course of action. By the early 1990s no new developments had taken place, with the exception of short term projects constructing roads and firebreaks. Consultation with the provincial Ministry of Natural Resources was planned, and development was expected to be community-based and multiple use-oriented. The key-word was "sustainable development" (Dean Jacobs, Nin.da.waab.jig Research Director, personal communication, April 19, 1991).

REGULATORY REGIMES AND NATIVE ACCESS TO OFF-RESERVE FOREST LANDS

Most Indian reserve forests are in sore need of rehabilitation and incapable of sustaining ongoing harvesting activities. The majority of Indian forests are also relatively small, too small even in a well-managed state for anything but a periodic harvesting opportunity. To create more viable forest management units, many bands endeavour to combine the management of their reserve forests with blocks of provincial Crown land. In this undertaking they encounter two major obstacles.

First, their reserves are enclaves of federal jurisdiction surrounded by lands under provincial laws and regulations. The outdated and incomplete forestry provisions of the Indian Act and the Indian Timber Regulations are clearly at odds with the more modern practices required by the provinces (Mactavish 1987:43). While this obstacle can be overcome, a second complication is more serious: In the most important forestry regions there are essentially no significant tracts which remain uncommitted to some form of tenure.

The Nuu-chah-nulth Tribal Council Forestry Study examined the latter problem thoroughly, by reviewing the existing tenure conditions in the whole area that would later become the Nuu-chah-nulth comprehensive claim territory, and concluded:

> The present political economy associated with the forest resource within the study area is characterized by large companies controlling 90 per cent of the cut and virtually all significant manufacturing within a context of legislation and regulation which reinforces this status quo. (West Coast Information & Research Group 1980:19)

Ninety per cent of the annual allowable cut of the region was allocated to three companies: MacMillan Bloedel, British Columbia Forest Products and Tahsis Company. The tenure these companies hold — Tree Farm Licences and Timber Sale Harvesting Licences — has been further entrenched by the latest Forest Act of 1978 by the introduction of so-called evergreen clauses. Thus, access to the resource base has been virtually put out of reach, not only for the native people but also for small-scale operators and newcomers to the industry in general. Woodlot Licences — shorter-term leases for exclusive cutting on 400 hectares or less — remain as almost the only opportunity for access but can hardly be viewed as a viable base for economic development. The Nuu-chah-nulth Tribal Council Forestry Study, after reviewing the situation, comes to the conclusion that

> ...the only broad strategy remaining for native people wanting access to the forest resource is essentially a political one. Some potential legal avenues may also be worth pursuing. (West Coast Information & Research Group 1980:10)

Nevertheless, there are cases where native groups successfully negotiated all obstacles. The most celebrated example is undoubtedly Tanizul Timber Ltd. of the Tl'azt'en Nation (Stuart Trembleur Lake Band) in central British Columbia. In 1981–82 Tanizul competed successfully with well-established companies for a Tree Farm Licence covering approximately 49,900 hectares, an area covering much of the band's traditional territory (Hopwood 1988:17). A Tree Farm Licence (TFL) provides the longest term of tenure available under the Forest Act: 25 years, subject to renewal every 10 years. Unlike a Forest Licence, the other major long-term tenure form in British Columbia, the TFL can and usually does include both Crown land and lands held by the licensee. All TFLs are designated as provincial forests. A TFL grants more than just cutting privileges; it entrusts the licensee with considerable resource management responsibilities.

> The band's plan for action developed during the 1970s.
> The logic of this choice flowed from the fact that we had abundant forest resources right on our doorstep. Non-Indian companies were logging in our backyard and yet provided little or no employment for our people. We wanted to change this. (Ed John, President of Tanizul Timber, 1985:113)

Tanizul Timber Company Limited was incorporated in 1981 because at the time the Indian Act did not allow a band to hold licences such as a TFL. Subsequently, the provisions of the Act have been changed to the effect that Indian bands are now permitted to apply for and receive timber tenures (John 1985:112; Hopwood 1988:16). The company's explicit purpose was the acquisition of the proposed TFL in order to create an employment base for the band and to bring the "Tanizul Triangle" lands — the band's traditional area of occupation and land use, which coincided with the proposed TFL's boundaries — under integrated resource management.

With no equity or past experience in forest management, the band focused its application on the social and economic benefits that would accrue to the local area. Their second draw was the fact that it had a land base in the vicinity of the TFL, which the two competing companies did not have. However, this land base also posed a problem. Granting of the TFL to the band was contingent on the federal government passing an Order-in-Council which transferred forest management rights and responsibilities on reserve lands from INAC to the band, so that these lands could be managed subject to provincial standards. The most significant section of the licence therefore reads as follows:

> The British Columbia *Forest Act*, *Ministry of Forests Act* and *Range Act*, as amended from time to time and regulations made from time to time thereunder, apply to reserve lands in respect of which any licence is granted as though the reserve lands were private lands within the meaning of the British Columbia *Forest Act*. (Ministry of Forests, 1981, Conditions for Tree Farm Licence 42, quoted in Cassidy and Dale 1988:109)

The importance of this development for the band cannot be overstated. Hopwood (1988:14) sums it up succinctly: "Other than Tanizul Timber Ltd., economic matters relative to the band are straightforward — there are almost none." In the late 1980s Stuart Trembleur Band forest operations provided employment for some 75 to 122 people each year, depending on the volume harvested and the amount of reforestation carried out (ibid.:22). Finally, Frank Cassidy and Norman Dale draw our attention to another important implication of the band's success.

> The Stuart Trembleur Band is a member of the Carrier-Sekani Tribal Council whose comprehensive claim was accepted by the federal government in 1983. It is the largest

> claim to a land area in the province and has aroused a great deal of concern in the Prince George area among forest officials and municipal leaders. While the statement of claim does not indicate how forest management would proceed after an agreement is reached, the Tanizul story provides an indication that the Carrier-Sekani peoples will strive to form co-operative commercial and administrative relationships when they have the chance to do so. (Cassidy and Dale 1988:110)

While the availability of additional TFLs in British Columbia or substantial blocks of timber land in other provinces is doubtful (Mactavish 1987:36), there are other success stories — though with some "mixed success" — where Indian bands gained access to off-reserve forest lands, either in agreement with the private sector or provincial governments: the Macleod Lake Indian Band, who in 1990 was successful in acquiring logging rights; Cariboo Indian Enterprises, holding a Forest Licence in central British Columbia (Cassidy and Dale 1988:101f; Cooper 1985:114); Hecate Logging, a co-venture between a Nuu-chah-nulth band holding a Forest Licence and a non-native company requiring access to timber (Cassidy and Dale 1988:102f); and Kiashke River Native Development Inc. of the Gull Band in Ontario, who obtained logging rights on the Great Lakes Paper Company's lease (Mactavish 1987:34f; Blair 1984). Overall, however, access to off-reserve timber lands is severely restricted and considered one of the major stumbling blocks for a successful and equitable participation by native people in forestry activities.

FORESTRY PRESSURES ON ABORIGINAL LANDS: PROBLEMS AND SOLUTIONS

So far we have mainly looked at forestry in the rather narrow sense of timber utilization and the opportunity for native people to utilize this resource for the advancement of their socio-economic goals. It is plainly evident that they are operating within an "environment of constraint" (Elias 1991:77), be it in their attempts to benefit from their reserve forests or their endeavour to gain access to off-reserve forest lands. But the forestry theme is by no means exhausted by these topics. The National Aboriginal Forestry Association Constitution states, "...forestry shall mean all uses of the forest lands within and affecting aboriginal territories."

Current forestry practices in Canada do much more than merely deny First Nations a fair share of the resource. In many cases, logging-related destruction or modification of forest ecosystems results in severe disruption of native people's lives. This conflict frequently takes place within the context of unresolved land claims.

British Columbia

Forestry-related conflicts come into sharpest focus in British Columbia. Nowhere else is the forest industry so important. Outside of the major southwestern urban centres, 30 per cent of all communities and regions are dependent solely on the forest sector for their economic well-being, and another 40 per cent rely on the forest industry as one of their top three employers (White, Duke and Fong 1989:9). While this dependence makes for extreme economic vulnerability, conflicting demands on the forest resource base are more pronounced here than in other parts of the country. With the advance of the practice of clear-cutting in the late 1950s and early 1960s — after the implementation of sustained-yield policy — it became evident that these forestry practices were having a severe impact on the salmon spawning streams in the areas being logged, thus affecting another major resource-based industry of the province. Things are not made easier by the fact that salmon come under the jurisdiction of the federal government, whereas forestry is a provincial concern. Thus the obvious physical resource conflict is further complicated by a bureaucratic and political one (Drushka 1985:144). All other species of fish, as well as the wildlife in the province, are under the jurisdiction of the provincial Fish and Wildlife Branch.

This economically unstable and politically volatile situation is placed within an overall climate of uncertainty due to the existence of unresolved native comprehensive claims covering the entire province. Groups like the Nisga'a, the Nuu-chah-nulth and the Gitksan-Wet'suwet'en have for many years linked the questions of aboriginal title and forestry management. The frequent confrontations between native people and logging companies are not caused by blanket opposition to forest operations on the part of native groups, but by Indian people's desire to be recognized as both an economic and a political factor in forestry, and their fear that forest lands are exploited at such a rapid rate that the resource will be exhausted before settlements are reached (Cassidy and Dale 1988:91). Opposition also grows out of a profound disapproval by First Nations of the manner in which forests are being managed, and some of their direct actions have been attempts to preserve special places from timber harvesting.

Gwaii Haanas

One of the longest-standing struggles in British Columbia between native people and loggers has taken place in the South Moresby (Gwaii Haanas) area of the Queen Charlotte Islands, particularly over logging plans on Lyell Island. The controversy lasted throughout the 1970s and 1980s and initially focused on the renewal of Rayonier Canada Limited's Tree Farm Licence #24.[4] In 1974 a group of young Haida and non-Indians formed an environmental group called "Islands Protection". These activists began to lobby for the permanent protection of a wilderness area on Moresby Island, including the southern portion of TFL #24 and adjoining areas. The Council of the Haida Nation and the environmentalists later joined forces in several unsuccessful petitions to the British Columbia Supreme Court to prevent renewal of Rayonier's licence. International attention was focused on the Queen Charlottes as a "northern Galapagos". During the next 13 years government reviews, studies, special commissions, and advisory committees debated the fate of the wilderness proposal, while logging continued unabated.

A most crucial element in this struggle was the role played by the Haida. In the 1970s there was no official Haida support for the wilderness proposal, nor were there any overt land claims activities. During those years, however, the Haida were keen observers of revelations about the realities of forest management on their islands (failure to comply with licence conditions, etc.). By 1981, under newly elected leadership, they were ready to act.

When they announced the registration of their formal land claim with the federal government in 1981 (accepted for negotiation in 1983), it was clear that their strategy was influenced by their perception of forestry practices in their homeland Haida Gwaii. They introduced a new argument: They based their claim not only on their ancestral occupation of the islands, but also on their moral obligation to manage the resources of the islands more responsibly than the provincial government and the lease-holding companies had done (May 1990b:59; Pinkerton 1983:69). In the same year they made several significant policy statements, among them a pronouncement on the necessity of reducing by one-half the rate of timber harvest on the entire Islands, a submission on the Management and Working Plan for TFL #24, and a policy paper on the management of all resources.

> Presently the Forests Ministry, in conjunction with the large companies, has nearly exclusive use over most of the prime lands on the Islands. The management practices are unacceptable to our people. The concept of multiple use has been mocked by the forest industry, making public input useless. (Pinkerton 1983:84)

---

[4] Various aspects of this struggle have been well documented by authors like May (1990b), Pinkerton (1983) and Shapcott (1989).

In 1985 matters came to a head when Rayonier's successor, Western Forest Products, directed its logging contractor, Frank Beban Enterprises, to proceed with logging on Lyell Island (located in the northern portion of the South Moresby area). The Haida proved that they were prepared to follow through with their assertion of a moral obligation, and blocked access roads to the intended cut area, tribal elders among them. Before the blockade ended, 72 Haida had been arrested.

In 1987 negotiations were concluded between the governments of Canada and British Columbia to create a new national park reserve encompassing the South Moresby area. For the environmentalists the battle was won; for the Haida its focus had merely shifted. "A national park is seen by the Haida as another intrusive if not so disruptive a use of lands which they claim are theirs." (Cassidy and Dale 1988:93).

Wah Nah Jus/Hilth Hoo Is

Meares Island (Wah nah jus/Hilth hoo is) off the West Coast of Vancouver Island at the mouth of Tofino Harbour is under claim by the Nuu-chah-nulth and has increasingly become a symbol of their claim to their ancestral lands. The controversy over logging this island bears certain similarities to the Gwaii Haana's situation. The Nuu-chah-nulth Tribal Council presented its claim to the west coast of Vancouver Island, its adjacent islands and surrounding waters to the federal government in 1980, the same year that MacMillan Bloedel obtained Timber Licence # T0140 covering a portion of Meares Island. Their claim was accepted for negotiation in 1983, the same year that the Provincial Cabinet's Environment and Land Use Committee announced clearance for logging activities on Meares Island with a 20-year delay on logging those parts visible from Tofino.

The following year the Tla-o-qui-aht Band, who along with the Ahousaht Band claims title to the island, asserted jurisdiction and declared Meares Island a Tribal Park. When cutting crews arrived on the island later in 1984, they were met by native and non-native protesters, occupying strategic landing areas. From there the battle was carried into the courts.

By January 1985 the British Columbia Supreme Court had upheld MacMillan Bloedel's rights and ordered protesters to cease interference with forestry operations. In his ruling Justice Gibbs argued that granting an injunction on behalf of the Nuu-chah-nulth would lead to a proliferation of similar applications throughout the province. The judge also decided that the province had authority to extinguish native land claims through the Terms of Confederation (ibid.). The Tla-o-qui-aht and Ahousaht Bands and environmental groups launched separate appeals. In March 1985 the British Columbia Court of Appeal overturned Justice Gibbs' decision and granted an injunction on behalf of the Nuu-chah-nulth preventing MacMillan Bloedel from logging pending trial on the issue of aboriginal title.

Nuu-chah-nulth legal counsel, Jack Woodward, anticipated that the province would argue that native people abandoned their title by accepting reserves and leaving the land unoccupied; another defence could be that native people had agreed to a legal system that is inconsistent with aboriginal title by complying with other provincial laws.

> Our point will be to show that the Indian people always considered that forest to be their private preserve for obtaining wood products.
>
> We want to show that Indian people treated Meares Island as their own private tree farm licence and that's inconsistent with MacMillan Bloedel's claim that they have a tree farm licence. (Jack Woodward, quoted in *Ha-Shilth-Sa*, April 29, 1986:3)

The *Wah nah jus/Hilth hoo is* court case began in the British Columbia Supreme Court in September 1991. It primarily focused on the issue of competing rights with regard to the trees on Meares Island (*Ha-Shilth-Sa*, September 12, 1991:4; November 13, 1991:1,3). In June 1992, however, court proceedings were replaced by negotiations, when the province and the Tla-o-qui-aht and Ahousaht Bands agreed to adjourn the court case until August 31, 1993, to give them time to work out an agreement.

While the court case had focused on the issue of ownership and jurisdiction of trees on the island, the ongoing negotiations are aimed at co-management of all resources on Meares Island. The province has signalled its willingness to recognize Ha Holthe and aboriginal title, which opens the door for negotiations envisaging a mutual integration of the Chiefs' Ha Holthe and provincial jurisdiction. Eventually the planned agreement is to be incorporated into the Treaty Process (*Ha-Shilth-Sa*, December 16, 1992:1,4).[5]

The Stein River Valley

The Stein River Valley is another cause célèbre where native groups and environmentalists joined forces in order to preserve wilderness areas from logging. The valley is the last expansive watershed in southwestern British Columbia, that has not been logged or penetrated by roads, the largest in the entire Fraser River drainage basin (M'Gonigle 1988:109).[6] The controversy started with the formulation of logging and road construction plans for the area in the early 1970s, which resulted in the formation of the Save the Stein Coalition, an environmental coalition of 17 groups representing about 45,000 members. The local Indian bands did not become directly involved for over a decade, until two events happened: In February 1985 there was a formal announcement that road-building would proceed immediately, and the native right to claim title to the land was openly challenged by the provincial Minister of Forests, Tom Waterland (Cassidy and Dale 1988:94). Immediately, the Lytton Band broke its long-standing silence on the Stein issue and announced official opposition to road construction and logging. Previously, the Mount Currie Band of the Lillooet Tribal Council had expressed its opposition. In 1985 the Tribal Council of the Nlaka'pamux Nation (of which the Lytton Band is a member) filed a comprehensive land claim which includes the Stein Valley (accepted by the federal government in 1987).

From then on the Lytton Band and the Lillooet Tribal Council took centre stage in the controversy over the Stein. Political activism over this issue increased dramatically in the mid-1980s, featuring various strategies undertaken jointly or simultaneously by native and environmental groups (M'Gonigle 1988:112ff). Among these "strategies for the assertion of control" (ibid.:112) were public and media events, most prominently the Stein Voices for the Wilderness festival, which has become an annual event now organized by the Lillooet Tribal Council and the Lytton Indian Band; advocacy research (ranging from cost-benefit analysis of diverse development options for the valley to native-sponsored ethnographic studies); assertion of public interest authority (construction of a hiking trail and institution of a "Rediscovery" program in the valley); and public negotiation (which resulted in a moratorium on road-building into the Stein Valley but not in conclusive consideration of the native claim).

> But with an injunction against logging on Meares Island, and a new national park reserve being established on the Queen Charlotte Islands, the Stein has also become the forest industry's symbolic last stand against what it perceives to be the theft of its land base. Economic or not, the Stein must be logged to demonstrate firm industry control over the province's forest lands. (M'Gonigle and Wickwire 1988:143)

In the late 1980s the future of the Stein remained in abeyance. In 1987, under persistent pressure from the Lytton Band, the Ministry of Forests signalled willingness to negotiate, but attempted unilaterally to limit the terms of reference of the discussions to the details of a road-building agreement. Native groups, on the other hand, have tried ever since to

---

[5] At press time, negotiations between the Ahousaht/Tla-o-qui-aht bands and the provincial government have reached a stalemate, and it appears that the issue will be decided by the courts after all (*Ha-Shilth-Sa*, July 15, 1993:1).

[6] This issue has been covered from various angles by Michael R.M. M'Gonigle (M'Gonigle 1988, 1989/90 and M'Gonigle & Wickwire 1988).

open up wider questions including alternatives to logging the Stein, the heritage and environmental values at stake, and finally, entitlement to land.

The occurrences surrounding South Moresby, Meares Island and the Stein have attracted the most attention, but they are by no means isolated incidents. In the late 1980s and early 1990s less publicized confrontations and struggles have continued, f.e. in Sulpher Pass in the Nuu-chah-nulth territory (*Ha-Shilth-Sa*, June 23, 1988); in the lower Tsitika Valley on the east coast of Vancouver Island, territory claimed by the Tlowitsis-Mumtagila Tribal Council (*Calgary Herald*, December 19, 1990); in the Pemberton area, in Lillooet lands (*Windspeaker*, March 15, 1991); and also in the interior of British Columbia, in the homeland of the Chilcotin Indians (*Calgary Herald*, June 16, 1990). Invariably, native people are trying to protect their fisheries, their traplines and game animals, burial grounds or sacred shrines from the effects of clearcutting and road construction.

In the summer of 1993 national and international attention of aboriginal people and non-native environmentalists was focused on clear-cut plans for Clayoquot Sound in the territory of the Central Region Bands of the Nuu-chah-nulth Tribal Council. The Clayoquot decision threatened the CORE (Commission on Resources and the Environment) process, the NDP government's innovative approach to developing a comprehensive land-use strategy, which supposedly guarantees open public involvement.

A Tenuous Alliance

All three of the high profile issues — South Moresby, Meares Island, and the Stein Valley — have featured an alliance of native and environmental groups. This collaboration, while mutually beneficial, does have its share of mutual distrust. Native groups have never left any doubt that their primary concern is the question of control and ownership, rather than a statement of the preferred state of the environment. In the Stein Valley case, for example, the Nlaka'pamux Tribal Council itself has been an active and successful developer throughout its territory, particularly in adjacent areas like the Nicola Valley. It is not as philosophically committed either to environmental values or to structural economic changes as are many other tribal councils throughout the province (M'Gonigle 1989/90:71). The Tahltan in northern British Columbia are the most notable example of a native group who explicitly rejects an environmental approach in favour of logging the Stikine River Valley, probably the most important national park campaign in British Columbia after Gwaii Haanas (M'Gonigle 1988:121; Hume 1990:14). Also, in Southeast Alaska, there is great concern among environmentalists about an overemphasis by native corporations on short-term profits in forestry development (Cassidy and Dale 1988:104–107). More typical, however, is the existence of "pro-development" elements in most native groups, including a strongly traditional development approach among some members of the Nlaka'pamux Tribal Council, of which the Lytton Band is a member. This has surfaced in differences with (and within) the Lytton Band over the character of alternative economic development strategies for the Stein (M'Gonigle 1988:121). As a result, in such a situation, environmentalists are distinctly uncomfortable with a "Just trust us!" approach.

Generally speaking, however, there is abundant evidence that among native groups there is a strong commitment to environmentally sustainable development, if not to explicit preservation. Such sustainable development in forestry would emphasize smaller-scale operations, adequate investment in intensive silviculture, stronger adherence to multiple use (especially non-extractive uses), and a greater local community role in forest use and management. All these elements appear in forestry plans and statements of groups such as the Lytton Band, the Nuu-chah-nulth and the Nisga'a (Cassidy and Dale 1988:99f).

> Native forestry is not necessarily different in practice than other forms of forestry, but one generalization that can be made is that aboriginal forestry will usually be different than an

> industrial timber company's version of forestry. The fundamental differences lie in different land ethics and value systems. (Merkel 1992:7)

Native people have legitimate concerns about the position of environmentalists, too (M'Gonigle 1988:121f). In the Meares Island case, with the Ahousaht Band's successful temporary injunction against the logging company, the environmental community had achieved its short-term goal, and moved on to the next crisis (the Stein), leaving Indian bands at Meares to carry on the protracted battle for a permanent injunction by themselves. Also, among some environmental organizations, preservation demands "park" designation, with no trapping or hunting allowed and little if any consideration being given to the implications of such a designation for native land claims or the opportunity for native people to have a voice in the management of that park. The protracted stalemate between the Haida and Parks Canada over the nature of ultimate authority in the management of the new Gwaii Haanas park reserve is a prime example for such situation.

For environmentalists, native claims have proven extremely useful in blocking unilateral action by the government, a fact borne out by the Stein, Meares Island and South Moresby. The absence of a strong native claim at Carmanah Creek on Vancouver Island has made this struggle all the more difficult for environmentalists (ibid.:118f). Another common element between native and environmental groups, ideological rather than pragmatic (and not shared by **all** native and environmental groups) is a shared belief in the need for a fundamental restructuring of social power and a common vision of sustainable development (ibid.:122). This applies in particular to those native groups described by Cassidy and Dale (1988) in the "homeland and hinterland" scenario, like the Nisga'a.

The Nisga'a

The Nisga'a have always been one of the most vocal and indefatigable of the province's native groups in the pursuit of land claims, and lately among their primary motivations has been the fear that the forests of the Nass River Valley will be irrevocably damaged by cutting practices under existing non-native tenure and provincial management (ibid.:119). In their comprehensive claim the Nisga'a demand compensation for forest resources already removed from the territory, and they also assert total ownership and control over the remaining forest resources. In 1978 the bands prepared a detailed forest plan. It proposed a strategy for sustained yield management involving a partnership between present Nass Valley operators, the province and the Nisga'a. During the transition to Nisga'a management, forest companies were to be guaranteed a timber supply sufficient to at least recover their investment in the region. The province rejected the plan.

In 1982 the Nisga'a Tribal Council commissioned a further study for a technical evaluation of forest management and practices in the Nass Valley (ibid.:120). The final report documented severe mismanagement of Tree Farm Licence #1, which dates back to the first commercial logging in the region in 1958 and includes large scale soil damage, timber highgrading, underutilization of felled timber and insufficient reforestation. The report also presented a more radical approach which remains the basis of the Nisga'a proposal for the forestry component of a comprehensive claims settlement. Most fundamentally, it called for taking over much of TFL #1 from the current licensee, Westar Timber, and implementing integrated resource management under a territorially based government. In a brochure designed to explain their proposal, "Forests for People: A Nishga Solution", the Nisga'a asserted: "Our solution is compatible with B.C. Law and is one that will share the resources of the Nass with the people of Canada." (ibid.:120).

While promoting its proposal, the Nisga'a Tribal Council also lodged a formal complaint with the British Columbia Ombudsman's Office, raising the issues of highgrading, overcutting and lack of reforestation. After investigating the situation the Ombudsman confirmed the Nisga'a findings and called for a fundamental restructuring of tenure conditions, designed specifically for the rehabilitation of poorly managed forests. On this basis the Nisga'a asked the Minister of Forests to transfer TFL #1 to them regardless of the status of the comprehensive claims question.

They were envisaging a comprehensive watershed-based planning approach with increased emphasis on value-added components of primary activities such as forestry.

> The key argument is that if one government has authority over all resource development for a watershed and has a constituency including both forest and fisheries users (many Nisga'a carry out both activities seasonally), there is less likelihood of resource conflicts. (Cassidy and Dale 1988:121f)

The Nisga'a also tried to purchase the licence from Westar but without success. Westar requested and was granted a reduction of its TFL. The Nisga'a Tribal Council attempted to combine the relinquished lands with higher quality areas to form a Timber Supply Area. Instead, the Ministry awarded the licence to contractors from Terrace and Vancouver.

> The picture formed of Nisga'a intentions in the forestry sector is one of using political strategies to increase their control over the resource. Like all other native groups the Nisga'a are concerned with unemployment and related social problems which could be alleviated by forest-based development. However, they have a stronger inclination than many other groups to seek these benefits by directly challenging existing management and tenure arrangements. This strategy proceeds both in the forum of comprehensive land claims and in efforts to secure TFL 1. It is an example of efforts on the part of native peoples to restore a sustainable homeland from lands which they perceive, at present, to be mere hinterlands. (ibid.:122)

The Gitksan and Wet'suwet'en

The neighbouring Gitksan and Wet'suwet'en people are taking an even more assertive stance, and their assertion of jurisdiction over their natural resources in accordance with their system of House Chiefs is a more radical departure from the status quo than in the Nisga'a case. Their various strategies of gaining control over their natural resources have already been described in some detail as they pertain to fisheries.

With regard to forestry, the bands have made it clear, that they are by no means "anti-development". "We are ready to do business, but companies have to understand that we want control over how that business is done." (Don Ryan, speaker for the Hereditary Chiefs of the Gitksan-Wet'suwet'en, quoted in Watt 1990:47). Like the Nisga'a, the Gitksan and Wet'suwet'en people are presently forced to witness how their ancestral lands are denuded of their forests and subjected to the same abusive practices of overcutting and high-grading as they prevail in Nisga'a territory (Glavin 1990:35f; 178ff).

The Gitksan-Wet'suwet'en and logging companies have tried to come to terms with each other. In 1988 Skeena Cellulose built a bridge across the Skeena River into the traditional territory of the Eagle clan. The land had been controlled for centuries by four hereditary chiefs. Clan members put up a blockade and stopped the company's progress. Managers from Skeena Cellulose met with the leaders of the Eagle clan and offered clan members training and equipment so they could do their own logging. The Eagles held a clan meeting and decided to turn the offer down. After studying Skeena Cellulose's 20-year plan, they decided there would be nothing left for future generations.

Instead, the Eagle clan has developed its own logging plan. Its members consider a 20-year plan as far too short-sighted and want to replace it with a 250-year plan. They want their land use plan to be a framework for selective logging, tourism development, hunting and trapping and preservation of culturally and environmentally sensitive areas.

> There are lots of opportunities for interaction with business. If the Eagles want to sell logs they've harvested selectively, the logging companies may want to buy. But the Eagles are going to harvest in ways that don't hurt the land. They are going to manage their own resources — not on the province's terms, not on the logging companies' terms — but

on their own terms, in their own territory. (Val Napoleon, Co-ordinator of the Gitksan-Wet'suwet'en Education Society, quoted in Watt 1990:47)

Control over the pace and style of resource development is one of the main elements of anticipated comprehensive land claims negotiations. Until a settlement is reached, the Gitksan and Wet'suwet'en are determined to do whatever it takes to make sure that there will be resources left, and they are not only employing political means. They have played havoc with the timber companies with a series of roadblocks and court injunctions which have halted the development of two new cutting areas. They successfully organized local logging contractors and politicians into a task force that insists that resource companies pay more attention to local opinions on resource extraction (Glavin 1990:29–47, 178–189; Watt 1990:47).

The March 1991 Supreme Court of British Columbia ruling that dismissed the Gitksan-Wet'suwet'en land title action against the provincial Crown (Delgamuukw v. The Queen) did nothing to ease the tension. Nevertheless, the McEachern decision may not have been totally devoid of positive elements. It required that the province fulfill the following:

- Give the House Groups adequate notice of impending developments;
- Disclose documents and information to the Indians;
- Give the Chiefs adequate time to respond and make alternative suggestions; and
- Provide the Chiefs with reasons for their resource management decisions. (Richard Overstall, Gitksan-Wet'suwet'en Chiefs' Meeting, June 24, 1992)

In practice, such adequate consultation and communication with the House Chiefs has been slow in coming. As Art Loring (Goo tsa gin) puts it, "Sending the Chief a letter is not enough." (Gitksan-Wet'suwet'en Chiefs' Meeting, June 24, 1992) The Hereditary Chiefs, on their part, countered such letters of notification with their own letters, which was what happened on June 19, 1992, when the Chief of the Eagle clan (Lax Skiik) politely informed Kitwanga Lumber Co. Ltd. that, regretfully, Lax Skiik must deny the company's request to log certain blocks in the Eagle clan's House Territory. However, the Chief offered the Eagle clan's assistance in finding an appropriate area in its territory to log in an ecologically responsible manner to produce an equivalent volume and quality of timber. Logging and business transactions would, however, be conducted under Lax Skiik control.

To arrive at a workable coexistence of all parties involved in resource use and management, the Gitksan and Wet'suwet'en are also negotiating with the provincial government. The Ministry of Forests' 1991 Integrated Resource Management Strategy falls far short of Gitksan-Wet'suwet'en expectations and has lacked meaningful aboriginal input. In Maas Gaak's (Don Ryan) opinion, management boundaries used in the Strategy fail to acknowledge ecological as well as cultural realities. Furthermore, with regard to a native presence, the Strategy merely recognizes cultural and archaeological features, rather than resource-related issues (Maas Gaak, personal communication, June 18, 1992). Nevertheless, a forestry-sectoral agreement between the province and the Gitksan-Wet'suwet'en is in preparation, and funding is sought for Gitksan-Wet'suwet'en research to improve the provincial approach to integrated resource management.

Where diplomacy and negotiations fail, however, the Gitksan and Wet'suwet'en people are as prepared as they have always been to assert their responsibilities out on the land, by what another culture would call "civil disobedience". It goes without saying, that such determination has its price. There is a potential for polarization among the Gitksan and Wet'suwet'en due to many individuals' dependence on forestry jobs and due to the forestry practices of some band-owned sawmills. So far there has been no open confrontation, but according to Wii Seeks (Ralph Michell), hereditary Chief of the Fireweeds (Giskaast) and one of the strongest proponents of an uncompromising protection of House Territories, such potential internal split is one of the most painful aspects of the House Groups' determination to take a stand against further deterioration of their Territories (Wii Seeks, personal communication, June 23, 1992).

The Prairie Provinces

During a forestry expansion process which started in the 1980s and is still ongoing, the boreal forests of the northern prairie provinces have been subjected to increasing forestry developments. White spruce, black spruce and lodgepole pine have always been important timber species, and "yesterday's weed", the aspen poplar, has become valuable for pulp and strandboard (McCord 1989:6). The late 1980s and early 1990s have witnessed an unprecedented giveaway of vast forest tracts in Forest Management Agreements (FMAs) in Alberta, and their equivalent in Saskatchewan and Manitoba to logging companies or pulpmills.

For northern native people these developments have been a mixed blessing. On one hand, the forest industry is an important employer in areas otherwise characterized by chronic unemployment problems. In Saskatchewan, in 1980, 18 per cent of the total forest industry labour force was of native ancestry; in the northern part of the province native participation in forest industry employment was as high as 80 per cent (Ondro and Williamson 1985:28). On the other hand, northern native communities are paying a high price for these opportunities, due to the damage sustained by their land-based economy. For this reason many native people are openly opposed to this forestry expansion; others are ambivalent; and some find themselves in a conflict of interest.

This happened in northwest Saskatchewan. On April 19, 1990, Treaty Indians and Metis met in Beauval to voice opposition to Miller-Western's Meadow Lake Pulp Mill, and to take a stand against what they viewed as "corporate exploitation of the North." (*New Breed*, April 1990) On the other hand, the Meadow Lake District Chiefs are half-owners of the company holding the forestry leases from which Miller-Western will obtain its trees. One Indian participant in the meeting probably spoke for the majority when he expressed support for native participation in saw-milling and selective logging, but uncompromising opposition to such practices as clear-cutting.

Two years later the internal conflict and division of the native community had by no means subsided as evidenced by a July 1992 incident north of Meadow Lake. Thirty native protesters were arrested after they set up a blockade to prevent logging trucks from travelling. The trucks were retrieving cut logs for Mistik Management, a native-owned company which manages forests in the area for NorSask Forest Products. The protesters' opposition was directed at clear-cutting, and they put pressure on Saskatchewan's Minister of Parks and Natural Resources to discontinue clear-cutting in the area by amending NorSask's forest management lease (*Vancouver Sun*, July 3, 1992:A6).

In Alberta the latest expansion of forestry development in the northern province has been one of the most controversial environmental issues in several years, with direct implications for northern native communities. This expanded development involved the establishment of seven major pulp mill projects — all of them located on a single river system, the Peace-Athabasca — and the disposition of huge tracts of land in Forest Management Agreements to supply these mills. Daishowa and AlPac, both bleached kraft pulp mills, were singled out for particularly strong public criticism, based on environmental concerns.

As a result, in an unprecedented move, in July 1989, a joint provincial-federal board was appointed to hold public hearings to review AlPac's Environmental Impact Assessment. Similarly, in anticipation of a large-scale disposition of forest lands by means of new FMAs, an Expert Panel on Forest Management was appointed by Alberta's Minister of Forestry, Lands and Wildlife, to review a variety of forest management issues. Both reports agreed on a fundamental issue: The province's drive for diversification by forestry expansion is not supported with adequate data, including baseline information about the rivers and the fish, fundamental data on the toxicity and other properties of dioxins, furans and other chlorinated organic compounds, timber and wildlife inventories, habitat information, etc. The AlPac Review Board recommended that the project not be approved at that time, principally because of the inadequate database. Both reports have something in common besides their conclusions: They were all but ignored by the provincial government.

The environmental impacts of pulp mill and timber harvesting activities have severe implications for the domestic economy pursued by northern Alberta's far-flung native communities, who find their settlements surrounded and their trapping and hunting territories covered by FMA's, or who depend on polluted river systems for their water supply and a major part of their diet. Many native leaders have voiced their concerns through the channels at their disposal, i.e. the AlPac Review Hearings and the media. The Dene Nation and the Metis Association of the Northwest Territories, as well as the Assembly of First Nations, were intervenors in the February 1991 Supreme Court hearing that determined the constitutional validity of the federal environmental assessment review process (EARP) which arose from the Oldman River dam dispute. Some native groups in northern Alberta reviewed the possibility of taking legal action against the province over the AlPac approval; for instance, the Fort Chipewyan Band (*Edmonton Journal*, August 18, 1990); the Cree Band at Fort McMurray (*Windspeaker*, January 4, 1991); and the Beaver Lake Band (Cree) near Lac La Biche (*Windspeaker*, January 18, 1991).

The Lubicon Lake Cree went a step further by asserting jurisdiction over their ancestral territory. They are in an exceptional situation since their band was "overlooked" by treaty commissioners for Treaty Eight in 1899. As a result, over several decades the band has been pursuing its 10,000-square-kilometre aboriginal title claim, which constitutes one-quarter of Daishowa's FMA area. The Lubicon Lake Cree left no doubt that they would not tolerate the removal of any resources from their land, be it timber or fossil fuels (*Grande Prairie Daily Herald Tribune*, October 9, 1990; *Alberta Report*, September 24, 1990; *Windspeaker*, January 18, 1991). On November 8, 1990, Chief Bernard Ominayak announced in Edmonton:

> We have given notice, effective today, they have to have proper authorization permits from the Lubicon people if they want to continue exploiting resources from unceded Lubicon lands....[Approval of such operating permits, licences and leases] will be subject to the payment of past and future royalties and to compliance with Lubicon environmental protection and wildlife management laws. (*Windspeaker*, November 23, 1990)

In other words "Deal with us or stay out." (*Windspeaker*, December 7, 1990).

The remainder of northern Alberta's Indian bands possess treaty rights to hunting, fishing and trapping on their surrendered lands. This particular issue was the most crucial point during the treaty negotiations in 1899 and 1900 (Fumoleau 1973:46–104; Daniel 1979:47:100). Nevertheless, since the turn of the century, these rights have been subject to constant erosion and progressive restriction, since the 1960s at an accelerated rate with the advent of the energy frontier (Fort McKay Band 1983:5–25). The resurgence in the forest industry is only the latest stage in a long process, and native groups like the Fort McKay people are running out of adaptive strategies.

Native communities in the Peace-Athabasca river system are already being severely affected by water pollution. While government and industry representatives try to belittle the impacts, community leaders report people getting violently sick after consuming fish (*Calgary Herald*, March 16, 1990). They also express concern about berries growing along the rivers and the entire aquatic food-chain. In the meantime, the provincial government, dissatisfied with the conclusions reached by its own appointed AlPac Review Board, hired a Finnish consulting firm to conduct yet another assessment of the data submitted to the AlPac Review Board (Edwards 1990:22). The resultant study was never made public, but the provincial government issued a statement based on this study to the effect that the health risk to native people from contaminated fish would be lower than anticipated, since natives eat less fish than the Canadian average! (*Windspeaker*, August 3, 1990; *Edmonton Journal*, August 18, 1990).

Some native groups in northern Alberta endeavour to profit from the inevitable, exemplified by a catering contract between AlPac and the Athabasca Native Development Corporation (ANDC), and a logging contract between Daishowa and Aboriginal Logging Ltd. Such participation is rendered somewhat tenuous by native environmental qualms, and Fort McKay was reconsidering its involvement as member of ANDC. Referring to employment opportunities, Loretta Gladue of Calling Lake said that people "don't make a fuss about the environmental concerns because the bread-and-butter issues override the environment." (*Windspeaker*, January 18, 1991). Statements like this are the exception, though, because for the majority of native people the environment is a "bread-and-butter issue". Most native leaders and their constituents — only too familiar with boom-and-bust cycles — seem to echo Fort Chipewyan chief Pat Marcel's feelings:

> We may very well be fighting a losing battle against the pulp mills and the governments that would approve such projects. But we are bound and determined to guarantee a safe environment for future generations to come. (*Fort McMurray Today*, April 11, 1990)

Ontario and Quebec

In the late 1980s shortly after confrontations between native groups and logging interests climaxed in British Columbia, similar stand-offs took place in northern Ontario and northern Quebec, again in the context of unresolved claims.

The **Temagami** controversy is another variation of a familiar theme. Once again, old-growth forest is the environmental resource in jeopardy, and various non-native user groups — environmental, recreational and timber interests — have for years been fighting over land which Indians believe does not even belong to the people of Ontario. The Teme-Augama Anishnabai were omitted from the Robinson Huron Treaty of 1850. As early as 1877, Chief Tonene asked for a treaty that would protect his people and their land from the encroaching lumbermen and settlers (Moise 1989:38). The Teme-Augama Anishnabai spent the following 113 years battling for recognition of their rights to their homeland N'Daki-Menan.[7] They are today occupying a small reserve on Bear Island on Lake Temagami, which was purchased for them by the federal government in 1943 and given reserve status in 1970, but which was never recognized by the tribal leadership as a resolution of their land claim.

By the late 1980s the Teme-Augama had exhausted the political route and the legal route. Having lost their land claims case before the Supreme Court of Ontario in 1985 and before the Ontario Court of Appeal in 1989, they appealed to the Supreme Court of Canada (which in 1991 upheld the lower courts' ruling). With logging-road construction into the last untouched remnant of their ancestral lands imminent, the Teme-Augama resorted to their last available tactics: They asserted their rights and responsibilities and set up a blockade, first in 1988 and again in 1989.

What sets Temagami apart from the other developments is the course of action subsequently taken by the Teme-Augama Anishnabai and the Government of Ontario. On April 23, 1990, both parties signed an agreement, providing for "joint stewardship" of about 40,000 hectares in the Temagami forest. The agreement was to be administered by a joint stewardship

---

[7] "The Temagami Experience", from its earliest beginnings, is described in detail by Hodgins and Benidickson (1989). The events preceding the stewardship agreement are discussed in journal articles by Moise (1989) and Hall (1990).

council. Half of its members were to be appointed by the provincial government, and half by the Teme-Augama Anishnabai. No timber licences were to be issued in the townships covered by the agreement without the approval of a majority of the council's members, which effectively gave the Teme-Augama a veto over logging in this area. Not surprisingly, there has been criticism of this agreement, mostly on the part of environmentalists, focusing on the relatively small portion of forests thus protected (18 per cent), and on the fact that the Ontario government, in separate negotiations, granted nine logging permits for vast sections of the Temagami area outside the areas included under the stewardship agreement (Hall 1990b:34; *Globe and Mail*, April 28, 1990).

But the Teme-Augama Anishnabai view the stewardship agreement as part of a larger agenda. It does not pre-empt the legal process (Mary Laronde, Bear Island, in an interview with Harris 1991:7), nor does it constitute part of a land claims settlement. The very fact that this agreement was signed **outside** the context of a claims settlement may have been advantageous for the Teme-Augama. As M'Gonigle (1980/90:78, 86) points out, under current policy, settlement of native land claims is usually arrived at by a competitive rather than a cooperative process, by the creation of a "lowest common denominator":

> ...give up what one must in order to achieve extinguishment of title and to safeguard access by the dominant society to important resources. Opportunities for cooperative action between central and local levels to achieve more sustainable resource management for the whole society are not envisioned. (ibid.:76f)

The fact that the Teme-Augama were not forced to surrender anything for the agreement is counterbalanced by the fact that the agreement is wholly imbedded in provincial administrative structures, and that it constitutes an implicit rather than explicit recognition of aboriginal rights and, therefore, is unlikely to be subject to constitutional protection. The Teme-Augama have expressed the hope of eventually expanding a shared stewardship structure to cover their whole claim area (Chief Gary Potts, quoted in Hall 1990b:34; Mary Laronde in an interview with Harris 1991:7).

> The stewardship council is one aspect of the Memorandum of Understanding and negotiations are another but they are inextricably linked. The creation of the stewardship council is premised on the fact that Ontario and the Teme-Augama Anishnabai agree to work toward a Treaty of Coexistence and that stewardship of the land is fundamental to coexistence. The stewardship council is the working model for coexistence and it is expanding this shared jurisdictional arrangement over the balance of the area, save for areas under municipal jurisdictions and those under exclusive Teme-Augama Anishnabai jurisdiction — that will be part of treaty negotiations.
>
> [In the event of a favourable ruling by the Supreme Court of Canada]...as the legally recognized owners of our homeland, and possessing the jurisdictional powers that accompany that, we would still pursue a shared decision-making regime on our lands. (Mary Laronde in an interview with Harris 1991:7)

Joint management of their land use area is also a vision pursued by the **Algonquin of Barriere Lake** in Quebec. The Mitchikanibikonginik or People of the Stone Weir are part of the Algonquin Nation (10 communities) which claims as its traditional territory all the land and water within the Ottawa River watershed, straddling the Ontario/Quebec border and including Parliament Hill. The Barriere Lake people pursue a largely land-based existence which is severely threatened by the consequences of clear-cut forestry, various silvicultural practices, such as chemical spraying and recreational hunting in the La Verendrye Wildlife Reserve.

Until the 1980s the Barriere Lake Algonquin employed mostly political means in their effort to draw attention to their plight. When in the late 1980s proceedings started to lock La Verendrye into 25-year Timber Supply and Forest Management Agreements with timber corporations, without any consideration of native interests, the Algonquin resorted to court challenges (in a futile attempt to win an injunction) and to civil disobedience. In contrast to the Meares Island case, their call for an injunction was not based on a pending comprehensive claim. At the time the Algonquin did not intend their actions to be an assertion of aboriginal rights, but rather as an attempt to alleviate immediate pressures on their subsistence economy (Chief Jean-Maurice Matchewan 1990:28). They were trying to force the Quebec Government and the federal government into negotiations aimed at a trilateral agreement on integrated resource management, which would take Algonquin land use into account.

The Barriere Lake Algonquin propose a model of "sustainable development", patterned after concepts of the 1987 Brundtland Report by the World Commission on Environment and Development. This report advocates an approach to development, where economic growth "must be based on policies that sustain and expand the environmental resource base." (World Commission on Environment and Development 1987:1) Aboriginal peoples have a singular role to play in this process.

> Tribal and indigenous people will need special attention as the forces of economic development disrupt their traditional life-styles — life-styles that can offer modern societies many lessons in the management of resources in complex forest, mountain, and dry land ecosystems. Some are threatened by virtual extinction, by insensitive development over which they have no control. Their traditional rights should be recognized and they should be given a decisive voice in formulating policies about resource development in their areas. (ibid.:12)

Under intense pressure the governments of Canada and Quebec eventually signalled willingness to participate with the Algonquin in a trilateral process. But in practice it soon became evident to the Indians that Quebec was approaching it as a unilateral process. In April 1991 the Barriere Lake Algonquin declared in a press release that negotiations had broken down due to Quebec's failure to allow them any meaningful input in the process. At the same time five Algonquin bands, under the leadership of Barriere Lake, decided to abandon their practice of pursuing their interests as a conservation issue, and instead to file a full-fledged land claim.

Nevertheless, in August 1991 a trilateral Agreement was reached with the province and the federal government, and the Algonquin entered into negotiations with the provincial government in order to develop an integrated resource management plan for the region. Implementation of the Agreement was plagued by numerous problems throughout the following two years, and in summer 1993 the potential for confrontation had not yet been dissolved (*Windspeaker*, July 5, 1993:R3).

CONCLUSION AND OUTLOOK

Forests are important to native people, and in the 1980s and 1990s native people have also become very important for Canada's forests. This interrelationship manifests itself in a number of ways.

Indian reserve forests potentially constitute a considerable resource for native people in the pursuit of their socio-economic goals. At present, however, due to their degraded state, Indian forests fall far short of their productive potential, and their owners are fully engaged in basic rehabilitation work. The only benefits thus created are training and employment. Due to program constraints there is little opportunity for native people to implement multiple use or to employ non-traditional forestry practices (i.e. practices not advocated by government foresters). With regard to access to off-reserve forest lands for native timber harvesting and forest management, the present regulatory regime has failed Indian people.

Ironically, it is on unsurrendered aboriginal lands — over which native people officially have no control — and outside the narrow confines of "native forestry activities", that the developments occurred which have had the greatest impact on Indian people as well as on forests. Like in the case of no other resource, the impact of non-native forestry practices and native people's perception thereof has served as a catalyst for the formulation and advancement of native claims and the assertion of aboriginal rights and control over aboriginal lands.

> The major, underlying issues in the forestry debate in British Columbia cannot be resolved within the framework of a forestry debate. The fundamental questions which need to be asked with respect to each area of land are:
>
> (1) Whose land is it?
>
> (2) Given present social values, what is the best use for the land?
>
> (3) As values will change in the future, how can options for the future be maintained?
>
> (Nuu-chah-nulth Tribal Council Presentation to the Forestry Commission. *Ha-Shilth-Sa*, May 3, 1990)

Canada's current forestry crisis brings us dangerously close to a point, where options may have been lost. The 1980s have brought a gradual acknowledgement of the fact that problems do indeed exist, and some tentative improvements in some areas. But a fundamental rethinking of basic premises by those in charge is still outstanding.

In the early 1990s we are focusing our hopes and expectations on statements of intent, proposals and suggestions. In the new National Forest Sector Strategy for Canada, the sixth recommendation (which, according to J. Stan Rowe [1992:14] should certainly be the first) advises that forest management should "focus on maintaining the long-term dynamics of healthy, stable, and well-balanced forest ecosystems." To this, in Stan Rowe's estimation, should be added, placing forest ecosystems in their proper context, "as healthy functional parts of the Ecosphere." (ibid.)

In 1991 Tin Wis — a coalition of British Columbia environmentalists, First Nations members, trade unionists, small business people and other activists — proposed a Forest Stewardship Act for the province, advocating a new, community-based, decision-making regime for British Columbia's forests, which would set new standards for citizen participation in resource management (Tester 1992:34ff).

In March 1992 a new Canadian forest strategy entitled "Sustainable Forests: A Canadian Commitment" was adopted by the Canadian Council of Forest Ministers. For the first time, an entire section within the strategy is dedicated to aboriginal issues.

Forestry innovations, if they do materialize, will face an onerous task in dealing with the legacy of past and present forestry practices and, furthermore, things are not always what they appear to be. In Alberta critics are constantly reminded that this province has the most extensive FMA reforestation requirements and the most stringent standards with respect to pulp mill technology in Canada. This may be true, but these achievements pale before the serious shortcomings made public by both the Expert Panel on Forest Management and the AlPac Review Board, whose reports were all but ignored by the provincial government. In a similar vein, a concept of integrated resource management is in place in Alberta, and the government's referral system permits Fish and Wildlife to make recommendations concerning FMAs. In practice this input remains primarily a reactive process in which Fish and Wildlife attempts to minimize the impacts of forest activities on the fish and wildlife resource **after** the Alberta Forest Service has done the planning and developed the ground rules. The Alberta Forest Service decides on whether the recommendations will be included in timber harvest planning and operating ground rules for an FMA (Expert Review Panel 1990:65).

Gross violations occur whenever industry and government do not play by their own rules, which happens not infrequently. One example is the period of "sympathetic administration" in British Columbia during the early 1980s. In an effort to help the industry maintain profitability, the British Columbia Forest Service decided not to hold the forest industry any longer to its normal "rigorous" standards. Part of sympathetic administration was "relaxed utilization of the overmature" which allowed levels of waste in clear-cutting that violated Forest Service regulations (May 1990b:53). And even without such open endorsement of violation of tenure conditions, the British Columbia Forest Service finds itself incapable of adequately enforcing its rules on the forest industry, as uncovered by the 1991 Auditor General's report on British Columbia's forestry.

Native people are usually the first ones to suffer the consequences of gross violations and standard practices of current forestry. They are also among the first to come forward to oppose destructive practices — often at great personal risk and expense — and to assert the right and the responsibility of land stewardship. What is most important is the fact that native groups have valid alternatives to offer, developed through generations of association with the ecosystem.

> The exercise of management rights...is most likely to succeed where they are imbedded in the experience of the place. The trend of centralization has historically run counter to this natural law, from the erosion of native folkways to the demise of the self-reliant rural farming community. The crisis of sustainability which we face today flows from this — where rights are separated from responsibilities, serious problems result. Absentee ownership and centralist mismanagement of the environment go hand-in-hand. Ultimately, the native title claim finds its justification in this naturalist perspective — in the social and ecological values which have traditionally been constitutive of native culture. This may be the essential difference which elevates native rights above those of just another special interest group. (M'Gonigle 1989/90:82f)

5

Wildlife

INTRODUCTION

> To hunt means to have the land around you like clothing.
> ...The focus of a hunter in a hunting society was not killing animals but attending to the myriad relationships he understood bound him into the world he occupied with them. (Lopez 1986:179)

In the area of aboriginal natural resource management, wildlife appears to be the most pervasive and ubiquitous concern expressed by native people. The harvesting of animals for food and/or fur remains the most important aspect of the renewable resource economy in the Northwest Territories (Sibbeston 1986:154), and similarly in Yukon. In the northern territories and in the provincial north, hunting, trapping and fishing remain central to the economic and social life of most small communities. Consequently, the sustainability of wildlife and its habitat is one of the most important determinants of the manner in which aboriginal people would like to see other renewable and non-renewable resources developed, by both native and non-native interests. This concern is also at the core of all northern land claims negotiations.

In the southern part of the country, northern native dependence on game animals is unmatched, but the protection of native hunting rights is anything but a non-issue. This may be attributed to the fact that these rights have a real as well as a symbolic value for aboriginal people.

This chapter starts out by discussing selected wildlife issues, such as native hunting rights, trapping and the controversy surrounding the commercialization of wildlife, as exemplified by game ranching and commercial hunting. It concludes with a discussion of the more comprehensive topic of aboriginal wildlife management, its practice and its potential.

HUNTING RIGHTS

Significance of Native Hunting Rights

Native hunting rights, whether derived from treaty, proclamation, statute or aboriginal title, are the classic example of rights peculiar to aboriginal people (Woodward 1989:317). The following passage, though quoted from a northern context, very well illustrates the significance of these rights for **all** aboriginal people, including those whose physical and socio-economic existence does not depend on them.

> Finally, native northerners universally understand that their aboriginal right to hunt and fish is the legal and political symbol of their special status in Canadian society. In a history shadowed by lost lands, cultural destruction and broken promises, the assertion of hunting rights is a means of exercising what is left of one's status. The maintenance of those rights is seen as the test of white society's good intentions and of the government's good faith. (Usher 1982:35)

This symbolic and ideological importance, however, is by far overshadowed by the very real dependence of native people in the Northwest Territories, Yukon and the northern parts of the provinces on the harvesting of wildlife for their diet. As Peter Usher explains, though native northerners now buy imported foods, game and fish continue to be of vital importance in their diet (Usher 1982:10). It is significant that socio-economic indicators, such as occupation, employment status and education, show no relationship to country food consumption (Wein et al. 1991:204). Studies conducted throughout the North have documented annual per capita country food harvests ranging from 109 kilograms to roughly four times that amount. For Canada as a whole, the comparable figure for meat and fish consumption was 79 kilograms. Estimates of the economic value of this food consumption indicate that it usually contributes the equivalent of several thousand dollars of income per family per year (Usher 1982:10).

Country food provides by far the major part of northern native people's protein requirements and most of the essential components of a balanced nutritious diet. Imported foods sold by the stores in small northern communities consist mostly of sugars, starches and canned fruits and vegetables, and they are costly. Dietary studies in these localities have shown that native people who depend largely on store-bought food items are frequently malnourished and more susceptible to diet-related health problems. "Reliance on country food, then, is a matter of health as well as economics." (ibid.:11)

As to the geographical area utilized for subsistence hunting, Indian and Inuit hunters continue to range widely in pursuit of food and furs. According to Usher (ibid.:10), there are indeed very few parts of northern Canada that are not being used for these purposes. It would simply be impossible for native hunters to restrict their harvesting activities to their reserve lands, which in the northern parts of the provinces are very small, and which do not even exist in the territorial north. Consequently, native people depend heavily on continued access to off-reserve resources, i.e. wildlife on Crown lands (ibid.).

The importance of wildlife to aboriginal people goes far beyond its food and economic value.

> It is the relations among people that hunting and fishing generate, not simply the relations between man and wildlife, which are important to native people. Despite the continued northward advance of industrial society, most native northerners continue to regard traditional activities as essential to the maintenance of their social structure and institutions, their culture, and the solidarity and cohesion of their community and family lives.
>
> Wildlife, in their perception, is also important for some less tangible reasons. One is security. Native people have seen many economic booms and busts, and know that even in the best of times they are the last hired, first fired and get the lowest paid jobs. Consequently, wage employment, even though people may want it, is not considered a permanent or secure source of livelihood. The land, on the other hand, provides exactly that anchor of security because, properly cared for, it will yield food forever. (ibid.:11)

While a prognosis for the future is always problematic, this situation is unlikely to change in the foreseeable future. David Pelly's observations for Pond Inlet characterize the circumstances in many northern communities.

> The future is not going to be easy. Today, half of the 1,000 residents of Pond Inlet are under 20 years of age. Given present birth rates, in 10 years the total population will be close to 1,500. The work force will double in size, but the number of jobs will probably

> increase only marginally. Hunting, it would seem, may become even more important as a source of food. (Pelly 1991:49)

Native people are aware of this and have in recent times intensified their endeavours to entrench and expand their hunting rights. At the same time, native hunting rights, whether derived from treaties or aboriginal title, have a history of being misunderstood, ignored or challenged.

> The significance of Treaty Indian hunting rights has long been under-estimated in wildlife management. There are reasons for this. It is a Canadian problem, largely unrecognized in wildlife journals, largely un-studied, essentially un-taught in schools of wildlife management and perceived by Canadian wildlife managers as an anomaly which they have been reluctant to accept. Historically, our efforts have been devoted to finding legal means to over-rule Treaty Indian hunting rights: these efforts have repeatedly failed. (Nepinak and Payne 1988:198)

Substance of Native Hunting Rights

Native hunting rights, which are protected by s.35(1) of the Constitution Act, 1982, fall under three broad categories: aboriginal rights, hunting rights confirmed by the Natural Resources Transfer Agreements of 1930 and treaty rights.[1] An additional category was created by contemporary treaties, where harvesting rights are incorporated in a broader category of resource-related rights and responsibilities.

The courts have generally held that **aboriginal title** does not imply ownership of land and wildlife, but rather "a right to occupy the lands and to enjoy the fruits of the soil, the forest and of the rivers and streams." (Justice Hall in the landmark case *Calder v. Attorney General of B.C. 1973*, quoted in Bartlett 1988:7). Native people, therefore, have no authority based on aboriginal title to regulate the allocation, harvesting and utilization of wildlife in accordance with their customary laws. This is the prerogative of the State (Usher 1982:36). In many instances, however, native people are wholly or partially exempt from the laws and regulations pertaining to hunting. The Yukon Act and the Northwest Territories Act, for example, both state that no territorial ordinance shall restrict or prohibit Indians or Inuit "from hunting for food, on unoccupied Crown lands, game other than game declared by the Governor in Council to be game in danger of becoming extinct." (Woodward 1989:335; Usher 1982:36). As a result native people there do not require licences to hunt for food, nor are they subject to bag limits or closed seasons.

Nevertheless, numerous contentious issues remain. What exactly constitutes "unoccupied Crown land"? In Yukon cases it has been held that mere scheduling of a tract of land as a game sanctuary does not constitute occupation (Woodward 1989:335). What impact do restrictions on commercial harvesting have on intersettlement trade in country food, an activity that is likely to become even more important in the future with the growing urban-village differentiation among native people in the North (Usher 1981:64)? The Governor in Council's power to abridge hunting rights on the basis of certain game species being threatened with extinction raises further questions; the inclusion on this list of "barren ground cariboo", a species which continues to be hunted regularly by the Inuit, is highly controversial (Woodward 1989:335). All these questions will not likely be resolved within the narrow framework of "hunting rights" as they are part and parcel of the more comprehensive issue of "wildlife management".

---

[1] Metis and non-status Indians have no special rights to wildlife resources even though they may be just as dependent on the resource in economic and cultural terms as status Indians. In northern Alberta, in "remote areas", outside cities, towns or villages, non-status Indians and Metis as well as non-Indians have the option of applying for a Subsistence Hunting Licence, which allows them one moose or deer, if a true need for wild meat to feed themselves or their families can be demonstrated, and provided there is a "surplus" of animals. Selection criteria and terms under the Licence are rather restrictive. (Government of Alberta, n.d.a)

In the area of aboriginal hunting rights, the 1990 Supreme Court of Canada decision in *Sparrow* is beginning to cast its shadow. In September 1990 the Nova Scotia government declared that it "recognizes and affirms that the Micmac have an existing Aboriginal right to harvest outside of reserves for wildlife and food and fur — subject only to the needs of conservation and public safety." (*Windspeaker*, September 28, 1990:3). As a result Micmac hunters were granted special seasons for moose and deer, as well as other considerations.

Sparrow's home province British Columbia was hesitant to follow suit, and it was not before 1993 that a higher court ruling established that the principles adopted in *Sparrow* apply to wildlife as well. In 1987 Harry Thomas Dick of the Mowachaht Band (of the Nuu-chah-nulth Tribal Council) was charged under the Wildlife Act of British Columbia for having elk meat in his possession without a licence or permit (*Ha-Shilth-Sa*, September 1, 1988). On October 7, 1988, Judge Sarich of the Provincial Court in Campbell River acquitted Thomas Dick and upheld his aboriginal right to possess wild meat.

> I find then that the people who were permanently resident in the settlement of Ahaminaquus had from time immemorial developed and enjoyed an aboriginal right to hunt elk on unoccupied lands adjacent to that settlement, and to possess the meat of those animals. (R. v. Dick [1989] 1 C.N.L.R.:137)

The Crown appealed to the British Columbia County Court, and the acquittal was set aside and Thomas Dick convicted (R. v. Dick [1989] 4 C.N.L.R. 120). An appeal of this decision by Thomas Dick to the British Columbia Court of Appeal was concluded in November 1991 and ruled upon (along with *Delgamuukw*) in June 1993. Harry Thomas Dick won his appeal with the recognition of his aboriginal right to hunt elk. During the same appeal procedure, another hunting case (R. v. Alphonse [1988] 3 C.N.L.R. 92 and [1989] 1 C.N.L.R. 121) was won by Shuswap Chief Willie Alphonse, Jr. of the Williams Lake Band, who had hunted mule deer off-reserve and out-of-season (*Windspeaker*, July 5, 1993:R1).

Just how anxious the Provincial Crown had been about the possibility of another decision like *Sparrow* was shown by the fact that it attempted to have the case dealt with prior to the Court of Appeal hearing. The provincial government expressed its consent to have Thomas Dick acquitted provided the Court of Appeal did not rule on the constitutional issues, i.e. aboriginal rights, raised by Thomas Dick in his appeal. The Crown's application was denied by the Court of Appeal (*Ha-Shilth-Sa*, August 1, 1991:17).

The release of new Interim Guidelines on Aboriginal Use of Fish and Wildlife by British Columbia's Ministry of Environment, Lands and Parks in March 1993 implied the acceptance by the province of an aboriginal right to wildlife harvesting for sustenance (*Ha-Shilth-Sa*, March 31, 1993:10; *Windspeaker*, April 12, 1993:9). These Guidelines confirm aboriginal priority of sustenance hunting and fishing in traditional territories, subject only to conservation concerns. They also suggest a self-administered permit system which would be helpful in gathering information on aboriginal harvesting for wildlife management purposes. Final guidelines for aboriginal use of fish and wildlife were to be developed in consultation with First Nations and other key stakeholders in the course of 1993, to be implemented in January 1994.

In the Prairie Provinces Indian hunting rights are circumscribed by the **Natural Resources Transfer Agreements**. These agreements merged and consolidated the treaty rights of the Indians in the area and restricted provincial power to regulate native rights to hunt for food. They also effected two important changes in the rights themselves.

> Under the treaties, hunting rights were general; under the agreements, hunting has been restricted to hunting for food. Under treaties, hunting rights were restricted to the tract of land surrendered by the treaty; under the agreements, hunting rights were expanded to the whole area of the prairie provinces. (Woodward 1989:319)

In the light of s.35(1) of the Constitution Act, 1982, the validity of restrictions to original treaty rights seemed questionable, but the May 1990 ruling of the Supreme Court of Canada in the *Horseman* case (R. v. Horseman [1990] 3 C.N.L.R.95) confirmed these restrictions. In 1983 Bert Horseman, a Horse Lake band member in the Treaty Eight area of northern Alberta, shot a grizzly bear in self-defence. He kept the hide until the next spring when, in need of money, he obtained a grizzly bear licence and sold the skin. Horseman thought he was exercising his Treaty Eight right to hunt for a living. Alberta Fish and Wildlife officers decided he was contravening the Wildlife Act and arrested him for trafficking (*Alberta Report*, May 21, 1990:23). The trial judge acquitted Horseman on the grounds that Treaty Indians were allowed to barter game as well as to use it to feed themselves and their families (*Grande Prairie Daily Herald Tribune*, May 4, 1990:1). But he was convicted by the Alberta Court of Appeal, and the conviction was upheld by the Supreme Court. The decision is made even more significant by the fact that the governments of Saskatchewan and Manitoba were both interveners supporting Alberta's position. The ruling states unequivocally that hunting rights under Treaty Eight, signed in 1899, had been changed by the Natural Resources Transfer Agreement of 1930.

Another seemingly never-ending controversy surrounds the question of what is meant by "unoccupied Crown lands" and "other lands to which the said Indians may have a right of access". In *R. v. Sutherland*, [1980] 2 S.C.R. 451 [Man.], the Supreme Court of Canada unanimously agreed that the provinces could not pass legislation designed to define the terms and rights under the Agreements. Section 49 of the Wildlife Act of Manitoba was drafted for that purpose and was declared to be *ultra vires*. The court also ruled that once any hunting at all was permitted in a certain territory, then a "right of access" within the meaning of the Agreements was established, and the province could not place restrictions on the season, method or limit of hunting. Indians may even hunt for food in provincial parks, if any other hunting is allowed in the parks (Woodward 1989:320f).

In practice, however, the situation is anything but clear-cut. Crown land is not considered to be "unoccupied" within the meaning of the Natural Resources Transfer Agreements, if it is declared a game preserve by the province (ibid.:323). In an Alberta case — based on precedents in Saskatchewan courts — it was ruled that the creation of a wildlife sanctuary by provincial regulation extinguished the hunting rights guaranteed by the Natural Resources Transfer Agreement (R. v. Twoyoungmen (1981), 10 Alta L.R. (2d) 15, affirming 6 Alta L.R. (2d) 220 (Dist. Ct.)). The wildlife sanctuary in question was the Sheep River Wildlife Sanctuary in Kananaskis Country which was set aside as critical winter habitat for 120 bighorn sheep. Three Stoney Indians were convicted of hunting offences after they killed a bighorn ram for food in the sanctuary.

Similarly, the creation of a National Park effectively prevents Indians from exercising their hunting rights. Decisions to this effect in the Prairie Provinces are at odds with certain Yukon cases that have held that mere scheduling of a tract of land as a game sanctuary does not constitute occupation. On the other hand, cases in Saskatchewan have maintained that forest preserves are considered unoccupied Crown land for the purpose of Indian hunting rights (Sanders 1973–74:55). Road corridor sanctuaries established by provincial governments remain another issue under constant debate (R. v. McIntyre [1991] 2 C.N.L.R.; *Calgary Herald*, February 28, 1990:B8).

The question whether leased Crown grazing land qualifies as "occupied land" was put to the test in Alberta courts in 1990. The case (R. v. Alexson [1990] 2 C.N.L.R. 98) involved George Alexson, a Treaty Indian who was charged with illegal possession of two elk shot on October 05, 1988, on leased grazing land southwest of Calgary (*Edmonton Journal*, February 4, 1990:A7). After having initially been acquitted by a provincial court justice in High River, on the basis of his hunting rights under the Natural Resources Transfer Agreement, he was convicted by a Court of Queen's Bench justice the following year.

Justice H.S. Prowse ruled that leased Crown grazing land is "occupied land," which gives lease holders the right to deny public access to it. The matter remains unresolved. After an appeal by Alexson, the Alberta Court of Appeal quashed his charges and ordered a new trial on the grounds that there was not enough evidence presented at the original trial to support a ruling whether grazing leases are occupied or unoccupied land.

The *Alexson* case attracted much attention not only from native groups, but also from the non-native public. Nearly 60 per cent of Alberta is publicly owned land covered by a variety of resource use agreements including grazing leases, cultivation leases, forest management agreements, mineral surface leases and others (*Edmonton Journal*, February 4, 1990:A7). Right of public access is spelled out in forest management agreements, but remains somewhat unclear in other Crown dispositions (*Calgary Herald*, April 4, 1990:A7). After the Alberta Court of Appeal decision, both sides claimed victory with Alexson vowing to continue hunting on Crown grazing land without permission, and the provincial government contending that ranchers are still empowered to order the public off their Crown grazing leases (*Calgary Herald*, April 5, 1990:A12).

Ironically, it appears that the real beneficiaries of *Alexson* are the licensed non-native hunters. When Alexson's counsel and Crown counsel filed their Factums (written summaries of their arguments), paragraph 10 of the Crown Factum contained what Bob Scammell terms a "short, amazing and historic sentence": "Hunting on land which is subject to a grazing lease is not an offence under the *Wildlife Act* or the *Public Lands Act* nor does it constitute trespass under the *Petty Trespass Act*." (Scammell 1990:14). But, the Crown goes on, a grazing leaseholder **might** be able to sue a "trespasser" civilly for damages, therefore, this possibility magically turns into an offence what provincial law seems to say is no offence (ibid.). To add to the confusion, the Crown also conceded in court that a licensed non-native hunter, lawfully in season, but without permission on this grazing lease, would not even have been charged (Scammell 1990:14; *Calgary Herald*, April 4, 1990). Why the court ordered a new trial remains an open question. The Alberta hunting lobby feels that, if there is a new trial, it will have to be limited to the native hunting question "of whether the unlicensed Indian, hunting for food, had the right to take the two elk with a rifle in a bow-only season." (Scammell 1990:14)

There is no common law right of access to private lands for the purpose of hunting. However, if the owner of a private land consents to hunting or does not object to it, a "right of access" within the meaning of the Agreements is established (Woodward 1989:321; Sanders 1973–74:55f).

As mentioned previously, **treaty hunting rights** usually extend only to the boundaries of the tract surrendered. The Douglas Treaties of Vancouver Island constitute an exception: The right guaranteed by these treaties to hunt "as formerly" includes the traditional hunting area of the tribe, even if it is located outside the tract surrendered (Woodward 1989:323).

It has been established in the courts that Treaty Indian hunting rights and those amalgamated by the Natural Resources Transfer Agreements prevail over provincial laws and regulations, but not over federal legislation or international treaties. The **Fisheries Act** includes regulations pertaining to marine mammals. The Beluga Protection Regulations afford native people (resident Indians, Inuit and persons of mixed blood) special access to belugas without a licence for domestic purposes. The Inuit are the only people permitted to hunt narwhal under the Narwhal Protection Regulations. Under the Seal Protection Regulations, native guides enjoy a monopoly on taking sport hunters hunting for seals in northern waters. And finally, under the Walrus Protection Regulations, native people are allowed to take walrus without a licence (ibid.:332f).

Besides the Fisheries Act, the **Migratory Birds Convention Act** is the other major federal piece of legislation that is relevant to native harvesting rights. Prior to the coming into force of s.35 of the Constitution Act, 1982, "it was clearly the law that the hunting of migratory birds by Indians, even if in exercise of an aboriginal right, was subject to controls imposed by Parliament." (Woodward 1989:334) The decisive case was *Regina v. Sikyea* [1964] S.C.R. 642, which dealt with the question whether the Migratory Birds Convention Act had taken away the treaty-protected hunting rights of an Indian in the Northwest Territories. With a decision that was subsequently upheld in the Supreme Court of Canada, the Appeals Court of the Northwest Territories ruled that the Migratory Birds Convention Act was inconsistent with the survival of native rights to hunt migratory birds: these rights had been extinguished (Sanders 1973–74:46).

In his ruling, Justice Johnson conceded that the Migratory Birds Convention Act constituted an "apparent breach of faith on the part of the government" which could not "be described as a minor or insignificant curtailment of these treaty rights, for game birds have always been a most plentiful, a most reliable and a readily obtainable food in large areas of Canada." (ibid.) After *Nowegijick* (1983) and *Simon* (1985), "The legal question at the heart of the controversy over abrogation of native hunting rights in Canada by the Migratory Birds Convention Act is 'legislative intent'". (Gottesman 1983:68) As Dan Gottesman notes, with regard to "legislative intent" the ruling remains entirely speculative.

> I cannot believe that the government of Canada realized that in implementing the Convention they were at the same time breaching the treaties made with the Indians. It is much more likely that these obligations were overlooked — a case of the left hand having forgotten what the right hand had done. (Justice Johnson, quoted in Gottesman 1983:69)

However, after a critical assessment of the political history of the Migratory Birds Treaty of 1916 between Canada and the United States and the Migratory Birds Convention Act of 1917, Gottesman concludes that there were, in fact, "clarity of motive and consistency of purpose." (Gottesman 1983:69) The Canadian policy-makers fully intended the Act to apply to native hunters and did not consider native rights a legal or moral obstacle to implementation.

> The wholesale sacrifice of North American wildlife to the passions of the capitalist marketplace was an exercise that, by the early twentieth century, was bound to recapitulate the range of anxieties that informed liberal society's conquest of a continent and domination (or annihilation) of its aboriginal peoples. These anxieties, heightened by guilt over the obvious costs to wildlife of over one hundred years of self-indulgent slaughter, generated an ideology of wildlife conservation that primarily served the psychological and economic interests of white "sport" hunters and their armourers. Native hunters were considered — and effects of their hunting "evaluated" — exclusively from this ethnocentric ideological perspective. The vices of the white hunter were simply written into the hunting of natives, and the solutions for one were automatically adopted as solutions for all. (ibid.:80f)

> The Act thus stands in the tradition of Canada's Indian Act as legislation of cultural deracination and disenfranchisement. (ibid.:85)

After the *Sikyea* decision other rulings, such as *Regina v. George* ([1966] S.C.R. 267) and *Regina v. Daniels* ([1968] S.C.R. 517), held that the Migratory Birds Convention Act applied to hunting activities on reserves as well as to Indian hunting rights in the Prairie Provinces under the Natural Resources Transfer Agreements (Sanders 1973–74:46f).

As a result of the coming into force of s.35 of the Constitution Act, 1982, however, there now may be limits to the applicability of the Act to native hunting. In many ways, the legal issues involved are identical with those which pertain to federal regulation of Indian fishing rights (Woodward 1989:334). In a discussion of constitutional issues, the Saskatchewan Justice Department comes to the following conclusion.

> As a result of the *Sparrow* decision there can be no doubt that the *Sikyea* case is no longer good law. The federal government can no longer override Treaty rights by ordinary legislation

> and regulations unless it meets the justificatory test set out in *Sparrow*. (Government of Saskatchewan 1990:10)

In *R. v. Eninew* (12 C.C.C. (3d) 365); *R. v. Bear* ([1984] 2 C.N.L.R. 126 (Sask. C.A.)), the Saskatchewan Court of Appeal found that s.35 does not exclude Indians from any "reasonable" conservation regulations under the Migratory Birds Convention Act (Woodward 1989:334). In his ruling, Justice Hall invoked the right to regulate contained in the Numbered Treaties.

> The rights so given were not unqualified or unconditional. In each case the right to pursue the avocation of hunting was subject to such regulations as may from time to time be made by the Government of Canada. Regulations made under the Migratory Birds Convention Act are the type of regulations which are contemplated in Treaties No.6 and No.10. The purpose of the Migratory Birds Convention Act is to conserve and preserve migratory birds including mallard ducks. (Government of Saskatchewan 1990:12)

The courts in Alberta and Manitoba have not been prepared to interpret the federal government's regulatory power as broadly. In both *R. v. Arcand*, [1989] 2 C.N.L.R. 110, (Alta. Q.B.) and *R. v. Flett*, [1989] 4 C.N.L.R. 128, (Man. Q.B.), it was decided that the regulations under the Migratory Birds Convention Act were not of the kind contemplated by the treaties. Both cases were appealed. As a result of the *Sparrow* decision, however, the Manitoba Court of Appeal refused to hear the Crown appeal in *Flett*. In October 1990 Manitoba stopped all charges against status Indians for violations of the Migratory Birds Convention Act and the Fisheries Act (Wagner 1991:26).

It is noteworthy that the reasoning in *R. v. Eninew*; *R. v. Bear* was expressly rejected by the Supreme Court of Canada in Sparrow.

> In *Eninew*, Hall J.A. found, at p.368, that "the Treaty rights can be limited by such regulations as are reasonable". As we have pointed out, management and conservation of resources is indeed an important and valid legislative objective. Yet, the fact that the objective is of a "reasonable" nature cannot suffice as constitutional recognition and affirmation of aboriginal rights. Rather, the regulations enforced pursuant to a conservation or management objective may be scrutinized according to the justificatory standard outlined above. (R. v. Sparrow [1990] 3 C.N.L.R.:186)

While this statement cannot be taken as expressly overruling *R. v. Eninew*; *R. v. Bear* (which dealt with "treaty" rather than "aboriginal" rights), it does imply that the Supreme Court of Canada may require a *Sparrow* type of analysis to determine if regulations are of the type contemplated by the treaties.

Whatever the legal outcome may eventually be, it appears that the Migratory Birds Convention Act has not been consistently enforced against native people, even before 1982. In the early 1970s D.E. Sanders remarked that "Michael Sikyea to this day believes that he won his case in the Supreme Court of Canada because no one restricts his rights to hunt" (Sanders 1973–74:61). In 1971, as a result of pressure from various native organizations, the federal government enacted a new set of Migratory Birds Regulations, which provided certain exemptions for Indians and Inuit. It appears that Indians and Inuit may hunt migratory game birds in any area of Canada, without a permit, but only during open season (Council for Yukon Indians 1984:431). A very important factor in the government's "tolerance" toward native hunting activities, such as spring hunting of waterfowl in the North, is without doubt the practical unenforceability of regulations under the Migratory Birds Convention Act, given the nature of harvesting activities (Berkes 1981:176). Government concessions on a practical or policy basis have always been easier to attain for aboriginal people than an explicit recognition of their rights.

The implementation of comprehensive claims agreements in the North has opened yet another venue to address the question of rights and legislation in a conciliatory, rather than confrontational manner. This is evidenced by the position of the Inuvialuit Wildlife Management Advisory Council with regard to migratory birds conservation in their settlement area. The American and Canadian federal governments are considering further adjustments to the hunting seasons, pursuant to the Migratory Birds Convention Act, and in anticipation of extensive public discussion of these amendments, the Wildlife Management Advisory Council has developed a set of principles, namely:

- conservation of migratory birds and their habitat is accorded highest priority;
- subsistence use by Inuvialuit is advocated subject to the conservation principle;
- a number of principles from the North American Waterfowl Management Plan are literally endorsed; and
- an overall approach characterized by "active communication and cooperation of all parties concerned" is recommended.

In its effort to establish general Inuvialuit by-laws, the Council consults with Inuvialuit communities and the Inuvialuit Game Council, as discussed later in this chapter, hoping to have the new government regulations and the community by-laws enacted simultaneously (Wildlife Management Advisory Council n.d.).

Implications of Native Hunting Rights

The constitutional development and the court rulings of the last decade have given rise to the emergence of new implications of native hunting rights. These implications have triggered hope and apprehension on the part of natives and non-natives respectively. After his 1978 ruling on the Stoney Indian hunting violations in the Sheep River Wildlife Sanctuary, Judge Cioni conceded that "traditional rights could be eroded by the sweep of a pen." (*Calgary Herald*, April 28, 1978). This opinion is no longer widely held. While the implications of the *Sparrow* decision for treaty rights (including rights under the Natural Resources Transfer Agreements) are far from clear, this matter is being given serious consideration by government departments and court judges (f.e. C.R. Fafard, P.C.J., in R. v. McIntyre [1991] 2 C.N.L.R.146).

> The recent decision of the Supreme Court of Canada in *Sparrow v. The Queen*...represents the dawn of a new era of judicial scrutiny of federal and provincial laws affecting the aboriginal peoples of Canada. The case provided the Court with its first opportunity to consider the meaning of section 35(1) of the Constitution Act, 1982, by which the existing aboriginal and Treaty rights of the aboriginal peoples of Canada were recognized and affirmed. As a result of the Court's decision many old rules with respect to the validity of these laws have disappeared and a new regime has been established in which laws affecting aboriginal and Treaty rights will have to be justified according to the test laid down by the Court. The effects of this decision will undoubtedly be seen first and foremost in the area of hunting and fishing regulation. (Government of Saskatchewan 1990:1)

As outlined in chapter 3, the justificatory test established by the Court is a two-step test designed to determine if any specific regulation affecting aboriginal or treaty rights is justified. The first step is the identification of a valid legislative objective, such as conservation and resource management, or the prevention of harm to society or to aboriginal peoples themselves. The Court makes it clear that the legislative objective must be "compelling and substantial" (R. v. Sparrow [1990] 3 C.N.L.R.:183).

The second step focuses on the question of whether the honour of the Crown in its dealings with aboriginal peoples is being upheld. The courts will consider the regulation in the light of the fiduciary obligations of the Crown to native people, and unless this standard is satisfied, the regulation will be invalid. Only valid conservation concerns are entitled to priority over the aboriginal right (R. v. Sparrow [1990] 3 C.N.L.R.:184).

It is generally understood that only federal legislation — such as the Fisheries Act or the Migratory Birds Convention Act — can possibly limit existing aboriginal and treaty rights. The *Sparrow* decision would, therefore, have no implications for the application of the Saskatchewan Wildlife Act, for example. As long as Indians are hunting for food on unoccupied Crown lands or other lands to which they have a right of access, they enjoy immunity from all provisions of the Act except those pertaining to public safety.

> Within this protected sphere of Indian hunting for food, no provincial game laws will be applicable, even game laws that could be justified as conservation measures pursuant to the *Sparrow* test. Indians hunting within the protection of paragraph 12 [of the Saskatchewan Natural Resources Transfer Agreement], could literally hunt a species into extinction and there is nothing that the Province could do. The responsibility to enact laws to protect endangered species that will be applicable to Indian hunting lies solely with the federal government. Conversely, if an Indian is hunting outside the protection of paragraph 12, he is subject to all of the provisions of The Wildlife Act and there is no need to justify those provisions on the basis of the *Sparrow* test or any other test. (Government of Saskatchewan 1990:8)

There are, however, "grey areas" in the application of provincial wildlife laws to Treaty Indians hunting for food, and it is in these "grey areas" that some court judges are looking to the *Sparrow* ruling to help them establish a new frame of reference. One of these twilight zones surrounds the question of the provinces' power to convert "unoccupied Crown land" into "occupied Crown land" and to deny Treaty Indians access to lands to which they used to have a right of access. The ruling on *R. v. McIntyre* provides an example. In this case a Treaty Indian was charged under the Wildlife Act with unlawful possession of wildlife, which was taken within a Road Corridor Game Preserve in northern Saskatchewan. In his decision in favour of the accused, Provincial Court Judge C.R. Fafard employs the *Sparrow* justificatory test to the question: "Did the Crown in creating this Road Corridor Game Preserve occupy the land in a constitutionally valid manner, that is, in a manner which respects the fiduciary duty of the Crown towards the Indians and which does not bring dishonour to the Crown." (R. v. McIntyre [1991] 2 C.N.L.R.:154f). Judge Fafard concluded that the provincial Crown failed this test by having neglected to consult with the Indians, who were the group most severely affected by the road corridor, and to grant them priority to the moose population available after conservation measures over resident and foreign sport hunters.[2]

The scope of constitutional protection of treaty and aboriginal rights is not the only contentious issue in current discussions; the very substance of native rights to the wildlife resource is anything but clearly defined to the satisfaction of native people.

> These existing aboriginal rights are limited only by the capacity of what the land and sea can produce, and defined again by the laws of nature and common sense which ensure we sustain those rights through successive generations. Degeneration of the land and sea will further reduce our rights; therefore we have a moral obligation to defend our resources and determine the fate of our tribal territories. (Percy Williams, Grand Chief of the Haida Nation, 1981, quoted in Pinkerton 1983:68)

These words make it very clear that native people view their rights to natural resources, such as wildlife and fish, as more than just a limited right of access for narrowly defined purposes. Barry Barton (1985:19) expresses the opinion that without adequate habitat protection, hunting, fishing and trapping rights would be useless, and that therefore Treaty

---

[2] N.F. McIntyre was later convicted by the Court of Queen's Bench [1992] 1 C.N.L.R. 129; his appeal was dismissed by the Saskatchewan Court of Appeal [1992] 3 C.N.L.R. 113; and his application for leave to appeal to the Supreme Court of Canada was denied.

Indians must possess implied rights to prevent damage to wildlife habitat. This interpretation is confirmed by the United States Boldt Decision (see chapter 3).

> The problem is that, with few exceptions, native people have no recognized legal interest in the resources on which they have relied historically. Aboriginal and treaty hunting rights have been viewed as providing the barest of interest in the land. All they mean, it turns out, is that the Indian or Inuk who is hunting or fishing on unoccupied Crown land is not actually trespassing (although he may be violating the game laws). The overseas oil company granted an exploration permit yesterday has greater standing before the law than the Indian whose ancestors used and occupied the land for 10,000 years. The reason is that such devices as the Dominion Lands Act, the Territorial Lands Act, and the Canada Oil and Gas Act, were all intended to convey rights in land from the Crown to individuals. All the while, aboriginal rights, which preceded those of the Crown, were never properly codified so as to give their holders a legally enforceable and practically useful defence. (Usher 1984:406f)

In the meantime, native people have interpreted the Constitution Act of 1982 and *Sparrow* as a means to defend their right to wildlife and fisheries not only against other parties with an interest in the same resources, but also against parties that have been granted competing interests in the land.

> One principle reinforced in *Sparrow* is that any regulation of or infringement upon aboriginal resource use requires consultation with the aboriginal peoples affected. If there is a loss of Aboriginal or Treaty rights, compensation must be considered.
>
> This is my understanding of the meaning of *Sparrow* and other recent case law as it bears on the issues before us.
>
> The Treaties provided for lands which may be taken up for settlement, mining and lumbering. The Treaties also assured that our right to hunt, fish and trap would remain unimpaired and we would be as free to hunt, fish and trap as we were before the Treaty: this is one of the rights that the Constitution Act and *Sparrow* recognized and affirmed.
>
> These assurances of the continuance of our vocations on the land, combined with the provision providing for the use of Crown lands for lumbering, say to me that the degree, nature and extent of any lumbering must be **consistent** with these rights and our use of resources.
>
> The degree, nature and extent of Repap's proposed operations in our area are not consistent with our rights and existing uses of land....
>
> Your proposals run contrary to the values of Aboriginal people: the government sees economic development, while we see land abuse. The Constitution Act is designed to protect our interests in a nation where these differences in values exist. The priority of the Province is forest harvesting; our priority is wildlife and the fishery.
>
> ...Treaty rights have been established as priority allocations which are protected in the Natural Resources Transfer Act and the Constitution Act and confirmed and further defined in *Sparrow*. Ensuring the protection of our rights in terms of Repap's plans must be dealt with on a bi-lateral basis. It is the responsibility of the Province to ensure that our rights are not further impaired. (Nepinak 1991a:1–4, emphasis in original)

This situation of competing land uses described by Chief Harvey Nepinak of the Waterhen First Nation in northern Manitoba recalls Daishowa and Alpac in northern Alberta, where the life of northern native communities is being disrupted by pulp mill developments and the disposition of huge tracts of land in forest management agreements. Peter Usher feels that the position of aboriginal people in such situations will only be strengthened if there is a fundamental change in the nature of property rights.

> A proprietary interest need not require full ownership of land in fee simple title, or of the resources themselves. A grant of interest in certain resources, in this case fish and wildlife, would suffice, but such a grant must carry with it something akin to a right of profit à prendre. This means not simply the right to hunt and fish, nor even the sole right to do

> so in the area of the grant, but also the right to enjoy the fruit (or "profit") of these resources, which is in principle measurable and predictable.
>
> Such an interest is an enforceable claim on that land, which cannot simply be ignored when the Crown expropriates the interest, or grants a competing interest to a third party, or when a third party interferes with the interest. It puts the native hunter or fisherman on an equal footing with the holder of an oil and gas exploration permit or a mineral claim.
>
> This arrangement is in stark contrast to the conventional system of hunting and trapping rights in which the licence holder (whether native or non-native) is deemed to have no interest in the land or resources as such, but a property right only in a fish or animal once it has been taken. If there are no longer any fish or animals to be taken, no right has been interfered with. What is proposed here is simply to raise hunting and trapping rights from the lowest form of interest in land to a higher, proprietary one. (Usher 1984:411)

Usher emphasizes, however, that there are two important differences between the concept proposed here and a conventional right of profit. Firstly, the notion of profit à prendre must encompass the subsistence interest. It must be recognized that subsistence resources represent value to aboriginal people, and that their loss has consequences that are, at least in part, measurable and compensable. (ibid.)

Secondly, these grants would have to be made on the basis of aboriginal title rather than the Crown's prerogative to maximize the revenue from its assets. Such grants would serve as the means by which a particular group is entitled to pursue its legitimate interests as recognized by the Crown, rather than the means by which the Crown implements economic development policy. (ibid.:412)

During the last decade native people have made it very clear that their stake in the wildlife resource is not adequately represented and protected by "hunting rights" in as narrow a sense as conventionally interpreted and enforced by governments and the courts.

> In the modern day native hunting rights must accomplish three practical ends. First, they should provide native peoples with a proprietary interest that constitutes an enforceable claim against all others. Secondly, they should provide a fair and effective system for compensation in the event of nuisance or trespass by a third party, or expropriation by the Crown. Thirdly, they should provide a framework within which local customary law can operate with respect to the harvesting and management of resources and within which native peoples can have effective input to the policies and administration that affect their interest in the resource base. (ibid.:411)

FUR-BEARER HARVESTING

Significance of Native Fur Harvesting

The trapping and hunting of fur-bearing animals is an activity of crucial importance for native people. The Canadian fur industry is one major industrial sector of the national economy, which allows native people to participate on a large scale and in a way which is socially and culturally relevant to them. While estimates of native participation in trapping are not entirely conclusive, Henderson and Herscovici (Todd and Boggess 1987:60) estimate the figure to be 50 and 60 per cent respectively. Publications of the Fur Institute of Canada and native organizations also give figures within this range. Considering the fact that native people constitute less than 5 per cent of Canada's total population, they show a singularly high participation in trapping.

This participation is highest in northern Canada. In the Northwest Territories, native people are by far the predominant group involved in trapping; in Yukon there is also a sizeable proportion of non-native trappers. One of the most important aspects of the fur harvest for aboriginal people is that it serves to capitalize the domestic economy as a whole. There are many misconceptions about the wild fur harvest in the North, misconceptions that are largely based on the different way in which trapping is perceived by aboriginal and non-aboriginal societies. For aboriginal peoples, trapping is usually just one component of their domestic economy (which has traditionally been described as "subsistence").

According to Peter Usher (1989:1), the domestic economy in the Northwest Territories consists of the harvesting (i.e. hunting, trapping, fishing and gathering) and processing activities by which people provide food, fuel, and other materials and services for household needs. These same activities also generate cash, such as the sale of furs and commercial fishing, and are often subsidized by other cash sources, such as occasional or seasonal wage work and government transfer payments. As a whole this type of economy is subsistence, rather than market-oriented and has a distinctive resource and cultural base.

In contrast, some observers consider trapping as a distinct, essentially commercial, and indeed imported activity, not as an integrated part of a coherent bush economy and society (Hutchins 1987:44). For this reason, opponents of trapping sometimes cite the small trapping incomes obtained by most trappers as evidence that trapping is no longer important or viable, but rather an anachronism that should be done away with as soon as possible. Such conclusion ignores the value of meat from fur-bearers, such as food, the personal use of furs and hides for clothing and handicrafts, and the low cost of living associated with the lifestyles of many trappers. It also disregards the fact that many native people prefer subsistence-oriented lifestyles to the regimentation of wage employment or the emptiness of social assistance. Testimony at the 1975 Berger Inquiry (Mackenzie Valley Pipeline Inquiry) left little doubt, that northern native people view their renewable resource-based domestic economy not only as a link with their past, but also as a basis for their aspirations for the future.

While there are trappers — both native and non-native — who derive their entire livelihood from the harvest of wild furs, this is the exception. Most trappers rely on another source (or other sources) of income, such as farming, commercial fishing, labour jobs or government transfer payments. Many trappers derive their entire winter income from trapping and then work at seasonal summer jobs. The total income to trappers from raw furs has ranged in recent years from $50 to 85 million (Fur Institute of Canada 1985). The few available estimates of gross annual incomes from trapping in different parts of Canada reveal that income means range from $533 to $1,596. Peak earnings in the range of $20,000 to 40,000 are the exception; such commercial trappers must be exceptionally skillful and well equipped, and high pelt prices would have had to coincide with high fur-bearer population levels.

It should be noted, however, that the trapping lifestyle, particularly in the North, has an economic value beyond revenue from fur sales. In such subsistence-oriented lifestyle a little income from trapping can go a long way. While living and working on the trapline, trappers often obtain other wild game as well as fur-bearers for food. The economic importance of the meat of fur-bearing animals for human consumption is great among native trappers; the most important species being beaver, muskrat, lynx and snowshoe hare. Meat obtained in this manner is also used as bait and dog food. Fur and leather goods are made for commercial and personal use.

Unfortunately, native trappers who pursue trapping as part of their domestic economy experience numerous problems in marketing their wild furs, and tend to by-pass auction houses (and optimum prices) to sell through private contract. Trappers lack organization at the community level (fur marketing co-ops), have few opportunities for trapper education (pelt preparation) and have little knowledge of the fur industry in general (Maracle 1988:12). Another obstacle is the requirement in most jurisdictions to have a trapping permit and a registered trapline. This requirement automatically captures the trapper in the web of income taxation. Payment of income tax is a drain on the very limited cash output of domestic activities. Thus the whole regulatory system of trapping and the marketing of wild furs and its resultant "paper trail" sometimes serve as a disincentive for trappers to market their furs at auction for the maximum possible price.

The importance of wild fur harvesting is reinforced by the fact that fur ranching has failed to establish itself in the North. In 1989 a fox farm was operating on an experimental basis in Eskimo Point, but prospects for development did not appear very bright (Usher 1989:43). As Peter Usher indicates, farming of fox or mink would require large quantities of local seal and fish. In order to be competitive, this feed would have to be purchased at very low prices that they would not be attractive to hunters. Imported feed supplements, such as cereals, would raise expenses considerably for northern producers. Given the well-known volatility of the fur market, the risk factor would be extremely high, since as high-cost producers they would be the first to disappear during market declines.

Some fox and mink ranching has recently been initiated by aboriginal people in Ontario (Richard Maracle, personal communication, December 6, 1989). One example is a fox ranch started on the Wikwemikong Reserve on Manitoulin Island in 1988. The ranch started with 600 foxes and is expected to expand to a capacity of 2,000 animals (*Northern Ontario Business*, February 1988). Another private fox ranch was initiated on the Nipissing Indian Reserve in 1988. The operators are hoping to reach soon a capacity for 300 foxes (Gabe Ferrazzi, personal communication, December 1989).

Native Trapping Rights in Jeopardy

Recent comprehensive land claims negotiations in the North have addressed the issue of trapping within the context of aboriginal economies with more clairvoyance and understanding than in the past. Nevertheless, indigenous trappers in Canada still find their rights inadequately protected by the law when faced with threats, such as regulatory restrictions imposed by provincial or federal legislation, or pressures on the land base and resources caused by competing and incompatible land uses. Until recently native trappers have been denied clear recognition of individual enforceable rights, both under aboriginal and treaty rights on one hand, and under government regulation and general property law on the other.

Since the 1930s a wide range of administrative and legislative measures have been introduced in Canada to ensure the responsible management of fur-bearer populations. Within a framework of registered and resident trapping areas, trappers are licensed or given permits by provincial authorities and, in most areas, royalties must be paid for fur-bearers which are taken. The money collected from licences and royalties helps pay for the scientific monitoring and control of wildlife. Royalties and licences also provide the basic statistical data which enable biologists to monitor trapping trends.

The most important management tool at the disposal of provincial fur managers is the regulation of trapping seasons. It ensures that fur-bearing animals are trapped only when their fur is "prime", allowing trappers to receive the best possible price for their efforts while preventing a waste of animal life for pelts with little market value. Controlled trapping seasons, moreover, allow fur managers to "fine-tune" wildlife management: Generally, the goal of good trapping is to take a high proportion of young male animals, which least affects the overall population strength.

Setting of quotas is another important management tool. Beavers, who are vulnerable because of their sedentary habits and whose colonies are easily detected, are the main example of quota management in Canada. With their high reproductive rates and few natural predators, however, they also pose the other side of the management problem: Too high populations can damage the habitat for themselves as well as other species. Therefore, trappers are often obliged to trap at least a minimum portion of their assigned quota, or it may be given to another trapper. Highly cyclical animal populations, such as lynx, must also be carefully managed with a quota system (Fur Institute of Canada 1986). Despite the improvement in scientific monitoring and fine-tuned management, trapping remains an activity with extremely volatile and variable returns.

When registered traplines were first introduced, this was purportedly done for the protection of wildlife and native interests. With regard to the latter, the effect was exactly the opposite, and native people viewed these measures as an open breach of their treaties.

> The decision in the 1930s to register traplines was viewed by government as a preferred solution to the problems of invasion of traditional lands and the growing problems between the Ft. McKay people and the "newcomers". The people of Ft. McKay view the registered trapline system as the first major attack by other governments to administer their lives and restrict them from practising their economy and culture. This system as well as reserves were promoted as being for their benefit but in fact they were to institutionalize and legitimize the presence of non-Indians within McKay territories and have contributed to the consistent erosion of their rights guaranteed by Treaty 8 and have restricted them in how they use their territory. (Fort McKay Band et al. 1983:9)

When the first registration of "lines" was undertaken, many band members were unable to secure registered lines "due to the bureaucratic slowness of Indian Affairs in protecting their areas from the encroachment of outsiders who had their money ready when registration was opened." (ibid.) As a result, traplines in the Fort McKay traditional territory were registered to non-Indians from as far away as Edmonton and Red Deer, while band members who had lost their lines had to double and triple up on traplines in the poorest part of their traditional area.

Hugh Brody describes similar developments for northeastern British Columbia during the 1920s to 1930s, where the whole region was divided into traplines, "the hunting equivalent to individual farms." (Brody 1981:90) He contrasts the native and non-native concepts of trapping land use.

> White settlers and trappers had clear notions of orderly land use that were based on well-tried patterns of frontier homesteading. They imagined that a trapping area they had claimed would be theirs alone, an area where they would have an exclusive right to harvest furs. The Indians' system was based on freedom of access, flexible use, and rotational conservation, which meant that some areas went untrapped for seasons on end. (ibid.:87)

The issue of conservation calls to mind another contrast. During the 1920s and 1930s, as a result of the Depression, the majority of white trappers in the North were itinerants who took up trapping as others had earlier joined the gold rushes (ibid.). As Father René Fumoleau puts it, "a white trapper was a stripper. He took all he could and left nothing behind. He was a transient ready to leave as soon as he had made his stake or found that it did not pay him to stay." (O'Malley 1976:129)

Another major disruption for native trappers in northern Alberta occurred in the 1960s, when the registered trapline system was "switched over" from linear traplines along creeks to registered trapping areas. Once again, this move occurred without native consultation and was viewed by local bands as another means of restriction and encroachment.

> First, more trappers could be squeezed into "areas" to accommodate the flood of requests from the growing population of Ft. McMurray, and from farther south, who wanted to trap in an area that was already overcrowded from the point of view of people at Ft. McKay. However, more revenue could be gained from licensing and fur taxes in this system. Secondly, the idea was prompted by Forestry and subsequently Fish and Wildlife (both Alberta government agencies) who took over its administration in 1970, that with "areas" the trapper was better able to manage and conserve the animals in his area by adapting his harvesting and shifting his trapping within the boundaries of its legal definition on the map. Further study of the problems within the registered trapping areas that are held by McKay people have [sic] revealed that the majority of their traplines have been infringed upon in a variety of ways, including: direct destruction of habitat by forestry roads; logging, seismic or truck

> trails; oil sands exploration lines and drill sites; campsites; airstrips and helipads; rights of way for pipeline or electric transmission and the like. (Fort McKay Band et al. 1983:13)

When trapline registration began in the early decades of this century, aboriginal people viewed the application of the system as a breach of their treaty rights. Over half a century later, by a strange twist of history, registered traplines have acquired a very profound meaning for native groups in the Treaty Eight area of British Columbia, as poignantly described by Hugh Brody.

> Even if a family is not using it, their trapline's existence through fallow years is a source of real security: it is important because it is there. Registered traplines are far more than areas in which an Indian can make money from furs; they are a stake in the land and its future. Moreover, the traplines taken together constitute a land base away from the reserve and, for nearly all reserves, traplines represent a large proportion of a hunting territory....For some individuals the fight in defence of a trapline is a fight for the possibility of making money from furs. For everyone, active trapper or not, it has become a struggle for the right to be an Indian. By twists of history and confusion over realities, the trapline has come to mean to the Indians something tantamount to the terms of the Treaty. Although they continue to insist upon and to exercise their right to hunt on Crown land wherever they can, it is registered traplines that they hold to be especially and irreversibly theirs. For a long time, the government had led them to believe this....For them it is the bitterest of ironies, therefore, to be told that in Canadian law, registered traplines grant no hunting rights and no protection against other activities that would destroy the wildlife on them. Only if the term "trapline" is fortified by the meanings that the Indians give the word can the importance of their traplines be grasped. (Brody 1981:98f)

One would logically assume with Alan Herscovici that registered traplines represent the Indians' strongest *de facto* claim to their traditional territories (Herscovici 1985:155f). But, paradoxically, the concept of registered traplines has failed native people just as miserably in the courts as out on the land. One example for this is found in the injunction proceedings on the James Bay project during the early 1970s (Chief Robert Kanatewat et al. v. James Bay Development Corporation et al. (15 November 1973) Montreal 05-04841-72 (C.S.), reported as Chef Max "One-Onti" Gros Louis c. Societé de développement de la Baie James, [1974] R.P.38). The Cree and Inuit petitioners seeking an injunction referred to the extensive coverage of the territory in question by traplines and to their links with historic family hunting territories.

The Quebec government and the Crown corporations, on the other hand, argued that the beaver-preserve system and the traplines had been instituted by the province during the 1930s, in response to resource depletion and with a view to assisting the Indian population. Because the government had formally established the system and was administering it, they argued, this was evidence for an abandonment of traditional ways and an administrative presence in the territory incompatible with the survival of aboriginal title.

Justice Malouf ruled in favour of the petitioners, citing the importance of trapping in the territory as evidence of the native dependence on the land. The Quebec Court of Appeal overturned this judgement, and it supported the government argument to the effect that the presence of a trapline system in the territory constituted an administrative presence by government incompatible with the continued existence of an aboriginal title (Societé de développement de la Baie James et al. c. Chef Robert Kanatewat et al. [1975] C.A. 166) (Hutchins 1987:33f). This matter was never ruled upon by the Supreme Court of Canada, as a result of the out-of-court settlement and execution of the James Bay and Northern Quebec Agreement in 1975. The *Bear Island* case (1985) provides a similar example of judicial irony, with the court inferring, that historical existence of family hunting territories implies "lack of organized society" and that contemporary existence of traplines implies "extinguishment" (Hutchins 1987:34).

There exist considerably more court decisions on fishing, the hunting of big game and the hunting of migratory birds by aboriginal people than on native trapping. Peter Hutchins (1987:31) hypothesizes that this may be attributed to a greater acceptance of legal constraints by aboriginal trappers, possibly as a result of underestimating the extent of legal protection available. Legal dissension over trapping has mostly focused on three points: the commercial aspect of trapping (perceived as divorced from subsistence activities), the question of its "aboriginality", and, finally, the individual (as opposed to collective) interest of a trapper in his/her trapline. While there are still unresolved problems, the 1980s have witnessed some encouraging developments.

First, there has been a growing tendency in the courts to acknowledge that barter, exchange and trade prevailed in aboriginal economies at the time of the historical treaties and that, as a result, treaties should be interpreted as recognizing and protecting the right to conduct these activities (ibid.:45). Contemporary treaties, such as the James Bay and Northern Quebec Agreement (1975) and the Inuvialuit Final Agreement (1984), explicitly recognize the commercial component of harvesting activities. Logically, this acceptance of a commercial component should apply not only to "treaty rights" but also to "aboriginal rights" recognized by the treaties. Both are recognized and affirmed by the Canadian Constitution.

Similarly, present-day legal doctrine, case law, and treaties seem to be accepting the long-standing pre-contact existence of a system of discrete hunting territories on the basis of anthropological evidence. These hunting territories were by no means, or indeed, are fixed parcels of real estate with frozen boundaries, but rather have to be understood as components of a dynamic system of changing people-land relationships based on effective occupation and use. The crucial point is that the system of discrete family hunting territories predates attempts by the government to "organize" both aboriginal and non-aboriginal trapping activity through the establishment of "registered traplines." (ibid.:45)

Finally, there remains the question, whether an individual interest survives the abolition of aboriginal title. In this context, the courts increasingly appear prepared to recognize a particular legal interest of a trapper in his or her trapline distinct from a public interest. In common law provinces and territories (i.e. everywhere in Canada except Quebec where, however, an equivalent is likely to exist), this individual interest is referred to by the notion of profit à prendre. The term refers to the right to take something, such as fish and game, off the land of another person. It is a right independent of ownership in the land and can be transferred. This legal concept accurately describes the interest of a trapper taking wild fur from a trapline or hunting territory situated on Crown or other lands and is clearly distinguished from a licence (ibid.:43).

> For all trappers, whether operating in a government-registered system or an aboriginal system, a recognition of an independent right in land rather than a tolerance through licence implies the ability to enforce the right against trespass or nuisance and, at least in the case of indigenous systems, to transfer traplines in accordance with traditional practice. Finally, as independent, transferable rights in land, trapline and trapping rights acquire an economic value that may be invoked in injunction or nuisance proceedings. (ibid.)

Animal Rights versus Native Rights

While native rights to harvest wild furs are being slowly and painfully defined within the Canadian legal and political system, aboriginal people are faced with another adversary more ominous and elusive than the State: the animal rights movement. The animal rights movement, or more specifically the anti-fur movement, poses a threat to the entire Canadian fur industry and rocks the very foundations of northern native domestic economies. This is a lesson already learnt at great expense by central and eastern arctic Inuit communities.

Commercial sealskin production was an important industry and, in many arctic villages, virtually the only source of cash income, besides government transfer payments. In the late 1960s, sparked by the controversy over the Newfoundland harp seal hunt, animal rights organizations launched a highly emotional campaign against seal hunting in general. This protest, primarily directed at stopping a non-native, commercial-industrial kill of newborn harp seals (whitecoats) in the waters of Atlantic Canada, had disastrous social and economic consequences for arctic villagers who used to hunt mature ringed seals.

According to George Wenzel, the ringed seal, in the Canadian central and eastern arctic, constitutes the single most reliable food-money resource species available throughout the winter to coast-dwelling Inuit. Within their "mixed economy", ringed seal harvesting could account for as much as 71 per cent of all utilizable biomass and 54 per cent of harvest-related cash income (Wenzel 1986:69, 71f). The 1982 European Community's voluntary boycott of all seal product imports resulted in the near-total collapse of the arctic sealing industry. This happened at a time when a broad external market for ringed seal pelts was just being developed, an important occurrence for the Inuit in view of the need to replace arctic fox — never an abundant or reliable resource — as an exportable commodity (ibid.:72). The Kitikmeot and especially the Baffin region were the most adversely affected areas, with fur dollars and income reduced by about 50 per cent in 1981–82 and further diminished by the same percentage in 1982–83 (Government of the NWT 1986:78). About 1,500 Inuit hunters and their families were involved; many were forced to leave the land for an uncertain future in communities with little wage employment. Loss of economic self-sufficiency and social alienation have resulted in an escalation of social and health problems.

> The effects of these campaigns are not simply the loss of cash income. The secondary effects on lifestyle and standard of living are far more dramatic. The sale of furs is how Native hunters finance their hunting. A modern hunting culture needs a cash input to support itself. An Inuit seal hunter, for example, needs at least $10,000 a year in order to go seal hunting. The same equipment he uses in the commercial hunt is used to hunt species whose only value is for food and domestic use for clothing and other basic necessities. This is a continuation and adaptation of a lifestyle that has supported Native people in the North for thousands of years. (Sibbeston 1986:154)

Travelling in the Pond Inlet area, David Pelly observed the effects on Baffin Island.

> It was the same in every camp we visited: at least one of the hunters had a wife back in town who was earning money to support the hunt. It is a formula that works, but it is possible for only a limited number of Pond Inlet's families. There are simply not enough jobs to go around.
>
> It used to be different. "Ten years ago," remembered Panipakoocho, "I saved and cleaned every sealskin to sell. I got about $35 a skin, enough to buy gas and bullets for the next trip." Since the collapse of the sealskin market following the 1983 European ban on imports of some pelts (particularly those of white-coat harp seal less than two weeks old), under one percent of the income in Pond Inlet comes from sealskin. The meat is still needed, but many of the skins are simply thrown away. Hunting is no longer a self-supporting operation. (Pelly 1991:48f)

After the destruction of the sealing industry the protest movement has expanded into a campaign against the fur trade in general. Among those involved were the International League for Animal Rights, I KARE Wildlife Coalition, International Fund for Animal Welfare, Greenpeace International, Animal Defense League and other organizations, supported by a generation of urban Europeans and Americans whose lives had been almost totally divorced from experience of the land and its resources. They united in a demand that the killing of fur-bearing animals be stopped. Graphic films, urban guerilla tactics, and a well-orchestrated and emotionally loaded political campaign made their mark. Great Britain has traditionally been the most vocal advocate of anti-fur politics, but British actions have tended to create a domino effect in other European countries, including Germany and Switzerland, the most important European markets for Canadian furs.

In 1988 pressure was brought to bear on the European Community (EC) to label all wild furs with a tag indicating that the animal may have been captured in a steel-jawed trap. A "cruelty" label, in other words (*Toronto Star*, April 4, 1990:B1). The British government announced its intention to go ahead with the tagging, despite protests from native leaders and then External Affairs Minister Joe Clark. While this plan never passed through the final stages of House of Commons approval, a precursor of the current EC Regulation on the importation of wild fur was introduced in the European Parliament in the same year. It was at one time intended to take effect in 1992, but then postponed to 1995.

Regulation No. 3254/91 in its current format was adopted by the Council of European Communities on November 4, 1991. One of its key elements is the provision that wild fur pelts and goods can be introduced into the Community only if it has been determined that the exporting country has in place

> (i) adequate administrative or legislative provisions to prohibit the use of the leghold trap;
>
> or
>
> (ii) trapping methods that meet internationally agreed upon humane trapping standards. (Standing Committee on Aboriginal Affairs 1993:10)

Initial drafts of the Regulation would have required exporting countries to comply with both conditions, but the preposition "and" was replaced by the preposition "or", an important modification which somewhat eased the requirements. The Regulation fails, however, to define "humane trapping standards", and it also appears that items (i) and (ii) are not mutually exclusive (ibid.:11). Even if these questions are resolved, Canada faces considerable political, legislative and practical challenges in meeting the 1995 deadline (which may be extended to 1996).

Native people have learnt from the experience of the anti-sealing campaign and are launching their own counterprotest. The cornerstone of their defence is Indigenous Survival International (ISI), "born out of the battle of the seals" as ISI Communications Director Cindy Gilday puts it (*Toronto Star*, June 11, 1988). Formed in 1984 as an alliance of aboriginal peoples from Canada, Alaska and Greenland, the organization is dedicated to preserving native harvesting rights and maintaining a market for fur and fur products. It also endeavours to relay the indigenous trapping message overseas and has succeeded in convincing Greenpeace to withdraw from the antiharvest movement. Although there is some scepticism about the wholeheartedness of Greenpeace's action, the move was a considerable political success for ISI (House of Commons 1986:50). In February 1990 ISI arranged a tour for an EC fact-finding delegation consisting of five members of the European Parliament, who came to Canada to learn about and experience trapping first-hand. This tour fostered somewhat revised opinions in the European Parliament on indigenous peoples and trapping, and was instrumental in reducing the original breadth of the EC Regulation and in delaying its implementation deadline (Standing Committee on Aboriginal Affairs 1993:10).

In 1985 the Aboriginal Trappers Federation of Canada (ATFC) was established to provide an umbrella organization for aboriginal hunters and trappers associations across the country. While ISI concentrates on counteracting the international antifur campaign, ATFC works at the domestic level to involve Canadian aboriginal trappers in the fur debate and to educate the Canadian public. More recent efforts have also been extended into the United States (Executive Director Bob Stevenson, personal communication, December 1989). The potentially valuable role of this organization is hampered by lack of funding and understaffing.

In its early stages, the anti-fur movement had been strongly focused on opposition to the leghold trap, which had been the principal holding device used by trappers since the

1800s. The perceived cruelty of this trap has been the subject of limited but persistent Canadian campaigns since the 1940s. The latest round of protest is not being taken lightly by the fur industry, as indicated by the establishment of the Fur Institute of Canada (FIC) in 1983. The membership of the FIC includes the processing, manufacturing and retailing sectors; trappers and ranchers; aboriginal groups; federal and provincial governments; and wildlife conservation and animal welfare organizations. Funds are provided by government, the industry (through the International Fur Trade Federation and the Fur Council of Canada) and the trappers (through a levy on the price received for pelts sold at public auction). The FIC promotes trapper education, often in cooperation with provincial trappers associations, and coordinates research and development of improved humane trapping systems. It administers a major humane trap research program, with principal facilities at the Alberta Environmental Centre at Vegreville, near Edmonton.

By the late 1980s the FIC had developed a set of trapping standards which are being incorporated in trapping legislation in every province and territory. These standards include the use of "humane" traps like the fast-killing Conibear trap, the prohibition of traps with metal teeth or metal serrated edges, restriction of foot-holding devices to larger species, more frequent checking of live-holding devices, mandatory trappers' education for novice trappers, and numerous other provisions (*Trappers News*, Spring 1990). In the Northwest Territories these standards are being phased in during the early 1990s, with the GNWT Department of Renewable Resources providing financial and technical assistance, trap exchange programs and trappers' education.

Native reaction to legislation and regulation of humane trapping technology has been mixed, since they are viewed as another infringement upon native rights. According to Dennis Cromarty (1988), a court case in northern Ontario has put in doubt the applicability of Ontario Ministry of Natural Resources humane trapping regulations in the case of Treaty Indians. As a result of this case, the Ontario Ministry of Natural Resources has discontinued the enforcement of the regulations against Treaty Indian trappers. While this is viewed as a victory for the treaty right to trap, the Nishnawbe-Aski Nation advised its member bands to proceed with great caution in their reaction to this ruling. It also took steps to educate the bands about the implications of the non-enforcement of the Ontario Ministry of Natural Resources humane trapping regulations (ibid.:38).

An ominous indicator for the future of trapping and the fur industry as a whole is the fact that increasingly the opposition to trapping appears to be based on ethical objections to killing animals, rather than on concerns about specific trapping methods. Just as the anti-sealing campaign started out as a conservation issue revolving around the question of whether the seal population was endangered (harp and ringed seals are not) and ended in total condemnation of killing any seals, the anti-leghold trap crusade is developing into a campaign that destroys the consumer market for furs and a general attack on any human use of fur-bearers (House of Commons 1986:41ff).

Alan Herscovici points out the short-sightedness of such campaigns.

> One of the most unfortunate aspects of the animal rights movement is that it unconsciously serves the interest of the mining, oil and gas and hydroelectric industries, which would like nothing better than to clear traditional hunters and trappers from the land. (Herscovici 1985:208)

It appears that the controversy calls for a reassessment of our place in nature.

> ...the greatest danger the philosophy of such groups pose [sic] is the concerted effort to separate humans, wildlife, and environment. They do not understand that in their desire to protect animals, they are destroying culture, spiritual and economic systems which have allowed humans and wildlife to be sustained over thousands of years. The western concept of protecting wildlife is only a hundred years old and the Animals First concept is only decades

> old. Theirs is based upon a belief that animals and humans are separate and they project human values unto animals. Ours is based upon the knowledge from hundreds of generations which allows us to understand that humans are part of all living things — and all living things are part of us. (Larry Merculieff, Commissioner of the Sea Otter Commission, at the ISI Sixth Annual Assembly, Anchorage, August 1990, reprinted in *IWGIA Newsletter* 62:12)

COMMERCIALIZATION OF WILDLIFE

Game Ranching

> Game ranching, without distinction as to type, is being advertised today as being a more efficient means of raising superior meat. It is praised as a means of diversifying a lagging farm economy, of making "marginal" lands productive, of giving "land to the landless", of putting land cheaply into the economic cycle, of creating jobs, of getting rid of native hunters from public land, of being a tool of conservation, and of saving "gene pools". (Valerius Geist, quoted in Keith and Saunders 1989:70)

This commentary by Valerius Geist[3] aptly summarizes the arguments put forward by proponents of the industry, an industry which since the 1980s has increasingly found itself the subject of one of the most serious environmental controversies in the Prairie Provinces. So far aboriginal people have mostly remained "sitting on the fence" of the game ranching issue, although the Indian Association of Alberta decided in 1990 to unanimously oppose the provincial government's plan to legalize the sale of elk meat, which it viewed as a threat to the wildlife resource and to native hunting rights (*Windspeaker*, June 22, 1990:8). On the other hand, the Kikino Metis Settlement in north-central Alberta set out as early as 1979 to form the Kikino Wildlife Ranching Association and to establish one of the largest game ranches on the prairies, based on elk and bison (McArthur 1986:167f; Struzik 1991a:36). Kikino was the first group that attempted to develop a wildlife ranch on marginal lands that cannot be utilized for regular agricultural purposes. Under the Alberta Wildlife Act, bison were considered "agricultural animals", but elk were not and, until 1991, could only be sold for breeding stock.

Geist further explained that "game ranching" must be distinguished from "game farming" in that the latter is a legal designation in Canada, denoting the raising of animals for the purpose of viewing or live sale. Game ranching involves the raising of big game to be killed for commercial sale (Keith and Saunders 1989:69). The status of game farming and ranching is anything but uniform in Canada. With the exception of Newfoundland, all provinces and territories have enacted or are considering legislation to allow game farming. In Alberta the Livestock Industry Diversification Act, Bill 31 was passed in summer 1991. This Act legalized the sale of elk meat and transferred the responsibility for overseeing game animal production from Alberta Forestry, Lands and Wildlife to Alberta Agriculture. Although domestication of wildlife in Alberta had been allowed since 1959, the legalization of trafficking animal parts did not occur until 1987. Prior to the 1987 regulations, 15 game farms existed in the province. Now there are 120 elk farming operations alone, most of them involved in selling antler velvet to the Far East, besides the sale of breeding stock (Ure 1990:14).

British Columbia allows the farming and sale of meat from fallow deer, red deer, bison and reindeer, but stops short of allowing elk and other indigenous animals to be raised for meat. Saskatchewan allows the raising and sale of meat from both native and non-native species, including elk. Game farming is prohibited in Manitoba, except for the raising of bison. Ontario permits only non-indigenous game animals to be farmed. In Quebec and the maritime provinces, indigenous as well as non-indigenous species are being reared. Yukon

---

[3] Valerius Geist is a Calgary biologist and well-known critic of game ranching.

and the Northwest Territories allow the raising of bison, reindeer and elk and permit meat sales for bison and reindeer (Karpan and Karpan 1989:25f; Renecker 1987:6; Government of Alberta n.d.b).

Game farming has been experiencing rapid growth since 1985. While the sale of meat may be a pleasant prospect, it is not what is driving the industry today (Struzik 1991a:36). The market for venison is still modest, and even the industry admits that it may take another ten years of work to develop it fully. For now the real profit is in selling either breeding stock or animal parts — which are traded to the Far East for use in traditional medicines and aphrodisiacs — or both. Furthermore, some ranchers are speculating on the possibility of paid hunting. Darrell Bellerose, manager of the Kikino Wildlife Ranch, suggested that once the market for breeding animals is saturated, and there is a healthy competition for the meat and parts market, the provincial government should consider legalizing paid-for hunts on private lands. Because of quirks in Alberta law which somehow defines bison as a domestic species, the Kikino Metis have already been able to host bow-and-arrow buffalo hunts on their ranch. Like some other ranchers, they would like to set up similar hunts for elk, moose and deer (ibid.:38).

The Kikino operators were the first in Alberta to commercially exploit the concept of an extensive ranch for game species. Although this type of large-scale operation requires a low input of labour because the range is stocked at carrying capacity, ranchers have little control over animal movements. Pastures are large and in this part of Alberta covered with forests of trembling aspen. This limits round-up opportunities and observation to winter when the animals can be baited into corral traps. For the game farmer or rancher, this entails a loss of economic opportunity because animals and their products are not available for harvesting and marketing when consumer demand is at its highest. As a result, the trend in commercial production is towards smaller farms or ranches, which are maintained at higher stocking rates with provision of supplemental feed and effective animal handling systems (Renecker 1987:5f).

Looking at the distribution of game farms or ranches in the three Prairie Provinces, it is interesting to note that 90 per cent of game farming activity has occurred in the white zone, i.e. agricultural area of the prairies, and only 10 per cent on the fringe between farmland and the boreal forest. A poll of game farmers in the late 1980s revealed that virtually all game farms replaced conventional farming and ranching operations: 41 per cent of the respondents stated that a portion or all of their game farm was previously tame pasture or a beef farm; 18 per cent had a portion or all of their game farm converted from cropland; the remaining 41 per cent reported that part or all of their game farm was previously range land or ungrazed native bush (ibid.:7).

Game ranching has also made its appearance in the far north, in the form of reindeer ranching. Of the five attempts to develop reindeer ranching in Canada, the Mackenzie Delta herd is the only one still in operation. This reindeer venture implemented in 1935 was intended to improve the economic situation of the native population by supplementing the herds of barren ground caribou and other wild mammals which had dwindled after the introduction of firearms. The original plan was to set up a government-owned main herd from which smaller herds would be turned over to interested Inuit herdsmen, each assigned to particular winter and summer ranges. As these herds increased, their holders would repay the number of beasts they had been given. The herds would eventually become self-supporting units (Scotter 1972:170). These objectives, however, were never reached. Between 1938 and 1954, six Inuit-owned herds of about 1,000 animals each were established. Most of these herds increased in numbers for a couple of years, declined, and finally reverted to government ownership.

The reasons for the failure of this experiment were many and complex. Although the food habits of reindeer and caribou are much the same, it does not necessarily follow that domesticated reindeer will thrive in a country that will support caribou (Porsild 1954:241). Whereas caribou may roam widely in search of food, the reindeer, in order to stay domesticated, must remain, at least to some extent, under constant supervision of the owner. Suitable reindeer country, therefore, must be sufficiently productive to permit the slow and leisurely grazing of large herds during winter and summer. Nevertheless, a reindeer industry is biologically feasible as proven by the maintenance of the herds to the present day.

The failure was primarily an economic and social one. Too little consideration was given to modern animal husbandry and range management practices, and the Mackenzie reindeer operation suffered from attempts to apply less modern Sami practices (Scotter 1972:171). Most importantly, few of the local Inuvialuit were interested in reindeer herding, and Indians were even less inclined to abandon their traditional domestic economy. These attitudes were reinforced by the fact that the herds were (and are) located near one of the best trapping grounds in Canada, the Mackenzie Delta.

By 1964 all of the reindeer had been returned to government ownership and control, where they remained for a decade (Nasogaluak and Billingsley 1981:87). In 1974 the federal government's entire reindeer enterprise — the animals and rights to a 47,000 square kilometre reindeer preserve (established near Inuvik in 1933) — were sold to a new company called Canadian Reindeer Ltd., which was owned by the former chief herder Silas Kanagegama. He, in turn, sold it to the present owner, William Nasogaluak, a hunter and trapper from Tuktoyaktuk, in 1978. After initial problems, mostly related to cash flow and marketing, the operation was turned into a million-dollar-a-year enterprise, particularly after a way was found to access the southern meat market, and after a new "cash crop" was discovered and capitalized upon, namely antlers for the oriental market (ibid.:86–95). Between 1974 and 1980 the herd increased from 5,200 to 13,000 animals. In the early 1980s Nasogaluak was speculating on the possibility of transplanting herds to a new locale (thus returning to one of the original objectives of the herd), of making his reindeer attractive for tourists and establishing a dairying industry (ibid.:89). He also foresaw potential problems, such as the consequences of oil and gas exploration on the Preserve and the impending settlement of the Western Arctic land claim, which might result in a change from the Crown land status of the Reindeer Preserve.

His latter concern was, indeed, borne out by the facts. The Inuvialuit Final Agreement of 1984 turned the Preserve over to the Inuvialuit and left Canadian Reindeer Ltd. without guaranteed free grazing lands. Moreover, the Reindeer Regulations, which prohibit the hunting of reindeer and caribou on the Preserve, are now viewed as having no force on Inuvialuit lands, and considerable killing of reindeer is alleged to be taking place (Scotter 1989:236). The failure of the new "landlords" to come to terms with Nasogaluak, and the federal government's refusal to mediate a solution, has led to concerted, but so far unsuccessful, attempts to sell the animals to a consortium of Asian interests. Such transaction would have sent the reindeer abroad or to northern British Columbia (Struzik 1991b:81).

Game ranching is an extremely controversial topic in Canada. This applies in particular to the introduction of non-native species. With regard to the Mackenzie Delta reindeer herd, George W. Scotter (1972:172) feels that the fact that an exotic species is replacing a native one, has caused insufficient concern. He suggests that game ranching with caribou might, in the long term, prove ecologically and economically more feasible.

But native or non-native species aside, there are other ecological threats invoked by game-ranching opponents. Biologist William Pruitt, once a proponent of the industry, lost his enthusiasm in the course of two sabbaticals to Scandinavia to study the winter ecology of reindeer. He discovered that management of game animals for profit will inevitably affect the well-being of wild animals in the same area. He stated that

> In order to maintain the highest productivity of the reindeer herds in the Scandinavian countries, the ecosystem has had to be simplified...every other animal which competes with

> the reindeer on the grazing lands, whether it is herbivore or carnivore must be eliminated. All predators — eagles, wolves, foxes, even jays and ravens — are shot because the reindeer herders see them as competitors. As a result, northern Scandinavia is an ecological desert. (Struzik 1991a:41)

Citing the current reindeer herding in northern Canada, and noting the territorial government's interest in establishing extensive reindeer and muskox operations there, Pruitt expresses great concern for the northern populations of barren ground caribou, grizzlies, black bears, wolves, wolverines, eagles and ravens (ibid.). This particular problem, associated primarily with the open-range concept practised on the northern tundra, would likely not occur to the same degree in the provinces, where legislation requires animals to be fenced.

But there are other equally serious problems associated with the commercial privatization of wild animals, ranging from the spread of disease to increased poaching. One of the most vocal opponents of the industry in Alberta is Valerius Geist, who after having been instrumental in laying the groundwork for game ranching in the early 1970s, walked away from the cause in 1975. Geist feels that commercialization of wildlife characterized by private ownership, the sale of meat and parts and the legalization of private, paid-for hunts would undermine the very foundations of what he considers "the most successful wildlife conservation and management system in the world" (ibid.:39). The groundwork for this system was laid in Canada and the United States in the early twentieth century with the creation of legislation and a publicly endorsed ethic which placed greater value on wildlife in the forest than dead wildlife sent to the market.

> The programme was based on four principles: first, that wildlife be maintained in the public domain; second, that only in the absence of markets could wildlife thrive and its true economic benefit be gained; third, that any material benefits deriving from wildlife should be allocated by law for the public good and not by the marketplace; and finally, that there should be no frivolous killing of wildlife. The last, given the popularity of sport hunting at the turn of the century, translated into an approval for subsistence meat hunting and a limited, well-regulated sport hunt. (ibid.)

The legalization of game ranching, on the other hand, places an economic value on dead wildlife and creates an infrastructure that can be infiltrated by poachers. Game ranchers maintain that their industry would, in fact, reduce poaching, because legal markets for meat and parts would be serviced fully by legitimate, regulated operators. The experience in the United States suggests, however, that the opponents are right: Poaching has increased dramatically wherever game ranching has been legalized (ibid.:41).

Disease infection and "genetic pollution" of purebred indigenous species are further threats to native wildlife, both occasioned by extensive trade and occasional escapes of captive animals. Studies had suggested that the confinement of game species, combined with regular exposure to humans and domestic species, encouraged disease (ibid.:43). This threat materialized in 1990 and 1991, with disastrous outbreaks of highly contagious and usually fatal bovine tuberculosis on game farms from Ontario to Alberta. In October 1990 Agriculture Canada stepped in to oversee the systematic destruction of more than 400 moose, elk, deer, yaks and wild boars on the Moravia Breeding International Inc. game farm near Sunridge, Ontario. By summer 1991 half of Alberta's elk herd was earmarked for eradication, as Agriculture Canada followed through with its policy of doing "the scientifically pure" (as Agriculture Canada veterinarian Maria Koeller put it on March 23, 1991 at the "Game Ranching and Indigenous Peoples" Conference in Saskatoon), namely destroying all TB-infected animals as well as those potentially exposed and susceptible to the disease, i.e. contact animals. By this time humans as well as cattle had been infected with tuberculosis. All this happened at a time when Canada was on the threshold of owning the world's first TB-free population of cattle.

Commercial Hunting

Some of the arguments advanced in opposition to game ranching may foster the belief that commercial hunting of indigenous game animals constitutes a more ecologically feasible mode of wildlife commercialization than game ranching of exotic or native species.

In January 1985 the Labrador Inuit Association (LIA) submitted a proposal to the provincial Department of Culture, Recreation and Youth for a commercial caribou hunt in northern Labrador, to be operated by the Labrador Inuit Development Corporation (LIDC). In the following spring, a pilot commercial hunt was conducted and, subsequently, measures were taken to "institutionalize" a commercial spring caribou hunt on a yearly basis. A quota of 1,000 animals was set over an eight-week period; government assistance was engaged for veterinary and meat inspection services; a former fish plant facility was used for processing; and an advertising and promotion campaign was launched for province-wide distribution, while interprovincial trade of caribou meat was envisaged for the future. In the late 1980s a permanent commercial caribou processing facility was constructed. It was anticipated, that once fully functional, the entire operation — including harvesters, base-camp and processing facility — would provide approximately 10 weeks' employment to 33 north coast Inuit during the most economically depressed time of the year (Popovitch-Penny, quoted in Keith and Saunders 1989:60).

Sadie Popovitch-Penny, the general manager of the LIA, feels that, in order to judge the success or failure of the commercial hunt, it should be analyzed with regard to its compatibility with traditional hunting and conservation principles and practices of the Labrador Inuit (Keith and Saunders 1989:61). First, she notes, that the most vital ingredient of the commercial enterprise is that it is both based in and controlled by the community.

> This indigenous management system, based on traditional Labrador Inuit experience, where the "village elders" made rules pertaining to hunting methods and areas, sharing of game, and regulations aimed at maintaining a balance between hunting and the availability of wildlife on which the Inuit depended for their survival, is seen as the key to successful management.
>
> The collective understanding that the Inuit shared with respect to the unofficial regulating of their hunting territories and basic wildlife management remains a curious but undeniably real carry-over to the modern era of snowmobiles and high-powered rifles. Local control over the commercial hunt is an important principle which must be maintained if the hunt is to succeed. (Popovitch-Penny, quoted in Keith and Saunders 1989:61)

A second important success variable for the commercial caribou hunt is its resemblance to the subsistence hunt, which the Inuit have pursued as an integral component of their seasonal cycle. The hunters felt that a hunt which involved going out on the land with snowmobiles, retrieving the caribou and eviscerating the animals in the country, as is done in the subsistence hunt, and then bringing them to the community for skinning and processing of the meat for shipment to the market, was entirely in keeping with their traditional resource-use practices. People felt that this, in fact, legitimized the commercial hunt.

The third factor invoked in favour of the commercial caribou hunt was the creation of a cash income, which replaced the opportunity lost with the disappearance of the market for seal pelts (Popovitch-Penny in Keith and Saunders 1989:62). The fragile domestic economy of the Labrador Inuit is under pressure during late spring, when the unemployment insurance benefits for the majority of fishermen and hunters are terminated and people lack the means to finance their next economic pursuit, the summer fishery. The fishery, in turn, is the economic foundation of the entire subsistence complex, as it is the only activity creating sufficient income to purchase vital capital equipment, such as snowmobiles and boats, without which none of their resource harvest activities could be pursued. Thus the commercial caribou hunt constitutes a vital link in a fragile chain of the land-based socio-economic existence of the Labrador Inuit.

Even though, the Inuit, in the preliminary planning stages for the Labrador commercial caribou hunt, made it clear that they did not want to see the commercial hunt take precedence over, or endanger, the subsistence hunt. The LIA secured a promise from the provincial government that, should the need arise to restrict harvesting for conservation purposes, the subsistence hunt would take precedence over the commercial hunt, and that the latter would have priority over the sport hunt. Thus, in the early stages of the Labrador Inuit commercial caribou hunt, commercial hunting was viewed not only as not interfering with the subsistence hunt, but also as complementing it in a remarkably positive manner (Popovitch-Penny in Keith and Saunders 1989:63).

Favourable conditions for the development of commercial harvesting activities also seem to present themselves in the western arctic, on Banks Island. Over the last two decades there has been a growing concern here among Inuvialuit hunters that the expanding muskox population might be detrimental to Peary caribou (Vincent and Gunn 1981:175; Struzik 1991c:42f; Gunn, Shank and McLean 1991:188f).

Banks Island has been the scene of rather extreme population cycles of muskoxen, manifesting themselves in the near disappearance of the animals throughout the first half of this century and their overabundance during the last decade. In the early 1990s there are approximately 35,000 muskoxen on the island, about one-third of the world's muskox population (Struzik 1991c:42). Hunting of muskoxen was prohibited from 1917 until 1976, when limited quotas were issued for specified zones. In 1979 the Wildlife Ordinance was amended to allow commercial sale of muskox meat, and provision was made for sport hunting of bulls under the quota (Vincent and Gunn 1981:177).

The potential impact of the expanding muskox population on the island's caribou is a long-standing matter of concern to the Inuvialuit hunters of Sachs Harbour since caribou is a preferred meat source. Government-sponsored studies have remained inconclusive as to the existence of competition between muskox and caribou (ibid.:178; Struzik 1991c:43f), but biologists are increasingly reluctant to dismiss indigenous knowledge outright, given the number of times it has proven scientists wrong in the past. Unless linked to the population increase of the muskoxen, the dramatic decline of caribou on Banks Island in recent years remains a puzzle. In 1970, for example, 12,000 caribou were counted. In 1988 there seemed to be only 2,500. The situation has reached a point where the inhabitants of Sachs Harbour have restricted their hunt, and they have convinced the Government of the Northwest Territories to hire hunters in Tuktoyaktuk on the mainland to shoot and fly up caribou meat for them. At the same time, a commercial culling of muskoxen on the island for trade to southern markets has been initiated.

According to Pedro Vanmeurs, head of the Inuvialuit Renewable Resources Development Corporation, the harvest of muskoxen "is as much a question of wildlife control as it is a much-needed economic boost for the Inuvialuit of Banks Island." (Struzik 1991c:43) According to Vanmeurs, the people of Sachs Harbour are convinced that the muskoxen are squeezing out the caribou, either by destroying their habitat or by intimidating them into moving off to less suitable locations. At least equally important, a commercial sustainable harvest of muskoxen is viewed as an opportunity to replace the income lost with the collapse of the sealing industry and the more recent decline in the fur trade (ibid:44).

Anne Gunn and her coauthors caution that a fully developed commercial harvest will require the establishment of markets and major investments in capital equipment, along with greater efficiency in procurement, processing and transportation. Investment is risky because of the uncertainty about the stability of population numbers, and it creates the additional risk of providing a momentum for harvesting, even if a population decline becomes apparent (Gunn, Shank and McLean 1991:192). All this is particularly true in view of our still inadequate understanding of the population dynamics of species such as caribou and muskoxen.

The necessity of replacing cash incomes lost to aboriginal domestic economies through the demise of the sealskin market and the downturn in the fur trade is a powerful and convincing argument in favour of commercial hunting. However, the discussion of the pros and cons of this issue has raised some serious ecological and economical pitfalls of this type of commercialization of wildlife use. It has also shown, that under certain circumstances, the boundaries between subsistence hunting and commercial hunting on one hand, and between commercial hunting and game ranching on the other hand, may become somewhat blurred.

At a fundamental level, Fikret Berkes expresses the concern that

> ...the commercialization of a subsistence hunt is probably one of the better documented mechanisms by which resources come to be overharvested. Incentive to create surplus breaks down the self-limiting principle of a subsistence operation, and together with it, the customary laws that regulate hunter-prey relations.... Commercialization of caribou hunting to serve the needs of over-wintering whalers at the turn of the century and commercialization of musk-ox hunting have been linked to the near-disappearance of various populations. The more recent developments of an Asian market demand for ungulate antlers may be viewed with alarm from this point of view. (Berkes 1981:171)

Similarly, Geist feels that commercial hunting, like game ranching, creates a retail market for wildlife meat and parts, with all its concurrent implications already discussed. While expressing sympathy for the situation of Canada's northern native communities, he nevertheless insists (particularly when interprovincial trade is involved) that

> ...Canada's parts cannot be considered in isolation from themselves or from its big southern neighbour when managing wildlife. Wildlife is managed with continent-wide policies, jointly developed by the United States and Canada early this century. These need particular attention when export markets are considered. (Keith and Saunders 1989:64)

Drawing further parallels between market hunting and game ranching, he remarks that both are incompatible with predators. Referring to the Labrador Inuit commercial caribou hunt, Geist envisages that "venison markets supplied by Quebec and Labrador caribou will lead ultimately to 'caribou ranching' from Gander to Nome" with disastrous consequences for the northern ecology (ibid.:71).

Peter Usher does not share Geist's objection in principle to commercialization of wildlife use by aboriginal peoples, but prefers to look at the issue pragmatically, on a case-by-case basis (Keith and Saunders 1989:80). He cautions, however, on the basis of economic considerations, against developing too great a dependency on marketable species. He warns that wildlife populations, particularly caribou, will not necessarily guarantee the regularity of supply that a market orientation is likely to demand. Usher also raises the important distinction between "outside markets" and local markets traditionally supplied by intra- and inter-settlement trade. These two types of markets make very different demands on local economies and exhibit very different degrees of flexibility.

This distinction raises the fundamental question of what is meant by commercialization. George Wenzel defines it as follows:

> Commercialization...is production from the land solely for the exchange value. My concern about this...is that, for the first time, the products that will produce exchange value from the South are so-called "traditional" items that have never before been evaluated that way. (ibid.:176)

Just how difficult it is to answer this question, without falling prey to cultural bias, is revealed by an aboriginal definition of "subsistence".

> Subsistence in our interpretation means we eat and we take for our own purposes. At the same time, subsistence could be interpreted as that which you take but you then exchange

> to survive. Does that conflict with harvesting for commercial purposes? I don't think so, though your interpretation is different from ours. (Charlie Watt, Senate of Canada, addressing a panel of the National Symposium on the North, quoted in Keith and Saunders 1989:78)

A Special Case: The Bison

The history of both subspecies (or ecotypes) of bison, the plains bison and the wood bison, over the last century has been colourful to say the least. After having been pushed to the brink of extinction one hundred years ago, the plains bison is today considered a "domestic species" and raised commercially for meat. The wood bison has also been removed from the endangered species list in Canada, but it has again become the subject of a heated conservation debate, which also concerns itself with the question of genetics. The fate of both types of bison has become closely intertwined, and aboriginal people have remained important players in shaping the current and future situation of these animals.

In the Prairie Provinces the plains bison is again contributing to the economic base of native communities. The Kikino Wildlife Ranch of the Metis in north central Alberta is, in part, a bison ranch. In Saskatchewan the Saskatchewan Indian Agriculture Program (SIAP) is undertaking a concerted effort to assist Indian bands in the development of bison ranches. SIAP is currently working on a plan of establishing a large herd of breeding stock to be placed on reserves on a share basis. The plan also envisages the construction of a central feedlot and the development of a marketing division. The Waterhen Bison Ranch at Waterhen, Saskatchewan, is a well-established cow-calf operation with a cow herd of 85 in 1991, a herd of 200 being the goal. In the early 1990s the Thunderchild Reserve was in the process of establishing the Angus Bison Ranch, and at least eight other bands in Saskatchewan were in various stages of negotiating purchases, laying the groundwork or acquiring information for bison-ranching enterprises (SIAP n.d.). There are other bands like the Stoneys in Alberta, for example, who own substantial herds of bison without deriving any economic benefits from them.

Aboriginal people's relationship with the wood bison is a more complex one: Currently native people are deriving subsistence benefits from wood bison; they are engaged in their commercial utilization; and they are involved in conservation efforts. Measures to protect the wood bison were first adopted in the 1890s, when their numbers had reached an all-time low due to a combination of natural factors and hunting pressure (Payne and Nepinak 1991:6). Wood Buffalo National Park (WBNP) was established in 1922, when the wood bison population had recovered to a number of 2,000. At that time conservation measures were distinctly at odds with native rights and native needs.

> Protection of animals took precedence over the protection of the Indian or his hunting rights. The Government sent more rangers, game wardens and veterinarians to the Wood Buffalo Park after 1923 than there were Indian agents or doctors in the entire Northwest Territories. (Fumoleau 1973:226)

Then, between 1925 and 1928, close to 7,000 tuberculosis- and brucellosis-infected plains bison from Buffalo National Park near Wainwright (dissolved in the early 1940s) were relocated to Wood Buffalo National Park, and totally disrupted the wood bison recovery (Michiel 1990:31). The newcomers passed on both diseases to the wild wood bison, and the two subspecies (or ecotypes) extensively hybridized. Within two decades the wood bison was considered extinct through genetic dilution.

In 1957, however, an isolated herd was discovered in the northwestern portion of the park, which was confirmed to exhibit pure wood bison characteristics. In the 1960s these wood bison remnants were threatened again, this time by an outbreak of anthrax in the park. Consequently, 18 healthy wood bison were relocated to what is now the Mackenzie Bison Sanctuary (MBS) in the Northwest Territories, where the herd now numbers in excess of 2,000 animals.

The Northern-Diseased Bison Issue

Wood Buffalo National Park (WBNP) is Canada's largest national park and home to approximately 4,000 to 5,000 bison which constitute the largest free-roaming herd of bison in the world, one reason why the park was designated a World Heritage Site by UNESCO. The resident bison, however, are neither pure wood nor plains bison, and 30 to 50 per cent of the animals are likely to be infected with bovine brucellosis and tuberculosis. Due to these facts, there is a strong lobby by Agriculture Canada, ranchers and some wildlife managers to destroy the entire herd.

One impetus for this drastic option is the proximity of the Mackenzie Bison Sanctuary to the northwest of the park, now home to more than 2,000 disease-free wood bison. This herd is growing rapidly and expanding its range southward. Should the two populations make contact, which is likely to happen sometime in the future, genetic and disease contamination of the MBS herd will inevitably occur. To prevent this, a bison-free zone is being maintained to the northwest of WBNP. As long as the park is inhabited by diseased animals, growth potential of the MBS herd is severely limited due to lack of suitable habitat into which it can spread. The Wood Bison Recovery Team and some wildlife managers consider this a serious impediment to the goal of removing the wood bison from the threatened species list (Aniskowicz 1990:35). Yet, given the events that have occurred since 1925, scientists generally agree that it is more than questionable that pure wood bison stock still exists.

Opponents to the elimination plan, many native people among them, feel that the government is less concerned about the welfare of "pure" wood bison than it is about encroaching cattle (*Kainai News*, October 04, 1990:2). This argument is convincing in view of the fact that the bison herd has been diseased for over sixty years. After the drought conditions of the 1980s, the proposition of shipping feed to cattle in southern Alberta became rather expensive. Instead, the government started subsidizing the shipping of cattle to the north for the summer. As agriculture (including game ranches for bison and elk) encroaches upon WBNP, the occurrence of brucellosis and tuberculosis in park bison is a great concern to livestock owners (Aniscowicz 1990:36; McCormack 1992:376). Since, prior to the events of 1991, the WBNP herd was the last reservoir of bovine tuberculosis and brucellosis in the country, and because the buffalo roam outside park boundaries, ranchers were afraid that Canadian cattle might lose their brucellosis-free status and never attain a tuberculosis-free designation, which would be a serious economic blow to the Canadian cattle industry. Consequently, Agriculture Canada wants to remove disease in bison the same way it removes disease from domestic cattle: by total elimination of the herd. Currently there is no treatment or effective vaccine for either disease in bison and cattle.

In 1989–90 a Northern-Diseased Bison Assessment Panel, which was formed under the Federal Environmental Assessment Review Office (FEARO), examined the socio-economic, resource conservation, environmental, and health issues associated with the diseased bison of WBNP. The panel's final report recommended the implementation of the slaughter/replacement/salvage option advanced by Agriculture Canada over any combination of the other alternatives: status quo, fencing of the entire park, bison-free buffer zones, and exclusive test/salvage measures. The FEARO panel recommendation included as a minor component the salvage of a small percentage of bison that test negative for the diseases and display wood bison characteristics. The principal goals were to exterminate the entire bison population of WBNP and to repopulate the park with wood bison from Elk Island National Park, after a four-year period to ensure that all bison were exterminated.

The eradication project met with vehement opposition from the native community. Residents of settlements like Fort Smith and Fort Chipewyan, immediately adjacent to the park, expressed open distrust of so-called "expert knowledge" as it pertains to the headcount of buffalo and the scope and perceived impact of the diseases (*Native Network News*, March

1990; *Kainai News*, October 4, 1990). Aboriginal people by and large had little appreciation for the concept of maintaining the purity of the wood bison subspecies, but rather they felt that "killing one bison population to make way for another is irrational." (*Fort McMurray Today*, October 15, 1990) They were very concerned about the extermination program's impact on their domestic economy, which includes the bison, and on the ecology of the area, particularly on the wolf population, which could be expected to resort to overkilling moose and scavenging traplines in the absence of its accustomed prey of bison (*Fort McMurray Today*, October 16, 1990). Native people who were used to encountering bison in their own habitat seriously doubted that it would even be possible to round up every single bison, and it would only take one missed animal to re-infect any new herds introduced to the range (*Fort McMurray Today*, October 17, 1990).

Native opposition to the "total elimination" proposal was an important factor in turning the tide in favour of a "new" plan, which was hardly less controversial. The alternative plan to "test and slaughter" infected bison was formulated after consultation between the federal Departments of Environment and Agriculture and local native people. According to this procedure, bison would be rounded up, tested for tuberculosis and brucellosis, and then the animals that tested positive would be slaughtered. Aboriginal people who customarily hunt bison on the periphery of WBNP would be directly involved in the entire process. This plan was still strongly opposed by conservation groups, such as the Canadian Parks and Wilderness Society, who feel that it is "political rather than scientific in nature." (Rasmussen 1991:43) Testing methods for tuberculosis and brucellosis are not totally reliable. Even this new plan would likely result in the elimination of the majority of the animals, without preventing infectious animals from passing through the system, while animals that test positive may not even be infectious. Viewed closely, the new "test and slaughter" plan appeared to be merely a "political reformulation of the original 'total elimination' plan. Inherent in both is a serious compromise of national park and ecosystem issues." (ibid.)

The Northern Buffalo Management Board

In the early 1990s the future of the WBNP bison population still remains in abeyance. Its fate is now in the hands of the Northern Buffalo Management Board (NBMB), which was established in June 1991 with funding from the federal departments of Indian Affairs, Environment and Agriculture. NBMB was conceived as a multistakeholder board, composed of native people, government and public representatives. The Board's mandate is the development of a management strategy which is to grow out of a community-based planning program. Its objective is to prevent the spread of the diseases and to ensure a healthy free-roaming buffalo population of the present genetic diversity. Data collection will involve both traditional knowledge and scientific methods, and the overall strategy will reflect an ecosystem approach, considering not only disease, but also predator-prey relationships and habitat threats.

This procedure which envisages a time frame of 10 to 15 years is a clear departure from the previous "drastic solution" approach. As a co-management institution, the NBMB exhibits unusual complexity. Its membership is comprised of representatives from nine native communities, Parks Canada, Indian Affairs, the Department of Agriculture, the Government of Alberta, the Government of the Northwest Territories, as well as three public representatives from an environmental organization, the Canadian Cattle Association and the Canadian Bison Association. This 17-member Board has two chairpersons: one aboriginal and the other, non-aboriginal. Despite this diversity, a consensual approach to decision-making is sought. It seems to be the general impression (Doug Stewart, WBNP Superintendent, personal communication, May 12, 1992) that the "true players" on the Board are the native members, the federal and territorial governments and the environmentalists. Agriculture Canada, the government of Alberta and the Canadian Cattle Association represent a purely agricultural perspective, whereas the Canadian Bison Association is mostly interested in turning bison into domestic stock.

George Kurszewski of Fort Smith, aboriginal chairperson of the Board, feels that the NBMB differs from other co-management institutions in several important ways because it

- Includes a native majority (9 native people out of 17 members)
- Recognizes native people as caretakers of the land
- Provides decision-making power[4]
- Recognizes explicitly the role of traditional knowledge (George Kurszewski, personal communication, May 13, 1992)

The envisaged management plan is to be developed by means of a community-based planning approach. According to Kurszewski (ibid.), there is no "WBNP bison herd", but each of the nine communities either has a herd of special significance to its people or is concerned with the reintroduction of bison to their region. The communities form committees to research and formulate specific management approaches for their herds. Of the nine native communities, only four have sizeable herds of bison in their proximity, and they are adopting quite different approaches to their management (Gilles Paquin, Coordinator, Fort Fitzgerald Buffalo Management Program, personal communication, May 15, 1992).

Fort Chipewyan favours a form of the test-and-slaughter option, placing much emphasis on local involvement, i.e. employment during the procedure. Fort Resolution also envisages testing and slaughtering (also described as the "maximum salvage method"), and aligns itself with the Wood Bison Recovery Team (see later section on the topic). The Fort Smith Native Band opts for what Chief Henry Beaver calls a "soft management plan", likely to include some testing and slaughtering (personal communication, May 11, 1992). The situation is complicated by the presence of the Hanging Ice Bison Ranch, which was established in 1990 with participation of the Fort Smith Hunters and Trappers Association (almost exclusively a Metis organization) and the Government of the Northwest Territories. This venture was closely tied to the prospect of the "total elimination" proposal being implemented. And finally, the Fort Fitzgerald Dene Band advocates a hands-off approach and an extended research period.

Of all the member bands of the NBMB, the Fort Fitzgerald Band is the most traditionally oriented. Its workplan advocates strong reliance on traditional environmental knowledge and unequivocally opposes any comprehensive management measure or disease eradication plan, which could result in the extermination of half the present bison population (Fort Fitzgerald Dene Band 1992:2f). The Band contests the assumption that disease is a major problem for the bison, but holds that other mortality factors are more important, and that above all, more research is needed before any management action is planned and implemented (ibid.:5). Their basic premise contends that the bison is sacred, and "We intend to work with the buffalo and learn from them as much as we can, by a respectful attitude." (ibid.:4)

The communities were expected to have their plans finalized by fall 1992. Then overlaps or conflicts would be determined before an overall management plan could be conceived. The situation is characterized by rare complexity, and the eventual outcome may very well be a "mosaic" of management approaches.

The Politics of Taxonomy

Conservationists express the hope that the problem will no longer be evaluated as if it was occurring on a cattle ranch or game farm, rather than in a national park. Should the park buffalo be eliminated in either guise, "test and slaughter" or "total elimination",

---

[4] Officially, the NBMB has only the power to make recommendations, but for "public image" reasons, the possibility that the Board's recommendations will not be followed by the Ministers is considered remote.

even though the animals are hybrids, such measure would effectively wipe out the single largest bison gene pool in the world (Rasmussen 1991:43; Aniskowicz 1990:36).

All the so-called wood bison now in existence are the descendants of some 37 animals removed from WBNP: the MBS herd originated from 16 animals while the Elk Island National Park wood bison are the progeny of 21 animals. All of today's plains bison in the United States and Canada originate from six primary captures of wild bison calves between 1873 and 1889, with a total of no more than 90 animals (Geist 1991:295). Thus all existing "pure" bison derive from very limited founding stock: "Because they passed through narrow genetic bottlenecks and have undergone extensive inbreeding, they now contain little genetic diversity." (Aniskowicz 1990:36)

In contrast, the WBNP herd numbered 1,500 to 2,000 indigenous wood bison when the plains buffalo were introduced in the 1920s. Therefore, the bison in the park and surrounding area have the broadest genetic base of any bison population in existence. They possess the largest and most diverse reservoir not only of wood bison genes but of all bison genes.

> The view that WBNP bison be killed off and replaced by genetically impoverished "wood bison" from EINP would destroy the largest continuous, well-tested gene pool of the species B. bison and give priority to the impoverished gene pool of an inbred phantom subspecies. (Geist 1991:297)

The argument of the desirability of maintaining genetic purity of the two bison subspecies has never been popular with most aboriginal people, but lately it has also come under increasing fire from the scientific community. Recent genetic studies indicate that plains bison and wood bison may not be distinct subspecies at all, but only geographical variants within a species (Aniskowicz 1990:35f). Geist calls "the so-called wood bison at best an ecotype." (*Fort McMurray Today*, October 18, 1990) Ecotypes are variations in a species due to adaptation to different ecosystems, but do not reflect genetic differences. If this is true, hybridization means little. In short, "There is no evidence for subspecies in B. bison, and no taxonomic justification for destroying the bison of WBNP." (Geist 1991:298)

The use of the genetic argument by special interest groups may have far-reaching implications for species and habitat protection. Also, it may influence native groups who view environmental protection as part of their comprehensive claims mandate. While in Canada the genetic argument has so far only surfaced in the discussion of the future of the WBNP bison herd, it has played a more ominous role in recent wildlife management questions in the United States (Krueger 1991:13). The United States National Cattlemen's Association adopted a policy supporting the claim that the wolf no longer exists as a genetic entity due to extensive crossbreeding with coyotes. The wolf is an endangered species in the United States, but it must exist in its historical genetic form (as preserved in zoos and research institutions) in order to earn protection. "The argument that endangered species may be more the victims of crossbreeding than the actions of man may have an impact on a number of wildlife management questions." (ibid.) This argument is being advanced, for example, by the United States logging interests in the Pacific Northwest, where a court ruling in 1990 prohibited timber harvesting over a wide are to protect the spotted owl. Forestry companies are appealing this ruling on the basis that the spotted owl no longer exists as a distinct species, but contains genetic fingerprints of several more common — and unthreatened — owl species.

Biologists argue that nature is not static and that, consequently, it is impossible to take a "genetic snapshot" of a so-called "pure wolf" or "pure spotted owl" and use it as a bench mark to measure animals against (Krueger 1991:14f). But until an ecosystem approach wins out over a species approach in conservation efforts and conservation legislation, we must be concerned about a future prospect as detailed by Steve Krueger.

For example, what if the bald eagles of the Churchill River basin in Saskatchewan and Manitoba are found to have different DNA fingerprints than captive bald eagles? Could corporations such as SaskPower (whose plan to build a hydroelectric dam on the river has been stalled for more than a decade) argue that there is no reason to protect the birds' breeding grounds? Or if captive whales are found to have a different genetic base than whales in the wild, could that be used to justify a resumption of full-scale commercial whaling?

In another time genetic fingerprinting could have been a useful tool for documenting evolutionary change in animals. Today, however, it has become an argument for preserving economic interests which are threatened by the habitat needs of competing species. If the real animal no longer exists, why sacrifice jobs and economic development to protect its habitat? (ibid.:17)

Native Participation in Wood Bison Recovery

Preservation of the "subspecies" is the basis for the efforts of the Wood Bison Recovery Team. This group of federal and western provincial biologists is attempting to rebuild wood bison stocks (or at least stocks of animals that are as close as possible to the original wood bison) and to re-establish wild populations. The present goal of the Team is the establishment of four geographically separate herds in Canada, numbering at least 200 animals (Michiel 1990:32). Since the team was organized in 1975, two herds have surpassed the 200-head number: the wild herd in the Mackenzie Bison Sanctuary and a semiwild herd in Elk Island National Park. Throughout the 1980s several smaller herds were shipped to various locations in the territories and northern Prairie Provinces.

In 1984, 34 wood bison arrived at Waterhen in northern Manitoba, which signalled the beginning of the involvement of the **Waterhen First Nation** in the rehabilitation project. One of the objectives of the Waterhen project is the release of young animals to the wild with the intention of establishing a free-roaming herd. Although it is uncertain that the wood bison was ever native to Manitoba due to lack of historical evidence, the habitat in the northern interlake area of the province seemed suitable for the animals (Suggett et al. 1988:10) and sufficiently removed from intensive agricultural development.

The animals are being kept in a large enclosure, where the environment is being modified to make it more suitable for wood bison in large numbers. More than 200 hectares of upland poplar forest have been cleared and seeded to pasture plants, such as alfalfa, clover and brome. In 1987 a drainage project was started to add further usable pasture (Nepinak 1990:4). During the winter, wild and tame hay is provided.

The Waterhen project operates within the frameworks of joint venture and co-management, with the province providing the land base and the Indian band providing management and labour. The bison and were provided by the federal government under a Northern Development Agreement. A management corporation was set up by the Waterhen Band to oversee daily operations and the preparation of the site, assisted by Manitoba Natural Resources Wildlife Branch staff and the Canadian Wildlife Service. After becoming operative, Waterhen Wood Bison Ranches Ltd. has provided numerous short-term and three long-term jobs for band members. After an increasingly satisfactory calf-crop in the late 1980s, 15 wood bison were released from the Waterhen herd in 1988. Unfortunately, rather than roaming northward into undeveloped areas, they moved south towards the agricultural zone and had to be recaptured. A more successful release effort further north was undertaken in spring 1991. It is hoped that these 13 released animals will establish the nucleus for a wild herd (Nepinak 1991b:12).

The present herd at Waterhen numbers 150 animals. It is expected to reach the desired structure and size for economic returns by 1995 (Payne and Nepinak 1991:12). The Waterhen Band's leadership feels that Waterhen Wood Bison Ranches Ltd. successfully combines commercial and conservation ambitions. With respect to the conservation goal, Chief Harvey Nepinak supports in principle the recommendations of the FEARO report on the "Northern

Diseased Bison". He is hopeful that should the FEARO recommendations be implemented, the Waterhen bison ranch, together with Elk Island National Park, will be called upon to assist in the repopulation of Wood Buffalo National Park (ibid.). In terms of commercial utilization, the Band envisages meat production and the sale of live breeding stock. Once a wild herd is established, there is also the possibility of developing a non-resident wood bison hunting program, and in an area already renowned for other species — pickerel fishing, duck hunting, bear hunting and white pelican viewing — the wood bison is also likely to serve as a tourist attraction (ibid.).

Another aboriginal wood bison conservation initiative, the **Hook Lake Wood Bison Management Plan**, is characterized by a somewhat different thrust. In contrast to the Waterhen First Nation, the native community of Fort Resolution to the northeast of Wood Buffalo National Park has a long-standing tradition of dependence on bison meat in its domestic economy. When the local herd dwindled to an estimated number of 200 animals during the 1970s and the 1980s, due to a several factors, the community of Fort Resolution decided to take action to restore its subsistence base. In 1989 community members voluntarily ceased hunting of the Hook Lake bison.

One year after this self-regulatory initiative, the local Deninoo Wildlife and Resources Committee entered into an agreement with the Department of Renewable Resources, Government of the Northwest Territories, to develop a co-management plan for the wood bison in the Hook Lake area. Under this agreement, the Deninoo Buffalo Steering Committee was established, which developed a management plan for the Hook Lake wood bison herd. This management plan is supported by the community of Fort Resolution and the South Slave Regional Council. The Hook Lake Wood Bison Management Plan has five goals:

- Restore a healthy herd of wood bison to the Hook Lake area;
- Preserve the genetic integrity of the Hook Lake wood bison;
- Salvage the existing healthy bison from the Hook Lake area;
- Preserve and enhance the Hook Lake ecosystem; and
- Explore and recognize the potential commercial opportunities for the Hook Lake wood bison herd. (Deninoo Wildlife and Resources Committee 1991:2)

A minimum time period of 10 years is anticipated to achieve these goals. The overall plan has the following major components:

- The establishment of 25.9 square kilometres of corrals and compounds;
- A round-up of the existing wood bison in the Hook Lake area and the implementation of testing, culling, quarantine and salvage programs;
- The acquisition of an alternative wood bison herd from the Mackenzie Bison Sanctuary or Elk Island National Park;
- An extensive wood bison breeding program;
- The implementation of a range enhancement program; and
- The insurance of a continuous supply of bison meat for the community of Fort Resolution. (ibid.)

Naturally, this management plan cannot be carried out in isolation from developments in Wood Buffalo National Park west of the Slave River, so the Deninoo Buffalo Steering Committee hopes to cooperate with the Wood Bison Recovery Team. Although this initiative is primarily concerned with one species, it also makes a strong statement of the community's commitment to the conservation and rehabilitation of its renewable resource base in general.

> The lands east of Slave River including North Prairie [location of planned bison enclosures] have always been used by the people of Fort Resolution. These lands are considered community lands. Similarly, people of Fort Resolution consider wildlife species in this area as community

> resources which should be managed by local people. This understanding has in large part provided the impetus for this Hook Lake Wood Bison Management Plan.
>
> Currently, the Deninoo Community Council is seeking formal recognition by other governments of the community's rights and interests to North Prairie. In the short term, the Council is seeking a grazing lease for the area while in the longer term, recognition of aboriginal title to the area is being considered.(Deninoo Wildlife and Resources Committee 1991:10f)

ABORIGINAL WILDLIFE MANAGEMENT

The discussion of hunting rights in the earlier part of this chapter concluded with the statement that in the modern context one of the practical accomplishments of hunting rights must be

> [the provision of] a framework within which local customary law can operate with respect to the harvesting and management of resources and within which native peoples can have effective input to the policies and administration that affect their interest in the resource base. (Usher 1984:411)

Recent developments effected by the Constitution Act, 1982, by case law and claims negotiations have produced gains in ensuring that aboriginal people possess more effective rights of access to renewable resources. There has, however, been minimal progress regarding native management rights over wildlife resources.

> Wildlife management is the application of ecological knowledge to populations of vertebrate animals and their plant and animal associates in a manner that strikes a balance between the needs of those populations and the needs of people. Ecological knowledge is applied in three basic management approaches: (1) preservation, when nature is allowed to take its course without human intervention; (2) direct manipulation, when animal populations are trapped, shot, poisoned, and stocked; and (3) indirect manipulation, when vegetation, water, or other key components of wildlife habitat are altered. (Robinson and Bolen 1989:2f)

Rick Riewe and Lloyd Gamble call our attention to another crucial aspect of wildlife management.

> "Wildlife Management" is actually a misnomer — it should be referred to as "people management" because most wildlife populations are actively manipulated by managing the harvesters, by setting seasons, quotas, bag limits, etc., and not by manipulating the wildlife species. (Riewe and Gamble 1988:31)

Peter Usher observes that one of the main reasons for the denial of aboriginal wildlife management rights is the fact that non-native Canadians (whether private citizens or government resource managers) feel that aboriginal rights, if interpreted as anything more than preferential access, would be an obstacle to the objectives of wildlife conservation (Usher 1987:3). Researchers like Usher, however, argue that, on the contrary, expanded and entrenched native management and property rights could be instrumental for the conservation of wildlife.

This controversy has sparked renewed interest in the questions of whether there exists an environmental ethic in traditional aboriginal societies, and how effectively systems of self-management have functioned in the past and at present. Research (Berkes 1981, 1987, 1988; Feit 1986, 1988; Nelson 1982; Brightman 1987) has shown that successful practices and systems of self-management do exist in aboriginal communities. These facts suggest that future management of wildlife populations particularly in the North can best be effected through joint participation of native wildlife managers and government-mandated wildlife managers. As William Robinson and Eric Bolen point out, "The practice of wildlife management is rooted in the intermingling of human ethics, culture, perceptions, and legal concepts." (Robinson and Bolen 1989:3) It follows that the combination and mutual accommodation of such dissimilar entities, as the indigenous and state systems of wildlife management in any form of co-management, is an extremely complicated and potentially frustrating process. Nevertheless, it is being attempted across the country. The settlement of comprehensive claims serves as one of the main vehicles of designing and implementing the co-management of renewable resources. Moreover, both the governments and aboriginal groups initiate co-management regimes as a means of dealing with crises and resolving conflicts.

Self-Management and Sustainability

A recognition by non-native Canadians of the existence of alternative philosophies and modes of utilization of the natural environment is a relatively recent phenomenon. With regard to the indigenous and premodern systems of wildlife management it was a commonly held belief "...that any ecological 'balance' between human and animal populations existed under no more effective control than human starvation and the inefficiency of the hunters' primitive technology." (Freeman 1985:266f) As late as the 1980s, this point of view was unequivocally expressed by A.H. Macpherson.

> There seems no evidence, then, that wildlife was purposefully managed by Amerindian populations in northern Canada at the time of contact. Instead we may conjecture that the impact of hunting on wildlife stocks was limited only by the low technological level of the hunters and the fact that their populations were small and insecure....Wildlife management for sustained yield is today a sophisticated, scientific activity which seeks to accommodate social desires in wildlife without damage to the resource. Historically, however, it is a product of the feudal society, and began as an imposition on the wanting by the wealthy. It is a craft rooted in privilege and not in poverty. (Macpherson 1981:104)

This narrow socio-cultural concept of wildlife management cannot be upheld in view of native resource harvesting facts in the past and in the present. The ability to use resources in a sustainable manner is derived from a combination of two factors: (a) the possession of appropriate ecological knowledge and suitable technology to exploit resources, and (b) a philosophy and environmental ethic to keep exploitive abilities in check and to provide ground rules by which the relationship between humans and animals may be regulated (Berkes 1988:7).

Historical Evidence for Boreal Forest Algonquin Groups

Historical evidence for the presence or absence of such conditions in native societies varies widely over time and place and is not devoid of cultural bias, since this evidence is non-aboriginal and originated mostly in the context of the fur trade. After his search of literature pertaining to boreal forest Algonquin groups, Robert A. Brightman comes to the following conclusions:

> It is clear that some groups were practising conservation in the seventeenth and eighteenth centuries while others were not, and that whatever conservation systems may have been in place broke down by the late 1700s and early 1800s, when the Crees in the Northern Department had overhunted beaver and big game to the point that reliance on hare and fish, migration south onto the plains, and starvation became humiliating and tragic consequences. (Brightman 1987:125)
>
> Paradoxically, the fur trade provided conditions conducive both to the inception of conservation systems where none may have existed and to the destruction of existing or emergent systems. The new market for animals susceptible to management would provide incentives for the innovation of management practices or for the perpetuation/elaboration of existing ones. However, competition for animals and large-scale population movements could result in increased pressure on game and also in disregard for boundaries between regional bands. Without such boundaries, hunters and trappers would have no practical incentive to conserve since the animals they spared might be taken by others, the commons dilemma. Yet, as

> Bishop (1974, 1984) suggests, limited-access land tenure and conservation later reappeared as adjustments to depleted environments and dependence on trade goods. (Brightman 1987:126)
>
> Game shortages came about not because Crees were killing more animals to obtain trade goods, but because they were reproducing under new technological conditions what was probably the aboriginal convention of killing as many animals as possible within the limits set by their assessments of costs and benefits. The potential for overhunting was already present. Steel traps, guns, and other tools made it easier. It was precisely in connection with the most efficient new hunting techniques that the major accounts of what Euro-Canadians defined as "waste" occurred. (ibid.:129)

Calvin Martin (1978) and Christopher Vecsey (1980) argue that in precontact times boreal forest Algonquins refrained from overkilling animals because of religious obligations to hunt selectively. Martin advances the theory that introduced diseases, in conjunction with missionary teachings and social disequilibrium, disrupted the Indian's covenant with game animals. This process not only resulted in a general despiritualization of the natural environment and a profanation of the hunt but, according to Martin (1978:146), Indians came to blame beaver and other animals for the new diseases that demolished Indian populations, and the overexploitation of wildlife that accompanied the fur trade was in part a revenge against disease-bearing animals.

Robert A. Brightman agrees with the relevance of "religious" ideas to game shortages but draws quite different conclusions, namely that traditional native belief systems may encourage, rather than proscribe indiscriminate hunting (Brightman 1987:130). He argues that a crucial precondition for conservation measures is the hunters' awareness of the fact that they can indeed influence the availability of animals in the future by harvesting selectively in the present. He contrasts such awareness with the boreal Algonquin idea that game animals killed by hunters spontaneously regenerate after death or reincarnate as fetal animals. Brightman (ibid.:131) reports such beliefs among Manitoba Cree in the 1980s, who call this process akwanaham otoskana ("[animal] covers its bones").

In comparing Indian and Western ecological knowledge, Charles A. Bishop discusses "respect", the complex of ritual attitudes towards animals, believed by Martin (1978) and others to have included rules limiting kills to immediate needs.

> A key difference between the two systems was the absence in the former [Algonquian] of a more general concept of animal population dynamics. And just as it is possible to practise conservation without "respecting" game, so it is possible to respect animals and simultaneously and perhaps unawaredly hunt them to extinction if the motives and means for obtaining them are present. (Bishop 1981:55)

Brightman hypothesizes that a transformation of Algonquin belief systems took place in the early nineteenth century, when the desperate game shortages became apparent to all.

> If hunters are unaware that animals can be managed, they may also be unaware that they can be hunted to depletion. It cannot be assumed that Crees and others involved in game depletions initially understood their own role as determinants. Rather than inhibiting overkill, religious definitions of the human-animal relationship encouraged it insofar as they premised an environment of primordial abundance in which game could not be destroyed but only temporarily displaced. (Brightman 1987:132)
>
> In the late eighteenth and early nineteenth centuries, however, it must rapidly become obvious that something was wrong: animals were not regenerating in proportion to the numbers killed. This disparity between convention and experience would eventually act back on Cree valuations of animals and hunting, leading to their adoption of conservation techniques. (ibid.:136)
>
> The religious interpretation of conservation by some contemporary Rock Crees and cultural transformations among other boreal [Algonquians] lead to conjecture that the game shortages motivated a reinterpretation of indiscriminate or "wasteful" hunting and trapping as offensive

> to animals and to the spirit entities regulating each species. The beings are understood to regulate the regeneration, movements, and distribution of animals as well as human access to them. Many Crees state explicitly that misimoswa ("Great Moose"), mistamisk ("Great Beaver"), misipisiw ("Great Lynx") and other beings interfere with the harvests of hunters who trap unselectively or waste the products of animals. (ibid.:138)

Conservation emerged at different times in different areas and undoubtedly under different circumstances. Even so, it was necessary that Crees redefine animals as manageable. (ibid.:137)

Historical Evidence from British Columbia

Georgina Ball (1985) describes what she calls the "monopoly system of wildlife management" practised by the Indians of British Columbia east and west of the Rocky Mountains at the time of contact and during the fur trade era. Tribal territories were divided into hunting territories and fishing sites, the possession rights of which were held by a clan, a smaller family group or an individual. Generally, these rights were passed on matrilineally from one generation to another. British Columbia's Indian hunting territories are viewed by Ball and earlier authors like D.S. Davidson (1928) as having originated in aboriginal times, and not in response to the European fur trade.

This monopolistic land and stream ownership provided the essential preconditions for the implementation of certain conservation measures and efficient management of important resources. According to Ball (1985:41), available records seem to indicate that only certain game and fish species were accorded such protection, in particular the beaver and the Pacific salmon. In precontact times the beaver was a reliable source of food and blankets for many tribes. Due to its sedentary lifestyle, it was particularly susceptible to careful management as well as to overexploitation. Realizing this, tribes who ascribed much importance to the beaver regulated their harvest through monopoly control (ibid.:44). Certain hunting methods, such as the use of trained dogs, discouraged indiscriminate killing of other game. Some aboriginal groups effected a measure of habitat improvement by controlled burning of forested land (ibid.:46).

The presence of prudent management practices among British Columbia's aboriginal groups did not, however, prevent the near extermination of the sea otter in the early nineteenth century as a result of the marine fur trade. Indiscriminate slaughter of these animals by Indians began well before rum and disease began their general erosion of coastal tribes' cultures. Ball (ibid.:48) suggests the possibility that native people participated in the extermination of the sea otter because this animal was not crucial to the survival of the coastal tribes. Its pelt was a luxury, not a necessity. Newly acquired tastes, acquisitiveness, and potlatch gift requirements created a demand for trade goods which, in the absence of any authoritative power to control the harvest, eventually resulted in the extermination of the sea otter on the British Columbia coast. Throughout their assault on the sea otter, the Indians kept their territorial rights and associated practices intact.

When the land-based fur trade entered British Columbia from the East, the resultant devastation of wildlife populations was initially less a result of the collapse of local aboriginal conservation practices than of the introduction of foreign eastern Indians as trappers by the fur companies. Iroquois and other eastern Indians had no vested interest in the resources of the Beaver and Sekanni and, therefore, made no effort to conserve them (Ball 1985:49). As Brightman (1987:134) observes, for similar situations in eastern Canada, "The game shortages were less tragedies of the commons than tragedies of invasion." Ruinous competition between the Hudson's Bay Company and the North West Company was eventually one factor that led to their amalgamation in 1821. The reorganized company held monopoly trading rights with native people west of the mountains for several decades and was, therefore, in a position to institute conservation measures in the devastated areas.

These examples of the evaluation of historical sources in eastern and western Canada show that non-native testimony about aboriginal conservation practices is varied and complex.

This is hardly surprising, since — cultural factors aside — all these observations took place during a crucial time in aboriginal peoples' lives, which was at best characterized by rapid evolution and at worst by upheaval and disruption. For our modern understanding, it is far more important to realize that among many aboriginal groups there is a living tradition of resource conservation and sustainable management which finds its expression in beliefs and practices fundamentally different from "scientific" management.

Current Examples of Sustainable Resource Management

Peter Usher observes that today the strongest evidence for effective self-regulation of resource use comes from the eastern Cree, who have relatively small, family-owned hunting territories and who harvest species with restricted ranges. In contrast, the eastern Dene and central Inuit depend on migratory species, such as caribou, whose ranges extend well beyond the bands' territories. In the latter case, the harvesting groups may not be in a position to know either the entire natural history of the animals or the extent of harvesting by other groups (Usher 1987:8).

The most extensive documentation of self-regulation in the management of living resources exists with regard to the **James Bay Cree** and was compiled by Fikret Berkes (for the Chisasibi Cree) and Harvey Feit (for the Waswanipi Cree). One of the key factors in the maintenance of this regulatory system is a form of land tenure which is believed by many to be aboriginal in origin, and which has found recognition by non-native government.

> The key institution that regulates the use of wildlife resources in the James Bay area is the trapline system. As recognized by the government, a trapline is a registered beaver trapping area in which a native tallyman has harvesting rights. As seen by the Cree people, a trapline is a traditional family hunting-trapping territory. Accordingly, any violations are dealt with by social pressures rather than by recourse to white man's law, and there are remarkably few such conflicts as long as traplines are not easily accessible. Only those people who are family members of the tallyman or who have been given permission by him can trap beaver on a trapline. Other people passing through the area can take animals which they encounter; by mutual agreement there is no permission requirement for such people, they can harvest animals, especially fish and small game, for their immediate food needs. (Berkes 1981:168)

> In addition to beaver, the Canada goose is hunted on a territorial basis in Chisasibi. Goose territories are only on the James Bay Coast (elsewhere geese are not abundant), and they are controlled by the paashchichaauchimaaw ("goose-shooting boss"). The goose territory system is not formalized and mapped. It is more fluid than the government-sanctioned beaver trapline system but just as real within the traditional management sphere. In Chisasibi the two kinds of bosses are not necessarily the same people, and the boundaries of the two kinds of territories do not necessarily coincide. (Berkes 1987:70)

> Hunting bosses in Chisasibi often talk about their ownership of the land and the animals. However, the word used, nitipaaihtaan, means "ownership to take care of" or "to control", and differs fundamentally from the term for ownership nitipiwaawsiiun, which is used for personal belongings, things that can be bought and sold. (ibid.:71)

A hunting boss thus assumes the responsibility for the distribution of the wealth of the land. He manages the harvesting activity for the benefit of band society as a whole: He leads the hunt, supervises the sharing of food and enforces customary laws with respect to harvesting. Management decisions for hunting territories are not only made with regard to access control, but are also expressed in the use of hunting territories on an intermittent or rotational basis, in order for the game to "grow" between harvests (Berkes 1988:16; Feit 1986:56). A hunting boss usually inherits the hunting territory from his father or from an uncle; he cannot buy it or sell it. If he fails to manage it for the community's benefit, he can be forced by social pressure to relinquish his authority (Berkes 1987:71).

Territoriality characterizes the harvest of some resources, but not others. The two species hunted on a territorial basis, beaver and Canada geese, are the most productive and predictable of all animals utilized by the Cree. But there are numerous other conventions and philosophical underpinnings which define the relationship between Cree hunters and trappers and their animal resources. One of the most significant features of this relationship is the fact that, unlike Western environmental values, those of the Cree are defined in social and moral terms.

> For the Waswanipi Cree, for example, the classification of animals involves a hierarchy which links animals to men and both to spirits and to God. Animals are social beings, not cut off from humans as part of a natural order separated from human society. And Waswanipi therefore interpret animal actions as the results of willful choice on the part of the animals. Animals in turn are interpreted as social beings capable of interpreting and understanding the actions of men. The Waswanipi hunters say that they only catch an animal when the animal gives itself to them, or is given them by God and the spirits. They are given animals because they respectfully ask for what they need to survive, and their requests are heard. And they are under reciprocal obligation for what they receive, and treat the animals with respect in the way they hunt, butcher, consume and use the animal bodies. This respect is expected and appreciated by the animals, whose souls survive to be reborn again....It is stated that hunters have the skill and technology to kill too many animals, and it is part of the responsibilities of the hunter not to kill more than he is given....Signs [from the animals and the spirits telling the hunter how many can be taken] involve complex observation and interpretation of weather, snow, vegetation and animal population parameters, all of which are considered as communications from animals and the spirits. (Feit 1988a:77)

Berkes (1988:17) is not aware of a notion of animal reincarnation among the Chisasibi Cree, but describes the same rules of conduct for hunters, most of which are aimed at showing respect to the animals as an indispensable means of ensuring a productive hunt.

He concedes that the question whether the Cree environmental ethic still truly operates, is not an easy one to answer. While the material he presented still represents the working environmental ethic of the recognized community leaders among hunters, Cree leaders themselves would be the first to admit that the system is under stress, and violations of the ethic are frequent and widespread (ibid.:18). On the other hand, Feit (1988a:81) concludes that a relative stability of both populations and harvests of beaver and moose over a ten-to-fifteen- year period are convincing evidence of a significant level of success of Waswanipi conservation and management practices.

> The land tenure system and these various ethical-cultural practices effectively constitute management by design. However, the analysis also suggests that management would break down if design criteria have been violated. Customary laws are mutually agreed upon by the whole community and remain viable as long as they are socially supported. If conditions change so that the ground rules no longer make sense, customary laws dealing with animal resources collapse. (Berkes 1981:170)

Current experiences show that the traditional system of self-management is fragile, as well as resilient and adaptable. Road construction on Chisasibi land during the 1970s severely disrupted the management of hunting territories by making these lands accessible to everyone. Privileged information was no longer necessary for access, and not even the beaver resource could be defended against overexploitation. Such disruption, however, is not necessarily permanent.

> Controversies over hunting rights reached some degree of stability after a few years. The new consensus was that anyone could hunt along the roads, but the position of the Cree Trappers Association local (an organization made up of tallymen) was that such rights would exclude beaver trapping. Thus, customary law had been re-defined to allow hunting in non-traditional areas, even muskrat trapping, as long as beaver rights of the tallymen were respected. Similar re-definitions of native customary law may be found in other communities which have experience with new road networks. (Berkes 1981:172)

Flexibility and adaptability of traditional Cree management systems, however, are of little consequence, if the land base itself is threatened. In view of Hydro Quebec's plans for the 1990s, this is the greatest challenge facing the James Bay Cree today.

> ...the Waswanipi system is based on building up a detailed knowledge of the land and the wildlife of a hunting territory over decades of personal use. Stewards say that they conserve and respect wildlife not only for their own benefit, but to be able to pass the land on to the next generation of hunters. This involves not only passing on the territory but educating the next generation, passing on to them the knowledge of the history of the land and of the game, so that they can continue to manage the wildlife. This knowledge is not learned in the abstract, but concretely by learning how to hunt a particular territory and particular game populations. This is how the Waswanipi reproduce the system of management, and it is this link in the social transmission of knowledge and skill from one generation to another which is broken when a trapline is cut over and must be abandoned for several years. The elders no longer have the specific knowledge and skills and history needed to manage the territory when it is again used. Both the social ties and the knowledge which are the very system of management are endangered. (Feit 1986:60f)

While northern Quebec is probably the most intensively studied region, similar evidence has been found in other parts of the country. Robert A. Brightman (1987:138f) describes the practice of conservation measures by Cree trappers and hunters in **northwestern Manitoba**. It usually includes more than the observation of provincial government rules about quotas and seasons. The term iskoh refers to the act of sparing animals that could easily be taken in order to save them for future harvesting; or, in the case of more mobile animals that may not be retrievable later, it refers to the religious proscription of overkilling. In contrast, the verb cāhkītā refers to the practice of overhunting an area to the point of depletion. Rotation of trapline sectors — the "resting" of land — is also practised. In Brightman's opinion, some trappers who do conserve have an essentially Western scientific understanding of sustained-yield game management. Others adhere to creative syntheses of Algonquin and Western conceptions. They perceive failure to trap and hunt selectively as exemplifying precisely the religiously proscribed act of cāhkītā, "overhunting", or mīstin, "waste", that is punished by the game spirits or the animals themselves. The depletion of game on a trapline is understood by them less as an actual decrease in the numbers of animals present than as a limitation on their visibility to the trapper/hunter and on his/her access to them (ibid.:139).

Richard K. Nelson (1982) describes how the **Koyukon of the Alaskan interior** have created an effective system for long-term resource management by combining empirical and supernatural knowledge. In their understanding, human interactions with natural things are governed by a moral code, which contributes to a proper spiritual balance between the human and nonhuman worlds (ibid.:218). Like the Cree, showing respect to the game is of paramount importance, and one of the most pervasive and potent themes that emerges in Koyukon ideology is a prohibition against waste of anything in nature. Nelson (ibid.:221) states that such ideologically founded avoidance of waste is unquestionably related to "conscious limitation of use". In addition to such religiously prescribed behaviour, there is also a pragmatic, empirically based approach to the conservation of natural resources. People make conscious efforts of self-regulation to enhance the productivity of species.

Nelson provides us with interesting observations by relating the conservation ethic and practices of the Koyukon Athapaskans to their natural environment. He points out that boreal forest species tend to be sedentary, non-herding, localized and subject to dramatic *in situ* fluctuations in abundance. The finite nature of such resource populations is quite evident, and it makes sense that Koyukon people have a very sophisticated comprehension of such ecological dynamics. Hunters who depend on migratory herding animals which are not confined to a local region are in a less favourable position to recognize the finite limits of living resources. It is significant that the Koyukon are most liable to violate their own rules on limiting harvests when they pursue the migratory caribou (Nelson 1982:225).

> Comprehensibility of the environment may be a key factor in the emergence of a conservation ethic and practices like those of the Koyukon. Subarctic peoples occupy an ecosystem that can be understood from their perspective even though the movements of individuals and groups are kept within a fairly specific and limited area of terrain. The prevalence of non-migratory, non-herding species allows them to see the consequences of their harvesting activities and to adjust these activities to serve their own best interests. And the spectre of severe shortages gives them ample cause to respond in practice to the clear implications of this knowledge. (ibid.:223)

Effective systems of aboriginal management of living resources have been documented by non-native academics for a finite number of cases, but it may be argued that they are as old as the hunter-prey relationship between humans and their animal resources on this continent, and as new as the recent abstinence from hunting wood bison by the Dene of Fort Resolution, the latest Inuit-initiated conservation efforts for polar bears (to be discussed below) or the innovative Eiderdown ventures on the Belcher Islands. Authors like Milton Freeman (1984) and Harvey Feit (1988a) argue convincingly that the co-existence of hunters with their principal food species over a long period of time is an a priori proof for conservation practices and sustainable management. Furthermore, as Feit explains,

> ...the fact that wildlife depletion has almost certainly intensified rather than declined, during the transition to urbanized state-level societies, is not just a result of demographic and technological changes, but of the changes in social organization and in particular of the increased social scale that is at a core of the declining capability for local self-regulation in industrialized societies. (Feit 1988a:76)

On the other hand, local systems of aboriginal resource management are in a constant state of flux and reorganization, not only to ward off new assaults on their integrity, but also to accommodate new modes of resource utilization which, in turn, may be vital for the system's continued existence. An example is the establishment of a commercial harvest of eiderdown by the Inuit on the Belcher Islands in the Northwest Territories. This new activity is being carefully designed to be "considerate" to the eiders, a non-migratory species, to be sustainable, and not to interfere with existing patterns of domestic harvesting (McDonald and Fleming 1991).

The previous discussions are not intended to argue that aboriginal people are "natural" conservationists, as if this were a matter of genetics. It cannot be denied that in some northern native settlements there is evidence of waste. As Peter Usher remarks, there are members of native communities who poach, waste, and trade in the black market their wildlife catch (Usher 1982:38). There are young native people who shoot animals for kicks, a form of vandalism that finds different outlets in the south. But there is evidence that such transgressions are more effectively dealt with by community action rather than by imposed legislation, as exemplified by the Igloolik elders waste committee (Riewe and Gamble 1988:34f). There is considerable proof to show that many aboriginal social and religious practices served, in outcome if not by conscious design, to conserve essential resources. And most native groups have had or still have a body of customary law governing the allocation, harvest and use of living resources, even though only a few have been committed to writing.

> The question that arises is whether these institutions are capable of solving new problems, such as commercialization, sport hunting and high efficiency gear. For this is what the decline of the traditional ethic is really about: the force and competence of customary law to deal with contemporary problems. And it is the tendency of management and enforcement

> officials to dismiss customary law that gives rise to much of the mistrust and hostility that native people now feel towards fish and wildlife departments. (Usher 1982:40)
>
> One of the causes of overharvesting, as well as of the destabilization of the traditional system, is that lands which were once by customary law closed to outsiders are now by territorial or provincial law open to all. (ibid.:42)

The necessity to deal with user groups — aboriginal and non-aboriginal — who are not susceptible to traditional or group-specific sanctions or control mechanisms, and to cope with influences on wildlife and habitat, which are totally out of control of local user groups, has demonstrated to aboriginal people the feasibility of coming to an understanding with state-mandated wildlife management. On the other hand, land claims negotiations and also plain common sense have convinced many state wildlife management officials that there has to be more user-group involvement in resource management. A logical solution appears to be a sharing of management responsibilities by means of co-management regimes.

Co-Management of Wildlife: The Concept

There is no widely accepted definition of co-management. The term broadly refers to various levels of integration of local- and state-level management systems. In their treatise on co-management, Berkes, George and Preston (1991a:12) use the term to describe "the sharing of power and responsibility between the government and local resource users." To come to grips with the concept, we have to focus our attention on two areas: the characteristics of the two different wildlife management systems that are to be combined or integrated, and the nature or level of this mutual integration.

> A model, or system, of wildlife management consists of at least the following elements: an information base and a paradigm, or set of mental constructs, that organizes and interprets it into useful knowledge; a set of practitioners with a distinctive worldview or culture that includes both this paradigm and certain normative values; a system of rules, norms, and customs that are intended to govern the behaviour of all who partake of wildlife and its benefits; and an overall set of objectives which are imbedded in the larger structure of values and goals of the society as a whole. (Usher 1986:70)

Usher (1986), Feit (1988a) and Berkes, George and Preston (1991a/b) provide us with insightful descriptions of the two wildlife management systems.

State management derives its legitimacy from the authority of the law of a nation state, usually from the constitutional powers exercised by the legislatures or the executives (Feit 1988a:75).

> The state system rests on a common property concept in which the state assumes exclusive responsibility and capability for managing a resource equally accessible to all citizens. The state manages for certain levels of abundance on a technical basis, and then allocates shares of this abundance to users on an economic and political basis. The system of knowledge is based on a scientific accumulation, organization, and interpretation of data, and management problems are resolved in a technical, a historical framework. This system of management is bureaucratic, which is to say, hierarchically organized and vertically compartmentalized. Managers become distinct from harvesters, authority becomes centralized and flows from the top down. The environment is reduced to conceptually discrete components which are managed separately. As these separate management units take on a life of their own, management objectives diverge and become focused on specialized objectives: maximizing fur production, trophy production or recreational expenditures. Not least, the management of fish and wildlife resources becomes separated from the management of the lands and waters that sustains them. (Usher 1986:71)

Indigenous local-level management systems are based on self-regulation (Berkes, George and Preston 1991a:12), and their legitimacy and authority is derived at the local level from community-based systems of knowledge, values and social conventions.

> The indigenous system rests on communal property arrangements, in which the local harvesting group is responsible for management by consensus. Management and harvesting are conceptually and practically inseparable. Knowledge comes from the experience of every aspect of harvesting itself — travelling, searching, hunting, skinning, butchering, and eating. It is accumulated by every individual, and shared intimately and constantly within the household, the family, or whatever is the social unit of production. It is also shared and exchanged within the larger society, and handed down in the form of stories from one generation to the next. In sum, these observations, like those of the state system's, become coded and organized by a paradigm or a set of paradigms that provide a comprehensive interpretation of them. The knowledge so produced becomes the cultural heritage of these societies, just as what we call science is part of ours.
>
> ...The indigenous system of management is a core feature of all northern Native cultures, and is therefore intimately linked with their values, ethics, and cosmology, which are generally based on an integrated, non-compartmentalized view of the environment. (Usher 1986:71)

Usher emphasizes that he describes two ideal types, the real examples of which are not necessarily as far apart as those models would suggest (ibid.:72). The fact remains, however, that the two systems are based on and operate within two profoundly different social realities, the protagonists of which have held each others' resource management systems in anything but high regard and have commonly failed to acknowledge the other as having any legitimacy. One of the fundamental challenges of co-management has also been the recognition of the strength and potential contributions of these two systems of knowledge (Berkes, George and Preston 1991a:12).

The reason for the lack of a single appropriate definition of co-management is the fact that there is a continuum of co-management arrangements, ranging from those that merely feature some local participation in government research, for example, to those that retain all the management power and responsibility in local communities. Berkes, George and Preston (1991a:12) suggest the use of a modified version of Arnstein's (1969) "ladder of citizen participation" to depict levels of co-management as rungs of a ladder that proceed through various stages of token power sharing to an increasing amount of real power-sharing. The seven rungs or stages may be characterized as follows:

1. **Information** constitutes the lowest level at which the management process is opened up to users — essentially one-way communication, often in technical jargon whereby information is supplied to user groups on rules and regulations, schedules and changes.
2. **Consultation** involves an explicit attempt to obtain the views of users. Although there is face-to-face contact, "Resource users may be heard but not heeded, and perhaps not even understood." (Berkes, George and Preston 1991b:7)
3. At the **cooperation** stage there is more than just talk. Local environmental knowledge is actively sought, and the use of native research assistants falls into this stage. Significantly though, the research being carried out follows the government agenda, and local users are involved at a low level as assistants or guides.
4. The **communication** stage marks the start of an actual information exchange. Local concerns begin to enter research agendas and resource management decisions . While community concerns are responded to, the government agency retains all power of decision-making.
5. The establishment of **advisory committees** marks the stage at which partnership in decision-making starts. There is an agreement to share power and responsibility for resource management through joint boards or committees. Such joint bodies often come about as the result of land claims negotiations or in an attempt to cope with a resource management impasse. While there is a search for common objectives, such initiatives are often ad hoc and sectoral. These committees have advisory powers only; they do not make decisions.

6. **Management boards** represent a higher rung if they have more than a merely advisory function. At this stage local users are actively involved in policy-making and in decision-making. Board decisions are usually binding.
7. At the last stage, joint decision-making is institutionalized, and there is a partnership of equals. Two alternatives present themselves: **community control** and **partnership**. Where resources are manageable locally (e.g. beaver), most or all management power is delegated to the community. In the case of resources that cannot be managed at the local level (e.g. caribou or Canada geese), resource users participate in decision-making as equal partners. This highest rung of the co-management ladder is characterized by the principle: "as much local-level management as possible; only so much government regulation as necessary." (Berkes, George and Preston 1991b:7–9; 36; 30 n. 9)

Over the past two decades a variety of co-management regimes were established in various parts of the country, which exhibited many if not all the above-mentioned features. Some were the result of land claims negotiations, others came about as a response to a perceived resource-management crisis. Some were area-specific, others focused on a particular species. Depending on their nature and on the severity of the tests they were subjected to, they have met with mixed success. The commonly perceived need for an innovative management approach was and still is the lowest common denominator of all co-management experiments.

> Neither the indigenous system nor the state system alone can protect northern wildlife and ecosystems, much less generate efficient and equitable wildlife management. Government agencies cannot implement and enforce their regulations without Native co-operation, Natives cannot protect the resources nor guarantee access to those resources without cooperation of government agencies. By creating co-management regimes that meld the two systems, both groups gain. (Osherenko 1988:102)

Co-Management of Wildlife: Examples

The James Bay and Northern Quebec Agreement

The James Bay and Northern Quebec Agreement (JBNQA) of 1975 provides for the native right to hunt, fish and trap all species of fauna, at all times, over all categories of land in the entire territory utilized by aboriginal groups. The only potential constraint on this aboriginal harvesting right is that it is subject to the principle of conservation, which is specifically defined in the Agreement.

> Conservation means the pursuit of the optimum natural productivity of all living resources and the protection of the ecological systems of the Territory so as to protect endangered species and to ensure primarily the continuance of the traditional pursuits of the native people, and secondarily the satisfaction of the needs of non-native people for sport hunting and fishing. (Feit 1989:77)

It was a fundamental assumption of the JBNQA negotiations that conservation was a shared priority goal, acceptable to and binding for all parties involved. Changes to the Agreement can only be made with native consent. The JBNQA was a legally binding contract between the aboriginal groups and the governments of Quebec and Canada. With the passing of the 1982 Constitution Act, the Agreement acquired constitutional protection, effectively denying the possibility of unilateral changes by either government.

One of the most important and constructive elements of the Agreement was the legal recognition of the Cree system of renewable resource management with its key structures: the system of hunting territories and the "owners" of these territories, now referred to as "traplines" and "tallymen". Feit remarks that the incorporation of the traditional aboriginal land tenure and resource management system in the JBNQA definition of harvesting rights was agreeable to all parties

> ...because it provided an acceptable series of compromises on several issues but especially those relating to sovereignty: (1) it recognized Cree rights but left open the question of the source of those rights, a form that did not make them dependent on a delegation of government authority but that also did not challenge government sovereignty by asserting an alternative source of legitimacy; (2) while not challenging sovereignty of government, the rights limited governments' claimed rights to unilaterally change Cree rights and thereby limited future exercise of government sovereignty; (3) both Cree and governments submitted themselves to a principle of protecting animals and wildlife; and (4) government recognized the indigenous Cree system of management of land and wildlife resources. (Feit 1989:78f)

As we noted earlier, in the late 1980s the system was still operative, serving both Cree resource utilization and conservation purposes well.

Another element of the Agreement — not strictly part of the co-management issue but affecting its relevancy — is the Income Security Program (ISP) for Cree hunters and trappers, which provides a guaranteed cash income to families following a "traditional" way of life, defined in the Agreement as spending at least 120 days per year on harvesting or related activities (Berkes 1989:192). As described in more detail by Feit (1988b:75–78; 1989:85–92) and Colin Scott (1984), this Program has effectively revitalized the indigenous land-based economy of the region. Furthermore, it has increased the number of Cree people who make hunting their main productive activity by about one-third. It has enhanced the traditional social organization of hunting, even though at the community level several changes in social organization and decision-making processes did occur. It is too early to comment on the potential threat of the development of a cycle of consumerism within Cree society. While consumer goods have increased, the emphasis has clearly been on goods and services that increase the efficiency or security of bush life. ISP has enabled the hunting sector of the Cree regional economy to expand during periods of recession in its commercial and administrative sector. After the insecurities of the 1960s and early 1970s, there has been an increased confidence in the viability of the hunting way of life, and this perception has been reflected in an increased and successful encouragement to young people to pursue that way of life. Finally, ISP has not resulted in any general overutilization or depletion of wildlife resources, since the traditional system of checks and balances has remained in place.

These undeniable accomplishments of the Agreement in general and the co-management regime in particular are counterbalanced by some significant problems and failures. Most of these can be related to one of the following: the functioning of the key co-management institution, the "Coordinating Committee on Hunting, Fishing and Trapping"; the failure of both governments to follow through with the implementation of various aspects of the Agreement; and the physical threat to the land and its renewable resources.

Problems with the Coordinating Committee — essentially "a white man's institution run by white man's rules" (Berkes 1989:195) — were already mentioned in the discussion of fisheries. The Committee is made up of representatives from the Cree, Naskapi and Inuit parties; the Quebec government; the federal government; and the developers. It supervises harvest studies, handles management-related information, recommends conservation measures, participates in environmental impact assessments, and generally provides a forum for native concerns. It functions strictly in an advisory capacity, and makes recommendations directly to the appropriate federal or provincial minister (Berkes 1989:192). The Coordinating Committee was a compromise from the outset.

> The major area of conflict was the relative authority of native and nonnative institutions in these regulatory structures and processes. Cree wanted final decision-making authority or shared authority; federal and provincial governments claimed such authority as an aspect of sovereignty. The idea of coordinating management through a joint committee developed in response to this confrontation but failed to settle the issue of who would control the joint system and have the authority to take and implement decisions.

> ...The provincial and federal governments retained a final decision-making authority for most, but not all issues; however their authority would be constrained. The goals and principles for management decisions, such as conservation and minimal impact on Cree activities, are legally binding on government decision makers, and a complex procedural system of consultation must be followed before advice of the joint committees can be set aside. This system respects government sovereignty while significantly constraining any exercise of that sovereignty which might negate Cree rights or benefits.
>
> Although key tests have not yet arisen, this system appears to be only partially workable in practice. The system is complex and bureaucratic; when it is not used in an atmosphere of goodwill, those using it can lose sight of issues in a plethora of procedures and rights. Furthermore, where there are significant conflicts between interests expressed by Cree and those expressed by governments, the system tends to inaction or slow action on the part of governments. Inaction has become a major tool of the governments for avoiding their legal obligations, thereby making it more difficult for Cree to bring court challenges based on contentions that government has acted in violation of the Agreement. Government does not, therefore, always respond effectively to Cree needs and sometimes undermines Cree rights.
>
> Beyond this, government has not always acted in the interests of conservation and has often responded primarily to political pressure from nonnatives rather than to conservation needs. To this extent, a fundamental assumption of JBNQA negotiations — that conservation was a shared priority goal — has not been systematically confirmed by experience with the implementation of the Agreement. (Feit 1989:82f)

The Committee has been plagued by problems of logistics, communication, insufficient funds, low-level government representation and a general lack of political clout. There has been a tendency on the part of governments to consult the Committee only casually and after major policy decisions have been made. Berkes (1989:202) feels that many of the problems are related to inconsistencies between the Agreement and existing government policies. While the Agreement seems to place top priority on aboriginal subsistence needs, the management regime for the area focuses on cash-oriented development, such as tourism and sport fishing. The main Quebec agency that receives recommendations from the Coordinating Committee is the Ministry of Recreation, Game and Fish. Its management policies are strongly oriented towards serving tourists and sport fishermen; there is hardly any provision in their plans to accommodate extensive native subsistence use of living resources. As a result, Coordinating Committee recommendations tend to be out of line with official policies, and they are frequently ignored.

The single most important factor, however, that places the aboriginal land-based economy and the co-management regime along with it in greatest jeopardy, is the physical threat to the land and its renewable resources by future hydro and related developments. Even in Category II lands, where aboriginal groups have exclusive harvesting rights, they do not hold subsurface rights, and these lands may be expropriated for development, subject to the provision of equal amounts of Category II lands elsewhere. Particularly in the southern portion of the region, commercial cutting of the forests occurs on a large scale and at a rapid pace, rendering affected hunting territories unusable for at least several decades. Large-scale industrial development projects are continuing on Cree lands (Feit 1989:96). Future phases of hydroelectric development are being delayed, but they are not abandoned.

Under the Agreement native people have achieved exclusive and preferential rights to living resources and a considerable degree of self-regulation, but they have no security of tenure on their land and, therefore, no guarantee for the future of a land-based way of life. At stake are a revitalized hunting economy and a fully operative aboriginal system of renewable resource management which put this situation into a particularly sharp focus.

The Inuvialuit Final Agreement

The Western Arctic or Inuvialuit Final Agreement (IFA) of 1984 was the first to be negotiated under the Comprehensive Land Claims Policy of 1974 and was, until recently (i.e. the ratification of the Gwich'in Agreement in 1992), the only one to have reached the stage of implementation. For a critical observation of wildlife co-management under the Agreement, it is important to know the goals being pursued by the signing partners of the Agreement. As Nancy Doubleday reminds us, "...the provisions of the Inuvialuit Final Agreement which deal with management of living resources are but one component of a cross-cultural compromise between Canada and the Inuvialuit." (Doubleday 1989:210)

The goals of the Inuvialuit with regard to their comprehensive claims settlement are spelled out in Section 1 of the Inuvialuit Final Agreement as follows:

- Preserve Inuvialuit cultural identity and values within a changing northern society;
- Enable Inuvialuit to be equal and meaningful participants in the northern and national economy and society
- Protect and preserve the Arctic wildlife, environment and biological productivity (Government of Canada 1984:1)

Doubleday (1989:211) summarizes these goals as cultural identity, integration and conservation.

The goals of the Government of Canada in regard to the settlement of comprehensive claims are detailed in its policy statement entitled "In All Fairness". The main thrust of this policy is "to exchange undefined aboriginal land rights for concrete rights and benefits." (Government of Canada 1981:19) With regard to wildlife, the statement specifically states:

> In addition to dealing with the protection of their rights to hunt, fish and trap the settlements should provide for the involvement of Native people in a much wider spectrum of activities affecting the whole area of wildlife. This could include, for example, fuller participation in wildlife management, such as making **recommendations to the government on the establishment and maintenance of wildlife quotas or providing advice** on the formulation of management policies and other related matters.
>
> Generally, the settlements may provide for prescribed **preferential rights** to wildlife on Crown lands. Exclusive rights would be limited to fee simple or the equivalent Native lands or to specified species elsewhere. **All areas, whether they include those for exclusive Native use or shared by the general public will continue to be subject to the existing general laws as they apply to hunting, fishing and trapping; they will be further subject to present and future sound conservation policies and public safety measures**. (ibid.:24, emphasis added)

Summarizing the overall governmental goals, Doubleday (1989:212) lists the following: fairness to native and non-native Canadians; specification of native rights under Canadian jurisdiction; and legal certainty.

The IFA created two principal management structures: the Inuvialuit Game Council (IGC) and the Inuvialuit Regional Corporation (IRC). The IGC is the body primarily concerned with renewable resources management. It is composed of a chairman and at least one representative from the Inuvialuit Hunters and Trappers Committees (HTCs) of Aklavik, Inuvik, Tuktoyaktuk, Paulatuk, Sachs Harbour and Holman Island. Its purpose is to "represent the collective Inuvialuit interest in wildlife" (Doubleday 1989:216), with one of its most important functions being the appointment of Inuvialuit members to all joint government/Inuvialuit bodies having an interest in wildlife. The IRC, on the other hand, is a development-oriented body, managing the IFA settlement lands and cash compensation. "It is, in effect, a large firm with business interests and an orientation to increasing the tangible value of the corporation." (Binder and Hanbidge 1991:4) The relationship between these two management structures, the IGC and the IRC, is not explicitly spelled out in the Agreement, but there seems to be a deliberate "dichotomy or tension" created under the IFA.

> ...the Inuvialuit Game Council and the Inuvialuit Regional Corporation are charged with what in western industrialized societies are fundamentally opposite mandates: conservation and economic development. (Robinson and Binder 1991:5)

Part of the task of resolving both the conservation and the development mandate falls to the various co-management bodies created under the IFA, collectively referred to as the Renewable Resources Committees. There are five of them: a Wildlife Management Advisory Council for the Northwest Territories and one for the North Slope of Yukon respectively (WMAC [NWT]/[NS], which includes DOE and GNWT/YTG); the Fisheries Joint Management Committee (FJMC, includes DFO); the Environmental Impact Screening Committee (EISC, which includes the Government of Canada, GNWT and YTG); and the Environmental Impact Review Board. Representation on each of these bodies is half Inuvialuit (IGC)-appointed and half government-appointed, with a chairman appointed by the government with Inuvialuit approval. The only exception to this is the FJMC, whose chairman is appointed directly by the Committee members (Binder and Hanbidge 1991:8).

The Wildlife Management Advisory Councils in particular are viewed by Doubleday as virtual models for joint management structures.

> ...their authority is broad, encompassing wildlife and habitat management, setting of quotas, and policy and legislative review. In theory, this body should have the capacity to make Inuvialuit views known from the local to the international level and at all levels in between, as well as ensuring equal participation by Inuvialuit in all wildlife matters. (Doubleday 1989:214f)

In her examination of the Agreement under the aspect of resources co-management, Doubleday reaches the conclusion that

> ...the Inuvialuit Final Agreement contains all the required ingredients for a co-management regime. It recognizes preferential or exclusive harvesting rights, control of access to the resource, participation in management, relevance of traditional knowledge, and modern scientific approaches to conservation — all of which represent elements of special status and self-government necessary for the survival of indigenous peoples. (ibid.:221)

However, it is also felt that the Agreement fails in one very important criterion which would truly reflect the aboriginal right to self-government in resource management: the deregulation of native rights subject to a conservation principle. "The weight within the joint management bodies will be on the side of regulation acceptable to government, rather than deregulation of native harvesting rights" (ibid.). Regulation is still not decentralized, and final decisions are invariably made by government ministers.

This is a very vital point which clearly sets the IFA apart from the JBNQA, where a considerable degree of self-regulation is being realized. But in the late 1980s the western arctic revealed some interesting examples of how local aboriginal management initiatives manifest themselves outside the narrow confines of community self-regulation and how they impact territorial and even international wildlife management.

In 1987 the Tuktoyaktuk HTC became concerned that there was overharvesting of grizzly bears. It suggested that a quota be established and the process of implementation began.

> The IFA requires cooperation between government, the joint bodies, the IGC and the HTCs to determine and establish harvest quotas. These activities are no longer the sole jurisdiction of government management agencies....With the WMAC (NWT) acting as a facilitator, consultations occurred between the government and the Inuvialuit until a consensus was reached. The WMAC (NWT) then made its recommendation to the Minister of Renewable Resources, who accepted them.
>
> It therefore became the responsibility of the IGC to designate the hunting area and quota recommended by the Minister. Once this was accomplished, the Tuktoyaktuk HTC drafted and passed a bylaw with the assistance of the Territorial Justice Department that set out the terms under which grizzly bear could be taken....The IGC approved the bylaw, making it applicable to all Inuvialuit. Concurrently, the government of the NWT adopted

> the bylaw as a regulation under the *Wildlife Act*, making it enforceable by Wildlife Officers as anticipated under section 14(77) of the IFA. At the same time the government passed a regulation under the *Wildlife Act* which was virtually identical to the HTC bylaw, making its terms enforceable as general law to non-Inuvialuit.
>
> ...**for the first time in Canada, a native organization (and user group) enacted wildlife regulations enforceable under government statutes.**
>
> At all times the WMAC (NWT) provided a forum for the government and the Inuvialuit to interact. The final result was a long-term management plan for grizzly bear and a potential economic benefit for Inuvialuit through guided sport hunting of this species. (Carpenter et al. 1991, quoted in Binder and Hanbidge 1991:13f, emphasis in original)

Polar bears constitute another example of a species, in whose protection and management aboriginal groups played a leading part. While the Banks Island subpopulation is managed in a similar manner as the grizzly bear described above, the Beaufort Sea polar bear subpopulation is shared internationally between the United States and Canada, and hunted by both the Inupiat of Alaska and the Inuvialuit of Canada. In Canada there are strict management regulations determining quotas, closed seasons and the protection of females with cubs and bears in dens. In Alaska, since the passage of the Marine Mammal Protection Act in 1972, aboriginal people are allowed to kill polar bears for subsistence purposes without restriction. Thus a potential for overharvesting exists, and it would be perfectly legal (Stirling 1988:206). As Ian Stirling points out, it could take decades for an international agreement to be negotiated between the United States and Canada, and it may not even be possible without changes in legislation. Furthermore, such an intergovernmental pact would likely be viewed by the aboriginal groups as just another imposition from the government, which would lack community support. Being concerned about the polar bear population, the Alaskan and Canadian aboriginal user groups instead negotiated an unofficial agreement between themselves to safeguard the polar bears of the Beaufort Sea. The Management Agreement for Polar Bears in the Southern Beaufort Sea was formally signed in Inuvik on January 29, 1988, by the Inuvialuit Game Council of Inuvik and the North Slope Borough Fish and Game Management Committee of Barrow, Alaska. It provides for harvesting regulations and habitat protection, as well as data collection and information-sharing.

There is also discussion of a joint Inupiat-Inuvialuit plan for management of shared Beaufort Sea beluga stock (Harwood and Adams 1991). The Alaska and Inuvialuit Beluga Whale Committee (AIBWC) was formed in 1988 to facilitate sustainable utilization, management and conservation of beluga whales in the Beaufort Sea. Representatives from coastal beluga-hunting communities in Alaska and the Mackenzie River Delta constitute half of the committee membership; the other half consists of U.S. federal and state representatives, scientists and technical advisors. The Canadian government has observer status. Since there are greater gaps in the database with regard to belugas than, for example, polar bears, the committee's activities are strongly research-oriented. To date the AIBWC has coordinated or assisted with the collection of samples for genetic, contaminant and basic biological studies; provided funding for DNA studies; supported beluga whale surveys; and commented on habitat issues related to oil and gas exploration. The fact that many of these research activities are planned and carried out by the local communities, has greatly contributed to research credibility with user groups. The AIBWC recently ratified its draft Alaska beluga whale management plan, a counterpart to the completed plan for beluga management in the western Canadian Arctic, and has initiated discussions of a joint Inupiat-Inuvialuit plan for the management of shared Beaufort Sea beluga stock.

The management situation of these smaller toothed whales, which figure most prominently in aboriginal subsistence whaling, is quite different from that of baleen whales. The former falls within national management regimes; with regard to the latter, aboriginal people have to deal with the international regulatory regime, more specifically with the designation of such species as the western Arctic bowhead whale as "endangered". Although Canada was one of the founder members of the International Whaling Commission (IWC), it withdrew from this organization in 1982 (Gambell 1991:2). Nevertheless, until 1991, Canada was reluctant to counteract the IWC guidelines with respect to severely depleted whale stocks, and to issue quotas for bowhead whales.[5]

Since the collapse of commercial whaling in the western Arctic in the 1930s, the Canadian Inuvialuit have been unable to continue their traditional hunt of the bowhead whale, unlike the Alaskan Eskimos, who in fact have developed an increasing dependence on this mammal in subsequent decades. In the late 1970s and early 1980s, the Inuvialuit began expressing deep concern about the abrogation of their traditional right to take bowhead whales (Doubleday 1989:223; 1991:13). The situation had deteriorated to the point where outside "experts" even denied the aboriginal whaling history of the Inuvialuit. Upon Inuvialuit request, an aboriginal tradition of bowhead whaling was verified by means of documentation of Inuvialuit traditional ecological knowledge of bowheads and bowhead whaling (Doubleday 1991:13).

Even then the Inuvialuit encountered a long and cumbersome process when they attempted to address this issue through the IFA and its co-management structures. As indicated by Doubleday (1989:224), the harvesting provisions of Section 14(29) of the Agreement give Inuvialuit priority with regard to marine mammals **where a harvestable quota exists**. Such quotas are to be "set jointly by the Inuvialuit and the Government according to the principles of conservation." As long as the western Arctic bowhead stock continued to be designated as "endangered species" stock by international interests, the provisions of Section 14 of the IFA were largely irrelevant. Before the international regulatory regime and the conventional scientific wisdom on which it was based, could be successfully challenged, the Inuvialuit could not act unilaterally on the basis of the Agreement to reopen the hunt.

That such opportunity eventually did present itself cannot be attributed to the Canadian government, for which the priorization of bowhead whale research has remained problematic due to its emphasis on commercial fisheries research (ibid.:225). It was primarily research initiated, commissioned or carried out by the Alaskan Eskimo Whaling Commission and its whaling communities, which served to seriously call in question prevailing scientific estimates of existing bowhead whale numbers. Canada reneged on its refusal to issue bowhead whale quotas, and in September 1991, the hunters of Aklavik attained one long-sought goal: the hunt of a bowhead whale for subsistence consumption (Binder and Hanbidge 1991:10).[6]

In the early 1990s the co-management regime which is being implemented in the Inuvialuit Settlement Region seems to be maturing. Earlier concerns — as, for example, expressed by Doubleday (1989:225f) — about potential conflicts between Inuvialuit objectives within the Agreement were not substantiated, once the environmental protection regime (which is an integral part of the co-management scheme) became fully operative. This concern had been sparked by the 1986 Inuvialuit decision to break away from the position of the Inuit Circumpolar Conference (ICC) which opposed the shipping of oil and gas by tanker, and to consent to such shipment by Gulf Canada from the Beaufort Sea, with no provision for environmental assessment and review. This decision, which was made before the co-management institutions

[5] See Freeman (1989a) for the response of Alaskan Yupik and Inupiat whalers to the 1977 decision of the IWC to place a moratorium on the taking of bowhead for subsistence purposes (i.e. to delete the aboriginal subsistence exception clause). The Eskimo whalers formed the Alaska Eskimo Whaling Commission (AEWC) and through legal proceedings and persistent lobbying persuaded the government of the United States to press for a modest take of bowhead whales to satisfy the domestic requirements of the Alaskan Eskimo. In 1981 these efforts resulted in a cooperative management agreement between the AEWC and the U.S. government.

[6] This momentous event is described in detail in Freeman, Wein and Keith 1992.

and procedures were fully established, did not augur well for the future in terms of environmental concerns.

However, one of the public reviews carried out by the Environmental Impact Review Board (EIRB) in 1990 provides a much better idea of Inuvialuit priorities. In this instance the EIRB recommended strongly against the approval of the Gulf Canada Resources Limited Kulluk Drilling Program (1990–1992) (EIRB 1990b and 1991; Gary Wagner 1991). The Gulf submission proposed a three-year program to drill a series of wells in the transition zone between the permanent-pack ice and the land-fast ice. The two principal reasons for the Board's recommendation against the proposal were the lack of preparation on the part of Gulf and the federal government to deal effectively with a major oil well blowout in the Beaufort Sea during the open water season, and the Board's inability, on the basis of the evidence, to make any sensible recommendation as to Gulf's potential liability in the event of a worst case scenario as required under s.13(11)(b) of the IFA (EIRB 1990b:16). The Kulluk decision resulted in some serious disagreements between the EIRB and the Canada Oil and Gas Lands Administration (COGLA, then acting as the government regulatory authority), but no developments took place.

To the Inuvialuit these events seem to show that the IFA environmental review process — as part of the co-management regime — does indeed "have teeth". There is also some confidence among the Inuvialuit that, even though legally the EIRB (like the other Renewable Resources Committees) has only an advisory function, for reasons of public image, the government is unlikely to approve developments or adopt measures in opposition to the Board (Gary Wagner, EIRB Secretary, personal communication, May 28, 1992).

The Beverly-Kaminuriak Caribou Management Board

The renewable resources co-management regimes which evolved under the JBNQA and the IFA are an integrated part of comprehensive claims settlements which were negotiated under the pressure of impending hydroelectric and non-renewable resource development. In contrast the Beverly-Kaminuriak Caribou Management Board owes its existence to a perceived crisis of the resource itself, one of the recurring "caribou crises." (Freeman 1989b:92) The Beverly and Kaminuriak barren ground caribou herds range over a vast area covering parts of northern Manitoba and Saskatchewan, as well as the southern Keewatin and southeastern Slave regions of the Northwest Territories. The animals constitute a crucial domestic resource for 18 Dene and Inuit communities around the edge of the caribou range, comprising a total population of approximately 13,000 (Usher 1991a:2).

In the late 1970s it was believed by biologists and government managers that both herds had been diminished to fractions of their previous populations, and were still declining at a precipitous rate. It appeared that the annual harvest exceeded natural recruitment into the caribou population. As a result, in 1979, representatives of five government agencies revitalized a long-standing Administrative Committee on Caribou Conservation as a Caribou Management Group, but concluded that they could not effectively manage the herds without involving aboriginal user groups. In 1981 representatives of these native communities proposed a users' caribou management board, with government officials having only advisory status (Osherenko 1988:95). In June 1982 these joint efforts resulted in the signing of the Beverly-Kaminuriak Barren Ground Caribou Management Agreement, which made possible the formation of the Beverly-Kaminuriak Caribou Management Board. It consists of 13 members: five representatives of the governments of Manitoba, Saskatchewan, the Northwest Territories and Canada; two community representatives each from northern Manitoba, and northern Saskatchewan; two representatives from the NWT Keewatin Wildlife Federation; and one each from the NWT Dene Nation and Metis Association. The overall objectives of the board may be summarized as follows:

- Coordinate the management of the herds primarily for traditional users on the caribou range;
- Establish a process of shared responsibility for the development of management programs between the agencies and traditional users; and
- Encourage communication between the agencies, groups, and public at large. (Monaghan 1984:422)

The Agreement did not transfer any jurisdiction or management authority to the Board; its function is purely advisory. Areas of recommendation (to the appropriate ministers) for herd management include such issues as the limitation of annual harvests and the allocation of those harvests between jurisdictions; the encouragement of traditional users to participate in management programs; and development and review of research proposals, harvest data collection systems, and predator management programs (ibid.). Further responsibilities of the Board include the monitoring of caribou habitat and conducting an information and education program.

Since its inception the Board has done much to reduce the polarization of opinions held by government and aboriginal parties, as each group has gained an appreciation and better understanding of different viewpoints (ibid.:425). A key component of the Board's relatively efficient operation has been the continuity of its membership and staff. Moreover, the Agreement calls for consensus decision-making whenever possible, acknowledging the value of the indigenous system (Osherenko 1988:98).

The Board tends to be seen in a positive light by governments as well as users (Usher 1991a:3–6). For governments it provides an effective venue for consultation with users and for coordination (particularly with regard to research) among jurisdictions. The Board's recommendations are generally viewed as sound, even if governments do not or cannot act on all of them. The Board itself is seen as realistic and relatively non-political. From the governments' viewpoint, caribou are no longer a high profile political issue, and the Board is seen as an important reason for that (ibid.:4).

Users favour the Board because it enables them to speak directly with managers and biologists about the resource, which is of vital concern to them. "Users feel that, while the Board is by no means perfect...the situation is a vast improvement over the days when management policy was made behind closed doors." (ibid.) Opportunities created by the Agreement are particularly appreciated by users in the provinces, where in the past they have had no input in resource management, and where, historically, treaty rights have been interpreted restrictively. The Inuit, in comparison, do not view the Board as so valuable an institution because they occupy a politically more powerful position in the Northwest Territories; also, their claims process offers alternative venues for conflict resolution.

> From an aboriginal political perspective, the Board certainly does not measure up to such objectives as self-government or self-management. The distinction between users and managers remains fundamental to the Board's structure and mandate, and in this sense, the Board is not fully an instrument of co-management. On the other hand, neither do the proposed claims-based management boards measure up to these ideals, since they are instruments of public government, not self-government. (Usher 1991a:6)

Despite its limited mandate, the Beverly-Kaminuriak Caribou Management Board is heralded by many as a model of successful co-management in the North (Osherenko 1988:95). This prompts Peter Usher to ask, whether the Board has really been such a success, a question which he answers with a qualified "yes, but within limits." (Usher 1991a:1) He credits this success only in part to the Board itself, and partly to good fortune.

The Caribou Management Board was born out of a crisis, which as it turned out, did not exist. Almost immediately after the Board's establishment, it became apparent that both herds were in fact more numerous than expected (Freeman 1989b:99; Usher 1991a:8).

Consequently, the Board did not find it necessary to start out by adopting unpopular management measures, but found it possible instead to start developing a cooperative atmosphere as well as a management plan. Numbers and productivity of the herds continue to be satisfactory, and there appears to be no immediate threat to this status quo. Usher (1991a:9) therefore concludes, the effect of this good fortune is that the Board has never been tested by a crisis of scarcity, which in the future may turn out to be the most crucial test.

Usher draws our attention to another favourable factor which undoubtedly has made the Board's task easier. While the Beverly and Kaminuriak herds are often characterized as a shared resource — not only among jurisdictions but also between Dene and Inuit hunters and communities — they are not really a shared resource in other important respects. The animals are used almost entirely for subsistence hunting by about 18 small aboriginal communities. The licensed resident and guided sport hunt are very limited, and there is virtually no commercial hunt. The exclusive focus by the Board on management for subsistence from the beginning has eliminated an element of competition, which constitutes a major source of conflict in the management context of most other large mammal populations (ibid.:2f).

Finally, Gail Osherenko (1988:97) states that the caribou co-management regime is imbedded in a favourable political climate. One of the government parties to the Agreement, the GNWT, represents a predominantly native population holding a majority of seats in the Legislative Assembly. In recent years aboriginal people have, at different times, held the minister and deputy minister posts in the Department of Renewable Resources of the GNWT, the agency responsible for the regulation of caribou hunting. Altogether, this circumstance has greatly contributed to the creation of a partnership between government and user groups.

As to the Board's achievements, Usher agrees that it has been an advocate for subsistence interests and a reasonably effective lobby with governments. The Board has had substantial input into allocation and regulatory decisions, "...however, these do not cost governments much money." (Usher 1991a:7) While governments have been willing enough to follow the Board's advice on matters of species management, the same cannot be said for habitat protection (Osherenko 1988:95). In fact, Osherenko (ibid.:98) feels that the biggest threat to the co-management regime comes from the apparent unwillingness of public authorities to act on the Board's recommendations with regard to habitat protection. Such protection would include fire management, as well as full protection of calving grounds from future industrial development (Usher 1991:7).

Furthermore, Peter Usher (1991a:11ff) raises the closely related concerns of successful communication and more effective incorporation of traditional knowledge in the management process. The use of English as the Board's working language tends to bar hunters with the most profound ecological knowledge from Board membership, although they do attend community meetings. Some of the principal terminology of the Board — wildlife, management, census, population — involves concepts which are not directly translatable from English to Chipewyan and Inuktitut, and do not even necessarily mean the same things in English to all members (Usher 1991a:12).

> However, if users do not fully understand what they are being told, or do not agree with it, they may either avoid seeking clarification, or state their concerns in a metaphor so unfamiliar to managers as to fail to promote useful dialogue. Consequently, approval of research agendas and proposals by user members may be more apparent than real. (ibid.:13)

> ...the criteria for co-management ought not simply to be user participation in the state system, or the appropriation of user knowledge by the state system, but rather a harmonization of the state and indigenous systems or approaches to understanding. What I have described is certainly progress, but it is not to say that the knowledge of aboriginal hunters has been adequately utilized, or that their views have been adequately understood and incorporated into the management process. (ibid.:14f)

Co-Management of Renewable Resources in Northern Manitoba

As expressed by Harvey Payne, formerly with the Manitoba Department of Natural Resources, "co-management in action" has actually a long tradition in northern Manitoba, if we classify the joint administration of the trapping regime by the provincial government and native communities as "co-management." (Payne, personal communication, October 1991) In this context the provincial government is perceived by native people as more responsive to trapping concerns in the past, than to resource-related aboriginal concerns nowadays. The "co-management story" for northern Manitoba is exemplified by the experiences of the Waterhen First Nation.

Like the Beverly-Kaminuriak Barren Ground Caribou Management Agreement, the Waterhen Moose Management Agreement was prompted by a crisis, a "real" crisis. In the 1970s it was discovered that the local moose population had drastically declined. A cancellation of licensed hunting in the mid-1970s did not effect a satisfactory recovery of the animals. The most important independent variable left was Treaty Indian hunting. As a result, in 1984 the Waterhen First Nation and the Manitoba government entered into a Moose Management Agreement, whereby the Waterhen Band agreed to voluntarily limit moose hunting in its traditional territory. Such restraint — which is still being advocated today (*Waterhen First Nation Resources Newsletter* 1, May 1991) — has resulted in a significant recovery of the local moose population. In view of this positive development, the Band is now intensifying its efforts to gain increased management control over the moose and to derive some revenue from their utilization by the acquisition of licences from the province for non-resident hunters, to be outfitted by the Band, which has met with partial success.

The immediate goal of the Moose Management Agreement — a recovery of the local moose population — was reached within a few years. However, this appears to be due to effective self-regulation on the part of the native community, rather than to the successful functioning of co-management processes or co-management institutions. As a result of the Agreement, the provincial government has undoubtedly been more forthcoming in sharing information with the Waterhen Band about conservation and resource management. The co-management institution created by the Agreement has remained a loosely structured advisory committee, half of which is appointed by the Band, the other half by the provincial government. Its activities and operation are informal and somewhat haphazard. Effective aboriginal input appears to be dependent on the political clout of individuals, rather than to flow from the design of the Agreement.

That the Agreement as it now stands is simply not effective in protecting Waterhen First Nation interests is proven by recent events. In 1990 the provincial government allocated to a major pulp and paper company most of the habitat targeted for moose and bison management, without any consultation and consideration of the Band. The Band's leadership declares that this is not acceptable.

> In the eyes of government and the company, the relationship between Repap and Manitoba is firmly established in the form of the Forest Act, the Forest Management Licence and the Share Purchase Agreement. Repap relies on the language of these agreements to protect its "rights" to harvest timber in our lands. The relationship between Waterhen, Pine Creek and Manitoba in these circumstances is much less clearly established. We seek a bi-lateral negotiation process with the Province to establish a co-management relationship. We are therefore not prepared to meet with Repap until such time as the commitment, principles and framework for our co-management agreement with Manitoba are as firmly established and binding in the eyes of government as is Repap's relationship with the Province. (Nepinak 1991a:4)

As in the 1980s a crisis provided the impetus for these renewed negotiations, which are being joined by the neighbouring Pine Creek First Nation. In the 1990s, however, it is not a conservation crisis, but rather co-management is viewed by the aboriginal parties as a potential means of conflict resolution and a tool to protect treaty rights. This time Waterhen does not seek a narrowly defined species-specific management agreement confined to Game Hunting Area #20, but rather a comprehensive, renewable resources co-management agreement, with a true element of power-sharing, and a scope extended to the ecologically and socially more relevant Fur Blocks.

The native negotiators want the co-management agreement to be treatylike in nature, recognizing and affirming treaty and aboriginal rights on the basis of the Constitution Act of 1982 and along the guidelines of the *Sparrow* ruling. Co-management is to be based on the principles of conservation and sustainable development, and there has to be an effective integration of "two bodies of wisdom". First Nations seek a joint role with the provincial Department of Natural Resources, and they will not be satisfied with an advisory capacity. Final decisions are to rest jointly with the Minister and First Nations (Waterhen and Pine Creek First Nations 1991).

The provincial government agrees to the overall guidelines and principles set out by the other party, and like the bands, envisages the joint appointment of a co-management board to administer the agreement. A potential source of friction is the recognition by the government of third-party interests (f.e. Repap), whereas the bands want local interests accorded the highest priority (Government of Manitoba 1991). The most glaring difference in viewpoint, however, concerns the matter of power-sharing and the question of authority in final decision-making. The government is adamant that the Minister retains final authority; First Nations are equally insistent on sharing this authority. There are tentative gestures of a rapprochement in this matter (*Waterhen First Nation Resources Newsletter* 2, June 1991), but the future will have to show the effectiveness of compromises.

Initiatives in Nunavut

Nunavut is subject to the Nunavut Land Claims Agreement, which was signed on May 25, 1993, by the Tungavik Federation of Nunavut (TFN) and Canada, and awaits passage into legislation in the immediate future. With respect to renewable resources management, the Agreement features a management structure that is similar in principle, if not in detail, to that of the Inuvialuit Final Agreement. The principal instrument of wildlife management is the Nunavut Wildlife Management Board, with equal Inuit and government/public membership plus a chairperson. The Board will oversee the harvest of wildlife, subject to the principle of conservation, and will be empowered to make management decisions, subject to disallowance by appropriate ministers (Government of Canada and the Tungavik 1993:28–37).

In the recent past, various wildlife management/co-management initiatives have sprung up on an ad hoc basis throughout the region. Their varied success is illustrated by two examples from Baffin Island.

In 1985 data collected by GNWT research programs suggested that the population of polar bears in the northeast Baffin area had been reduced by overharvest. In other words, the quotas set for that region were apparently too high. As a result, the wildlife managers set out to reduce the polar bear quotas for the communities of Broughton Island and Clyde River through a negotiated agreement between the community Hunters' and Trappers' Associations and the Government of the Northwest Territories (Lloyd 1986:108).

The reduction in quotas envisaged was substantial: The number went down from 45 bears to 15 in one community; and from 22 to 10 bears in another. According to Freeman (1986:31), the community that reduced its bear harvest by 67 per cent was one of the Inuit communities hardest hit by the European boycott of sealskins, and hardly able to afford any further reduction in its domestic income. Nevertheless, the communities voluntarily complied with the new quotas, as they shared the concern about the state of the bear population and had developed a satisfactory working relationship with government resource managers and scientists. The process that led to this positive result was a lengthy and costly one.

Kevin Lloyd summarizes the evolution of the Agreement with the following sequence of events:

1. Agreement that there was a problem;
2. Agreement that the Inuit had more to lose than anyone else, if there was overharvest and a prolonged recovery;
3. Agreement that the Department of Renewable Resources and the Inuit would work together to identify a solution to the problem. (Lloyd 1986:115)

He attributes the success of the negotiations to several factors, namely:

1. Independent evidence from the hunters' own experience which corroborated the possibility of overharvest;
2. Repetition of meetings with adequate time between meetings for acceptance of the nature of the problem and proposed solutions;
3. Negotiation with the hunters by the individual who had the benefit of direct experience in the research, the Polar Bear Biologist;
4. Trust by the hunters in the Biologist. This grew throughout the process and was based on several years of dialogue about polar bears and on the Biologist's natural attribute of being forthright and honest; and
5. Ongoing contact between the wildlife officer and the HTA. This kept the issue "alive" and also ensured quick responses to questions from hunters. (ibid.)

The Agreement between the Government of the Northwest Territories and the people of Broughton Island and Clyde River was in the form of a Letter of Understanding, rather than a formal co-management agreement. The Letter of Understanding was signed in 1985 by the presidents of the two HTAs and the Minister of Renewable Resources for the GNWT. In addition to the reduced quotas, it provided for other conservation measures, such as the sparing of breeding females and family groups, and emphasized that the Agreement was in no way prejudicial to the comprehensive claim settlement.

This Agreement was not a co-management agreement resulting in the creation of its own co-management institutions and procedures. Rather it was a cooperative effort by the government and user groups, which resulted in the successful mobilization of self-regulation on the part of the aboriginal community, based on a mutually agreed upon purpose. The Agreement was renewed in 1992.

In the winter of 1991/1992 another informal agreement concerning polar bears was worked out, this time with the communities of Grise Fjord, Arctic Bay, Pond Inlet and Resolute Bay. It was similar in principle to the NE-Baffin polar bear Letter of Understanding.

The brief history of the SE Baffin Beluga Committee and the federal government's conservation efforts for this species demonstrates that not all joint management initiatives meet with success. The SE Baffin beluga whale stock is viewed by the federal DFO as a strongly pressured group, in sore need of conservation measures. A revival of a quasi-commercial whale fishery for intersettlement trade resulted in a peak harvest of 178 belugas in 1977 and prompted the government's concern. After an initial quota reduction, a Beluga Management Committee was formed in 1986, with joint representation from the communities of Pangnirtung, Iqaluit, Lake Harbor and the federal government. However, the functioning of the Committee remained very ineffective, and a satisfactory working relationship among communities and between user groups and government was never established.

In 1989 the Nunavut Wildlife Management Advisory Board was created and its assistance was enlisted for beluga-conservation measures. The Board agreed to an annual quota of five belugas per community. Funding shortages severely limited its effectiveness, and appropriate community consultation was not realized (Pike, Richard and Goodman 1991).

Things came to a head in the fall of 1990, in the wake of the Oka crisis, with outright defiance of quota regulations by Iqaluit hunters and the seizure of one beluga by DFO officials. By then the beluga issue had become an extremely emotional subject, not so much because belugas are an important staple, but because they are a delicacy and a "cultural icon" (Bob Longworth, Manager of the Iqaluit Research Centre, personal communication, August 5, 1992). In an outburst of protest highly unusual for the community of Iqaluit, people marched in the streets protesting the quota regulations, and a radical section, Qalugiaq, tried to disrupt a meeting of the Nunavut Wildlife Management Advisory Board.

At this point the NWT government leader intervened and suggested that the NWT Science Institute become involved as a mediator. As a northern institution the Institute had credibility and a track record of acknowledging traditional as well as western scientific knowledge. The SE Baffin Beluga Committee was reorganized under the chairmanship of the Executive Director of the Science Institute, with representation from the HTAs of the three communities, a representative from the Baffin Regional Council and the DFO, and with two unofficial observers, namely a consultant and the manager of the Iqaluit Research Centre.

The Committee met in January 1991, reviewing scientific as well as traditional knowledge of the SE Baffin beluga stock and conducting community meetings. In conclusion, the Committee was dissatisfied with DFO assumptions which it found "shaky" on several grounds. It drafted a unanimous report to the Minister of Fisheries and Oceans, who accepted all of the Committee's recommendations (including an increased quota). One of the most important recommendations concerned the establishment of a new beluga co-management institution. This co-management board is constituted by representatives from the communities, a representative from the Baffin Regional Council, the regional DFO Superintendent and a second DFO representative (who was a member of the original SE Baffin Beluga Committee). This board has been functioning since.

Dan Pike and his coauthors point to several reasons for the failure of the original conservation efforts for SE Baffin beluga whales.

1. The initiative was prompted by an externally perceived stock crisis, which is always a dubious starting point for conservation. "Hunters hate being told what to do";
2. The DFO felt compelled to act fast because of the conservation problem, without sufficient time to establish a satisfactory working relationship with the user groups;
3. The aboriginal communities were not directly involved in research and decision-making; and
4. The language barrier was a serious obstacle to communication. (Pike, Richard and Goodman 1991)

In 1991 and 1992 there were successful beluga harvests without incident. Even though the situation has stabilized somewhat in the last two years, beluga management currently constitutes by far the most volatile issue DFO has to deal with (Tim Suretti, DFO Area Manager, Iqaluit, personal communication, August 7, 1992). Dissension within the native community constitutes a major problem. SE Baffin Inuit are by no means united in their perception of the beluga situation or the manner in which this situation should be handled. Such internal friction is more pronounced in Iqaluit than in more stable and traditional communities, such as Pangnirtung and Lake Harbour. From the point of view of government officials, the inability to deal with representative leaders creates unsurmountable problems (ibid.). Nevertheless, DFO is making concerted efforts to involve aboriginal user groups in research and decision-making. Beluga surveys in the summer of 1992 constitute an example where biologists yielded to Inuit advice in the choice of their survey methods, adopting cliff surveys rather than aerial surveys.

Co-Management of Wildlife: Observations

The previous examples have shown that wildlife co-management regimes have evolved under a variety of conditions and circumstances. The settlement of comprehensive claims serves as an important vehicle for designing and implementing co-management. Not surprisingly, the conditions under which claims are negotiated and the goals incorporated in their overall settlement have an important impact on the evolving co-management regimes. The James Bay and Northern Quebec Agreement was essentially accomplished to clear the way for large-scale hydro developments, and this is reflected in the current threat to the Cree land base, without which renewable resources co-management, however successful, is futile. The Inuvialuit are faced with a certain dichotomy in the objectives expressed in the IFA and the institutions created by it, which presents a special challenge for their co-management regime. The people of Nunavut may find themselves in a similar situation, once their Agreement reaches the stage of implementation. Lancaster Sound faces similar environmental threats (necessitating political decision-making) from oil and gas exploration, production and shipping as the Beaufort Sea.

Co-management regimes that are not part of a comprehensive claims settlement were usually initiated by the government in response to a perceived or real resource crisis. These are exemplified by the Beverly-Kaminuriak Barren Ground Caribou Management Agreement, the Waterhen Moose Management Agreement, and the initiatives on Baffin Island to protect depleted polar bear and beluga whale stocks. In such cases, governments lack any real control over aboriginal harvesting activities, and aboriginal peoples may or may not, of their own accord, become party to joint management agreements, which may limit their harvesting as a group (Wagner 1991:27). Such "emergency responses" are usually species-specific.

An exception to this pattern is the Hook Lake Wood Bison Management Plan, which was initiated by the native community with self-regulatory measures that evolved into a co-management plan. Though focused on the wood bison, this initiative also exhibits strong elements of a feeling of land stewardship born out of an aboriginal title claim.

In the 1990s yet another category of co-management initiatives made its appearance. These initiatives are considered emergency measures, too. They are undertaken by aboriginal groups in an attempt to use co-management regimes for conflict resolution and as a means to protect treaty and aboriginal rights. The ongoing negotiations between the Waterhen and Pine Creek First Nations and the Province of Manitoba clearly fall into this category. The same is true for the Teme-Augama Stewardship Agreement and the tripartite agreement of the Algonquin of Barriere Lake (see chapter 4). Co-management as envisaged by these initiatives is without exception area-specific and comprehensive in nature, encompassing all renewable resources.

No matter how, why and under what circumstances negotiations take place, co-management for aboriginal groups is about power-sharing. "The degree of power-sharing is the element that separates co-operative management from co-management." (Payne and Nepinak 1990:14)

> For many, the issue of rights is at the top of the agenda: northern natives are not merely one of the "user-groups" in the manager's parlance, they are the owners of the resources of "their" land. "Devolution" in the sense of government giving rights to native groups is a wrong-headed way of posing the issue. According to one Mushkegowuk region native leader, "I already **have** rights; you cannot give me rights but you can **recognize** them." In this view, the issue of co-management is one of the more tangible aspects of sovereignty and the applicability of the laws of the land, over and beyond the boundary of the reserve. Genuine co-management is possible only with native self-government over the land traditionally held by the native group: "co-management has to recognize co-jurisdiction." (Norman Wesley,

> Mushkegowuk Council, Moose Factory, Ontario, quoted in Berkes, George and Preston 1991b:26, emphasis in original)

But power, sovereignty and jurisdiction are exactly what governments — be they federal, provincial or territorial — have been unwilling to relinquish, whether by devolution or recognition. Co-management institutions, such as committees and boards, invariably have advisory functions only, and the responsible ministers retain the power to make the final decisions.

But there are other ways for aboriginal user groups to exert strong influence over the management of resources they depend upon, namely by the retention of at least an element of self-regulation and by successful integration of indigenous knowledge systems into the co-management process.

> While a co-management system is likely to be given legal force within the structures of the state, co-management which is capable of being recognized as legitimate and effective in the North will in most cases have to be based on and express forms of pre-existing self-management. (Feit 1988a:85)

> But there is one area in which real and beneficial progress could be made. That is in the effective incorporation of native customary law into the management of fish and wildlife, and into the regulation of hunting and fishing. (Usher 1982:40)

The James Bay and Northern Quebec Agreement scores high in this respect with the legal recognition of aboriginal management systems and structures. But even the Inuvialuit Final Agreement has revealed surprising examples of how aboriginal ways of doing things have left their mark on the overall management of species and habitat. The Beverly-Kaminuriak Barren Ground Caribou Management Agreement and others similarly designed, such as the Porcupine Caribou Management Agreement of 1985 (Therrien 1987), provide for the determination of the overall quota/sustainable yield by government, but the allocation of the aboriginal share is left to local and regional user group organizations.

Co-management regimes tend to show their true colour in crisis situations. In this context it is of major importance whether we are dealing with an internally (by user groups) or externally (by government-mandated managers) perceived crisis. This is particularly true for migratory and/or herding animals, such as caribou or whales, whose life and natural history are not as easily comprehensible as those of beaver, muskrat or moose. Whenever aboriginal user groups refuse to cooperate with government-initiated conservation measures, this usually does not imply that they are less concerned about the species in question. Rather they do not share the same assumptions as government managers, since they operate from a different knowledge base. In some cases they are also openly suspicious of government motives. When the Alaskan Yupik and Inupiat pressured the United States government for a bowhead quota, after the IWC had placed a moratorium on the harvest of this species, they did so because they disbelieved the official bowhead population estimates due to methodological limitations. The SE Baffin beluga conservation and co-management initiative never got off the ground because users and managers did not share the same assumptions and did not take the time to communicate. The opposite is true for the successful NE Baffin polar bear management initiative and the Waterhen Moose Management Agreement.

The most dramatic variance of knowledge and its interpretation between users and managers undoubtedly occurs with respect to caribou. Milton Freeman describes the phenomenon of the recurring "caribou crisis".

> The "crisis" is noted by state managers of the resource, whose population surveys periodically indicate progressive decline in the numbers of one or other of the migratory barren ground caribou herds. The traditional users, having a longer association with caribou, frequently view caribou demography quite differently — often in far less alarmist terms. In the latest "caribou crisis", the state management agencies predicted the virtual extinction of two

> formerly very large caribou herds occupying an extensive range immediately to the west of Hudson Bay. This "extinction" was to occur within a very few years unless remedial actions were taken immediately by way of harvest restriction and wolf removals. As in earlier "caribou crises", the state management biologists claimed to have diagnosed the problem, predicted the inexorable outcome, and devised a solution, all with quantitatively precise intelligence. (Freeman 1989b:92f)

With regard to the 1980 "caribou crisis" (disbelieved by the Inuit from the start), the biologists' assertions of overharvesting and imminent "extinction" of the herds were seriously upset in 1982, when the supposedly most endangered herd, the Kaminuriak herd, magically multiplied from an estimated 40,000 animals in 1980 to more than 200,000 in 1982 (Riewe and Gamble 1988:33). Freeman blames not only the shortcomings of scientific research for such obviously faulty data, but also the deliberate misinformation of the public in the employ of state managers' self-interest (Freeman 1989b:98ff, 105).

Even where there is agreement on numbers between users and managers, their interpretations may differ. Under some sustained yield harvesting programs, it is assumed that maintaining a stable population is desirable for caribou, that it is their natural population condition. But caribou biologists do not agree on this issue at all, and some suggest that like other arctic mammals, caribou experience population oscillations with cyclic peaks and lows in numbers. The role of hunting in influencing caribou population levels is equivocal (Freeman 1985:269), and the substantial amount of information accumulated by harvesters in the form of lengthy time-series of data by species, season and locality, remains vastly underutilized. Scientific and state management has tended to cut itself off from a significant source of knowledge (Feit 1988a:83).

What does the future hold for co-management? In view of the governments' political agendas, a change in the power structure for aboriginal user groups is highly unlikely. A lack of real political power within the management system will have to be compensated for by improved communication and mutual integration of systems of knowledge and decision-making. That this is problematical even under optimum conditions — with an abundant and healthy resource, lack of competition, and an atmosphere of good will and considerable mutual understanding — is demonstrated by the Beverly-Kaminuriak Caribou Management Board.

It seems there is no alternative to co-management. Most initiatives currently underway are less than 10 years old. Another decade or two will go a long way in showing us whether First Nations will be satisfied with their lack of real power, and how far mutual understanding and integration of knowledge and organizational design can be carried in practice.

CONCLUSION AND OUTLOOK

Wildlife is at the core of many aboriginal communities' socio-economic aspirations. Its continued utilization, especially in the northern part of the country, constitutes an essential prerequisite for the economic, social and political development of native communities. In southern Canada wildlife-related concerns are not as ubiquitous and dominant as in the North, but even here the utilization of wildlife has some economic relevance and powerful symbolic and ideological implications.

Aboriginal wildlife-related activities include such ageless pursuits as hunting and trapping as well as innovative initiatives in the areas of game ranching and recovery programs for endangered species.

During the last decade the focus of aboriginal aspirations has shifted from the question of preferential access to wildlife to that of management power over wildlife species and their habitat. Not surprisingly, the political scene and Canadian jurisprudence have been hesitant to follow this trend.

The status quo in most parts of the country is characterized by a situation where there is a sharp dichotomy between aboriginal wildlife users and wildlife managers and legislators. This results in tremendous difficulties in the enforcement of laws and regulations, since they are not understood and sanctioned by user groups. "Aboriginal people learn the law...through being charged with offences: whatever is left over, constitutes their right." (Payne and Nepinak 1990:14)

The political nature and cultural entrapment of wildlife management, as we know it, is lost on many of its main advocates.

> But the management problem has an economic and political side that not all scientists (despite the fact that many of them become managers) are willing to see. Many wildlife professionals see themselves as custodians of a conservation ethic which is above politics. "We are responsible for resource management, not social programs", "politics should be kept out of resource management", "resource management is a scientific problem" are ideas that are commonly expressed by employees of fish and wildlife administrations, and shared by many other Canadians.
>
> ...Scientific management is based not only on the precepts of conservation and common property, but often as well on neo-classical economics. The notions of optimum use and maximum benefit, as measured by harvest statistics, performance data and dollar valuations, also do not sit easily with native concepts. (Usher 1982:38)

Ironically, the political and cultural limitations of resource management do not even seem to have been apparent to such enlightened individuals as the creators of the *Sparrow* ruling. This ruling is being heralded as a landmark case for the protection of treaty and aboriginal rights, and justly so. Inadvertently, it may even serve in the future not only as a safeguard of preferential and guaranteed rights of access to wildlife resources for aboriginal groups, but it may also be employed to substantially revise wildlife management as a whole.

In the *Sparrow* ruling the Supreme Court regarded the justification of conservation and resource management as "surely uncontroversial" and "consistent with aboriginal beliefs and practices, and...the enhancement of aboriginal rights." (R. v. Sparrow [1990] 3 C.N.L.R.:183)

> Yet, in fact, there is much that is controversial about conservation and management. Conservation of what, for whom and to what ends, and by what means? How do we decide on appropriate conservation objectives, how do we know the chosen methods are the best ones, and how do we know when and if the objectives are being achieved? There are few agreed-upon answers to these questions, even among natural scientists, let alone between the state and indigenous models of management.
>
> ...A strong case can be made that fish and wildlife management, and the economic objectives associated with it, have been used as a means of social control and engineering of aboriginal people, with no less disruptive effect than Indian administration itself. This process has been lent a veneer of objectivity by the rise of scientific management, but *Sparrow* opens the way to challenging the state management system through the first three tests, especially the test of least infringement.
>
> ...In sum, tests one, two and three call into question the conventional wisdom on conservation and management. If future court challenges can show that the indigenous management system is on balance at least as effective as the state's, the case for self-government with respect to natural resources will have been greatly advanced. (Usher 1991b:21)

6

Land

INTRODUCTION

> It is very clear to me that it is an important and special thing to be an Indian. Being an Indian means being able to understand and live with this world in a very special way....It means saying the land is an old friend and an old friend your father knew, your grandfather knew, indeed your people always have known....we see our land as much, much more than the white man sees it. To the Indian people our land really is our life. Without our land we cannot — we could no longer exist as people. If your people ever take our land you will be taking our life. (Richard Nerysoo of Fort McPherson before the Berger Inquiry, quoted in Berger 1977:94)

> My children are like the caribou — they belong to this land, not the land of the south, but the land that is rightfully theirs. This land is rightfully theirs by birth and by choice. Please do not take that choice away from them. (Elizabeth Kaye of Old Crow, quoted in Fuller and McTiernan 1987:18)

> In the culture of Western Canadian Indians, the land is the gift of the Great Spirit, the common legacy of all. The true owners are the children yet unborn. The Indians naturally view their land as a trust with a permanent sign on the corner-post, "Not for Sale". (Indian Chiefs of Alberta 1970:31)

> Land is the ultimate multiple resource. With the exception of offshore oil, all the significant renewable and non-renewable natural resources important to society are intricately associated with the land. This is true even of most important marine fisheries, whose larval or juvenile stages are dependent on inshore marshy or estuarine environments. An incredible variety of landforms and geological and ecological processes provides humankind with everything from basic foodstuffs to the material basis of all wealth and economic activity. Raw landscape was probably also the primeval origin of pure aesthetic pleasure, and it continues as a major source of artistic inspiration and recreative release. (Rees 1987:3)

It is difficult if not impossible to overemphasize the importance of land to aboriginal people. Land is one of the most important (if not the most important) sources of self-identification for native people. As so poignantly expressed by Elizabeth Kaye from Yukon and by Richard Nerysoo from the Northwest Territories, this is certainly true for northern native people, but this attitude is by no means confined to the North. Marie Marule of the Blood Tribe in southern Alberta speaks for many Treaty Indians when she states: "The elimination of reserve lands inevitably means the termination of status and rights for Indian people. The easiest way to destroy the distinctiveness of Indian people and their cultural heritage is to eliminate the land base." (Smallface Marule 1978:111) As will be shown later on in this chapter, land also plays an important part in the self-identification of Metis people.

Ironically (and no doubt involuntarily), this attitude is being reinforced by government policy. As Robert Groves (1991:224) points out, even though less than half of Canada's aboriginal people (350,000 out of at least 750,000, as enumerated by Statistics Canada) are currently "landed" in the sense of residing on lands officially recognized by federal or provincial authorities as being wholly or essentially governed by either aboriginal authorities or by the Crown on their behalf, it is generally assumed by all parties involved, that territoriality — "the actual or secured potential for control or jurisdiction over a defined land base" (ibid.:225) — is a precondition for aboriginal self-determination.

> To us land without jurisdiction, or having a say about what happens to the land, is pointless. You can't have a paper form of government without land, and you can't have land without us having a say over what happens on the land. Why settle it if somebody else is going to control our land and our resources? (Joe Mathias, Squamish Chief, on "Centre Point", *CBC Sunday Magazine*, November 4, 1990)

Self-determination in this sense seems to find its most concrete expression in governance by a people or group over a defined population in a defined land area. "The obstacles facing a non-territorial conception of indigenous self-government often seem overwhelming." (Groves 1991:224)

Even though government practice has in the past resisted programs for land acquisition, the pressure for such initiatives outside of claims processes is mounting. For example, in 1989 the Canadian Bar Association issued a recommendation that Parliament establish an Aboriginal Land Acquisition Commission for Metis and off-reserve Indians (ibid.:226).

> Official government policies on self-government stand in sharp contrast to governmental resistance to the acquisition of lands for the majority of aboriginal peoples and it is fair to say, take the existence of an exclusive land base for effective self-government as a *sine qua non* in most government thinking. Indeed, the alternative is so unknown as to resist public pronouncements even in the presence of formal policies....Thus while the theoretical right or need of all aboriginal peoples to be self-governing is generally granted in Canada, Canadian policy and law has connected self-government very tightly to the one attribute — land — that Canadian governments show the least willingness to provide. (ibid.:227)
>
> Ironically, the strong link between self-government and territoriality at the level of precedent and policy may come to haunt State representatives. Aboriginal peoples are not only demanding but are being supported in the call for self-government as a "stand-alone" right. The first item on the agenda of many non-landed groups has invariably been lands and resources. These groups have been told that self-government will be negotiated with them, and this general assurance may in the not distant future be concretized in law. But governments have been ill-equipped to deal with the logical consequence of their own presumptions about territoriality, or with the political consequences of reneging on what aboriginal peoples see as a natural corollary of self-government: the provision of a territory over which to govern. (ibid.:241)

Thus land has not only been a primary source of self-identification for aboriginal people, it is also the prime attribute for their identification by other parties. This is even expressed in the Indian Act. Under Section 2(1) of the Act a "band" is defined as a body of Indians, having lands (or moneys) in common that are being held in trust for them by the Crown.

Since the mid-19th century Canadian Indian policy has exhibited a uniquely territorial focus by using the manipulation of the Indian land base as its major tool to further its political goals.

> Legislation outlining the goals of the reserve system and establishing the procedure for assimilation was passed in the Legislature for Upper Canada in 1857 in "an Act to encourage the gradual civilization of the Indians in this province..." In 1869 essentially the same bill

> with a slight change in emphasis was passed by the Parliament of Canada and entitled "an Act for the gradual enfranchisement of Indians..." Both laws were based on the assumption that the reserve was the place where the Indians could be "civilized", meaning Christianized, educated and be made a farmer. (Tobias 1977:89)

The confinement of Indian people on widely scattered reserves, which provided them with a communal land base was only the first step. Then Indian society was to be "atomized" (ibid.:94). Thus the government would be dealing with individuals, rather than bands. The Canadian government never went as far as the American General Allotment Act, but the Location Ticket[1] (introduced by the Indian Act of 1876) was a step in the same direction and was deemed to be a halfway house to private ownership. It was intended to undermine long-standing communalism, and especially to discourage cooperative farming and ranching. After a three-year probationary period the individual might be enfranchised and be given title to his/her land. Land title was also offered as a reward to individuals who obtained a university degree or became a lawyer, priest or minister, and as a result automatically lost their Indian status and became enfranchised. As Squamish Chief Joe Mathias puts it, "The message was simple: 'We will reward you with Indian land if you give up your Indian ways.'" (Mathias and Yabsley 1991:39)

By the turn of the century, the reserve system was being questioned as a means of assimilation, and consequently the following years featured massive assaults on the Indian land base. In 1907 the government revised the Indian Act to make it simpler and more attractive for bands to surrender their reserves. Many reserves, particularly in the newly established prairie provinces Alberta and Saskatchewan, lost vast quantities of land, some of it through fraudulent procedures (Notzke 1985:17, 43f; Raby 1973). In 1918 the Indian Act was amended once more, this time to empower the Department of Indian Affairs to lease reserve land without a previous surrender, even if the band council actively opposed such action "...through some delusion, misapprehension or hostility..." (Indian Affairs Annual Report 1918:20).

For over a century the government employed territoriality in its efforts to control and assimilate aboriginal people. Today's situation shows that aboriginal people have successfully used the same means to resist these efforts. Active and passive resistance of native people have rendered the tool of land management in the service of enfranchisement an ineffectual one (Tobias 1977:97). The settlement of specific claims has in some cases reimbursed Indian bands for land lost through fraudulent surrenders. Throughout history and up to the present, Indians have consistently promoted reserves as their ethnic homelands.

The settlement of comprehensive claims opens the door for aboriginal people to realize the potential of their relationship with their land and their designs for their territory more

---

[1] The Location Ticket was an innovation of the original Indian Act (1876). The government regarded it as an essential feature of the "civilization" process and a necessity for enfranchisement. It was a means by which the Indian could demonstrate that he/she had adopted the European concept of private property, which was an additional test of whether he/she had become "civilized". The Superintendent General had the reserve surveyed into individual lots, which the band council could assign to individual band members. As a form of title the Superintendent General would then give the band member a Location Ticket. But before a ticket was issued, the individual had to prove that he/she was "civilized" (according to earlier legislation: literate in either English or French, free of debt, and of good moral character — standards that few of the colonists would have been able to meet!). In passing this first test, and receiving a Location Ticket, the Indian entered a three-year probationary period during which he/she had to demonstrate that he/she would use the land as a Euro-Canadian might. If he/she passed these tests, he/she was enfranchised and given title to his/her land. Thus the land became part of the surrounding municipality. This process was mostly designed for the Indians east of Lake Superior, who were considered more advanced. Marie Marule (*Kainai News*, October No.2, 1981) points out that the Location Tickets or Certificates of Possession (if issued after 1951) resulted in serious problems on various eastern reserves. Enterprising individuals would buy off other people's certificates and then disproportionately control the band's land base; 10 per cent of a community might control 50 per cent of the land.

fully than has been the case for the historical treaties. The envisaged creation of Nunavut shows just how far the idea of an aboriginal homeland can be carried.[2]

> The point at which material production and cultural reproduction meet is with the notion of territory. Indigenous peoples all over the world share a fundamental understanding of the importance of this concept. Territory is the term used more frequently by indigenous peoples because of the notion of continuous area combined with access to resources. Land, however, is the word with which indigenous peoples articulate their relationship with the earth.
>
> There are two aspects to this relationship....On the one hand indigenous peoples' relationship with their territories rests on the importance of resources to the continuing existence of the group. On the other hand, the territory is an area deeply associated with the identity of the people as a whole which each generation keeps in trust for the future.
>
> The first element is an indigenous expression of the use or ecological relationship between indigenous peoples and the environment we noted above, while the second aspect covers the cultural reproduction and management of an ecosystem. Whereas for non-indigenous peoples these factors are separated into "economic" and "cultural" domains, for indigenous peoples they are aspects of the same phenomenon, where time, space, resource use, management and conservation are all part of the same complex, linking identity to production and reproduction. (Gray 1991:22)

THE ABORIGINAL LAND BASE IN THE PROVINCES

> Indian lands are lands held in the name of the Crown, but which Indians have a legal right to occupy and possess. This form of land ownership is in a class by itself in Canadian law.
>
> There are two kinds of Indian lands in Canada: reserve lands (within the meaning of the Indian Act) and aboriginal title lands. The Indian interest in the land is the same in both cases, with the consequence that rights to aboriginal title lands are as enforceable in the courts as are rights to reserve land. (Woodward 1989:196f)

> Lands which are subject to aboriginal title are lands "reserved for the Indians" under Canadian law. (ibid.:201)

Only a proportion of those lands perceived by aboriginal people as being subject to aboriginal title is explicitly recognized as such by law. In most of British Columbia and parts of eastern Canada, aboriginal title as claimed by native groups has not been recognized by provincial governments nor verified by the courts. In terms of resource management, constraints on the physical possession of land or territory limit aboriginal people's rights of access to resources contained within the territory. Previous chapters have illustrated that on all categories of aboriginal land — territory subject to recognized or unrecognized aboriginal title as well as reserve lands — there are numerous constraints on native people's use of natural resources, let alone native jurisdiction over resources. The most elaborate apparatus of external control is operating on those lands where native people have the greatest security of tenure: the reserves.

Indian Reserve Lands: Problems and Issues

The federal government has exclusive jurisdiction over Indian reserve lands and resources. In its ability to legislate with respect to "Indians and Lands reserved for the Indians" it is restrained only by Section 35 of the Constitution Act, 1982 (Bartlett 1990:133). Explicit recognition of the management prerogative of the minister is spelled out in Section 60 of the Indian Act.

---

[2] The closely interrelated topics of aboriginal title and native claims will not be dealt with in this chapter. There is a comprehensive body of literature in this area: Clark 1991; Cumming and Mickenberg eds. 1972:13–50; Elias 1989a & b; Elliot 1985; Grant 1991; Usher, Tough and Galois 1991; Woodward 1989:196–222; to name but a few.

> 60. (1) The Governor in Council may at the request of a band grant to the band the right to exercise such control and management over lands in the reserve occupied by that band as the Governor in Council considers desirable.
>
> (2) The Governor in Council may at any time withdraw from a band a right conferred on the band under subsection (1).

Robert Groves goes so far as to state:

> In contrast to the American system of recognizing Tribes as distinct and dealing with their lands as consequential subjects for jurisdictional contest, Canadian legislation has all but ignored Indian political existence in favor of regulating with minute precision all aspects of the essentially "federal" property that reserves constitute. The *Indian Act* in this sense is more properly styled "an Act for the administration of federal reserve lands", with the Indian people connected to those lands being effectively reduced to mere adjuncts and agents for the convenient administration of those lands. The American experience has been to place tribal recognition first and deal with the territorial realities after, while the Canadian trend has been to legislate territoriality closely and leave recognition of aboriginal peoples as political entities as an afterthought. (Groves 1991:230f)

There are approximately 2,300 Indian reserves in Canada, out of which more than 1,600 are located in British Columbia. These reserves vary considerably in size, as well as in the nature of the Indian interest in them. These variations stem from the different ways in which Indian reserves have been set apart — either by treaty or agreement or by executive action — and the different extent to which federal-provincial arrangements override the initial grant or treaty promise (Bartlett 1990:129). Not surprisingly, reserves established as the result of a treaty or an agreement tend to be much larger than those set aside by executive action. The beneficial interest of aboriginal people in their reserves has been affected by the degree of control of the various provinces over public lands.

It has already been illustrated that in British Columbia, due to provincial control of public lands, the Indian interest in reserves set aside by both treaty and executive action has been severely curtailed to serve provincial interests. In the Prairie Provinces and in Ontario, the Indian interest has also been limited, but to a much lesser extent, because the provinces exerted less control over the setting apart of reserves on public lands. The Nova Scotia and New Brunswick agreements with Canada in 1958 constitute a partial exception to this pattern, since they recognize the full beneficial entitlement of the Indians to their reserve lands, but they do so within the context of an arrangement entrenching the rights of squatters and settlers, thereby restricting Indian people to a minuscule fraction (0.2 per cent) of their traditional lands (ibid.:130).

The Indian Act provision that confers the greatest degree of power and discretion over reserve lands to the Crown is subsection 18(1). The first part of this subsection states that reserves are held "for the use and benefit" of the Indians; the second part empowers the governor in council to "...determine whether any purpose for which lands in a reserve are used or are to be used is for the use and benefit of the band."

No reserve land can be disposed of or leased without a surrender of the land to the Crown having taken place. A surrender generally requires the consent of the majority of the electors of the band. The right to withhold consent to a surrender or to attach conditions to it is the only means at a band's disposal to exercise any power in this matter (ibid.:137).

The minister is also entitled to issue permits for the use of reserve lands up to one year and to issue leases of lands held by individual band members under certificates of possession without band council consent or a surrender. Band council consent is only required in the case of longer term permits or where leased lands are held by the band in common (Bartlett 1990:137).

The question whether to surrender reserve lands for a lease or to issue a permit for non-Indian use sometimes constitutes an important issue for band governments. This was the case for the Peigan in southern Alberta in the early 1980s. The controversy surrounding the location of facilities of the Lethbridge Northern Irrigation District (LNID) on reserve land was already discussed in chapter 2. It focused on the question of who owns the Oldman River water bed and was apparently resolved in 1981 when the Peigan's rights were acknowledged in an agreement with the provincial government. One of the major accomplishments of this agreement as the Peigan leadership saw it, was the Peigan's successful resistance to an expropriation by means of a land surrender and subsequent lease in favour of a permit system, where the band retained ownership of the land in question and would regain control when/if the LNID works were no longer needed (Notzke 1985:43). Provincial claims to "ownership" of the land in question, in conjunction with Lonefighter leader Milton Born With A Tooth's trial in Fort Macleod Court of Queen's Bench in March 1991, raise numerous questions, including the question whether it would not have been to the Peigan's advantage to have settled the question of ownership of the river bed in the courts.

Section 28 of the Indian Act provides that a permit may be issued allowing a non-band member to occupy or use reserve lands. There is no express limitation in the section on either the duration of the permit (providing the band council has consented) or on the use of land which can be allowed. In practice, however, departmental policy used to be much more restrictive. When the Peigan were negotiating their agreement with the province, DIAND was reluctant to issue permits in situations where, in other contexts, a lease could be seen as the normal method of transferring land use rights. In order for reserve land to be leased, the band must surrender the land to the Crown, whereupon the federal government leases the land to the nonband member. Section 38(2) of the Indian Act provides that a surrender may be absolute or qualified, conditional or unconditional. There are no ground rules in the Indian Act or in the judicial system outlining the appropriate division of revenues. All lease moneys are payable to the Crown.

The 1988 amendment to the Indian Act (Bill C-115, often referred to as the Kamloops Amendment) introduced an important change with regard to surrendered lands. It created the category of "designated lands" constituting those lands that are surrendered for leasing rather than sale. This amendment was designed primarily to extend the exemption from taxation of personal property to lands surrendered for leasing (Woodward 1989:265). Furthermore, the definition of "reserve" was amended in over 30 sections of the Act to include "designated lands". In some areas this has far-reaching implications. According to Jack Woodward (ibid.:267f), it remains an unresolved constitutional question, which level of government has legislative jurisdiction over the use of designated lands, more specifically over the non-Indian interest during the duration of the lease. The provinces seek to extend laws, such as land use legislation and taxation statutes, to leased reserve lands. On the other hand, the Musqueam Band drafted a taxation by-law in 1990 in preparation for taxing leaseholders on Indian land in the City of Vancouver (*Kainai News*, November 22, 1990:3). The resolution of this question is crucial for future developments on these lands.

Richard H. Bartlett suggests that the only significant power of the Band Council under the Indian Act, with respect to reserve land, is the power to allot possession of that land to individual band members (Bartlett 1990:138). Such allotment is, however, subject to the approval of the minister, who issues a certificate of possession when approval is given, and a certificate of occupation when the approval given is conditional (Section 20[1-6]). An allottee may transfer his/her right of land possession to another band member or to the band but this, too, is subject to ministerial approval.

Many bands, particularly on the Prairies, choose to use neither the certificates of possession nor any of the Indian Act provisions for internal Indian land holding on reserves. They adhere to what may be called "customary" or "traditional" land allotment patterns. These bands allot land to individual band members at the discretion of the Band Council. They avoid any ministerial validation of the allotment. The allottee, on the other hand, has no more legal security of tenure than the Band Council is prepared to permit. The practice of this land policy and the problems encountered vary from reserve to reserve.

On the Peigan Reserve in southern Alberta, 244 square kilometres, or 57 per cent of the reserve's land base, have been individually allotted (Notzke 1987:121ff). Much of today's distribution pattern goes back to the 1920s, when the Peigan population numbered around 500 (one-sixth of today's population). The educational policy of that period placed particular emphasis on manual training and agricultural instruction, and band members interested in agriculture were allocated a parcel of land by the Indian agent. Yet in the 1950s small-scale agriculture experienced a serious relapse, when mechanization and related changes intensified, and traditional farming became just too uneconomical. Many of the older individuals on the reserve, interviewed by the author during a sample survey in 1982, recalled working their land with a horse-drawn plough until the late 1950s. Then they resorted to leasing their plots to non-Indian farmers and ranchers because they saw no other way of making a living. While reserve land had been leased before, it was only at this time that band members started leasing out their small individual plots to off-reserve enterprises. With the onset of "self-government" in the 1960s, political factors gained importance in the process of land allocation.

In the 1980s there were about 170 landholders on the Peigan Reserve. The average size of a large holding was 390 hectares, while small holdings averaged 65 hectares. Small plots accounted for 75 per cent of all individual land holdings. Sixty per cent of the individually allocated grazing land, and 90 per cent of the arable land were leased out. This appears logical when we consider the land-people ratio. An economic unit for an Indian dryland farmer would require a minimum of 500 hectares. With regard to ranching, it is assumed that a satisfactory living could be made on a pasture capacity of 250 animal units. Based on a general carrying capacity of 10.1 hectares per animal unit per year, this translates into 2,525 hectares per ranch.[3] Even if this acreage were reduced by the use of a six-month grazing system, supplementary feed and use of the community pasture, the discrepancy between the actual holdings and economic units is still evident.

Not even the large holdings on the reserve, which constituted only a small percentage of the individual plots, reached minimum economic unit size. The resultant pattern was the exorbitant leasing out of valuable land, with two-thirds of the revenue leaving the reserve and only one-third being paid to the "owner". Almost all of the reserve's arable land was farmed by non-band members on a share-cropping basis, and a sizeable portion of the reserve's pasture was grazed by off-reserve cattle. A survey (Notzke 1985:49) indicated that 66 per cent of the landowners interviewed leased their land; of these, only two leased it to fellow band members. All socio-economic strata were represented among these "armchair farmers". While a few individuals argued that they were just not interested in either farming or ranching, the majority expressed considerable inclination for full-time ranching if more land and capital were available. The leasing of land seemed to be a legitimate and socially acceptable way of contributing to one's living on the Peigan Reserve. If there was a degree of resentment among the landless (which is likely), it did not manifest itself in the way it did a few years ago on the neighbouring Blood Reserve, where a landless band member demonstratively erected his tipi beside the band's administration building, and where political pressure groups tried to force the Band Council to set up a workable land policy. The land question was for a long time the most controversial and emotional subject on that reserve.

---

[3] These are absolute minimum numbers, which do not necessarily guarantee a "comfortable" living (Ken Nicol, personal communication, July 20, 1993).

There is no defined land policy on the Peigan Reserve; the Council handles disputes over land individually. The main source of contention seems to be the question of inheritance. Normally, this matter is decided within the family, and the parcel of land is transferred to the surviving spouse or handed down to one child. But increasingly, people appeal to Council to settle arising disputes, and in some cases the land returns to the band to be transferred to a new applicant.

Individual land tenure on the Stoney Reserve in the Rocky Mountain foothills west of Calgary, is subject to the same customary system. Here, however, it is even more flexible and informal. The division between "landowners" and landless band members is less pronounced than on the reserves of the Blackfoot Confederation, as every family by custom has the right to fence off or use a parcel of land to graze some livestock. There are "acceptable" limits as to the size of holdings an individual may fence off for himself/herself, the majority measuring under 65 hectares. Sixty-nine per cent of a Stoney sample (Notzke 1985:53) claimed a parcel of land, with the majority being uncertain about its exact size. Only two of the twenty-two landholders utilized larger areas, in the neighbourhood of 260 hectares. There is no land registry, and as a result there are no data regarding the number of landholders or size of holdings. No land has been formally designated as band land (except the band ranch). Although some unsettled areas have a tradition of communal use, theoretically individuals are allowed to take their share of this land. About 60 per cent of the main Morley Reserve have been taken up individually. Naturally certain holdings have come to be associated with certain families, and the land distribution pattern goes back a long time in history. With over 400 households on the Morley Reserve, and its physical features imposing limitations on settlement and utilization of some parts, there is a pronounced land shortage. The individual holdings are uneconomically small, especially in view of the fact that the wooded character of a major part of the reserve necessitates larger ranch units to make a living than on the Peigan Reserve. Nevertheless all the individually used land is utilized for grazing livestock, and none is leased to non-band members. Although leasing was practised before self-government, it was discontinued two decades ago as a matter of policy, and thanks to their gas royalties, part of which are distributed on a per capita basis, band members do not depend on this source of income. There is no defined land policy; disputes arising over questions of inheritance and transactions are handled individually by the Council.

Thus the land situation on these reserves is characterized by a peculiar tension caused by the combination of hard economic facts, perceived and/or real political favouritism, and the enduring Indian holistic concept of land ownership. Referring to supposedly communal ownership of the land base, the landless feel justified in asking where their profit from this resource is likely to occur. Due to population increase and historically established distribution patterns, only a limited number of families can reap the major benefits. In view of the acute land shortage on these two Treaty Seven reserves, we have to bear in mind, that southern Alberta has Canada's largest Indian reserves.

Despite numerous inroads by provincial legislation into the resource management of Indian reserves, these areas constitute islands of distinct legislation within the provinces. In *Dick v. R.* [1985] 4 C.N.L.R. 55 (S.C.C.), the Supreme Court of Canada recognized the power of Parliament to deny the application of provincial laws to Indian reserve lands and resources — the protection that Section 91(24) always envisaged (Bartlett 1990:135). Indian reserve lands are protected from seizure and exempt from taxation. All these are characteristics which are viewed as privileges by non-Indians, and which have caused envy and suspicion.

In the early 1990s a new land management regime for aboriginal lands is being discussed, namely an optional First Nations' Chartered Land Act (FNCL Act). This draft legislation was developed by a group of chiefs from across Canada who established an interim First Nations' Lands Board. The proposed act is intended to enable First Nations to choose between remaining under the land administration sections of the Indian Act or opting into a new land management regime under the FNCL Act. This new regime would essentially place control and decision-making power in regard to land management with First Nations governments, rather than the federal government. Along with this, as lawyer Louise Mandell explains in a letter to the Penticton Indian Band (February 26, 1993), the act would devolve federal fiduciary obligations from Canada to First Nations governments in the area of land management.

The Act would also involve a profound change in the nature of title to the land. Although the legal title would remain with the federal Crown

> First Nations ownership of reserved lands will pass from a communal title, held in trust for the benefit of First Nations citizens by Canada, to a title called "chartered lands", which are held and defined pursuant to the enactment of a Charter which must be consistent with Federal law. (ibid.:2f)

Such "chartered lands" may include not only reserve lands, but also fee simple lands and land obtained under a claim settlement or treaty entitlement. Needless to say, there are numerous legal implications and possible scenarios for what could happen to chartered lands, which must be explored. Furthermore, this initiative must be viewed in a wider context of devolution of other federal fiduciary obligations.

The proposed FNCL Act has met with an overall hostile reaction from such organizations as the Assembly of First Nations, the Union of British Columbia Indian Chiefs and the Coalition Against First Nations Genocide. Its opponents are concerned about the possibility of land alienation, and they tend to view the Act in the same light as the Dawes General Allotment Act, which by 1934 had effected the loss of two-thirds of reserve lands in the United States. Although the Act was to proceed to the House of Commons for first reading in spring 1993, the First Nations' Lands Board decided to postpone this step in order to revise and clarify it (*Windspeaker*, June 7, 1993:3).

Uneasy Neighbours

In the previous section we have looked at selected aspects of land management on Indian reserves. To understand the attributes of land as a resource for native people, we have to appreciate the problems they encounter in endeavours to expand their reserve land base. Two occurrences, one in Alberta and the other in British Columbia, are quite educational in this respect. They show that in addition to "normal" legislative and bureaucratic hurdles, aboriginal people are faced with tremendous political opposition from their white neighbours.

In 1987 the Peigan settled a specific land claim with the federal government. The basis for this claim was an improper surrender of the northwest corner of their reserve in the early 1900s. The case had been before the courts since 1980, when the federal government opted for an out-of-court settlement. Under the terms of the agreement, the government agreed to pay for the replacement of 4,168 hectares of land for the Peigan and added $2.115 million in cash. In the spring of 1990 the Peigan prepared to purchase the 3,370 hectare Big Coulee Ranch, on sale on the outskirts of their reserve. The following are just a few samples gleaned from the local press.

> Reserve status for the land could split the "thriving" community of Spring Point, may depreciate land values and, the brief [prepared by local residents and delivered to the federal and provincial governments] says, "will no doubt cause some families to leave.
>
> The brief states that statistics reveal a higher incidence of alcohol and drug abuse along with violence among the native population than in adjacent populations in southern Alberta and points out that, "many families have located here to avoid the cities where these problems are plagueing [sic] non-natives as well." (*Fort Macleod Gazette*, May 23, 1990)

> We do not dispute the right of the Peigan to buy land. What we do dispute is their right to turn it into a "foreign country" by giving it reserve status.

> Reserves in themselves should be a thing of the past, as they have proved more of a detriment to both the Indian and the white population allowing them both to live separately with total disregard for each others [sic] welfare. It is time for our native population to stand on its own two feet in the real world and its [sic] time for our government to stop kowtowing to special interest groups at the expense of others. (*Fort Macleod Gazette*, May 23, 1990, Editorial)

The local population in general strongly objected to the lack of public input into the matter, and expressed its fears about a "worst case scenario" as a result of the anticipated loss of government control over the land: unregulated development, increased population, unregulated hunting and vehicular traffic, random garbage dumping, restricted access, complications for obtaining rights of way and the potential loss of a municipal tax base. In the end the Peigan did not buy Big Coulee Ranch, apparently due to bureaucratic delays in obtaining the Minister's signature.

On the west coast of Vancouver Island, in spring 1991, the Tla-o-qui-aht First Nation of the Nuu-chah-nulth Tribal Council declared a boycott of Tofino businesses and services, following numerous futile attempts to gain support from the Tofino Village Council for its application to DIAND to confer reserve status upon the Tin-Wis site. The Tla-o-qui-aht held a 35-year lease on the site, which was federal Crown land. Tin-Wis, meaning "calm water", has traditionally been a whaling station for the Tla-o-qui-aht, who are now interested in developing this traditional land into a native theme resort (*Ha-Shilth-Sa*, June 14, 1991:1).

The Tla-o-qui-aht had been informed that their application would be accepted by DIAND (The site was given reserve status through an Order-in-Council in July 1993). This step did not need the approval of the Tofino Council but, for the sake of "good community relations," the band approached the Council anyway, because the land falls within its municipality. They met with stiff opposition particularly from tourism enterprise operators. A local motel association brought forth a petition opposing the Tla-o-qui-aht application.

> Our concerns are about Indian Reserve Status being granted for this prime piece of property right in the middle of tourist commercial land. These concerns outnumber any possible advantages to the area....The tourist commercial zoning could not be enforced and in fact the property could be used for housing or whatever their (Tla-o-qui-aht) needs require. This property is serviced by water and sewer, how can the municipality enforce payment of these services or taxes if residents of an Indian reserve default? ...This causes concern to all tourist-oriented businesses in the area. (ibid.)

As in the Peigan case, a major concern was fear of loss of control over the land by the municipality, but another factor was anticipation of "unfair competition", since the band would not have to pay the taxes that other non-native resorts are obliged to pay. Band representatives did their best to assuage these concerns. The Tla-o-qui-aht envisaged the establishment of a lease agreement between the Tin-Wis Society, which plans the development of the site, and the band. The designated property under this agreement would be subject to all municipal by-laws and taxes. Further meetings did nothing to sway the Council in its opposition, even though numerous Tofino residents supported the Indian initiative. This situation does not bode well for the political climate in which British Columbia's comprehensive native claims will be settled.

Indian Land under the Sechelt Act

In 1986 the Sechelt Indian Band of British Columbia became the first aboriginal group in Canada to develop its own constitution and to formally withdraw its reserve lands from the jurisdiction of the Indian Act. The Sechelt land base of some 1,000 hectares is spread over 33 separate reserves in the vicinity of the Sechelt Peninsula, 50 kilometres northwest of Vancouver. Large portions of the band's land have been developed and leased to non-native residents (Etkin 1988:78). This constitutes a substantial portion of the Sechelt economic base, in addition to fishing, logging, gravel extraction, a salmon hatchery and tourism. Consequently, an important function of Bill C-93 (the Sechelt Act) was to place reserve lands under a different management regime.

The most crucial departure from the previous situation for the Sechelt Indian Band was the fact that Bill C-93 made the band owner in fee simple of its reserve lands. This has important economic implications for the Sechelt people. It enables the band to buy and sell land and use it as collateral to finance development projects.

On the other hand, it is also important to consider what the Sechelt Act did **not** change. Section 38 of the Act, like Section 88 of the Indian Act, recognizes and extends provincial jurisdiction to Indian lands. The Act provides that the band's title to the land and its interest with respect to the resources are subject to the province's interest in the minerals of the reserves and the provincial powers of management, as recognized in the British Columbia Indian Reserves Mineral Resources Act. It also affirms the conditions attached to the provincial conveyance with regard to expropriation, water rights, construction materials and highways. The province does not relinquish any of these powers as a result of the Sechelt Act (Bartlett 1990:163).

Thus the transfer to the Sechelt Indian Band of title in fee simple to their reserve lands is subject to this provincial interest. In order to allow the registration of the title under the provincial land titles system, many provisions of the Indian Act are no longer applicable. This includes provisions of the Act relating to management, possession, inalienability and surrender, and exemption from seizure. As Richard H. Bartlett sees it, essentially "The Band has obtained the power to manage its land, subject to the powers which remain in the province, but has lost the protection of the lands provided by the Indian Act." (ibid.)

One may argue, however, that the Indian Act protection has been replaced by new safeguards for Sechelt Indian land tenure built into the Sechelt Constitution and the Sechelt Act.

> In light of the wording of s.25 [which notes that the lands are to be held for the "use and benefit of the Band and its members"], one might argue that Sechelt land title is vested not just in a legal entity (the Band) but in some more amorphous collectivity. One might argue that the form of ownership by the Sechelt people is *sui generis* in nature; it is not the same as ownership by a corporation. This consideration might arise if there is a dispute over how Sechelt lands are being used. In resolving this issue, a court might find that the provisions of the Band constitution governing land use are ambiguous. The court would then look to s.25 of the Act for further guidance. The interests of the amorphous collectivity referred to above may be found to be paramount over the interests of the Sechelt Band as a legal entity. (Hyatt 1986:11f, quoted in Etkin 1988:90)

The communal ownership of Sechelt lands is reflected in the decision-making process pertaining to issues that could potentially lead to an alienation of land or resources. The Sechelt Constitution holds that

> ...no Sechelt lands may be mortgaged, sold, or otherwise have the title to them transferred, unless the mortgage, sale or title transfer has been first approved in a referendum by a vote 75% in favour by all the Band electors. (Division 4:1, quoted in Etkin 1988:92)

Similarly stringent rules apply to the disposal of resources, such as timber, gravel, sand, clay or other substances. For these resources to be developed by non-Band interests, consent of the Band electors is required by referendum, if the term of the permit is more than five years, or the permit "is in respect of Sechelt lands that were previously in a natural and undeveloped condition." (3:3,a of Band Constitution; Etkin 1988:93). In all other cases, a two-thirds majority vote of Council is required.

Further powers of the Band under the Sechelt Act include the following:

- power to make by-laws with respect to access, residence, zoning and land use planning;
- expropriation for community purposes;
- use and construction of buildings and roads;
- protection and management of fur-bearing animals, fish and game on Sechelt lands;
- taxation for local purposes of interests in Sechelt lands, and of occupants and tenants of Sechelt lands;
- the administration and management of property belonging to the band;
- the preservation and management of natural resources on Sechelt lands; and
- matters related to the good government of the band, its members, or Sechelt lands (Bartlett 1990:163).

As Richard Bartlett (ibid.:164) explains, powers involving the management of natural resources, expropriation, taxation and good government could not have been conferred under the Indian Act. He also notes that the power with respect to natural resources is somewhat illusory because of the extent of provincial powers and interests. Of major significance, however, is the power to levy local property taxation. This right is subject to the approval of the Governor in Council which, in turn, is conditional upon the province withdrawing or suspending the taxation of non-Indian tenants on Sechelt lands. The province agreed to suspend taxation of tenants, where the band desires to provide municipal services. About 350 non-Indians lease land from the Sechelt Band, whose interest could be taxed.

In conclusion, Bartlett feels that

> The significance of the Act resides not so much in the ambit of powers conferred upon the Sechelt as in the absence of federal superintendence....
>
> The ambit of powers which could be conferred under the Sechelt Act is not insubstantial, but the affirmation of provincial power over the lands and the limited ambit of the power to tax suggest that self-government is not a proper description. The regime is more properly termed self-management and community government. (ibid.)

It should finally be noted that the Sechelt Act does not abrogate aboriginal rights. Section 3 explicitly states that nothing in the Act will "abrogate or derogate" from any existing aboriginal or treaty rights of the Sechelt people or any other native people under Section 35 of the Constitution Act, 1982. The band has protected itself from losing any rights that might accrue to native people in the future as a result of constitutional negotiations (Etkin 1988:87).

A Land Base for the Metis

In the context of aboriginal lands in Canada, Metis settlements constitute an anomaly: they were established on provincial lands under provincial jurisdiction even though jurisdiction over Indians and lands reserved for Indians has always resided in the federal government. A historical perspective helps explain this anomaly.

> The concept of a Metis land-base in the sense of a large territory or Metis reserve land has surfaced repeatedly since the early nineteenth century. This idea is historically based on two different and conflicting notions. The first of these is the concept of aboriginal rights, i.e. that the Metis, because of their part Indian ancestry, can claim the land as an aboriginal people. This is the commonly understood basis of Metis land claims today, having been asserted by North-West Company officials in the second decade of the nineteenth century. In 1870, Prime Minister John A. MacDonald accepted the argument that the Metis had a valid land claim as an aboriginal people. Therefore, Section 31 of the Manitoba Act set aside 1.4 million acres for the extinguishment of Metis title to the land. This meant

> that the **part** Indian Metis were to receive **full** land compensation (160 acres per person) just like the Indians.
>
> Another Metis claim at the Red River and beyond was based on the argument that the Metis "nation" had established demographic dominance over Red River as a civilized community that functioned as "wardens of the plains" to protect the region against encroachment by the Plains Indians. (Kienetz 1988:14, emphasis in original)[4]

Numerous authors (f.e. Flanagan 1983; Taylor 1983) have thoroughly discussed the details of land allocations to the Metis in Manitoba and the North-West, following the Manitoba Act of 1870 and the Dominion Lands Act in 1879. These grants never resulted in a lasting land base for the Metis because they were issued on an individual basis as (land or money) scrip and could be sold to white settlers and land speculators.

> Half-breed scrip, although a recognition of Metis title, was quite different from the treaty recognition of Indian land title. Scrip policies were tied in with the survey system used in western Canada and the policies of the Dominion Lands Act. The Metis interest in land was conceived of as an individual proprietary interest which could be exchanged for money or individual lots. Reserves were not obtainable under scrip procedures and policies were not discussed or negotiated. Although the Metis hunted, trapped and fished, and often had an economy indistinguishable from Treaty Indians, scrip policies provided no resource rights. (Usher, Tough and Galois 1992:120)

While Metis are one of the three aboriginal peoples of Canada whose aboriginal rights and treaty rights are recognized and affirmed by Section 35(1) of the Constitution Act, 1982, the Act provides no definition of Metis. Furthermore, Canadian law at present remains silent as to the nature of Metis rights that were constitutionalized in 1982 (Woodward 1989:56). Consequently, Metis organizations have endeavoured since the 1980s to clarify both these questions, and the concept of a land base is a focal point in this effort.

Historically the meaning of the word "Metis" has changed repeatedly, and while Metis people always maintained a strong sense of self-identification, prior to 1982 they never concerned themselves with a narrow identity definition. However, from the 1980s on, Metis organizations found it necessary to formulate their own identity criteria in order to be recognized by the governments of Canada (Krosenbrink-Gelissen 1989:40). In 1984 the Metis National Council (MNC) addressed the First Ministers' Conference on Aboriginal Constitutional Matters with a clarification on this point. The MNC definition was based on the following criteria: self-identification, community acceptance as a Metis, aboriginal ancestry, and historical and/or legal proof that the person has descended from those Metis who had aboriginal title that had to be extinguished by either the Manitoba Act of 1870 or the Dominion Lands Act of 1879.

> While using Canadian legislation as a precondition for claiming Metis identity, the Metis have created two groups of Metis: the "status" Metis who can establish a link with the land, whereas the "non-status" Metis cannot. The connection between land, aboriginal title, and aboriginal rights is of crucial importance for those who claim to be, or are recognized as aboriginal people. (Krosenbrink-Gelissen 1989:41)

For the Metis, recognized aboriginal title is a heritage as well as a right. Consequently, land and resource rights figure prominently in the MNC's categories of rights that the organization wants identified as Metis aboriginal rights (Krosenbrink-Gelissen 1989:40).

---

[4] For a brief yet comprehensive history of Metis identity, Metis migration and the concept of a Metis land base see, Krosenbrink-Gelissen 1989. On Metis aboriginal rights and Metis claims, see Driben 1983, Taylor 1983, and Chartier 1985.

In the past, the federal government has denied any responsibility for the Metis, and it continues to deny that it has jurisdiction over them (Bartlett 1990:165). Consequently, the Metis have traditionally been compelled to approach provincial governments for access to their rights. Only in Alberta have these efforts resulted in a communal land base for the Metis. In 1936 Metis political pressure induced the Alberta government to establish an inquiry into the conditions of the Metis in Alberta. The recommendations of the Ewing Commission were implemented in the Metis Betterment Act of 1938/1940. The Act provided for more than 500,000 hectares of communal land for the Alberta Metis, hunting and fishing permits and socio-economic and health programs.

Under the Act, if Metis people formed Settlement Associations in various parts of northern Alberta and adopted a common constitution that outlined how the settlements would be run, the government would set aside areas of land for settlement by the Associations. Twelve settlements were established in this manner, five of which have been dissolved since (*Windspeaker*, June 23, 1989, Settlement Anniversary Section:1). The Alberta government viewed the Metis Betterment Act as a welfare provision rather than a land grant (Krosenbrink-Gelissen 1989:38).

In the 1940s Saskatchewan followed Alberta's example on a much smaller scale. These lands, which were administered under general land and welfare legislation, were described as being set apart

> ...for the purpose of settling or re-establishing on such lands certain Metis who are eligible to be so settled or re-established by the Northern Areas Branch of the Department of Municipal Affairs with the view of providing such Metis with permanent homes and the opportunity of earning a livelihood. (O.C.706/44, Sask. July 4, 1944, quoted in Bartlett 1990:59)

Part of the land was used for the establishment of training farms. Both provinces, however, denied the Metis title to the land as well as the mineral resources, and they reserved the power to rescind the setting apart of lands and to abolish entire settlements without any surrender or consent by the Metis (Bartlett 1990:165).

It was only in the mid-1980s, upon recommendations of the 1984 MacEwan Committee, that the Alberta provincial government resolved to endow the Metis settlements with more permanence by granting them title in fee simple to their settlement lands, but excluding mineral and water rights and existing third-party interests. This was realized by the Metis Settlements Land Act of 1988 (Bill 65) and the Alberta-Metis Settlements Accord of 1989. These measures would be entrenched by an amendment of the Alberta Act that would preclude any alteration or revocation without Metis consent. The Accord grants control over mineral development on the settlement lands to the Metis, yet denies them ownership and principal economic benefits (ibid.:101). The grants were to be made to a corporation, known as the Metis Settlements General Council, on behalf of the eight Metis settlements.

The entire legislative package, which granted limited self-government, 506,250 hectares of land and a financial package of $310 million over 17 years to Alberta's Metis, was introduced in the provincial legislature on May 30, 1990. In return the Metis agreed to discontinue their long-standing lawsuit against the province over oil and gas revenues from their traditional lands.

In 1992 the Metis and the Government of Alberta worked out the details of provincial resource ownership on Metis lands and Metis control over the development of these resources. Metis communities control access to their lands and are thus in a position to negotiate agreements with prospective developers, addressing royalty payments, training and hiring clauses as well as environmental protection. In 1993 Alberta's eight northern Metis settlements are considering the possibility of establishing their own oil and gas exploration company, partly in order to put a business structure in place to negotiate with other developers (*Windspeaker*, January 4, 1993:8).

ABORIGINAL LANDS NORTH OF SIXTY

Aboriginal People and Northern Land Use Planning

The 1980s were an important formative period for the evolution of a northern land use planning concept. Even though the federal government decided to terminate its Northern Land Use Planning (NLUP) policy in 1991, the events leading up to its formulation and implementation in two cases played an important role in paving the way for current and future land use planning practices in claims areas.

What is involved in land use planning? Each of the words — "land", "use", "planning" — has different connotations for different people with varying backgrounds, but generally speaking, what is implied

> ...is the idea of making considered decisions about how people should make use of (or leave unused) some part of the earth's surface, having regard to known and expected circumstances and to given aims and/or criteria. (Richardson 1989:5)
>
> Regional land-use planning deals with the allocation of land and resources, usually among competing uses and users, and outlines the conditions or rules under which the environment may be used. The terms and conditions that are appended to land-use and water-use permits should reflect planning goals. Planning functions in the often ethereal world of values, norms, and goals, but is of use only when it helps to solve everyday and week-by-week problems. (Fenge 1987:25)

Until the 1970s almost all the land in the Northwest Territories and Yukon was owned by the Crown and managed essentially by means of a system of land use permits, licences and leases by the Department of Indian Affairs and Northern Development (Richardson 1989:23). While the land ownership situation has changed little, the management framework has grown considerably more complicated during the last decade.

The concept of regional land use planning for the North is not an entirely new one, but it took Justice Thomas Berger's landmark inquiry into the social, economic and environmental implications of the proposed Mackenzie Valley gas pipeline to make the idea popular and to include it in the political agenda (Fenge 1987:26). Justice Berger felt that regional land use planning in the North would emerge only from the settlement of native claims, "...indeed, a settlement of native claims is the keystone of land use planning in the North." (Berger 1977, Vol. 2:119).

Following the Berger Inquiry, virtually all northern native peoples' associations started advocating regional land use planning through land claims negotiations as one means of protecting their livelihood based on the renewable resource sector (Fenge 1987:27). In 1978 the Inuvialuit of the western Arctic, represented by the Committee for Original Peoples' Entitlement (COPE), signed a land claims agreement-in-principle with the federal government.[5] This agreement promised a land use planning commission for the western Arctic. The following year the Inuit Tapirisat of Canada (ITC), representing the Inuit of the eastern Arctic, developed an official plan to guide all land and resource uses in the proposed territory of Nunavut.[6] In 1980, the Council for Yukon Indians (CYI) signed an agreement-in-principle committing the federal government to comprehensive land use planning in Yukon.[7] This agreement guaranteed Yukon Indians 25 per cent representation on all planning bodies (Staples 1987:86).

---

[5] Inuvialuit Land Rights Settlement Agreement-in-Principle, signed 31 October, 1978.

[6] Political Development in Nunavut. Ottawa: Inuit Tapirisat of Canada, 1979.

[7] An Agreement-in-Principle with Respect to Land Use Planning and Environmental Assessment in Yukon, signed 12 December, 1980.

It took DIAND three years, from 1980 to 1983, to develop a northern land use planning policy that was acceptable to territorial governments and native organizations. This tortuous process has been recounted in detail by Terry Fenge (1987). It must suffice here to say that DIAND started out with a land use planning policy that was rigidly structured, strongly centralized and almost exclusively geared towards the interests of the hydrocarbon industry, while it subordinated the territorial governments and excluded native organizations. Despite the federal government's previous commitments and promises to aboriginal groups, the policy made no connection between native claims and land use planning. "Thus, in December 1981, DIAND had a Cabinet-approved northern land-use policy with which virtually no one in the North agreed." (ibid.:35).

By 1983 DIAND finally felt compelled to negotiate a planning program with the territorial government, and within three months DIAND and the GNWT agreed on a planning system that reflected the existing division of jurisdictional responsibilities but allowed the GNWT meaningful participation in formulating, approving and implementing land use plans. The Dene Nation, the Metis Association of the NWT and the Tungavik Federation of Nunavut (TFN) had agreed early in 1983 to negotiate land use planning outside the forum of land claims, even though TFN was negotiating land, resource and environmental matters with the federal government at the land claims table at the same time (ibid.:45). The native organizations were not signatories to the draft agreements between DIAND and the territorial government, but they were invited to negotiate their involvement in land use planning. Aboriginal people would be represented on policy advisory committees and land use planning commissions. Furthermore, both governments agreed to use eight principles proposed by the native people's organizations to guide land use planning. Two of these planning principles were particularly significant:

> The primary purpose for land use planning in the N.W.T. must be to protect and promote the existing and future well-being of the permanent residents and communities of the N.W.T. taking into account the interest of all Canadians. Special attention shall be devoted to protecting and promoting the existing and future well-being of the aboriginal peoples and their land interests as they define them.
>
> The planning process must ensure land use plans reflect the priorities and values of the residents of the planning regions. (Tungavik Federation of Nunavut, Dene Nation, and Metis Association of the NWT 1983:197f)

The Agreement acknowledged that in the future land use planning may be conducted differently in the regions of the NWT, to reflect land claims settlements and constitutional developments (Fenge 1987:43).

After DIAND, the GNWT and the NWT aboriginal organizations reached an agreement on the implementation of a Northern Land Use Planning (NLUP) Policy in July 1983, and after a similar agreement had been concluded with the YTG and the CYI in September 1983, the planning initiative ground to another ten-month halt, when DIAND encountered opposition after reporting back to Cabinet. The Prime Minister's Office felt that DIAND had given up too much federal power over northern land and resources, and that the agreements were tantamount to constitutional change (ibid.). It was not before May 1984, that the prime minister finally approved the agreements on the condition that the territorial governments and DIAND sign letters of understanding to the effect that their agreement "is in no way intended to supplant or modify the current jurisdictional authorities and responsibilities of the parties involved."[8]

---

8 Letter of Agreement on Northern Land Use Planning, which was signed by N. Cournoyea, Minister of Renewable Resources, GNWT, and J. Munro, Minister of Indian Affairs and Northern Development on June 18 1984, quoted in Fenge 1987:43.

The GNWT was agreeable to implementing the planning policy on this basis while continuing its endeavour for greater authority over land and resource management in other forums. The YTG, on the other hand, refused to sign this letter and argued that land use planning was indeed a step in altering jurisdictional responsibilities and that land, once planned, should be transferred to the territorial government for administration and management.

> The YTG approach to land-use planning has been markedly different from that of the Government of the Northwest Territories (GNWT). The two governments share the objective of achieving increased jurisdictional responsibility, but differ in their perceptions of the means to achieve it. For the GNWT, jurisdiction is perceived to apply primarily to management responsibility, and, therefore, this government has pursued a more equitable and more active role for itself in the development and administration of land-use planning mechanisms with the federal government. Land ownership is an important but secondary consideration. In contrast, the YTG has linked increased jurisdictional control directly to land ownership and, therefore, has sought to develop a mechanism for block land transfers. At the same time, the YTG has pursued a strong place for itself in any management exercise. (Staples 1987:80)

This situation puts a potential aboriginal land base in Yukon into much greater jeopardy than is the case in the NWT. Not surprisingly, Indian people in Yukon are adamantly opposed to any land transfers to the territorial government prior to the settlement of their claim, and they are supported in this position by the federal government.

In 1982 the YTG unilaterally passed its own Yukon Land Planning Act. Upon closer investigation, this Act appeared to be no more than a thinly disguised intended vehicle for land transfers (ibid.:80–83). It gave excessive discretionary authority to the Yukon Cabinet, failed to discuss categories of land ownership and jurisdictional conflicts or to set out a policy framework to guide planning; it did not guarantee public participation in the planning process, nor did it offer any commitment to the protection of the environmental integrity of the land or to the people who depend on it. The contents of the Act also contravened the 1980 land use planning agreement-in-principle that guaranteed Yukon Indians 25 per cent representation on all planning bodies.

After three more years, characterized by a climate of increasing uncertainty and suspicion on the part of Yukon's native people, a Land Use Planning Agreement was finally reached between the federal government and the Yukon Territorial Government in 1987.

The Northern Land Use Planning Policy and Native Claims

From the outset the three major parties to the Northern Land Use Planning Policy Agreement in the NWT had been in favour of the concept of land use planning, but they had very different ideas about its scope and purpose (Fenge 1987:46). In 1980–81 DIAND perceived land use planning primarily a means to implement the federal interest in the North, i.e. to prepare the way for energy and non-renewable resource development. Northern groups felt that a focus of land use planning on non-renewable resource development alone would perpetuate the colonial relationship between Ottawa and the territories. During the 1983 negotiations, northern participants were not satisfied with just seeking stronger representation on planning institutions, but they also sought to refocus planning such that it would deal with wildlife harvesting, habitat protection and environmental conservation (ibid.).

Several critics commented that the NLUP Policy Agreements were essentially political statements, almost akin to treaties, dealing primarily with the sharing of power (Fenge 1987:45; Richardson 1987:55; Staples 1987:73). They went into great detail in defining the interests of the three principal parties — the federal government, the territorial governments, and the native organizations — the roles of the ministers, the advisory committees, and the land use planning commissions; and the representation of each party on the committees and commissions. Far less attention was paid to technical planning questions, such as boundaries for planning areas or data needs, or the results expected from planning.

The evolving land use planning system in the NWT was built around a territorial Land Use Planning Commission, comprising a nominee from each of the four aboriginal organizations together with two federal and two territorial government nominees. The responsibility for policies and goals was conferred on the federal Minister of Indian Affairs and Northern Development and the territorial Minister of Renewable Resources, on behalf of their governments. "In other words, in the final reckoning, government policy will prevail." (Richardson 1987:58f) It was assumed that the two ministers would be able to reach an agreement or at least an acceptable compromise. In the exercise of their responsibilities, the ministers were to consult with an Advisory Committee, consisting of senior federal and territorial government officials and native representatives. "Thus the two advisory committees [for Yukon and NWT] will be in an excellent position, if not primarily responsible, for setting the policy framework within which the planning for each region will be carried out." (Richardson 1987:59)

However, there was a serious shortcoming. As Nigel H. Richardson (ibid.:60; 63f) points out, there was no provision for public participation and local involvement. In both agreements negotiations resulted in the establishment of territory-wide planning bodies, which left a potentially serious gap at the planning area level.

> Given the powerful role of the advisory committees, however, there is some cause for concern that the goals of northern land-planning will turn out to be the goals of government and the native peoples' organizations, rather than the goals of the people who live in the planning regions. These goals need not be completely different, but neither must they be identical. Most important, there is no provision in the system established by the agreements for local residents to be involved in the setting of goals, except to the (limited) extent that they are represented by some of the committee members. (ibid.:60)

Once the actual land use planning process got under way, in the Lancaster Sound and Beaufort Sea-Mackenzie Delta regions, it was essentially taken over by regional "sub-commissions" consisting mainly of Inuit in the former case and Inuvialuit and Dene in the latter. The Yellowknife-based NWT Land Use Planning Commission was subsequently abolished in the late 1980s in favour of three regional commissions based on land claim areas (Richardson 1989:23).

The Lancaster Sound Regional Land Use Plan was the first to be prepared under the NLUP Policy, and was approved by the federal and territorial governments in November 1990 (Government of Canada Press Release of November 28, 1990). It was developed by the Lancaster Sound Regional Land Use Planning Commission, which was established in 1986, and whose members were nominated by the federal and territorial governments and the Tungavik Federation of Nunavut. The Plan covers an area of 1.5 million square kilometres, all the lands used by the communities of Clyde River, Pond Inlet, Nanisivik, Arctic Bay, Resolute Bay and Grise Fjord. It is an area rich in wildlife resources, but also subject to ongoing mining and oil production. Lancaster Sound itself is part of the Northwest Passage and the tanker route south from arctic oil and gas fields.

The Mackenzie Delta-Beaufort Sea Regional Land Use Planning Commission was appointed in 1987 and completed its work in 1991. The land use planning area covered the Inuvialuit and Gwich'in settlement regions. When the planning process took place, the IFA was already being implemented and the Gwich'in Agreement was in its final stages of ratification.

> The Gwich'in and Inuvialuit Agreements have several implications for land use planning in the Mackenzie Delta-Beaufort Sea region. First, the land management systems established by the agreements are the reality within which any land use plan must operate. The agreements

> are an effective means of furthering the objectives of all Canadians, and the Commission's recommendations have been framed in consideration of these agreements.
>
> Second, the plan can have only the force of recommendations to the appropriate private and public land management authorities. Implementation of the plan as it pertains to private or public lands must rest with the established authorities. Approval of the plan is up to the Inuvialuit and Gwich'in planning partners, as well as the territorial and federal governments. (Mackenzie Delta-Beaufort Sea Regional Land Use Planning Commission 1991:7)

The Tungavik Federation of Nunavut (TFN) envisages its Nunavut Planning Commission (NPC) with a powerful role in the review process. The TFN considered the provisions on implementation in the NWT Agreement as vague and inadequate. Two provisions of the NWT Agreement were relevant in this context. Section 4.2 stipulated that "Once plans are approved, implementation and monitoring mechanisms shall serve to ensure that compliance occurs." In addition, Section 5.3.4 stipulated that the ministers would seek "commitment and approval" from Executive Council and Cabinet. Section 5.3.5 further provided that:

> The joint commitment and approval sought is the collective determination to ensure that policies, guidelines and programs which fall under the respective jurisdictions of all the various Ministers will conform with the goals, objectives and policy guidelines outlined in the plans. (NWT Agreement, quoted in Bankes 1987:108f)

The TFN planning agreement,[9] as amended by the water agreements of 1985,[10] goes beyond this. It stipulates that all proposals for "development" shall be referred to the Nunavut Planning Commission, which is to determine whether the proposal conforms with the land use plan. Proposals that do not conform will not be submitted for further review unless a ministerial exemption is issued, in which case the minister shall give written reasons for granting such exemption (Bankes 1987:109). Thus the Nunavut Planning Commission is to function as a screening mechanism for proposals before they even reach government departments, the Nunavut Water Board or the Nunavut Impact Review Board.

According to Nigel D. Bankes, the DIAND land use planning initiative could not have come at a better time for TFN. Without it, the Inuit would have faced lengthy negotiations alone with the federal government at the claims table. Instead, they were able to join forces with the territorial government and other northern native groups to present an almost united front. The final result may not have been entirely satisfactory to TFN, but it was a useful stepping stone to facilitate its own negotiations. The gains that it did produce may have been unattainable in claims negotiations because of the rhetoric of political devolution (ibid.).

Land use planning is likely to be effected in different ways in the various claims regions. People may not even call it "land use planning". In the Inuvialuit Settlement Region, for example, the various land and resource administration committees and screening and review boards constitute the most important means to realize Inuvialuit planning aspirations (Bayly 1987:128).

The IFA of 1984 provides that the Inuvialuit surrender all their aboriginal claims, rights, title and interest of any kind.[11] In return, they were granted title in fee simple, including all minerals, to blocks of 1,813 square kilometres at each of the six Inuvialuit communities, and a block of 2,072 square kilometres in Cape Bathurst. A further 77,700 square kilometres were granted to them in fee simple, but excluding minerals other than building materials, carving stones and valuable clays and earths. The Inuvialuit have exclusive wildlife harvesting rights over the entire Settlement Region. The land grants are subject,

---

[9] "Land Use Planning Provisions of an Agreement-in-Principle" between Tungavik Federation of Nunavut and the Department of Indian Affairs and Northern Development, July 1984, Frobisher Bay.

[10] Tungavik Federation of Nunavut, "Water Provisions of an Agreement-in-Principle", January 18, 1985.

[11] The following is mostly summarized from Bartlett 1990:171–175.

however, to existing surface and subsurface interests and government reservations for public works (Bartlett 1990:119). The total area of 90,650 square kilometres amounts to approximately one-third of the territory traditionally occupied by the Inuvialuit.

While the Agreement provides for Inuvialuit self-management of Inuvialuit lands and resources, it does not provide for local government or separate legislation, but rather entrenches federal and territorial jurisdiction.

> 7(97) Except as otherwise provided in this Agreement, Inuvialuit lands shall be subject to the laws of general application applicable to private lands from time to time in force, including, without restricting the generality of the foregoing, territorial laws and ordinances that apply or are made to apply generally to private lands. (Government of Canada 1984:13)

In the event of the transfer of full legislative jurisdiction to the NWT, Inuvialuit lands will not be protected under Section 91(24) of the Constitution Act. The Agreement declares that "...the Inuvialuit lands shall be considered, accepted and deemed not to be lands reserved for Indians." (ibid.) Nevertheless, in some respect, the legal regime resembles that for reserve lands. Title to Inuvialuit lands may only be conveyed to Inuvialuit or Inuvialuit corporations, or to the federal Crown. The land may not be taxed.

The fee simple lands are owned by the Inuvialuit Land Corporation, all of the shares of which are held by the Inuvialuit Regional Corporation (IRC). The IRC does not have its own share capital and is controlled by the Inuvialuit community corporations. The lands are administered by an IRC division, the Inuvialuit Land Administration. As previously mentioned, administration and disposal of lands and resources are subject to laws of general application which include, for example, legislation pertaining to environmental protection and land use. The Agreement expressly allows the Inuvialuit to set higher, but not lower, standards for environmental protection, when disposing of non-renewable resource rights.

The Inuvialuit have advisory power but not control over developments in the Settlement Region outside Inuvialuit lands. They are guaranteed equal participation to that of government on any land use planning agency to be established, and they are represented on an Environmental Impact Screening Committee and on an Environmental Impact Review Board.

Even though Inuvialuit lands include the beds of rivers, lakes and other water bodies, the offshore is not included in the land grants. Furthermore, all waters in the settlement region are reserved to the Crown. The Environmental Impact Screening Committee and the Review Board have no jurisdiction with regard to off-shore development. Accordingly, in order to exert any influence over off-shore activities, the Inuvialuit must rely on the operation of any land use planning agency on which they have representation, on the advisory powers of the Wildlife Management Advisory Councils and on the Fisheries Joint Management Committee. The Inuvialuit lack any effective control or veto-power over off-shore development.

Northern Land Use Planning Policy has come a long way since the Ottawa-based bureaucrat-dominated planning scheme originally proposed in the early 1980s. Aboriginal people, particularly at an organizational and political level, have been strongly motivated to push for a planning approach and for their active participation in it, because they are only too familiar with the consequences of a lack of planning as it characterized northern development for far too long. Particularly at the local community level, however, land use planning is likely to encounter some of the same problems discussed earlier with regard to co-management regimes, because, as Thomas Gallagher reminds us, "Native participation in land planning almost always requires cross-cultural communication." (Gallagher 1988:96) Drawing mainly on experiences with Athabaskan people in Alaska, Gallagher points to fundamental cultural differences in how some native people may view planning as compared to western industrialized society.

> This difference may stem from a "world view" in which the future is perceived as uncertain and beyond control. With this view the native person "conditions" the future when talking

> about it, saying "if" something happens rather than "when". In this world view, to speak of the future with great certainty is to be presumptuous.
>
> If native people are concerned about the propriety of planning, the impact on participation could be profound. When agencies ask people to participate in shaping the future, they may be asking them to do something that is not appropriate or normative....
>
> This difference in world view may pose a fundamental problem in involving native people in land management planning. (ibid.:95)

When the federal government's Northern Land Use Planning Policy was terminated in 1991, funding considerations were without doubt an important factor. But there is also a possibility that the policy had fulfilled its task and outlived its usefulness, in view of the proliferation of resource, land management and planning agencies under the claims process. The Lancaster Sound Regional Land Use Plan states explicitly that the establishment of the Nunavut Planning Commission will permit the dissolution of the Lancaster Sound Land Use Planning Commission. The Nunavut Planning Commission will be responsible for monitoring, amending and reviewing the land use plan, and if necessary, for conducting land use planning exercises in response to changing land use patterns (Lancaster Sound Regional Land Use Planning Commission 1991:43). Similarly, the Gwich'in Agreement (s.24.2) provides for ongoing land use planning in the Gwich'in Settlement Region. The Inuvialuit, too, have a well-established system of land management under the IFA. While land use planning was in progress, the opinion was voiced among the Inuvialuit, that the Commission's work constituted a duplication of efforts (Norm Snow, Joint Secretariat, personal communication, May 30, 1992).

CONCLUSION AND OUTLOOK

Access to and control over a land base is a prerequisite for economic development in most societies, but with aboriginal people in particular, land is a constantly recurrent theme. Many aboriginal people feel that any degree of self-determination is only meaningful with a sound economic base, i.e. the opportunity for native people to gain the advantage from their own natural resources — resources that the land provides.

Benefits derived from the land can be manifold. A land base may enable aboriginal communities to continue their timeless land-based pursuits, that have for so long sustained their domestic economies and nurtured their social and cultural life. Land may also enable aboriginal people to pursue contemporary development strategies in terms of commercial resource exploitation in a manner that suits their particular purposes and needs. These two strategies are by no means mutually exclusive, and they may be carried even further by means of equity participation by native people in joint ventures, as described by Peter Douglas Elias (1991:40–42). By means of their secure interest in lands and resources, native people may be able to contribute something to the business relationship, thus enabling them to derive not only cash benefits from the venture, but also allowing them an element of control over such matters as socio-economic goals and environmental practices.

> Simply put, ownership or rights to resources confers the greatest bargaining strength on aboriginal people seeking equity participation. Substantial equity participation may in turn lead to real decision-making capabilities and advancement towards broader socio-economic goals. (Elias 1991:41)

When we glance across the country it appears that, despite a history of subjugation of native land and resource rights, the concept of aboriginal homelands has been gaining strength. For close to a century, reserve Indians have steadfastly resisted any attempts by the government to do away with their reserve lands, which have failed as a vehicle for assimilation. In 1990 Oka and the stand-off on the Oldman River were drastic reminders of just how sensitive Indian people have become to what they perceive as encroachment on their homelands. In their efforts to enlarge their reserve lands, Indians are facing considerable obstacles. Even in those rare cases where circumstances are favourable and government agencies are cooperative, Indian people's white neighbours tend to make it quite clear just how uncomfortable they are with a "foreign country" on their doorstep. The "Sechelt-solution" in some ways reduced the "foreign country" character of Sechelt lands, but even while adopting corporate features in their land ownership, the Sechelt also incorporated culturally and socially conditioned safeguards to ensure their land base as a future homeland.

Of Canada's aboriginal peoples, the Metis look back on the longest struggle for a land base, and only Alberta has been prepared to grant their settlements any degree of permanency, along with devolution and a financial package. The substance of their aboriginal rights, however, (and the question whether these rights include an aboriginal land base) remains unclear at the present time.

In the North aboriginal people have made rapid progress since the 1970s in asserting their land rights and promoting their interests. The land base provided by the IFA seems to be fully in accord with the concept of a homeland for the perpetuation of the Inuvialuit way of life. The future will tell how effective the management institutions created by the claims process are in safeguarding these interests.

The Tungavik Federation of Nunavut carries the concept of an aboriginal homeland even farther with its plan to create a new political entity: Nunavut. As John Amagoalik puts it

> Wildlife harvesting rights and economic rights to the land contained in our land claim must go hand-in-hand with political authority over those ancestral lands. The land claim, on its own, deals with some of our immediate needs, such as job creation and economic development, but for long-term solutions, we must have self-government. (Amagoalik 1992:20)

One of the numerous hurdles "on the road to Nunavut" was the agreement on the western boundary of the new territory (Rueggeberg and Thompson 1984), rendered particularly problematic since the collapse of the Dene/Metis Final Agreement in 1990. The boundary was finalized by a plebiscite on May 4, 1992, when it was approved by 54 per cent of NWT voters. The boundary plebiscite took place in an atmosphere of animosity between the Inuit and the Dene, since the line grants the Inuit traditional Dene hunting areas. While the Sahtu Tribal Council negotiated an agreement on land use in the overlap area with the TFN (*The Press Independent*, May 8, 1992:8), three Dene bands in northern Saskatchewan initiated court action, a step also considered by Dene National Chief Bill Erasmus (Pool 1992:7).

Having "to place boundaries on a land where none exist" (Griffith 1987:30) is not an easy task for northern aboriginal people. This applies to the land selection process within claims areas as well as to boundaries separating claims regions.

> The maintenance of territorial integrity and access to resources, was effected chiefly through the defence of social boundaries rather than of the territorial perimeter itself. The key to survival was access to and control of resources rather than the control of land per se. Since the core of the territory, and especially its key resource sites, were the primary concern, boundaries were seldom physically demarcated, and were apt to be somewhat permeable, according to social rules.
>
> ....
>
> Aboriginal tenure systems thus incorporate two seemingly contradictory principles: permission must be sought to use another's territory, but no one can be denied sustenance. The key is the acceptance of the obligations that go with the right. (Usher, Tough and Galois 1992:112)

Interestingly enough, boundary issues, such as land use overlap (Wonders 1983) and shared/migratory resources like caribou, are handled in exactly the same way today. The

IFA, for example, contains various provisions acknowledging reciprocal land use and occupancy claims. In the case of a species that is harvested by other native groups, it provides membership on the co-management bodies (WMACs) to non-Inuvialuit native wildlife harvesters. This membership is temporary, used only for the duration of a specific issue of mutual concern, and conditional on reciprocity: these groups must provide, in their land claim settlement, for equivalent Inuvialuit membership on their wildlife boards. This is the case, for example, for the Gwich'in Final Agreement (GFA) south of the Inuvialuit Settlement Region (ISR), which has reciprocal provisions for the Inuvialuit (Binder and Hanbidge 1991:21).

In a similar vein, the Inuvialuit and the Gwich'in signed an Overlap Agreement in 1984 that temporarily accommodated wildlife harvesting by Gwich'in within the ISR, and by Inuvialuit south of the ISR, until the settlement of the Gwich'in claim. This was done by identifying the individual Inuvialuit and Gwich'in who had traditionally harvested wildlife in the other group's area and confirming their and their immediate family's right to continue. The Overlap Agreement was to be updated when the GFA was finalized.

Another item addressed in the Overlap Agreement recognized the Gwich'in claim to the ownership of a block of land within the ISR and dealt with the principles for mutual consultation in its management and development.

The future will show how successful innovative employment of traditional aboriginal land management practices will be in other parts of the country. In this context British Columbia probably has a long way to go, since the Hereditary Chiefs of the Gitksan-Wet'suwet'en people, for example, have been asserting their ownership and jurisdiction over their House Territories in an extremely hostile political climate.

7 Non-Renewable Resources

INTRODUCTION

> We do not see a difference between the gas and the buffalo. It is all part of our world. As we once were helped by the buffalo and used them wisely, so we can now be helped by the gas, if we use it wisely. We believe it is best to take the goods of the earth with care, and not spend them recklessly. We are no longer alone in believing that the earth will not provide for people forever unless every resource that is used is spent with consciousness of the future. (Chief John Snow 1977:141)

> A culture can be destroyed as effectively by money as by disease or war. The influx of money at Hobbema was an invasion by a foreign value system into a culture that had been based on hunting, fishing, and a subsistence economy for most of its history....The invasion of the oil money was the culmination of a century of turmoil, just one more way in which the harmony of an Indian community was destroyed by powerful outside forces. (York 1990:89,91)

> First the white men came and trapped all the mink and otter and beaver, then they came back for the trees and all we had left were the rocks. Then the s.o.b.'s came back for the rocks. (Gilbert Oskaboose, Serpent River, Ontario, quoted in *Windspeaker*, June 7, 1991:9)[1]

These quotes eloquently summarize the mix of impacts that non-renewable resource development has had on aboriginal communities across the country. As expressed by former Chief John Snow of the Goodstoney Band of Stoneys, Alberta, if wisely used and effectively controlled, non-renewable resources constitute another gift of the land that sustains native people's lives. As painfully experienced by the Cree Indian people of the Hobbema area, the overabundance of monetary returns from some non-renewable resources has had a deadly impact on native communities. And finally, as in the case of uranium, non-renewable resources may exert a "fatal attraction" to non-native interests to exploit them, the most likely fatalities being the environment and aboriginal communities depending on it.

In the context of aboriginal natural resource development, non-renewable resources fundamentally differ from renewable resources. Native peoples have been sustained by the land, sea and waterways since time immemorial and they look back on a long tradition of harvesting fish and wildlife and using the forest. Such long-established precedent does not exist in the non-renewable resources sector. Granted that aboriginal groups did use metals

[1] For the complete story, see Appendix of this book.

in small quantities for weapons, and the people of the northwest coast hammered placer copper into large plaques called "coppers" that figured prominently in trade and ceremony, there is no aboriginal tradition for extractive mining. Soon, however, native people began to appreciate the value of these resources, and to experience the immediate impact of their exploitation on renewable resource-based economies.

As with other natural resources, the rights of aboriginal people to minerals and hydrocarbons are poorly defined and quite variable from jurisdiction to jurisdiction. There are no treaty or aboriginal rights to non-renewable resources not located on reserve land, nor does the Indian Act provide for such an interest. Even with regard to on-reserve minerals, native people do not enjoy a comprehensive interest. Their benefit from these resources is determined by the bilateral agreements entered into by Canada and the provinces with respect to reserve lands and minerals thereon. These agreements were based on the bilateral understanding of treaty rights, the usufruct and the Crown prerogatives, and in no way incorporated Indian opinions (Bartlett 1985:537).

Treaty Indians have often claimed that they retained all interest in the subsurface of ceded lands, including minerals.

> Information obtained through the oral testimony [for a research project of the Treaty and Aboriginal Rights Research wing of the Indian Association of Alberta] in the Treaty Six region concentrated on the questions of what the Indians gave up or did not give up and what they were to receive in return. The understanding which runs through all of the testimony is that the Indians gave up limited rights in the land, namely, the surface rights. This was explained as being land required for farming. It is most often expressed in terms of depth, informants varying on the actual depth, from six inches to two feet. (Taylor 1979:42)
>
> A notable difference in the Treaty Seven testimony from that given in Treaty Six is that none of the informants saw the treaty as an instrument of land surrender at all. It is most characteristically viewed as a peace treaty. (ibid.:44)

In their defence of mineral rights, however, aboriginal people are faced with even more serious obstacles than with respect to renewable resources. This is partly due to the time-honoured legal construct of usufructuary rights, which until recently (till *Guerin v. R.* [1984] 6 W.W.R.) was used to describe the aboriginal title interest in land and resources (Woodward 1989:221). The application of this concept to the aboriginal context dates back over a century to the *St. Catherine's Milling* case (St. Catherine's Milling etc. Co. v. R. (1888), 14 A.C. 46 at 54 (P.C.) [Ont.]), where the Privy Council called the Indian interest in their land a "personal and usufructuary right" (Woodward 1989:220). It was also used to characterize the Indian interest in reserve lands in the provinces that were parties to Confederation in 1867 and was applied to reserves set apart in British Columbia. Any reversionary or residual interest in these lands was vested in the provinces by Section 109, British North America Act, 1867.

The concept of the usufruct was highly significant in shaping the agreements between the federal and provincial governments with regard to reserve lands (Bartlett 1985:537). As no such agreement was signed in Quebec, the content of the usufruct remains important in this province. Traditionally, the usufruct has been interpreted as not extending to minerals, which were accordingly vested in the provinces. In 1976 the Nova Scotia Court of Appeal clearly limited the extent of a usufructuary right.

> A "usufructuary right" to land is, of course, merely a right to use that land and its "fruit" or resources. It certainly must include the right to catch and use the fish and game and other products of the streams and forests of that land. For the primitive, nomadic Micmac of Nova Scotia in the 18th century, no other use of land was important. (Regina v. Isaac (1976), 9 APR 460, 478)

Obviously this precludes any possibility of a Micmac interest in minerals. More recently, however, in the *Guerin* case, 1984, the meaning of the word "usufructuary" has been reinterpreted as having nothing to do with defining the nature of the rights to be enjoyed, but as being intended to indicate who the beneficiaries of those rights are (Woodward 1989:222).

> The court called the interest "a possessory estate, inalienable except to the Crown". This shift in emphasis from the right of use to the right of possession is significant. The modern view is that the Indian interest in land is "more than a simple right of occupancy, it entails the absolute and exclusive possession, use and enjoyment of the land and all its economic resources",[2] subject to the restriction on alienation. (ibid.:220f)

This reinterpretation of the usufruct will undoubtedly have a more significant impact on aboriginal title lands than on reserve lands, where aboriginal benefits from non-renewable resources are primarily determined by federal-provincial agreements.

The development of non-renewable resources on reserve lands is governed by the Indian Act, the Indian Oil and Gas Act, the Indian Oil and Gas Regulations and the Indian Mining Regulations (except in British Columbia). Before any mineral or hydrocarbon development can take place on Indian land, the land and resources in question must be surrendered to the federal Crown. Once the mineral rights are surrendered, they are administered by the Indian Minerals Directorate of DIAND under the Acts and Regulations identified above.

The Indian Mining Regulations fail to provide for any meaningful input by Indian band governments into the development of on-reserve mineral resources. Under the Regulations the chief of the Indian Minerals Division is responsible for the administration and disposition of the minerals. The only reference to the band council in the Regulations deals with the council's approval of, and consent to, the terms and conditions of the surrender. The Department of Indian Affairs is empowered to issue permits and leases on the basis of public tender without consultation with, let alone approval of, the band council. The only way in which the band can exercise control over the management and disposition of minerals on its lands is by refusing to surrender the minerals and thereby vetoing development, or by imposing conditions on the surrender (Bartlett 1990:142). Section 53 of the Indian Act requires that the management and disposal of surrendered lands, including minerals, be in accordance with the terms of the surrender. The Regulations require compliance with provincial standards and laws as long as they do not conflict with the Regulations. Although in practice Indian band governments are encouraged to participate in negotiations and decision-making on mineral development, they are not entitled by law to do so.

Where the non-renewable resource is oil or gas, the Indian Oil and Gas Act and Regulations thereunder come into play. Their administration and implementation manifest numerous similarities to the Indian Mining Regulations. The Regulations under the Oil and Gas Act also require adherence to relevant provincial laws, and place control only over the terms of the surrender of resource rights with the band in question. Bartlett feels that the Regulations confer somewhat greater control over the development of oil and gas on reserves than over the development of other resources (ibid.:143).

Non-renewable resources are distributed quite unevenly among reserves across the country. In 1980 the major portion of Indian revenue derived from minerals came from oil and gas, namely 97 per cent. Five Alberta reserves accounted for more than 80 per cent of total Indian oil and gas revenues (Government of Canada 1980:68), with 17.7 per cent coming

---

[2] John Hurley, "Aboriginal Rights, the Constitution and the Marshall Court" (1982–83), 17 La Revue Juridique Themis 403 at 422.

from the remaining Alberta reserves. Compared to fossil fuel production, mining development on Indian reserves has been relatively insignificant, due in part to strong economic disincentives from the viewpoint of reserve residents (see below) and the potential disruption to band members (Frideres 1984:54).

The 1991 DIAND National Inventory of the Mineral Resource Potential of Indian Reserve Lands rates 132 out of 2,267 Indian reserves as having a good overall potential for mineral development, and 553 as having moderate potential. The Indian Land Registry indicates that 136 reserves have surrendered their minerals (Government of Canada 1991:6).

> Different federal/provincial regimes affect the surrender of minerals because of outstanding mineral ownership issues. Where the ownership is claimed by a province, the minerals may revert to the province when they are surrendered. In these provinces, the issue is a strong disincentive for affected bands considering mineral development on their lands.
>
> Surrenders are also unpopular because of the reluctance that bands have to participate in "surrenders" with the unpopular connotations associated with that word. The scarcity of mineral developments requiring surrenders is due to such factors as poor knowledge base, confusion and disincentive relating to ownership of the mineral rights, and a lack of a means or mechanisms to effectively take advantage of mineral opportunities as they arise. (ibid.)

Actual or potential benefits to be derived from non-renewable resources by aboriginal people, and the impact of resource development by native or non-native interests on aboriginal communities vary widely across the country depending on a number of variables. They include the kind of non-renewable resource involved; the presence or absence of outstanding claims; the nature of the federal-provincial agreement with respect to minerals on reserve lands; and the resulting aboriginal interest in the resources.

THE EASTERN PROVINCES: FRUSTRATED OPPORTUNITIES

Overview

The Constitution Act of 1867 empowered the then existing provinces — Quebec, Ontario, New Brunswick and Nova Scotia — to administer and control their own natural resources under Section 109. The same Act, under Section 91, gave the federal Crown legislative powers with respect to Indians and lands reserved for Indians. The regime governing mineral development on reserve lands evolved only several decades later. The provinces of New Brunswick and Nova Scotia agreed in 1959 that any benefits derived from mineral development on Indian land would go to the Indian residents of the reserve (Frideres 1984:55). There is no such agreement with the province of Quebec, which claims all interest to minerals, once a band surrenders this interest. Therefore there is little incentive for Indian bands to even consider developing mineral resources until they are able to receive some benefits from them. There are some exceptions to this rule, as some Indian reserves are exempt from Quebec's claim depending on how and when the reserve was established (Cumming and Mickenberg 1972:231f). Areas covered by the James Bay and Northern Quebec Agreement and the Northeastern Quebec Agreement are also exempted: Community consent is required for mineral-related activities, and compensation for surface rights must be paid. Like Quebec, the provinces of Prince Edward Island and Newfoundland lack agreements with the federal government respecting mineral development on Indian reserve lands.

The situation of Indian mineral rights in Ontario is of particular interest. This province has historically ranked as the leading producer of minerals, in addition to oil and gas, in Canada. This general picture sharply contrasts with the underdeveloped state of mineral resources on Indian lands in Ontario. Out of Ontario's 189 Indian reserves, 44 per cent are located within the Greenstone Belt, which alone accounted for approximately $7 billion worth of mineral production in 1989 (Government of Canada 1991:6). A recent government study rates 38 (20 per cent) of Ontario's Indian reserves as having good mineral development potential, and 69 reserves (37 per cent) as having a moderate potential (ibid.:3). The same study shows that mineral extraction is occurring on 30 reserves. This includes small-scale developments and cases of production of materials with a low commodity rating. By and large, mineral resources on reserve lands in Ontario have failed to confer any meaningful benefits upon the Indian people of that province (Bartlett 1983:246). An important reason for this state of affairs is the 1924 Canada-Ontario Indian Reserve Lands Agreement.

The Canada-Ontario Indian Reserve Lands Agreement

The Canada-Ontario Indian Reserve Lands Agreement entitles the province to receive one-half of all proceeds from the disposition of reserve mineral rights. This provision is of particular significance, as it became part of the Natural Resources Transfer Agreements for Manitoba, Saskatchewan and Alberta. Reserves excepted from this provincial claim are those set apart by Treaty No. Three in 1873 and several reserves conveyed in fee simple or by letter patent (Bartlett 1983:266). In his investigation of Indian mineral rights on reserves in Ontario, Bartlett comes to the conclusion that

> ...the 1924 Canada-Ontario Indian Reserve Lands Agreement may represent a substantial denial of the Indian mineral rights promised by treaty and a confiscation of existing beneficial ownership of Indians in minerals, precious and non-precious, in reserves. (ibid.:263)

The original ownership of minerals on Indian reserves is dependent on the manner in which reserves were established. Indian reserves were set apart by an executive act, by agreement under a treaty, and by purchase. In each case it is important to determine the interest that was intended for the grant, and the rights that resulted from the process (ibid.:247). In the evaluation of these issues, the principles of interpretation as established by *Nowegijick* and *Simon* (see chapter 2) must be employed. "The adoption of such principles of construction to the instruments whereby reserves were established in Ontario dictates the full beneficial ownership of minerals by the Indians." (ibid.:255)

The Six Nations Reserve, for example, was established in recognition of the Indian alliance during the American Revolutionary War. The land was purchased from the Mississaugas in 1784, and the Six Nations Indians were granted "the full and entire possession, use, benefit and advantage of the said district or territory, to be held and enjoyed by them in the most free and ample manner." (Logan v. Styres (1959) 20 D.L.R. (2d) 416 (Ont.H.Ct.) quoted in Bartlett 1983:255). More commonly, reserves were established by means of a treaty. Treaties negotiated in southern Ontario between 1780 and 1850 customarily provided for the reservation of "tracts of land". As Ontario's mining industry had yet to begin at that time, a reservation of land would have presumed to carry with it any benefits that the land might provide (ibid.). Minerals were not specifically referred to because they were not considered significant at that time.

This view changed in the 1840s which witnessed the origins of the Ontario mining industry, upon the discovery of silver, copper, and other precious and non-precious minerals in the vicinity of Lakes Superior and Huron. After the brief but colourful "Mica Bay Affair" (Wightman 1991), which was illustrative of an increasingly confrontational climate between Indian people and mining interests, the Robinson Treaties of 1850 were negotiated, primarily motivated by mining prospects. These treaties explicitly provided that "mineral or other valuable productions" on reserve lands were to be disposed of only for the exclusive benefit of the Indians.

Treaty No. Three of 1873 provided for the setting aside of "reserves for farming lands" and "other reserves for the benefit of the said Indians". The written terms of the treaty make no express provision for non-renewable resources, but an exchange during treaty negotiations reported by Treaty Commissioner Alexander Morris indicates that aboriginal people were well aware of the significance of these resources.

> Fort Francis Chief:
>
> Should we discover any metal that was of use, could we have the privilege of putting our own price on it?
>
> Governor Morris:
>
> If any important minerals are discovered on any of their reserves the minerals will be sold for their benefit with their consent, but not on any other land that discoveries may take place upon; as regards other discoveries, of course, the Indian is like any other man. He can sell his information if he can find a purchaser.
> (Morris 1880 [1971]:50,70)

"To prevent complication", Morris urged that "no patents should be issued, or licences granted, for mineral or timber lands, or other lands, until the question of the reserves has first been adjusted." (ibid.:52) The surveyors, however, whose task was the setting aside of the reserves, were instructed to exclude any "known mineral lands" from within reserve boundaries (Grand Council of Treaty No. Three 1981:24,26, quoted in Bartlett 1983:253). The written terms of Treaty No. Nine, 1905, were almost identical to those of Treaty No. Three. The land surrendered by this treaty was rich in minerals. Similar to Treaty No. Three, signed over three decades earlier, Bartlett again observes that "It would seem that the Commissioner assured the Indians of their entitlement to all the minerals on the reserve lands, but did their [sic] best to ensure that reserve lands were not located where there were mineral deposits." (Bartlett 1983:253)

Thus, while there was an "inofficial" policy of excluding aboriginal people from mineral-rich lands, there can be little doubt that reserve lands set apart by either statute or treaty included mineral rights for native people. Bartlett further suggests that Indian legislation enacted by the Pre-Confederation Province of Upper Canada and by the Dominion supports the conclusion that minerals on reserve lands, precious and non-precious, are generally vested for the benefit of the Indian bands (ibid.:257). The first Indian Act of 1876 is a point in case, as it defines a "reserve" so as to include "...all the trees, wood, timber, soil, stone, minerals, metals or other valuables, thereon or therein." (Statutes of Canada, 1876, c.18 (39 Victoria) S.3, quoted in Bartlett 1983:257). Until 1919 minerals could not be disposed of without a surrender to the Crown (see later section on 1919 amendment).

The claim of the Province of Ontario to ownership of an interest in resources on Indian reserves is based on Section 109 of the British North America Act, 1867:

> All lands, mines, minerals and royalties belonging to the several provinces of Canada, Nova Scotia, New Brunswick at the Union, and all sums then due or payable for such lands, mines, minerals or royalties shall belong to the several provinces of Ontario, Quebec, Nova Scotia, and New Brunswick in which the same are or arise, subject to any trusts existing in respect thereof, and to any interest other than that of the Province in the same.

During the following decades some key court cases dealt with the fate of Indian resource/mineral rights on reserves set apart before and after Confederation: *St. Catherine's Milling and Lumber Co. v. The Queen* (1889) 15 A.C. 46 (P.C.); *Ontario Mining Co. v. Seybold* (1903) A.C. 73; and the *Star Chrome Mining* case (Attorney General of Quebec v. Attorney General of Canada (1920) 1 A.C. 40).[3]

> The 1920 decision of the Privy Council in *Star Chrome Mining* cast a cloud upon the Indian entitlement to minerals on reserves set apart by executive act. No such doubt could be said to exist with respect to the Indian entitlement to minerals, precious and non-precious, under the Robinson Treaties, Treaty #3 and in lands to which the fee simple title was granted

[3] For a discussion of these cases see Bartlett 1983:258–263.

> upon purchase or otherwise before 1913. Moreover, the better opinion suggests, although it is not beyond controversy, that such entitlement arises under Treaty #9 and the agreements and treaties entered into the first half of the nineteenth century. Such determination suggests that the 1924 Canada-Ontario Indian Reserve Lands Agreement may represent a substantial denial of the Indian mineral rights promised by treaty and confiscation of existing beneficial ownership of Indians in minerals, precious and non-precious, in reserves. (Bartlett 1983:263)

Under these circumstances, it is hardly surprising that Indian bands have refused to accept the terms of the Agreement, which in turn has discouraged mineral development on Indian lands.

> A number of Indian bands have been deeply concerned about the lack of benefit under the present Agreement and have refused to allow mineral development on their reserves. A few examples are the Garden River, Muncey, Chippewa, and Oneida Bands. Other bands have permitted development expecting that the Province will trim back its share of revenue to them. This is not possible till the Agreement has been amended. (Government of Canada 1971, quoted in Bartlett 1983:247)

Negotiations to amend the Agreement began in the 1960s, and in 1970 proposals to cancel Ontario's share of mineral revenues were tabled. These proposals were not acted upon at that time, however. It was not until recently that a partial amendment of the Agreement took place. First Nations can now collect the full amount of the revenue from mineral exploitation if the province agrees to waive its claim to half of the revenues (Native People's Circle on Environment and Development 1991:11). However, this does still not constitute a realization of aboriginal people's full entitlement to the benefits from their own resources. It also fails to consider claims with respect to the denial of rights over more than half a century.

THE PRAIRIE PROVINCES: NON-RENEWABLE RESOURCES — BLESSING OR BLIGHT?

Overview

In the Prairie Provinces the history of Indian land alienation, reserve allocation and resource ownership patterns contrasts sharply with that of Eastern Canada and British Columbia. Here the federal government not only exercised jurisdiction over "Indians, and Lands reserved for the Indians", but it also retained control over public lands of the provinces until 1930 (Bartlett 1986:203). As a result, it was able to extinguish aboriginal title and provide for the establishment of reserves without being compelled to accommodate local settlers' or developers' interests. Consequently, prior to 1930, the regime that was established with respect to resource disposition and development recognized full Indian beneficial interest in reserve lands and resources, as negotiated in the treaties.

The treaty negotiations may have recognized Indian ownership of minerals on reserve lands explicitly or implicitly, but as in Ontario, the Department of the Interior sought to purposefully avoid the setting apart of lands with significant mineral potential. Mineral claims were always excluded from reserve lands, even when located in the traditional territory of a band. Accordingly, the federal Minister of Mines and Resources expressed surprise when substantial oil deposits were discovered on Indian reserves in Alberta.

> [I]t was not expected that developments of minerals or coal or of oil so far as Alberta is concerned would take place on Indian reserves. (Hon. T.A. Crerar, House of Commons, Debates, 30th May 1938, at 3349, quoted in Bartlett 1986:204)

The vast majority of today's Indian reserves in all three Prairie Provinces had been set aside by 1930, although the reserve land treaty entitlement of Indian people had not been fully met at that time, particularly in the northern parts of the provinces. The Natural

Resources Transfer Agreements stipulate that the provinces make available further reserve lands to meet outstanding treaty entitlements, if required to do so. They also provide that the Indian interest in those reserves set apart in the Prairie Provinces after 1930 would be governed by the same resource ownership regime imposed in Ontario under the 1924 Canada-Ontario Indian Reserve Lands Agreement. Upon surrender, one-half of the proceeds of all mineral dispositions are payable to the provinces.

> It is suggested that provincial entitlement to one-half of the proceeds of mineral dispositions in reserves set apart after 1930 violates treaty promises. The entitlement of the province of Ontario had arisen out of a refusal of the province to recognize the Indian interest in the precious metals, no matter what the federal government had promised. The federal government had, of course, no power to impose recognition of such an interest. In the Prairie provinces, however, the federal government could impose recognition of the **entire** beneficial interest of the Indians upon the provinces since it had the sole administration of the public lands. The federal government did secure recognition of the entire beneficial interest of the Indians in reserves set apart before 1930 but failed to do so with respect to reserves set apart thereafter. There is, of course, no difference between the treaty entitlement of reserves set apart before 1930 and those set apart thereafter. Accordingly, yet paradoxically, the Prairie provinces are obliged to transfer the precious metals when setting apart reserve lands, but they are entitled to one-half of the proceeds of mineral dispositions.
>
> The explanation for this denial of the treaty entitlement of Indians in reserves set apart after 1930 is found in the declared purpose of the transfer: to place the Prairie provinces in a position of equality with the other provinces of Confederation with respect to the administration and control of their natural resources, notwithstanding the promises made to the Indians. (Bartlett 1990:122, emphasis in original)

Only a small amount of land has been set aside as reserve land since 1930. The provinces have successfully exercised their control over public lands to oppose and retard the establishment of new reserves. They have also insisted on their entitlement to a 50 per cent share of mineral revenues from those reserve lands (ibid.). In the yet unresolved dispute with the Lubicon Band, the Province of Alberta initially refused to transfer any minerals to the Indians in their oil-rich claim area. However, in October 1988, an agreement was reached whereby the province would reserve title to minerals in the area which contained producing oil wells but would transfer title where non-renewable resource development had yet to occur (*Globe and Mail*, October 20, 1988:A1–2; October 24, 1988:A8). Since this agreement did not lead to a settlement of the claim, the Lubicon Cree on their part slowed oil production in their claim area by threatening sabotage. The resulting closure of numerous producing wells for over a year created a loss in revenue of close to $11 million (*Windspeaker*, January 18, 1991:1).

Oil and Gas in Alberta

The major proportion of income accruing to native people from non-renewable resources in Canada is derived from oil and gas in the province of Alberta. There are two reasons for this: (a) the unforeseen rich deposits of fossil fuels under selected reserves (Stoney, Sarcee and Blackfoot in southern Alberta; reserves in the Hobbema and Edmonton District); and (b) the comparatively favourable economic regime governing resource development on Alberta's Indian reserves, insofar as native people enjoy the full beneficial interest of all resources on their reserve lands, provided these were established prior to 1930. Over the past fifteen years, more than $2 billion in oil and gas revenue has poured into Alberta Indian bands' bank accounts. The bulk of this money has gone to just a handful of bands: the Sawridge Band at Lesser Slave Lake, the Enoch Band near Edmonton, the four Cree Bands at Hobbema, and the Stoney and Sarcee near Calgary (York 1990:89). The impact of fossil fuel development on these reserve communities has ranged from relatively beneficial to disastrous.

Natural Gas Production on the Stoney Reserves

Substantial natural gas reserves, distributed in several fields, underlay the Stoney Reserves west of Calgary. During the last two decades, royalties from this resource have contributed to a considerable rise in the Stoneys' standard of living. They have had a major impact on all other sectors of the reserves' economy. John Snow, former chief of the Goodstoney Band, used to point out an analogy by saying: "We do not see a difference between the gas and the buffalo. It is all part of our world. As we once were helped by the buffalo and used them wisely, so we can now be helped by the gas, if we use it wisely." (Snow 1977:141) Just as the buffalo was the staff of life in the Stoney's traditional subsistence, gas has eased their transition into modern times. Both are considered gifts of the land they are living on.

An amendment to the Indian Act in 1919 made it possible to extract minerals on Indian reserves without the land being surrendered by the band in question. Prior to this amendment, no lease of surface rights for the purpose of exploiting non-renewable resources could be given without a surrender thereof by the band. The original purpose of this amendment was to enable the British Columbia government to exercise its rights to precious metals on reserve lands (see later section on British Columbia in this chapter).

> Owing to local conditions, misapprehension or hostility on the part of a band, it is not always possible to secure a surrender for mining rights. This obstacle has been effectively overcome by the amendment. (Indian Affairs Annual Report 1919:30)

At that time major finds of minerals and fossil fuels on Indian reserves in the Prairie Provinces were not anticipated, and in any case, the amendment makes no reference to subsurface rights. More recent amendments in 1938 and 1951 (amendment of the Indian Act to its present form) provided for the disposition, upon surrender, of subsurface rights, and without surrender, of surface rights in respect of all minerals (Bartlett 1983:258).

The Indian Oil and Gas Regulations provide for the issuance of dispositions by the manager of the Indian Minerals Division of DIAND. The band council's prior approval of the disposal and its terms and conditions must be obtained, however. The disposition of rights to produce oil and gas may be effected by public tender or by ad hoc negotiation. The Regulations oblige the operator to comply with provincial requirements, such as being in the possession of a provincial exploratory licence or a provincial well licence, and adhering to provincial standards relating to the environment, health and safety, methods of exploration, development and treatment, and "conservation and equitable production". This last condition subjects Indian oil and gas production to the allowable production level set by the Energy Resources Conservation Board of Alberta and the Department of Energy and Mines of Saskatchewan (Bartlett 1990:143).

On the Stoney Reserves permit and lease parcels are offered for public tender. The Stoneys retain control over the routing of pipelines and the position of gas wells, taking care that service corridors are established within existing cutlines and other disturbed areas. The Stoneys have the option of taking their royalty share in dollars, as they are at the present time, or taking it in kind and processing their own gas which so far has seemed to be less economical.

The revenue derived from the gas is shared within the community in a variety of ways. Part of the money is invested in the future, in terms of revenue- and employment-creating projects. Gas money is also used to subsidize the reserve's livestock economy, thus enabling band members in the protective environment of the reserve — and benefitting from a tribally owned resource — to engage in an activity that would prove uneconomic under off-reserve competitive conditions (Notzke 1985:76). Another portion of the royalties is regularly distributed among the population on a per capita basis and has served to make the Stoneys independent from the government's social assistance programs. It has been argued that these payments create the same syndrome as the welfare system — payment without gainful employment. But for the people on the reserve, there is a crucial difference between the traditional sharing of a communally owned natural resource and, as they see it, the perpetuation of dependence on a paternalistic government. Nevertheless, it cannot be denied that these payments have served to curb economic activity, be it handicraft production (for the market) or taking advantage of available employment opportunities in band enterprises, such as a ranch, a sawmill and a restaurant. This may simply be "human nature", but it must not be forgotten that like other native groups, the Stoneys look back on a long "welfare tradition" which is not easily overcome (Notzke 1985:97).

Like the buffalo of earlier years gas has helped the Stoneys in a variety of ways. But unlike its predecessor, it has not provided its beneficiaries with that wholesome way of life which satisfies not only their material needs but also their social and spiritual needs. Social pathologies seem to have been aggravated, rather than alleviated, by recent wealth derived from non-renewable resources. These dismal consequences of resource development have become nowhere more appallingly visible than in Hobbema, the administrative centre of four Cree Indian reserves, 80 km south of Edmonton.

Oil Production at Hobbema

The oil money that started flooding into the unprepared native communities of the Samson, Ermineskin, Louis Bull, and Montana bands in the mid-1970s was considerably more substantial and overwhelming than the gas revenue received by the Stoney Indian bands in the 1970s and 1980s. By 1983, at the peak of the oil boom, the four bands (with a population of just over 6,000) were receiving $185 million in annual royalties.

> In the history of Canada, very few communities have ever been transformed from poverty to wealth so suddenly. As the oil money poured into Hobbema, the social upheaval was traumatic. Alcoholism increased, cocaine arrived on the four reserves, families broke apart, and the suicides mounted steadily.
>
> From 1985 to 1987, there was a violent death almost every week at Hobbema, and the suicide rate for its young men was eighty-three times the national average. There were as many as three hundred suicide attempts by Hobbema Indians every year....
>
> A culture can be destroyed as effectively by money as by disease or war. The influx of money at Hobbema was an invasion by a foreign value system into a culture that had been based on hunting, fishing, and a subsistence economy for most of its history. (York 1990:89f)
>
> How could an influx of money precipitate an increase in suicides? It might be logical to assume that the wealth would lead to stability and fewer social problems. However, the link between Hobbema's high suicide rate and its new-found wealth can be understood if the oil money is recognized for what it was: a crisis for the Cree community. A crisis can be caused by economic disaster or by sudden prosperity. The circumstances are different, but the result is the same. Almost a century ago, the French sociologist Emil Durkheim described collective crises as "disturbances of the collective order" — and he found a strong connection between suicide and collective crises. Regardless of whether the crises is caused by a sharp upturn or a sharp downturn in social circumstances, the disruption can be traumatic — and it can sometimes lead to an epidemic of suicides. (ibid.:94)

When the bands were confronted by their sudden wealth, the Department of Indian Affairs adopted a "hands-off policy". There was no counselling or training to help the bands with investments or budgeting, or to guide them in coping with the accompanying social changes. By the late 1980s, however, the four bands had proven themselves to be fast learners in both these areas. Following the slump in international oil prices in 1985, Hobbema Indian leaders successfully resisted pressure from band members for greater monthly royalty payments and proceeded with long-range investment and economic development strategies (ibid.:104). More importantly, in 1987, the Hobbema bands hired an addiction expert and created a comprehensive treatment program for the entire community. Within two years the suicide problem at Hobbema was almost eliminated. Thus the destructive consequences of the influx of oil money were a temporary phenomenon for the people of the four Cree reserves of Hobbema, though it exerted a terrible toll. It provides another sad example of the federal trustee's failure to provide even a minimum amount of guidance in an unmanageable situation.

Hydrocarbon Resource Development Concerns

Indian people have expressed considerable dissatisfaction with the federal government's handling of their oil- and gas-derived revenue. Resource companies send royalty and lease payments directly to the Department of Indian Affairs, which then deposits the money into the trust fund. According to Charles Wood, then head of the national Council of Chiefs, bands have been paying dearly in lost interest dollars for the government's bureaucratic delays in depositing payments in the trust account (*Kainai News*, October 1981, No.2). For this reason, the idea was conceived in the early 1980s to form a political organization modeled after the Council of Energy Resource Tribes (CERT) in the United States.

Studies conducted throughout the 1980s paint a rather dismal picture of the overall impact, development and administration of Indian hydrocarbon resources. In 1984, Joe Dion, former chief of a band with significant oil and gas reserves, reported to the Department of Indian Affairs on the social impact of petroleum-related activities.

1. The general (Indian) community and most of the leaders are dreadfully uninformed regarding how their resources assets can and should be developed; and
2. With only a few exceptions, the Indian community receives little enduring benefit from development. Technical and managerial learning does not take place. (Dion 1984:41, quoted in Bartlett 1990:143)

Among his recommendations were the following:

1. A new set of legislative and administrative practices for oil and gas development on Indian lands should be established; and
2. A specific plan for resource development by Indians must be consistent and built upon any broader set of policies for Indian self-government. (Dion 1984:42f, quoted in Bartlett 1990:143f)

During the mid-1980s the operation of the Indian Minerals West directorate became subject to close examination. Indian Minerals West was found lacking in even the most fundamental prerequisites necessary to fulfill its mandate for the Indian bands of western Canada. It was in urgent need of restructuring. In 1987 a task force, chaired by Joe Dion and composed of representatives of the affected Indian bands and the departments of Indian Affairs and Justice, issued an interim report.[4] One of its most important recommendations concerned revisions to the Indian Oil and Gas Regulations so as to provide for joint management of Indian oil and gas by the bands and the Crown, with the ultimate goal of transferring more and more management responsibility to the Indian resource owners. The report also proposed that an Indian oil and gas resource council be established. The council would be jointly responsible with the Minister of Indian Affairs for the appointment of a new director of the restructured Indian Minerals West agency. The agency would report to and work with the council to insure that Indian issues and concerns were dealt with. The report also addressed a very real conflict in the future design of Indian oil and gas management. On the one hand, it expressed a strong commitment to the transfer of full oil and gas resource control to Indian people within a decade. On the other hand it recognized the necessity of

---

[4] Government of Canada, Department of Indian and Northern Affairs, Interim Report to the Chiefs. Indian Oil and Gas Task Force. January 1987.

resolving the issues of trust responsibility, liability and financial support. During the task force meetings, the Deputy Minister had made it clear that as long as native people insisted that the Crown bear a trust responsibility, the Crown must play a role in the management of the resource (Bartlett 1990:144f).

An Indian Oil and Gas Resource Council (IRC) was in fact set up in March 1987, and Indian Minerals West was renamed Indian Oil and Gas Canada. In the task force's final report, Chief John Snow of the Stoneys expressed his view that the IRC

> would assume a significant element of control of Indian Oil and Gas Canada to ensure that Indian interests are followed — and to act as a necessary initial step in attaining full Indian control of resource management and development. (Chief John Snow, quoted in *Kainai News*, April 16, 1987)

Six years later, resource and revenue management problems persist, arising as it appears, from the dichotomy between native control and governmental trust responsibility. In January 1992 Federal Court of Canada Justice James Jerome ordered representatives of the Samson Band and the federal government to work out a trust fund transfer agreement by the end of February. The Band wants the money transferred to its investment company Peace Hills Trust. Indian Affairs broke off the talks the day before the deadline, raising questions about the viability of Peace Hills Trust and a suit by 14 women who want to be reinstated into the Band under Bill C-31. The Samson Band started a lawsuit against the federal government in 1989, claiming that the trustee had mismanaged the fund. The main thrust of the case is control of the trust fund, to be given either to the band or its trust company, Peace Hills Trust, and a claim of $575 million compensation for lost revenues (*Windspeaker*, March 2, 1992:2).

Many aboriginal communities in the northern parts of the Prairie Provinces must deal with non-renewable resource-related problems of a different kind. The Stoneys, the Sarcee, the Cree Bands at Hobbema and several other bands in Alberta are striving for a more active role in the management of their oil and gas resources and the revenue derived therefrom. At the same time they are trying to come to terms with the social consequences of these developments. Native groups, like the Fort McKay Band, have to deal with the impact of non-renewable resource development outside their reserves, but within their traditional harvesting areas. These developments have proven extremely disruptive to aboriginal community life in general, and potentially disastrous to renewable resource-based domestic economies in particular. The damaging impact has been social as well as environmental in nature.

> During the construction phase of the Great Canadian Oil Sands (now Suncor) from 1963–1967, there was an invasion of Ft. McKay territory by sportshunters who had come to work on the project. This was also true during the Syncrude construction phase from 1973–1978. Between the men living in camp and the town of Ft. McMurray the construction work force reached 8,000 by mid 1977. Fish and Wildlife estimates of numbers of hunters in the game management units which correspond to McKay hunting and trapping territory for the 1974 big game season was almost 2,000 hunters. These, in the main, were newly arrived "locals" who came to work in the oil sands industry. These statistics were estimates based on voluntary returns of questionnaires and are gross underestimates of the numbers of sportshunters that actually were in the bush that season. It was during this time that horses belonging to the people of Ft. McKay began to get shot. Subsequently, sportshunting has gotten so bad that it is not even safe to be in the bush during the open season....
>
> Needless to say the Athabasca River Valley and particularly along its banks are the most important areas for the moose in the whole area according to Fish and Wildlife's own maps of critical areas for important species. This is where Great Canadian Oil Sands (now Suncor) and later Syncrude were built, and where the provincial government has designated the lands as an energy and transportation corridor — right through the most critical area for the moose. Fish and Wildlife, while claiming to be interested in the conservation of the animals, pursues a totally inept policy with drastic consequences for McKay's

> hunting, trapping, fishing and gathering rights, particularly as McKay's territory becomes taken up by further natural resource and energy development. (Fort McKay Band et al. 1983:13,25)

Uranium Production in Northern Saskatchewan

In neighbouring northern Saskatchewan aboriginal communities are also faced with the impact of non-renewable resource development over which they have neither control nor any beneficial interest in. The situation is further complicated by two facts: (a) there are outstanding treaty land entitlements; and (b) the non-renewable resource in question is uranium.

Canada is the most important uranium supplier in the world. "The first country ever to mine and refine uranium on a large scale, Canada remains the undisputed world leader in uranium exports." (Edwards 1991:10) Unfortunately for native people, uranium mines in Canada are, for the most part, located in areas where they constitute a substantial if not the predominant portion of the resident population. These are northern Ontario, northern Saskatchewan, and the Northwest Territories. Nowadays, "Northern Saskatchewan is...the major front-end location of the nuclear system." (Harding 1988:1) Saskatchewan's uranium reserves account for over 90 per cent of those discovered in western Canada and the Northwest Territories. They supply the major portion of Canada's uranium production, which is now more than 30 per cent of the world market (ibid.:2). Aboriginal concerns about the presence of uranium mines in areas which have for generations constituted harvesting areas for communities, and where aboriginal groups continue to assert title, become more undertstandable when we consider the unavoidable hazards inherent in uranium mining, no matter how proficiently it is carried out.

> The greatest risks to the environment are: (1) contamination of groundwater, river systems and lakes with dissolved radioactive materials; (2) catastrophic failures of tailings containment; (3) the dispersal of radioactive dust, which finds its way into water, plants, animals, fish and humans; (4) releases of radon gas into the air, which will deposit radon progeny on the ground for many kilometres in all directions; (5) pollution of surface and ground water by chemical pollutants in tailings, notably heavy metals, acids, ammonia and salts.
>
> In the short term, chemical pollution has caused by far the most damage. Whole groups of organisms have disappeared downstream from some old uranium tailings areas because of acidification. Radiation hazards are more subtle and will take longer to become manifest. (Edwards 1991:15)

> One of the central problems in the debate about the nuclear fuel cycle is ignorance. Scientists simply do not know what the effects of chronic exposure to low-level radiation are, either in people or in other biota. We can guess, based on extrapolations from victims of high-level radiation such as atomic bombs and nuclear reactor accidents like Chernobyl. We will only begin to know for sure after several more decades have passed and a large population of exposed people has been studied. In the meantime, we have to ask: "Do we really want to live in this uncertainty? What risks are we willing to accept as a society?" (Dr. Stella Swanson, research scientist, in 'Uranium', National Film Board of Canada, quoted in Edwards 1991:17)[5]

During the latest expansion of uranium mining in northern Saskatchewan, aboriginal people of the region have made it abundantly clear that they are unwilling to take the risk, neither for their environment, nor for themselves. The Cluff Lake Board of Inquiry (CLBI) established in 1977 is often held up as the legitimization for the massive expansion of uranium mining in northern Saskatchewan. It is significant that in the CLBI's 300-page report there is only a half-page reference to aboriginal rights.

---

[5] For an extensive bibliography on all aspects of uranium development, see Edwards 1991:22–24.

> Our terms of reference are not sufficiently broad to permit a thorough investigation of that issue and indeed, to have made the issue a part of the present Inquiry would have been a mistake, for, the very nature of the issues dictates that if there is going to be an investigation at all, it should be subject of a separate investigation. (CLBI, Final Report, p.204, quoted in Harding 1988:4)

This reasoning does not stand up to critical examination. As Jim Harding (1988:4f) points out, the Mackenzie Valley and Alaska Highway Pipeline Inquiries with a similar mandate both considered aboriginal rights. The former recommended a 10-year moratorium and the latter a four-year postponement of the pipeline so that aboriginal claims could be addressed. Richard H. Bartlett argues in a similar vein:

> The Board is clearly empowered to review and recommend conditions regulating the social and economic impact of the project. Such a review necessarily entails a study of the rights in law of the Indian and native people of Northern Saskatchewan, who represent a significant element in the social and economic structure of the region....the CLBI was remiss, and in error, in construing its terms of reference so as to deny consideration of what Mr. Justice Berger termed "the urgent claims of northern native people." (Bartlett 1981:14f)

Native people actually constitute more than a "significant element...of the region". When the CLBI was formed, aboriginal people constituted 19,000 of 25,000 northerners in the province. If the three northern mining and administrative centres of Uranium City, Creighton and LaRonge are discounted, over 90 per cent of the northern provincial population are native people. Approximately 10,000 of these people are Metis and non-status Indians, and the rest status Indians (Harding 1988:5). It is not surprising under the circumstances that the Federation of Saskatchewan Indians (FSI) did not participate in CLBI hearings, because the Board refused to address aboriginal rights. The Meadow Lake and Prince Albert District Chiefs of the FSI felt that "...the Inquiry is not dealing with the question of whether or not uranium mining should expand in northern Saskatchewan but simply with the question of how." Therefore

> ....to participate in an inquiry having such limited terms of reference would mean that Indian people and their governments (Chiefs and Councils) have already concluded that further uranium development is an acceptable and desirable course of action for the Indian people of northern Saskatchewan. This is not the case.
>
> ....
>
> Regardless of our future conclusions about these unresolved questions (about the environmental, social and economic impacts of further uranium mining on the Indians of Northern Saskatchewan) no further uranium development is acceptable to Indians until:
>
> (a) land selection by Bands with unfulfilled Treaty land entitlement is completed;
> (b) the Treaty Rights of hunting, fishing, trapping and gathering are guaranteed against violation;
> (c) the Treaty Rights for health, economic development and resources management are assured; and
> (d) we have the time and resources to carefully examine the many serious questions related to the uranium industry.
>
> (Meadow Lake and Prince Albert District Chiefs, Statement of October 7, 1977, quoted in Harding 1988:7f)

In a similar vein the Association of Metis and non-Status Indians of Saskatchewan (AMNSIS) declared their aboriginal rights directly to the CLBI, and expressed opposition to the proposed uranium development at Cluff Lake in the strongest possible terms (Harding 1988:9f).

Across-the-board opposition from native people against uranium mining expansion was not only prompted by environmental and social concerns for the land base and communities in view of unsettled claims, but it was also dictated by the experience of a history of exclusion of native people from even the short-term benefits of mining. This history continues into the present as Allan Blakeney, Saskatchewan Premier from 1971–1982, declared that permits to explore for uranium on Crown lands automatically rendered these lands "occupied" and not available for any agreements on land entitlement. This occurred when the push was on for uranium mining (Harding 1988:18).

In 1985 the Prince Albert District Chiefs commissioned a study of the impact that uranium mining has had on northern employment, economic development, health and the environment. The results revealed a growing disenchantment by northerners with the reality of the promised "sharing" of economic benefits of the uranium industry, and a substantial increase in opposition to uranium mining since the time of the Inquiry. The attitude of many native people had shifted from support for a moratorium to outright opposition to uranium mining per se. Despite some marginal improvement during the 1980s, it had become obvious that it is the suppliers of technology and capital, not labour and northerners, who reap the major benefit from uranium mining (Harding 1988/1989:132).

In spite of the tangible benefits that do exist, aboriginal people have become increasingly concerned about the possibility of unmanageable environmental problems that may confront future generations. The circumstances surrounding the 1989 Wollaston spill at the Rabbit Lake uranium mine and its handling by the Provincial Court (Cameco — the world's largest uranium producer — was fined a mere $50,000.) have shocked many local native residents, who also detected environmental changes affecting their livelihood (*Caribou News*, October 1989:8). According to Marie-Rose Yooya of the Prince Albert District Chiefs, mitigation and reclamation efforts at the Rabbit Lake mine site have fallen far short of the company's promises (ibid.:9). "In reality, it boils down to how much risk we are prepared to accept in order to have economic benefit." (Prince Albert District Chiefs 1985:217)

> One of the main reasons there was a "boom" in the uranium industry in northern Saskatchewan was because the fundamental issues of aboriginal rights and land claims were not addressed in the public inquiries. The CLBI not only concurred with the government when it refused to declare a moratorium on uranium mining, but also when it refused to include aboriginal rights in its own terms of reference. This meant the expansion of uranium mining was unimpeded once it was legitimized through the public participation process. (Harding 1988:37f)

BRITISH COLUMBIA: RESOURCES, PEOPLE AND THE PROVINCE — IRRECONCILABLE DIFFERENCES?

In British Columbia we encounter a fundamentally different scenario with regard to aboriginal people and non-renewable resources. On reserve lands the situation is characterized by an overall denial of Indian interest and jurisdiction over minerals. Due to the existence of unsettled comprehensive claims in this province, potential aboriginal interest in non-renewable resources outside established reserve lands is also of major importance. This fact creates an overall climate of uncertainty for mineral production in British Columbia.

Mineral Production on Indian Reserve Lands

The regime governing mineral development on Indian reserves in British Columbia is mostly determined by the federal-provincial British Columbia Indian Reserves Mineral Resources Agreement of 1943. This Agreement confers on the province the administration, control and disposition of metallic minerals on reserve lands (i.e. excluding coal, oil, gas and construction material). Exploration, development and disposal of these resources are governed by provincial laws, and the Indian Mining Regulations are not applicable to Indian reserves in British Columbia. Application of provincial mineral legislation to reserves, however, is conditional upon the surrender of the base mineral interest to the Crown in accordance with the Indian Act. In the event of mineral production, the province retains 50 per cent of any revenues received from the disposition of minerals. The remaining 50 per cent is to be paid to the federal government in trust for the band concerned.

A major issue of contention is the use of the term "revenues" in the Agreement (Bartlett 1990:148; Cassidy and Dale 1988:133). The province interprets it as including rents, royalties and fees but not mineral taxes; this interpretation substantially reduces the amount of revenues accruing to Indian bands as a result of mineral development on reserve lands. Consequently, Indian bands in British Columbia have been reluctant to develop mineral resources on their reserves, and the federal government has not promoted non-renewable resource development on reserve lands other than for oil and gas.

> The 1943 agreement was supposed to promote development; it has effectively stopped it by its denial of Indian interests. The lack of regard for Indian interests in the agreement may in part be explicable by the governance of the Indian Affairs Branch at that time: between 1936 and 1949 the Indian Affairs Department was a branch of the Ministry of Mines and Resources. (Bartlett 1990:149)

This status quo has been entrenched by more recent arrangements. When lands were conveyed to the Fort Nelson Band in 1961 in fulfilment of the terms of Treaty No. Eight, the province reserved the minerals in clear violation of the Treaty (ibid.:116, 149). The 1977 Fort Nelson Indian Reserve Minerals Revenue Sharing Agreement between the federal and provincial governments purported to resolve this long-standing issue by providing "...for ownership, administration and control by the Province of coal, petroleum and any gas or gases underlying the Reserve and for equal sharing between Canada and the Province of the net profit and gross revenue from the disposition of coal, petroleum and any gas or gases." (S.C.1980-81-82-83, c.38, quoted in Bartlett 1990:149). The Fort Nelson Reserve is above a natural gas pool. The 1977 Agreement effectively extends the 1943 regime to hydrocarbons. Oil, gas and coal resources are administered and disposed of under provincial law, while other mineral resources on the reserve within the meaning of the 1943 Agreement are also administered as though subject to the Agreement.

> The 1977 Fort Nelson Agreement provides the greatest degree of provincial control, jurisdiction and entitlement over mineral development on any reserve lands in Canada. The agreement was made between Canada and the province, but was conditional upon a surrender by the band of its mineral interest and the approval of the band council. The surrender and approval were induced by the refusal of the province to transfer the mineral rights except on these terms. This represents a gross violation of Treaty No.8. (Bartlett 1990:150)
>
> It was concluded in violation of Treaty Eight, the 1912 McKenna-McBride Agreement, the 1916 *Report* and article 13 of the Terms of Union. It is suggested that the agreement could not have been secured after the enactment of the Constitution Act, 1982, and the entrenchment of treaty and aboriginal rights in section 35....A consequence of this furtherance of local interests in British Columbia is the manifest absence of any agreement with the Indians providing for the extinguishment of aboriginal title and establishment of reserves. This is likely to cost the province far more in the long run than it has gained in any short term advantage. (Bartlett 1986:203, emphasis in original)

In recognition of the fact that the current framework discourages non-renewable resource development on reserve lands, an effort was launched in 1986 to redefine the mineral management regime on British Columbia's Indian reserves. This initiative involved tripartite discussions among native leaders, the federal government and the province. There was agreement by all three parties that the provincial mining regulatory approach should be retained, since it seemed to be working as a means of ensuring environmental protection and safety (Cassidy and Dale 1988:158). The working group developed two options for administration and control. One possibility was an amendment to the 1943 Agreement to allow bands which are legal entities (like Sechelt) to assume full responsibility for and control over reserve mineral development and to determine with the province and developers how provincial mining regulations will apply to reserve land. The second option was to repeal the Agreement and to amend the Indian Mining Regulations to include British Columbia. This would still make allowance for the application of provincial legislation unless it conflicts directly with the Indian Mining Regulations.

Furthermore, three revenue-sharing options were proposed to modify the unsatisfactory status quo. One would involve a 50 per cent sharing of mining taxes and royalties between the province and the bands. A second option would allocate the entire amount of these moneys to the bands, similar to the regime in the Prairie Provinces. The third option would be to transfer 100 per cent of all mining taxes and revenues plus federal and provincial income taxes to the Indian bands (Cassidy and Dale 1988:158).

> While it is no small feat that these groups have been able to generate a discrete set of alternatives, the discussions have underscored how far the parties remain apart. The attempt to design province-wide regulations has come up against contending jurisdictional concerns on the part of the parties involved as well as a diversity of native perspectives. Not only do native governments differ in their attitudes towards mineral development, but they also vary in the likelihood that significant discoveries will be made on their lands. The incentive to conclude negotiations is much less for native bands whose lands are not especially promising in terms of minerals....
>
> To date, there has been no resolution of the issues involved....The diversity on the native side presages situations in which many rather than one negotiating forum may be required for non-renewable resource management if comprehensive claims settlements take place.
>
> Perhaps the broadest implication of this attempted amending process is that the native drive for subsurface ownership is not premised on a desire to shut down mining or for radical changes in how mining is regulated once the decision has been made to proceed. It suggests that, although comprehensive claims settlements might change the administration and distribution of the benefits of non-renewable resource development, at least some native governments would have a keen interest in seeing that development continues. (ibid.:158f)

Mineral Production and Outstanding Aboriginal Claims

The existence of unsettled comprehensive native claims in British Columbia creates a considerable element of uncertainty for the province's mining industry, which is second only to forestry among the natural resource sectors of the provincial economy in aggregate economic impact. The provincial government has traditionally not considered the use, management or the derivation of revenues from non-renewable resources as subject to native rights. On the other hand, while native people speak with many voices, when expressing their views on non-renewable resource development, their common concern may be summarized in one word: "control". Aboriginal people want control over non-renewable resource management.

> They see control as direct decision-making about development and management and not as the indirect giving of advice to other decision-makers....
>
> Fears of environmental damage from non-renewable resource development to the renewable resources which are the cornerstone of native traditions are, many native peoples assert, grounded in experience. The Haisla at Kitamaat, for example, say that their food source was the price they paid for the aluminium smelter at Kitimat....
>
> ...Several native leaders...emphasized the point that the difference between native peoples and non-renewable resource companies is that natives must live in the country after development. (ibid.:138f)

Furthermore, native people want broader participation in the economic aspects of non-renewable resource development, i.e. not only jobs and training, but participation in all phases of resource development by means of joint ventures, equity participation, etc.

When we look at current developments in British Columbia involving aboriginal people and non-renewable resources, a broad spectrum of possible future arrangements presents itself. Fort Nelson represents an example, where native people participate in natural gas development exclusively in terms of revenue sharing. After years of acrimony an agreement was reached between the band and the province in 1980 which resulted in the passage of the Fort Nelson Indian Reserve Minerals Revenue Sharing Act (SC 1980-81-82, c.38). Under the Act revenues from all non-renewable resources are to be shared equally between Canada, on behalf of the band, and the province. The Agreement, however, did not change the nature of proprietary rights and administrative responsibilities, nor did it grant to the band any voice whatsoever about the pace of development or the control of social and environmental impacts (Cassidy and Dale 1988:145). While it has resulted in increased prosperity and a diversified economic portfolio for the Fort Nelson Band, the Agreement has attracted much criticism from native organizations like the National Indian Brotherhood and the Union of B.C. Indian Chiefs. They viewed the arrangement as a dangerous precedent — as a process enabling the provincial government to, in effect, "buy off" Indian bands and the federal Crown (ibid.:146).

In a sharply contrasting scenario, in the late 1980s the Tahltan Tribal Council (TTC) and Gulf Canada Resources Limited were engaged in negotiations regarding a potential coal mine at Mount Klappan in northwestern British Columbia. Mount Klappan is located within territory included by the Tahltan in their comprehensive claim. Frank Cassidy and Norman Dale (ibid.:154) feel that the outcome of these negotiations could be highly significant for future developments in British Columbia, since "this case appears to be the most advanced and formalized interaction at present in British Columbia between a native government and a corporation in the non-renewable resource sector." Furthermore, northwestern British Columbia is currently the most attractive area in the province for new non-renewable resource developments.

In the late 1980s the Mount Klappan project was subjected to the province's mine development review process. Native people who might be affected by any proposals are now routinely identified by the provincial government, under consultation with DIAND, and relevant information material submitted to the provincial Mine Development Steering Committee is also circulated for comment to aboriginal governments. The Tahltan have been particularly interested in and responsive to this opportunity of participation.

Negotiations between the TTC and Gulf began in 1986.

> The goal, at least for the Tahltan, is to achieve a comprehensive project participation agreement dealing with a wide range of issues. These include avoidance of irreparable environmental damage, assurance that land claims will be unaffected, provision of job and training opportunities for all phases of the development, consideration of equity participation in the project, provision of maximal opportunities for Tahltan businesses as well as financial and managerial assistance from Gulf. (ibid.)

While Gulf is aware of the fact that a comprehensive claim has been filed and accepted for negotiation in the territory that includes Mount Klappan, the corporation does not consider its dealings to be with a governmental or quasi-governmental body. Gulf views its involvement with the Tahltan as consistent with general corporate policies of improving relationships with local communities and avoiding confrontation. While the company at best envisages a modest partnership with the Tahltan as evidenced primarily in economic benefits accruing to the native community, the Tahltan's goal is the assumption of a co-management role in resource decisions and management within the claimed territory (ibid.:155).

In April 1987 the Tahltan Tribal Council issued a policy statement on resource development in its territory, which probably constitutes the most explicit statement on co-management of non-renewable resources made by a British Columbia native group (ibid.).

We wish to make it very clear that Tahltan people and the Tahltan Tribal Council are not inherently opposed to any specific type of business or resource development within our country. However, we do feel strongly that any development within our tribal territory must adhere to some basic principles that the Tahltan Tribal Council has developed.

We appreciate that most private developers "just want to conduct their business". They do not want to have any discussions or participate in any actions that have overtones of aboriginal rights or native politics. We in one sense sympathize with that wish of developers because we, as businessmen, also experience frustration when politics begin to directly affect our business endeavors. However, the reality is that if our tribal objectives of achieving substantial participation in business development within our country is to be realized within a reasonable time, we must combine politics and business when dealing with developers wishing to establish themselves within Tahltan country. Developers will have to come to terms with this reality if they expect to function successfully within our territory.

Before a resource development project can commence within Tahltan tribal territory, it will be necessary for the developer and the Tahltan Tribal Council to enter into a project participation agreement that encompasses the following elements and basic principles:

1. assurance that the development will not pose a threat of irreparable environmental damage;
2. assurance that the development will not jeopardize, prejudice or otherwise compromise the outstanding Tahltan aboriginal rights claim;
3. assurance that the project will provide more positive than negative social impacts on Tahltan people;
4. provision for the widest possible opportunity for education and direct employment-related training for Tahltan people in connection with the project;
5. provision for the widest possible employment opportunities for Tahltan people with respect to all phases of the development;
6. provision for substantial equity participation by Tahltans in the total project;
7. provision for the widest possible development of Tahltan business opportunities over which the developer may have control or influence;
8. provision for the developer to assist the Tahltans to accomplish the objectives stated above by providing financial and managerial assistance and advice where deemed necessary.

(Tahltan Tribal Council 1987:2–5, emphasis in original)

As Cassidy and Dale point out (1988:156f), neither Gulf nor provincial representatives necessarily accept the above as an agenda for negotiations. But the principles and requirements outlined therein may be a good indicator of the kinds of provisions aboriginal leaders may be seeking "after native claims".

Current developments in northern British Columbia seem to indicate that, even prior to the settlement of native claims, native people may be close to achieving goals similar to those targeted by the Tahltan. Curragh Resources Inc. has been involved in negotiations with the Kaska Dena Tribal Council since the late 1980s. The Council has member bands in north-central British Columbia as well as in southern Yukon. Curragh has come to an agreement with the Kaska Dena Nation with regard to the construction and operation of the Sä Dena Hes Mine in Yukon. The company is also involved in negotiations with the Fort Ware Band and the Tsay Kay Dena Band in British Columbia with regard to the Stronsay Mine.

The terms of the Sä Dena Hes Mine agreement can be summarized as follows:

1. The Kaska have an option to acquire a 5 per cent equity position in the Sä Dena Hes project;
2. The Kaska have preferential rights to training, employment and spin-off business opportunities;
3. A jointly funded scholarship fund was established for post-secondary education of Kaska members;

4. Minimum employment and apprenticeship targets were set for Kaska members;
5. Compensation was arranged for trappers;
6. A cooperative environmental review process was developed involving the Kaska and CRI;
7. Kaska Inc. was given an advisory position on the Sä Dena Hes management committee; and
8. CRI agreed to establish an office on Kaska land. (Jean Gleason, Kaska Dena Council, Forum for Aboriginal Involvement in British Columbia's Industry, November 26, 1991)

THE NORTH: CHANGING GROUND RULES FOR DEVELOPMENT

The development of non-renewable resources by outside interests has had a tremendous impact on the lives of northern aboriginal people. The Klondike goldrush of 1898 created the first of many "boom frontiers". Close to one century later, the inquiry into another non-renewable resource project, the Mackenzie Valley Pipeline, ushered in a new era of northern native political activism, and a government commitment to the settlement of comprehensive native claims.

The Pre-Berger Era

Non-renewable resource development in the territorial north did not start in earnest until after World War Two. The mining frontier did not proceed slowly or in a closed front, but rather in leap-frog fashion, jumping far beyond the settled areas to isolated points of concentrated wealth in the northern Cordilleran and the Canadian Shield. The exploitation of these isolated resources necessitated the construction of so-called company towns to accommodate workers and their families, each built around a single resource-based industrial enterprise. These townsites were transplants of southern culture and society in the northern environment, bearing no relationship whatsoever to their hinterland. As a result they were accompanied by a process of marginalization of the neighbouring native populations. Norman Wells, Port Radium and Faro are significant examples.

The Pine Point Mine

Too many of the large scale northern economic development projects in the 1960s and early 1970s were characterized by a lack of foresight and consideration concerning their environmental and socio-economic impact. A typical example is the Pine Point Mine (1964, now closed) south of the Great Slave Lake. By the time development decisions were being made regarding Pine Point, the native community of Fort Resolution had suffered severe economic decline. Both the territorial and the federal government were well aware of this situation, since a preliminary survey of the Great Slave Lake area had concluded that "development programs were needed and were feasible" and had identified Fort Resolution as "an area of immediate need" (Macpherson 1978a:85). The territorial government tried to provide an economic base for the settlement by establishing a lumber co-operative (which closed down in 1968). The Indians and Metis of Fort Resolution were well adjusted to a wage economy, and many of them welcomed the opening of a mine in the hope that it would provide the economic base they so badly needed.

Yet despite the clear recognition of the economic stagnation of the area, and despite the enormous financial backing which the federal government provided to Cominco, no measurable social benefits accrued to the native people of Fort Resolution. The primary impediment to native employment at the mine was the lack of a road from Fort Resolution to Pine Point. The second deterrent was the housing situation, single men's bunkhouses being the only accommodation available to native people. Besides, Cominco's hiring practices (as well as fringe benefits) were geared towards southern workers, since hiring for Pine

Point was usually conducted through the Alberta and Northwest Territories Chamber of Mines, and through centres in Vancouver and Edmonton. Indian and Metis employment, therefore, was minimal during construction as well as operation of the mine. Within a couple of years the relationship between Fort Resolution and Pine Point deteriorated, and when in the mid-1970s Cominco finally made belated efforts to encourage native employment, people were not interested any more. Further negative impacts of the mining development were experienced by the community when, after a ten-year delay, the Fort Resolution road was completed in 1974: availability of alcohol and drugs, invasion by outsiders with abuse and vandalism, and depletion of fish and game resources. The Pine Point case shows, that if native employment is considered a desirable goal, it must be conceived as an integral part of project development, and not as an afterthought.

The Cyprus Anvil Mine

In the development of the Cyprus Anvil Mine in Yukon during the mid-1960s, the federal government tried to avoid some problems encountered with the Pine Point project and attempted to ensure native participation in the operation through negotiation of a "development agreement". But since these goals were only articulated and not enforced, the record of native employment at the Anvil Mine was also a poor one (Macpherson 1978b:128). In addition, no analysis was made of the effects of exploration and development upon the Indian community of Ross River, located approximately 70 kilometres from the mine. A road to Ross River had existed since World War Two, but the community had never been subjected to pressures directly related to development until exploration began in the Anvil region.

Though the mine had its company town, Faro, the community of Ross River was practically taken over by whites. Boom conditions in Ross River began around 1966. The following years saw the establishment of all kinds of businesses, owned and managed by white entrepreneurs and catering to non-natives, as well as an expansion of the transportation infrastructure in the Anvil-Ross River region. In addition to other detrimental impacts of the mining operation, the region became overhunted due to additional roadside hunting by whites from Faro and Ross River. In Ross River a southern urban white community structure was superimposed on the original community, while new modes of education, consumption and production were pressed upon the native population. New needs and dependences were artificially created and old skills forgotten. The affected people had no control whatsoever over the agents of change.

The Post-Berger Era

Two 1977 inquiry reports were instrumental in changing this condition. Both commissions of inquiry were set up by the federal government to investigate the likely consequences for the land and peoples of northwestern Canada, affected by pipelines proposed for the delivery of Alaskan natural gas to American markets. The more extensively publicized of these two reports was the Mackenzie Valley Pipeline Inquiry under the chairmanship of Justice Thomas Berger (Berger 1977). The second report resulted from the Alaska Highway Pipeline Inquiry (Lysik et al. 1977), which was to assess the social and economic implications of the Alaska Highway routing of the pipeline.

These inquiry hearings in many ways set new standards for consultation with communities on northern development. They were unprecedented in their holistic approach to analysing the impact of a project. Both inquiries did not treat the building of a pipeline as a mere technical or engineering problem, nor did they restrict themselves to economic feasibility studies or standard environmental impact assessments. They went further to study the consequences of possible ecological changes for the people's land-based economy (for instance, Old Crow's reliance on the Porcupine caribou herd), and examined the general social and economic impact of large-scale development on northern people: the negative social impacts of short-term wage labour — family disruption and the "decapitation" effect on small communities, whereby the most able members are drawn off (Usher 1977:213); the disruptive effect of the enormous influx of transient workers from the south with its associated problems of alcohol, sex, drugs and racism; and the increased overall sense of alienation on the part of native people, when they lose control over their own destiny. In addition the inquiries were a clear departure from the blind reliance on "expert" opinion, as they offered a chance for local people to share their experiences and to express their feelings and expectations. They also provided a forum for native politicians to express their concerns and to articulate their claims, which in general gave rise to the evolution of greater political awareness by aboriginal people.

These developments established new ground rules for industrial corporations.

> It seems that the reality of having everything to lose by dealing falsely with native peoples and their legitimate claims has only become an important consideration since native peoples have started to gain, through politicisation, a voice which is heard beyond their communities and across the country. The growing concern of southern Canada over the social and environmental impact of unmonitored exploitation of energy and mineral resources, provided native peoples with a channel for voicing their concerns; a channel which also helped to acquaint them with the extent of what was actually happening, and showed that non-involvement would be fatal. Politicisation became necessary for native peoples, in order to enable them to retain, or rather regain, some control over their land, livelihood and their future. As long as no-one publicly objected to the mode of activity of industries in the north, there was no need for companies working there to be concerned about the consequences of dealing falsely, or rather, of exploiting resources without regard for the extent of negative impact on the north. (Orzechowska and Mueller-Wille 1981:212)

This changed political landscape resulted in a modified approach to non-renewable resource development in the 1980s and 1990s. Not surprisingly, changes are most apparent in areas subject to finalized comprehensive claims settlements, such as the Inuvialuit Settlement Region. But even in those parts of the northern territories where claim settlement has yet to reach the implementation stage, a changed "development climate" is very much in evidence. This is exemplified by the Chevron-Fort Good Hope Agreement.

The Chevron-Fort Good Hope Agreement

In June 1987 Chevron Canada Resources Limited of Calgary and the community of Fort Good Hope, a Dene-Metis community in the Northwest Territories, negotiated a joint venture agreement for oil and gas exploration on a 405,000-hectare block of land adjacent to the settlement.[6] As a result of the Berger Inquiry, the lands around Fort Good Hope had been withdrawn by the federal government from disposition under prevailing oil and gas legislation. Speculation that these lands might have a geology similar to that of the adjacent, productive Norman Wells field, prompted British Petroleum Limited (BP) to endeavour to free the lands in question from the freeze. Hoping that the local community's consent would aid in relaxing the Order-in-Council preventing the disposition, BP negotiated an agreement with Fort Good Hope in 1985. Strong industry opposition to this deal, on the grounds that BP's actions contravened the principles of the free market, prompted the Minister of DIAND to eventually put up the lands for bid. Chevron ended up as the successful bidder.

> The key feature of the community benefits part of Chevron's bid was an offer to assist the community in establishing a gravity and seismic company which would be given the contract for that portion of the work. Having been selected, Chevron then had to enter into negotiations with the community and, as a result, the scope of the proposed benefits was broadened dramatically, most importantly by the development of an equity participation proposal. An

---

[6] The following material on the Chevron-Fort Good Hope Agreement is mostly summarized from Cassidy and Dale 1988:147–149.

> agreement was ultimately finalized in June 1987 after lengthy negotiations funded by Chevron and the federal government.
>
> This agreement provides that the community will have the right to acquire a 20 percent interest in any production licences. The first 10 percent will be available on a very favourable basis since the cost will be fixed on the basis of prior investment costs. The second 10 percent is based on the value of the lands and facilities. In both cases the acquisition will be paid for from a portion of production revenues. The government gives the community an important say in the project management through an Operating Management Committee and various sub-committees. There is equal representation on all committees. Deadlocks are resolved by arbitration. The agreement continues to provide for a community seismic company getting all seismic-related contracts. All other contracts go through an Education, Training and Business Development Sub-committee and have to be issued on a competitive basis, but with a community, northern and then Canadian order of preference. (Cassidy and Dale 1988:148)

Chevron viewed this agreement as a joint-venture agreement, separate and apart from the exploration agreement issued by the federal government. The corporation contributed geological and technical expertise as well as risk capital. The community of Fort Good Hope had two things to offer: the value of cooperation and the veto that could arise from the withdrawal of the lands from disposition. It is worth emphasizing what the community did not contribute: Fort Good Hope did not contribute the land, for the land base is still classified as federal Crown land disposed of under the Canada Oil and Gas Act and the Canada Petroleum Resources Act. More importantly, the native community did not contribute its aboriginal title which remained untouched by the Agreement.

After spending in excess of $42 million in the Fort Good Hope area between 1987 and 1991, Chevron came up "dry" and surrendered its exploration rights. The Dene from Fort Good Hope (as well as from Norman Wells, Yellowknife and Inuvik) received many economic benefits from their joint venture with Chevron and remain receptive to further exploration activity, if it occurs (Hancock 1992b:40).

The Norman Wells Pipeline and Oilfield Expansion Project

While the circumstances surrounding the Fort Good Hope agreement are somewhat unique, its accomplishment reflects an overall change in the development climate that is much in evidence in other projects. This is illustrated by the community development initiatives set in motion by the Norman Wells Pipeline and Oilfield Expansion Project (Gorman 1987). Notwithstanding Berger's recommendation for a 10-year moratorium on major non-renewable resource projects, the Mackenzie Valley was again targeted for a pipeline only three years after Thomas Berger submitted his report. In public hearings conducted by the federal Environmental Assessment Review Panel and by the National Energy Board to consider the Norman Wells proposal, native and non-native northerners insisted that special initiatives were needed to enable communities to cope with the socio-economic impacts of the anticipated development. When the Norman Wells Pipeline and Oilfield Expansion Project was approved in 1981, the federal government committed over $20 million for programs to ensure jobs, training and business opportunities for northerners and imposed a two-year project delay to allow time for these programs to be organized (ibid.:10).

The launching of community and social development programs prior to the actual construction phase had been one of the major goals of the Dene groups. The Dene Nation defined community development as

> ...a process whereby community members respond to control and manage their own needs by developing strong and healthy environments according to their own values and culture and, in turn, are able to respond accordingly to outside forces affecting their lives. Under this premise, the social problems accompanying rapidly changing environments can only be dealt with in the Dene context; the solutions must arise out of Dene traditions and way of life if they are to be effective for the Dene themselves. (quoted in Gorman 1987:11)

> During the Norman Wells Project, the Dene called for training that would not only enable communities to respond to economic opportunities, but also allow them to enhance their traditional renewable resource economy and to protect their cultural and social life, to ensure that, once the project was over, they would still have families and viable communities to live in.
>
> ....
>
> The overall Dene Community Development Programme was designed for 26 communities with different concerns and priorities. The concept was to provide human and financial resources to allow communities to identify their own needs, concerns and impacts. Following this needs assessment, more specific programmes would be designed to meet the identified requirements. (ibid.)

The impact of the Dene Community Development Program encompassed Dene settlements along the Mackenzie, from Fort Resolution in the south to Arctic Red River in the North. It resulted in the realization of a vast variety of socio-economic initiatives and projects. Even though throughout its history it was plagued by chronical problems associated with the funding process, and the Dene were denied any meaningful input into decisions related to the project itself, the Program seems to constitute an effective and innovative example of community impact management.

Hydrocarbon Development in the Inuvialuit Settlement Region

Obviously, socio-economic impact control, economic participation and environmental monitoring can be most effectively realized where comprehensive claim settlement agreements are being implemented. This situation can be observed in the Inuvialuit Settlement Region. The oil and gas industry has been active in this area for about two decades. The Prudhoe Bay oil discovery in Alaska's North Slope in 1968 resulted in extensive exploration activity, first on the mainland and by the late 1970s, in the offshore. The latter yielded the Amauligak oil field below the Beaufort Sea in 1984, where Gulf Canada subsequently carried out some production which was transported by tanker to markets in Japan (Keeping 1989:7). The Amauligak wells are not on Inuvialuit lands (the Inuvialuit received title only to onshore areas), but they are located within the Settlement Region. Accordingly, the provisions of the Final Agreement pertaining to environmental assessment for impact on wildlife harvesting apply to exploration and development of the field.

Oil and gas have also been discovered on Inuvialuit lands, for example, on the Tuktoyaktuk Peninsula by Esso Resources Canada. On Inuvialuit fee simple lands with mineral rights, 7(1)(a) lands, Inuvialuit rights and power essentially replace those of the federal government as landowner. As a result the Canada Oil and Gas Act and its successor legislation, the Canada Petroleum Resources Act no longer apply to Inuvialuit 7(1)(a) lands. In other words, the federal Crown no longer retains the right to exploit and dispose of the land's resources (ibid.:117). On the other hand, the Oil and Gas Production and Conservation Act continues to apply to Inuvialuit lands, since this statute is applicable not only to Crown lands in the North, but more generally

> ...applies in respect of the exploration and drilling for and the production, conservation, processing and transportation of oil and gas in [the Yukon and the Northwest Territories, amongst other areas]. (Oil and Gas Production and Conservation Act, R.S.C. 1985, c.O-7, ss.3–5, quoted in Keeping 1989:118)

The Act falls within the category of "laws of general application applicable to private lands" which are held to apply to Inuvialuit lands.[7]

[7] For implications of the applicability of the Oil and Gas Production and Conservation Act to Inuvialuit lands, see Keeping 1989:118–122.

An important feature of the Inuvialuit Final Agreement is the treatment of third party existing non-renewable resource rights and the conditions for continued and new access and subsurface activity. While oil and gas rights to Inuvialuit lands granted prior to the Final Agreement are protected and "access on and across Inuvialuit lands" is guaranteed these rights holders, such access is subject to compensation charges and conditional upon the negotiation of what the Final Agreement calls "Participation Agreements". A Participation Agreement

> ....may include specific terms and conditions respecting the nature and magnitude of the land use for which the access is being sought. Without limiting their generality, the terms and conditions may also include:
>
> (a) costs associated with any ILA inspection of the development work sites and the nature and scope of such inspection;
> (b) wildlife compensation, restoration and mitigation;
> (c) employment, service and supply contracts;
> (d) education and training; and
> (e) equity participation or other similar types of participatory benefits.
>
> (Government of Canada 1984:15) s.10(3))

Participation Agreements thus provide considerable latitude for conveying socio-economic benefits on the Inuvialuit. This is even more so when it comes to granting new non-renewable resources rights on Inuvialuit lands.

This is accomplished by means of Concession Agreements which grant subsurface rights for the exploration and production of coal, oil, gas and minerals on 7(1)(a) lands. For oil and gas, they replace the exploration agreements under the Canadian Oil and Gas Lands Administration (COGLA, disbanded in 1991). They may prescribe stronger but not weaker environmental and safety standards. The federal licensing agency retains its responsibility for monitoring and enforcing the national drilling regulations on all lands in the Settlement Region (Cassidy and Dale 1988:162).

Participation Agreements and Concession Agreements are governed by the Rules and Procedures (1986) of the Inuvialuit Land Administration (see chapter 6).

> The Rules read very much like delegated legislation, and their legislative flavour seems to appeal to the Inuvialuit, perhaps because as has been observed by some who have dealt with the Inuvialuit in connection with the Final Agreement, they tend to view themselves as a sovereign body, not as a group of private citizens. On the other hand, the legislative character of the Rules has troubled industry. One part of this problem, from industry's point of view, is that the Rules can be amended unilaterally by the Inuvialuit without necessarily preserving existing rights. (Keeping 1989:138f)
>
> As well, the Inuvialuit can agree to something that fails to satisfy the Rules if they so choose. They are, after all, **their** Rules. Hence, in the Concession granted to the Esso consortium....the Rules are overridden by certain articles of the Concession and made inapplicable to certain other matters critical to both the Inuvialuit and industry — most importantly, the nature of the interest granted by the Inuvialuit under the Concession. (ibid.:140, emphasis in original)

The 1986 Concession Agreement allowing Esso Resources Canada Limited to explore and produce oil and gas on Inuvialuit 7(1)(a) lands south of Tuktoyaktuk replaced Esso's Exploration Agreement with the federal government under the Canada Oil and Gas Act, which otherwise would not have expired until June 1987. The Concession Agreement was preceded by two years of increasingly specific negotiations and agreements and involved a lengthy community-based ratification process. The more salient elements of the Agreement have been summarized by Frank Cassidy and Norman Dale.

> The Inuvialuit attached several new conditions to the agreement including the exclusion of almost 130 square kilometres of land for environmental reasons and the inclusion of the Inuvialuit Petroleum Corporation as a co-signatory. The concession agreement has a 30-year term with provision for successive cooperation agreements, renewable every two to five years. Also included are arrangements to govern surface access for Esso and its contractors, access fees, land relinquishment, royalties, work requirements and review as well as appeal procedures. Four elements of the agreement are particularly interesting.
>
> First, in accordance with the 1984 Final Agreement, the Esso lease is governed by Canadian and Territorial laws and its operation and management may be amended to conform to additional Inuvialuit rules. Such amendments may trigger re-negotiation, which if unsuccessful, could be referred to arbitration. Second, Esso and its associates are required to prevent, mitigate and compensate for present and future wildlife harvest loss. Third, the concession agreement provides for direct Inuvialuit involvement in exploration and production through the Inuvialuit Petroleum Corporation. Finally, the petroleum corporation is granted the preferential right to buy oil and gas for local use over and above its share of production. In other words, through the agreement, local residents are to have a small oil refinery and cheaper fuel. (Cassidy and Dale 1988:162f; see also Keeping 1989:142–148)

In addition to the negotiation of Participation and Concession Agreements, the Inuvialuit wield considerable power to endorse or prevent the go-ahead of non-renewable resource development by means of their representation on the Environmental Impact Screening Committee and the Environmental Impact Review Board. This influence extends to the offshore as illustrated by the Environmental Impact Review Board's successful stalling of Gulf's Kulluk Drilling Program 1990–1992 in the Amauligak Field in the Beaufort Sea. This interesting case will be further explored in chapter 9.

Potential Renewable/Non-Renewable Resource Use Conflicts

Even though northern native people are obviously coming to terms with the non-renewable resource-based industry and vice versa, a potential for conflict with renewable resource activities remains in many cases. "Oil in the Wilderness" is "an Arctic Dilemma", as Douglas B. Lee (1988) puts it. He is referring to a transboundary issue, namely the United States administration's 1987 proposal to explore for oil and develop Alaska's Arctic National Wildlife Refuge, adjacent to Canada's Northern Yukon National Park.

The U.S. Department of the Interior's draft environmental assessment of the proposal concluded that "a population decline and change of distribution of 20 per cent to 40 per cent of the [Porcupine] caribou would occur" (McNamee 1989:76), a loss of up to 72,000 animals. Drilling in the "nursery" of the Porcupine Caribou Herd would have disastrous effects on the herd and erode the base of the domestic economy for 7,000 aboriginal people in northern Canada and Alaska. While many North Slope Eskimos — shareholders of the Arctic Slope Regional Corporation — were in favour of the anticipated development, others were ambivalent about it, and Alaska's Gwichin as well as Canada's aboriginal communities and the federal and territorial governments registered strong objections. In November 1991, at least a reprieve was gained when the bill failed to win sufficient Congressional support to go to debate (no author 1992:11). But unless the Refuge is legally designated as "wilderness", oil industry lobbyists are more than likely to resurrect the proposal (ibid.; Struzik 1992:115).

A Canadian parallel to this example is the prospect of mining exploration and development in the Thelon Game Sanctuary, part of which is used by the Beverly Caribou Herd as calving grounds (*Caribou News*, December 1987:1,3; December 1988:4f).

CONCLUSION AND OUTLOOK

The relationship between aboriginal communities and non-renewable resources is a complex one for several reasons: the comparative lack of aboriginal traditions for non-renewable resource extraction; the inconclusive nature of aboriginal and treaty rights with regard to minerals and fossil fuels; the often problematic relationship between renewable and non-renewable resource-based activities; and the vast potential for positive as well as negative social and socio-economic impact of non-renewable resource development on native communities.

The issues that aboriginal people are confronted with in regard to non-renewable resources vary considerably across the country. In the eastern provinces Indian people have been frustrated by the denial of their beneficial rights to their own mineral resources. This status quo has essentially stifled development and can only be remedied by legislative changes and a recognition of aboriginal people's entitlement to compensation for the denial of their rights in the past.

The situation is quite different in the Prairie Provinces. On some reserves in the Province of Alberta, abundant resources — oil and gas — coincide with reserve communities' full entitlement to the benefits from their exploitation. Due to the disruptive effect of sudden wealth, this outwardly positive situation has inflicted suffering among its beneficiaries by way of rampant social pathologies. While there are indications that people are learning how to cope, further disruption is anticipated once their non-renewable resources run out. This outcome is already foreshadowed on some reserves.

Indian people in northern Saskatchewan are faced with an even less manageable situation. They have to contend with the environmental and social impact of uranium mining, within the context of traditional domestic economies and outstanding treaty land entitlements. Most people are frustrated with the dwindling prospect of a settlement of their land entitlement, and almost everyone is deeply concerned about the potential environmental impact of uranium mining in general. Not surprisingly, these feelings are being communicated to the Northwest Territories. When FEARO panel members, who were reviewing the proposal for a uranium mine in the Kiggavik area near Baker Lake, visited northern Saskatchewan on an information-gathering trip, the province's northern native communities presented them with arguments expressing strong opposition to the proposal. These arguments were based on their experience and disillusionment with uranium mining, and their concern about the potential impact of mining activities on caribou habitat (*Caribou News*, October 1989:1f,9).

In a referendum held in Baker Lake in 1990, 397 residents voted against uranium mining, with 43 in favour of the proposed Kiggavik project (*IWGIA Yearbook*, 1991:33).

Furthermore, as a result of the lichen-caribou food chain, caribou in northern Saskatchewan and parts of the Keewatin have extraordinarily high levels of polonium-210 (a carcinogen) in their flesh. Indians and Inuit depending on these animals for their diet tend to have up to 80 times more polonium-210 in their bodies than other Canadians. Uranium mining can only exacerbate this situation, because increased amounts of airborne polonium-210 will be deposited on the lichens as fallout from the tailings and abandoned ore bodies (Edwards 1991:15).

Like the eastern provinces, British Columbia is characterized by a legislative framework that discourages non-renewable resource development on reserve land. Presently, resource-based industries in general face a climate of uncertainty in British Columbia due to outstanding aboriginal claims. While aboriginal groups have different agendas in respect to mining and hydrocarbon development, most exhibit a common element:

> From the native viewpoint a non-renewable resource development project should not be assessed in isolation, but rather, it should be assessed according to its potential place in a native economic system which attaches more than a monetary value to renewable resources. Because of their ties to the territory and their salient responsibility to future generations, native peoples express an unwillingness to rely upon a single resource. They are especially leery of negative and irreversible impacts resulting from development. This attitude led to strong opposition by all coastal native groups towards the lifting of the moratorium on offshore petroleum exploration. At the 1985 hearings of the West Coast Offshore Exploration Environmental Assessment Panel, groups such as the Nuu-chah-nulth, Nisga'a, Kwakiutl

> and the Offshore Alliance of Aboriginal Nations repeated the same major concern: If risks to the marine environment can not be fully assessed, development should not proceed. Such outright native opposition usually occurs when they perceive that renewable resources are threatened by non-renewable resource developments. (Cassidy and Dale 1988:140)

The same theme is reiterated by northern aboriginal communities. The direct and indirect impact — actual and potential — of non-renewable resource development on northern native communities' society and economy can hardly be overstated. Recently we have witnessed a profound change in the ground rules for development of minerals and hydrocarbons in the North which has been beneficial to native people.

> There is a greater spirit of cooperation now between politicians, miners, natives, non-natives and environmentalists than existed in the early 1970's, the days of the Berger Report. Nowadays, all sectors are trying harder to find ways to keep the land, the culture, **and** the jobs...
>
> The industry is beginning to see that land claims negotiations could be a boon. In fact, miners and mining investors are welcoming each ratification to help bring about stability in the industry...
>
> ...Native northerners seem to want to win at the mining game too....
>
> Natives are seeing for themselves that mining can foster more jobs, cheaper living costs, more convenient transportation routes, substantial financial compensations, and opportunities to strike new partnerships. (Hancock 1992a:30f, emphasis in original)

Due to market conditions and the transportation factor, non-renewable resource development in the North remains a "waiting game", especially in the oil and gas patch (Hancock 1992b:37). There has been a renewed interest in mining, however, particularly after the election of Nellie Cournoyea as Government Leader of the Northwest Territories Legislative Assembly and Minister of Mines and Petroleum Resources. There has also been a resurrection of John Diefenbaker's "Roads to Resources" vision of the 1950s, with the territorial government's 1990 release of an ambitious multibillion dollar Transportation Strategy, which is planned to particularly benefit the mining industry (Hancock 1992a:31). The industry received a major boost with the discovery of diamonds in the Snare Lake-Lac de Gras-Point Lake area, about 320 km northeast of Yellowknife, which gave rise to a staking rush in the early 1990s.

With regard to hydrocarbons, Esso, Gulf and Shell (the producers) and Foothills, Polar Gas and Interprovincial (the transporters) have formed a consortium to construct a gas pipeline down the Mackenzie Valley from the Beaufort Sea. Due to the unpredictability of market conditions, there is no particular drive to put this plan into action (Hancock 1992b:37; Watt 1991:18f). In the wake of the Exxon Valdez spill, aboriginal groups and both territorial governments remain strongly opposed to tanker transportation of crude oil through arctic waters, despite contrary objectives of industry and the federal government (Hazell 1990).[8]

No gas production is currently taking place in either the Beaufort Sea or the Mackenzie Valley. Oil production is confined to Norman Wells, from where the oil is sent south via Interprovincial's pipeline to Zama, Alberta. As Lyn Hancock (1992b:37f) puts it, "There's lots of gas up North but nobody to sell it to." and "...there's lots of people to sell it to but not enough oil." Nevertheless, for the first time in over two decades, new lands have been made available for exploration in the Beaufort Sea and Mackenzie Delta, and more

---

[8] Canarctic currently operates the only crude oil tanker in the Eastern Arctic, the M.V. Arctic, which each summer carries crude oil from Panarctic's Bent Horn field to southern markets.

Calgary-based Panarctic Oils Limited has announced a plan "that Jules Verne might have drafted" (Hazell 1990:47), namely to draw oil from a production facility on the seabed and transport it beneath the ice in huge submarine tankers.

are becoming available — Crown land as well as Inuvialuit land — as Shell Canada pursues further agreements with the Inuvialuit Development Corporation.

Whatever the future holds for non-renewable resource development in the North, with comprehensive claims negotiations approaching finalization in the Mackenzie Valley and Yukon, aboriginal people will have their regulatory bodies in place, and they will be in a better position now to negotiate a fair share of the benefits — as they see them — and to manage the impact of developments on their communities and environment.

To maximize the benefit from non-renewable resources to people and the environment, it seems appropriate to extend the concept of "sustainable development" to these resources. Naturally, sustainable development has different implications for non-renewable than for renewable resources (Osberg and Hazell 1989:22). It does not imply that minerals or fossil fuels should not be used because such use reduces availability for future generations. But sustainable development does imply wise use of these resources and the revenues derived from them as well as a holistic resource use planning approach. As further explored by Osberg and Hazell,

> Current thinking about how the sustainable development approach applies to non-renewables is indicated by the following goals:
>
> 1. Maximizing long-term as well as short-term benefits to communities affected and involved with resource use and development.
> 2. Conservation of non-renewable resources through energy efficient technologies and practices.
> 3. Increased recycling and re-use of mineral resources and industrial wastes.
> 4. Elimination of adverse environmental impacts in the exploration, extraction, production, processing and transportation of oil, gas and mineral resources and products.
>
> (ibid.)

8

Native People and Protected Areas

INTRODUCTION: PROTECTED AREAS, ENDANGERED SPACES AND SACRED PLACES

> Most of the land we designate as formal wilderness or set aside in national parks is land passed on to us by people who considered it to be, in part at least, their homeland. We consider it to be of national park quality because they did not treat it the way we have treated land. Too often they have gone, and our legal designations, our wardens and patrols, take their place. Something seems to have gone wrong, somewhere along the way. (Dasmann 1984:668)

> ...native and environmental interests may diverge more often than is realized by others. This is illustrated by the difficulties associated with the establishment of northern national parks during the past decade. It is not just a matter of native organizations and the responsible agency reaching agreement on traditional use and occupance in protected areas; rather southern and northern approaches to wilderness and wildlife conservation are based on different philosophies and systems of knowledge of man-made relationships....The preservation philosophy which underlies the setting aside of national parks and excluding man is antithetical to the holistic view of native peoples and their relationship to the land. With the establishment of the North Yukon National Park, pursuant to the 1984 Western Arctic (Inuvialuit) Land Claims Agreement, there now may be precedent and example for a mutual accommodation of native interests and conservation efforts. (Sadler 1990a:xixf)

Canada comprises a land and freshwater area of 997,061,000 hectares. Protected natural heritage areas set aside by the federal and provincial/territorial governments constitute 68,617,987 hectares or 6.9 per cent of Canada's land and freshwater area. Federal protected areas, represent 43.2 per cent, provincial/territorial areas 56.8 per cent of the national total (Ward and Killham 1987:viii).

In 1989 the World Wildlife Fund Canada and the Canadian Parks and Wilderness Society launched the Endangered Spaces Campaign, which has been joined by more than 90 conservation organizations across Canada, forming the largest conservation coalition in the country's history (Hackman 1990:27). Its goal is the completion of a network of protected areas (parks, wilderness areas, ecological reserves, etc.) by the year 2000, which represents each of the roughly 300 ecological regions of Canada. This concept is based on the realization that species extinction can only be halted by the protection of the entire ecosystems. "Fifty per cent of the natural ecosystems in Canada are not protected, and we have only 10 years to duplicate the more than a century of effort it took to protect the first half." (Hackman

1990:28) The most important elements of this campaign were endorsed by Canada's Green Plan which commits the federal government to the creation of five new national parks by 1996 and 13 more by the year 2000. It also establishes the idea of protecting 12 per cent of Canada as a national goal.

Of the legislative devices available to set aside protected natural areas, the designation of an area as national park is the oldest and the most effective and refined tool. In most countries, national parks afford the greatest degree of protection to the natural environment, and in western society, the national parks idea is probably the oldest and most thoroughly developed conservationist concept. Though the idea of "parks" goes back a long time in history (Jubenville 1976:25–27), the national parks concept as we know it today originated in nineteenth-century North America. The first thrust was the Yosemite Grant Act of 1864, which turned over to the state of California the Yosemite Valley and the Mariposa Grove of Big Trees for preservation and recreational use (ibid.:37). The language of the Yosemite bill established an intent — use and preservation — which was incorporated into the Yellowstone National Park Act. The Yellowstone National Park Act of 1872 created the legal precedent for preserving large areas for public benefit, use and enjoyment. The national parks idea quickly caught on, and the late nineteenth century witnessed the establishment of further national parks not only in North America but also in Australia and New Zealand. Canada created its first national park in 1885 with Banff National Park, then Rocky Mountain Park. By the turn of the century the national parks movement was well underway.

Today the International Union for the Conservation of Nature (IUCN) lists approximately 3,500 protected areas in more than 125 countries. Of these protected areas, more than 1,000 are national parks. The remainder include a variety of game reserves, protected landscapes, scientific reserves and landmarks. In Canada, provincial parks that prohibit resource extraction are included in the IUCN's national parks category (Eidsvik 1989:33). This IUCN definition is presently the one most widely recognized (Machlis and Tichnell 1985:9).

> A national park is a relatively large area:
>
> 1) where one or several ecosystems are not materially altered by human exploitation and occupation, where plant and animal species, geomorphological sites and habitats are of special scientific, educative and creative interest or which contains a natural landscape of great beauty; and
> 2) where the highest competent authority of the country has taken steps to prevent or eliminate as soon as possible exploitation or occupation in the whole area and to enforce effectively the respect of ecological, geomorphological or aesthetic features which have led to its establishment; and
> 3) where visitors are allowed to enter, under special conditions, for inspirational, educative, cultural and recreative purposes.
>
> (IUCN 1975:Preamble)

The maintenance of national parks (and other protected areas in the same mold) is beset by numerous problems. One set of problems is inherent in the concept itself. Gary E. Machlis and David L. Tichnell described it in a nutshell.

> We must always remember that national parks, for all their seeming wildness and the apparent dominance of Nature are partly social creations. They are conceived, established, maintained, and in turn threatened by society. Lost in the philosophical debates between "environmental protection" and "resource development" is the fact that the perpetuation of national parks does not depend upon one or the other; it depends on both. (Machlis and Tichnell 1985:95)
>
> The conflict originates from the paradoxical mandate that parks provide opportunities for public enjoyment in environments that are to be preserved. (ibid.:22)

National park problems arising from this dual mandate are universal and well known. Another set of problems, however, is caused by circumstances which until recently had received far less attention. The national parks idea is a product of western industrialized society. Without any adjustment this concept has been transplanted into different cultural and social environments. In the process, aboriginal populations have either been physically displaced or their socio-economic base has been severely disrupted. Such cultural insensitivity and failure to integrate protected areas into regional socio-economic systems may not only have disastrous consequences for local indigenous populations but, in the long run, will also jeopardize the very resources protection areas are designed to preserve. It is, under this aspect, that the management of existing protected areas in Canada and the establishment of new ones shall be examined.

Not only do aboriginal people lack a concept in their languages for what is commonly referred to as a "park", but the two main ingredients of the park idea — preservation and recreation or leisure — are utterly alien concepts in aboriginal cultures.

> This distinction between work and leisure is largely an artifact of industrial society. Leisure, however, requires not only time but also space and resources. The need for wilderness parks, and for the recreational use of wildlife, well known to wildlife managers, is that of an industrial as opposed to an agrarian or a foraging society....What is more-or-less unified in aboriginal cosmology is fragmented in our own. The division of knowledge into branches such as law, political theory, economics, and biology, the distinctions between work and leisure, between man and nature, among the attributes of land and the incidents of property, are essentially foreign to aboriginal tradition. (Usher 1984:400)

This is no less true for the concept of preservation which is based on a notion of "apartness" between man and nature. "Preservation" and "conservation" are often taken to mean exactly the same thing, namely to keep things undisturbed or in an unchanged condition. In practice, however, and in particular with regard to the natural environment, the two terms have assumed quite different meanings. Preservation is most commonly used in reference to non-use of a resource and non-interference with the processes of nature. In contrast, the concept of conservation is entirely compatible with sustainable utilization of resources.

> Conservation and development-policy-making and -planning often seem to assume that we, the aboriginal peoples, have only two options for the future: to return to our ancient way of life or to abandon subsistence altogether and become assimilated into the dominant society. Neither option is reasonable. We should have a third option: to modify our subsistence way of life, combining the old and the new in ways that maintain and enhance our identity while allowing our society and economy to evolve. As original conservationists, we now aim to combine development and conservation, and to put into practice the concept of equitable, culturally appropriate, sustainable development. As such, the goal of the World Conservation Strategy is our goal too. (Erasmus 1989:93f)

These words by George Erasmus, former National Chief of the Assembly of First Nations and also a director of World Wildlife Fund Canada, indicate that a meeting of the minds between indigenous people and society at large may be possible after all. This is also suggested by a neologism which the Inuit use to describe a park, namely "mirnguiqsirvik", "a place to rest and relax" (Bruce Rigby, personal communication, July 26, 1993). The fact that numerous places, which have been designated as parks, also have sacred value and special significance for native people, has a potential for complicating as well as facilitating such understanding. Mount Rainier in Washington State, the Banff Hot Springs and Gwaii Haanas (South Moresby) are examples. Whereas the ingredients of the Euro-American parks concept are alien to aboriginal ways of thinking, veneration for and protection of special places are not.

> Holy places are well known in what have been classified as primitive religions. The vast majority of Indian tribal religions have a centre at a particular place, be it river, mountain,

plateau, valley, or other natural feature. Many of the smaller nonuniversal religions also depend on a number of holy places for the practice of their religious activities. In part the affirmation of the existence of holy places confirms tribal peoples' rootedness, which Western man is peculiarly without. The development of shrines in the religious life of the practitioners of world religions would seem to indicate that this spatial dimension cannot be avoided as men seek religious experiences. (Deloria 1973:81)

Modern people still do value the sacred in their lives, as evidenced by the abundance of churches, synagogues, and mosques of the world, but modern society seems to disavow the potential of natural places as being capable of arousing sacred feelings in us. In the Indian mind, sacred places in nature not only represent physical touchstones for evoking sacred values, but they also hold an important key to personal power. This power is called wakonda by the Lakota, orenda by the Iroquois, pokunt by the Shoshone, manitou by the Algonquins, yek by the Tlingit, naula by the Kwakiutl, sgana by the Haida, and mana among the Hawaiians. (Swan 1990:70)

Due to the power of social convention, there was no need for "protective legislation" with regard to special places in the aboriginal past, but such need does exist in today's multicultural societies of Canada and the United States. Lawyer Jack Woodward makes the connection between the protection of native religions and the protection of the environment which sustains these religions.

Native religion is afforded two sorts of constitutional protection under Canadian law. Firstly, the right to practise and follow a native religion is guaranteed by the Canadian Charter of Rights and Freedoms, the Canadian Bill of Rights, and the other constitutional principles or enactments that protect the religious freedom of Canadians. Secondly, native religion may be afforded special and additional protection by the entrenchment of aboriginal and treaty rights by s. 35(1) of the Constitution Act, 1982. **The practical effect of this dual system of protection for native religions is that the material conditions necessary for the exercise of native religion may be guaranteed as "aboriginal and treaty rights", over and above the personal freedom to carry on the practices.**

Generalization about native religions in Canada is difficult, considering the diversity of our native cultures. Many native people are Christians. Indeed, many native communities were Christianized before the assertion of British sovereignty. Even within Christian native communities, however, elements of native religion may remain. And it is generally true that native religions in Canada involve some special relationship with the natural world. **Preservation of the natural environment may be a precondition for the exercise of native religion. An assertion of aboriginal rights or title may be an effective method of preventing industrialization of wilderness areas required for the practice of native religion.** (Woodward 1989:339f, emphasis added)

The principle outlined in the above citation has not yet been tested in Canadian courts. Jack Woodward argues, that in comparison, American courts have assumed a far more activist stance in protecting the natural environment upon which some native religions depend than have Canadian courts (ibid.:340). An example was an injunction granted in 1985 to permanently prohibit the U.S. Forest Service from logging in the sacred "high country" of the Yurok, Karok and Tolowa Indians of northern California. Another point in case is the 1978 American Indian Religious Freedom Act, which gave birth to a new land use category, "the sacred place in nature". After over a decade, however, this act has not lived up to native expectations. There has been much frustration in attempts to validate the ultimately unprovable, and sacred places still are on trial (Swan 1990:131).

Thus the stage that is set for a cooperative effort by aboriginal and non-aboriginal Canadians to improve and expand the system of protected areas, is cluttered with a multiplicity of concepts, deeply ingrained in respective cultures and societies, and more often than not incomprehensible to the other party. Furthermore the situation is complicated by legal and political factors, and by the question of legal and moral rights.

LEGISLATIVE AND CONCEPTUAL FRAMEWORK OF PROTECTED AREAS

Federal Level

The roots of the Canadian National Parks Act are found in the 1885 Order in Council establishing Rocky Mountain Park in Banff, Alberta. The National Parks Act was not passed by the Government of Canada until 1930, and with the exception of a few amendments in 1974 and Bill C-30 in 1988, the Act has remained virtually unchanged (McMillan 1986:1). Its general purpose is set out in Section 4:

> The National Parks of Canada are hereby dedicated to the people of Canada for their benefit, education and enjoyment, subject to this Act and the regulations, and the National Parks shall be maintained and made use of so as to leave them unimpaired for the enjoyment of future generations.

The procedure for creating a new national park in a province involves a federal-provincial agreement setting out the terms and conditions of transferring control and administration of the required lands from the province to the federal government. In the northern territories this process includes federal land withdrawal (Ward and Killham 1987:20) and special provisions for native people who have an unextinguished aboriginal claim to the area in question.

> 1.3.13 Where new national parks are established in conjunction with the settlement of land claims of native people, an agreement will be negotiated between Parks Canada and representatives of local native communities prior to formal establishment of the national park creating a joint management regime for the planning and management of the national park.
>
> 1.3.14 Boundaries of national parks would not be finally established in legislation until a settlement of relevant native claims is reached. As an interim measure such areas may be set aside as "national park reserves". (Government of Canada 1982b:40)

National park reserves are practically "parks in waiting": their boundaries are provisional, they do not compromise native land claims, but they are subject to national park legislation in all other respects.

Commercial exploration, extraction or development of renewable and non-renewable resources in national parks is prohibited.[1] Prior to the 1920s aboriginal people were not allowed to hunt, fish or trap within national park boundaries. Indeed, in the early 1900s, Banff National Park was expanded in order to prevent Stoney Indians from hunting bighorn sheep (Foster 1978:60f). The establishment of Wood Buffalo National Park in 1922 brought the first departure from this traditional policy. An exemption to the National Parks Game Regulations authorized the Superintendent of Wood Buffalo to issue permits to Treaty Indians, who had hunted and trapped in the area prior to the creation of the park. Non-natives who had previously hunted and trapped there were granted similar rights (Hunt 1979:606f).

Provisions for the retention of traditional hunting, fishing and trapping rights by aboriginal people are part of the 1974 amendments to the Act, under which Auyuittuq, Nahanni and Kluane[2] national park reserves were established. These amendments find their expression in parks policy.

---

[1] This prohibition did not prevent decades of logging in Wood Buffalo National Park, with the last renewal of a timber lease by Ottawa in 1981. In February 1992 the Canadian Parks and Wilderness Society with help from the Sierra Legal Defence Fund took legal action against the environment minister to stop logging in the Park. In May 1992 the Federal Court ruled that logging in WBNP is illegal and invalid under the National Park Act.

[2] In the case of Kluane National Park Reserve, even though it was established under the 1974 amendments to the National Parks Act, aboriginal people are not allowed any harvesting activities. The government takes

> 3.2.11 Certain traditional extractive activities will be permitted in the following circumstances:
>
> i) In new national parks, guarantees will be provided so that **certain traditional subsistence resource uses by local people will be permitted to continue in parts of national parks for one or more generations when such uses are an essential part of the local way of life and when no alternatives exist outside the park boundaries**. These exceptions will be agreed to at the time of formal establishment of a new national park and will be outlined in the park management plan.
> ii) Selected activities which are of cultural value in portraying to visitors traditional relationships between man and the land in the park area as part of the park experience may be permitted.
> iii) In new national parks, the treaty rights of Indian people and those rights recognized in native land claims settlements will be honoured and extractive activities which are the subject of such rights can only be terminated after agreement has been reached with the people concerned.
> iv) Controlled sport fishing of naturally regenerating populations of native species will be permitted.
>
> All such activities will be subject to the requirement to protect the ecosystems and maintain viable populations of fish and wildlife species. (Government of Canada 1982b:42, emphasis added)

The language used is both vague and restrictive and potentially damaging to native interests. Subsection (ii) alludes to a "human zoo". Application and interpretation of the 1974 amendments has varied widely (Hunt, Miller and Tingley 1979:81). But even though the amendments fall far short of the recognition of native interests in perpetuity, this change in legislation and policy has opened the door to an innovative approach to the design and management of new national parks. Native people still have no rights to pursue traditional harvesting activities in the older established parks.

Provincial Level

The legislative and conceptual framework for protected areas varies somewhat from province to province, and so does the terminology for designated protection areas. All provinces have provincial parks, and many feature ecological reserves. Furthermore there is a variety of wilderness areas, wilderness parks, natural areas, wildlife sanctuaries, regional parks, conservation areas, game preserves, etc. enjoying widely varying degrees of protection.

Provincial parks are administered under the Provincial Parks Acts of the respective provinces (with the exception of Prince Edward Island, where they are administered under the Recreation and Development Act). They exhibit similarities to national parks in that they have a dual mandate: preservation and outdoor recreation. They do not, however, enjoy the same degree of protection from resource extraction as do national parks (though these are by no means immune, either). The situation in Ontario is indicative of this shortcoming. In the late 1970s, 15 per cent of Ontario's provincial park system were being logged, and a much larger percentage had been logged in the past (Reid 1979:110). Circumstances in Algonquin Provincial Park seem to mock the very idea of a park, and cause the Canadian Parks and Wilderness Society to ask: "When is a park not a park?"

---

the view that native people have not traditionally hunted or trapped in the park, because prior to the withdrawal of the area as a national park reserve, Kluane formed part of the Kluane Game Sanctuary. Consequently, no hunting had been allowed within the area since 1942 when the Sanctuary was established. Apparently Parks Canada does not view hunting as an element of native culture that can survive a one-generation lapse (Hunt et al. 1979:35).

The prohibition of hunting and trapping in sanctuaries however, seems to contravene Section 17(3) of the Yukon Act, which prohibits the Governor in Council from enacting ordinances "restricting or prohibiting Indians or Eskimos from hunting for food, on unoccupied Crown lands, game other than game declared by the Governor in Council to be game in danger of becoming extinct." (Theberge et al. 1980:76). For a detailed history of the establishment of the Kluane National Park Reserve, see Theberge 1978.

(Locke 1991:1) In Algonquin, logging has been permitted in the park since 1893 and is now carried on in 75 per cent of it (*Globe and Mail*, April 11, 1991). More than 60 commercial hunting camps operate in the southern section of the park. The discussion of hunting rights in chapter 5 has already shown that aboriginal people's rights of access to designated protection areas for traditional harvesting purposes are anything but conclusive or clear-cut. By and large they are excluded. There does not appear to be any concerted effort to accommodate native rights and practices in provincial legislations and policy formulations, as there has lately been at the federal level. Recent developments in Ontario though show an inclination in that direction as discussed later in this chapter.

A second important category of protected areas found in many provinces is ecological reserves. Ecological reserves are the product of an international initiative, the International Biological Program (IBP). This 10-year program, adopted by Canada and 57 other nations and carried out between 1964 and 1974, was a response by scientists and governments to the worldwide problems of human population explosion, food shortages and environmental destruction. Its key action was the setting aside of natural areas.

> Rational use and management of the earth's limited resources can only be based on sound scientific knowledge. Research ecologists who must provide that knowledge, lack basic information on the earth's ecosystems. Without such data, they are not able to explain how man's activities affect the environment. In recognition of this, the International Biological Programme established a subcommittee for the Conservation of Terrestrial Communities (IBP-CT). This was an international effort to preserve samples of the world's ecosystems for present and future biological research, as datum points by which to measure man-made changes in ecosystems and for educational and demonstration purposes. (Taschereau 1985:1)

> An Ecological Reserve is a legally protected natural area where human influence is kept to a minimum. Change, itself a natural phenomenon, is not interfered with, but is allowed as far as possible to proceed uninterrupted by man. (ibid.:5)

Paradoxically, in spite of the IBP being an international program, the federal government never provided any leadership in its execution, and the progress that did occur in the establishment of ecological reserves was made at the provincial level (Foster 1979:261). In 1971 the government of British Columbia enacted the first Ecological Reserves legislation, and by 1972 it had established 54 ecological reserves. Most of the other provinces followed suit, and only two provinces, Ontario and Prince Edward Island, do not have an Ecological Reserves Act. Similarly, the northern territories under federal jurisdiction do not have any form of Ecological Reserves legislation.

British Columbia still has the largest number of ecological reserves, namely 113. However, the areas are small and endangered by competitive resource use and encroachment, and their management and protection is plagued by understaffing and lack of funds (Taschereau 1985:35f). Saskatchewan and Nova Scotia have no ecological reserves, though they do have appropriate legislation, and the remainder of the provinces have a small number. Ecological reserves are politically less attractive than other types of protected areas, since they are perceived as natural areas with distinctly restricted use, namely research and education, while use for recreation is deliberately de-emphasized and resource extraction prohibited (ibid.:81). These factors account for the extremely slow pace of their establishment.

International Level

National parks, provincial parks and ecological reserves accommodate the perceived needs of non-aboriginal Canadians to varying degrees, which accounts for their different political popularity and support. To aboriginal people they all appear unaccommodating and exclusive, since none of these concepts embraces the idea of man as integral part of the ecosystem. One type of area departs from this traditional notion: the biosphere reserve.

In 1970 the General Conference of UNESCO launched an international ecological program on Man and the Biosphere (MAB). Its goals were to

> ...develop within the natural and social sciences a basis for the rational use and conservation of the resources of the biosphere and for the improvement of the relationship between man and the environment; to predict the consequences of today's actions on tomorrow's world and thereby to increase man's ability to manage efficiently the natural resources of the biosphere. (IUCN 1979:1)

An International Co-ordinating Council guides and supervises the program through national committees established in 110 countries. The planning, financing and implementation of MAB field projects and the establishment of biosphere reserves are the responsibility of these committees (Taschereau 1985:10; Inglis 1990:142). Bernd von Droste zu Huelshoff explains how biosphere reserves are distinct from other designated protection areas.

> A biosphere reserve constitutes a representative example of one of the world's major ecosystems and thus conserves genetically viable plant and animal populations in their natural habitats; provides sites for long-term research on the structure, functioning and dynamics of ecosystems; combines research and monitoring, environmental education, training and demonstration; and seeks the support and participation of the local people, in part through research contributing to their social and economic development. A biosphere reserve is not an enclosed, inaccessible sanctuary. It blends with the surrounding human landscape. Finally, biosphere reserves form an international network linked up with other networks in MAB, thus offering a vast framework for comparative research for a continuum reaching from undisturbed natural areas to man-made systems.
>
> ...MAB emphasizes man's partnership with nature. A biosphere reserve is open and interacts with its region. The local people can be its guardians. (von Droste zu Huelshoff 1984:690f)

Ideally, biosphere reserves include a protected core of relatively undisturbed land to serve as a reference against which to assess the effects of human use. Designated areas, such as national parks or ecological reserves, are suitable to provide such core. To date there are four biosphere reserves in Canada: Waterton Lakes (Alberta), Riding Mountain (Manitoba), Long Point (Ontario) and Mont St. Hilaire (Quebec). There are no such reserves yet in the North, but there is a pronounced interest in this program on the part of some northern native people. Furthermore, the circumpolar MAB Northern Science Network has adopted the issue of northern protected areas and biosphere reserves as one of its three main themes for research and collaboration emphasis (Slaughter 1990:152).

> In fact, biosphere reserves have been with us for many years and, through a natural convergence of concepts and ideas, are more relevant now than at any time in the past. In the final analysis, biosphere reserves could play an important role in demonstrating, as they have done in many Third World countries, the ecological and economic advantages of integrating management of all important resources in a region. This convergence comes at a time when northerners, in planning for the sustainable development of their resources, are seeking new or better models, and fresh ideas. (Inglis 1990:144)

Julian T. Inglis provides us with an extensive list of characteristics of biosphere reserves which appear to make them particularly well suited for northern Canada.

1. The fact that they do not require land withdrawal or alienation: the core would already be protected by national, territorial or settlement legislation. In fact, the need for a withdrawal of large areas may be lessened, by eliminating the need for withdrawal of surrounding "buffer" zones as part of the core conservation areas;
2. The proposal to establish a reserve comes from northerners — it is not imposed from outside. The initial proposal comes from residents, HTA's, councils, territorial governments, or non-government organizations;

3. Management is by local committees, with residents involved in research, monitoring, training and resource management. This fits well with new institutional arrangements emerging through the land claims process and land use planning;
4. Biosphere reserves are internationally recognized as part of a global system. Monitoring within the reserves contributes to a worldwide appreciation of environmental change; but it also contributes to residents, understanding of how external forces act on their resources;
5. Biosphere reserves provide an opportunity to conserve resources in a cooperative fashion over very large areas. They can be established in land, marine and freshwater areas, retaining the notion of the unity of land and sea in the Canadian Arctic Archipelago;
6. Future options are retained; reserves are adaptable to changing patterns of resource use and management; and
7. Biosphere reserves provide a vehicle for transboundary cooperation on ecosystem protection (e.g.) North Yukon-Alaska North Slope. (Inglis 1990:145)

ABORIGINAL PEOPLE AND PARKS: LESSONS FROM ABROAD

The nineteenth century Euro-American national parks idea created a conceptual precedent that has come to dominate conservation strategies throughout the world. Worldwide, more than 3,500 national parks and wildlife reserves cover 400 million hectares (Lewis 1990:18). Ecologist Raymond Dasmann strikes at the core of the problem that aboriginal people have, with the imposition of designated protection areas, when he points out a fundamental contradiction between the approaches of "ecosystem people" — peoples who depend for their subsistence primarily on the ecosystem(s) in which they live — and "biosphere people" who have the whole biosphere at their disposal (Dasmann 1974, 1976, 1984).

> Local catastrophes that would wipe out people dependent on a single ecosystem may create only minor perturbations among the biosphere people, since they can simply draw more heavily on a different ecosystem....The impact of biosphere people upon ecosystem people has usually been destructive....Biosphere people create national parks. Ecosystem people have always lived in the equivalent of a national park. It is the kind of country that ecosystem people have always protected that biosphere people want to have formally reserved and safeguarded. But, of course, first the ecosystem people must be removed — or at least that has been the prevailing custom. (Dasmann 1976 [1988]:305f)

All over the world aboriginal people are trying to come to terms with modern concepts of conservation and protected areas, and they are attempting to modify these concepts in a way that enables them to derive benefits and sustenance from them. Three examples will be briefly discussed. They are selected because they represent different parts of the spectrum of what may be called the "internalization" of the idea of protected areas on the part of indigenous people, and as well because they contain interesting lessons for Canada's aboriginal people.[3]

African Experiences with a Foreign Concept

The teeming herds of wildlife of an African Eden have always exerted a strong force on the European mind, and in turn, European imagination became a decisive factor in shaping the fate of Africa's land, animals and people.

> The problem is rooted in the nature of the colonial relationship itself, which allowed Europeans to impose their image of Africa upon the reality of the African landscape. Much of the emotional as distinct from the economic investment which Europe made in Africa has manifested itself in a wish to protect the natural environment as a special kind of "Eden",

[3] For an interesting discussion of relevant ideas and case studies of protected areas in Africa, Asia and Latin America, see Wells and Brandon 1992.

> for the purposes of the European psyche, rather than as a complex and changing environment in which people have actually had to live. The desire to maintain and preserve "Eden" has been particularly pronounced in eastern and southern Africa, where European ambitions have extended to permanent settlement. Here, at its crudest, Africa has been portrayed as offering the opportunity to experience a wild and natural environment which was no longer available in the domesticated landscapes of Europe....Much of conservation thinking in Africa, as defined and exercised by Europeans, has therefore been directed to sustaining an image of Africa which forms a part of a European mythology. Europe no longer exerts direct political control over Africa, but the mythology of the African environment and the symbol of Africa as a yet unspoilt Eden continues to stimulate many of those who wish to intervene in the way the environment is managed in Africa.
>
> ...The image of Africa as a refuge from the technological society of Europe has frequently been reinforced by the broad notion that the conservation of the African environment is an entirely apolitical affair, a global value that no prejudice could undermine.
>
> ...This naive and idealized picture of apolitical conservation in Africa, or anywhere else for that matter, is faintly absurd. As a rallying call to humanity to gather round the standard of environmentalism it has proven to be fatally flawed, failing to appreciate that, to rural societies in Africa, conservation is a **very** political issue. Attempts to manage the African landscape for conservation or development invariably involve direct interventions in the relationship between man and his environment (i.e. between rural man and his means of production). (Anderson and Grove 1987:4–6, emphasis in original)

Rural African people have paid and are still paying a high price for such interventions. In many cases, ethnic or tribal minorities are the hardest hit, for example, pastoral groups in eastern Africa and the San in southern Africa. One of the most notorious examples is without doubt the case of the Ik, nomadic hunters of the border area of Uganda, Kenya and Sudan, who were displaced from their main hunting grounds by the establishment of Kidepo Valley National Park (Uganda). The result was starvation and cultural and social dissolution (Turnbull 1972).

In neighbouring Kenya and Tanzania, Maasailand has for decades been under considerable pressure from conservation interests (Naingisa 1991; Homewood and Rogers 1984, 1987; Collett 1987; Lindsay 1987; Western 1982). The Maasai-case illustrates another dubious phenomenon in postcolonial Africa, namely that of the state manipulating environmental interests to its own ends. Moving and "villagising" hunters and gatherers, pastoralists or shifting agriculturalists in the name of conservation is intended to have the effect of integrating these indigenous groups into the national society (Gray 1991:25).

When Amboseli National Park was established in critical Maasai grazing lands in southern Kenya in 1974, the Amboseli Maasai looked back at seven decades of progressive confinement and restriction in the name of pacification, clearing the land for European settlers and conservation of wildlife. By the late 1960s they had resorted to "political" spearing of wildlife as a form of social protest against the impending loss of their dry season grazing lands, and they demanded formal ownership of the land in the Amboseli basin (Western 1982:97; Lindsay 1987:155f). To resolve this conflict, the government and county council entered into negotiations with the Maasai, which were concluded in 1977 with a Park Agreement.

In a nationwide program of land adjudication, the local Maasai became joint owners of the surrounding bushlands in a number of "group ranches" organized roughly along clan/subsection lines and traditional grazing areas. Furthermore, the park plan stipulated that the group ranches receive a number of benefits from the National Park in their midst: guarantee of an adequate water supply outside the Park area for their cattle; compensation for the "opportunity costs" of tolerating wildlife grazing on their group ranch lands; direct economic benefits from tourism development on ranch lands; and additional direct benefits in terms of social and educational services. In 1977 the Maasai agreed to vacate the Park land in return for these benefits.

> The overall policy was to integrate the Park with surrounding livestock grazing lands so that the effective area for wildlife was much larger than the central protected areas, while the local herdsmen enjoyed improved living standards and developed a vested interest in the Park. (Lindsay 1987:158)

After apparent initial success, the situation started deteriorating again in the early 1980s, as evidenced by an increasing disillusionment with the Park Agreement on the part of the Maasai, and a resurgence of poaching. As discussed in more detail by Lindsay (ibid.:158–165), this failure must be attributed to various factors, such as unsatisfactory implementation of the Agreement, the unpredictable nature of the tourism industry, a number of wrong assumptions about Maasai society, and the failure to keep up an ongoing process of consultation with the local population. "But perhaps the chief drawback to all the programmes in Amboseli was that they approached the issue by attempting to graft conservation onto a changing pastoralist society, without addressing the nature of the change itself." (ibid.:164)

Maasai in Tanzania are faring worse. A current controversy focuses on the Ngorongoro Conservation Area (NCA). The NCA is a joint wildlife conservation/pastoralist land use area in northern Tanzania, adjacent to the Serengeti Plains and part of the ecological unit utilized by the Serengeti wildlife population migrations (Homewood and Rodgers 1987:123). After the creation of Serengeti National Park in 1951 the local Maasai accepted a compromise. They forfeited their grazing rights in the Serengeti in return for a continued guarantee of user rights in the Ngorongoro Conservation Area. They were also promised an improved water supply in the latter. During the three decades of its existence, the NCA has not seen a comprehensive management or development plan, it has been managed strictly on an ad hoc basis (Naingisa 1991:55). Due to a shortage of water and pasture and the prohibition of cultivation in Ngorongoro, recent years have witnessed a dramatic impoverishment of Ngorongoro Maasai, a population of 23,000 with 120,000 head of cattle. Furthermore, there is a strong lobby for expelling the Maasai from Ngorongoro altogether.

There is no lack of detailed studies of pastoralist ecology in the area. Their conclusions may be summarized as follows:

> 1. Pastoralists, livestock and wildlife have coexisted in the area for over 2,000 years; pastoralist grazing and burning activities have helped to shape the area's present highly valued landscape;
> 2. Livestock numbers monitored for over 20 years have fluctuated but show no overall trend of increase;
> 3. Wildlife populations have undergone a dramatic increase over the same period, making the idea of adverse competitive impact of livestock dubious if not untenable;
> 4. Disease interactions between cattle and wildlife populations favour the latter;
> 5. There is no evidence to bear out suggested changes in vegetation composition whether in pastoralist-occupied areas or in areas from which pastoralist stock have been excluded for 10 years or more; and
> 6. The NCA shows negligible erosion. Rates are lower than for all surrounding areas despite the greater geomorphological and topographic predisposition of the area to erosion. (Homewood and Rodgers 1987:124)

These observations show that plans to remove the Maasai from their traditional territory are not based on fact, but are "image-related" or simply politically expedient.

Maasailand accounts for more than 50 per cent of the total game population found in Kenya and Tanzania. In Maasai traditional belief wild animals are the cattle of the creator, and a reserve to be harvested only in times of extreme need and loss of livestock (Naingisa 1991:54).

> The mere fact that the wildlife populations of Mara and Amboseli are dependent on access to grazing in the Maasai areas, means that the Parks, on their own, are not an effective conservation strategy. The acceptance by the Maasai of wildlife in their grazing areas is

> therefore central to the maintenance of tourism in Kenya. In this way they make an enormous contribution to Kenya and its development simply by being Maasai and not sedentary ranchers. But perhaps the Maasai could confer the ultimate gift on humanity if the Parks were abolished: they could provide a model of man coexisting with wildlife. It is the destruction of this alternative image, the Maasai as pastoralists who are able to coexist with wildlife in a way that pastoralists have done in this area for at least 2,500 years, that is the ultimate irony of conservation policy in Kenya Maasailand today. (Collett 1987:146)

The relocation of the San (Bushmen, Basarwa) from the Central Kalahari Game Reserve (CKGR) in Botswana is no less controversial. Ironically, the CKGR was not originally conceived as an exclusive park, but was established upon the recommendation of an anthropologist, George Silberbauer, in 1961, in order to preserve the people, wildlife and habitats of the central Kalahari region. Today the Reserve is still inhabited by approximately 1,200 San, although the number of people utilizing it varies with rainfall and resource availability, and as many as 3,500 people claim to have land rights in the Reserve (Hitchcock 1991:10). The majority of these people no longer follow a "pure" hunting and gathering way of life, but rather they subsist in a mixed economy that involves hunting and gathering as well as some livestock raising and crop cultivation and Botswana government drought relief assistance.

In 1985 the government of Botswana called for a commission of inquiry to assess future options for the Game Reserve. This commission recommended that portions of the Reserve be turned into a "Wildlife Management Area", where people would be allowed to continue to reside and utilize local resources. These recommendations were rejected by the Ministry of Commerce and Industry, which oversees parks and reserves in Botswana. Instead, the Minister argued that the San population "is undermining the integrity of the Game Reserve" (*Botswana Daily News*, December 2, 1986:1, quoted in Harden 1989:9). It was stipulated that the residents of the Reserve would be "encouraged" to move to areas outside the boundaries of the CKGR where they would be provided with facilities. This move was presented as being in the national interest as well as in the best interest of the San. Not surprisingly, the San refuse to move from their ancestral lands. So far the government has not required anyone to leave and has yet to stop providing assistance to the people in the Reserve.

The reasons behind the pressure for relocation of the San are complex and have very little to do with their actual impact on the wildlife of the Kalahari. The resettlement plans are part of a strategy to pacify environmentalists, who have been pressuring the European Community to withdraw its subsidies to Botswana's cattle industry (Harden 1989:10f; Hitchcock 1991:12). The environmental community's outcry, however, had not been caused by the Game Reserve's human population, but rather by the death of hundreds of thousands of antelope on account of disease-control fences blocking their migration routes out of the CKGR to water and dry season grazing (Owens 1985:292–308, 319–321). In the late 1980s pressure to turn the CKGR into a "true" game reserve or national park, where people would not be allowed to live or hunt and gather, somewhat subsided but did not disappear completely, while a modest degree of political mobilization occurred in the San communities. In November 1990 Botswana government planners suggested that the CKGR be nominated as a biosphere reserve under UNESCO's Man and Biosphere Program. Within its framework continued residence and sustainable utilization of resources in the Reserve would be permitted (Hitchcock 1991:12).

While minority populations have been particularly adversely effected by national parks and game reserves in Africa, African society at large does not feel either that it has a stake in protection areas for game. Not only is there the problem of resource competition, but there is also a lack of opportunity for Africans to visit parks, even if they had the interest. Entrance fees are beyond the reach of many local people, and the mandatory requirement of a vehicle is prohibitive. Moreover, Walter J. Lusigi suggests that the type of recreation represented by parks is a low priority for most people, even for those who can afford it, an opinion that Richard H.V. Bell does not share (Lusigi 1979:40, 1984:141; Bell 1987:95). As a result, protected areas have come to be viewed as alien institutions to be identified with tourists, and the wildlife as state property and not as a resource people have a stake in.

The way some Namibians celebrated independence from South African rule in 1990 may be extreme, but it is indicative of the way people feel and act towards what they perceive as an alien and imposed institution: They raced into the Etosha Game Reserve with guns and trucks and poached as much wild game as they could. South Africa has already learnt its lesson. In its newest reserve, Richtersveld National Park in the arid northern Cape, seminomadic pastoralists have been allowed to stay; limited stock raising will be permitted in the park; and agreements have been negotiated to protect unique plant species (Koch 1991:54).

What is the "Canadian connection" of these African experiences? In brief, they should serve as a warning. Africa exemplifies the unfortunate situation where by and large the institution and the concept of natural protected areas have remained external to African life. The process was started in a colonial context but has been perpetuated long after independence by the national governments for the sake of tourist dollars as well as for political expediency. While there have been conservation successes, the process has also caused human and environmental degradation. Today's uncontrollable poaching activities in many parts of Africa, which threaten wildlife species and populations with extinction, are partly based on hard economic facts. But it is suggested here that a debilitated African environmental attitude is another contributory factor. If people are effectively excluded from the management and utilization of resources, they will eventually feel that they have no stake in the resources, and there is no harm in defiling state property. Experiences in Zimbabwe seem to indicate that such attitudes can be effectively reversed, if people are given a reason to care (Child 1984:120).

It has been shown that the force of European imagination has been an important factor in creating this situation. With regard to Canada, the European mythology of the African environment has a powerful counterpart in the southern mythology of the North: the North as a frontier, or more recently, the North as yet another Eden. It is no mere coincidence that the vast lands of northern Yukon and northeastern Alaska are often called North America's Serengeti for their huge concentrations of wildlife and pristine condition (Lee 1988:861f; McNamee 1989:76). Northern aboriginal people have good reason to want to make sure that northern parks or reserves will protect resources with northern life in mind.

Aboriginal Landlords of Australian Parks

While in Africa expropriation of indigenous people for the purpose of park establishment seems to be the rule of the game, in Australia and Oceania native control and ownership sometimes serve as an enabling force for the creation of protected areas.

In New Zealand there is a well-established practice of Maori tribes gifting the nation with land for the establishment of national parks. The country's first national park owes its existence to such gift by elders of the Ngati Tuwharetoa at Tongariro in 1889. New Zealand's legislation (the National Park Act of 1952 and the Reserves Act of 1977) promotes gifting of land for conservation purposes, and the management of "multiple use reserves" (which includes indigenous use) permits interesting alternatives to public ownership of land (Clad 1985:54). Some of the indigenous uses, which are being accommodated by New Zealand's national parks and reserves, include herb and food gathering in the North Island's Urerewa National Park, mutton-bird hunting on Kaitoreti Spit and the practice of traditional fishing rights on Lake Waikeremoana by the local tribe, who also rents the lake to the surrounding national park (ibid.:54f). New Zealand is passing its experiences on by assisting in the management design of Nepal's Sagarmatha National Park.

In Australia indigenous lands have been transferred into national park status as well, but Aboriginal people remain the owners.

Australia's Northern Territory (NT) exhibits numerous similarities to Canada's northern territories: both regions have historically been treated as "hinterlands"; they have become the focus of mineral development activity; and they contain large indigenous populations who are actively engaged in attempts to retain control over their land and resources in order to safeguard traditional lifestyles. In Australia's Northern Territory, Aboriginal people comprise 22 per cent of the population, and Aboriginal land, held under unalienable title, totals nearly half a million square kilometres or about 34 per cent of the NT (Altman 1989:457). The territorial economy is characterized by an extremely narrow base (focused almost entirely on the public sector, mining and primary industries) and its extremely high dependency on federal funding. Tourism constitutes the Territory's second largest and fastest growing industry, contributing 4.6 per cent of Territory product (ibid.:457f).

The NT capitalizes on two major drawing cards in terms of tourist attractions: the environment and Aboriginal culture. This is of double significance, as the two most important tourist destinations, Kakadu and Uluru National Parks, are owned by Aboriginal people, and leased back to, and run, by the federal Australian National Parks and Wildlife Service (ANPWS). This creates a peculiar tension: the NT Government is vehemently opposed to Aboriginal land rights and the management of some of its national parks by the federal government (Australian national parks are usually managed under state legislation), but, on the other hand, is dependent on Aboriginal interests for the implementation of its "developmentalist" policies in the tourism field (ibid.:460).

Consultation with Aboriginal people is required in Australian Northern Territory legislation for park agency management of:

> (a) Land vested in an Aboriginal or Aboriginals, or in a body corporate that is wholly owned by Aboriginals; (b) Land held upon trust for the benefit of Aboriginals, or (c) Any other land occupied by Aboriginals. (Territory Parks and Wildlife Conservation Ordinance of 1976 and National Parks and Wildlife Conservation Act of 1975, quoted in Gardner and Nelson 1981:341)

Furthermore, the terms of the leases clearly define a native role in Kakadu and Uluru.

Uluru National Park was originally founded as the Ayers Rock — Mount Olga National Park in 1958. It was transferred into Aboriginal ownership in 1985, after a prolonged political struggle, with the passage of the Aboriginal Land Rights (Northern Territory) Amendment Act. A condition of the 1985 land grant provided that the National Park be leased back to the Australian National Parks and Wildlife Service. The Park comprises 1,325 square kilometres and is surrounded by aboriginal land except for an enclave of some 104 square kilometres north of the Park, excised for the Yulara township site in 1976. In the mid-1980s the Aboriginal population of the Park fluctuated between 120 and 150. Tourism to Uluru has increased rapidly with over 200,000 visitors in 1987. This was greatly facilitated by the development of accommodation facilities outside the Park in the tourist village at Yulara.

> While Uluru National Park is now managed on a day-to-day basis by the ANPWS, policy is formulated by a board of management (the Uluru-Kata Tjuta Board) with an Aboriginal majority. This means that while the Park has been leased back to ANPWS for 99 years, decisions about visitor use of the Park are determined by the Board. However, the NT Government and private sector interests own and control Yulara where almost all tourist facilities are located. This gives them economic control over regional tourism. (Altman 1989:462)

The establishment of Kakadu National Park was linked to the Ranger Uranium Environmental Inquiry, which promoted National Park designation for the original sanctuary. But, as reported by Michael Hill (1983:166), the traditional Aboriginal owners were the first to suggest that if they were successful in their claim to the land covered by the proposed park, they would be willing to lease the land to the Director of the Australian National Parks and Wildlife Service. Their motivation was not so much based on a clear understanding of what the national park concept was all about as on the fear that alone they might be powerless to protect the land from competing interests (i.e. uranium mining), and the feeling that the establishment of a national park in the area was likely to create a management regime sympathetic to their aspirations and interests. As one traditional owner put it: "Whatever this national park thing is, whatever else it does, the land will be safer." (Fox 1983:163)

> Under the terms of the Lease Agreement the Director accepted certain obligations. These include commitments to train local Aboriginals in skills necessary to enable them to assist in Park management; to employ as many traditional Aboriginal owners as is practicable under conditions that recognize their special needs and their culture; to promote among non-Aboriginals a knowledge and understanding of Aboriginal traditions, culture and languages; to engage Aboriginals in park interpretation programs; to consult regularly with the NLC [Northern Land Council] about policy so that the opinions of the traditional owners are taken into account; and (as part of the Plan of Management), to have due regard for the needs of the Aboriginal owners in their use of and movement throughout the Park. In accordance with the Agreement, Aboriginals are involved in planning for and managing the Park at both the consultative and employment levels.
>
> Aboriginal agreement is required before any development or management action affecting them may proceed. Depending on the project or action that is proposed, consultation may take place with individual traditional owners, a group of owners, the Gagadju Association to which all traditional owners of the Park belong or the Northern Land Council. The traditional owners determine the level at which the consultation takes place. They also use the consultative process to put forward their own proposals for the Park. (Hill 1983:166)

In contrast to Uluru, there is no formal institutional structure (such as a management board with an Aboriginal majority) in Kakadu to safeguard Aboriginal interests. Instead, this function is assumed by the Northern Land Council (land councils in general are becoming para-governmental institutions), which represents the interests of traditional owners, and undertaken through informal consultative processes.

When Kakadu National Park was proclaimed in 1979, no more than 20 per cent of its traditional owners lived there, but by 1982 the proportion had risen to 75 per cent. This is not only an indication of people's confidence in the management of the area, but it also relates to the more effective servicing of the outstations (communities) by the Gagadju Association, now responsible for utilizing the royalty payments from uranium mining (Fox 1983:165).

The Park's Aboriginal population numbers between 260 and 280 and is distributed among 15 communities in the Park. Kakadu National Park cannot be viewed in isolation from the large Ranger uranium mine and its mining town which occupy an enclave within the Park. Of great significance for the Aborigines is the payment of mining royalty equivalents of about $3 million per annum to the regional Gagadju Association under the Land Rights Act. In the period 1982 to 1987, the number of visitors at Kakadu quadrupled from 45,800 to 195,000. Growth can be linked to improved ANPWS facilities and transport links associated with the Ranger mine as well as to the World Heritage listing of the Park (Altman 1989:462f).

What benefits do Aboriginal people derive from the existence of the parks in general and their ownership of the land in particular? Obviously, there are a variety of economic benefits derived from different kinds of involvement in the tourism industry: employment, ownership of or shares in enterprises, sale of artifacts, commoditization of culture and the lease or sale of resources (Altman 1989:465–468). At Uluru, for example, tourism-related employment in 1986 provided 18 per cent of household income, and the manufacture of artifacts, another 6 per cent. At Kakadu the impact of the uranium mine and its royalty payments must be borne in mind. In general, local Aborigines do not work at the mine, but prefer employment with ANPWS and the Gagadju Association. Overall, it was estimated that 26 per cent of regular household income in 1986 was derived from ANPWS employment alone.

Jobs, such as ranger, hold other less tangible benefits for Aboriginal people, as they allow them to continue in their function as land stewards. On the other hand, the combined expectations of tribal elders and the park service put a heavy burden on the shoulders of these individuals. As one Kakadu ranger, Jonathan Yarramarna, puts it

> There are two sets of laws for us here — Aboriginal law and government law. That means we have to look after the country in two ways, which is pretty hard for us....But we can do it. (Breeden 1988:287)

The sale of hunting and ritual culture features prominently in tourism marketing by the NT, but there is little evidence that Aboriginal people are interested in supplying it (Altman 1989:467).

One of the more surprising facts is that Aboriginal parties receive only a small proportion of the tourism rent (or profits) generated by the resources they own. This is most apparent in the case of Kakadu. The leaseback agreement concluded with ANPWS in 1978 stipulated an annual lease payment of $7,502. Jon Altman hypothesizes that this "peppercorn rental" was probably acceptable to traditional owners, because they receive over $3 million per annum in mining royalty and rental payments from the Ranger uranium mine (ibid.). At Uluru National Park, under the memorandum of lease signed between members of the Uluru-Kata Tjuta Land Trust and the Director of ANPWS in 1985, Aboriginal owners are paid $75,000 annually plus 20 per cent of any gate fees. In 1986 this amounted to more than $100,000.

> It is of interest that while Aboriginal people are provided with a statutory guarantee of a share of mineral rent raised on Aboriginal land, there is no such guarantee with tourism rent. This distinction might be based on an assumption that mineral resources are finite, whereas tourism resources are inexhaustible. However, such an assumption may prove false in situations when excessive tourism pressure results in environmental (and associated cultural) degradation. (ibid.:474)

Aboriginal people at Kakadu and Uluru are feeling the tourism pressure and associated economic and non-economic costs. Land use by tourists potentially reduces Aboriginal access to land for hunting, gathering and fishing, and thus reduces Aboriginal income-in-kind. Some Aborigines in Kakadu feel that their hunting and fishing rights are not adequately protected (Kesteven 1984:17 quoted in Altman 1989:472). Their position as landowners enables Aboriginal people at least to close communities and sacred sites to visitors, and where they are able to gain a majority of policy formulating bodies, like the Uluru-Kata Tjuta Board, they can regulate tourism within the park to a certain extent.

The Aboriginal experience in Uluru and Kakadu National Parks has shown, that even where parks are revenue generating tourist destinations, property rights do not necessarily translate into financial returns. Jon Altman also advises that it is absolutely crucial for Aboriginal people to ensure that their interests are given statutory recognition and protection before, and not after, tourism growth (Altman 1989:474). In their struggle for recognition of their land rights, the Gagadju at Kakadu and the Pitjantjatjara at Uluru were compelled by circumstances to place their ancestral lands within the confines of a concept they only vaguely understood. While Aboriginal people as "park landlords" have a degree of leverage in these locations, they still find themselves in a situation where the concept of a national park and the phenomenon of mass tourism have been imposed on them.

> [A] factor working against success is an apparent narrowness of the management authority's understanding of the term management. For instance, Aboriginals have always voiced their fear of tourism throwing large numbers of Europeans against the Arnhem Land boundary at the East Alligator River [in Kakadu]. Yet they see ANPWS improving access roads, setting up attractive facilities, producing colorful brochures and displays, all primarily aimed at controlling visitor use but in fact increasing demand. Aboriginals are involved in discussing the proposed developments, in guiding visitors, and in providing information for signs and leaflets. They are involved in the implementation of management but not in the management decision-making process itself. This is not to say that ANPWS didn't want to allow full involvement but that the political climate did not allow time for traditional consultative processes to work. Often short-term political solutions caused destabilization for the traditional people and it is in the field of middle management decisions that the Aboriginals perceive the Service excluding them most of all. (Fox 1983:165)

The transferability of similar arrangements to Canada is purely hypothetical at the present time, since in contrast to Australian (and United States) federal agencies, Parks Canada requires outright public ownership of national park land (Gardner and Nelson 1981:209). But, particularly in the North, there may be room for innovative thinking.

Kuna Yala: Indigenous Biosphere Reserve in the Making?

This title is taken from a journal article by R. Michael Wright, Brian Houseal and Cebaldo de Leon (1985), because it characterizes best the unique initiative that is evolving in Panama. After observing the African scene, where national parks and reserves were superimposed on the natural and social environment and have remained alien to both, and Australia, where a somewhat uneasy and incomplete mutual accommodation has been reached, we have come full circle: in Kuna Yala, indigenous people have developed their own concept of a protected area for their own purposes, and they are now searching for an appropriate designation to give it national and international status and credibility.

The Kuna have been called one of the most autonomous and independent indigenous groups in the world (Wright et al. 1985:352) and "a model example of a successful self-defense movement" (Nietschmann 1984:271). They staged a brief armed rebellion in 1925 against the newly formed and still weak nation of Panama, and were granted an autonomous status within the Panamanian state. The Comarca de Kuna Yala became a Kuna-controlled political division along the northeastern Caribbean coast of Panama, extending from the crest of the continental divide to the offshore islands. The Comarca Kuna run their affairs through a highly organized political system of island and regional leaders, and Kuna representatives are members of the Panamanian National Assembly (ibid.:279).

The Comarca de Kuna Yala is an isolated stretch of lush tropical forest, about 200 kilometres long and averaging 27 kilometres in width. Approximately 30,000 Kuna Indians live in 60 villages on some of the 350 tiny offshore coral islands, supporting themselves with fishing and complex multi-crop agriculture on the flat alluvial soils of the mainland coast. The Kuna have always placed high priority on the protection of their forest lands which they view as the abode of spirits and a source of medicinal plants. Even among their agricultural plots they maintain untouched "spirit reserves" where the spirits are appeased and curers can gather medicinal herbs (Breslin and Chapin 1984:32). Traditionally, the mountain divide had served as an effective buffer to protect Kuna lands from the ravages of the slash-and-burn agriculture and cattle grazing economies that characterize Panama's interior, and which have already devastated the western slope of the divide.

This situation changed in the early 1970s, when the government proceeded with the construction of a road into the western end of the reservation from the Pan-American Highway to the Caribbean coast. Concern grew among some Kuna, that unless a permanent presence could be established where the road penetrated Kuna lands, squatters would inevitably flow into the reservation (Wright et al. 1985:354; Byrne Swain 1989:100). As a result, in 1975, a group of young Kuna set up an experimental agricultural station at Udirbi, where the road entered Comarca lands. This station was intended to create a presence for control of non-Kuna immigration and to develop appropriate uses for the land. The agricultural experiment failed, however. The tropical mountain environment proved unfit for permanent agriculture or livestock raising, and after a frustrating five years, the Udirbi group adopted a different approach.

They developed the concept of a forest park, which was to combine the elements of tourism, scientific research and a protected area (modeled on the traditional Kuna spirit reserves) to enlist the support of the outside conservation and scientific community in their cultural and natural preservation goals (Wright et al. 1985:355). They sought advice from CATIE, a regional agricultural research centre in Costa Rica and the Smithsonian Tropical Research Institute in Panama, and soon developed an international network for technical and financial support. The project has grown considerably in scope since its inception.

> The conservation success of the project depends, as does its ecological aspect, on the link between the mountains and the coast, the young defenders of the reservation and the traditional knowledge base of the islands, the balance of scientific tourism and the cattle culture of the interior. The project has now received the blessing of the Kuna General Congress and every other week volunteers from the island communities come to Pemasky to help demarcate the border of the reservation, returning with an awareness of the devastated landscape beyond the mountains. The Pemasky — or Kuna Wildlands — Project also provides a link between the population of Kuna at both ends of the reservation and is seen as a model for resource management and defense of the Comarca as a whole. The goals of the protected area complex have now grown beyond merely holding the line along the border of the 60,000 ha (148,260 ac[res]) study area in the western sector of the reserve to the possibility of including the entire Comarca and perhaps some adjacent protected areas in subsequent phases of the project. As a result, the Kuna have begun to seek a classification appropriate to the mixed objectives of their initiative. The protected area designation should not threaten the Kuna culture by injecting national institutions into the Comarca, but, instead, should recognize the unique legal protection provided by the Kuna's land title (by law non-Kuna are prohibited from holding land in the reservation).
>
> For the moment the biosphere reserve is the only category of protected area that seems appropriate to this project. Interestingly enough, the concept of the biosphere reserve, which seeks to conserve representative samples of the world's biogeographical regions and man's traditional relationships to them, coincides directly with the Kuna Indian concept of "Kuna Yala" (Kuna place, or territory) being an integral part of "Abia Yala" (the mother earth, biosphere) and thereby worthy of conservation for cultural and spiritual reasons. (ibid.)

While the future of the project as a whole remains open, the Kuna have encountered serious problems in their attempts to promote ecotourism. In part this is due to a lack of easy transportation to their park centre, but of greater importance is the wider national context. Despite its natural splendours, Panama has never promoted nature tourism of any kind, but rather focused on its hotels, casinos and nightlife. As a result the country lacks even the most basic infrastructure for ecotourism, which creates an extremely unfavourable environment for the Kuna park. This situation starkly contrasts with neighbouring Costa Rica, which during the late 1980s has become **the** nature centre of tropical America (Chapin 1990:44f).

NATIVE PEOPLE AND PARKS IN THE PROVINCES: CONFLICT AND COMPROMISE

Under Section 6 of the National Parks Act, as amended in 1974, Parks Canada wields considerable power with regard to the establishment of national parks:

> The Governor in Council may authorize the Minister [of Indian Affairs and Northern Development] to purchase, expropriate, or otherwise acquire any lands or interest therein for the purpose of a park....Public lands within the Parks shall not be disposed of or located or settled upon, and no person shall use or occupy any part of such lands, except under the authority of this Act or the regulations. (National Parks Act of 1930, Amended 1974)

This section makes it perfectly clear that prior to the passage of the Constitution Act, 1982, Parks Canada was in a position to ignore both treaty rights and aboriginal rights in its pursuit to establish new national parks. A precedent was established by Canada's first national park at Banff, which effectively reduced the Stoney Indians' hunting grounds and also barred them from sacred sites and pipestone quarries (Snow 1977:46, 68, 87; Chief Frank Kaquitts, quoted in Scace and Nelson 1986:137f).

Provincial treatment of aboriginal people with regard to designated protection areas has tended to be even more arbitrary, as exemplified by the case of the Brunswick House Ojibwa in the Treaty Nine area of Ontario. The establishment of the Chapleau Crown Game Reserve in 1925 deprived this band of its trapping and hunting livelihood, and eventually resulted in its enforced relocation. In 1968, Missinaibi Lake Provincial Park was created in place of the game reserve, and including the band's old reserve lands.

> While very diligently working at preserving ancient native cliff paintings, [the Ontario Ministry of Natural Resources] denies access by the descendants of the artists. Similarly, the Ministry permits the trapping of nuisance beaver and some subsistence hunting in the game preserve by more "traditional-looking and behaving" Cree Indians from James Bay, while it denies access by those Indians who are the rightful and legitimate heirs to the preserve lands under the pretext that, as one Ministry official put it, "There aren't any real Indians around Chapleau anymore". (Greenberg 1985:29)

More recently, under its new NDP government, Ontario has adopted a more conciliatory stance towards its native population. In 1991, in anticipation of claims negotiations with the Golden Lake Algonquin (closely associated with Quebec's Barriere Lake Algonquin, see chapter 4), the Ontario Ministry of Natural Resources directed Algonquin Provincial Park rangers not to enforce most hunting and fishing regulations against Golden Lake Algonquin band members. This happened shortly after the band had decided to back up its claim to the park by open violations of the law (*Globe and Mail*, March 1, 1991:A4). In October 1991, an Interim Agreement on Hunting was concluded between the government and the Algonquin of Golden Lake (Clairman 1993:16). This step has attracted much criticism on the part of conservationists, who claim that it was politically motivated and without the support of scientific data as to the potential impact on the park, which is already severely stressed by logging, pollution and recreational development.

By and large, however, any actual or potential system of co-management or even cooperative utilization and administration of designated protection areas in the provinces is limited to the special case of Wood Buffalo National Park, which is in part located in the Northwest Territories, and to areas subject to unsettled aboriginal claims, best exemplified by British Columbia.[4]

Wood Buffalo National Park: The Evolution of Co-Management

Wood Buffalo National Park constitutes the first example of a Canadian designated protection area, where native rights and practices were taken into account (Hunt et al. 1979:79), and it is the only one in the country with a long standing-tradition of native subsistence use and involvement (East 1986:87). The overall picture presented is one of

---

4 See also Stix 1982 on Labrador.

rare complexity, not only because of the number of interest groups involved, but also because some native groups are considered merely as a matter of Parks policy, whereas the involvement of others is based on the recognition of legally protected rights.

> The history of Native involvement in Wood Buffalo is not unlike the efforts to establish resource-based economic ventures in the park — well meaning but not effective. For almost the first fifty years of its existence, the park was characterized by government officials acting in what they perceived to be the best interests of local Native people. The very first act of the park management, probably in the form of the local Indian Agent, was to determine who could continue to hunt and trap in the park and who could not. There is very little evidence that this was done other than arbitrarily and the results remain contentious to this day. The rules and regulations regarding hunting and trapping in the park were made largely without consultation and enforced, it would appear, with inconsistency and even whimsy. The "style" of management fostered a climate of distrust and cynicism which continues to exist today. (ibid.:87f)

Although accorded national park status in 1922, Wood Buffalo was — for over four decades — not managed by Parks Canada or its predecessors, but by the Northern Affairs arm of the Department of Indian Affairs and Northern Development. For much of its early history, the Park's mandate remained somewhat unclear. In his history of the Park, B. Potyondi (1981) uses the term "dual allegiance" to describe a management regime targeted ostensibly for preservation but also geared towards economic development and native interests (East 1986:87).

When the National Parks Branch assumed authority for WBNP in 1964, it focused its attention on reconciling the "dual allegiances", and it also made efforts to establish structures which would permit local people, in particular native people, effective input into the management process. There was regular consultation with band councils about proposals that would affect their members. Attempts were made to establish a park-wide hunters and trappers organization, which would serve as the primary communication and management participation tool. Trapping areas were consolidated into "Group Trapping Areas" and members of these groups were given influence over decisions affecting their area. Ken East, former WBNP Superintendent, describes the experience from a Parks perspective.

> The effectiveness of these efforts to introduce an informal "joint management" regime to Wood Buffalo was jeopardized by two factors: a failure to agree on a practical definition of "consultation" and the diversity of interests expecting and deserving to be consulted. "Consultation" in the mind of the government is the process of seeking a range of contributions which will be considered when decisions are made. In the minds of many interest groups, however, "consultation" ought to be the process of seeking direction. "Ask us what we want and implement it." If the response is not implemented, consultation is deemed not to have occurred. For Native groups with a proprietary perspective on the land about which decisions are made, the distinction is critical. (ibid.:88)

The diversity of interests presents a major complication. The size of the Park, the number of different communities in and around the Park, and the number of different native organizations have created a considerable array of separate interests which all pertain to aboriginal involvement in management decisions. These organizations include the following:

- Fitz Smith Native Band
- Fort Chipewyan Cree Band
- Fort Smith Metis Association
- Fort Resolution Dene Band
- Wood Buffalo Park HTA (Fort Chipewyan)
- Little Red River Band

- Fort Chipewyan Metis Association
- Hay River Dene Band
- Fort Smith HTA
- Group Area Leaders
- Registered Trapline Area Holders (East 1986:88, Table 1)

While there is a certain homogeneity of interest, it would be a mistake to assume that all these groups and organizations share common goals and aspirations just because they are native.

> The Group Trapping Area approach used in Wood Buffalo is an example of where there might be conflict between entities which both have legal status....Trapping in each Group Area is essentially co-managed by the Group Area members and Park Officials. Legal status for the Group Trapping approach is provided under the Wood Buffalo Game Regulations and, as the trappers have a somewhat proprietary perspective toward their areas, Group Area Leaders tend to be very serious in assuming their responsibilities. But the Group Area members are also Band members in most instances. This raises the question as to where the Group Area responsibilities stand and Band responsibilities start — or vice versa.
>
> The challenge comes in determining who should be involved in what decisions and what the degree of influence ought to be. For example, the Fitz Smith Native Band and the Fort Smith Metis Local have indicated that they ought to represent the interest of Native hunters and trappers in much of the north end of the park. The Group Area Leaders have given no indication that they are prepared to accept that their interests are to be represented by those two organizations. In fact, they have provided signals to the contrary. Meanwhile, the hunters in the north end are completely unorganized and seem, at least individually, to feel that no other body is appropriate to represent them. At the same time, the Dene-Metis are negotiating a land claim which will impose an entirely different joint management structure on the north end of the park but the Dene-Metis participants represent only a portion of those presently eligible to hunt and trap in that section of the park. It's hard to tell the players without a program and nobody has printed up a program yet. (ibid.:89)

The 1987 settlement of the treaty land claim of the Fort Chipewyan Cree Band was imposed on this complex situation. The principal provisions of this settlement as they pertain to joint management of the Park can be summarized as follows:

1. Guarantees of hunting, trapping and fishing rights for all Cree Band Members in the "traditional area of interest";
2. Establishment of a Wildlife Advisory Committee to advise the Minister on many aspects of the management of the "traditional area of interest". The Cree Band will have a majority of the voting members on the committee;
3. According to the Wildlife Advisory Committee, the authority to determine who, amongst Cree Band members, will receive hunting and trapping permits for the "traditional area of interest" in any given year and, by implication, to determine how many permits will be issued;
4. "Rights of first refusal" on any economic activities which might be developed in the "traditional area of interest";
5. Preferential access to training and employment opportunities in the park and particularly the southern end of the park; and
6. A commitment that the Government of Canada will make its best efforts to re-establish the natural water regime in the Peace Athabasca Delta — thought to be disrupted by construction of the Bennett Dam. (East 1986:89, 92; see also *Kainai News*, January 14, 1987:2)

Ken East, then Park Superintendent, raises several potential benefits and concerns regarding the finalization of this claim settlement. Most of the benefits as he sees them relate to the elimination of uncertainty with regard to rights and privileges, the integrity of the land base, and the question of who to consult with on what issues. One of his major concerns is the fact that joint management/co-management as applied to general purpose land management, rather than to a specific wildlife species, is an essentially untried concept in Canada.

Similar to other co-management regimes discussed earlier, the emphasis in the Cree Land Claim settlement is clearly on the advisory function of band representatives, and the fact that the Minister retains control. The settlement is equally unambiguous about the primary function of the land in question. The relevant clause reads as follows:

> Parks Canada will continue to manage the lands and resources within the Park including the Traditional Lands according to the National Park Act, Regulations, Parks Canada Policy and Park Management Plans. Emphasis will continue to be placed on protection and conservation of natural resources in the park. (East 1986:93).

Nevertheless, East anticipates a discrepancy between diminished authority of Parks Canada and its undiminished responsibility and accountability.

> It would seem in principle that all parties to a co-management regime must be prepared to share responsibility and accountability to the degree that they share authority. Those that operate national parks are responsible and accountable to the Canadian people. Band administrations with whom co-management agreements are struck are responsible and accountable to their members. There is significant potential conflict implicit in this dichotomy. (ibid.:94)

Chief Archie Waquan of the Fort Chipewyan Cree Band, on the other hand, feels that the interests of his people and those of Parks Canada need not be at odds: "Co-management acknowledges that with intelligent planning, mutually beneficial arrangements for resource protection and resource use can be implemented." (Waquan 1986:82) The implementation experience of this claim settlement will be crucial, since the Cree claim is but the first in a series of native land claims that will affect the Park.

In 1992/1993 the Parks Service is engaged in a WBNP Management Plan Review. In this process, "regional integration" addressing land claim agreements and cooperative management of traditional landuse is one of the main concerns (*WBNP Management Plan Review Program*, Newsletter No.1, March 1992:5). Doug Stewart, WBNP Superintendent, feels that "in many ways WBNP is a 'southern' park in a truly cross-cultural situation, unlike the newly established 'northern' parks." (Personal communication, May 12, 1992). With regard to northern parks, even in the absence of a true understanding of northern parks issues by high-ranking Parks Canada officials, Parks Canada negotiators are comparatively free to negotiate parks terms in a wider claims and federal context, and park superintendents and wardens are free to implement those terms. In WBNP, due to the large number of stakeholders (with different formal and informal relationships with Parks Canada) and much "historical baggage", the situation is immeasurably more complicated. A frustrated Henry Beaver, Chief of the Fort Smith Native Band, claims that there are just too many rules and regulations in the Park, and he expresses the hope that possibly the Northern Buffalo Management Board (see chapter 5) can be used as a means of transforming parks administration from within (personal communication, May 11, 1992). Even under optimum conditions a holistic management approach to WBNP may prove problematic in the future.

Aboriginal Lands in British Columbia: Assertion of (Co-)Management

Theoretically, the situation in British Columbia with regard to the establishment of new protection areas should exhibit similarities to that of the northern territories, since in both cases we are dealing with areas subject to unsettled aboriginal claims. This is not the case. In fact, it took the Province of British Columbia until 1990 to as much as acknowledge the validity of aboriginal claims. Until very recently, in British Columbia, there was a pronounced lack of political will and flexibility on the part of both the federal and provincial governments to sit down with aboriginal people and to discuss truly innovative designs and management regimes for parks. This has not, however, prevented native people from protecting their special places as they see fit.

The discussion of forestry-related conflicts in British Columbia in chapter 4 has already dealt with the nature of the alliance among native and environmental groups in connection with high profile issues like Gwaii Haanas, Meares Island and the Stein Valley. In all three situations the concept of parks or protection areas has played an important role in determining the fate of the lands in question. The idea of a park was used and sometimes carried as a banner by both native and environmental groups, but this does not necessarily imply that both sides are talking about the same thing.

Meares Island has become a symbol of the Nuu-chah-nulth claim to their ancestral lands on the west coast of Vancouver Island. In order to protect this land from logging interests, the Clayoquot Band, who along with the Ahousaht Band claims title to the island, asserted jurisdiction and declared Meares Island a Tribal Park in 1984.

> The Clayoquot Band do declare Meares Island a Tribal Park and we call for:
>
> 1. Total preservation of Meares Island based on title and survival of our native way of life.
> 2. Preserve Meares Island, as the island is an economic base of our people who harvest natural unspoiled native foods, including all (a) seafoods and shellfish, (b) protect our traditional hunting rights of deer and water fowl, etc., (c) protect the rights of our Elders to continue the gathering of their Indian medicines, (d) protect the right of native artists to continue the gathering of their needs — cedar bark, cedar for canoes and paddles and masks, etc.
> 3. Protection of all herrings, spawning grounds around the island.
> 4. Protection of salmon streams on the island.
> 5. Protection of all traplines.
> 6. Protection of all sacred burial sites on Meares Island.
>
> The native people are prepared to share Meares Island with non-natives, provided that you adhere to the laws of our forefathers, which was [sic] always there. On that basis we recognize your needs for:
>
> 1. Watershed, as they (Tofino residents) already have in place their water system on Meares Island.
> 2. Hunting of waterfowl in Lemmens Inlet, existing aquaculture leases. We would permit access to our island for recreational purposes — hiking, camping, fishing, whale watching, gathering restricted amounts of seafood and shellfish.
> 3. Recognize our Land Claims, that there be no resources removed from Meares Island excluding watershed.
>
> Signed by the Clayoquot Band Council and Hereditary Chiefs. (Declaration reprinted in *Ha-Shilth-Sa*, April 29, 1986:5)

Since 1984 a circuit trail has been constructed on the island by the Western Canada Wilderness Committee (*Hah-Shilth-Sa*, April 28, 1988:8), and the Park has welcomed numerous non-native visitors, while its traditional aboriginal use has continued. Nevertheless, the island's future is in abeyance pending the settlement of the Nuu-chah-nulth claim.

When it was decided in 1987 to declare Gwaii Haanas, the South Moresby portion of the Queen Charlotte Islands, a national park reserve, the battle was won for the environmentalists and a concerned public. But it was only the beginning of a new struggle for the Haida Nation. While protection of the land from resource extraction was being realized, the issue of land ownership was by no means resolved, and with the cessation of logging, the Haida had also lost their only leverage for generating public support (May 1990a:4). The federal-provincial Memorandum of Understanding on South Moresby (and the subsequent 1988 Agreement) did not include the Haida Nation as a party to the Agreement, although the federal government and in particular Tom McMillan, then federal Minister of the Environment, had repeatedly pledged full involvement of the Haida in every aspect of national park management. Yet these promises were slow to materialize. John Broadhead, one of the many individuals instrumental in saving Gwaii Haanas, contemplates what happened after 1987.

> ...could the national park reserve actually be a political manoeuvre to avoid altogether the Haida and the aboriginal-rights issue that they represent?
>
> The questions arise because, a year and a half later the promises spoken by Canadian politicians to the Haida remain no more than words. On the contrary, government agencies are systematically deleting all acknowledgement of the Haida's aboriginal rights from official documents related to South Moresby. Also, negotiations to share responsibility for managing the proposed park reserve have been stalemated by a federal refusal to agree to anything more than a token role for the Haida.
>
> The Haida have made it clear that until a framework for management that respects their interests and responsibilities is reached, there will be no South Moresby "park", and they will continue to manage Gwaii Haanas without Parks Canada. (Broadhead 1989:62; see also May 1990b:310–313)

And that is exactly what they have done. Even before the national park reserve idea was finalized, the Haida had created two "tribal parks", dedicating all of Gwaii Haanas as well as northern Duu Guusd (NW Graham Island) as permanently protected areas (May 1990a:3). Since the mid-1970s, they had been running their own program for the protection of important abandoned village sites and other significant places. "Haida Watchmen" were stationed at the village of Ninstints — which was recognized in 1981 by UNESCO as a World Heritage Site — and at a handful of other special locations, in order to warn tourists about the vulnerability of the remaining poles and longhouses. They charged each tourist a fee of $25 for a permit to visit important archaeological sites.

Throughout the 1980s the number of visitors had increased steadily, and the creation of a national park reserve brought a tourism surge before any management plan or infrastructure were in place to deal with the deluge of visitors. Two years after the establishment of a park reserve, an estimated 23,000 people ventured into the area salvaged from loggers. Even though Parks Service staff called the fee imposed by the Haida "illegal", they did nothing to stop it. They recognized that the Haida Watchman Program was effective in guarding village sites and monitoring bacterial counts in the Hot Springs, as well as providing visitor information and emergency search-and-rescue services. Even prior to the official park reserve creation, the program had expanded to include a tour service offering escorted visits to Gwaii Haanas and feasts at the community hall in Skidegate.

> Just why it is that the Haida Watchmen remain the only visible management presence within a Canadian national park has to do with an appropriate degree of caution on the part of the Canadian government mixed with its nearly maddening inability to negotiate a plan with the Haida Nation.
>
> With the various levels and departments of government involved, draft proposals acceptable to the Haida Nation and the Canadian Parks Service have been nixed by the Department of Justice. Two summers have come and gone since the park was officially created and yet there are still no park wardens, no visitor information centers, none of the usual trappings of a park. The Parks Service has respected the Haida and the commitment made by Tom McMillan, the federal minister of the environment, when the deal was struck — that not a penny would be spent until an agreement with the Haida could be reached. (May 1990a:5)

The stalemate was finally broken in 1990. It had become clear that the Haida were not agreeable to the management of Gwaii Haanas as a "National Park Reserve under the National Parks Act" by a co-management committee with advisory role only to the Minister (*Haada Laas*, Journal of the Haida Nation, October 1988:4). What they did consent to was essentially "an agreement to disagree", as Roger Hamilton, Superintendent of the South Moresby/Gwaai Haanas National Park Reserve, puts it (Personal communication, July 2, 1992), or "a parallel statement of ownership" (Guujaw, personal communication, July 1, 1992). The Canada-Haida Agreement (Bill C-59) was ratified by the Haida Nation in May 1990 (McNamee 1993:45), but it was not approved by the government and passed into legislation before January 1993.

The Agreement contains parallel statements on the two parties' divergent positions on sovereignty, title and ownership to the land, but also expresses their willingness to work together. It contains mechanisms to address disputes and is characterized by built-in flexibility (Roger Hamilton, personal communication, July 2, 1992). The Agreement resulted in the creation of an Archipelago Management Board, comprised of two Haida and two Parks Canada representatives. Neither of the two parties can take actions to manage or develop the park reserve without consent of the other party. The Board must agree on all issues before it can proceed, and its approval is mandatory for any legislation. Parks Canada is responsible for financing all aspects of tourism development, including the Watchmen Program. The Agreement acknowledges continued use of the area by the Haida, without placing the Haida under the authority of the National Parks Act, nor does it prejudice the Haida claim (Andy Thompson, lawyer, written commentary, 1990). Michael Jackson (UBC Faculty of Law, written commentary, no date) goes so far as to call the Agreement "a contemporary version of the Iroquois two row Wampum Belt", signifying the relationship between two peoples.

Developments in Haida Gwaii may have important implications for other wilderness areas that involve aboriginal title issues. Michael M'Gonigle suggests a locally based management strategy along the lines of the Haida "Watchmen" program for the Stein Valley (M'Gonigle 1988:125; M'Gonigle and Wickwire 1988:171). There are ongoing negotiations between the Nisga'a Tribal Council and the British Columbia Ministry of Parks to create Nisga'a Memorial Provincial Park in the Nass River Valley. A third participant in the negotiations is Skeena Cellulose Inc. with logging interests in the area (Parkin 1991:25f).

The gradually changing political climate in British Columbia is also evidenced in an improved relationship between aboriginal people and established parks. Under a July 1992 agreement between the Ditidaht Band (of the Nuu-chah-nulth Tribal Council) and the Government of Canada (DOE), the Ditidaht will receive $9.5 million in compensation for the rights to harvest timber on reserve lands included in Pacific Rim National Park. The Ditidaht will retain a right to harvest trees for cultural purposes. Furthermore, in March 1993, they were to begin negotiating a long term co-management plan for the Park with Parks Canada (*Ha-Shilth-Sa*, June 30, 1992:10; September 2, 1992:7).

With regard to new protected areas, not only the federal government, but also the provincial government, is committed to including aboriginal people as partners in the process. This was expressed in British Columbia's "Protected Areas Strategy", announced in spring 1992, essentially a response to the Endangered Spaces Campaign (John Broadhead, personal communication, July 1, 1992).

PARKS NORTH OF SIXTY: NEW HORIZONS

It was suggested earlier that the North has always exerted a strong influence on the southern imagination — and vice versa. For the longest time the North was primarily viewed as a last frontier, mostly in terms of resource exploitation. If we associate not only exploitation with the concept of a frontier, but also new ideas and innovative designs, the North may very well become — in terms of our southern imagery — a last frontier for conservation. At this stage it has become clear even to southerners, that the old approaches to park planning just don't work north of sixty. Here the settlement of comprehensive aboriginal claims is a foregone conclusion if not an established fact, and forms an integral part in the establishment of new protection areas. Simultaneously, necessary compromises are focused on the dichotomy between the conventional "parks" concept and traditional resource users' priorities. What counts is not southern imagery but northern reality.

> Protected sites are seen as a tool for achieving conservation and sustainable development goals and not as ends in themselves. For this reason considerable thought must be given to the type of designation and therefore, protection, conferred. The intention is not to further separate Inuit from lands, but rather to promote sustainable use within a living landscape. (Doubleday 1990:87)

> It is good that some areas are set aside to protect wildlife and it is good that there are controls on industries and road building, but the southern ideas of excluding all human activities from all wilderness areas are not ideas that my people can ever agree to. (Norma Kassi, M.L.A., Old Crow, Yukon, 1990:95)

In the northern territories the federal government is the principal agency responsible for the establishment and management of protected areas, since it still owns the overwhelming percentage of the land surface in both territories. As a result, the territorial park network is small. In the Northwest Territories it comprises no more than 5,300 hectares, serving primarily to provide facilities for local residents (community parks) or to support tourism (wayside parks). Yukon has one territorial park: Herschel Island in the Beaufort Sea (Bregha 1989:213; Vaughan 1984:321). The responsibility for the development and operation of the territorial park system in the Northwest Territories lies with the Department of Economic Development and Tourism, which reflects the GNWT conviction that parks be established for the use and benefit of the people (Vaughan 1984:322). From this perspective the GNWT views Parks Canada's activities — excluding the Crown itself, the largest single private or government agency using NWT lands — with many reservations.

> Historically, many northerners have viewed the national parks as a salve to the southern environmental conscience. They see lands in the Northwest Territories as being used to meet southern needs, with the Northwest Territories left to bear the significant problems (and costs) but to receive few, if any, offsetting benefits. Existing national parks are viewed traditionally by residents of the Northwest Territories as causing the loss of opportunities for business and resource development, making only a minimal contribution to the economic health of nearby communities, and being managed under policies and guidelines that perhaps are more applicable to southern national parks. (Vaughan, Superintendent of Parks, GNWT, 1983:329)

In the 1980s the dialogue between the Government of the Northwest Territories and Parks Canada improved, as an agreement was signed in 1981 providing the GNWT with a more meaningful voice in the selection, establishment and development of new national parks. Rather than accepting a transplant of southern-based conservation concepts and priorities, the GNWT pursues a system of protected areas which contributes directly to the goals of an overall integrated resource management system. (Livingston and Bastedo 1990:71). Furthermore, the establishment of national parks has become integrated into the claims process.

There are two national parks within the Inuvialuit Settlement Region. The establishment of Aulavik National Park on Banks Island was announced in August 1992. The design of a co-management regime for this park was part of an "establishment agreement".

In contrast, Northern Yukon National Park (NYNP) was a direct result of the Inuvialuit Final Agreement of 1984. Section 12(6) of the IFA states explicitly that

> ...the planning for the National Park and the management thereof shall have as their objects to protect the wilderness characteristics of the area, maintaining its present undeveloped

state to the greatest extent possible, and to protect and manage the wildlife populations and the wildlife habitat within the area. (Government of Canada 1984:18)

An Inuvialuit role in the management and administration of the Park is firmly entrenched in the IFA. In addition to the role which Inuvialuit co-management bodies play in the management of land and resources in the Inuvialuit Settlement Region in general, several sections of the IFA pertain specifically to rights and privileges for Inuvialuit beneficiaries inside the Park. These provisions cover a variety of items including:

- Sec. 12(8): the right of prior Inuvialuit consent to affect a change in the character or removal of park lands;
- Sec. 12(9): the right of Inuvialuit involvement, through the mechanism of a Wildlife Management Advisory Council detailed in subsection 46, to advise the Minister of the Environment on park planning and management;
- Sec. 12(24): the exclusive right to harvest and dispose of game in the park;
- Sec. 12(42): the predominant employment preference in the operation and management of the park;
- Sec. 12(43): the preferred right to economic opportunities arising from park operations and management;
- Sec. 12(44): the right of first refusal for wildlife related guiding opportunities; and
- Sec. 12(45): the right to enter into bilateral agreements with the Council for Yukon Indians to share rights and privileges afforded beneficiaries in the Yukon North Slope. (Government of Canada 1988:3f)

Initially, Northern Yukon National Park was administered out of Kluane, before a Parks Office was opened in Inuvik in 1987. Only then, was a closer contact established with the Inuvialuit co-management bodies, particularly the Wildlife Management Advisory Council (North Slope) (WMAC/NS) and the Fisheries Joint Management Committee (FJMC). The Park is currently being managed under Interim Guidelines which provide management directives for a new park during the period between park establishment and the preparation of a Park Management Plan. For the development of a Park Management Plan, a Planning Advisory Committee was established. Its members include two representatives from Aklavik (the Inuvialuit community closest to and most concerned with the Park), one each from the Inuvialuit Game Council (IGC) and from Parks Canada, and a planning facilitator (Bill Smith, Chief Park Warden NYNP, personal communication, June 4, 1992).

At present, consultation and management decision-making is very much an ad hoc process with relevant people being consulted whenever necessary. According to Chief Park Warden Bill Smith, co-management of the Park is taking place at different levels:

- Most productively in consultation with the Hunters and Trappers Committees, particularly in Aklavik;
- More formally through the Wildlife Management Advisory Council/North Slope, who reports to the Inuvialuit Game Council; and finally
- Through a working level agreement between DFO and CPS, with CPS managing the sports fishery, and DFO (in cooperation with FJMC) managing the commercial (char) fishery adjoining the Park.

Bill Smith views the renewable resources committees under the IFA as "empowered rather than advisory committees", a perception which is reinforced by recent developments with regard to the Inuvialuit Settlement Region environmental protection regime. In his opinion, one of the most important goals of co-management is "to push down decision-making to the lowest possible level." According to Smith, Parks Canada is fully committed to co-management in this sense, as well as to an ecosystem perspective.

Once completed, the Park Management Plan for NYNP will be presented to the WMAC who advises the Minister regarding the accceptance of the Management Plan. The Inuvialuit leave their mark on Northern Yukon National Park in yet another way: In spring 1993 the Park's name was changed to "Ivvavik National Park". Ivvavik means "birthing place" or "nursery". This name was chosen after a competition by an Elders committee and the WMAC.

Another national park was finalized and proclaimed in summer 1993, on the Old Crow Flats, south of Ivvavik National Park. Vuntut National Park, although adjoining Ivvavik, is a separate entity and part of the Vuntut Gwich'in Final Agreement.

Co-management is also being realized for those protected areas which have only attained national park reserve status. Auyuittuq National Park Reserve on Baffin Island is an example. In the face of considerable Inuit opposition the Park Reserve was established in 1974. Park Reserve boundaries were still being adjusted in the 1990s. Nothing was finalized, prior to the ratification of the Nunavut Land Claims Agreement.

The Park Reserve's impact on the two communities adjacent to its boundaries, Pangnirtung and Broughton Island, has been somewhat different from the beginning, with Pangnirtung deriving significantly more benefits from the Park Reserve's presence than Broughton Island. This is due partly to Pangnirtung's greater prosperity and more enterprising and politicized character, but also enhanced by the fact that the territorial government intended Pangnirtung as a "demonstration community for tourism" (Bruce Rigby, Superintendent, Eastern Arctic District National Parks, personal communication, August 11, 1992).

In Pangnirtung a Park Advisory Committee (with representatives from various community groups, such as the HTA, Elders, the Hamlet etc.) has been in existence since 1981, and it has become increasingly active and visible during the past couple of years. After almost two decades characterized by communication problems and numerous misunderstandings, the Park Reserve's presence is today viewed positively by the community of Pangnirtung: Auyuittuq's aboriginal employment record is 80 per cent (aiming for 100 per cent); local resource harvesting is allowed; people appreciate the cash income derived from tourists and have retained full control over tourism activities outside the Park Reserve; and the local Parks Office (designed in consultation with the community) has become a focus for community activity with regard to broader environmental issues. It is presently being transformed into an environmental resource centre for the local population (Interviews with Japodee Akpalialuk, Mayor of Pangnirtung; Sakiasie Sowdlooapik, Visitor Service Officer CPS; Rebecca Mike, Pangnirtung MLA; and Bruce Rigby, August 10–11, 1992). As Japodee Akpalialuk, Pangnirtung Mayor, sums up the situation, "It is worth it for both sides."

As Ivvavik was a creation of the IFA, Northern Baffin Island National Park will result from the finalization of the Nunavut Land Claims Agreement. This was announced by the Canadian Park Service and the Tungavik Federation of Nunavut in April 1992 (Borealis 3(3):50). The negotiation of an Inuit Impact and Benefits Agreement began after the proclamation of the Nunavut Land Claims Agreement on July 9, 1993, and must be completed within three years of this date (Bruce Rigby, personal communication, July 26, 1993). Local concern in Pond Inlet and Arctic Bay about the future of the polar bear sport hunt suspended work on an originally planned marine park, but there is strong local support for the terrestrial park.

Bruce Rigby, Eastern Arctic District National Parks Superintendent, eventually envisages a Parks Advisory Committee for the entire Eastern Arctic (Nunavut) Region. This committee would be an amalgamation of individual local committees, thus making possible an information exchange among different park areas. The fact that northern parks generally cater to the same clientele would make such an initiative very feasible.

While there are many positive signs, and Parks Canada has assumed an increasingly accommodating position towards aboriginal interests, this does not necessarily imply that the completion of a northern national parks network which accommodates a native presence on the land will be an easy task. This is illustrated by the persistent impasse regarding the National Park Proposal for the East Arm of Great Slave Lake, caused by an adamant refusal of the Dene community of Snowdrift to see its extensively used subsistence lands transformed into a park. The people of Snowdrift are deeply suspicious of parks, an attitude reinforced by "advice" from the Fort Smith Native Band (Chief Henry Beaver, Fort Smith Native Band, personal communication, May 11, 1992). It took 15 years and the involvement of the Dene Nation to convince the community to participate in the park consultation process. Theoretically, Snowdrift's objectives and those of Parks Canada could be mutually supportive, but in practice this would require concessions regarding control and title on both sides.

> Snowdrift's general concerns about their area are that the Dene retain title to the land; that they exercise effective control over all development in the area; that they do not suffer infringements upon the traditional culture; that conservation and wildlife protection be of utmost importance and that they exercise jurisdiction over it; that locally-initiated, small-scale economic development take place; that the traditional economy be nurtured by every means available; that their environment remains a good place to live and raise children in a traditional manner; and that any changes are improvements to their way of life rather than encroachments on it.
>
> These concerns have raised basic questions in discussions surrounding park development. Some of these questions specifically include Snowdrift's option in choosing structures of land management; available options for Snowdrift's involvement in the administration and management of the park; whether Snowdrift wants tourism development and, if so, the particular economic opportunities that would be open to the community; and, more importantly, whether tourism can be controlled. (Griffith 1987:30)

The people of Snowdrift were eventually induced to examine the park proposal by another development that was externally imposed on them: the land selection process in the Dene/Metis claim negotiations. They began to consider the possibility of augmenting their settlement lands by protecting an extended area for conservation and subsistence use. The initiative ground to another halt with the rejection of the Dene/Metis Final Agreement in 1990. The future of this national park proposal is now caught up in the South Slave Region land claim.

In the 1980s the U.S. National Park Service was faced with the same problem as Parks Canada: a redefinition of the national parks concept for the state of Alaska (Shaver 1985:51). The ten national parks, preserves and monuments created by the Alaska National Interest Lands Conservation Act (ANILCA) in 1980 are the largest and most diverse parklands yet incorporated into the U.S. National Parks System. The intention from the outset was not only to protect the ecosystem but also to provide for continued subsistence harvest opportunities on federal lands in Alaska. It is significant that ANILCA's protection of "customary and traditional" subsistence uses of park resources is extended to both native and non-native people.

"Subsistence resource commissions" were instituted principally to guarantee an input by domestic harvesting interests into the park management process. The commissions, comprised mainly of local resource harvesters, are each required to devise and recommend to the Secretary of the Interior a "subsistence hunting program" for their respective parks (Caulfield 1988:55). Their congressional mandate makes these commissions fundamentally different from management advisory boards/committees in Canada. It requires the Secretary of the Interior and the National Parks Service to promptly implement their recommended program for subsistence hunting unless it

> ...violates recognized principles of wildlife conservation, threatens the conservation of natural and healthy populations of wildlife...is contrary to the purposes for which the park....is established, or would be detrimental to the satisfaction of subsistence needs of local residents. (U.S. Congress 1980, quoted in Caulfield 1988:55)

Not surprisingly, since the passage of ANILCA, controversy surrounding subsistence activities in new park units has centered upon the definition of key terms and phrases used in the legislation, such as "customary and traditional" and "natural and healthy". In the late 1980s most of the commissions were nearing completion of their subsistence hunting programs. The manner in which the Secretary of the Interior and the National Park Service will respond to these recommendations will be crucial in determining the political climate in which ANILCA's provisions will be implemented. With regard to the future role of Alaska's subsistence resource commissions, we may ask the same question about Canada's various co-management institutions: Whether they

> ...are simply to be an extension of the existing "state system" of resource management or whether their congressional mandate will result in the meaningful inclusion of the views of local people in park management. In short, will they be vehicles for cooperation or co-optation? (Caulfield 1988:62)

ABORIGINAL PARKS: INNOVATIVE CONCEPTS

Northern Community Conservation Initiatives

It has been shown that the cooperation between aboriginal people, as resource users, and government-mandated parks officials requires flexibility and imagination on both sides. This is even more true in situations where native groups design unique solutions to their conservation concerns, and outside agencies are placed in a position where they (ideally...) should respond in a constructive way.

One of the most intriguing examples is the Clyde River Proposal for a Bowhead Whale Sanctuary at Igalirtuuq, on northeastern Baffin Island.[5] The initiative started in 1983, when the community entered into a cooperative bowhead research program with World Wildlife Fund Canada (WWF), the Department of Fisheries and Oceans (DFO), the Department of Renewable Resources (DRR of GNWT) and the Department of Indian Affairs and Northern Development (DIAND). The community and WWF were primarily interested in the relationship between bowhead whales and the Isabella Bay (Igalirtuuq) feeding and breeding grounds. The people of Clyde River had traditionally hunted bowheads and felt a strong affinity for the animals. The research of the WWF was part of its "Whales Beneath the Ice" program, which was aimed at the recovery of the whale populations. The research stimulated a high level of community interest and generated a joint body of knowledge which combined traditional and scientific elements. The findings led both the people of Clyde River and the WWF to conclude that Igalirtuuq required protection to assist the bowhead population recovery.

After this research period, the Clyde River Hamlet Council and the Hunters and Trappers Association jointly set up a Special Committee on Igalirtuuq to develop a conservation plan based on local knowledge, the research findings and community concerns. Concurrently, WWF and a DRR technical advisor prepared supporting background documents. After weighing various options and combinations thereof, the Special Committee produced a proposal that went beyond mere habitat protection. It recommended that a biosphere reserve be established surrounding a whale sanctuary under the UNESCO Man and Biosphere Program, which would at the same time protect Inuit archaeological and historical European whaling sites.

---

[5] Credit for the following information must be given to Bourque and McCullum 1990, and to Joellie Sangoya, Clyde River, who talked about his community's initiative at the IASCP (International Association for the Study of Common Property) Common Property Conference in Winnipeg, Manitoba, September 26–29, 1991.

The main goals set out in the Proposal are to:

1. Protect the Bowhead and its critical habitat at Isabella Bay from human disturbance and pollution;
2. Aid recovery of the Bowhead through research and conservation at Isabella Bay and its surroundings;
3. Protect an important cultural heritage resource of Baffin Inuit; and
4. Enable direct involvement of Clyde River in decisions and work related to the conservation plan. (Clyde River 1990, quoted in Bourque and McCullum 1990:17)

The Proposal also includes specific objectives:

1. To secure government leadership to protect critical Bowhead whale habitat through the establishment of a Whale Sanctuary, archaeological sites and a Biosphere Reserve at Isabella Bay; and
2. To draw public attention to the urgent conservation needs of the Bowhead whale by sharing the knowledge and concerns of Clyde River. (Clyde River 1990, quoted in Bourque and McCullum 1990:17)

Further elements of the proposal were detailed recommendations for protection, buffer zone establishment, modest tourism development, continued research and community involvement. The community has submitted the proposal to the appropriate government agencies: DFO (whale sanctuary), DIAND and GNWT (archaeological sites), as well as other departments which could assist in implementation.

> The Proposal provides a good description of the values it would protect: the whales, their habitat, Inuit and whaler archaeology and potential whale hunting in the future. It sets out the stresses on the Bowhead: tourism, pollution, resource development, defence activities and natural factors. It describes the opportunities to set up a Sanctuary: community support, fulfillment of government commitments to Arctic conservation and international attention. The conservation plan component sets out the protection goals and describes how the Whale Sanctuary, Biosphere Reserve and archaeological site protection can be implemented. The management policies cover boats, aircraft, hunting, research, tourism, non-renewable resource development, defence exercises and garbage. The implementation plan identifies DFO as the responsible government department for implementing the Whale Sanctuary while committing the community to assist in any way possible. In particular they recommend: DFO accept the proposal and appoint a project coordinator, set up a steering committee with community representation to work out the details, submit a Biosphere Reserve proposal to UNESCO, set up a shelter for wardens and researchers on Cape Raper near Isabella Bay and set up an informal whale migration monitoring network. (Bourque and McCullum 1990:20)

In 1992 Clyde River was still waiting for a response to the Proposal from DFO, DIAND and DRR. Its only measure of success so far is the development and implementation of its own management policies. The community has unanimously endorsed the Proposal and plan and is restricting its own use of Isabella Bay, while the whales migrate through. While more research was funded for 1992 (*Working for Wildlife*, Winter 1992:3), no steps seem to have been taken to accord Isabella Bay protected-area status.

Clyde River's initiative may be the most ambitious and elaborate one, but it is not the only one. The Inuit community at Resolute has expressed an interest in setting aside Cunningham Inlet (crucial beluga habitat) as a special protection area within the claim settlement process (Struzik 1991d:25).

Paulatuk's community conservation plan includes the recommendation that the Bluenose caribou calving grounds be protected through the establishment of a national park (The Community of Paulatuk and The Wildlife Management Advisory Council 1990:20). Discussions are under way between the community and Parks Canada on this proposal. The proposed national park will include the entire Hornaday watershed. The proposal is complicated since it is not confined to the Inuvialuit Settlement Region, but extends into the claims areas of TFN and Sahtu (Gordon M. Hamre, CPS Yellowknife, personal communication, May 7, 1992).

The Kaska Dena in southern Yukon intend to set aside a vast stretch of wilderness as an ecological reserve. This area will be home and breeding ground for caribou, goats and sheep. No hunting, resource extraction or human habitation will be permitted. This land will come from the Kaska Dena's settlement lands under the Yukon land claim agreement, and represents a long-term investment in renewable resources (Peter Douglas Elias, personal communication, 1991).

Mission Mountains Tribal Wilderness in Montana

The Confederated Salish and Kootenai Tribes (CSKT) in Montana made a strong statement with the land use on their reservation: more than one-quarter of the Indian-owned land on the Flathead Reservation has protected area status. The majority of this protected land is occupied by the 36,220-hectare Mission Mountains Tribal Wilderness, representing a probably unique concept in North America.

> The Mission Mountains have served as a guide, passage way, fortification and vision seeking ground, as well as a place to gather medicinal herbs, roots and a place to hunt for food for the Pend d'Oreille and Salish Indians since they have lived at the foothills of the Missions. (Flathead Culture Committee 1978)

As early as 1936 the Tribal Council voted unanimously to set aside about 40,000 hectares of the Mission Mountains as an Indian-maintained and -managed national park. No results came from this resolution, but a year later, Bob Marshall, then Chief Forester for the Office of Indian Affairs, drafted an order that established twelve "roadless areas" and four "wild areas" on twelve Indian reservations across the country. The west side of the Mission Range was included in the order as a roadless area. Bureau of Indian Affairs Commissioner John Collier signed the order which differed from U.S. Forest Service wilderness regulations and the Wilderness Act of 1964 in at least one of its stated purposes:

> If on reservations, where the Indians desire privacy, sizeable areas are uninvaded by roads, then it will be possible for the Indians of these tribes to maintain a retreat where they may escape from constant contact with white men. (CFR 1937, quoted in CSKT 1982:78)

The only management restriction was that these areas would not have roads passable for motorized vehicles. In the late 1950s most of these roadless and wild areas were declassified, and only one remains in existence today: the Wind River Roadless Area on the Wind River Reservation in Wyoming. The areas were declassified for two reasons: they had been created without the consent or input of the tribes involved, and some of the tribes had economic development plans for the areas (CSKT 1982:79).

The Mission Range Roadless Area was declassified in the Federal Register in 1959. The Confederated Tribes had also objected to its inclusion in a National Wilderness Preservation System, since they would not have been involved in its establishment and management, and they were concerned about the protection of their rights.

Throughout the 1970s, however, there were several initiatives and proposals by tribal members directed toward effecting their own wilderness designation for the Missions. In 1979 the Tribal Council officially established the Mission Mountains Tribal Wilderness, and a year later the Tribal Wildland Recreation Department was founded, which developed a wilderness management plan.

The ordinance establishing the tribal wilderness in some ways parallels and even includes language from the 1964 Wilderness Act, but it specifically omits significant parts of the Act and places greater emphasis on others.

> **Section 1 — Statement of Policy**
>
> Wilderness has played a paramount role in shaping the character of the people and the culture of the Salish and Kootenai Tribes; it is the essence of traditional Indian religion and has served the Indian people of these Tribes as a place to hunt, as a place to gather medicinal herbs and roots, as a vision-seeking ground, as a sanctuary, and in countless other ways for thousands of years. Because maintaining an enduring resource of wilderness is vitally important to the people of the Confederated Salish and Kootenai Tribes and the perpetuation of their culture, there is hereby established a Mission Mountains Tribal Wilderness Area and this Area, described herein, shall be administered to protect and preserve wilderness values.
>
> ....
>
> **Section 4 — Use of the Mission Mountains Tribal Wilderness**
>
> a. It is the principal objective of this Ordinance to protect and preserve an area of land in its natural condition in perpetuity. This Wilderness shall be devoted to the purposes of recreational, scenic, scientific, educational, conservation, cultural, religious and historical use only insofar as these uses are consistent with the spirit and provisions of this ordinance. Human use of this Area must not interfere with the preservation of the Area as wilderness. (The Tribal Wilderness Ordinance, CSKT 1982:7f)

Tom McDonald, Program Manager of the Wildland Recreation Program, puts it unequivocally: "The ecosystem comes first, man comes second." (Personal communication, February 26, 1992). This protective attitude is exemplified by the tribal concern about the area's grizzly bear population. Each year since 1982, a sizeable portion of the wilderness is closed to all human use for two and a half months, because grizzlies concentrate in this particular area to feed on ladybugs and army moth larvae. Nontribal members are allowed access to the Wilderness with a permit, available for a fee. "Improvements and facilities, which include trails, campsites, bridges, signs, fences, hitch racks, etc. will be provided only where they are necessary for protection of the wilderness resource. They will not be provided primarily for the comfort or convenience of the visitor." (CSKT 1982:21).

It may come as a surprise to many that use of the Wilderness Area by tribal members is relatively insignificant; they are the minority users of their own Wilderness.

> There is, however, an intense appreciation and love for the Wilderness that more than compensates for the lack of direct recreational use....
>
> It is one part of the Indian culture that remains as it was. The need for preservation, then, is more out of a reverence for the land, its community of life, and what it means to the Indian culture than out of a need to enjoy the benefits of direct use. This is a dimension that is unique to the Tribal Wilderness and it is reflected in the Council's action. (ibid.:82f)

A further indication of the Tribes' commitment to the Tribal Wilderness concept is the establishment of a Mission Mountains Tribal Wilderness Buffer Zone in 1986 (CSKT 1986).

One reason for the relatively light use that the Tribal Wilderness receives from tribal members may be the fact that there are other protected areas on the reservation which are open only to tribal members. The 24,000-hectare South Fork Primitive Area (bordering on the Mission Mountains Tribal Wilderness) was established in 1974 and, with overwhelming support from the tribal membership, considerably expanded in 1991. A second slightly smaller Primitive Area is located in the northwest corner of the reservation. Until 1979 not even non-member spouses and children of tribal members were admitted into these areas.

CONCLUSION AND OUTLOOK

A mutual understanding between aboriginal and non-aboriginal people regarding the issue of protected areas will not be arrived at easily. On both sides there are too many concepts involved which are deeply ingrained in respective societies, often incomprehensible to the other party, and sometimes mutually exclusive. Native people's understanding of and interaction with their environment is viewed by many of them as the foundation of their culture and society, and in large parts of Canada, constitutes the basis for their socio-economic existence. Attitudes grown out of such reality are not easily compromised.

In comparison to other resource uses, the issue of protected areas is further complicated by the fact that on the non-native side it is not just economical and political considerations that enter into the picture, but ideas and images which have no grounding in fact. This does not make them any less powerful, on the contrary.

Superimposed on this dichotomy are unresolved questions of legal rights and sovereignty.

Canada is but a microcosm of a worldwide dilemma. A look at other countries demonstrates a whole gamut of possible relationships between protected areas and indigenous peoples. In many African countries, national parks have remained essentially alien institutions, which not only have barred local people — indigenous groups most prominent among them — from their resources but have also fostered hostile and wasteful attitudes towards these resources. Northern Australia provides us with examples where aboriginal people retained their titles to protected lands and entered into tentative relationships of accommodation with the foreign institutions. And finally, in Panama, an autonomous indigenous group has designed a concept of protection area uniquely its own.

This spectrum of situations and relationships is also found within Canada. In the older established parks in most of the provinces, native people have been effectively excluded from protected lands, to which they had originally retained user rights if not ownership. Wood Buffalo National Park is an exception to this rule, since it constitutes the only example where aboriginal people have a history of participation in the use and management of the park.

Large parts of Canada anticipate both the settlement of comprehensive native claims and the establishment of new national parks. As exemplified by Gwaii Haanas, and, on a smaller scale, Meares Island, aboriginal groups in British Columbia proceeded with the establishment of their own protection areas. This was done partly because protection from resource exploitation could not wait for governmental action (which was not forthcoming in any case); it also constituted the assertion of jurisdiction. These actions in no way preclude access by non-natives to the protected areas, but they establish aboriginal systems of visitor guidance and control.

In the northern territories it is too early to discern a pattern of parks co-management. Developments so far show or predict co-management by means of existing wildlife co-management bodies, as well as through native and native/non-native parks advisory or joint management institutions. Current examples are confined to Inuit and Inuvialuit, and it remains to be seen how acceptable this scheme will be to the Dene and Metis.

Finally, there are innovative initiatives by aboriginal people to establish protection areas for their own purposes and, in some cases, of their own design. The community of Paulatuk seems to be looking towards the concept of a national park to protect the calving grounds of the Bluenose caribou herd. Without doubt such special mandate will necessitate a revision of the conceptual framework of a national park. The people of Clyde River — like the Kuna Indians — devised their own special plans for areas they wanted to protect and in what manner, and decided that these plans fitted into the concept of a biosphere reserve which would enable them to benefit from an international network. Such initiatives, however, rely on the cooperation of outside agencies, which is not always readily forthcoming. As J.W. Bourque and John McCullum (1990:28) noted, "Creative solutions require innovative responses," and many of these new projects recommend some change in the present resource management framework, which would effect a greater degree of community control over the decision-making process. Only in a few isolated cases — where a project can be carried out exclusively on an aboriginal land base — does such dependency on outside agencies not exist. This would be the case, if the Kaska Dena, after the settlement of their claim, executed their plans. It also applies to the Tribal Wilderness and Primitive Areas of the Confederated Salish and Kootenai Tribes in Montana.

Undoubtedly, the establishment and management of new designated protection areas with the involvement of aboriginal people will be even more difficult than parks creation and maintenance have been in the past. The dual mandate of preservation and recreation alone creates numerous problems which is unlikely to change.

> Recreation always has been important in Canada's national parks. It is a justification for them, land use of and an environmental impact on them, an economic cost-benefit measure of them, and a cause of management problems in them. (Marsh 1979:151)

Whatever aboriginal people will bring to the parks context in terms of management input and motivation for park establishment, be it for protection of a renewable resource base or less tangible elements, such as cultural and spiritual values, it will, in most cases, necessitate a revision of the preservation mandate — in favour of a conservation mandate — and will create a whole new interface with the recreation element. The relationship between these two user groups will have to be considered with regard to its impact both on the resource base and on the aboriginal population. The recent initiative by Parks Canada to establish a task force to specifically look into the issue of aboriginal people and parks shows that Parks Canada takes the matter seriously.

It will take the wisdom and knowledge of both native and non-native society to guarantee a future for conservation areas in Canada that will safeguard the well-being of the entire ecosystem, man included.

9

Native People and Environmental Impact Assessment

INTRODUCTION: EIA AT A CROSSROADS

> Environmental impact assessment in Canada, as elsewhere, is a socio-political phenomenon. It is grounded in the perceptions and values of society which find expression at the political level through administrative procedures of governments. Science is called upon to explain the relationship between contemplated actions and these environmental perceptions and values. Although the views of the general public may not be supported by the findings of scientific investigations, their collective aspirations cannot be ignored. It must be recognized, therefore, that decisions resulting from environmental impact assessments may be based as much on subjective judgements involving values, feelings, beliefs and prejudices, as on the results of scientific studies. (Beanlands and Duinker 1983:37)

> Any consideration of the significance of environmental effects must acknowledge that environmental impact assessment is inherently an anthropocentric concept. (ibid.:44)

> It's a big sham — a front....It's to ease people's consciences. They can say we did a study and the people didn't object. A lot of decisions aren't made by the people on the panels, but the guys who control the stock market. They're not likely to listen to someone who's been fishing for 40 years, but someone who can do experiments in a tank. That's called scientific. (Frank Collison, Vice-President, Council of the Haida Nation, quoted in Shapcott 1989:62)

> Neither the courts nor the British Columbia Environmental Appeal Board can factor the social values of another culture into their decision-making. The values of the dominant culture are so imbedded in the process of EIA (including that administered by the Environmental Assessment Review Process at the federal level), that alternative values cannot even be considered. As noted earlier, the underlying values — both of the culture and the process — must be changed to make environmental impact assessment meaningful to Native people. (Shapcott 1989:68)

In the early 1990s Canada's aboriginal people have figured in the controversy surrounding environmental impact assessments of major new resource development projects, such as the Oldman River Dam in Alberta and the Great Whale Project in northern Quebec. Native people have also initiated their own retrospective impact assessments for resource developments which took place in the 1960s and early 1970s, when environmental attitudes and ideas of social justice were different from what they are today, and when as a result, no environmental or socio-economic impact assessments whatsoever were conducted even for mega-projects. Developments like the Churchill-Nelson Hydro Project in Manitoba (see chapter 2) and the

Cyprus Anvil Mine in Yukon (see chapter 7) dealt devastating blows to local and regional native societies and economies, consequences with which all parties concerned have yet to come to terms. These facts illustrate the necessity of making aboriginal concerns an integral part of current endeavours to redefine and restructure environmental impact assessment in Canada.

> The basic idea of EIA is quite straightforward: to scrutinize a development scheme while it is still in the planning stage (sometimes by examining an "impact statement" prepared by the proponent) in order to ensure that the expected effects on the environment are acceptable and to require such corrective or mitigative measures to be incorporated as seem necessary; or, in extreme cases, to reject the project altogether. Initially, "environment" meant mainly the natural environment (the original U.S. statute was enacted a few years after the publication of Rachel Carson's *Silent Spring*, on the flood tide of the "environmentalist" movement), but later expanded to include the social, cultural and economic milieu as well. Ontario's Environmental Assessment Act defines "environment" to include, effectively, everything. (Richardson 1989:28)

Thus historically, the concern with the social impact of projects emerged out of the concern with the analysis of impacts on the physical environment. Today both are incorporated in most legislative and administrative impact assessment regimes, and the general analytic strategy used in assessments is essentially similar in both cases.

> Social impact assessment is an approach to the study of social change which has as one objective anticipating the future consequences of intentional interventions (projects) in the present. A second objective of SIA is to help shape policies which will guide these intentional interventions in such a way that desirable impacts will be maximized and undesirable impacts will be minimized. The most central steps in SIA research are (1) describing the social activities in an area prior to a project, (2) describing the activities associated directly with the project itself, and (3) forecasting the patterns of social activity which will result from the interaction of pre-project activities and project activities. If SIA research is to be influential in shaping the design of projects, social impact considerations must be institutionally incorporated into the full range of decision making processes which govern project development. (Bowles 1979:134)

Environmental impact assessment[1] as we know it in North America was introduced in the United States by the National Environmental Policy Act (NEPA) of 1969, and adopted by the Canadian government in 1973 in the form of the Environmental Assessment and Review Process, or EARP. During the following decade most of the provinces introduced at least a rudimentary form of environmental impact assessment (EIA) process, the most comprehensive and stringent being established in 1975 by Ontario's Environmental Assessment Act.

Significantly, in contrast to the United States, EARP was introduced in Canada as an administrative rather than legislative procedure, which can be explained by the political culture of both countries.

> Compared to the United States, the political culture of Canada is marked by a lesser degree of citizen activism, wide latitude traditionally granted to administrative discretion, and restricted rights to participate in decision making or to challenge the process in court. Conversely, the public inquiry system in Canada has no real counterpart in the United States. The linkage of this tradition with EIA in the review of major projects has been an important catalyst for the growth and diversification of the process in this country. (Sadler 1990b:103)

EARP has been used to assess the potential environmental effects of proposals requiring a federal government decision. The process was updated in 1977 and reinforced in 1984

---

[1] In this chapter, the term "environmental impact assessment" (EIA) will be used as follows: If used alone, EIA may be assumed to be concerned with impacts on both the physical environment and the social environment. If used in conjunction with "social impact assessment" (SIA), it refers primarily to the physical environment.

when the EARP Guidelines were issued by Order-in-Council. As already noted, EARP has no statutory base. It is an administrative procedure which federal ministers may, but are not obliged to, require as a precondition of their approval or authorization of a project which falls in some way under their jurisdiction. This may be any proposal which:

- Is to be undertaken by a federal department or agency;
- May have an environmental effect or directly related socio-economic effect on an area of federal responsibility;
- The federal government makes a financial commitment to; or
- Is located on lands, including the offshore, that are administered by the federal government. (Kansky 1987b:2)

The impact assessment process is essentially a self-assessment process. In other words, the responsibility for considering the potential environmental effects of a proposal rests with the initiating government department which has the decision-making authority regarding the proposed project. The EARP Guidelines require that the initiating department consider the following:

- The potential environmental effects including effects on foreign territory;
- Social effects directly related to potential environmental effects including effects on foreign territory; and
- Concerns of the public regarding the proposal and its potential environmental effects. (ibid.:3)

Furthermore, with the approval of the Minister of the Environment and the initiating department, the review may include general socio-economic effects, technology assessment and the need for the project (EARP Guidelines s.4[2]).

The EARP process is administered by the Federal Environmental Assessment Review Office (FEARO). FEARO is not part of the Department of the Environment, although its Executive Chairman reports directly to the Minister of the Environment. The EARP process can by subdivided into two phases: the initial assessment and the public review by an EARP panel (Kansky 1987b:4). During the first phase the initiating government department reviews the proposal. If the department concludes that adverse environmental effects are unlikely, there is no further review. If in the department's opinion there is a potential for significant adverse environmental impacts, the proposal is automatically referred to the Minister of the Environment for public review by an EARP panel. If the proposal is likely to have some environmental effects, the initiating department has the discretionary power to decide, whether the proposal is to proceed with changes; whether further study is required; whether the proposal should be modified by the proponent for reassessment; whether it should be referred to an EARP panel for public review; or whether it should be rejected altogether (EARP Guidelines s.12 and 13).

Once a proposal is referred to the federal Minister of the Environment for review by an EARP panel, terms of reference are drafted by FEARO in consultation with the initiating department and submitted to the Minister of the Environment. These terms of reference define the scope of the review. The panel, whose members are suggested by FEARO and appointed by the Minister of the Environment, issues guidelines, after consultation with the public, to the proponent for preparation of an Environmental Impact Statement (EIS) (s.30). The proponent is obliged to submit to the Panel copies of the EIS in local Indian or Inuit languages, as stipulated by the Panel (s.34[b]). The EIS is subsequently made available to the public.

When the Panel is satisfied with the EIS, public hearings are held. The EARP Panel may hold two types of hearings: community hearings, which are usually of an informal nature and held in affected rural areas, and general hearings in urban centres, focusing on the technical aspects of a proposal and its potential impact. Once the Panel has completed its review, it prepares a report containing its conclusions and recommendations (s.31). These are limited to those options contained in the terms of reference. The Panel may not be in a position to recommend rejection of the proposal, but rather be confined to proposing terms and conditions to minimize adverse environmental effects. The Panel Report is submitted to the Ministers of the Environment and the initiating department, who make the final decision. They are not legally bound to follow the Panel's recommendations. Once a proposal is approved, the proponent must ensure that appropriate post-assessment, monitoring, surveillance and reporting required by the initiating department are carried out (s.34[b]).

This is a mere skeleton outline of the EARP process. One effect of the 1984 Guidelines may have been a tightening of the initial screening process (Hunt et al. 1985:21). Critics of EARP have often argued that too many projects were "screened out" at an early stage, thus escaping an environmental review. One innovation introduced by the 1984 Guidelines is s.13, which stipulates that a proposal must be subjected to EARP "if public concern about the proposal is such that a public review is desirable", notwithstanding that the screening/initial assessment of the project under s.12 would normally not have resulted in a public review. There is no suggestion as to how such "public concern" is to be measured.

The 1984 Guidelines also refined the determination of the scope of the EARP Panel's review. The terms of reference, as established by the Minister of the Environment in consultation with the minister of the department initiating the project, must be made public. But as already mentioned, it is only with the approval of the ministers that the public review may include "such matters as the general socio-economic effects of the proposal and the technology assessment of and need for the proposal" (ibid.:22).

The 1984 Guidelines have done nothing to deal with the problem of delay in the review processes. The only reference to time is found in s.3 which states that environmental implications of a project are to be considered "as early as possible and before irrevocable decisions are taken." This is in contrast to the requirements of some legislated processes, for example, in Newfoundland with regard to oil and gas related projects, where a "clock" begins to run as soon as a proposal is submitted to the government (ibid.).

EARP is the most important federal framework for environmental impact assessment and review. As previously mentioned, all provinces have their own legal frameworks for environmental impact assessment, some of which are legislated, while others are a matter of provincial government policy.[2] Responsibility for public review processes also falls to such regulatory bodies as the National Energy Board (NEB), the Ontario Energy Board and Alberta's Energy Resources Conservation Board (ERCB) and Natural Resources Conservation Board (NRCB), who conduct formal, quasi-judicial reviews. Not surprisingly, there is significant duplication and overlap not only between the federal and provincial governments but even between different agencies of the same government. Frequently, participants are unaware of such facts as, for example, that EARP functions in a merely advisory capacity, whereas the NEB has regulatory responsibilities.

Independently from its institutional and legislative framework, environmental impact assessment has reached an important crossroads.

> While the process has undergone remarkable growth to become firmly institutionalized, serious reservations remain about the impact of impact assessment on project planning and decision making in general. It seems generally accepted that the application of EIA plus SIA has resulted in greater protection of resource potentials and community health and well-being, when necessary economic development takes place, than otherwise would be

[2] For more detail on provincial regimes, see Mitchell and Turkheim 1977:50–62; Waiten 1981:14–17; for Ontario and Manitoba, see also Richardson 1989:29.

> the case. The fundamental worry is that impact assessment is a pro-forma exercise which occupies a marginal place and is of peripheral influence within the development process. In the final analysis, EIA is often characterized more by a capacity to delay and frustrate than to shape positively the course of proposed action. (Sadler 1990b:104)

Several crucial issues are being focused upon in current discussions of environmental impact assessment. One of these issues is the role of science.

> Impact assessment was and still is founded upon the predictive capabilities of the natural and social sciences. Given the natural variability of ecosystems and the social dynamism which characterize communities, this is a difficult task. Much remains unknown about the processes that govern the structure and response of particular systems to project-induced change. Uncertainty is therefore a fundamental characteristic of impact assessment. From a scientific perspective, the crucial challenge is how to cope with this condition. (ibid.:105)

While the essential unknowability of some environmental impacts is problematic enough, impact assessment is rendered even more difficult by the fact that it is a thoroughly anthropocentric and socio-political process. This is obvious as it pertains to social impact assessment, but subjective value judgements play no less a role when it comes to the consideration of potential impacts on the physical environment. Subjective value judgement is bound to enter into the identification of what is referred to as VEC's or Valued Ecosystem Components, and it also plays a role in determining just what constitutes a "significant" impact.

> It is impossible for an impact assessment to address all potential environmental effects of a project. Therefore it is necessary that the environmental attributes considered to be important in project decisions be identified at the beginning of an assessment. This will normally require some form of public consultation or social scoping exercise to determine the values attached to various ecosystem components. Both the views expressed by the general public and those of the professional community should be considered when determining these values.
>
> ....
>
> Every assessment ultimately focuses on the question of whether the predicted impacts are significant....
>
> Three interpretations of impact significance have been identified for environmental assessment purposes: (i) statistical significance (related to problems of isolating project-induced changes from natural variation), (ii) ecological considerations (related to the importance of project-induced changes from a purely ecological perspective, independent of social values), and (iii) social importance (related to the acceptability of project-induced changes in valued ecosystem components). An overriding consideration is the degree to which project-induced changes are expected to affect project decisions. (Beanlands and Duinker 1983:92f)

Progress of environmental impact assessment as an applied science has been severely hampered by its static and reactive character. It usually takes place after a project has been defined and a site or route has already been selected (Sadler 1990:108). An evaluation of the validity of the prediction of project impacts has usually not been considered part of the process; assumptions and hypotheses about developmental effects typically go untested and methods that would allow for more accurate predictions do not evolve.

> The purpose of SIA is to ascertain how and to what extent specified social groups will become better or worse off as a result of certain externally generated actions. This is done first of all by means of projection or prediction. If claims of change are to be verified, however, there must also be a process of hypothesis testing and post-project evaluation. Hypothesis testing occurs through monitoring. (Usher and Weinstein 1991:5)

> The process of environmental impact assessment should not end with the production of a report. It is our contention that an EIS must become as much a document of future commitment and responsibility as it is a summary of past and predicted environmental events. Given the relatively undeveloped state-of-the-art in accurately predicting long-term biological consequences of proposed activities, post-EIS monitoring programmes must be undertaken

> for environmental impact assessment to develop beyond the current rudimentary guessing game. The EIS should incorporate detailed statements of commitment by both government and industrial agencies to follow through with carefully selected environmental monitoring programmes. (Beanlands and Duinker 1983:34)

While environmental monitoring and auditing activities are an emerging area of research interest and their benefits more and more recognized, they have not yet become an established part of environmental impact assessment (Davies and Sadler 1990:7).

Closely related to the problem of incompleteness and discontinuity of the environmental impact assessment process is its ill-defined relationship to land use planning. Gordon E. Beanlands and Peter N. Duinker (1983:21) feel that in the long term impact assessment will have to move away from the conventional project focus "along the path toward comprehensive environmental planning." Currently, environmental impact assessment is designed to be part of planning and not the equivalent of it, yet, for the most part, the planning frameworks necessary for systematic impact assessment are very poorly developed in Canada (Sadler 1990b:108). As a result, EIA is frequently stretched to the limit in acting as a surrogate. A typical example occurred in the early 1980s in conjunction with hydrocarbon development in the Beaufort Sea-Mackenzie Delta. Part of DIAND'S expectations for the EARP hearings was that the proponents (Dome Petroleum Limited, Gulf Canada Resources Inc. and Esso Resources Canada Limited) would produce an environmental impact statement that would serve also as a regional planning document (Baily 1987:124).

> These weaknesses could have been largely avoided when EIA was adopted by provincial governments had the procedure been treated, as in some European countries, as an elaboration of the land use planning system. On the one hand this would have given EIA the context and continuity which it now generally lacks, while tending to simplify and expedite the process; on the other, it could have given the implementation of land use plans greater effectiveness combined with greater flexibility. (Richardson 1989:29)

As an interim step of improvement of the process, Barry Sadler proposed "area-wide assessment".

> This approach, broadly defined, involves the systematic documentation of regional environments to identify the nature and range of potentials and constraints on proposed courses of action....Regional screening and evaluation of the relationship between development scenarios and environmental capacities yields a space and time framework for the comparison and analysis of cross-linkages among site-specific impacts from both similar and unrelated types of activity.
>
> The instrumental value of this form of assessment rests on the possibilities for early and extensive incorporation of environmental considerations into decision-making, in a proactive rather than reactive manner....
>
> Candidate areas for this type of study may be based on administrative, resource, ecological or socioeconomic boundaries, or some combination thereof. (Sadler 1990b:119)

While the potential for such approach seems to have been recognized in Canada, its translation into practice has remained embryonic. Examples for a move in this direction are a comprehensive regional planning exercise resulting from recommendations by the Lancaster Sound Environmental Assessment Panel, and planning and assessment studies undertaken by the British Columbia Ministry of the Environment (ibid.:120).

The changes proposed at the federal level by Bill C-78, the Canadian Environmental Assessment Act (1992), address only some of these issues. First efforts to plan a reform of the environmental assessment procedure were undertaken by the federal government in 1987. Two subsequent court decisions, namely the rulings on Rafferty-Alameda[3] and the

[3] Canadian Wildlife Federation Inc. v. Canada (Minister of the Environment) [1989] 3 F.C.309

Oldman River Dam[4], added momentum to the reform process. Before the decision on Rafferty-Alameda, the EARP Guidelines were considered an informal, non-enforceable mechanism for reviewing resource developments that might have an adverse impact on the environment. In its May 1989 ruling the Federal Court of Canada decided that EARP is in fact a legally enforceable law of general application, which imposes additional responsibilities on the federal government. The Oldman River ruling is a direct outcome of this decision. In January 1992 the Supreme Court of Canada confirmed a 1990 Federal Court of Appeal ruling to the effect that Ottawa has the constitutional power and obligation to conduct environmental impact assessments of any project that involves aspects of federal jurisdiction.

> It broadens the application to any federal authority, not just the Department of the Environment (as was the case with Rafferty-Alameda), and to any type of decision making, not just the issuing of permits or licences. This is an enormous expansion on Rafferty-Alameda. That's the victory in the (Oldman) decision. (Martha Kostuch, Vice President, Friends of the Oldman River, quoted in Bryson 1991:14)

The EARP Guidelines, however, had not been drafted with strict legal interpretation in mind, a fact that has augmented the need for reform. According to a fact sheet by FEARO (Government of Canada 1990b, Fact Sheet No.2), the reform package consists of three key elements:

- New EA legislation;
- A new process for policy and program assessment;
- A program for funding participants in public reviews.

The Canadian Environmental Assessment Act (CEAA, passed by the House of Commons and the Senate in 1992) will for the first time set out in an Act passed by Parliament the federal government's responsibilities and procedures for the environmental assessment of projects. The legislation establishes a new agency, the Canadian Environmental Assessment Agency. It will report to the Minister of the Environment, but will be separate from Environment Canada, as well as from other federal departments and agencies. Bill C-78 clearly transfers decision-making powers to the environmental portfolio. Under the current Guidelines it is the minister responsible for the project who decides whether there is a need for public review; the new legislation makes this a decision of the Environment Minister.

> Critics give the legislation high marks for the way it handles public reviews, mediation, monitoring of projects, transborder issues and policy review. However, many insist that C-78 does not clear up the confusion over which level of government is responsible for what kind of projects. Regulations that list the pieces of federal legislation that C-78 will apply to were not released with the bill. Thus questions about the scope of federal government regulations remain largely unanswered. (Bryson 1991:18)

Critics of the Bill also point out that C-78 does not give rise to new regulatory measures. Substance as well as wording of the CEAA rather tend to increase the element of discretion, which places environmental assessment in the political realm rather than firmly rooting it in legislation. The Bill will not effect any changes in the basic premises of environmental impact assessment and review. As Frank J. Tester points out, in 36 cases which were subjected to public panel review between the inception of the process in 1973 and January 1992, questioning of the underlying development issues was consistently discouraged and most deliberations were focused on the mitigation of negative effects. Only one proposal (a fuel barge facility planned for Vancouver Airport in 1989) was clearly rejected, and in only two other cases did the panel reviews appear to convince the proponent not to proceed.

---

[4] Friends of the Oldman River Society v. Canada (Minister of Transport) [1992] 1 S.C.R.3

Thus, while the review process has provided a forum for citizen participation, it has not offered an opportunity for successful challenges to conventional "development projects" (Tester 1992:39).

Environmental impact assessment in Canada is at a crossroads. Theory and practice of environmental review as well as its place in legislation are being challenged by the public, by the scientific community and by the courts. Contents and process of environmental impact assessment have also been put in question by aboriginal people, but their involvement or lack of involvement seem to have attracted less attention than the numerous other critical elements of the issue.[5]

EIA AND ABORIGINAL PEOPLE: PROBLEMS AND ISSUES

General Concerns

To consider the relevance of environmental impact assessment to aboriginal people, one must take into account their socio-economic reality, their political agenda and their cultural context. We have already discovered that impact assessment is a complex socio-political and anthropocentric process with ample room for subjective value judgement. The accommodation of different interest groups even within "mainstream society" is an ongoing challenge. Native people have made it very clear that they do not want to be treated as mere special interest groups (Kansky 1987a:47), but as people with special rights, with their own level of government, a distinct culture and economy and their own goals and aspirations for the future. In a system where much decision-making power is at the discretion of governments, or where regulatory powers are vested in quasi-judicial bodies like Alberta's ERCB and NRCB, whose focus is on ensuring resource development, rather than on the conservation of resources or on social concerns, political and economic power are decisive factors determining the degree to which groups can make themselves heard in the review process. To date this situation has put aboriginal people at a distinct disadvantage. A culturally and socially inappropriate setting of public hearings has often added to the alienation of native people.

Even the basic question of whether or not to participate in environmental impact assessment procedures has not always been an easy one to decide for aboriginal people.

> For many Native people across the North, and for the Haida, the settlement of claims to territory is central to the examination of whether environmental impact assessment can be a meaningful process. Participation in the process is rejected by some Natives as a legitimization of the status quo that asserts foreign sovereignty, laws and regulations over their land. To not participate, however, means even less control. Either way, they have reason to anguish. (Shapcott 1989:64)

As the last bastions of non-recognition of aboriginal claims are gradually falling in Canada, shortcomings of the contents and procedure of environmental impact assessment, as aboriginal people perceive it, need to be examined more closely. One of the most serious requests made by native people with regard to environmental impact assessment has been to be given an opportunity to provide input in the terms of reference of EIA studies which

---

[5] These pages have provided a brief and sketchy introduction to the exceedingly complex topic of environmental impact assessment, but there is a voluminous literature on this topic. A volume edited by M. Plewes and J.B.R. Whitney (1977) highlights a variety of aspects of EIA. Gordon E. Beanlands and Peter N. Duinker (1983) focus on a discussion of "An Ecological Framework for Environmental Impact Assessment in Canada", but provide a host of other useful information. Kurt Finsterbusch and C.P. Wolf (1977) edited a comprehensive "Methodology of Social Impact Assessment". In 1980, Kurt Finsterbusch introduces us to the concept of Social Impacts with his "Understanding Social Impacts". Barry Sadler (1990) discusses the transitional state of EIA in Canada. All these references provide information and extensive bibliographies but fail to shed light on an aboriginal context.

are usually far too restrictive (Kansky 1987:58, 93). Also, the kind of knowledge sought by those engaged in environmental impact assessment research is often at odds with aboriginal concepts.

> It's a big sham — a front...It's to ease people's consciences. They can say we did a study and the people didn't object. A lot of decisions aren't made by the people on the panels, but the guys who control the stock market. They're not likely to listen to someone who's been fishing for 40 years, but someone who can do experiments in a tank. That's called scientific. (Frank Collison, Vice President, Council of the Haida Nation, quoted in Shapcott 1989:62)

> Current federal and provincial processes are externally created with little meaningful input by Native people. When they are imposed on Native organizations, they often don't accomplish what they seek to. EIA and the bodies of expertise are exclusively government, university or science community issues. I think there is a huge pond of traditional wisdom in Native communities about stewardship, resources and practical realities. (Michael Robinson, Executive Director of the Arctic Institute of North America, quoted in Shapcott 1989:63)

Native people have expressed many other concerns about the prevailing practice of impact assessment, too numerous to discuss in detail (Kansky 1987a). Many of these concerns are shared by non-native Canadians. Most importantly, aboriginal communities affected by resource developments want to be involved in the EIA/SIA process from start to finish, and they want to participate in its design and implementation. "Whistlestops" by review panels in native communities are simply not enough (ibid.:6). Only if impact assessment evolves into a truly cross-cultural process can aboriginal benefits from this procedure be realized.

> Neither the courts nor the British Columbia Environmental Appeal Board can factor the social values of another culture into their decision making. The values of the dominant culture are so imbedded in the process of EIA...that alternative values cannot even be considered. As noted earlier, the underlying values — both of the culture and the process — must be changed to make environmental impact assessment meaningful to Native people. (Shapcott 1989:68)

There have been efforts to rethink social impact assessment to make it more relevant to native communities. After an exhaustive review of SIA literature and criticism, Rachel Corbett (1986) concludes that social impact assessment "has tried to be something it cannot be; that is scientific, objective, predictive and comprehensive...." (quoted in Shapcott 1989:70). She argued for an alternative approach.

> According to this approach, the purpose of SIA is not to serve decision-makers but affected communities by empowering them to make their own decisions and manage social and economic impacts themselves....As a bargaining tool, SIA enables communities to negotiate programs for impact mitigation, monitoring, and development; employment and economic benefits, and joint ventures....As a consciousness-raising and educational tool, SIA promotes open communication, helps communities learn about themselves. As a community development tool, SIA helps establish goals, build local leadership, motivate residents to participate, make decisions, manage resources, and increase its capacity to formulate, implement and evaluate policy. (Corbett 1986, quoted in Shapcott 1989:70)

This approach does not conceive of social impact assessment as a project-specific activity, but as a comprehensive community planning tool.

An integral element of this view would also be the adoption of socially and culturally appropriate forms of process and practice. To some degree this was illustrated by the Haida's participation in information hearings and public meetings of the Joint Canada/British Columbia West Coast Offshore Exploration Panel in 1984 and 1985 (Shapcott 1989:67). On one hand, they played the environmental impact assessment "game" by the rules, producing their own expert witness who gave a technical submission on impacts. On the other hand, they conducted their own internal studies and held hearings in a form and forum that was uniquely Haida.

> The Haida process...is community-based, relies heavily for direction on views of the traditional chiefs and allied elders, is holistic, dynamic, flexible, political and confrontational in a balanced way. Above all, it is the Haida way; it was not developed to fit into a southern notion of EIA. It is capable of fitting a myriad of situations, ranging from court appearances, public hearings and workshops to discussions on wharves and fishboats. (Michael Robinson, Executive Director of the Arctic Institute of North America, quoted in Shapcott 1989:69)

If social and environmental impact assessment is conducted by outsiders, it must be performed within the social and cultural context of the people involved (Waiten 1981:4). One such approach was developed in the late 1970s in connection with impact assessment for the Polar Gas Pipeline in the Keewatin District, by the staff of the Keewatin Inuit Association and the Kananaskis Centre for Environmental Research (University of Calgary). This "ethnographic" method focused primarily on an unstructured information exchange and the consensual nature of Inuit society (Tester 1980, quoted in Waiten 1981:21).

During the international Environmental Impact Assessment Workshop in Wellington, New Zealand, in 1985, aboriginal representatives (Canada's Walpole Island Band among them) offered the following recommendations:

> 1. Environmental data must be shared in a form that is both easily accessible **and** comprehensible to community members;
> 2. Native people must have full involvement in the whole process of E.I.A. planning, area-wide;
> 3. Native people have valuable knowledge and expertise and they should be involved in the development process;
> 4. Compensation, when appropriate, must contribute to the self-reliance of the Native community. It should not be just monetary but also in the form of employment in all phases of development, thus channelling the benefits back into the community again;
> 5. Native peoples must be directly involved in the decision-making process which affects their lives and their communities; and
> 6. There must be improved post-project auditing and monitoring to ensure that objectives are met and interests are protected.
>
> (Tooshkenig and Jacobs 1985:16f, emphasis in original)

For environmental and social impact assessment to be effective and relevant for aboriginal communities, native people must be involved from start to finish, and every phase and aspect of the process must be tuned in to the socio-cultural environment in which it takes place. Furthermore, there are selected issues which have been of particular significance for impact assessment in the native context: a) the preservation of native heritage values; b) basic assumptions about subsistence-oriented societies and economies which underlie impact assessments; and c) subsistence harvest studies. The first has mostly been relevant for native communities in southern Canada, the two latter are crucial for northern resource development.

Resource Development and Native Heritage Values

The consideration of resource development impacts on native heritage sites occupies a special place within the context of social and environmental impact assessment. The Stein River Valley issue in southwestern British Columbia, which was already discussed in chapter 4, is a case in point. In the extended struggle of the Lytton Band, the Lillooet Tribal Council and non-native groups to protect the Stein from logging, native heritage sites in the valley played a crucial role. These sites, consisting of pictographs and culturally modified trees, featured prominently in the logging opponents' argument for protection of the valley, and furthermore, were to constitute an important basis for alternative development options, such as low impact tourism.

The area had been subject to archaeological and ethnographic research for almost a century, and throughout the 1970s and 1980s both proponents and opponents of logging commissioned several heritage impact assessment studies for planned logging-related developments.

> A socio-historical analysis of past archaeological/ethnographic research in the Stein reveals two distinct approaches to culture and land. The first (1897–1961) was rooted in the academic and museum community, and focused on culture as a study-object, complete in and of itself. The second, beginning in the 1960s, focused on culture as a component of resource development. Unlike its earlier counterpart, this later phase of research was undertaken outside of the academic institution. Initially it focused on the popular educational and recreational potential of its subject-matter. By the 1970s, however, archaeological research became aligned with provincial land-mapping activity, itself a component of land allocation and development planning. Beginning in 1979, archaeological and ethnographic research had begun to play a role in land and resource development through the new field of impact assessment. By 1988, archaeology and ethnography had become key players in environmental/resource conflicts. (Wickwire 1991/92:54)

Wendy C. Wickwire (1991/92) provides us with an interesting analysis of how conceptual and ideological orientation affects the outcome of impact assessments. Both "sides" to the controversy used ethnographic and archaeological information to construct their argument. In the case of British Columbia Forest Products (BCFP), archaeological and ethnographic work was undertaken to comply with Section 7 of the British Columbia Heritage Conservation Act. This section required that prior to any major developments which would alter the landscape and thus endanger heritage sites, a site survey or site investigation had to be carried out to locate and evaluate heritage resources in the area, and to assess the impact on these of the proposed development. The proponent (in the case of the Stein Valley, BCFP) was responsible for funding the study and for submitting it for review to the Heritage Conservation Branch (HCB), then the department within the Ministry of Tourism, Recreation and Culture designated to manage provincial heritage resources (now the Archaeology Branch [AB] under the Ministry of Tourism and Ministry Responsible for Culture).

In the late 1980s the Lytton and Mt. Currie Indian Bands compiled their own ethnographic and archaeological reports, first in response to the BCFP study and later as a basis for their own alternative development proposal for a Stein tribal heritage park (Wickwire 1991/92:53f). Two Vancouver-based organizations, the Institute for New Economics and the Western Canada Wilderness Committee, also took part in this heritage study. Their explicit objective was to challenge the logging agenda.

Although supposedly objective and independent, the conclusions reached by the researchers retained by the respective parties in fact support the respective interests of those parties.

> ...the BCFP consultants examined the archaeological sites along the proposed haulroad and concluded that few were in danger of impact, and that where there was potential impact, this could be successfully mitigated. Meanwhile, the consultants for the native bands examined the same sites and concluded that some sites, especially pictographs, would be affected. The BCFP researchers studied the Stein trail and concluded that it was used only sporadically for battling, while the band consultants examined the trail and concluded that it was a well-used trail for a variety of peaceful cultural purposes. The Western Canada Wilderness Committee examined the heritage and culturally modified trees along the haulroad and concluded that many were in danger of damage from road-building. The BCFP archaeologists looked at the same trees and concluded that many trees should actually be cut down for scientific purposes. (ibid.:70f)

The reason for such divergent conclusions lies in two very different ideological approaches to the interpretation of heritage sites, and in the varying degree to which archaeological and ethnographic findings are mutually integrated (or fail to be integrated). British Columbia's heritage review process defines landscape narrowly as "an inventory of sites" within a development zone. Such approach arbitrarily separates individual sites from each other and from their larger context, and furthermore, reduces them to the physical remains which were left at specific locations sometime in the past. The Archaeology Branch is charged with "managing" archaeological (not ethnographic) sites and "resources", and consequently excludes ethnographic interpretation as a factor in the impact assessment except as an aid to locating sites or as providing a "setting" for the archaeological data (Wickwire 1991/92:72).

> A major weakness of the inventory approach to heritage assessment is its reliance upon tangible physical remains, to the exclusion of all else. In areas where there are habitation sites and burial sites, there will naturally be tangible remains to be assessed. In a valley like the Stein, however, which was utilized over a wide territory for hunting, fishing, spiritual, and travel purposes, tangible remains may be few and often difficult to uncover. Low archaeological visibility does not necessarily mean low archaeological significance. Because major decisions are being made on the basis of low site-density and therefore low heritage value, the criteria for defining significance need rethinking. (ibid.)

Researchers associated with the Indian bands used a more holistic approach to their assessment of the heritage value of the Stein, fully realizing the embedment of physical sites in the past and present life of the native community. Consequently they arrived at very different conclusions about the potential impact of resource development on the native heritage sites of the Stein Valley.

> An ideological choice clearly underlies the positions taken by the two parties involved in this work. For the one, protection of a living culture was key. Although changed, culture was viewed as something present and ongoing, its meaning still evident in the many sites in their living context. For the other, making an inventory of the remnants of a dead and dying culture was all that was necessary to fulfill the objectives of the formal guidelines of the Heritage Conservation Branch....
>
> While the BCFP ethnographic field study was being done in Lytton during the fall of 1985 and later in 1988, the native community was actively asserting its sovereignty over the valley in the form of an official land claim, Stein festivals, and public declarations. And yet, the BCFP ethnographic reports produced during this period declined to consider this living, vital community voice in its "use and occupation" study. This approach, which focuses on a static past to the point of failing to recognize the present in the field situation, is simply unacceptable in contemporary anthropology. (ibid.:75f)

The fact that the Nlaka'pamux Tribal Council had filed a comprehensive land claim which included the Stein Valley, and which was accepted by the federal government in 1987, is a major factor in the logging opponents' success in at least stalling resource development in this watershed. Aboriginal people are not always in a position to protect their cultural heritage resources as effectively, and sometimes have to settle for less than satisfactory mitigation measures.

Peigan resistance to the Oldman River Dam in southern Alberta ranged from negotiation over litigation to the Lonefighters' civil disobedience (see chapter 2). In addition to the unsettled state of their water rights, the threat to cultural resources in their traditional territory was a major factor prompting Peigan opposition to the project. In seeking an injunction in 1988, the Peigan invoked their right to religious freedom, as the valley contains religious sites as well as flora and fauna essential for Peigan religious practices.

In Alberta, the government department responsible for the protection of historical resources in the province is Alberta Culture. In the case of the Oldman River Dam and reservoir, Alberta Environment prepared and submitted a Historical Resources Impact Assessment and Mitigation Plan, which had to be approved by Alberta Culture. Like British Columbia's Archaeology Branch, Alberta Culture adopted a piecemeal approach focusing on the documentation of sites and on salvage archaeology, whereas the Peigan concerned themselves more about the river as a whole, which they regard as a link between themselves and the Creator.

> The Oldman River has been our link to life itself. As far as our legends go the Creator gave the Oldman River to the Peigans and the river provides intercedence between the people and the Creator and has been the base of our cultural and spiritual beliefs and values. (Chief Leonard Bastien, quoted in *Kainai News*, May 10, 1990:10)

Unless endowed with sufficient political clout to halt a project, aboriginal people usually do not find themselves in a position to enforce their holistic conservation viewpoint. But they may be able to realize selective conservation of heritage sites, a process which has been documented for the United States, and is referred to as "cultural triage" (Stoffle and Evans 1990).[6]

> Indian people make two general types of responses: **holistic conservation** ("this land is mine, go away") and **cultural triage** ("if you go ahead with the project then these are the cultural resources that require most protection"). (ibid.:91, emphasis in original)
>
> Indian people initially take a preservationist position regarding traditional cultural resources and development projects, expressing this viewpoint through holistic conservation statements. Holistic conservation positions, however, are only effective in protecting cultural resources when taking the position causes a project not to occur. If a project proceeds despite a holistic conservation position (and many projects have already been approved before Indian people are asked for a response), then Indian people must assume alternative positions in order to reduce adverse impacts and work for positive impacts. These alternative positions involve prioritizing cultural resources that are perceived to be equally valuable. This raises an ethical and intellectual dilemma, termed here the "holistic conservation — triage dilemma," for Indian people. (ibid.:94)
>
> "Cultural triage" should be defined as a forced choice situation in which an ethnic group is faced with the decision to rank in importance cultural resources that could be impacted by a proposed development project. Through this ranking the probability of certain cultural resources being protected is increased. On the other hand, it is understood that by selecting some cultural resources for special status, it relegates others to less-than-special status. Those defined as less-than-special, then, are placed at greater risk from the proposed project.
>
> Medical professionals who triage patients accept the principle that all human life is valuable and similarly, Indian cultural experts...who triage cultural resources accept the principle that all traditional cultural resources are of equal importance. Triage occurs when a threatening situation precipitates a forced choice in the allocation of limited resources, a choice that must be based on some criteria. (ibid.:95f)

It goes without saying that cultural triage involves considerable risk to cultural resources as well as to aboriginal people who agree to participate in the process. The requirements of the process and all parties involved are onerous, indeed.

In California there is an agency specifically charged with safeguarding religious and cultural heritage rights of First Nations: The Native American Heritage Commission (NAHC) which was created by the Governor of the State of California under AB-4239 in 1976. The Commission's task is to identify and catalogue places of cultural significance, to develop protective measures for sacred places and to ensure appropriate native American access for ceremonial activities to those places located on public lands (Evans 1981:1). The nine commissioners are appointed by the Governor with the consent of the Senate. Five or more

---

[6] " 'Triage' is a Euroamerican medical term that refers to 'screening of patients to determine their priority for treatment' (Stedman 1982:1322). Triage is the process of rationing life-saving medical resources among patients who have varying levels of need (Winslow 1982). Patients are ranked according to criteria that reflect an agreed-upon value position, such as 'the greatest good for the greatest number.' A choice can be forced when war creates more wounded than a medical facility can assist at one time, or when a new medical advance, such as the artificial heart, is more limited in supply than in demand. **The crux of medical triage is that professionals must develop a corollary rule that partially violates the general principle from which it derives.**" (Stoffle and Evans 1990:95, emphasis added)

appointees are native elders, traditionalists or spiritual leaders nominated by Indian organizations or tribes within the State. Customarily commissioners have been California Indians. The Heritage Commission's primary responsibility is responding to requests for assistance from Indian communities. In this capacity it often functions as a mediator or facilitator between government agencies and local communities.

During its years of activity the Commission has come to realize the importance of understanding and involving itself with federal and state environmental protection laws, such as the National Environmental Policy Act (NEPA) of 1969 and the California Environmental Quality Act (CEQA) of 1970 (ibid.:4). In 1980 the Commission published a Cultural Resources Handbook, which provides a step-by-step analysis of the laws protecting cultural resources and guidelines how to use them effectively. The Native American Religious Freedom Act (PL-95-341), passed in 1978, acts as an additional safeguard reinforcing constitutional protection of free exercise of religion by aboriginal people.

While appropriate legislation appears to be in place in California, much still depends on timely action and effective communication on the part of native people. Uncertainty and differences of opinion between Indians and heritage impact assessment researchers persist, particularly when it comes to the documentation of current land use or the identification of sites lacking artifactual material. There may also be disagreement between archaeologists and native people about the mitigation measures they would recommend for human burials and ceremonial sites.

In order to improve the review process, the Commission has strongly recommended the presence of a local native American monitor on archaeological crews, and in long-term projects, the formation of a native American advisory council. These recommendations have been successfully implemented. The Heritage Commission operates a county referral system, which puts development agencies into contact with Indian monitors for archaeological crews, elders and other cultural resource persons. In order to safeguard responsive action in the long-range future, the Commission initiated a Sacred Lands Study in the 1980s. This project inventoried and catalogued all places of religious or social significance to California Indians. It was designed as a proactive rather than reactive measure which would serve the needs of both the native American community and government agencies (ibid.:6).

> The confidential nature of this material is of primary concern to California Indians who have suffered for more than a century from deliberate and unintentional destruction of those places most meaningful to them. Secrecy has often been the only means of protecting them. But now that energy related projects, such as pipelines and geothermal, wind, and nuclear facilities are proposed for previously remote and unspoiled areas, they are realizing that registering these sites with NAHC may by a more successful means of protection.
>
> The inventory provided by the Sacred Lands Study will allow the NAHC to function as a clearinghouse for energy-related projects. Bringing a regional inventory to the attention of public agencies at the announcement of a project and, at the same time, alerting those Indian communities and individuals whose heritage is involved, will make possible mitigation measures which are discussed and agreed upon by both parties. (ibid.:7)

Aboriginal Communities and Impact Assessment: The Need for a New Paradigm

The importance of perception and ideology has been noted in regard to heritage impact assessment, but this factor is equally important as it pertains to social and environmental impact assessment in general. It has far-reaching implications for northern aboriginal communities. Social impact assessment research and the evaluation of its results are inextricably tied to the researchers' and evaluators' perception of the society they are operating in and their general paradigm of social change.

> The origins of SIA as a practical technique lie in cost-benefit analysis, economic assessment, and social indicator research. As an applied form of social science, the subject matter of SIA is **social change**. So we must also ask, what is our theory of social change, and how does that influence the questions we ask, the data we gather, and the hypotheses we test. SIA is inevitably informed by the general theories or paradigms of social change that have developed in the social sciences (and become part of popular convention), whether these are explicitly acknowledged, or implicit in the terms of reference and the choice of variables assessed. These paradigms may be reduced in essence to two, which in the present context may be labelled acculturation/modernization, and subsistence/response (although they are rarely identified explicitly as such and there is no standardized terminology for them). (Weinstein et al. 1992:8f, emphasis in original)

These two models (the latter of which they term "subsistence/adaptation") are described in more detail by Peter Douglas Elias and Martin Weinstein.

> The modernization/acculturation model assumes there is an essential similarity between the impact assessments required for northern aboriginal communities and other Canadian populations. The model assumes that hunting, trapping, and fishing will be replaced by wage-labour and business as the means for making a living and that this process represents an inevitable and universal step in human progress. In this view, bringing development to the "door-step" of an Indian band represents an opportunity to modernize and share in the benefits of progress. Concerns about impacts to land and resources are limited to recreation use and sentimental values. Environmental impacts are not seen as economic issues because hunting and fishing and gathering are not considered economic activities; trapping has validity as an economic activity only because it results in the production of a saleable commodity. This model assumes that Indian people hunt and fish for their livelihood because other opportunities are not available and, if they were, hunting and fishing would become recreational activities. The model is distinctly ethnocentric.
>
> The modernization/acculturation model was created to guide development and change in agricultural societies. The theory behind the model does not take into account fundamental differences between agricultural societies and hunter-gatherer societies. The subsistence/adaptation model for impact assessment is more appropriate, at least for northern aboriginal communities. This model assumes that land and resource use is a primary value for aboriginal societies, one of the valued things that needs to be assessed. The model treats subsistence as a system inextricably linking the natural environment, the biology and productivity of animal and plant resources, the history of the human occupation. Local culture is based on hunting, trapping, fishing and gathering, including critical elements of satisfaction and meaning in life, economic well-being, and recreational preferences. Ideas of how life should be lived are fundamentally tied to being on the land. We cannot assume aboriginal resource harvesters will eagerly give up their way of life in exchange for wages. Rather, in northern aboriginal communities, wage earners typically combine rather casual employment and resource harvesting, by deciding how best to use and manage lands, time and cash. The result is the mixed economy. (Elias and Weinstein 1992, Vol. 1:5f)

Traditionally, social impact assessment in northern communities (where it was conducted at all) has been patterned after the modernization/acculturation model, and as a result has ultimately failed to accurately predict or successfully manage socio-economic impacts of resource developments. The past two decades have shown that the effects of industrial resource developments on small, northern aboriginal communities are fundamentally different from those on non-aboriginal communities. Studies conducted in various communities from Labrador and James Bay to Yukon and Alaska show the enduring importance of wildlife, fish and plant resources in the livelihood of native people. The reason for this is that renewable resources do not merely constitute the economic base for aboriginal communities, but their harvesting provides **the** major integrative social force. The environment people depend upon for their livelihood provides the very matrix for their society.

> This way-of-life is distinguished not simply by reliance on the natural productivity of habitat, but by social linkages, institutions and values which are mediated through resources....
>
> Subsistence is, at its most fundamental level a system of social relations. The system of relations embracing production, distribution, and consumption in mixed economies are typically organized in households. More elaborate kin relations, political alliances, or shared land interests are often the basis for more-or-less enduring arrangements of several households. The principles of kinship, alliance, and land tenure organize economic relations on a household, inter-household, and community basis and help to set the mixed economy apart from market economies. Households and alliances of households also form pools of labour, capital and technology necessary for the successful operation of the mixed economy. Harvesting requires particular, well-polished skills and earning cash may require a quite different set of skills. The household serves as a pool bringing together the skills needed for effective economic operation....
>
> ...Subsistence societies tend to be conservative because of their concern with system stability and maintenance. Consequently, environmental change is viewed with deep concern since the land lends ultimate stability to social order and security. The social system is maintained and reproduced through institutions that organize work and mutual aid centered on harvesting, food and fur preparation, gifting and sharing, ceremonialism, feasting, and ritual observance. These institutions are wholly adapted to the local environment and constraints of resource productivity, abundance and distribution. (Elias and Weinstein 1992, Vol. 1:7f)

For social and environmental impact assessment to be constructive under these conditions, it is of paramount importance that researchers, assessors and decision makers develop a thorough understanding and appreciation of subsistence (domestic, mixed — the terminology varies) economies. A generic model of the socio-economic system in question is still being elaborated by practitioners, there is no textbook version (Weinstein et al. 1992:10). Nevertheless, advanced attempts at such modelling are currently in use in social impact assessments in the North, as exemplified by Peter J. Usher's report for the Grand Council of the Crees (of Quebec) in conjunction with the Great Whale Project impact study (Usher 1992a) and by Peter Douglas Elias' and Martin Weinstein's study for the Kaska Dena Council in northern British Columbia (Elias and Weinstein 1992; see section on Development and the Indian Peopele of Fort Ware of this chapter).

Just as native culture must be viewed as something living and ongoing when it comes to native heritage impact assessment, northern aboriginal mixed subsistence economies must be conceived of as socio-economic systems which can develop and change, while still retaining their essential material and institutional features.

Subsistence Harvest Studies

Resource harvesting is a central and integrative activity in northern native communities. As the "science" of environmental impact assessment is coming to terms with the ideological issue of perceiving subsistence as a viable and ongoing socio-economic system, it is faced with another problem, this time of a technical nature: native harvest surveys. Quantitative estimates of native harvests are crucial for impact assessment, mitigation and compensation, and they are also important for basic research in the social and biological sciences, resource management and allocation, and economic planning.

Harvest statistics are counts, or estimates, of the number of a particular species of fish or wildlife taken over a specified period of time in a specific area by a particular group of people. The resulting data may thus be presented as totals for either a geographical area or a category of harvesters (Usher and Wenzel 1987:145). According to Peter J. Usher and George Wenzel (ibid.), the term "native harvest survey" seems to have come into common use as a result of the implementation of the James Bay and Northern Quebec Agreement of 1975. This Agreement stipulated five-year surveys of the Cree and Inuit harvests to provide a basis for minimum preferential allocations on a species-by-species basis to these two aboriginal groups. Similar surveys were conducted in anticipation of Inuit claims in the eastern and central Northwest Territories. These repetitive and comprehensive surveys rely exclusively on harvester recall for their harvest data, and have usually been conducted with a considerable degree of local initiative and control.

Where for some reason it is not possible to collect original data, there are two other, less satisfactory sources of information. One consists of a number of administrative data sets, such as those compiled by fish and wildlife agencies for the purpose of licensing, Fur Export Tax returns, etc. While these are usually characterized by historical depth and wide geographic coverage, they are of doubtful reliability due to poor design, lack of reporting incentive and the possibility of deliberate misrepresentation of catch (ibid.:148).

The second possible source of harvest information is provided by estimates of native harvests in biological and social scientific literature. However, the purposes of these estimates and the methodology vary widely and tend to be idiosyncratic. They do not lend themselves to comparison over time and space (ibid.:146).

Over the last two decades industry and government have become reluctant to rely on conventional wildlife agency statistics as the sole basis for estimating native harvests and, like the native organizations, have come to employ hunter recall surveys in their studies. Due to the special nature of this research, obtaining and interpreting data is anything but unproblematic.

> Biologists, like social scientists, have relied mainly on hunter recall surveys to obtain native harvest data. These surveys are in principle no different from any other kind of social survey. Even though the resulting data may be of primary use to wildlife scientists and management agencies, the data themselves are social in nature: they are reports by human beings about their own activities and their consequences. There seems to have been inadequate recognition on the part of biologists that harvest surveys are not biological but social in nature and consequently require the application of social scientific techniques for their conduct and interpretation. (ibid.:152)

With regard to any set of harvest data, five parameters need to be specified: harvest, categories, time, area and harvesters. Considering the various objectives of harvest data collection, in particular the somewhat divergent needs of wildlife management and socio-economic analysis, we may assume that these parameters may be defined differently in each case. This, however, tends to be done implicitly rather than explicitly (ibid.). Anne Gunn and her coauthors comment on this problem in conjunction with the Kitikmeot Harvest Study during the 1980s, which was cooperatively conducted by the Kitikmeot Hunters and Trappers Association and the NWT's Department of Renewable Resources.

> More discussions with the fieldworkers are planned through a workshop in fall 1986 to evaluate and define exactly what is being reported. For example, the role of trap loss, non-retrieval, and non-consumption or use of different species may be significant but are only partially reported. From a wildlife management perspective, it is the total number lost to a population regardless of use or non-use (non-retrieval, etc.) that is important in evaluating a harvest. The extent and causes of non-retrieval or non-consumption of harvested wildlife are becoming more important to wildlife managers as the ethics of hunting come under increasing public scrutiny. From a perspective of evaluating subsistence levels, it is the consumptive use of game that is important. Discussions with fieldworkers would refine the definition of terms and possibly lead to measures of some of the possible discrepancies between kill and use. Some data such as a measure of trap loss of foxes could be used as the basis for more effective use of renewable resources. (Gunn et al. 1986:258)

Each parameter thus requires careful attention to detail and purpose. The same is true for various aspects of the survey methods, particularly in a cross-cultural situation. Sampling methods need to be accounted for, and the possibility of a non-response bias as well as a response bias must always be borne in mind. The former refers to the possibility that those individuals who choose not to participate in a survey, may in some significant way differ from those who do — for example, that they are the top harvesters, or that they do not harvest at all (Usher and Wenzel 1987:154). Response bias, on the other hand, arises from the fact that in any social survey there may be a discrepancy between the true answer to a question and the respondent's answer to it. There are many possible reasons for this, such as poor questionnaire/interview design, recall failure, bias introduced by the interviewer, or strategizing on the part of the respondent (ibid.).

In a study concerned with assessing the effects on native resource harvesting of the Lake Winnipeg Regulation (LWR) and the Churchill River Diversion (CRD) in northern Manitoba, Peter J. Usher and Martin S. Weinstein point to the problem of choosing the right indicators to assess the impact. In retroactive impact assessments, harvest data often fail to reveal adaptive strategies on the part of the harvesters.

> LWR/CRD appears to have had adverse effects on commercial fishing in each of the NFA [Northern Flood Agreement] zones. The effects vary: the Cross Lake fishery has experienced a sharp decline in production, the Nelson House fishery has been partially contaminated by mercury, and the cost of fishing has increased at Norway House and possibly also at Split Lake. The respective domestic fisheries have probably been affected in the same ways.
>
> These effects are only partially revealed by the indicators used here — volume, value, and participation — for which administrative and monitoring data are available. The response by fishermen to adverse physical and biological effects has, in some cases, been the intensification of individual effort to maintain production levels. This adaptive strategy in response to declining catch per unit of effort was documented at South Indian Lake by Waldram (1983), using the following indicators: capital equipment, net utilization, frequency of net relocation, travel distance, length of working day, and gasoline consumption. No such indicator data are available and no monitoring system has been devised to measure this response in NFA communities. (Usher and Weinstein 1991:33)[7]

SELECTED NATIVE EXPERIENCES AND GOVERNMENT PROCEDURES

Dismal Beginnings

Until well into the 1970s major resource development projects were undertaken without any consideration for their environmental and social effects. In other cases, crash environmental and social studies were conducted as an afterthought, once the projects were underway.

The first category is exemplified by hydro-power developments, such as the W.A.C. Bennett Dam in British Columbia (1968) and the Churchill-Nelson River Hydro Project in Manitoba (1974) (see chapter 2) and by mining projects like the Cyprus Anvil Mine in Yukon (mid-1960s) (see chapter 7). Invariably these projects had severe environmental and socio-economic consequences, and it has mostly been up to aboriginal communities "to pick up the pieces". Decades later, they are still trying to do just that. The implementation of the Northern Flood Agreement in northern Manitoba has been an ongoing struggle ever since its signing in 1977, and in the early 1990s, researchers like Peter J. Usher and Martin S. Weinstein are only beginning to assess the effects of river diversion and lake regulation on native resource harvesting, coming not even close to a comprehensive socio-economic impact assessment (Usher and Weinstein 1991:1). With regard to the Cyprus Anvil Mine, the Ross River Dena Council commissioned a retrospective impact assessment study to provide a basis for possible mitigative and compensatory measures (Weinstein 1992).

In the eastern Arctic, in the North Baffin Region, spring 1976 witnessed the construction of the Nanisivik lead and zinc mine. R. Gibson investigated the decision-making process

[7] For further information on fisheries harvest studies, see Berkes 1990 and Usher 1992b.

for the Nanisivik mine to determine its efficiency, effectiveness and its sensitivity to northern and native interests.

> The federal government failed to ensure meaningful consultation with the people to be affected and proceeded without a thorough assessment of potential social impact, despite the spirit and letter of its own official northern development policy and the advice and recommendations of its own experts. Similarly, the government failed to carry out an environmental impact assessment or even to collect essential baseline data prior to the decision, in contravention of an explicit Cabinet directive which required such an assessment before any commitments or irrevocable decisions were made. (Gibson 1978:149f, quoted in Jacobs and Fenge 1990:277f)

The terms and conditions for operation of the mine provided for a socio-economic impact study once the mine had been in operation for several years. Upon pressure from the Baffin Regional Inuit Association (BRIA) this study was carried out in 1978, focusing primarily on the effectiveness of the native employment program and on the impact of mine employment on native workers and their families. The research procedure was cooperatively designed by representatives from INAC, Government of the NWT, Nanisivik Mines and BRIA. The methodology employed included interviews and questionnaires. The study's outcome can only be characterized as ineffectual. The response rate was extremely low, which was due in part to the unavailability of people away on hunting and trapping trips, but also to the general impression that little would come of the study, and finally, to the incomprehensibility of the questionnaires (Waiten 1981:115f). As Cathy Waiten points out, such dismal response record appears to lend support to a culturally more sensitive method such as Tester's ethnographic approach (see earlier section of this chapter; Waiten 1981:116).

The dismal impact assessment record in the Lancaster Sound region continued with the establishment of the Polaris mine on Little Cornwallis Island in the early 1980s. As in the Nanisivik debate, the Inuit played a very limited and mostly reactive role in the decision-making process for the mine. The environmental assessment and review process of the project was waived by the Minister of Indian Affairs and Northern Development, as it had been for Nanisivik (Jacobs and Fenge 1990:278f).

> In summary, both the Nanisivik and Polaris projects were portrayed by the Federal Government as economically beneficial to the North but the federal view of northern needs was overly narrow. Social impacts of the projects, including their effects on the renewable resource economy, were not major concerns in federal-industry decision making. (ibid.:280)

Formative Years

Justice Thomas Berger's Mackenzie Valley Pipeline Inquiry was instrumental in changing the character of northern development and also ushered in a new era of environmental review processes. Not surprisingly, it was in the Mackenzie Valley and the Beaufort Sea Region where innovative frameworks for social and environmental review first became manifest.

One example is the use of Canada benefits requirements to assist in managing the impacts of hydrocarbon development on northern native communities. It started with the formation of the Canada Oil and Gas Lands Administration (COGLA) as a regulatory agency in 1981. For project authorization COGLA required that a resource company submit a benefits plan prior to commencing work and an annual report for each year the project was active. COGLA consulted with other federal departments and with provincial, territorial and local organizations when it reviewed documents submitted by the companies.

A typical action plan, as exemplified by Dome Petroleum's 1984 plan for the Beaufort activities, included detailed intentions with regard to northern employment, northern training, northern business development, community consultation and information, northern cultural and social programs, and social and environmental monitoring (The DPA Group Inc. 1986:22).

The emphasis of these plans was clearly on economic impacts, with considerable attention to detail. Little effort was directed at monitoring socio-economic trends or social change, however (ibid.). According to DPA, the COGLA requirements generated definite benefits to the Beaufort region, including an impressive northern employment record, stimulation of local businesses and the provision of community infrastructure. A particular innovation in the North has been the use of a variety of approaches to support local business development, such as joint ventures, offering administrative and technical support, technology transfer, and the provision of long-term contracts to stabilize the cash flow of northern companies. Observers have interpreted COGLA's regulatory power as an important factor for the commitment of the oil industry to northern development. This situation contrasts with the absence of any significant policies or action on the part of oil companies in the provinces where regulations are much less stringent. Furthermore, reports to COGLA were made public which allowed each company's performance to be compared to the industry as a whole. This added an important public relations element (ibid.:22f).

The strategy employed by COGLA as a regulatory agency resulted in a review process which was concerned with the monitoring and management of impacts rather than with their forecasting. The same is true — with regard to the physical environment — for the Beaufort Environmental Monitoring Program (BEMP), an interdisciplinary program geared to facilitate research and management decisions for the Beaufort Sea Region.

As previously mentioned, exploration for offshore oil and gas in the Canadian Beaufort Sea has been underway for approximately two decades. Promising results led to serious consideration of hydrocarbon production possibilities in the region. The potential development activities were referred to the Federal Environment Assessment and Review Office (FEARO) in 1980. An environmental impact statement was produced and extensive public hearings were held under the EARP process in both northern and southern Canada.

Native people's reaction to the development proposals and the EARP process seems to have been rather mixed. Virtually all groups (Council for Yukon Indians, Inuit Tapirisat of Canada, the Dene Nation) expressed reservations about development decisions prior to the settlement of comprehensive claims, and they also criticized the absence of a comprehensive land use plan. Furthermore, community residents were unhappy with the "whistlestop" character of the consultation process, and they desired more appropriate consideration of their land-based economy in the assessment process (Kansky 1988:5–7; 13–15; 23–40).

> The EIS should indicate the value of hunting using the following indicators: an individual's worth in his eyes and in the community, the function of harvesting activities in family relationships and the community, the length of time invested in learning about hunting and survival skills, the length of time in passing on skills to younger Inuit and the cash and in-kind value of harvesting activities. These are important in assessing cultural and socio-economic impacts that may result from impacts on the environment. (Baffin Regional Inuit Association at Beaufort Sea Environmental Assessment Panel, 1983, quoted in Kansky 1988:21)

People also expressed a desire to be involved in future surveillance and compliance monitoring of development projects (ibid.:26).

In 1984 the EARP panel released its report with the recommendation that a phased development of Beaufort Sea hydrocarbons could be compatible with sound environmental management, conditional upon the implementation of a substantial number of mitigative measures. While EARP did provide a mechanism to deliver a recommendation on whether or not to proceed with Beaufort Sea production, it was unable to reliably predict the impacts of development, which was in part due to the limited understanding of Arctic ecosystem processes, compounded by uncertainties about innovative technologies proposed by the industry (Everitt et al. 1990:252).

To resolve this problem, Indian and Northern Affairs and Environment Canada cooperatively introduced the Beaufort Environmental Monitoring Program (BEMP) as an interdisciplinary tool to facilitate impact management decisions for the Beaufort Sea region. The general approach adopted by the project was the use of Adaptive Environmental Assessment and Management (AEAM) techniques to create a computer simulation model of the biophysical processes of the Beaufort Sea. The conceptual model which underlay the simulation model provided the framework for the creation of a set of impact hypotheses. These hypotheses, rigorously evaluated and refined in several workshops, became the basis for the proposed monitoring and research (ibid.:253).

Robert R. Everitt and his coauthors remain silent as to local native involvement in design and execution of the monitoring program. As a whole it appears to have been highly technical and mostly lacking in cross-cultural interchange of knowledge. Nevertheless, in the definition of valued ecosystem components (always a subjective judgement call), local aboriginal communities were considered.

> In the context of BEMP valued ecosystem components are **those resources or environmental features that are important to local human populations**; or have potential national or international profiles; and if altered from their existing status, will be important in evaluating the impacts of development and in focusing management or regulatory policy. **The final list of VECs reveals the subjective judgement of the participants in BEMP that the harvests, populations and habitat for fish and wildlife were of primary concern**. (ibid.:255; emphasis added)

BEMP's success as an adaptive management tool prompted the federal government and the Government of the NWT in 1985 to initiate a similar on-shore program — the Mackenzie Valley Environmental Monitoring Program (MEMP) for the delta and potential pipeline corridor. Similar in concept to BEMP, MEMP was undertaken to recommend a scientifically defensible monitoring and research program, which would address the potential impacts of oil and gas development in the Mackenzie Valley and Delta. While MEMP was primarily a biophysical monitoring program, it also had a substantial resource harvesting component (Everitt 1986:45). The inclusion of such a component necessarily meant that native northerners would have a strong voice in MEMP. Native community residents from the Mackenzie Valley, the Great Bear Region, the Mackenzie Delta and along the Beaufort Sea had an important influence over the direction of the project and the development of the impact hypotheses.

> During MEMP, it became clear that trained scientists and Native communities have differing views about what constitutes a significant effect. A careful review of all the MEMP hypotheses will show that those hypotheses not concerned with harvesting are species specific and look at regional impacts; and the resource harvesting hypotheses are not species specific but are concerned with community level effects. Most of the hypotheses that look at the direct effects on fish and wildlife are unconcerned with local effects that do not have an effect at the population level. However, it is local effects that are of prime concern to a community. What this shows is that monitoring to determine the effects on resource harvesting must be community based. For resource harvesting, local effects are all important. (ibid.)

For several years, aboriginal communities have argued for a strong role in the monitoring of the effects of energy development in the North. Native people have been hired by the oil companies to act as surveillance monitors on seismic operations, and as polar bear monitors for offshore drilling activities. In general, however, the communities have had little say in the design and conduct of monitoring programs to assess the environmental impact of hydrocarbon developments (Everitt 1986:44).

> The experience with MEMP shows that Native people should be involved right from the start in the design of the program. There are two reasons for this. First, success of the

> monitoring will likely depend on Native cooperation; early involvement is a test to ascertain the degree of cooperation to be expected. Second, Native involvement is a valuable source of information on monitoring priorities.
>
> Northern communities should be given contracts to undertake surveillance and local effects monitoring. Native groups should undertake surveillance monitoring programs for those energy development activities that have direct effect (e.g. seismic activity) on the land and its resources. Monitors should be responsible to the community and not the development companies as is currently the case. While monitoring to determine the local effects may require scientific expertise, the community should direct the programs. It needs to be emphasized that data from scientific sampling projects is only one source of the information available on local effects. The people themselves are often the most effective monitors because they are present at all times.
>
> The role of Native groups in monitoring programs designed to determine the regional effects is less clear....It seems likely that the conduct of programs to look at the regional impacts will likely remain in the domain of the scientific community, particularly those concerned with wildlife management. However, the role of the Native groups will be in setting the scope and priorities of these programs. This too may change dramatically in the near future as Native control of wildlife management increases as a result of land claims. (ibid.:47)

COGLA's regulatory measures, BEMP and MEMP, clearly show that in the 1980s and 1990s the North is no longer treated as an economic hinterland of southern Canada. In impact assessments on the biophysical environment, aboriginal subsistence resources are accorded the respect and consideration they deserve. When it comes to economic benefits, northern communities have come to recognition as respected partners and as beneficiaries deserving of special consideration. But a closer look at impact assessment and review procedures reveals that the northern mixed economy and the culture that supports it and is supported by it, have not yet been fully integrated in the process and in the contents of contemporary impact assessment in northern Canada. This final step seems to have been reserved for those impact assessment and review procedures that are initiated and guided by the aboriginal communities themselves.

ABORIGINAL INITIATIVES IN IMPACT ASSESSMENT AND REVIEW

Oil Sands Development and the Cold Lake Indian Band in Northern Alberta

In 1978 Esso Resources Canada Limited applied to the Alberta government to build a heavy oil extraction and upgrading facility on 143 square kilometres of leased land within six kilometres of the Cold Lake Indian Reserve. Esso and the Alberta Energy Resources Conservation Board were of the opinion that regional and national benefits to be derived from this project outweighed any negative impacts within the project area. The Cold Lake Band did not share this view and, as a means of assessing the validity of Esso's position, decided to undertake an evaluation of the effects of similar developments (Suncor, Syncrude and Amoco Oil sands plants) on comparable native communities in the Athabasca Oil Sands Region (in particular Fort McMurray and Fort McKay) (Waiten 1981:107).

> The study project may be viewed as a model for increasing tribal or band control over the SIA production process and as an Indian community's response to the usually serious deficiencies of company or proponent-funded and controlled socio-economic and community impact assessments of their projects as they relate to Native Indian communities. The study project represents a rather unique approach to social impact assessment formulation and implementation. (Justus and Simonetta 1982:239; consultants retained by the Cold Lake Band)
>
> It was the first occasion where one Indian community **anticipating** major impacts undertook its own analysis and evaluation of impacts **already incurred** by other Indian communities

> in the same region from heavy oil sands development. Also unique to this study approach was the central importance placed on the perceived impacts expressed by the Indian people directly affected by existing oil sands development as it was revealed **through research conducted in the Indian languages of the area by researchers who share a common cultural and linguistic background and a legitimate "need to know"**. The degree of "fit" between the perceived impacts of those directly affected in the communities was also assessed against agency statistics and interviews with key personnel in public agencies and industry in the area. Overall, this assisted in the development of local strategies to more effectively deal with situations produced by rapid development before, during and after implementation. (Justus and Simonetta 1982:241; emphasis in original)

A steering committee of band members and Indian Affairs representatives was formed to draft the terms of reference for this study. A major constraint was a delay in securing the necessary funding. By the time it was in place, the project had already been approved, and the "no-go" option no longer existed. Consequently, the Band concentrated its efforts on strategies to prevent or minimize adverse impacts and to enhance potential benefits (ibid.:240).

The reason for selecting the Athabasca Tribal Council communities of Fort McKay, Fort McMurray and Fort Chipewyan for comparison was that, like the Cold Lake Band, they were composed of Cree and Chipewyan people, and they were hunting and trapping societies based on family production units. All the bands were extensively involved in the traditional land-based economy as well as in seasonal wage employment. Just as the Cold Lake Band was the closest human settlement to the proposed Esso project, the Fort McKay Band was the closest community to the Syncrude project. Both development projects occupied traditional hunting, trapping and food gathering lands of the respective bands. Since the 1960s the Fort McKay Band had directly experienced the impact of oil sands plant development and was, therefore, selected at the outset of the fieldwork for particularly intensive research (ibid.:240f).

The Fort McKay people were also in a position to relate their own experiences with the Alberta Oil Sands Environmental Research Program (AOSERP), a 10-year program established by agreement between the governments of Alberta and Canada in 1975, to direct and coordinate research projects concerned with the environmental impact of Athabasca Oil Sands in Alberta. By 1983, after having spent more than $19 million on its four components — land, water, air and human systems — the program had concluded that a) there had occurred no detectable environmental changes in the oil sands area, and b) that any changes that might have taken place, did not constitute a problem (Fort McKay Band et al. 1983:21). The people from Fort McKay considered the whole research project a farce, not only because of more than a decade of delay in establishing a baseline data bank, but also because of the ultimate failure to consult those people most intimately associated with the land.

> It would seem that the most logical decision would have been to consult the McKay people who live in the closest proximity to the projects and whose Indian economy depends on resource harvesting. The Athabasca River, their primary source of drinking water since time immemorial, became so polluted that they could not even wash their clothes in it without breaking out in skin rashes, so the assertion that there have been "no detectable" environmental changes in the area is bizarre. Ft. McKay hunters and trappers have detailed knowledge of the changes in the plants and the animals, the water and the air and yet they were never asked if they had noticed any changes over the years. These hunters and trappers are dependent on nature when they are out in the bush, yet McKay requests for information on the results of AOSERP research in terms of answering the question, "Is it safe to drink the snow melt water?" were met instead with a presentation on the structure and function of the research program by an Alberta Environment AOSERP representative that visited the community.
>
> In short, there is a total lack of fit between the McKay observations and experiences of environmental impacts since the coming of the oil sands plants and the apparent belief by governments and industry that everything is fine in the Athabasca Oil Sands area....Perhaps

> one of the most frightening omissions of the programs was that not one cent was spent on research into the implications of oil sands for human health in the area, and particularly for the health of McKay people, who depend so much on the land and water that are being polluted for their well-being. Not to mention alcohol and drug abuse problems in the community which are a direct result of people being forced to rapidly adopt a new way of life and new value system without being given time to assess whether they wished to enter this alternative system and if so on what terms. (Fort McKay Band et al. 1983:21f)

The research of the Cold Lake Band focused on project-related effects on the community's ability to manage itself and to provide a high quality of life for its members as defined by the community (Justus and Simonetta 1982:244). As a starting point, baseline profiling of the Cold Lake Band prior to the proposed Esso project served four distinct purposes:

> 1. It showed the past impacts of other developments in the area since 1950 to have been largely negative;
> 2. It showed that the Cold Lake Band was already at a critical level of stress;
> 3. It provided a baseline from which to predict future impacts from the Esso project; and
> 4. It provided a baseline from which to measure actual impacts as the Esso project proceeds. (ibid.:247)

Afterwards the impacts of the Suncor, Syncrude and Amoco projects on affected Indian communities were identified, assessed and evaluated, through the perception of people directly affected by the developments and the analysis of agency records and the views of agency personnel with first-hand knowledge of the communities. Of particular interest was the advice to the Cold Lake Band given by those with fifteen years of experience of the effects of oil sands projects on their doorstep:

> 1. Safeguard the environment, resources and wildlife;
> 2. Take all the benefits it is possible to get from the company;
> 3. Assure that Band members will get jobs with the company;
> 4. Be wary of and deal carefully with non-Natives and restrict their entrance to your lands;
> 5. Secure adequate education and training for Band members so that they qualify for good jobs;
> 6. Be aware of all the implications before you make any agreements;
> 7. Secure business development opportunities for the Band;
> 8. Assure that a company liaison representative with decision making authority is permanently available to the Band to provide information on all developments before they happen;
> 9. Ensure transportation is provided by the company for all Band members who may be employed;
> 10. Watch out for problems with the unions;
> 11. Secure all promises in writing;
> 12. Ensure that environmental impact information is provided to the band in language that can be easily understood;
> 13. Maintain Indian control of all Band lands and resources; and
> 14. Keep Band members informed of all developments and involved in the decision making. (Justus and Simonetta 1982:248)

The impacts of the Suncor, Syncrude and Amoco projects on the native communities in the region may be summarized as follows.

> 1. Deterioration of the social fabric of the community, as evidenced by increased alcohol and drug abuse, increased violence, decreased sense of security, increased family breakdowns, loss of kin support and overall lack of community solidarity;
> 2. Lack of improvement in the standard of living, in terms of infrastructure, health conditions and transportation;
> 3. Degradation of the physical environment and the natural resource base;
> 4. Deterioration of economic stability with the loss of access to and reduced yields from hunting, trapping, fishing, gathering and resultant increased debt loads;

5. Until very recently, relatively little participation in potential employment opportunities with Suncor, Syncrude or Amoco, as evidenced by the number of local Indian employees and the degree of dependence on social assistance payments;
6. Lack of effective access to career or trades job opportunities as evidenced by the high number of labour or menial jobs held;
7. Lack of meaningful long-term job opportunities as evidenced by the overall short average length of employment; and
8. An overall decline in the ability of the Indian communities to manage themselves and provide for the basic and essential needs of their members. (ibid.:249)

These findings clearly indicated that there had been serious disruptions in the social fabric of the aboriginal communities in the Athabasca Oil Sands area which tended to be most severe for those communities closest to the plant facilities.

> Changes in the biophysical and human environments of these communities and their attendant costs were significant, adverse and not fully understood....
>
> The main conclusion to be derived from the experience of the Athabasca Tribal Council communities and their advice to the Cold Lake Band faced with the massive Esso project is that in order to derive any lasting benefits from the proposed project the community must deal from a position of strength. A strong and dedicated leadership is required. Infrastructure, social services and related programs must be in place prior to any development and the Indian bands must maintain **full control** over their lives, lands and resources. (ibid.:249f; emphasis in original)

Based on these conclusions, the Cold Lake Band leaders and their consultants proceeded to develop a list of mitigative measures that would help safeguard Band interests and the integrity of the community. These proposed measures covered a wide range of areas: the biophysical environment, community health, education and training, employment and business development, reserve infrastructure and social services, transportation and the negotiation of a company-band agreement (ibid.:250–252). While the Band was interested in project-related employment, it did not want to be tied to the rise and fall of the Esso-project. Its major concern was the development of the community to a stage of self-sufficiency, while retaining different options for its members to pursue their livelihood.

According to Roger Justus and JoAnne Simonetta, by the 1980s federal government support for Indian bands likely to be affected by major resource development projects had considerably increased, compared to the 1960s and 1970s. Not only Indian and Inuit Affairs, but also Health and Welfare Canada and Environment Canada had accepted an increasing amount of responsibility for supporting Indian band efforts at impact identification, assessment and management through research, training, negotiations and interventions in the regulatory hearing process (Justus and Simonetta 1982:253). The authors also detected a new trend toward long-term formal negotiations with regard to project modification and impact management as an alternative to direct confrontation and costly project delays. Such an innovative attempt is being undertaken by the Kaska Dena Tribal Council in northern British Columbia.

Development and the Indian People of Fort Ware: Predicting and Managing Consequences

This was the title of a study undertaken by Peter Douglas Elias, in cooperation with Martin S. Weinstein for the Kaska Dena Council and the Fort Ware community in 1992. The circumstances surrounding this study exhibit some interesting differences and similarities with regard to the research undertaken by the Cold Lake Band. The Cree and Chipewyan people of northern Alberta are Treaty Indians, who view the encroachment on their land-based economy by major resource development projects as a breach of their treaty right to hunt and trap on unoccupied Crown land. Their attempt to participate more effectively in impact assessment and management is an effort to rectify this situation.

In contrast, British Columbia's First Nations find themselves on the threshold of a new relationship with mainstream society. The provincial government's 1990 decision to acknowledge the validity of comprehensive aboriginal claims and the rise to power of the New Democrats the following year set the stage for a redefinition of the relationship not only between the province's Indian people and government, but also between native people and industry. The course which is being charted by the Kaska Dena for their accommodation of industrial enterprise in their ancestral territory, could very well be precedent-setting for other aboriginal communities in the province.

While their political environment is quite dissimilar, both the Cold Lake and the Fort Ware studies exhibit important similarities. They are intended to empower the respective Indian community to negotiate the best possible future for its members. Equally important, both studies are distinctly empirical in nature. Cold Lake opted for inferring the likely future impacts of resource development on its people from the experience of other selected communities in a comparable situation.

In the case of Fort Ware, the Kaska handpicked their researchers: the senior author with a background in the social sciences (anthropology), the second author with a background in the physical sciences (biology). Both were empirical in their approach, and they both were long-time practitioners in the field, looking back on a long-time association with the Kaska in particular and northern native communities in general. The time factor and the funding situation ruled out a full-blown environmental and socio-economic impact assessment at this stage, forcing the authors to fall back on their familiarity with the local situation at hand and their experience with comparable situations elsewhere in the North. However, this study was also intended as a first step in laying the groundwork for a future extensive research and monitoring program.

In 1992 the Kaska community of Fort Ware was faced with immanent and dramatic change from regional resource development. Two forestry enterprises and three mining corporations were vying for access to the lands and resources contained within the community's traditional territory. The corporations had gone through the motions of impact statements as prescribed by British Columbia's 1971 Environment and Land Use Act, but not surprisingly, had failed to address many concerns most crucial to Fort Ware's future.

> All stakeholders have agreed to do their best to meet the needs and concerns of the people at Fort Ware, within limits. These limits are broadly set by the government's legislative capacities and political interests, industry's profit, and recent court decisions. Within these limits must be found opportunities for local benefit, given limits on how far the community can go in accommodating outside interests and activities. At present, the limits of community accommodation are unknown. Until the community possesses necessary, sophisticated information, local people will be at a distinct disadvantage in the whole development situation. In ideal circumstances, fullblown environmental and sociocultural impact assessments would be launched. This was not done. To a large extent, we are still living with the history of native rights in British Columbia. In this view, industrial development furthers the job of human settlement and the proper place for Indians is to join in or get out of the way. In this model of rights and resource development assessment was only required to determine impact on public infrastructure and employment opportunities. The Fort Ware community and the Kaska Dena people are the inheritors of earlier notions of progress which saw no urgent need to assess the impact of industry on their interests and culture. All stake holders are anxious for developments to proceed in a timely fashion. The band and the tribal council feel there are potential benefits that far exceed the negative effects, providing all stakeholders can reach agreement on managing certain aspects of development. This study is offered as an alternative to more traditional social impact assessment. Given limited time and money, the best that can be accomplished is an attempt to predict impacts using the body of literature

dealing with economic organization and history of other northern communities, along with limited data bearing on the Fort Ware situation. (Elias and Weinstein 1992, Vol. 1:1f)

Of necessity, therefore, the study commissioned by the Kaska Dena Council had to be a compromise, a compromise between "hard" facts and "soft" values, and between what could realistically be assessed and what people desperately needed to know.

> Our **goal** is to predict change in the quality of life of the people at Fort Ware, given pending change in their natural and social environment. Our **purpose** for this prediction is to identify what should be done to minimize undesirable changes in the quality of people's lives and what should be done to maximize desirable change. (Elias and Weinstein 1992, Technical volume: 1; emphasis in original)

In order to formulate their hypotheses, Peter Douglas Elias and Martin S. Weinstein relied on their version of the subsistence/adaptation model for northern mixed economies, enhanced by their familiarity with socio-political and cultural idiosyncrasies of Fort Ware Kaska society and their empirical knowledge of resource development-induced change in comparable northern native communities. In theory, a model comprising a dependent variable (quality of life) measurable by certain indicators, and an independent variable (condition of the environment), also measurable by a system of appropriate environmental indicators, would appear straightforward. In reality, it quickly becomes clear that the possible outcome is mediated by such factors as the community's predisposition to environmental and economic change, its political efficacy and its social coherence.

> In the model of the mixed economy changes in the natural environment take precedence as the cause of general cultural change and, to be sure, the companies do promise changes to the natural environment. We believe the most significant change in the natural environment will appear as change in the quality and quantity of resources available to the people of Fort Ware. The most notable social consequences of change in the quality and quantity of available resources will be reflected as changed patterns of activity on the land. As well, companies and governments are promising changes in the social environment; in effect, they will increase the intensity and broaden the basis of economic, institutional and cultural relations with people at Fort Ware. We believe the most significant change in the social environment will appear as change in people's cash income, the effectiveness of local institutions, and the quality of cultural experience in the community. In turn, these fundamental changes in land use activities, cash income, political effectiveness, and cultural experience will ramify throughout the socio-cultural system at Fort Ware. (ibid.:10)

The study at hand is not an attempt to accurately predict the environmental and socio-economic impacts of impending resource developments, because the necessary data simply do not exist. Rather the authors' predictions and recommendations "based on theory and intuition, backed with comparative literature and scant local data" (Elias and Weinstein 1992, Vol. 1:3) are intended to enable the Kaska to make informed decisions when they negotiate the details of their relationship with industry and the conditions for granting industry access to their claim territory.

> If development is to take into account the community's interests, the need for information cannot stop at pre-development assessment. A regular monitoring program is needed if development and planning are to proceed together. Assessment, monitoring and planning are required to track the consequences of change. Stakeholders should be prepared to alter their activities and deal with problems that will become apparent only as things proceed. Because all problems cannot be foreseen, important decisions will be made regularly in the future. The community must have considerable ability to determine the outcome of future management decisions. The monitoring service will become the chief management tool available to all stakeholders.
>
> Refined information is of little use to decision makers if they do not know where their decisions should take them. As part of the monitoring service, the community should undertake

> to state clearly their goals for the future. Managing and controlling change implies going in a certain direction, and this direction must be known. (Elias and Weinstein 1992, Vol. 1:3)

This study for the Kaska Dena Council clearly marks the beginning of a long process. It serves as a tool of empowerment and precedes a mission statement of the community and the negotiation of an adaptive management process for resource development on Kaska lands.

EIA AND COMPREHENSIVE CLAIMS AGREEMENTS

So far we have considered aboriginal people's involvement in impact assessment within the framework of federal, provincial or territorial environmental legislation. Such legislation is not designed to be particularly responsive to the special nature and full scope of native interests, and frequently native actions are relegated to no more than obstructionist and delaying tactics (Feit 1982:291). On the other hand, comprehensive land claims agreements result in the establishment of new resource management regimes, which include frameworks for environmental impact assessment and review procedures. Thus native people have the opportunity to be involved in the design and implementation of environmental and social impact assessment and protection regimes, which in contents and context are more commensurate with their interests and lifestyle.

The James Bay and Northern Quebec Agreement[8]

The incorporation of a social and environmental protection regime in the 1975 JBNQA becomes all the more significant when we consider that, at the time of the negotiation of the Agreement, the federal and provincial governments had only very weak environmental and social protection regimes in place. Furthermore, there was no explicit social component in either the Canadian or the Quebec procedure, nor was there any general obligation to conduct public assessment and review. However, this lack of a precedent enhanced the opportunity for the Cree to design new and appropriate provisions (ibid.:297).

> [Their observations in other jurisdictions] led the negotiators to reject a regime simply composed of an impact assessment and review procedure, and to negotiate a two-component social and environmental regime. On one hand, they sought a social and environmental impact review procedure which would apply to all new development, defined as projects consisting of any work, undertaking, structure, operation or industrial process which might affect the environment or people of the territory.
>
> On the other hand, they sought a procedure whereby social and environmental (including land use) regulations and policies could be reviewed and/or adopted to minimize the negative impact of development on aboriginal peoples and their wildlife resources of the region.
>
> The Cree thus negotiated a joint, government-Cree committee with a mandate for reviewing existing legislation, policy and regulations, and for conducting mandatory reviews of any proposed changes to these. The committee was empowered to initiate needed additions or changes to the existing legislative, regulatory or policy framework by recommending such to a government authority. It also supervised the implementation of the entire JBNQA social and environmental protection regime, thereby assuring that the results and experience with impact assessment and review can be "fed-back" into the legislative and regulatory regime. In effect, it generally provides a surveillance of both environmental quality and the quality of life in the region. (Feit 1982:298f)

---

[8] The following section relies primarily on Feit (1982) and as a result only describes the impact review regime established for the Cree portion of the James Bay and northern Quebec territory. The Inuit regime differs from this in several respects, due in part to the establishment of a non-ethnic regional government in the Inuit areas in contrast to the ethnically defined Cree Regional Authority (Feit 1982:297).

In addition to this committee, three joint Cree-government bodies were established to implement the impact assessment and review process. The first is an evaluation committee, whose task is to decide whether or not a project is to be subjected to an assessment and, if so, to recommend timing, nature and extent of the assessment. Furthermore, there is a review committee and a review panel; these constitute parallel Cree/Quebec and Cree/Canada bodies which consider projects respectively falling under the jurisdiction of the provincial or federal governments (ibid.:300).

In some cases, a developer may be required to prepare only a detailed impact-assessment statement. In the event that there are important project location or design alternatives to be considered, both preliminary and detailed impact assessment statements must be produced. In the case of a preliminary impact statement, the review bodies recommend which development option should be further pursued by the developer and subjected to a detailed impact-assessment. In regard to a detailed impact assessment statement, they recommend whether or not a project should be authorized to proceed, and, if so, under what terms or conditions, which may include modifications and mitigative measures (ibid.).

It is important to realize that, final decision-making power rests with the respective federal or provincial ministers, under whose jurisdiction the project in question falls. The Cree have ultimate authority only over their reserve lands (Category I lands). In view of their geographically limited jurisdiction, the Cree have endeavoured to have incorporated in the Agreement certain mechanisms that would lend additional weight to Cree interests. One such provision was the formulation of a number of principles that are legally binding on the governments with decision-making authority, with regard to resource development. These principles are essentially geared towards protecting Cree society, economy and resources, thereby involving the Cree in the decision-making process. A second mechanism is constituted by the legal framework and the character of the consultative committees: "...while the committees are consultative, such consultation and their recommendations are made more effective and "weighty" by being obligatory, exclusive, joint, permanent, expert, formal, authoritative, and accessible to the Cree." (ibid.:304)

During the initial years of operation of the social and environmental protection regime, certain areas of concern emerged. They involved the relationship between proponents and the Cree, and between proponents and the regime; certain ambiguities arising from Cree-initiated projects; and finally and most essentially, the question of how effective the regime really was in influencing government decisions (ibid.:309f).

The first problem stems from the fact that development proponents had come to perceive that they had two avenues for attempting to deal with Cree interests, namely bilateral negotiations and proceeding through regime committees. The relationship between the two is a complex one. The regime has been found not only to permit bilateral negotiations but also to encourage them, even though project authorization can only be given by the responsible government departments after completion of the regime proceedings.

> The official Cree policy is therefore one of pursuing extensive bilateral negotiations with certain proponents as well as pursuing full participation in the operation of the regime. Because negotiations, when successful, involve agreements on remedial measures and especially on compensation, they can compliment the regime process by providing agreements on issues not likely to be settled so satisfactorily through assessment and review. The regime is potentially strongest in the areas where negotiations are weakest — namely rejection of a project, project design modifications and choice of site locations, preventive measures, monitoring procedures, and specific remedial works undertakings by the proponents. Negotiations are the best arenas for financial compensation and funds for Cree controlled remedial works.
>
> Initial experience with the regime has shown conflicts, however, because if negotiated agreements can compliment review procedures, they may also be perceived by proponents as a means to pre-empt the latter as well. Thus, some proponents have clearly hoped to negotiate agreements with the Cree on remedial measures, funds and compensation in the

> hope that this will facilitate authorization of their projects through the regime. This could happen through convincing government authorities that Cree concerns have already been met in a bi-lateral agreement and that the regime procedure need be nothing more than a rubber stamp. Or, it could happen by the Cree accepting a trade-off of compensation and funds for remedial measures, for not opposing the project or seeking modifications, preventive measures, specific remedial works, or monitoring, through the regime. Proponents have explored both avenues to pre-empt the regime. (Feit 1982:311f)

A second potential problem to be addressed by the regime is its application to Cree-initiated projects. The protection regime was designed as a universal one with applicability to all projects in the territory. It was assumed that Cree-initiated projects on Cree reserve lands would be reviewed, the same way as other projects, with recommendations being sent to the respective local Cree governments, who have final decision-making power for Category I lands. In practice, however, most Cree projects were concerned with community infrastructure and housing programs, which generally had extensive community input and clear community support. As a result, the application of the regime procedure was perceived as pointless and in fact, counterproductive due to delays caused by the authorization process. This was the situation in the early 1980s. Harvey A. Feit points out, however, that in the future, as the Cree population and communities grow, and Cree administrative and corporate organizations diversify and grow in scale, projects proposed in the settlements will become more specialized and of less universal benefit. Under those conditions the protection regime would serve as an appropriate and Cree-controlled means of public assessment and review (ibid.:313).

Finally, we must ask, how effective the regime has been in controlling development in the territory. The real test is constituted by those types of development which have the greatest impact on the regional environment and on Cree land use, namely forestry operations and hydroelectric projects.

With regard to the former, after initial difficulties, Feit (ibid.:314) describes the regime in the early 1980s as being quite successful in introducing an innovative and joint approach to the regulation of impacts of forestry developments. Cree hunters had input in the selection of areas to be cut or preserved, which enabled them to protect important moose, fish and beaver habitats and populations. Their instructions were communicated to local departmental offices and incorporated into the locally issued government cutting permits (ibid.).

In the early 1990s the overall picture does not appear as positive. According to Jeannette Lajois, senior environmental analyst, and Robert Beaulieu, forest engineer for the Cree Regional Authority, the consultation process is rather unsatisfactory, even with regard to Category II lands, where the Cree have exclusive harvesting rights (Personal communication, July 6, 1993). The formal consultation channels provided for by the Agreement allow for advisory input only; and while the authorities must respond to committee suggestions within a period of 90 days, these suggestions tend to be ignored. The 1986 Quebec Forestry Act has introduced some general improvements in provincial forestry practices, such as adherence to the sustained yield principle, but even these improvements are sometimes more apparent than real (ibid.). Furthermore, Robert Beaulieu feels that there is a lack of adjustment of forest management units and Cree traplines. Cree traplines should be taken into account in the calculation of sustained yield.

The situation is even more problematic where hydro developments are concerned. Here we are faced with a much more overt conflict between the Cree and government interests.

> The crown corporations promoting the developments are large and powerful organizations within the provincial bureaucracy. The potential conflicts between them and the department charged with regulating the environmental and social impacts of their projects tend to push decision-making high up in the bureaucracy into the political arena. This tends to remove key considerations and decisions from the joint Cree/Quebec committees and locates them with internal Quebec committees, or with senior civil servants or politicians. In any case,

> there is a tendency for the decisions to be removed from Cree view and participation. The middle level and senior civil servants appointed to the joint committees sometimes sit without effective mandates, and no effective discussion, compromise or consultation takes place. Joint committees tend to be treated as adjuncts to the internal governmental committees, as mere formalities, where discussions taken elsewhere in government get reported and cursorily rubber stamped before being finally approved and implemented. This is contrary to the intent, process, structure, and legal provisions of the regime. (Feit 1982:316)

Furthermore, there is not always agreement on which hydro projects are exempt from environmental scrutiny, because they already have the blessing of the JBNQA as an integral part of the La Grande Complex. This was exemplified by dissension over the Eastmain project in 1991 (*Globe and Mail*, July 7, 1991:A3). The situation is aggravated by the federal government's practice to keep a low profile in its involvement in development issues in Quebec. This reflects a minimalist reading of the federal mandate under the JBNQA to which the federal government is bound (Feit 1982:315).

The situation finally came to a head in 1991 in conjunction with the controversial Great Whale Project. Hydro Quebec had hoped to start road and airport construction in fall 1991. In order to adhere to this schedule the corporation opted for a "fast track approach" to the environmental impact assessment. The assessment was to be segmented into two parts: first, the access infrastructure and subsequently the complex itself (*IWGIA Newsletter*, November/December 1991:57). This action intensified opposition to the project. Not only were members of a provincial environmental review commission physically prevented from conducting hearings in Kuujjuarapik/Whapmagoostui (*Windspeaker*, July 5, 1991:3), but the Cree took the provincial corporation and FEARO to Federal Court, demanding strict adherence to the environmental assessment provisions of the JBNQA and the involvement of the federal government in the process with regard to its jurisdictional areas of responsibility.

While the court proceedings were still in progress, the federal government announced in July 1991 that the Great Whale Project would be subjected to the EARP process. In September 1991 the Federal Court ruled in the Cree's favour, demanding that the Great Whale Project be submitted to both a federal and provincial review (*Globe and Mail*, September 11, 1991:A1f).

In January 1992 a Memorandum of Understanding was signed between the governments of Quebec and Canada, the Cree Regional Authority, the Grand Council of the Cree, Makivik Corporation and the Kativik Regional Government. This aimed to coordinate and provide direction to the environmental assessment and review process. (Fenge 1992:2) The process started in late January 1992 with public hearings into the scope of the assessment. The scope of assessment may be viewed as the most crucial part of the whole procedure, since, simply put, it determines what an EIA is going to look at (Pannell 1992:7). It provides the basis for the guidelines for the proponent's Environmental Impact Statement (EIS) and for the terms of reference of the review panel.

Despite the importance of the hearings, the federal government was conspicuously absent and submitted only written briefs. Its actions belied its multiple responsibilities for aboriginal people and concerns for fish and fish habitat, migratory birds, and the waters and islands of Hudson and James Bay (belonging to the NWT). They also sharply contrasted with the active and critical federal participation in the same type of hearings for Manitoba Hydro's Conawapa hydroelectric dam, which raised very similar concerns (ibid.).

Nevertheless, the EIS Guidelines released in September 1992 are unusually comprehensive and present Hydro Quebec with a difficult task. They tackle the thorny issue of economic justification and need for the project, and require the proponent to present and evaluate the proposal from the viewpoint of sustainable development, considering the "carrying capacities of ecosystems and human societies." Furthermore, the examination of potential environmental impacts is to employ not only scientific approaches but aboriginal knowledge and values.

And finally, Hydro Quebec is expected to address the cumulative impacts of the Great Whale Project in the context of other hydro developments, both planned and completed, in northern Quebec, Ontario and Manitoba (CARC 1992:10).

The Great Whale environmental impact assessment and review process has the potential for laying new ground rules for environmental impact assessment, as the Mackenzie Valley Pipeline Inquiry did almost two decades ago. It remains to be seen whether this potential will be realized.

The Inuvialuit Final Agreement

One of the principal goals expressed in the Inuvialuit Final Agreement (IFA) of 1984 is the protection and preservation of the Arctic environment (s.1[c]). The IFA created two joint management structures to guarantee this protection: the Environmental Impact Screening Committee (EISC) and the Environmental Impact Review Board (EIRB). The EISC and the EIRB have the same structure: Each is comprised of seven permanent members with three appointed by the Government of Canada and three appointed by the Inuvialuit Game Council. Of the three government appointees, the governments of the Northwest Territories and Yukon each have one designated member. The Chairman, who cannot vote except in the event of a deadlock, is appointed by Canada with the consent of the Inuvialuit.

The jurisdiction of the EISC and the EIRB extends to all developments in the Inuvialuit Settlement Region (ISR), and to any proposed developments that might have a significant adverse impact on present and future wildlife harvesting in the Inuvialuit Settlement Region. The latter category includes developments in the offshore and outside the Inuvialuit Settlement Region (s.11[1] and s.13[7]).

The concept of "development" is defined quite comprehensively in the IFA.

> ..."developer" means a person, the government or any other legal entity owning, operating or causing to be operated any development in whole or in part in the Inuvialuit Settlement Region, and includes any co-contractant of such owner or operator. For greater certainty, "developer" includes any Inuvialuit developer;
>
> "development" means:
> (a) any commercial or industrial undertaking or venture, including support and transportation facilities relating to the extraction of non-renewable resources from the Beaufort Sea, other than commercial wildlife harvesting; or
> (b) any government project, undertaking or construction whether federal, territorial, municipal, local or by any Crown agency or corporation, except government projects within the limits of communities not directly affecting wildlife resources outside those limits and except government wildlife enhancement projects; (IFA s.2, Government of Canada 1984:1)

As Magdalena A.K. Muir (1991:11) suggests, a legal interpretation of "development" could be quite expansive. The use of terms such as project, undertaking, venture or construction suggests some physical event or entity. On the other hand, Janet M. Keeping (1989:45) argues that "development" may even include intangibles, such as government policy. This would allow the Inuvialuit joint structures to assess developmental thrusts at their earliest, that is policy stages, rather than when particular implementation schemes have already gained momentum.

The first stage of the environmental review process is carried out by the Environmental Impact Screening Committee. In 1987 the Inuvialuit Game Council made a blanket referral of all development projects in the offshore and onshore on Crown lands in the Inuvialuit Settlement Region to the EISC. This action has not been challenged by the federal government, even though the referral made s.11 applicable to the offshore waters in the ISR, instead of the theoretically more limited screening prescribed for wildlife compensation in s.13 (This limitation is more apparent than real, since the protection of wildlife harvesting necessitates viable habitat). Before the screening process is even started, the EISC expects the proponent to have consulted with the Hunters and Trappers Committees, whose communities might be affected by the proposed development (Marshall Netherwood, EISC Secretary, personal communication, May 28, 1992). Development proponents are required to submit a project description to the Screening Committee containing the following information:

1. Purpose of the project;
2. Nature and extent of the proposed development;
3. Rationale for the site selection; and
4. Information and technical data in sufficient detail to permit an adequate preliminary assessment of the project and its environmental impact. (IFA s.11[12], Government of Canada 1984:17)

When screening a project description, the EISC has three options in rendering a decision: a) the development will have no significant negative environmental impact and may proceed; b) the development could have significant negative impact and is subject to further assessment; or c) the development proposal has deficiencies of a nature that require the submission of another project description.

The Screening Committee's 1990–1991 Annual Activity Report tells us that during this period the EISC held nine meetings during which they reviewed and rendered decisions on thirty submissions. In 28 cases it was decided that the proposal would not have any significant negative environmental impact on the ISR; one proposal was referred to the EIRB for further environmental impact review; and one submission was determined to be deficient, returned to the proponent, and was not resubmitted. The list of 30 submissions covered a wide variety of projects: geological and palynological fieldwork, biological research, mapping, road construction, a tourism proposal, a dredging project, a Beaufort Sea Drilling Program Update, and so forth.

During the past couple of years, there has been a significant increase in tourism and scientific research activities in the ISR. Many of these activities could have had an environmental impact and required screening. The EISC members encountered considerable difficulty in their endeavours to develop practical criteria for assessing the potential impacts of such activities on the environment and on wildlife. In the early 1990s, meetings were planned with government regulators and special interest groups involved in tourism and other organizations involved in research activities to discuss these issues (EISC 1990:5).

If the Screening Committee decides that a project proposal must be subjected to an environmental review process, it has the discretionary power to refer it to the EIRB or any other review agency it considers competent. The EISC will most likely refer development proposals to the EIRB because this body includes the Inuvialuit (Gary Wagner, EIRB Secretary, personal communication, May 28, 1992). Once the Review Board has reviewed the project, it decides whether or not the development should proceed and, if so, on what terms and conditions, including the mitigative and remedial measures. The Board may also recommend further assessment (s.11[24]).

The Review Board's recommendation is then transmitted to the government agency under whose jurisdiction the authorization of the development falls. If the governmental authority chooses to reject the Review Board's recommendations or to modify them, it has to give reasons for this decision in writing within thirty days. While EIRB recommendations are not binding on the government departments authorizing the developments, the process set out in the IFA (s.11[31]) states unequivocally: "No licence or approval shall be issued that would have the effect of permitting any proposed development to proceed unless the provisions of this section have been complied with." The IFA is silent as to the legal ramifications, if reasons for non-acceptance of EIRB recommendations are not given within thirty days. One interpretation of s.11(29) is that in such case the government authority may be assumed to have accepted the recommendations of the EIRB.

Nothing in the IFA prevents the government from carrying out environmental impact assessment and review under its own laws and policies (s.11[32]). The IFA does not, however, specify any integration of its procedures with the EARP Guidelines Order or successor legislation. In this respect it contrasts with the recently finalized Gwich'in Agreement, where s.24.3.8 makes allowance for such arrangement.

In 1989 the EIRB carried out its first public review which resulted in the approval of the Esso Chevron et al. Isserk I-15 Drilling Program. The approval was subject to 10 conditions and three major recommendations, all of which were accepted by the Canada Oil and Gas Lands Administration (COGLA) (EIRB 1989 and 1990a).

Things did not go as smoothly in 1990, when in its second review the EIRB recommended strongly against the approval of the Gulf Canada Resources Limited Kulluk Drilling Program (1990–1992) (EIRB 1990b and 1991; Wagner 1991). Unlike Esso's Isserk I-15 project which concerned the drilling of one specific exploration well in the land-fast ice-zone, the Gulf submission proposed a three-year program to drill a series of wells in the transition zone between the permanent-pack ice and the land-fast ice, which presented a very different scenario. The two principal reasons for the Board's recommendation against the proposal were the lack of preparation on the part of Gulf and the federal government to deal effectively with a major oil well blowout in the Beaufort Sea during the open water season, and the Board's inability on the basis of the evidence to make any sensible recommendation as to Gulf's potential liability in the event of a worst case scenario as required under s.13(11)(b) of the IFA (EIRB 1990b:16). The Board's conclusion also raised some serious questions about Beaufort Sea hydrocarbon development in general and about the federal government's exercise of its regulatory responsibilities.

> In the opinion of the Board, the chief fault in the company's submission was Gulf's professed inability to project what the actual onshore impacts anticipated from a major oil well blowout would be. It is incomprehensible that after drilling in the Beaufort Sea/Mackenzie Delta area for 25 years a reliable body of information does not exist to enable Gulf to provide the Board with estimates, assumptions, models, or data on the crucial areas of shoreline impacts, shoreline responses and cleanup standards.
>
> If Gulf is correct in claiming that reliable information is not available, then there has been a failure on the part of both government and industry to adequately address issues of environmental protection and wildlife preservation in connection with drilling in the Beaufort Sea. The Board's conclusion was that:
>
> > Perhaps no other element of the review has proven to be more disconcerting and disturbing to the Board than the inescapable conclusion that, based upon the information available to the Board, the regulatory authorities of the Government of Canada responsible for offshore oil and gas exploration, have failed to discharge their mandated obligations in a responsible and effective manner. (Environmental Impact Review Board Press Release 3/90, issued June 29, 1990, quoted in Wagner 1991:37)

The Kulluk decision resulted in a serious disagreement between COGLA and the EIRB over the interpretation of s.11(29) of the IFA. The EIRB and its legal counsel were of the opinion that if COGLA officials are unable or unwilling to accept the recommendations of the Board, their reasons for this rejection must be made public, in writing, within thirty days of release of the EIRB decision. COGLA countered that the 30-day response period started only once they, as the government regulatory authority, decided to accept, modify or reject the Board's recommendations. In other words, COGLA's approach has no time limit at all (EIRB 1991:1). COGLA was disbanded in 1991; in 1993 there still have been no further developments on this issue.[9]

[9] "The Minister of Indian Affairs and Northern Development created the Beaufort Sea Steering Committee (BSSC) to respond to the recommendations of the EIRB. The BSSC involved more than 100 people and

In the early 1990s the environmental review process in the ISR appears to be evolving. To the Inuvialuit the developments surrounding Gulf's Kulluk proposal seem to show that the IFA environmental review process does indeed "have teeth". There is some confidence among the Inuvialuit that, even though legally the EIRB has advisory function only, for reasons of public image the government is unlikely to approve developments in opposition to the Board (Gary Wagner, EIRB Secretary, personal communication, May 28, 1992). Wagner feels, that in this context, it is important to realize, that the review process is truly a joint effort in co-management and not an "Inuvialuit process", even though the EISC and the EIRB are creatures of the IFA. The departure from the "us-them" image is difficult to accomplish for all parties involved.

Not surprisingly, a public review process is an ongoing educational challenge to the population at large, who is unaccustomed to the opportunity of having an impact on developments. Poor understanding of concepts and procedures involved in the review process is still a widespread problem, particularly because in their public meetings and hearings the Inuvialuit lean towards a somewhat "judicial" style for fear of legal challenges on procedural grounds (ibid.). "Committee burn-out" within a relatively small pool of competent people is another problem faced by many northern native communities.

Some hypothetical questions remain to be resolved in the future, should they ever become an issue, for example, the application of the EARP process in the ISR or on Inuvialuit lands (under "laws of general application applicable to private lands from time to time" — IFA s.7[97]); disagreement on developments between the Inuvialuit Game Council and the Inuvialuit Regional Corporation; or differences of opinion between the EISC and the EIRB on one hand and the IRC on the other hand over the screening of development proposals concerning Inuvialuit Private Lands.

CONCLUSION AND OUTLOOK

Environmental and social impact assessment can be a very important force in the life of aboriginal people. In too many cases impact assessments have disregarded and alienated native communities, but in other instances they have truly empowered them. In a session of the international Workshop on Environmental Impact Assessment Procedures in Wellington, New Zealand, in 1985, aboriginal participants reached an important conclusion:

> EIA is an activity of the power culture which offers the minority culture a direct access to the decision-making process. EIA is seen in this context and is used by the minority culture as a device to influence power culture decisions outside the intended scope of EIA. (Rob Owen and Dean Jacobs, quoted in Tooshkenig and Jacobs 1985)

Justice Thomas Berger's Mackenzie Valley Pipeline Inquiry was a classical example of just how this happens. That the message is spreading, is shown by the fact that almost two decades later, Thomas Berger is conducting a similar independent review at the request of the World Bank, this time among India's indigenous people whose land base and livelihood is threatened by the $11 billion Sardar Sarawor Dam in the Narmada Valley, which would displace an estimated 100,000 people (McIlroy 1992).

In order to serve any beneficial function for aboriginal communities, however, impact assessment has to be adjusted in contents and procedure to a different cultural and socio-economic milieu.

> The language of formal EIA — "experts", "objectivity", "technique", "number-crunching", "quantitative analysis", "data", "cost/benefit analysis", — betrays the bias and exposes the

laboured for eight months before issuing over 700 pages of comment in eight volumes, plus several technical appendices. The budget expended on this exercise is a closely guarded secret." (Wagner 1991:37) limitations of Western environmental science. It is the language of the technocratic fixers; of rigorous, rational inquiry; of a world view which holds the economic as the highest value. As such, it is foreign to Natives whose language and expertise are based upon knowledge of custom, experience accumulated by wise elders over centuries, and a spiritual sense of unity with nature. (Shapcott 1989:79)

Traditional SIA has been guided by the same Euro-Canadian cultural values and assumptions about native life and northern native communities which have resulted in many of the present conflicts between native and non-native society. There is an essential self-interest in both sets of assumption (i.e. the positive effects of replacement, on the one hand, and unexamined compatibility, on the other). The assumptions promote the north as a development frontier and native people as a potential work force. The change required in SIA methodology is to be able to answer questions about how northern development should proceed if it took into account the north as a sustainable native homeland. (Weinstein et al. 1992:3)

Only a band or tribally controlled and directed SIA effort can be of use to the band/tribe for the purposes of their own planning as well as strategy development for dealing with major projects which are proposed on or near their lands. (Justus and Simonetta 1982:255)

Progress is being made in this area. To a lesser degree this is even true for externally controlled, government-mandated environmental review procedures, but this positive note particularly applies to those impact assessments which are primarily guided by aboriginal interests and concepts. Of particular relevance among the latter are those environmental review procedures, which form an integral part of native resource management regimes resulting from comprehensive claims settlement agreements.

10

Synthesis and Outlook

INTRODUCTION

This book has attempted to shed some light on the complexity of the environment in which aboriginal people must operate in their endeavour to utilize natural resources and to partake in their management. During the last decade in particular, native people have fine-tuned different tactics in their pursuit of both goals. Their efforts have resulted in a re-examination of native rights to resources on the part of the government, the courts and non-aboriginal resource managers, and have given rise to a wide variety of co-management regimes across the country. These latest developments have also ushered in an era where it is no longer only aboriginal resource use which is circumscribed by constraints imposed by non-native society, but where native people are now able to exert influence over the way non-aboriginal people use the land and its resources.

MEANS FOR GAINING CONTROL OVER RESOURCES

As Peter Douglas Elias (1991:45–53) has illustrated with the example of water resources, and as can be gleaned from most of the chapters in this book, native people are resorting to a wide variety of tactics in their efforts to accommodate, avoid or eliminate the many external constraints on their ability to gain access to and/or management power over natural resources. Some of these tactics can be accommodated by the status quo; others are deliberately designed to change this condition.

Making use of the provisions of the Indian Act to the fullest extent possible may be viewed as occupying one end of the spectrum of options available to native people. This type of initiative is best illustrated by the fishing by-laws passed by several member bands of the Gitksan-Wet'suwet'en during the 1980s, which were designed to strengthen the management power of the hereditary chiefs. However, these by-laws were either disallowed by the Minister of Indian Affairs, or their implementation was prohibited by Supreme Court of British Columbia injunction. These developments illustrate one major weakness of this option: While validly enacted by-laws potentially increase Indian regulatory power over reserve resources as well as override federal and provincial regulations, they have been routinely disallowed by the Minister or successfully challenged in court. A second drawback of band by-laws is their limited territorial scope: By-laws are only effective on reserve lands. This particularly limits their usefulness for fisheries and water rights-related issues.

Instances where aboriginal people gained a share of control over off-reserve resources by means of negotiations are numerous. Most negotiated arrangements must, however, be viewed in the context of valid aboriginal rights (tested in court), a perceived resource crisis, or the threat of physical confrontation. Many co-management, joint management or joint stewardship agreements fall into this category: Temagami, the tripartite agreement of the Algonquin of Barriere Lake, and virtually all fish and wildlife-related co-management regimes which were not created by a claims settlement. Arrangements which resulted from British Columbia's Joint Stewardship Agreement initiative in the 1990s form a subgroup of their own.

There are very few cases where aboriginal people have successfully achieved legislated delegation of power over resources. Notable examples are the Metis Settlements Land Act of 1988 and the Alberta-Metis Settlements Accord of 1989. These legislations granted Metis settlements title in fee simple to their settlement lands but excluded mineral and water rights and existing third party interests.

The importance of court decisions for aboriginal resource-related rights can hardly be overstated, but "going to court" is a costly and long drawn-out process. Supreme Court of Canada decisions on *Sparrow* and *Sioui* have had momentous implications for aboriginal and treaty rights in First Nations' favour, but the opposite is true for *Horseman*. The outcome of litigation is usually precedent-setting which is another factor often inducing aboriginal and non-aboriginal parties to opt for an out-of-court settlement or to remain at the negotiating table. But frequently native people are unable to negotiate protection of their interest either in advance of damage caused by competing users or in retrospect, when seeking after-the-fact compensation for damages, and they are forced into the courts. This has been a common occurrence in the case of aboriginal communities suffering the impacts of hydroelectric developments, such as the Churchill-Nelson River Project in Manitoba, the E.B. Campbell hydro dam in Saskatchewan, the Bighorn Dam in Alberta and the W.A.C. Bennett Dam in British Columbia. As borne out by the experiences of the affected communities in the latter two cases, taking recourse to the legal system does by no means guarantee any degree of success. In yet another scenario, native people may be seeking a precedent-setting ruling to define their rights, as exemplified by the Peigan seeking legal clarification of their water rights.

The claims process contrasts with the above-mentioned options in its comprehensiveness. The settlement of contemporary aboriginal claims does not merely establish preferential or exclusive harvesting rights, but as a rule puts in place a new resource management regime, in which native people are actively participating parties. As Elias points out, a vitally important feature of resource rights thus obtained, is the fact that they are protected by the Constitution Act of 1982, since the terms of a land claim settlement become the operational definition of aboriginal rights (Elias 1991:51).

A final tactic employed by aboriginal people to gain control over land and resources is the assertion of rights. When "ordinary" measures such as by-laws, negotiation, litigation or constitutional challenge have failed (or take too long to produce results), native groups may resort to extraordinary tactics, namely defy established authority and assert their own control. Selected examples that demonstrate these actions are the following: initiatives of the Haida to control recreational fisheries in Haida Gwaii and to assume "management" of Gwaii Haanas; Gitksan-Wet'suwet'en actions to reclaim their traditional House Territories; and the activities of the Peigan Lonefighters to thwart the purpose of the Oldman River Dam.

While the above-mentioned tactics — creating by-laws, negotiation, attempts at legislative changes, litigation, the claims process and assertion of control — are clearly distinguishable avenues for achieving increased control over natural resources, they rarely occur in isolation. More commonly, any number of these means will be used by aboriginal people concurrently, with individual manoeuvres constituting part of an overall strategy. Throughout the past decade, for instance, the Gitksan and Wet'suwet'en could be observed pursuing their overall goal, ownership and jurisdiction over their House Territories, on many different fronts: manipulation of the Indian Act, negotiation, litigation, the claims process and assertion of rights.

CO-MANAGEMENT — THE WAY OF THE FUTURE?

Co-management is the theme which permeates virtually all chapters of this book. Co-management regimes for renewable resources between native and non-native parties are being established in all parts of Canada under very different circumstances and for different purposes. With the exception of the co-management scheme created by the 1975 James Bay and Northern Quebec Agreement, no co-management effort is older than a decade, and only some of the co-management regimes created by claims settlements or initiated by the government in crisis situations have a "historical depth" of several years.

To date three northern comprehensive claims agreements are being implemented in the territorial north, but other agreements, such as the Sahtu claim and claims in Yukon are likely to reach this stage in the near future. All these settlements will result in the establishment of resource co-management regimes.

The co-management of northern national parks is closely tied to the settlement of comprehensive claims, and the future is likely to witness a proliferation of co-management structures in this area. Crisis-oriented co-management structures are also still being created, as exemplified by the 1991 Northern Buffalo Management Board.

The *Sparrow* ruling gave rise to a very different category of co-management initiatives, which were not contingent upon a particular resource or event, but which were prompted by a fundamental rethinking of rights and relationships. Those initiatives have been largely confined to British Columbia, but there are indications that a similar process of "rethinking relationships" is taking place in the other provinces and within the federal government. While the implications of the *Sparrow* decision for treaty rights (including rights under the Natural Resources Transfer Agreements) are far from clear, this matter, too, is being given serious consideration by government departments and court judges.

The most recently proposed application of co-management structures pertains to the cooperative environmental management of industrial resource extraction areas (Elias and Weinstein 1992, Vol. 1:32) Peter Douglas Elias describes this process as "strategic co-management" (Personal communication, December 7, 1992). This application is a step in the long overdue process of empowerment of aboriginal peoples, whose legitimate interests as stakeholders in the environment are given recognition by the establishment of joint management regimes.

Co-management as a means of crisis resolution, a result of comprehensive claims settlements, a matter of policy and a tangible expression of native people's empowerment — these categories continue to exist contemporaneously and cannot always be clearly distinguished. They also represent an evolution still in progress. The Charlottetown Agreement has failed, but whenever constitutional talks are resumed, it is unlikely that the clause pertaining to aboriginal people's inherent right to self-government will be weakened. The last proposal for constitutional change contained a contextual statement within which the inherent right to self-government would operate.

> The exercise of the right of self-government includes the authority of the duly constituted legislative bodies of Aboriginal peoples, each within its own jurisdiction:
>
> ....
>
> b) to develop, maintain and strengthen their relationship with their lands, waters and environment so as to determine and control their development as peoples according to their own values and priorities and ensure the integrity of their societies.

Judging from recent experiences, it is more than likely that aboriginal people's future involvement in resource management will feature exclusive as well as shared rights and responsibilities. If this occurs, future co-management regimes may draw their legitimization not from necessity, common sense, legislation, policy or a sense of social justice, but from a constitutionally entrenched right.

OUTLOOK

In the field of aboriginal natural resource use and management, much of our interest has been focused on the numerous constraints which define native people's options in resource development. There are indications, however, that changes are underway, and that increasingly First Nations may be in a position to exert influence over the way non-aboriginal people use the land and its resources.

At the lowest level this is happening in all joint management regimes, which are specifically designed to constitute a sharing of power and responsibility and a merging of different types of environmental knowledge and management styles. Nevertheless, aboriginal influence on the broad range of society's resource-based activities becomes more tangible in areas subject to the settlement of comprehensive claims. As exemplified by the Inuvialuit Final Agreement, the claims process gives rise to a new resource management regime with its own environmental protection regime. The IFA expressly allows the Inuvialuit to set standards higher than the federal government for environmental protection, when disposing of non-renewable resource rights on their own lands. It guarantees Inuvialuit representation on the Environmental Impact Screening Committee and the Environmental Impact Review Board, with regard to controlling developments throughout the Inuvialuit Settlement Region outside Inuvialuit lands. The Kulluk decision has shown that the IFA environmental review process does indeed "have teeth". While the Renewable Resources Committees officially have advisory function only, their real and political power may be much greater than such wording would imply. As the Paulatuk Conservation Plan puts it, adherence to Inuvialuit conservation standards should simply be recognized "as a cost of doing business" in the region (Community of Paulatuk and WMAC [NWT] 1990:16).

British Columbia, too, is bracing itself for the impact of the claims process. The negotiation and implementation of contemporary treaties will be taking place in an economic and political environment which is fundamentally different from the territorial north. In common with Yukon and the Northwest Territories, however, British Columbia will feature many powerful aboriginal players in the natural resource game. Resource companies will have no choice but to accommodate themselves to new landlords. This accommodation will be more difficult in some cases than in others. As Gitksan spokesman Don Ryan (Maas Gaak) puts it, "We're ready to do business. But companies have to understand that we want control over how that business is done." (Watt 1990:47). British Columbia's First Nations have widely different political agendas, environmental practices and economic priorities, but undoubtedly aboriginal influence will change certain resource use practices and effect the discontinuation of others.

Clearly it will be in those areas subject to unsettled comprehensive claims, where aboriginal impact on resource management will be experienced most profoundly. But even in the Prairies and Eastern Provinces such influence cannot be ruled out. Not only are there unsettled comprehensive claims as illustrated by the Lubicon Cree and the Algonquin of Barriere Lake. There are also innumerable specific claims, which have in the past been consistently prohibited from considering treaty rights to harvesting and related environmental quality issues (Wagner 1991:25). Indian treaty rights are constantly being re-examined and re-interpreted, and the last word on Metis rights remains unspoken. In this context it is hard to ignore Barry Barton's important suggestion that without adequate habitat protection, fishing, hunting and trapping rights would be useless; therefore Treaty Indians must possess implied rights to prevent damage to wildlife habitat, including the aquatic habitat (Barton 1985:19). The implications can be observed in the U.S. Pacific Northwest as a result of the Boldt Decision. There is thus a possibility that Treaty Indians, equipped with their constitutionally protected treaty rights, may in the future exert a far stronger influence on land and resource use in the provinces than ever before imagined.

Finally, there is yet another less tangible side to possible native influences on natural resource use and management. In this era of environmental crisis, society is searching for alternative models of sustainable development to avoid a large scale "tragedy of the commons". It has been observed that elements of effective communal resource management still function in many aboriginal communities. Communally-based responsible environmental management is something, those native communities may be able to teach us all.

Peter Douglas Elias concludes his book *Development of Aboriginal Communities* with the observation that there is a certain irony in observing late 20th-century Indians, Inuit and Metis establish new frontiers in Canadian social, political and economic life (Elias 1991:228). This certainly holds true in the field of natural resources. In a country that owes so much of its national character to resource frontiers created by immigrant society, it is now aboriginal people who advance into "new territory" by reclaiming lands and resources as well as management power over them. But perhaps we may carry the image a step farther. The newly evolving partnership between aboriginal and non-aboriginal resource users and managers may open up another frontier which both parties can advance together: towards more responsible and sustainable environmental management.

Appendix

The Serpent's Eggs

Gilbert Oskaboose

Long ago and far away — when the world was young — a great Serpent came down from the north, and by its passing carved a mighty river through the rugged Cambrian Shield in a land now called Northern Ontario.

Anishnawbek elders say it is so.

As she moved ponderously south she searched with a growing sense of urgency for her great body was ripe with new life and her time was near.

In the wild barren lands between Elliot and Quirke Lakes she laid millions of tiny eggs, dark ominous nodules that sank away from the light, deep into the bedrock, to lie dormant for millennia, waiting for their time to come.

And all around life went on. Her passing had created a river and the rains came and the river took on a life of its own. Schools of pickerel and bass swarmed through its cool depths; silver trout knifed through its eddies; giant northern pike patrolled the warm shallows. On shimmering wings great dragonflies foraged up and down its length and on glossy surfaces of still backwaters black whirligig beetles spun in delirious circles.

Sleek otter and mink prowled its banks, and in the air above, the tumbling flights of teal and mallards floated with the wind.

In time a wandering Ojibway scout found the sacred river and brought his people there, to live in peace and harmony with the land and wild creatures that made the river their home. The men hunted bear and moose, the women gathered blueberries and acorns and the tiny strawberries that grew wild and sweet in the meadows at the river's edge; the children ran with wolves and the elders spoke with eagles. In the moon of Popping Trees they sat around their fires in warm lodges and listened to the elders tell of the great Serpent.

It was a good life, the way the Creator meant it to be. But only the mountains live forever, it is said. For the First People change came in the forms of The Others — a new race of humans that moved into the territory, strange people with pale faces, cold icy eyes and hair the colour of dead grass.

The newcomers said they were trappers and in no time at all they had trapped all the beaver and otter and muskrats in the territory. After that they went away and left the people with only the trees and the rocks. A few years later they were back again. This time they said they were loggers, and that was true as well because soon they had logged all the big timber. They took all the white pine and red pine and jackpine and went away again, leaving the People on the rocks.

Everyone thought The Others were gone for good and the elders burned tobacco...and thanked the Creator for small mercies.

But it wasn't meant to be. Somebody discovered a thing called uranium and The Others came back — for the bare rocks.

They called themselves miners and they came armed with little black boxes that chattered like angry squirrels whenever they walked near the Serpent's nest. That made them happy and they started digging there, and didn't stop until they had found the Serpent's eggs.

The elders tried to warn them not to bother the eggs but they sent the elders away, and called our people foolish old men and stupid Indians.

They kept digging and wouldn't listen to anyone, not even their own medicine men who told them something was very wrong, that men were starting to die from a strange disease that made their lungs black and made them cough up blood.

They kept digging and what they couldn't sell they threw into the river and some of the lakes. The river and the lakes died and nobody paid any attention.

The miners ground up the Serpent's eggs into a fine yellow powder they called "yellowcake" and sold it for a lot of money to their pale brothers south of the medicine line.

Those brothers in the south were from a different tribe. They were called "military tacticians" and "nuclear technicians" and they cooked up the yellowcake in big pots and made strong medicines from it. Many of the technicians became sick and died after handling the yellowcake and some of the other medicines. Nobody seemed to notice.

One of the medicines was called "radium" and they had their women paint it on the dials that went into the cockpits of tanks and airplanes so that their warriors could see the dials and fight at night. The women used tiny brushes that they put into their mouths to wet and sharpen into fine points, so that they could paint fine, neat lines. After a while the power of the Serpent's eggs came out of the radium and ate away their faces and those women died too, just like the technicians.

Two minor tribes known as the "peace-niks" and the "anti-nukes" became worried and tried to stop the military tribe but they were too small and weak.

The military tribe was very strong and they had powerful friends to help them. Some of those allies were called the strategists and they believed that something called an "acceptable loss factor" make it okay that a few people might die from the medicines.

Another thing they made from the yellowcake was "nuclear bombs". The best way to describe the bombs is that they were long and slim and cold — just like the Serpent — and whenever they dropped one on another tribe, that tribe disappeared in an instant, just as if the sun had fallen on it.

The Others dropped two of them on the Japan tribe a few years ago.

They called one of the bombs "Fat Boy". Fat Boy must have been very heavy because when they threw him off the airplane and he landed on the Japan tribe, 100,000 people died instantly.

When the other tribes saw this, they became very frightened and asked The Others not to make any more bombs but they wouldn't listen and kept on making what they called "bigger and better bombs".

They even taught the new bombs how to fly so they wouldn't need airplanes anymore.

When they wouldn't stop making the bombs, other tribes figured they had better make some too, just to be on the safe side, and pretty soon there was a big race to see which tribe could make the biggest and the most bombs.

Very soon many of the tribes had many bombs, enough to totally destroy the Earth thirty or forty times over, even if a powerful medicine man could bring it back each time it was destroyed.

In all of their recorded history The Others had never invented a weapon that they didn't come to use on each other — sooner or later.

And so, that's the way the final war was started. The military tribe got into a big fight with the communist tribe. It started off with a lot of bad words that led to threats that ended up with them shooting their flying bombs at each other.

It wouldn't have been too bad if they just shot a few and then quit. Maybe their "acceptable loss factor" would have worked and only a few hundred thousand would have died, with a few hundred thousand more dying later when the Serpent's breath settled down to the ground. But it didn't work out that way, they just kept shooting more and more.

One or two fires might have gone out by themselves or they could have been put out but ten thousand fires raged in a nuclear inferno that took on a life of its own. Giant freak firestorms never even dreamed of by the military and strategy tribes created winds up to 1,000 miles an hour that screamed and writhed and sucked whole cities and entire tribes into the gaping maw of the Serpent.

She had returned, lingered, and was gone — and the Earth was gone with her forever.

And in a galaxy far away a tiny planet hung in deep space, a single dewdrop that sparkled and shone in the gossamer web of another solar system, waiting for the white light from an incinerated planet as it sped across the dark chasm of a billion light years.

It was the dead of winter when the light arrived and on the southern hemisphere of that tiny green planet, peaceful men tending their flocks on rocky hillsides looked up, and lo, a great shining light appeared in the eastern sky, and they were afraid, and stood in fear and awe, and wondered what this great sign could mean.

——— THE BEGINNING ———

References

Altman, Jon. 1989. Tourism Dilemmas for Aboriginal Australians. Annals of Tourism Research 16(4):456–476.

Amagoalik, John. 1992. The Land Claim and Nunavut: One without the Other Isn't Enough. Arctic Circle 2(4):20.

Ancona, Douglas M. 1985. Northwest United States Indian Fishing Rights: Multi-Jurisdictional Resource and Harvest Management Problems and Solutions. In: Native Self-Reliance through Resource Management. Proceedings of International Conference "Towards Native Self-Reliance, Renewal and Development" held in Vancouver, August 19–24, 1984. William F. Sinclair et al. eds. Vancouver: Hemlock Printers. pp.52–53.

Anderson, David, and Richard Grove. 1987. The Scramble for Eden: Past, Present and Future in African Conservation. In: Conservation in Africa. People, Policies and Practice. David Anderson and Richard Grove eds. Cambridge: Cambridge University Press. pp.1–12.

Aniskowicz, B. Theresa. 1990. Life or Death? A Case for the Defense of Wood Buffalo National Park's Bison. Nature Canada 19(2):35–38.

Arnstein, Sherry A. 1969. A Ladder of Citizen Participation. Journal of the American Institute of Planners 35:216–224.

Assembly of First Nations, Forest Policy Committee. 1983. A Proposal by Indian Governments for: An AFN-Canada Forest Development Agreement. Ottawa: AFN, November 30, 1983.

Ball, Georgina. 1985. The Monopoly System of Wildlife Management of the Indians and the Hudson's Bay Company in the Early History of British Columbia. B.C. Studies 66:37–58.

Bankes, Nigel D. 1987. The Place of Land-Use Planning in the TFN Claim. In: Hinterland or Homeland? Land-Use Planning in Northern Canada. Terry Fenge and William E. Rees eds. Ottawa: Canadian Arctic Resources Committee. pp.95–112.

Bartlett, Richard H. 1981. Indian and Native Rights in Uranium Development in Northern Saskatchewan. Saskatchewan Law Review 45(1):14–29.

———. 1983. Mineral Rights on Indian Reserves in Ontario. The Canadian Journal of Native Studies 3(2):245–275.

———. 1984. Indian Reserves in Quebec. Saskatoon: University of Saskatchewan, Native Law Centre. Studies in Aboriginal Rights N.8.

———. 1985. Reserve Lands. In: Aboriginal Peoples and the Law: Indian, Metis and Inuit Rights in Canada. Bradford W. Morse ed. Ottawa: Carleton University Press. pp.467–578.

———. 1986. Provincial Jurisdiction and Resource Development on Indian Reserve Lands. In: Managing Natural Resources in a Federal State. J. Owen Saunders ed. Toronto, Calgary, Vancouver: The Carswell Company Ltd.

———. 1988. Aboriginal Water Rights in Canada: A Study of Aboriginal Title to Water and Indian Water Rights. Calgary: The Canadian Institute of Resources Law.

———. 1989. Hydroelectric Power and Indian Water Rights on the Prairies. Prairie Forum 14(2):177–193.

———. 1990. Indian Reserves and Aboriginal Lands in Canada: A Homeland. A Study in Law and History. Saskatoon: University of Saskatchewan Native Law Centre.

Barton, Barry. 1985. Water Resources and Native Peoples. Calgary: The Canadian Institute of Resources Law.

Bayly, John U. 1987. Large Scale Oil and Gas Extraction from the Beaufort-Mackenzie Delta Region: Can Land-Use Planning Help the Native Residents? In: Hinterland or Homeland? Land-Use Planning in Northern Canada. Terry Fenge and William E. Rees eds. Ottawa: Canadian Arctic Resources Committee. pp. 113–137.

Beanlands, Gordon E., and Peter N. Duinker. 1983. An Ecological Framework for Environmental Impact Assessment in Canada. Halifax: Dalhousie University, Institute for Resource and Environmental Studies, and Hull: Federal Environmental Assessment Review Office.

Beaudry, Michel. 1992. Searching for Sockeye. Equinox 66:52–62.

Bell, Richard H.V. 1987. Conservation with a human Face: Conflict and Reconciliation in African Land Use Planning. In: Conservation in Africa. People, Policies and Practice. David Anderson and Richard Grove eds. Cambridge: Cambridge University Press. pp. 79–101.

Bennett, David. 1982. Subsistence v. Commercial Use. The Meaning of these Words in Relation to Hunting and Fishing by Canada's Native Peoples. Ottawa: Canadian Arctic Resources Committee.

Berger, Thomas R. 1977. Northern Frontier, Northern Homeland. The Report of the Mackenzie Valley Pipeline Inquiry. Two Volumes. Toronto: James Lorimer and Co., Publishers.

Berkes, Fikret. 1977. Fishing Resource Use in a Subarctic Indian Community. Human Ecology 5(4):289–307.

———. 1981. The Role of Self-Regulation in Living Resources Management in the North. In: Proceedings of the First International Symposium on Renewable Resources and the Economy of the North. Milton M.R. Freeman ed. Ottawa: Association of Canadian Universities for Northern Studies. pp. 166–178.

———. 1982. Preliminary Impacts of the James Bay Hydroelectric Project, Quebec, on Estuarine Fish and Fisheries. Arctic 35(4):524–530.

———. 1985. The Common Property Resource Problem and the Creation of Limited Property Rights. Human Ecology 13(2):187–208.

———. 1987. Common Property Resource Management and Cree Indian Fisheries in Subarctic Canada. In: The Question of the Commons. The Culture and Ecology of Communal Resources. Bonnie J. McCay and James M. Acheson eds. Tuscon: The University of Arizona Press. pp. 66–91.

———. 1988. Environmental Philosophy of the Chisasibi Cree People of James Bay. In: Traditional Knowledge and Renewable Resource Management in Northern Regions. Milton M.R. Freeman and Ludwig N. Carbyn eds. Edmonton: Boreal Institute for Northern Studies. Occasional Publication No. 23, pp. 7–21.

———. 1989. Co-Management and the James Bay Agreement. In: Co-Operative Management of Local Fisheries. Evelyn Pinkerton ed. Vancouver: University of British Columbia Press. pp. 189–208.

———. 1990. Native Subsistence Fisheries: A Synthesis of Harvest Studies in Canada. Arctic 43(1):35–42.

Berkes, Fikret, Peter George and Richard Preston. 1991a. Co-Management: The Evolution of the Theory and Practice of the Joint Administration of Living Resources. Alternatives 18(2):12–18.

———. 1991b. Co-Management: The Evolution of the Theory and Practice of the Joint Administration of Living Resources. Hamilton: Program for Technology Assessment in Subarctic Ontario, McMaster University. TASO Research Report, Second Series, No. 1.

Berkes, Fikret, and D. Pocock. 1983. The Ontario Native Fishing Agreement in Perspective, A Study in User Group Ecology. Environments 15(3):17–26.

Bielawski, Ellen. 1992. Inuit Indigenous Knowledge and Science in the Arctic. Northern Perspectives 20(1):5–8.

Binder, Lloyd N., and Bruce Hanbidge. 1991. The Inuvialuit of the Western Arctic and Resource Co-Management under a Land Claims Settlement. Paper presented at the IASCP (The International Association for the Study of Common Property) Common Property Conference, September 26–29, 1991, Winnipeg, Manitoba.

Bishop, Charles A. 1974. The Northern Ojibwa and the Fur Trade: An Historical and Ecological Study. Toronto: Holt, Rinehart and Winston of Canada.

———. 1981. Northeastern Indian Concepts of Conservation and the Fur Trade: A Critique of Calvin Martin's Thesis. In: Indians, Animals, and the Fur Trade: A Critique of Keepers of the Game. Shepard Krech III ed. Athens, Georgia: The University of Georgia Press. pp.39–58.

Blair, John H. 1984. Producing and Providing: The Story of Kiashke River Native Development Inc. Report prepared for the Ontario Royal Commission on the Northern Environment.

Bourque, J.W., and John McCullum. 1990. Northern Canadian Community Conservation Initiatives. A Report from the Community Perspective. Yellowknife: Department of Renewable Resources, Government of the Northwest Territories.

Bowles, Roy T. 1979. Social Impact Assessment in Small Canadian Communities. Peterborough: Trent University, Department of Sociology.

Breeden, Stanley. 1988. The First Australians. National Geographic 173(2):266–289.

Bregha, Francois. 1989. Conservation in the Yukon and the Northwest Territories. In: Endangered Spaces. The Future for Canada's Wilderness. Monte Hummel ed. Toronto: Key Porter Books Ltd. pp.211–225.

Breslin, P., and M. Chapin. 1984. Conservation, Kuna Style. Grassroots Development 8(2):26–30.

Brightman, Robert A. 1987. Conservation and Resource Depletion. The Case of the Boreal Forest Algonquians. In: The Question of the Commons. The Culture and Ecology of Communal Resources. Bonnie J. McCay and James M. Acheson eds. Tuscon: The University of Arizona Press. pp.121–141.

British Columbia Aboriginal Peoples' Fisheries Commission. n.d. British Columbia Indian Aquaculture Development Program. A Discussion Paper. Vancouver: British Columbia Aboriginal Peoples' Fisheries Commission.

Broadhead, John. 1989. The All Alone Stone Manifesto. In: Endangered Spaces. The Future for Canada's Wilderness. Monte Hummel ed. Toronto: Key Porter Books Ltd. pp.50–62.

Brody, Hugh. 1981. Maps and Dreams. Indians and the British Columbia Frontier. Vancouver: Douglas and McIntyre.

Bryson, Connie. 1991. Rafferty-Alameda. The Public Found a Key and Opened a Door. Environment Views 13(4):12–19.

Busby, Chris. 1991. James Bay: the Sequel. Bourassa's Dream for Quebec. Borealis 2(4):8–13.

Byrne Swain, Margaret. 1989. Gender Roles in Indigenous Tourism: Kuna Mola, Kuna Yala, and Cultural Survival. In: Hosts and Guests. The Anthropology of Tourism. Valene L. Smith ed. Philadelphia: University of Pennsylvania Press. Second Edition. pp.83–104.

Canada, Saskatchewan, Cluff Lake Board of Inquiry. 1978. Final Report of the Cluff Lake Board of Inquiry. Hon. Mr. Justice E.D. Bayda, Chairperson. Regina: Cluff Lake Board of Inquiry.

Canadian Arctic Resources Committee. 1987. Interview: Pierre Asselin. Northern Perspectives 15(4):6–7.

———. 1988. Changing Times, Challenging Agendas. National Symposium on the North. Ottawa: Canadian Arctic Resources Committee.

———. 1992. The EIS Guidelines: Pushing Hydro-Quebec into the 21st Century. Northern Perspectives 20(2):7.

Canadian Bar Association. 1988. Aboriginal Rights in Canada: An Agenda for Action. Ottawa: Canadian Bar Association. Chapter 2 Reprint. Conference Program "The Economic Bridge to Self-Reliance. Aboriginal Land Claims", sponsored by Native Investment and Trade Association, Vancouver, May 12–14, 1990.

Cassidy, Frank, and Norman Dale. 1988. After Native Claims? The Implications of Comprehensive Claims Settlements for Natural Resources in British Columbia. Lantzville, B.C.: Oolichan Books and Halifax, N.S.: The Institute for Research on Public Policy.

Caulfield, Richard A. 1988. The Role of Subsistence Resource Commissions in Managing Alaska's New National Parks. In: Traditional Knowledge and Renewable Resource Management in Northern Regions. Milton M.R. Freeman and Ludwig N. Carbyn eds. Edmonton: Boreal Institute for Northern Studies. Occasional Publication No.23. pp.55–64.

Chapin, M. 1990. The Silent Jungle: Ecotourism Among the Kuna Indians of Panama. Cultural Survival 14(1):42–45.

Chartier, Clem. 1985. Aboriginal Rights and Land Issues: the Metis Perspective. In: The Quest for Justice: Aboriginal Peoples and Aboriginal Rights. Menno Boldt and J. Anthony Long eds. Toronto: University of Toronto. pp.54–61.

Cheslatta Carrier Nation. 1990. The Story of the Surrender of the Cheslatta Reserves on April 21, 1952. Burns Lake: Cheslatta Carrier Nation.

Child, Graham. 1984. Managing Wildlife for People in Zimbabwe. In: National Parks, Conservation and Development. The Role of Protected Areas in Sustaining Society. Jeffrey A. McNeely and Kenton R. Miller eds. Proceedings of the World Congress on National Parks. Bali, Indonesia, 11–22 October, 1982. Washington, D.C.: Smithsonian Institution Press. pp. 118–121.

Clad, James C. 1985. Conservation and Indigenous Peoples: A Study of Convergent Interests. In: Culture and Conservation: The Human Dimension in Environmental Planning. Jeffrey A. McNeely and David Pitt eds. London, Sydney, Dover, N.H.: Croom Helm Ltd. pp. 45–62.

Clairman, Cara L. 1993. First Nations and Environmental Groups in Ontario's Parks — Conflict and Cooperation? Canadian Native Law Reporter (1993) 1:1–19.

Clark, Bruce A. 1987. Indian Title in Canada. Toronto, Calgary, Vancouver: The Carswell Company Limited.

Clement, Wallace. 1986. The Struggle to Organize. Resistance in Canada's Fishery. Toronto: McClelland and Stewart Ltd.

Clyde River. 1990. Igalirtuuq: A Conservation Proposal for Bowhead Whales at Isabella Bay, Baffin Island, NWT. Clyde River, NWT: Community of Clyde River.

Cohen, Fay G. 1986. Treaties on Trial. The Continuing Controversy over Northwest Indian Fishing Rights. Seattle: University of Washington Press.

Collett, David. 1987. Pastoralists and Wildlife: Image and Reality in Kenya Maasailand. In: Conservation in Africa. People, Policies and Practice. David Anderson and Richard Grove eds. Cambridge: Cambridge University Press. pp. 129–148.

Columbia Lake First Nation. 1991. Statement on Columbia Lake Band Water Rights. Columbia Lake Band.

Confederated Salish and Kootenai Tribes. 1982. Mission Mountains Tribal Wilderness Management Plan. CSKT: Wildland Recreation Department.

———. 1986. Mission Mountains Tribal Wilderness Buffer Zone Management Plan. CSKT: Wildland Recreation Department.

Coon-Come, Matthew. 1992. Canada: Great Whale River — James Bay II Hydroelectric Project. Case Document presented at the Second International Water Tribunal, Amsterdam, Holland, 17–22 February, 1992. IWGIA Newsletter 2, April/May/June 1992:4–10.

Cooper, Jim. 1985. Caribou Indian Enterprises. In: Native Self-Reliance through Resource Management. Proceedings of International Conference "Towards Native Self-Reliance, Renewal and Development" held in Vancouver, August 19–24, 1984. William F. Sinclair et al. eds. Vancouver: Hemlock Printers. p. 114.

Corelli, Rae. 1990. Fateful Consequences. MacLean's, May 21, 1990:56–57.

Corke, C. Phillip. 1985. The Determination of Indian Water Rights in the United States. In: Native Self-Reliance through Resource Management. Proceedings of International Conference "Towards Native Self-Reliance, Renewal and Development", held in Vancouver, August 19–24, 1984. William F. Sinclair et al. eds. Vancouver: Hemlock Printers. pp. 142–144.

Council for Yukon Indians. 1984. Submission on Renewable Resources Management. In: National and Regional Interests in the North. Third National Workshop on People, Resources, and the Environment North of 60. June 1–3, 1983, Yellowknife, NWT. Ottawa: Canadian Arctic Resources Committee. pp. 427–433.

Council of the Haida Nation. 1991. Haida Fisheries Program. Massett: Council of the Haida Nation. October 1991.

———. 1992. Management Plan for the Commercial Recreational Fishery of Haida Gwaii. Massett: Council of the Haida Nation. June 1992.

Crerar, A.D. 1969. Fisheries in the Atlantic Provinces. Ottawa: Atlantic Development Board. Background Study No. 3.

Cromarty, Dennis. 1988. Summary of the Activities of the Nishnawbe-Aski Nation, June 1985–June 1988. Nishnawbe-Aski Nation, June 28, 1988.

Cumming, Peter A., and Neil H. Mickenberg. 1972. Native Rights in Canada. Second Edition. Toronto: The Indian-Eskimo Association of Canada in Association with General Publishing Co. Ltd.

Daniel, R. 1979. The Spirit and Terms of Treaty Eight. In: The Spirit of the Alberta Indian Treaties. Richard Price ed. Toronto: Butterworth and Co. (Canada) Ltd. pp.47–100.

Dasmann, Raymond F. 1974. Difficult Marginal Environments and the Traditional Societies which Exploit Them: Ecosystems. Symposium on the Future of traditional primitive Societies. Cambridge, UK. Survival International News 11:11–15.

———. 1976. National Parks, Nature Conservation, and "Future Primitive". The Ecologist 6(5):164–178. Reprinted in: Tribal Peoples and Development Issues. A Global Overview. John H. Bodley ed. Mountain View: Mayfield Publishing Company, 1988. pp.301–310.

———. 1984. The Relationship between Protected Areas and Indigenous Peoples. In: National Parks, Conservation, and Development. The Role of Protected Areas in Sustaining Society. Jeffrey A. McNeely and Kenton R. Miller eds. Proceedings of the World Congress on National Parks. Bali, Indonesia, 11–22 October, 1982. Washington, D.C.: Smithsonian Institution Press. pp.667–671.

Davidson, D.S. 1928. Family Hunting Territories in Northwestern North America. New York: Museum of the American Indian.

Davies, Matthew, and Barry Sadler. 1990. Post-Project Analysis and the Improvement of Guidelines for Environmental Monitoring and Audit. Ottawa: Minister of Supply and Services.

Deloria Jr., Vine. 1973. God is Red. New York: Dell Publishing Co., Inc.

———. 1978. The Lummi Indian Community: The Fishermen of the Pacific Northwest. In: American Indian Economic Development. Sam Stanley, ed. The Hague/Paris: Mouton Publishers, distributed in the USA and Canada by Aldine, Chicago. pp.87–158.

Denevan, William M. 1992. The Pristine Myth: The Landscape of the Americas in 1492.
Annals of the Association of American Geographers. 82(3):369–385.

Deninoo Wildlife and Resources Committee. 1991. Hook Lake Wood Bison Management Plan. Fort Resolution: Deninoo Wildlife and Resources Committee.

Dion, Joe. 1984. Social Impact of Petroleum Activity. Ottawa: Department of Indian and Northern Affairs, October 1, 1984.

Doran, Janis. 1982. History of Water Rights on Indian Reserves in British Columbia (circa 1850–1930). Public and Intergovernmental Relations, British Columbia Region, Indian and Northern Affairs Canada.

Doubleday, Nancy C. 1989. Co-Management Provisions of the Inuvialuit Final Agreement. In: Co-Operative Management of Local Fisheries. Evelyn Pinkerton ed. Vancouver: University of British Columbia Press. pp.209–227.

———. 1990. The Inuit Regional Conservation Strategy: Sustainable Development in the Circumpolar Region. In: Sustainable Development through Northern Conservation Strategies. Elaine Smith ed. The Banff Centre for Continuing Education. Calgary: The University of Calgary Press. pp.83–90.

———. 1991. Competing Value Systems: Evolution of Norms, State Control and Traditional Ecological Knowledge. Paper presented at the IASCP (The International Association for the Study of Common Property) Common Property Conference, September 26–29, 1991, Winnipeg, Manitoba.

The DPA Group Inc. 1986. Alternative Approaches to Social Impact Assessment. Prepared for: The Northern Alberta Development Council, April 1986.

Driben, Paul. 1983. The Nature of Metis Claims. The Canadian Journal of Native Studies 3(1):183–196.

———. 1987. Fishing in Uncharted Waters. A Perspective on the Indian Fishing Agreements Dispute in Northern Ontario. Alternatives 15(1):19–26.

Drushka, Ken. 1985. Stumped: the Forest Industry in Transition. Vancouver: Douglas and McIntyre.

East, Ken. 1986. Resource Co-Management in Wood Buffalo National Park: The National Park's Perspective. In: Native People and Renewable Resource Management. The 1986 Symposeum of the Alberta Society of Professional Biologists. Edmonton: Alberta Society of Professional Biologists. pp.86–95.

Edwards, Gordon. 1991. Uranium: a Discussion Guide. Montreal: National Film Board of Canada.

Edwards, Paul. 1990. The AL-PAC Review Hearings: A Case Study. Edmonton: Environmental Law Centre.

Eidsvik, Harold. 1989. Canada in a Global Context. In: Endangered Spaces. The Future for Canada's Wilderness. Monte Hummel ed. Toronto: Key Porter Books Ltd. pp.30–47.

Elias, Peter Douglas. 1989a. Aboriginal Rights and Litigation: History and Future of Court Decisions in Canada. Polar Record 25(152):1–8.

———. 1989b. Rights and Research: The Role of the Social Sciences in the Legal and Political Resolution of Land Claims and Questions of Aboriginal Rights. Canadian Native Law Reporter 1:1–43.

———. 1991. Development of Aboriginal People's Communities. North York: Captus Press Inc.

Elias, Peter Douglas, and Martin S. Weinstein. 1992. Development and the Indian People of Fort Ware: Predicting and Managing Consequences. A Study for the Kaska Dena Council and the Community of Fort Ware. September 1992.

Elliot, David W. 1985. Aboriginal Title. In: Aboriginal Peoples and the Law: Indian, Metis and Inuit Rights in Canada. Bradford W. Morse ed. Ottawa: Carleton University Press. pp.48–121.

Environmental Impact Review Board. 1989. Public Review of the Esso Chevron et al. Isserk I-15 Drilling Program. Inuvik: Joint Secretariat.

———. 1990a. Annual Activity Report 1989–1990. Inuvik: Joint Secretariat.

———. 1990b. Public Review of the Gulf Canada Resources Limited Kulluk Drilling Program 1990–1992. Inuvik: Joint Secretariat.

———. 1991. Annual Activity Report 1990–1991. Inuvik: Joint Secretariat.

Environmental Impact Screening Committee. 1990. Annual Activity Report 1988–1990. Inuvik: Joint Secretariat.

———. 1991. Annual Activity Report 1990–1991. Inuvik: Joint Secretariat.

Erasmus, George. 1989. A Native Viewpoint. In: Endangered Spaces. The Future for Canada's Wilderness. Monte Hummel ed. Toronto: Key Porter Books Ltd. pp.92–98.

Etkin, Carol E. 1988. The Sechelt Indian Band: An Analysis of a new Form of Native Self-Government. The Canadian Journal of Native Studies 8(1):73–105.

Evans, Nancy H. 1981. The Native American Heritage Commission and Energy-Related Issues. In: Native Americans and Energy Development II. Joseph G. Jorgensen ed. Irvine: University of California. (Manuscript)

Everitt, Robert R. 1986. Native Roles in Monitoring of Energy Developments. In: Native People and Renewable Resource Management. The 1986 Symposium of the Alberta Society of Professional Biologists. Edmonton: Alberta Society of Professional Biologists. pp.44–48.

Everitt, Robert R., D.A. Birdsall and David Stone. 1990. The Beaufort Environmental Monitoring Program. In: Integrated Approaches to Resource Planning and Management. Calgary: The University of Calgary Press. pp.251–266.

Ewers, John C. 1958. The Blackfeet. Raiders on the Northwestern Plains. Norman: University of Oklahoma Press.

Expert Panel on Forest Management in Alberta. 1990. Forest Management in Alberta. Report of the Expert Review Panel. Edmonton: Alberta Energy/Forestry, Lands and Wildlife.

Feit, Harvey A. 1982. Protecting Indigenous Hunters: The Social and Environmental Protection Regime in the James Bay and Northern Quebec Land Claims Agreement. In: Indian SIA: The Social Impact Assessment of Rapid Resource Development on Native Peoples. Charles C. Geisler, Rayna Green, Daniel Usner and Patrick West eds. Ann Arbor: University of Michigan. pp.290–321.

———. 1986. James Bay Cree Indian Management and Moral Considerations of Fur Bearers. In: Native People and Renewable Resource Management. The 1986 Symposium of the Alberta Society of Professional Biologists. Edmonton: Alberta Society of Professional Biologists. pp.49–65.

———. 1988a. Self-Management and State-Management: Forms of Knowing and Managing Northern Wildlife. In: Traditional Knowledge and Renewable Resource Management in Northern Regions. Milton M.R. Freeman and Ludwig N. Carbyn eds. Edmonton: Boreal Institute for Northern Studies. Occasional Publication No. 23, pp.72–91.

———. 1988b. The Power and the Responsibility: Implementation of the Wildlife and Hunting Provisions of the James Bay and Northern Quebec Agreement. In: James Bay and Northern Quebec: Ten Years After. Sylvie Vincent and Garry Bowers eds. Montreal: Recherches Amerindiennes au Québec. pp.74–87.

———. 1989. James Bay Cree Self-Governance and Land Management. In: We Are Here. Politics of Aboriginal Land Tenure. Edwin N. Wilmsen ed. Berkeley: University of California Press. pp.68–98.

Fenge, Terry. 1987. Land-Use Planning in Canada's North: A Wind of Change or a Bag of Wind? In: Hinterland or Homeland? Land-Use Planning in Northern Canada. Terry Fenge and William E. Rees eds. Ottawa: Canadian Arctic Resources Committee. pp.19–51.

———. 1992. The Great Whale Review and the Federal Government's Disappearing Act. Northern Perspectives 20(2):2–5.

Findley, Rowe. 1990. Will We Save Our Own? National Geographic 178(3):105–136.

Finsterbusch, Kurt. 1980. Understanding Social Impacts. Assessing the Effects of Public Projects. Beverly Hills, London: Sage Publishers.

Finsterbusch, Kurt, and C.P. Wolf eds. 1977. Methodology and Social Impact Assessment. Second Edition. Stroudsburg, Pennsylvania/Woods Hole, Massachusetts: Hutchinson Ross Publishing Company.

Flanagan, Thomas. 1983. Riel and the Rebellion: 1985 Reconsidered. Saskatoon: Western Producer Prairie Books.

Flathead Culture Committee. 1978. Position Paper on the Mission Mountains. St. Ignatius, Montana.

The Fort Fitzgerald Dene Band. 1992. Workplan for a Community-Based Plan for Management of Buffalo in Wood Buffalo National Park. March 1992.

Fort McKay Band, R. Justus and J. Simonetta. 1983. From Where They Stand: Progressive Restriction, Natural Resource Exploitation and the Fort McKay People in North-East Alberta, Canada. World Council of Indigenous Peoples Newsletter 3:5–25.

Foster, B. 1979. Ecological Reserves in Canada with Emphasis on British Columbia. In: The Canadian National Parks: Today and Tomorrow. Conference II: Ten Years Later. October 8–13, 1978, Banff, Alberta. J.G. Nelson, R.D. Needham, S.H. Nelson, and R.C. Scace eds. Waterloo: University of Waterloo. Volume 1. pp.261–266.

Foster, Janet. 1978. Working for Wildlife. Toronto: University of Toronto Press.

Fox, Allan. 1983. Kakadu is Aboriginal Land. Ambio 12(3–4):161–166.

Francis, Kathy. 1992. First they Came and Took our Trees, now they Want our Water too. Presentation by Chief Kathy Francis to the Water Export Conference, "Should British Columbia's Water be for Sale?", Vancouver, B.C., May 7–8, 1992. Squirrel Cove: Klahoose Indian Band.

Franks, Martha. 1991. The Uses of the Practicably Irrigable Acreage Standard in the Quantification of Reserved Water Rights. Natural Resources Journal 31(3):549–585.

Freeman, Milton M.R. 1984. Arctic Ecosystems. In: Handbook of North American Indians. D.J. Damas and W.C. Sturtevant eds. Washington, D.C.: Smithsonian Institution. Volume 5, pp.36–48.

———. 1985. Appeal to Tradition: Different Perspectives on Arctic Wildlife Management. In: Native Power. The Quest for Autonomy and Nationhood of Indigenous Peoples. Jens Brosted et al. eds. Bergen, Oslo, Stavanger, Tromso: Universitetsforlaget AS. pp.265–281.

———. 1986. Renewable Resources Economics and Native Communities. In: Native People and Renewable Resource Management. The 1986 Symposium of the Alberta Society of Professional Biologists. Edmonton: Alberta Society of Professional Biologists. pp.29–37.

———. 1989a. The Alaska Eskimo Whaling Commission: Successful Co-Management under Extreme Conditions. In: Co-Operative Management of Local Fisheries. Evelyn Pinkerton ed. Vancouver: University of British Columbia Press. pp.137–153.

———. 1989b. Graphs and Gaffs: A Cautionary Tale in the Common Property Resources Debate. In: Common Property Resources. Fikret Berkes ed. London: Belhaven Press. pp.92–109.

Freeman, Milton M.R., Eleanor E. Wein and Darren E. Keith. 1992 Recovering Rights. Bowhead Whales and Inuvialuit Subsistence in the Western Canadian Arctic. Canadian Circumpolar Institute and Fisheries Joint Management Committee.

Frideres, James S. 1984. Government Policy and Indian Natural Resource Development. The Canadian Journal of Native Studies 4(1):51–66.

Fuller, Stephan, and Timothy McTiernan. 1987. Old Crow and the Northern Yukon: Achieving Sustainable Renewable Resource Utilization. Alternatives 14(1):18–25.

Fumoleau, René. 1973. As long as this Land shall Last. Toronto: McClelland and Stewart Limited.

Fur Institute of Canada. 1985. With Respect to the Fur Industry (Information Pamphlet). Toronto: Fur Institute of Canada

———. 1986. On Nature's Terms (Information Pamphlet). Toronto: Fur Institute of Canada.

Gallagher, Thomas J. 1988. Native Participation in Land Management Planning in Alaska. Arctic 41(2):91–98.

Gambell, Ray. 1991. International Management of Aboriginal Subsistence Whaling. Paper prepared for the IASCP (The International Association for the Study of Common Property) Common Property Conference, September 26–29, 1991, Winnipeg, Manitoba.

Gardner, J.E., and J.G. Nelson. 1981. National Parks and Native Peoples in Northern Canada, Alaska and Northern Australia. Environmental Conservation 8(3):207–215.

Geist, Valerius. 1991. Phantom Subspecies: The Wood Bison "athabascae" Rhoads 1897 Is Not a Valid Taxon, but an Ecotype. Arctic 44(4):283–300.

Getty, I.A.L., and J.W. Larner. 1972. The Kootenay Plains and the Big Horn Stoney Band — An Oral and Documentary Historical Study, 1800–1970. Unpublished Research Report. Morley: Stoney Tribal Council.

Getty, Wayne E.A. 1975. A Case History and Analysis of Stoney Indian-Government Interaction with Regard to the Bighorn Dam: The Effects of Citizen Participation — A Lesson on Government Perfidy and Indian Frustration. Unpublished M.S.W. Thesis. Calgary: The University of Calgary, Faculty of Social Welfare.

Glavin, Terry. 1990. A Death Feast in Dimla-Hamid. Vancouver: New Star Books Ltd.

Gorman, Margaret. 1987. Dene Community Development: Lessons from the Norman Wells Project. Alternatives 14(1):10–12.

Gorrie, Peter. 1990. The James Bay Power Project. Canadian Geographic 110(1):21–31.

Gottesman, Dan. 1983. Native Hunting and the Migratory Birds Convention Act: Historical, Political and Ideological Perspectives. Journal of Canadian Studies 18(3):67–89.

Government of Alberta. 1986. A Guide to Native Communities in Alberta. Edmonton: Native Affairs Secretariat.

———. n.d.a. Subsistence Hunting (Information Pamphlet). Forestry, Lands and Wildlife.

———. n.d.b. Livestock Industry Diversification in Alberta (Information Pamphlet). Alberta Agriculture.

Government of British Columbia. 1992. Policy Framework — Joint Stewardship (Draft). Information Package, B.C. Environment.

Government of Canada. 1971. Statement on Proposals to Amend Ontario Indian Land Agreement, 1924. Department of Indian Affairs, July 16, 1971.

———. 1980. Indian Conditions. A Survey. Ottawa: Indian and Northern Affairs Canada.

———. 1981. In all Fairness: A Native Claims Policy, Comprehensive Claims. Ottawa: Department of Indian Affairs and Northern Development.

———. 1982a. A Policy Statement for Forest Renewal. Ottawa: Environment Canada.

———. 1982b. Parks Canada Policy. Parks Canada.

———. 1983. Canadian Forestry Service Policy for Indian Land Forestry Programs. Ottawa: Agriculture Canada.

———. 1984. The Western Arctic Claim: The Inuvialuit Final Agreement. Ottawa: Department of Indian Affairs and Northern Development.

———. 1986. A Policy Proposal for a B.C. Indian Community Salmon Fishery. Released for Discussion by the Minister of Fisheries and Oceans and the Minister of Indian Affairs and Northern Development (March 13, 1986). Ottawa: Department of Fisheries and Oceans.

———. 1988. Northern Yukon National Park. Interim Management Guidelines. Environment Canada: Canadian Parks Service.

———. 1989. 1988 Indian Reserve Community Profiles. Manitoba Region. Ottawa: Department of Indian Affairs and Northern Development.

———. 1990a. First Northern Regional Land Use Plan Approved. Press Release, November 28, 1990. Indian and Northern Affairs Canada.

———. 1990b. Federal Environmental Assessment: New Directions. Fact Sheets Nos. 1–13. Ottawa: Federal Environmental Assessment Review Office.

———. 1991. A National Summary of Mineral Resources Potential of Indian Reserve Lands. Mineral Inventory Report. Ottawa: Indian and Northern Affairs Canada, June 5, 1991.

Government of Canada and the Tungavik. 1993. Agreement Between the Inuit of the Nunavut Settlement Area and Her Majesty the Queen in right of Canada. Ottawa: Department of Indian Affairs and Northern Development and the Tungavik.

Government of Manitoba. 1991. Outline of Joint Principles and Guidelines for Co-Management, Waterhen/Pine Creek Bands and Manitoba Natural Resources. (Draft) Department of Natural Resources, June 13, 1991.

Government of the Northwest Territories. 1986. NWT Data Book 1986–87. Yellowknife: Outcrop Limited.
———. 1990. Renewable Resources: Building on a Tradition. Yellowknife: Government of the Northwest Territories.
Government of Ontario. 1990. News Release. Province and Teme-Augama Anishnabai sign Historic Stewardship Agreement. Ontario Ministry of Natural Resources.
———. 1991. Interim Enforcement Policy on the Aboriginal Right to Hunt and Fish for Food. Ontario Ministry of Natural Resources, May 28, 1991.
Government of Saskatchewan. 1990. Implications of Sparrow v. the Queen for Wildlife and Fisheries Management in Saskatchewan. A Discussion Paper prepared by the Constitutional Branch, Saskatchewan Justice, September 1990.
Government of Yukon. 1986. Yukon Data Book 1986–87. Whitehorse: Outcrop (Yukon) Ltd.
Grant, Peter. 1991. Delgamuukw and Others v. The Queen, the Gitksan-Wet'suwet'en Land Claims Case in British Columbia: Pushing the Boundaries of the Recognition of the Content of Aboriginal Jurisdiction. In: Commission on Folk Law and Legal Pluralism. Proceedings of the 6th International Symposium. Ottawa, August 14–18, 1990. Harald W. Finkler ed. Volume 1. pp.248–255.
Gray, Andrew. 1991. Between the Spice of Life and the Melting Pot: Biodiversity Conservation and its Impact on Indigenous Peoples. IWGIA Document No.70. Copenhagen: International Work Group for Indigenous Affairs.
Greenberg, Adolph M. 1985. Game Conservation and Native Peoples in Northern Ontario. Cultural Survival Quarterly 9(1):26–30.
Griffith, Ray. 1987. Northern Park Development: The Case of Snowdrift. Alternatives 14(1):26–30.
Groves, Robert. 1991. Territoriality and Aboriginal Self-Determination: Options for Legal Pluralism in Canada. In: Commission on Folk Law and Legal Pluralism. Proceedings of the 6th International Symposium. Ottawa, August 14–18, 1990. Harald W. Finkler ed. Volume 1. pp.224–245.
Gunn, Anne, K. Jingfors and P. Evalik. 1986. The Kitikmeot Harvest Study as a successful Example for the Collection of Wildlife Harvest Statistics in the Northwest Territories. In: Native People and Renewable Resource Management. The 1986 Symposium of the Alberta Society of Professional Biologists. Edmonton: Alberta Society of Professional Biologists. pp.249–259.
Gunn, Anne, Chris Shank and Bruce McLean. 1991. The History, Status and Management of Muskoxen on Banks Island. Arctic 44(3):188–195.
Gwich'in Tribal Council, Comprehensive Claims Branch (DIAND), Aboriginal Rights and Constitutional Development (GNWT). 1991. Comprehensive Land Claims Agreement between Her Majesty the Queen in Right of Canada and The Gwich'in as Represented by the Gwich'in Tribal Council. July 13, 1991.
Hackman, Arlin. 1990. Endangered Spaces: Ten Years for Wilderness in Canada. Borealis 1(4):27–29.
Hall, Nancy. 1990a. Temagami. The Battle to Protect "Deep Water" Country. Borealis 1(4):14–21.
———. 1990b. Temagami Agreement Reached — Environmentalists Unhappy. Borealis 2(2):34.
Hancock, Lyn. 1992a. Mining in the North. Above and Beyond 4(2):29–36.
———. 1992b. Oil and Gas...A Waiting Game. Above and Beyond 4(2):37–40.
Hansen, Lise C., and David T. McNab. 1986. Historical Summary with Respect to Fishing as an Indian Treaty Right in Ontario. Toronto: Ministry of Natural Resources.
Harden, Blaine. 1989. Botswana: Goodbye to the Kalahari — San Forced to Abandon their Territory. IWGIA Newsletter 58:8–19.
Harding, Jim. 1988. Aboriginal Rights and Government Wrongs: Uranium Mining and Neocolonialism in Northern Saskatchewan. Regina: Prairie Justice Research, University of Regina.
———. 1988/1989. Indigenous Rights and Uranium Mining in Northern Saskatchewan. IWGIA Document No.62. Copenhagen: International Work Group for Indigenous Affairs. pp.116–136.
Harper, Janet. 1985. Washington State Indian Settlement: Treaty Fishing Rights. In: Native Self-Reliance through Resource Management. Proceedings of International Conference "Toward Native Self-Reliance, Renewal and Development" held in Vancouver, August 19–24, 1984. William F. Sinclair et al. eds. Vancouver: Hemlock Printers. pp.74–75.
Harris, Judith. 1991. Temagami Stewardship Council. An Interview with Mary Laronde, Bear Island, Lake Temagami, Ontario, August 30, 1990.
Harwood, Lois, and Marie Adams. 1991. Alaska and Inuvialuit Beluga Whale Committee (AIBWC) — A Case Study. Paper presented at the IASCP (The International Association for the Study

of Common Property) Common Property Conference, September 26–29, 1991, Winnipeg, Manitoba.

Hazell, Stephen. 1990. The Icetanker Cometh. Crude Oil in the Arctic. Arctic Circle 1(1):47–48.

Heartwell, Colin. 1988. A Forest Tenure System for Yukon. Victoria: Forestry Canada, Pacific Forestry Centre.

Heber, R.W. 1986. Fish and Oil: The Cultural Ecology of Offshore Resource Activities in Nova Scotia. In: Fish versus Oil: Resources and Rural Development in North Atlantic Societies. J.D. House, ed. St. John's: Institute of Social and Economic Research, Memorial University of Newfoundland. pp. 162–175.

Hecky, Robert E. 1987. Methylmercury Contamination in Northern Canada. Northern Perspectives 15(3):8–9.

Henderson, L.A. 1985. Trapping as a Management Tool — An Overview. Can. Dep. Indian North. Aff. Rep. Contract 84-458.

Herscovici, Alan. 1985. Second Nature. The Animal Rights Controversy. Montreal: CBC Enterprises.

Hildebrand, Lance. 1985. Woodland Utilization Plan for the Public Bush on the Walpole Island Indian Reserve. Wallaceburg: Walpole Island Research Centre (Nin.Da.Waab.Jig) Occasional Paper No. 10.

Hill, Michael. 1983. Kakadu National Park and the Aboriginals: Partners in Protection. Ambio 12(3–4):158–169.

Hitchcock, Robert K. 1991. Game Park vs. the San. Conservation and Sustainable Development in Kalahari. IWGIA Newsletter 1:7–12.

Hobson, George. 1992. Traditional Knowledge Is Science. Northern Perspectives 20(1):2.

Hodgins, Bruce W., and Jamie Benidickson. 1989. The Temagami Experience. Recreation, Resources, and Aboriginal Rights in the Northern Ontario Wilderness. Toronto, Buffalo, London: University of Toronto Press.

Homewood, Katherine M., and William A. Rodgers. 1984. Pastoralism and Conservation. Human Ecology 12(4):431–441. Reprinted in: Tribal Peoples and Development Issues. A Global Overview. John H. Bodley ed. Mountain View: Mayfield Publishing Company, 1988. pp. 310–320.

———. 1987. Pastoralism, Conservation and Overgrazing. In: Conservation in Africa. People, Policies and Practice. David Anderson and Richard Grove eds. Cambridge: Cambridge University Press. pp. 111–128.

Hopper, M., and G. Power. 1991. The Fisheries of an Ojibwa Community in Northern Ontario. Arctic 44(4):267–274.

Hopwood, Allen. 1988. The Social and Economic Returns from Investment in Forest Management Programs on Indian Lands — Two Case Studies. Victoria: Forestry Canada. FRDA Report 049.

House of Commons. 1986. The Fur Issue. Cultural Continuity, Economic Opportunity. Report of the House of Commons Standing Committee on Aboriginal Affairs and Northern Development. Ottawa: Queen's Printer for Canada, December 1986.

Hume, Mark. 1990. Stikine. The Great River. Borealis 2(2):8–15.

Hundley Jr., Norris. 1985. The Winter's Decision and Indian Water Rights: A Mystery Reexamined. In: The Plains Indians of the Twentieth Century. P. Iverson ed. Norman and London: University of Oklahoma Press. pp. 77–199.

Hunt, C.D. 1979. People and Parks: Selected Legal Issues in Canada. In: The Canadian National Parks: Today and Tomorrow. Conference II: Ten Years Later. October 8–13, 1978, Banff, Alberta. J.G. Nelson, R.D. Needham, S.H. Nelson, and R.C. Scace eds. Waterloo: University of Waterloo. Volume 2. pp. 605–624.

Hunt, Constance, Rusty Miller and Donna Tingley. 1979. Wilderness Area. Legislative Alternatives for the Establishment of a Wilderness Area in the Northern Yukon. Ottawa: Canadian Arctic Resources Committee.

Hunt, Constance, H. Ian Rounthwaite and J. Owen Saunders. 1985. Environmental Protection and Resource Development: Legislation, Policy and Institutions. In: Environmental Protection and Resource Development: Convergence for Today. Barry Sadler ed. The Banff Centre for Continuing Education. Calgary: The University of Calgary Press. pp. 11–46.

Hutchins, Peter W. 1987. The Law applying to the Trapping of Furbearers by Aboriginal Peoples in Canada: A Case of Double Jeopardy. In: Wild Furbearer Management and Conservation in

North America. M. Novak, J.A. Baker, M.E. Obbard and B. Malloch eds. Ontario Ministry of Natural Resources. Published by the Ontario Trappers Association.

Hyatt, David. 1986. The Sechelt Indian Band Self-Government Act. Unpublished Paper.

Indian Chiefs of Alberta. 1970. Citizens Plus. A Presentation by the Indian Chiefs of Alberta to Right Honourable P.E. Trudeau, Prime Minister and the Government of Canada. June 1970. (The "Red Paper").

Infolink Consultants Inc. 1989. Native Forestry: Ethic to Reality. Conference Proceedings, November 22–24, 1989, Vancouver Trade and Convention Centre. Ottawa: Infolink Consultants Inc.

Inglis, Julian T. 1990. The UNESCO Canada/Man and the Biosphere Program. In: Sustainable Development through Northern Conservation Strategies. Elaine Smith ed. The Banff Centre for Continuing Education. Calgary: The University of Calgary Press. pp.141–148.

International Union for the Conservation of Nature. 1975. World Directory of National Parks and other Protected Areas. Gland, Switzerland: IUCN.

———. 1979. The Biosphere Reserve and its Relationship to other Protected Areas. A Report prepared for UNESCO by the Commission on National Parks and Protected Areas of the International Union for Conservation of Nature and Natural Resources.

Intertribal Forestry Association of British Columbia. 1990. A Brief Scenario on the Creation of the Intertribal Forestry Association of B.C. Kelowna: IFABC.

Jackson, E.T. 1984. Community Economic Self-Help and Small-Scale Fisheries. Ottawa: Department of Fisheries and Oceans.

Jacobs, Dean M. 1986. A Co-Operative Study of Socio-Economic and Environmental Factors in Resource Management on the Walpole Island Indian Reserve — Final Report. Wallaceburg: Walpole Island Research Centre (Nin.Da.Waab.Jig) Occasional Paper No.24.

Jacobs, Peter, and Terry Fenge. 1990. Integrating Resource Management in Lancaster Sound: But on Whose Terms? In: Integrated Approaches to Resource Planning and Management. Reg Lang ed. The Banff Centre for Continuing Education. Calgary: The University of Calgary Press. pp.267–291.

Jenness, Diamond. 1932. The Indians of Canada. Ottawa: National Museum of Canada.

John, Ed. 1985. The Tanizul Timber Company Ltd. In: Native Self-Reliance through Resource Management. Proceedings of International Conference "Towards Native Self-Reliance, Renewal and Development" held in Vancouver, August 19–24, 1984. William F. Sinclair et al. eds. Vancouver: Hemlock Printers. pp.112–114.

Johnson, Martha. 1992. Dene Traditional Knowledge. Northern Perspectives 20(1):3–5.

Jubenville, Alan. 1976. Outdoor Recreation Planning. Philadelphia, London, Toronto: W.B. Saunders Company.

Justus, Roger, and JoAnne Simonetta. 1982. Oil Sands, Indians and SIA in Northern Alberta. In: Indian SIA: The Social Impact Assessment of Rapid Resource Development on Native Peoples. Charles C. Geisler, Rayna Green, Daniel Usner and Patrick West eds. Ann Arbor: University of Michigan. pp.238–257.

Kansky, Marilyn. 1987a. Native Indian and Inuit Views on the Federal Environmental Assessment and Review Process. A Research Project for the Indian Association of Alberta. Edmonton: Environmental Law Centre.

———. 1987b. Summary of the Federal Environmental Assessment and Review Process Procedures. Prepared as a Background Paper for a Project to Determine Native Indian and Inuit Concerns. Edmonton: Environmental Law Centre. November 1987.

Karpan, Robin and Arlene. 1989. Fair Game? To raise, or not to raise, wild animals as livestock. Canadian Geographic 109(3):24–29.

Kassi, Norma. 1990. Conservation in the Northern Yukon: Planning for Sustainable Development. In: Sustainable Development through Northern Conservation Strategies. Elaine Smith ed. The Banff Centre for Continuing Education. Calgary: The University of Calgary Press. pp.91–97.

Keeping, Janet Marie. 1989. The Inuvialuit Final Agreement. Calgary: The University of Calgary, Canadian Institute of Resources Law.

Keith, R.F., and A. Saunders eds. 1989. A Question of Rights. Northern Wildlife Management and the Anti-Harvest Movement. National Symposium on the North. Ottawa: Canadian Arctic Resources Committee. Volume 2.

Keith, Robert F., et al. 1987. Arctic Fisheries: New Approaches for Troubled Waters. Northern Perspectives 15(4):1–5.

Kesteven, S. 1984. Summary of Report to the Minister of Aboriginal Affairs on a Fieldtrip to Kakadu National Park to Discuss Tourism with Aboriginal Traditional Owners and Residents of the Park Area, 21–31 March 1984. Unpublished Report, Department of Aboriginal Affairs (File 83/465), Darwin.

Kienetz, Alvin. 1988. Metis "Nationalism" and the Concept of a Metis Land Base in Canada's Prairie Provinces. Canadian Review of Studies in Nationalism 15(1–2):11–18.

Koch, Eddie. 1991. People Preserves. Scientific American, December 1991:54.

Krosenbrink-Gelissen, Lilianne E. 1989. The Metis National Council: Continuity and Change among the Canadian Metis. European Review of Native American Studies 3(1):33–42.

Krotz, Larry. 1991. Dammed and Diverted. Canadian Geographic 111(1):36–44.

Krueger, Ralph R., and Bruce Mitchell eds. 1977. Managing Canada's Renewable Resources. Toronto, London, Sydney, Wellington: Methuen Publications.

Krueger, Steve. 1991. What would Darwin say? Special Interest Groups are attacking endangered Species from an evolutionary Angle. Nature Canada 20(1):12–17.

Kubish, Glenn. 1990. The Peace River War. Alberta Report, January 8, 1990:24–25.

Kuiper, Bob. 1985. Nuu-chah-nulth Forestry Program: A Case Study of Community-Based Planning and Implementation Project Model. Vancouver: INAC Planning Section.

Lancaster Sound Regional Land Use Planning Commission. 1991. The Lancaster Sound Regional Land Use Plan. March 1991.

Lane, Robert, and Barbara Lane. 1978. Recognition of B.C. Indian Fishing Rights in Formal Treaties with the Indians and with Foreign Governments. Mimeograph prepared for the Union of B.C. Indian Chiefs, Vancouver.

Lawson, Michael L. 1985. Federal Water Projects and Indian Lands: The Pick-Sloan Plan, a Case Study. In: The Plains Indians of the Twentieth Century. P. Iverson ed. Norman and London: University of Oklahoma Press. pp. 169–185.

Lee, Douglas B. 1988. Oil in the Wilderness. An Arctic Dilemma. National Geographic 174(6):858–871.

Legislative Assembly of the Northwest Territories. 1989. The SCONE Report: Building Our Economic Future. Yellowknife: Legislative Assembly of the NWT.

Lewis, Damien. 1990. Conflict of Interests. Geographical Magazine, December 1990:18–22.

Lindsay, W. Keith. 1987. Integrating Parks and Pastoralists: Some Lessons from Amboseli. In: Conservation in Africa. People, Policies and Practice. David Anderson and Richard Grove eds. Cambridge: Cambridge University Press. pp. 149–167.

Linton, Jamie. 1991. "The Geese have lost their Way". Nature Canada 20(2):27–33.

Livingston, Ron, and Jamie Bastedo. 1990. Northwest Territories Conservation Strategy. In: Sustainable Development through Northern Conservation Strategies. Elaine Smith ed. The Banff Centre for Continuing Education. Calgary: The University of Calgary Press. pp. 67–81.

Lloyd, Kevin. 1986. Cooperative Management of Polar Bears on Northeast Baffin Island. In: Native People and Renewable Resource Management. The 1986 Symposium of the Alberta Society of Professional Biologists. Edmonton: Alberta Society of Professional Biologists. pp. 108–116.

Locke, Harvey. 1991. When is a Park not a Park? Circular Letter, Summer 1991. Toronto: Canadian Parks and Wilderness Society.

Lopez, Barry. 1986. Arctic Dreams. Imagination and Desire in a Northern Landscape. New York: Bantam Books.

Lusigi, Walter J. 1978. Planning African National Parks — An Example from Kenya. In: Nationalpark Bayerischer Wald. 2. Tagungsbericht. Forschung in Mitteleuropaeischen Nationalparken. Grafenau, Bayerischer Wald, 25.–27. Mai, 1978. Schriftenreihe des Bayerischen Staatsministeriums fuer Ernaehrung, Landwirtschaft und Forsten. pp. 37–48.

———. 1984. Future Directions for the Afrotropical Realm. In: National Parks, Conservation, and Development. The Role of Protected Areas in Sustaining Society. Jeffrey A. McNeely and Kenton R. Miller eds. Proceedings of the World Congress on National Parks. Bali, Indonesia, 11–22 October, 1982. Washington, D.C.: Smithsonian Institution Press. pp. 137–146.

Lysyk, Kenneth M., Edith E. Bohmer and Willard L. Phelps. 1977. Alaska Highway Pipeline Inquiry. Minister of Supply and Services Canada.

Lytwyn, Victor P. 1990. Ojibwa and Ottawa Fisheries around Manitoulin Island: Historical and Geographical Perspectives on Aboriginal and Treaty Fishing Rights. Native Studies Review 6(1):1–30.

Machlis, Gary E., and David L. Tichnell. 1985. The State of the World's Parks. Boulder and London: Westview Press.

MacKay, Donald. 1985. Heritage Lost: the Crisis in Canada's Forests. Toronto: MacMillan of Canada.

Mackenzie Delta-Beaufort Sea Regional Land Use Planning Commission. 1991. A Community-Based Regional Land Use Plan for the Mackenzie Delta-Beaufort Sea Region. October 1991.

MacLaine, Craig, and Michael S. Baxendale. 1990. This Land is our Land. The Mohawk Revolt at Oka. Montreal, Toronto: Optimum Publishing International Inc.

Macpherson, A.H. 1981. Commentary: Wildlife Conservation and Canada's North. Arctic 34(2):103–107.

Macpherson, Janet E. 1978a. The Pine Point Mine. In: Northern Transitions. Volume 1. Northern Resource and Land Use Policy Study. Everett B. Peterson and Janet B. Wright eds. Ottawa: Canadian Arctic Resources Committee. pp.65–110.

———. 1978b. The Cyprus Anvil Mine. In: Northern Transitions. Volume 1. Northern Resource and Land Use Policy Study. Everett B. Peterson and Janet B. Wright eds. Ottawa: Canadian Arctic Resources Committee. pp.111–149.

Mactavish, John S. 1987. Review of Indian Forest Resources Management and Development. Prepared for the Department of Indian Affairs and Northern Development, March 1987.

Mandell, Louise. 1993. Letter to Penticton Indian Band. February 26, 1993.

Maracle, Richard R. 1988. Fur Industry Marketing Study for Indigenous People. Deseronto: Richard R. Maracle and Associates.

Marchak, Patricia. 1987a. Uncommon Property. In: Uncommon Property: The Fishing and Fish Processing Industry in British Columbia. Patricia Marchak, Neil Guppy and John McMullan eds. Toronto: Methuen Publications. pp.3–31.

———. 1987b. Organization of Divided Fishers. In: Uncommon Property: The Fishing and Fish Processing Industry in British Columbia. Patricia Marchak, Neil Guppy and John McMullan eds. Toronto: Methuen Publications. pp.223–248.

Marchand, Susan J. 1986. Environmental Impacts on the Lake St. Clair Fishery: A Case Study of Mercury Pollution and its Effects on Walpole Island Indian Reserve. Wallaceburg: Walpole Island Research Centre (Nin.Da.Waab.Jig.) Occasional Paper No.11.

Marsh, J.S. 1979. Recreation and the Wilderness Experience in Canada's National Parks, 1968–1978. In: The Canadian National Parks: Today and Tomorrow. Conference II: Ten Years Later. October 8–13, 1978, Banff, Alberta. J.G. Nelson, R.D. Needham, S.H. Nelson, and R.C. Scace eds. Waterloo: University of Waterloo. Volume 1. pp.151–177.

Martin, Calvin. 1978. Keepers of the Game. Indian-Animal Relationships and the Fur Trade. Berkeley: University of California Press.

Matchewan, Jean Maurice. 1990. Mitchikanibikonginik: Algonquins of Barriere Lake: Our long Battle to create a sustainable Future. Rapid Lake Indian Reserve: Barriere Lake Indian Government.

Mathias, Joe, and Gary R. Yabsley. 1991. Conspiracy of Legislation: The Suppression of Indian Rights in Canada. B.C. Studies 89:34–45.

Maxfield, P.C., M.F. Dieterich and F.J. Trelease. 1977. Natural Resources Law on American Indian Lands. Boulder, Colorado: Rocky Mountain Mineral Law Foundation, University of Colorado.

May, Elizabeth. 1990a. Tourism to the Rescue? Cultural Survival Quarterly 14(2):2–5.

———. 1990b. Paradise Won. The Struggle for South Moresby. Toronto: McClelland and Stewart Inc.

McArthur, David. 1986. Renewable Resources and Native Economic Development in the Lac La Biche Region. In: Native People and Renewable Resource Management. The 1986 Symposium of the Alberta Society of Professional Biologists. Edmonton: Alberta Society of Professional Biologists. pp.158–170.

McCord, Barbara. 1989. What is the Boreal Forest? Environment Views 12(2):5–10.

McCormack, Patricia A. 1992. The Political Economy of Bison Management in Wood Buffalo National Park. Arctic 45(4):367–380.

McCullum, Hugh, and Karmel. 1975. This Land Is Not For Sale. Toronto: Anglican Book Centre.

McDonald, Miriam, and Brian Fleming. 1991. The Role of Traditional Knowledge in Community-based Management of an Eiderdown Industry Developing in Northern Canada. Paper presented at the

IASCP (The International Association for the Study of Common Property) Common Property Conference, September 26–29, 1991, Winnipeg, Manitoba.
McIlroy, Anne. 1992. India's Narmada: Déjà Views. Arctic Circle 2(6):28–31.
McMillan, Tom. 1986. Preserve and Protect. An Overview of Amendments to the National Parks Act. Environment Canada, Parks.
McMullan, John. 1987a. The Organization of the Fisheries: An Introduction. In: Uncommon Property: The Fishing and Fish Processing Industry in British Columbia. Patricia Marchak, Neil Guppy and John McMullan eds. Toronto: Methuen Publications. pp. 35–45.
———. 1987b. State, Capital, and the B.C. Salmon Fishing Industry. In: Uncommon Property: The Fishing and Fish Processing Industry in British Columbia. Patricia Marchak, Neil Guppy and John McMullan eds. Toronto: Methuen Publications. pp. 107–152.
McNamee, Kevin A. 1989. Fighting for the Wild in Wilderness. In: Endangered Spaces. The Future for Canada's Wilderness. Monte Hummel ed. Toronto: Key Porter Books Limited. pp. 63–82.
———. 1993. Debating the Future of Gwaii Haanas. Nature Canada 22(1):42–49.
Merkel, Garry. 1992. What is Aboriginal Forestry? NAFA (National Aboriginal Forestry Association) Quarterly 1(1):7.
M'Gonigle, R. Michael. 1988. Native Rights and Environmental Sustainability: Lessons from the British Columbia Wilderness. The Canadian Journal of Native Studies 8(1):107–130.
———. 1989/90. Developing Sustainability: A Native/Environmentalist Prescription for Third-Level Government. B.C. Studies 84 (Winter 1989/90):65–99.
M'Gonigle, R. Michael, and Wendy Wickwire. 1988. Stein. The Way of the River. Vancouver: Talon Books.
Michiel, Patrick. 1990. The Bison Saga. Nature Canada 19(2):29–34.
Mitchell, Bruce, and Richard Turkheim. 1977. Environmental Impact Assessment: Principles, Practice and Canadian Experiences. In: Managing Canada's Renewable Resources. Ralph R. Krueger and Bruce Mitchell eds. Toronto: Methuen Publications. pp. 47–66.
Moise, Ben. 1989. Temagami Wilderness under Siege. Canadian Geographic 109(1):28–39.
Monaghan, Hugh J. 1984. The Caribou Management Board and its early Growth. In: National and Regional Interests in the North. Third National Workshop on People, Resources, and the Environment North of 60. June 1–3, 1983, Yellowknife, NWT. Ottawa: Canadian Arctic Resources Committee. pp. 417–426.
Morell, Mike. 1989. The Struggle to Integrate Traditional Indian Systems and State Management in the Salmon Fisheries of the Skeena River, British Columbia. In: Co-Operative Management of Local Fisheries. Evelyn Pinkerton ed. Vancouver: University of British Columbia Press. pp. 231–248.
Morris, Alexander. 1880 (1971). The Treaties of Canada with the Indians of Manitoba and the North-West Territories. Reprint. Toronto: Coles Publishing Co.
Morris, C. Patrick. 1985. "As Long as the Water Flows...." United States Indian Water Rights: A Growing National Conflict. In: Native Power. Jens Brosted et al. eds. Oslo: University of Oslo Press. pp. 239–261.
Muir, Magdalena A.K. 1991. Impact of Aboriginal Claims Agreements on Environmental Review in the Northwest Territories. Journal of Environmental Law and Practice, August 1991. (Manuscript)
Murray, A.R., and J.W. Clouthier. 1986. Involvement of People of Indian Ancestry in Saskatchewan's Fisheries. Regina: Saskatchewan Parks and Renewable Resources. Fisheries Branch.
Naingisa, Shomet. 1991. Statement of KIPOC, NGO for Pastoral Peoples, Northern Maasailand, Tanzania. IWGIA Newsletter 2:54–57.
Nasogaluak, William, and Douglas Billingsley. 1981. The Reindeer Industry in the Western Canadian Arctic: Problems and Potential. In: Proceedings of the First International Symposium on Renewable Resources and the Economy of the North. Milton M.R. Freeman ed. Ottawa: Association of Canadian Universities for Northern Studies. pp. 86–95.
Native People's Circle on Environment and Development. 1991. Draft Report. Toronto: Ontario Round Table on Environment and Economy.
Nelson, Richard K. 1982. A Conservation Ethic and Environment: The Koyukon of Alaska. In: Resource Managers: North American and Australian Hunter-Gatherers. Nancy M. Williams and Eugene S. Hunn eds. Boulder: Westview Press, Inc. pp. 211–228.
Nepinak, Harvey. 1990. The Waterhen Wood Bison Project. Smoke Signals 1(1):4–6.

———. 1991a. Notes for a Meeting with the Manitoba Department of Natural Resources and Chief Harvey Nepinak, Waterhen First Nation, and Chief Clifford McKay, Pine Creek First Nation. Dauphin, Manitoba, January 16, 1991.

———. 1991b. Waterhen Wood Bison Project. Paper presented at the CIC (Conseil International de la Chasse et de la Conservation du Gibier) Conference, May 16, 1991, Quebec City, Quebec.

Nepinak, Harvey, and Harvey Payne. 1988. The Hunting Rights of Indian People in Manitoba: An Historical Overview and a Contemporary Explication toward Enhanced Conservation through joint Management. Alces 24:195–200.

Nietschmann, Bernard. 1984. Miskito and Kuna Struggle for Nation Autonomy. Paper presented at the Annual Meeting of the American Association for the Advancement of Science, New York. Reprinted in: Tribal Peoples and Development Issues. A Global Overview. John H. Bodley ed. Mountain View: Mayfield Publishing Company, 1988. pp.271–280.

Noble, Kimberley. 1991. Water Follies. Report on Business Magazine, May 1991:61–68.

Northern Diseased Bison Environmental Assessment Panel. 1990. Report of the Environmental Assessment Panel. Federal Environmental Assessment Review Office. Minister of Supply and Services Canada.

Notzke, Claudia. 1985. Indian Reserves in Canada. Development Problems of the Stoney and Peigan Reserves in Alberta. Marburg/Lahn: Marburg University, Department of Geography.

———. 1987. Indian Land in Southern Alberta. In: A Cultural Geography of North American Indians. Thomas E. Ross and Tyrel G. Moore eds. Boulder and London: Westview Press. pp.107–126.

Okrainetz, Glen. 1992. Towards a Sustainable Future in Hudson Bay. Northern Perspectives 20(2):12–16.

O'Malley, Martin. 1976. The Past and Future Land. An Account of the Berger Inquiry into the Mackenzie Valley Pipeline. Toronto: Peter Martin Associates Limited.

Ondro, W.J., and T.B. Williamson. 1985. The Forest Industry in the Economy of Saskatchewan, 1979–80. Edmonton: Northern Forest Research Centre, Canadian Forestry Service, Information Report NOR-X-270.

Orzechowska, Monika, and Ludger Mueller-Wille. 1981. Non-Renewable Resources in Canada's Arctic: Developments, Issues and Concerns in the 1980s. Suomen Antopologi 4:202–223.

Osberg, Zella, and Stephen Hazell. 1989. Towards a Sustainable Approach. Natural Resource Development and Environmental Protection in the Northwest Territories. A Background Study for the Special Committee on the Northern Economy of the Legislative Assembly of the Northwest Territories. May 1989.

Osherenko, Gail. 1988. Wildlife Management in the North American Arctic: The Case for Co-Management. In: Traditional Knowledge and Renewable Resource Management in Northern Regions. Milton M.R. Freeman and Ludwig N. Carbyn eds. Edmonton: Boreal Institute for Northern Studies. Occasional Publication No.23, pp.92–104.

Owens, Mark and Delia. 1985. Cry of the Kalahari. Glasgow: William Collins Sons and Co. Ltd.; Fontana PB.

Parkin, Tom W. 1991. Rim of Fire. Aiyansh Volcano: B.C.'s Avenging Mountain. Borealis 2(3):22–26.

Pannell, Brian. 1992. When They Don't Show up to Play the Feds are on the Proponent's Team. Northern Perspectives 20(2):7.

The Community of Paulatuk and the Wildlife Management Advisory Council (NWT). 1990. Paulatuk Conservation Plan. A Plan for the Conservation and Management of Renewable Resources and Lands around Paulatuk, Northwest Territories. March 1990.

Payne, Harvey, and Harvey Nepinak. 1990. Wildlife Co-Management. Paper presented at the "People and Land in Northern Manitoba" Conference, May 1990, Winnipeg, Manitoba.

———. 1991. Waterhen Wood Bison Project. Paper presented at the "Game Farming and Aboriginal Peoples" Conference, March 21–23, 1991, Saskatoon, Saskatchewan.

Pearse, Peter. 1982. Turning the Tide. The Commission on Pacific Fisheries Policy. Final Report. Vancouver: Department of Fisheries and Oceans.

Pelly, David F. 1991. Pond Inlet. An Inuit Community caught between two Worlds. Canadian Geographic 111(1):46–52.

Pike, Dan, Pierre Richard and Dan Goodman. 1991. Eastern Canadian Arctic Beluga and Narwhal Management: History, Status and Future Challenges. Paper presented at the IASCP (The International Association for the Study of Common Property) Common Property Conference, September 26–29, 1991, Winnipeg, Manitoba.

Pinkerton, Evelyn. 1983. Taking the Minister to Court: Changes in Public Opinion About Forest Management and Their Expression in Haida Land Claims. B.C. Studies 57:68–85.

———. 1987a. Indians in the Fishing Industry. In: Uncommon Property: The Fishing and Fish Processing Industry in British Columbia. Patricia Marchak, Neil Guppy and John McMullan eds. Toronto: Methuen Publications. pp.249–269.

———. 1987b. The Fishing-Dependent Community. In: Uncommon Property: The Fishing and Fish Processing Industry in British Columbia. Patricia Marchak, Neil Guppy and John McMullan eds. Toronto: Methuen Publications. pp.293–325.

———. 1987c. Intercepting the State. In: The Question of the Commons. The Culture and Ecology of Communal Resources. Bonnie J. McCay and James M. Acheson eds. Tuscon: The University of Arizona Press. pp.344–369.

———. 1989. Introduction: Attaining Better Fisheries Management through Co-Management — Prospects, Problems, and Propositions. In: Co-Operative Management of Local Fisheries. Evelyn Pinkerton ed. Vancouver: University of British Columbia Press. pp.3–33.

———. 1992. Translating Legal Rights into Management Practice: Overcoming Barriers to the Exercise of Co-Management. Human Organization 51(4):330–341.

Plewes, M., and J.B.R. Whitney eds. 1977. Environmental Impact Assessment in Canada: Processes and Approaches. Proceedings of a Symposium held at The Institute for Environmental Studies, February 1977. Pub. No.EE-5, September 1977.

Pool, Annelies. 1992. The Death and Birth of Dreams. Dividing the NWT. Above and Beyond 4(3):6–9.

Porsild, A.E. 1954. Land Use in the Arctic. Canadian Geographical Journal 48(6):232–243 (Part 1) and Canadian Geographical Journal 49(1):20–31 (Part 2).

Potyondi, B. 1981. Dual Allegiance; A History of Wood Buffalo National Park, 1929–1965. Parks Canada Microfiche Report Series No.104. Ottawa.

Price, Steve. 1984. Carolinian Canada Fact Sheet. Toronto: World Wildlife Fund Canada.

Prince Albert District Chiefs. 1985. Study of the Uranium Industry. Prince Albert, April 1985.

Raby, Stewart. 1973. Indian Land Surrenders in Southern Saskatchewan. The Canadian Geographer 17(1):36–52.

Randall, Alan. 1981. Resource Economics. An Economic Approach to Natural Resource and Environmental Policy. New York, Chichester, Brisbane, Toronto, Singapore: John Wiley and Sons Inc.

Rasmussen, Ray. 1991. The Politics of Bison Slaughter. Borealis 2(3):43.

Reed, F.L.C. 1980. Importance of the Forest Industry in the Canadian Economy. In: The Forest Imperative, Proceedings, Canadian Forest Congress, Toronto, September 22–23, 1980. pp.17–21.

Rees, William E. 1987. Introduction: A Rationale for Northern Land-Use Planning. In: Hinterland or Homeland? Land-Use Planning in Northern Canada. Terry Fenge and William E. Rees eds. Ottawa: Canadian Arctic Resources Committee. pp.1–17.

Reid, R.A. 1979. The Role of National Parks in Nature Preservation. In: The Canadian National Parks: Today and Tomorrow. Conference II: Ten Years Later. October 8–13, 1978, Banff, Alberta. J.G. Nelson, R.D. Needham, S.H. Nelson, and R.C. Scace eds. Waterloo: University of Waterloo. Volume 1. pp.106–113.

Renecker, Lyle A. 1987. Game Production Developments in Canada and Alberta. In: Focus on a new Industry. Proceedings of the 1987 Alberta Game Growers' Association Conference, October 22–24, 1987, Red Deer, Alberta. Lyle A. Renecker ed. pp.5–8.

Richardson, Miles, and Bill Green. 1989. The Fisheries Co-Management Initiative in Haida Gwaii. In: Co-Operative Management of Local Fisheries. Evelyn Pinkerton ed. Vancouver: University of British Columbia Press. pp.249–261.

Richardson, Nigel H. 1987. The Northern Land-Use Planning Agreements: A Commentary. In: Hinterland or Homeland? Land-Use Planning in Northern Canada. Terry Fenge and William E. Rees eds. Ottawa: Canadian Arctic Resources Committee. pp.53–70.

———. 1989. Land Use Planning and Sustainable Development in Canada. Ottawa: Canadian Environmental Advisory Council.

Riewe, Rick. 1991. Inuit Use of the Sea Ice. Arctic and Alpine Research 23(1):3–10.

Riewe, Rick, and Lloyd Gamble. 1988. The Inuit and Wildlife Management Today. In: Traditional Knowledge and Renewable Resource Management in Northern Regions. Milton M.R. Freeman

and Ludwig N. Carbyn eds. Edmonton: Boreal Institute for Northern Studies. Occasional Publication No.23, pp.31–37.
Robinson, Mike, and Lloyd N. Binder. 1991. The Inuvialuit Final Agreement and Resource Use Conflicts: Co-Management in the Western Arctic and Final Decisions in Ottawa. Calgary: Canadian Institute of Resources Law.
Robinson, William L., and Eric G. Bolen. 1989. Wildlife Ecology and Management. New York: Mackmillan Publishing Company. London: Collier Macmillan Publishers. Second Edition.
Rostlund, Erhard. 1952. Freshwater Fish and Fishing in Native North America. Berkeley and Los Angeles: University of California Press.
Rowe, J. Stan. 1992. No Environment = No Development. Implications of the Brundtland and National Task Force Reports to Canadian Forest Management. Parks and Wilderness 9(1):12–15.
Rueggeberg, Harriet, and Andrew R. Thompson. 1984. Resource Management Boundary Problems. Yellowknife: Western Constitutional Forum.
Ryan, Don. 1985. The Inland Salmon Fishery. A Viable Solution to the Mixed Stock Problem. Brief to the House of Commons Standing Committee on Fisheries and Forestry. Gitksan and Wet'suwet'en Tribal Council.
Sadler, Barry. 1990a. Sustainable Development, Northern Realities and the Design and Implementation of Conservation Strategies. In: Sustainable Development through Northern Conservation Strategies. Elaine Smith ed. The Banff Centre for Continuing Education. Calgary: The University of Calgary Press. pp.ix–xxviii.
———. 1990b. Impact Assessment in Transition: A Framework for Redeployment. In: Integrated Approaches to Resource Planning and Management. Reg Land ed. The Banff Centre for Continuing Education. Calgary: The University of Calgary Press. pp.99–129.
Sanders, D.E. 1973/74. Indian Hunting and Fishing Rights. Saskatchewan Law Review 38:45–62.
Saskatchewan Indian Agriculture Program. n.d. Bison Ranching on Indian Reserves. (Information leaflets) Craven: Saskatchewan Indian Agriculture Program.
Savard, Remi. 1979. Destins D'Amérique. Les Autochtones et nous. Montreal: L'Hexagone.
Scace, R.C., and J.G. Nelson eds. 1986. Heritage for Tomorrow. Proceedings of the Canadian Assembly on National Parks and Protected Areas. Volume 1. Ottawa: Minister of the Environment and Minister of Supply Services Canada.
Scammell, Bob. 1990. We should spring the Claptrap! Western Canadian Outdoors, June/July 1990:14.
Scott, Colin. 1984. Between "Original Affluence" and Consumer Affluence: Domestic Production and Guaranteed Income for James Bay Cree Hunters. In: Affluence and Cultural Survival. 1981 Proceedings of The American Ethnological Society. Richard F. Salisbury and Elisabeth Tooker eds. Washington, D.C.: American Ethnological Society. pp.74–86.
Scotter, George W. 1972. Reindeer Ranching in Canada. Journal of Range Management 25:167–174.
———. 1989. Reindeer Husbandry in North America. In: Wildlife Production Systems. Economic Utilization of Wild Ungulates. Robert J. Hudson, K.R. Drew and L.M. Baskin eds. Cambridge: Cambridge University Press. pp.223–241.
Shapcott, Catherine. 1989. Environmental Impact Assessment and Resource Management, a Haida Case Study: Implications for Native People of the North. The Canadian Journal of Native Studies 9(1):55–83.
Shaver, C. Mack. 1985. National Park Values and Living Cultural Parks. Conflicting Management Demands in Alaska's New National Parklands. Cultural Survival Quarterly 9(1):51–53.
Sibbeston, Nick. 1986. Economic Development and Renewable Resources in the Northwest Territories. In: Native People and Renewable Resource Management. The 1986 Symposium of the Alberta Society of Professional Biologists. Edmonton: Alberta Society of Professional Biologists. pp.153–157.
Simon, Mary. 1991. Statement by the Inuit Circumpolar Conference. United Nations Conference on Environment and Development. PrepCom III, Geneva, Switzerland, September 2, 1991. Presented by Mary Simon, President.
Slaughter, Charles W. 1990. Recent United States and Circumpolar Initiatives toward Northern Conservation and Development. In: Sustainable Development through Northern Conservation Strategies. Elaine Smith ed. The Banff Centre for Continuing Education. Calgary: The University of Calgary Press. pp.149–158.

Smallface Marule, Marie. 1978. The Canadian Government's Termination Policy: From 1969 to the Present Day. In: One Century Later. Western Canadian Reserve Indians since Treaty 7. Ian A.L. Getty and Donald B. Smith eds. Vancouver: University of British Columbia Press. pp. 103–116.

Snow, John. 1977. These Mountains Are Our Sacred Places. Toronto and Sarasota: Samuel Stevens, Publishers.

Standing Committee on Aboriginal Affairs. 1993. Canada Fur Watch: Aboriginal Livelihood at Risk. Fifth Report of the Standing Committee on Aboriginal Affairs. Larry Schneider M.P. Chairman, House of Commons, May 1993.

Staples, Lindsay. 1987. Land-Use Planning in the Yukon: A Struggle for Constitutional Development. In: Hinterland or Homeland? Land-Use Planning in Northern Canada. Terry Fenge and William E. Rees eds. Ottawa: Canadian Arctic Resources Committee. pp. 71–94.

Stevenson, Shawn. 1988. Wild Rice Report 1987. Northwestern Region of Ontario. Kenora: Ontario Ministry of Natural Resources, July 1988.

Stirling, Ian. 1988. Polar Bears. Ann Arbor: The University of Michigan Press.

Stix, John. 1982. National Parks and Inuit Rights in Northern Labrador. Canadian Geographer 26(4):349–354.

Stoffle, Richard W., and Michael J. Evans. 1990. Holistic Conservation and Cultural Triage: American Indian Perspectives on Cultural Resources. Human Organization 49(2):91–99.

Struzik, Edward. 1990. Stopping the River's Flow. Nature Canada 19(1):30–37.

———. 1991a. Wild Harvest. Equinox 56:33–43.

———. 1991b. Review of Arctic Exodus by Dick North. Canadian Geographic 111(4):80f.

———. 1991c. The Magical Mystery Tour. Nature Canada 20(3):37–44.

———. 1991d. High Tech in the High Arctic. Nature Canada 20(1):18–25.

———. 1992. Arctic Victory. Equinox 62:115.

Suggett, G.D., H. Payne and R.D. Hurst. 1988. In Search of the North American Bison. Winnipeg: Manitoba Natural Resources, Conservation Comment No. 125, September 1988.

Swan, James A. 1990. Sacred Places. Santa Fe: Bear and Company, Inc.

Swanson, Stella. 1991. What do Scientists know about the long-term Effects of Uranium Mining on the Environment? In: Uranium: a Discussion Guide. Gordon Edwards. Montreal: National Film Board of Canada. pp. 16f.

Swift, Jamie. 1983. Cut and Run: the Assault on Canada's Forests. Toronto: Between the Lines.

Tahltan Tribal Council. 1987. Resource Development Policy Statement. Signed by Vernon Marion, President Tahltan Tribal Territory. April 7, 1987.

Taschereau, Pierre Michael. 1985. The Status of Ecological Reserves in Canada. Ottawa: The Canadian Council on Ecological Areas.

Taylor, John Leonard. 1979. Two Views on the Meaning of Treaties Six and Seven. In: The Spirit of the Alberta Indian Treaties. Richard Price ed. Toronto: Butterworth and Co. (Canada) Ltd. pp. 9–45.

Taylor, John L. 1983. An Historical Introduction to Metis Land Claims. The Canadian Journal of Native Studies 3(1):151–181.

Tester, Frank J. 1992. Reflections on Tin Wis. Environmentalism and the Evolution of Citizen Participation in Canada. Alternatives 19(1):34–41.

Theberge, John B. 1978. Kluane National Park. In: Northern Transitions, Volume 1: Northern Resource and Land Use Policy Study. Everett B. Peterson and Janet B. Wright eds. Ottawa: Canadian Arctic Resources Committee. pp. 151–189.

Theberge, John B., J. Gordon Nelson and Terry Fenge eds. 1980. Environmentally Significant Areas of the Yukon Territory. Ottawa: Canadian Arctic Resources Committee.

Therrien, Beverly K. 1987. Native Participation in Public Policy Making and the Advancement of Native Interests in Northern Canada: A Case Study of the Porcupine Caribou Management Board. Unpublished M.A. Thesis. Edmonton: University of Alberta.

Thurston, Henry. 1992. The Rush to Rice. Equinox 62:24–32.

Tobias, J.L. 1977. Indian Reserves in Western Canada: Indian Homelands or Devices for Assimilation. In: Approaches to Native History in Canada. Papers of a Conference held at the National Museum of Man, October 1975. D.A. Muise ed. Ottawa: National Museum of Canada.

Todd, W.W., and E.K. Boggess. 1987. Characteristics, Activities, Lifestyles and Attitudes of Trappers in North America. In: Wild Furbearer Management and Conservation in North America. M. Novak, J.A. Baker, M.E. Obbard and B. Malloch eds. Ontario Ministry of Natural Resources. Published by the Ontario Trappers Association.

Tooshkenig, William, and Dean M. Jacobs. 1985. Report on the Workshop on Environmental Impact Assessment Procedures. March 27–29, 1985, Wellington, New Zealand. Wallaceburg: Walpole Island Research Centre (Nin.Da.Waab.Jig). Occasional Paper No. 8.

Topolniski, Dan, Sydney Kerwan and Allan Kristofferson. 1987. Economic Opportunities in the Commercial Fisheries of the Northwest Territories. Northern Perspectives 15(4):8–10.

Tough, Frank. 1985. The Establishment of a Commercial Fishing Industry and the Demise of Native Fisheries in Northern Manitoba. The Canadian Journal of Native Studies 4(2):303–319.

Tungavik Federation of Nunavut, Dene Nation, and Metis Association of the Northwest Territories. 1983. Press Release, May 5, 1983. In: National and Regional Interests in the North. Third National Workshop on People, Resources, and the Environment North of 60. June 1–3, 1983, Yellowknife, NWT. Ottawa: Canadian Arctic Resources Committee. pp.197–198.

Turnbull, Colin M. 1972. The Mountain People. New York: Simon and Schuster.

The United Chiefs and Councils of Manitoulin. 1988. The Treaty of Manitoulin Island. A Question of surrounding Islands? West Bay: The United Chiefs and Councils of Manitoulin.

Usher, Peter J. 1977. Northern Development: Some Social and Political Considerations. In: Managing Canada's Renewable Resources. Ralph R. Krueger and Bruce Mitchell eds. Toronto: Methuen Publications. pp.210–218.

———. 1981. Sustenance or Recreation? The Future of Native Wildlife Harvesting in Northern Canada. In: Proceedings of the First International Symposium on Renewable Resources and the Economy of the North. Milton M.R. Freemen ed. Ottawa: Association of Canadian Universities for Northern Studies. pp.56–71.

———. 1982. Fair Game? Nature Canada 11(1):5–11, 35–43.

———. 1984. Property Rights: The Basis of Wildlife Management. In: National and Regional Interests in the North. Third National Workshop on People, Resources, and the Environment North of 60. June 1–3, 1983, Yellowknife, NWT. Ottawa: Canadian Arctic Resources Committee. pp.389–415.

———. 1986. Devolution of Power in the Northwest Territories: Implications for Wildlife. In: Native People and Renewable Resource Management. The 1986 Symposium of the Alberta Society of Professional Biologists. Edmonton: Alberta Society of Professional Biologists. pp.69–80.

———. 1987. Indigenous Management Systems and the Conservation of Wildlife in the Canadian North. Alternatives 14(1):3–9.

———. 1989. Towards a Strategy for Supporting the Domestic Economy of the Northwest Territories. Ottawa: P.J. Usher Consulting Services.

———. 1991a. The Beverly-Kaminuriak Caribou Management Board: An Experience in Co-Management. Paper presented at the IASCP (The International Association for the Study of Common Property) Common Property Conference, September 26–29, 1991, Winnipeg, Manitoba.

———. 1991b. Some Implications of the Sparrow Judgement for Resource Conservation and Management. Alternatives 18(2):20–21.

———. 1992a. Modelling Subsistence Systems for Social Impact Assessment. A Report prepared for the Grand Council of the Crees (of Quebec) as an Attachment to Evidence presented by the Social Impacts Panel at the public Consultation on the Scope of the Great Whale Project Impact Study, Environmental Assessment Review Panels and Committees, at Montreal, 18 March 1992. Ottawa: P.J. Usher Consulting Services.

———. 1992b. Estimating Historical Sturgeon Harvest on the Nelson River, Manitoba. Prepared for Cross Lake Band of Indians and Savino and Co., Winnipeg. Ottawa: P.J. Usher Consulting Services.

———. 1992c. Socio-Economic Effects of Elevated Mercury Levels in Fish on Sub-Arctic Native Communities. In: Contaminants in the Marine Environment of Nunavik. Proceedings of the Conference, Montreal, September 12–14, 1990. Quebec: Université Laval, Centre d'Etudes Nordiques. pp.45–50.

Usher, Peter J., Frank J. Tough and Robert M. Galois. 1992. Reclaiming the Land: Aboriginal Title, Treaty Rights and Land Claims in Canada. Applied Geography 12:109–132.

Usher, Peter J., and Martin S. Weinstein. 1991. Towards Assessing the Effects of Lake Winnipeg Regulation and Churchill River Diversion on Resource Harvesting in Native Communities in Northern Manitoba. Ottawa: Minister of Supply and Services.

Usher, Peter J., and George Wenzel. 1987. Native Harvest Surveys and Statistics: A Critique of their Construction and Use. Arctic 40(2):145–160.

Van Dyk, Jere. 1990. Long Journey of the Pacific Salmon. National Geographic 178(1):3–37.

Van West, John J. 1990. Ojibwa Fisheries, Commercial Fisheries Development and Fisheries Administration, 1873–1915: An Examination of Conflicting Interests and the Collapse of the Sturgeon Fisheries of the Lake of the Woods. Native Studies Review 6(1):31–65.

Vaughan, A. 1984. The History and Future of Parks in the Northwest Territories: A Government of the Northwest Territories Perspective. In: National and Regional Interests in the North. Third National Workshop on People, Resources, and the Environment North of 60. June 1–3, 1983, Yellowknife, NWT. Ottawa: Canadian Arctic Resources Committee. pp.319–335.

Vecsey, Christopher. 1980. American Indian Environmental Religions. In: American Indian Environments. Ecological Issues in Native American History. Christopher Vecsey and Robert W. Venables eds. Syracuse: Syracuse University Press. pp.1–37.

Vennum Jr., Thomas. 1988. Wild Rice and the Ojibway People. St. Paul: Minnesota Historical Society Press.

Vincent, D., and A. Gunn. 1981. Population Increase of Muskoxen on Banks Island and Implications for Competition with Peary Caribou. Arctic 34(2): 175–179.

von Droste zu Huelshoff, Bernd. 1984. How UNESCO's Man and the Biosphere Programme is Contributing to Human Welfare. In: National Parks, Conservation, and Development. The Role of Protected Areas in Sustaining Society. Jeffrey A. McNeely and Kenton R. Miller eds. Proceedings of the World Congress on National Parks. Bali, Indonesia, 11–22 October, 1982. Washington, D.C.: Smithsonian Institution Press. pp.689–691.

Wagner, Gary. 1991. Remarks Relevant to the Public Review of the Gulf Canada Resources Limited Kulluk Drilling Program 1990–1992. June 1991. Inuvik: Joint Secretariat.

Wagner, Murray W. 1991. Footsteps Along the Road. Indian Land Claims and Access to Natural Resources. Alternatives 18(2):23–27.

Waiten, Cathy M. 1981. A Guide to Social Impact Assessment. Prepared for Research Branch, Corporate Policy, Indian and Northern Affairs Canada, Ottawa.

Waldram, James B. 1988. As Long as the Rivers Run: Hydroelectric Development and Native Communities in Western Canada. Winnipeg: The University of Manitoba Press.

Waquan, Archie. 1986. Resource Co-Management in Wood Buffalo National Park: The Cree Band's Perspective. In: Native People and Renewable Resource Management. The 1986 Symposium of the Alberta Society of Professional Biologists. Edmonton: Alberta Society of Professional Biologists. pp.81–85.

Ward, E. Neville, and Beth Killham. 1987. Heritage Conservation — The Natural Environment. Waterloo: University of Waterloo. Prepared and Funded by Environment Canada, Lands.

Waterhen and Pine Creek First Nations Chiefs and Councils. 1991. The Nature and Scope of Co-Management. Waterhen and Pine Creek First Nations, May 1991.

Watt, Erik. 1991. Mackenzie Pipeline or Pipe Dream? Northwest Explorer, October/November 1991:18–23.

Watt, Keith. 1990. Uneasy Partners. Report on Business Magazine, December 1990:42–49.

Wein, Eleanor E., Jean Henderson Sabry and Frederick T. Evers. 1991. Food Consumption Patterns and Use of Country Foods by Native Canadians near Wood Buffalo National Park, Canada. Arctic 44(3):196–205.

Weinstein, Martin S. 1992. Just like People get lost: A Retrospective Assessment of the Impacts of the Faro Mining Development on the Land Use of the Ross River Indian People. A Report to the Ross River Dena Council. June 1992.

Weinstein, Martin S., Adrian Tanner, Peter Usher and David Denton. 1992. Great Whale River Project. Environmental Review: Social Impacts Panel. Testimony on behalf of the Grand Council of the Crees (of Quebec). Presentation of the Social Impacts Panel.

Wells, Michael, and Katrina Brandon with Lee Hannah. 1992. People and Parks. Linking Protected Area Management with Local Communities. Washington, D.C.: The World Bank, The World Wildlife Fund, U.S. Agency for International Development.

Wenzel, George W. 1986. Canadian Inuit in a Mixed Economy: Thoughts on Seals, Snowmobiles, and Animal Rights. Native Studies Review 2(1):69–82.

West Coast Information and Research Group. 1980. Nuu-chah-nulth Tribal Council Forestry Study. Volume 1. Port Alberni, B.C.: West Coast and Information and Research Group.

Western, David. 1984. Amboseli National Park: Human Values and the Conservation of a Savanna Ecosystem. In: National Parks, Conservation, and Development. The Role of Protected Areas in Sustaining Society. Jeffrey A. McNeely and Kenton R. Miller eds. Proceedings of the World Congress on National Parks. Bali, Indonesia, 11–22 October, 1982. Washington, D.C.: Smithsonian Institution Press. pp.93–98.

Wheeler, Polly. 1988. State and Indigenous Fisheries Management: The Alaska Context. In: Traditional Knowledge and Renewable Resource Management in Northern Regions. Milton M.R. Freeman and Ludwig N. Carbyn eds. Edmonton: Boreal Institute for Northern Studies. pp.38–47.

Whillans, Thomas H., and Fikret Berkes. 1986. Use and Abuse, Conflict and Harmony: The Great Lakes Fishery in Transition. Alternatives 13(3):10–18.

White, W.A., K.M. Duke and K. Fong. 1989. The Influence of Forest Sector Dependence on the Socio-economic Characteristics of Rural British Columbia. Victoria: Forestry Canada, Pacific Forestry Centre.

Wickwire, Wendy C. 1991/92. Ethnography and Archaeology as Ideology: The Case of the Stein River Valley. B.C. Studies 91–92:51–78.

Wien, Fred. 1986. Rebuilding the Economic Base of Indian Communities: The Micmac of Nova Scotia. Montreal: The Institute for Research on Public Policy.

Wightman, Nancy M., and W. Robert. 1991. The Mica Bay Affair: Conflict on the Upper-Lakes Mining Frontier, 1840–1850. Ontario History 83(3):193–208.

Wildlife Management Advisory Council (NWT). n.d. Principles for the Conservation of Migratory Birds in the Inuvialuit Settlement Region. (Information pamphlet) Inuvik: Wildlife Management Advisory Council.

Wonders, William C. 1983. Overlapping Land Use and Occupancy of Dene, Metis, Inuvialuit and Inuit in the Northwest Territories. Ottawa: Department of Indian Affairs and Northern Development.

Woodward, Jack. 1989. Native Law. Toronto, Calgary, Vancouver: The Carswell Company Ltd.

Woodward, Jack, and Donna Jordan. 1993. Native Law Fax News. Issue No. 20. May 6, 1993.

World Commission on Environment and Development. 1987. Our Common Future. Oxford University Press.

Wright, R. Michael, Brian Houseal and Cebaldo de Leon. 1985. Kuna Yala: Indigenous Biosphere Reserve in the Making? Parks 10(3):25–27. Reprinted in: Tribal Peoples and Development Issues. A Global Overview. John H. Bodley ed. Mountain View: Mayfield Publishing Company, 1988. pp.352–356.

Wuerscher, Rose Boyko. 1982. Title to the Water Bed: The Legal History of the Ad Medium Filum Aquae Rule. Prepared for Research Branch, Indian and Northern Affairs Canada.

Wylynko, David. 1991. State of the Industry. How well are we managing our Forests? Nature Canada 20(1):26–34.

Yaremchuk, G.C.B., and B. Wong. 1989. Issues in the Management of Native Domestic Fishing in the Northwest Territories. Canadian Manuscript Report of Fisheries and Aquatic Sciences No.2010. Fisheries and Oceans Canada. Minister of Supply and Services Canada.

York, Geoffrey. 1990. Life and Death in Native Canada. London: Vintage U.K.

Zimmerman, Erich W. 1964. Meaning and Nature of Resources. In: Introduction to World Resources. Henry L. Hunker ed. New York: Harper and Row. pp.1–29.

No Author. 1992. Safe for the Time Being. Arctic Circle 2(4):11.

IWGIA (International Work Group for Indigenous Affairs) Yearbook 1991. Copenhagen 1992.

Newspapers / Newsletters

Akwesasne Notes

Alberta Report

The Calgary Herald

Caribou News

CRITFC (Columbia River Inter-Tribal Fish Commission) News

Dryden Local Express

The Edmonton Journal
Environment Law Centre Newsletter
The First Perspective
Fort Macleod Gazette
Fort McMurray Today
The Globe and Mail
Grande Prairie Daily Herald Tribune
Haada Laas, Journal of the Haida Nation
Ha-Shilth-Sa
IWGIA (International Workgroup for Indigenous Affairs) — Newsletter
Kainai News
Manitoulin Expositor
NAFA (National Aboriginal Forestry Association) Quarterly
Native Network News
New Breed Northern Ontario Business
The Press Independent
Timberlines
Toronto Star
Trappers News
The Vancouver Sun
Waterhen First Nation Resources Newsletter
Weekender
Windspeaker
WBNP Management Plan Review Program Newsletter
Working for Wildlife

FILM

Incident at Restigouche, Alanis Obomsawin (Producer and Director), National Film Board of Canada, 1984.

Radio

"Our Native Land". Centre Point. CBC Sunday Magazine, November 4, 1990.

Index

Credits

Cover
Use of the photograph on the cover (taken by the author) was graciously permitted by Joe Crowshoe, Donald Shade (son of the late Harry Shade) and Nelbert Little Moustache.

Chapter 2 (p. 7)
Donald Jacobsen, Assistant Library Director, American Museum of Natural History, New York, granted the copyright for "Map recording a Battle" in *Social Organization and Ritualistic Ceremonies of the Blackfoot Indians*. Clark Wissler, 1911/1912, Anthropological Papers of the American Museum of Natural History, New York, p. 44.

Chapter 3 (p. 33) and Chapter 8 (p. 227)
Vancouver artist Joe David granted the copyright for his prints depicting a salmon and "Life of Meares Island". The latter silkscreen print was produced for fundraising purposes in 1985.

Chapter 4 (p. 81) and Chapter 7 (p. 197)
Tom Duncan of Woodland Studios, Serpent River Indian Reserve, gave permission to reproduce two pieces of artwork by Stanley Panamick. They were originally featured in the booklet *Ojibway Legends* (No. 1) by Gilbert Oskaboose, the Birch Tree on page 1 and the Serpent on page 5.

Chapter 5 (p. 111)
This polar bear hunting scene was executed by an Inuit artist, Ekootak, and featured on pp. 88–89 of *I, Nuligak. The Autobiography of a Canadian Eskimo*. Edited and translated by Maurice Metayer. Copyright 1966, Peter Martin Associates Ltd. Pocket Book edition published by Simon Schuster of Canada Ltd. Richmond Hill, Ontario. Neither publisher had any records on file for this book.

Chapter 6 (p. 173)
The Many Spotted Horses Medicine Wheel was featured in Alberta Culture's pamphlet *Medicine Wheels in Alberta*. Reprint permission was obtained from J. Rod Vickers, Provincial Museum of Alberta (for Archaeological Survey, Provincial Museum of Alberta).

Appendix
Gilbert Oskaboose, Ojibway writer, kindly granted me permission to reprint his story "The Serpent's Eggs" from *Ojibway Legends* (No. 1) by Gilbert Oskaboose. Woodland Studios, 1988. pp. 5–10.